Zones of Focused Ambiguity in Siri Hustvedt's Works

Buchreihe der ANGLIA/
ANGLIA Book Series

―

Edited by
Lucia Kornexl, Ursula Lenker, Martin Middeke,
Gabriele Rippl, Hubert Zapf

Advisory Board
Laurel Brinton, Philip Durkin, Olga Fischer, Susan Irvine,
Andrew James Johnston, Christopher A. Jones, Terttu Nevalainen,
Derek Attridge, Elisabeth Bronfen, Ursula K. Heise, Verena Lobsien,
Laura Marcus, J. Hillis Miller, Martin Puchner

Volume 52

Zones of Focused Ambiguity in Siri Hustvedt's Works

Interdisciplinary Essays

Edited by
Johanna Hartmann, Christine Marks,
and Hubert Zapf

DE GRUYTER

For an overview of all books published in this series, please see
http://www.degruyter.com/view/serial/36292

ISBN 978-3-11-057869-0
e-ISBN (PDF) 978-3-11-040772-3
e-ISBN (EPUB) 978-3-11-040776-1
ISSN 0340-5435

Library of Congress Cataloging-in-Publication Data
A CIP catalog record for this book has been applied for at the Library of Congress.

Bibliographic information published by the Deutsche Nationalbibliothek
The Deutsche Nationalbibliothek lists this publication in the Deutsche Nationalbibliografie;
detailed bibliographic data are available on the Internet at http://dnb.dnb.de.

© 2016 Walter de Gruyter GmbH, Berlin/Boston
This volume is text- and page-identical with the hardback published in 2016.
Typesetting: Konrad Triltsch, Print und digitale Medien GmbH, Ochsenfurt
Printing and binding: CPI books GmbH, Leck

♾ Printed on acid-free paper
Printed in Germany

www.degruyter.com

Table of Contents

Johanna Hartmann, Christine Marks, and Hubert Zapf
Introduction —— 1

Literary Creation and Communication

Siri Hustvedt
Why One Story and Not Another? —— 11

Gabriele Rippl
The Rich Zones of Genre Borderlands: Siri Hustvedt's Art of Mingling —— 27

Diana Tappen-Scheuermann
Reality Bites: Fractured Narrative and Author-Reader Interaction in Siri Hustvedt's Work —— 39

Caroline Rosenthal
"A carnival in hell": Representations of New York City in Siri Hustvedt's Novels —— 51

Alfred Hornung
The Shaking Woman in the Media: Life Writing and Neuroscience —— 67

Psychoanalysis and Philosophy

Lucien Mélèse
~~The~~ **No Truth about Siri** —— 83

Françoise Davoine
Siri's Timequakes —— 99

Jason Tougaw
The Self Is a Moving Target: The Neuroscience of Siri Hustvedt's Artists —— 113

Klaus Lösch and Heike Paul
Dimensions of Tacit Knowledge and the Art(s) of Explication in Siri Hustvedt's Work —— 133

Mark C. Taylor
Wounding Words —— 153

Medicine and Narrative

Rita Charon
The Great Glazed Tank of Art: From the Real to the Imaginary with Siri Hustvedt —— 185

Carmen Birkle
"No self is an island": Doctor-Patient Relationships in Siri Hustvedt's Work —— 193

Britta Bein
Mysterious Illness and the Acceptance of Ambiguity —— 225

Petra Gelhaus
In Search of a Diagnosis: Siri Hustvedt's *The Shaking Woman* —— 237

Susanne Rohr
"The image makers": Reality Constitution and the Role of Autism in Siri Hustvedt's *The Blazing World* —— 249

Vision, Perception, and Power

Carla Schulz-Hoffmann
"What fascinate me are the journeys that begin with looking and only looking": Siri Hustvedt's Visual Imagination —— 265

Astrid Böger
"I look and sometimes I see": The Art of Perception in Siri Hustvedt's Novels —— 281

Birgit Däwes
"Openings that can't be closed": Patterns of Surveillance Culture in Siri Hustvedt's Novels —— 295

Anna Thiemann
Portraits of the (Post-)Feminist Artist: Female Authorship and Authority in Siri Hustvedt's Fiction —— 311

Trauma, Memory, and the Ambiguities of Self

Jean-Michel Rabaté
History and Trauma in Siri Hustvedt's *The Sorrows of an American* —— 329

Katharina Donn
Crisis of Knowledge: Trauma in *The Sorrows of an American* —— 341

Katja Sarkowsky
"The wounded psyche is not a broken leg": Illness, Injury, and Writing the Self in Siri Hustvedt's Work —— 357

Christopher Schliephake
Embodied Memories, Embodied Meanings: Mind, Matter, and Place in the Works of Siri Hustvedt —— 373

Heike Schwarz
"We have different selves over the course of a life, but even all at once": The Multiple Self and Cultural Multiple Personality in Siri Hustvedt's *The Blazing World* —— 389

Interview with Siri Hustvedt

Susanne Becker
"Deceiving the reader into the truth": A Conversation with Siri Hustvedt about *The Blazing World* (2014) —— 409

List of Contributors —— 423

Johanna Hartmann, Christine Marks, and Hubert Zapf
Introduction

Siri Hustvedt's reputation and public presence have been growing steadily in the 21st century. She is recognized internationally as one of the most widely read and appreciated contemporary American writers. She has drawn manifold responses to her work from different disciplines and areas of thought and has been a frequent contributor to literary, artistic, and scholarly events. In her significance and stature as a public intellectual, she is not merely an American writer but a transnational, cosmopolitan author, who develops new forms not only of literary narrative but of interdisciplinary thought and writing, bringing together otherwise separated genres and branches of knowledge in a broad spectrum between literature and philosophy, historiography and art, psychoanalysis and neuroscience, narrative and medicine. One hallmark of her works is an intermedial approach to literary production, in which different forms of art and their complex mutual relationships with language and narrative are constitutive of her style and her specific analysis of human perception, identity, and communication in contemporary societies.

In view of Siri Hustvedt's presence and international reputation in literary and intellectual culture, academic response to her work in terms of systematic scholarly analysis and research has so far lagged behind. While her writings have been extremely well received in the general public, they still await more sustained attention in academia. There are signs, however, that this is currently changing. Several monographs on her work have been published recently,[1] and the number of Ph.D. projects and research networks connected with her work is increasing steadily. The present volume further highlights Siri Hustvedt as an important literary figure and her impact on interdisciplinary research in literary studies and the humanities more generally. The volume comprises a collection of essays by scholars from various interdisciplinary fields and perspectives, illuminating the wide range of topics, ideas, forms, genres, and aesthetic modes that Hustvedt employs to convey her complex analyses of contemporary life both in her narratives and her essays.

---

[1] Christine Marks. 2014. *"I am because you are"*: *Relationality in the Works of Siri Hustvedt*. American Studies 244. Heidelberg: Winter; Corinna Sophie Reipen. 2014. *Visuality in the Works of Siri Hustvedt*. Frankfurt: Peter Lang; Johanna Hartmann. 2016. *Literary Visuality in Siri Hustvedt's Works: Phenomenological Perspectives*. text und theorie. Würzburg: Königshausen & Neumann.

Siri Hustvedt comes from a background that is both recognizably American and yet also transatlantic and cosmopolitan in orientation. She grew up in the bilingual household of a family of Norwegian immigrants in which language and literary culture played a significant role. Her mother was a French instructor and librarian, and her father taught Norwegian language, literature, and history at St. Olaf College in Northfield, Minnesota. During high school, Hustvedt wrote her first poems and lived for a time in Norway, and later studied history at St. Olaf College in Minnesota. She went on to study at Columbia University in New York, where she received her Ph.D. in English literature with a thesis on Charles Dickens titled *Figures of Dust: Language and Identity in Charles Dickens*. In recent years, she has been a frequent guest in Europe, giving readings, participating in conferences, and delivering keynote lectures at prestigious events, such as the Schelling Lecture in Munich, the Freud Lecture in Vienna, and the Kierkegaard Lecture in Copenhagen. In addition to her literary production, she has continuously published essays and papers in academic and scientific journals, including *Contemporary Psychoanalysis*, *Seizure: the European Journal of Epilepsy*, *Neuropsychoanalysis*, and *Clinical Neurophysiology*. She also received major prizes, such as the Gabarron International Award for Thought and Humanities 2012, which was conferred on her "for her tireless investigative work that has allowed her to integrate with a single voice highly original ideas of philosophy, neuroscience, psychology or psychoanalysis in her literary, creative and documentary work. The Jury has also wanted to underscore her contribution to the understanding and discovery of Fine Arts, through her many essays and articles."[2]

Hustvedt's literary works include the novels *The Blindfold* (1992), *The Enchantment of Lily Dahl* (1996), *What I Loved* (2003), *The Sorrows of an American* (2008), *The Summer without Men* (2011), and *The Blazing World* (2014). Her autobiographical analysis of her illness in *The Shaking Woman, or, A History of My Nerves* (2010) has drawn attention from different fields and has helped to revitalize interdisciplinary scholarly interest in the connections between literary life writing and the life sciences.[3] She has published a collection of poems, *Reading to You* (1981), and the essay collections *Yonder* (1998), *Mysteries of the Rectangle: Essays on Painting* (2005), *A Plea for Eros* (2006), and *Living, Thinking, Looking* (2012).

---

[2] The Gabarron. 2012. Press Release October 29. <http://gabarron.org/Awards/Awards/Awards2012/Winners/ThoughtandHumanities/PressRelease/tabid/1738/Default.aspx> [accessed 15 March 2015].

[3] See the newly instituted graduate training college *Life Sciences / Life Writing* at Mainz University, in which Hustvedt serves as cooperating external expert.

The roles of writer and scholar can in fact not be clearly separated in her work, since she includes a wide range of scientific material from various disciplines in her narratives, not only in her neurological memoir *The Shaking Woman* but in novels like *What I Loved, The Sorrows of an American,* or *The Blazing World* as well. By integrating scientific knowledge with highly personal stories, her texts combine rational analysis with psycho-emotional energy as the two vital sources of human creativity which have been identified both by traditional literary theory and by contemporary neuroscience.

This volume approaches Hustvedt's work from a range of perspectives in order to engage with an oeuvre that is hallmarked by a wide variety of styles, themes, forms of narration, and aesthetic features. The overarching themes of the essays crystallized the categories that organize the volume: "Literary Creation and Communication," "Psychoanalysis and Philosophy," "Medicine and Narrative," "Vision, Perception, and Power," and "Trauma, Memory, and the Ambiguities of Self." The collection opens with an essay by Siri Hustvedt herself on the creation of imaginative texts and closes with an interview with the author by Susanne Becker, in which Hustvedt elucidates her personal conception of the processes of writing and reading literary texts – processes that for Hustvedt are intricately intertwined.

The first part of the collection, "Literary Creation and Communication," examines how communication through and in the form of fictional and non-fictional literature can take place. The section opens with *Siri Hustvedt*'s essay "Why One Story and Not Another," in which she illuminates concepts of creativity involving the individual's body and mind. She points out how her artistic freedom as an author of fiction is nevertheless always guided by the intrinsic imperatives of what "feel[s]" like "fictional truth." Imaginative storytelling evolves not from arbitrary invention but from a complex interplay between conscious and unconscious factors that produces a distinctive form of knowledge including not only the intellectual and reflexive dimensions but emotionality, memory, imagination, and the embodied existence of every human being in the creative process. Hustvedt's essay is followed by *Gabriele Rippl*'s contribution, "The Rich Zones of Genre Borderlands: Siri Hustvedt's Art of Mingling," which explores how the prevalent theme of "mixing" can be utilized for an analysis of the novel's aesthetics in which confining genre conventions are constantly transcended. Rippl calls this phenomenon "genre hybridization" and traces it in Hustvedt's three most recent novels. *Diana Tappen-Scheuermann* approaches Hustvedt's fiction through the lens of reader-response theory. Her contribution, "Reality Bites: Fractured Narrative and the Author-Reader Interaction in Siri Hustvedt's Work," especially focuses on and compares the autobiographical/autofictional dimensions in both the memoir *The Shaking Woman* and the novel

What I Loved. Caroline Rosenthal's article "'A carnival in hell': Representations of New York City in Siri Hustvedt's Novels" looks at the representation of New York in *The Blindfold* and *What I Loved*. Rosenthal conceptualizes New York as a metropolis that is central to the "cultural imaginary of the nation" (51) and a setting which is intricately related to the development of both themes and characters of Hustvedt's fiction, claiming that "Hustvedt not only uses the space of New York to render repressed and hidden aspects in her figures' psyche, [...] but demonstrates how bodies are informed by spatiality." (52) As the last contribution within this section, *Alfred Hornung*'s essay "*The Shaking Woman* in the Media: Life Writing and Neuroscience" analyzes how the public discourse and discussion of Hustvedt's memoir and the described migraines differ in various TV and interview formats in Europe and the US and thus reads Hustvedt's books as interacting with the wider public and media landscapes.

Part II, "Psychoanalysis and Philosophy," opens with contributions by the French psychoanalysts *Lucien Mélèse* ("The No Truth about Siri") and *Françoise Davoine* ("Siri's Timequakes"), who in very different ways trace the impact Hustvedt's fiction has had on their work in the field of psychoanalysis but also their personal lives. Mélèse explores the transitional space between author and reader by sharing excerpts from his correspondence with Hustvedt and connecting the novels with personal associations and fragments of his own life experience. Davoine interweaves reflections on *The Sorrows of an American* with a rich tapestry of psychoanalytic theory, drawing on her own experience as well as works linked to trauma. In the next chapter, "The Self Is a Moving Target: The Neuroscience of Siri Hustvedt's Artists," *Jason Tougaw* traces the intersubjective forces at work in visual representation from within a neuroscientific framework. In his essay, he connects the author's use of ekphrasis, which he reads as "contiguous with forms of 'self representation' our brains engage in" (113), to ideas developed by neuroscientists such as Jaak Panksepp and António Damásio. Tougaw pursues the "moving targets" of Hustvedt's ideas on self-representation and identity by examining the portrait artists who populate Hustvedt's novels. *Klaus Lösch and Heike Paul* analyze Hustvedt's writings from the angle of the "tacit knowledge" that forms an implicit but nevertheless influential dimension in the lives and psychology of Hustvedt's characters. As the authors point out, "[t]he tacit may bring forth pathologies, trigger extreme physical responses, store negative experiences, affirm dominant ideologies, and stabilize symbolic and social order; at the same time, it may also be the origin/touchstone of protest and resistance" (149). In *Mark C. Taylor*'s "Wounding Words" the impact of Søren Kierkegaard's works is the focus of attention, especially concerning questions of authorship (e.g. the choice of narrative voice or the use of pseudonyms) and the influence of psychoanalytic, especially Freudian, concepts. In this way Taylor establishes connections that are prevalent in Hustvedt's *The Sorrows of an American* and *The Blazing World*.

In Part III, "Medicine and Narrative," the theme of illness and its literary representation and discussion in Hustvedt's oeuvre stand at the foreground. *Rita Charon*, Director of the Program in Narrative Medicine at Columbia University, begins this section by sharing her impressions from Hustvedt's previous visits to the program to teach literature to health care practitioners and her participation in the Narrative Medicine Rounds. Charon views Hustvedt's literary endeavors as "surgeries," "live-saving interventions" that "had opened a clearing for others who shared her brand of uncertainty, others who had experienced symptoms on those borderlands between things" (189). *Carmen Birkle*, in "'No self is an island': Doctor-Patient Relationships in Siri Hustvedt's Work," examines fictional representations of doctor-patient relationships, claiming that "representing these encounters in narrative offers insights into Hustvedt's perception of the medical profession and, at the same time, allows her to situate herself and her illness within the medical discourse as a form of therapy" (194). Also from the perspective of literary studies, *Britta Bein* looks at the phenomenon of "Mysterious Illness and the Acceptance of Ambiguity in *The Blindfold* and *The Summer without Men*." Bein conceives of illnesses as crises that – in analogy to literature – allow for forms of reading and interpretation that can serve as "possible strategies to cope with 'mysterious illnesses'" (227). From a medical perspective, *Petra Gelhaus* in her article "In Search of a Diagnosis: Siri Hustvedt's *The Shaking Woman*," follows the author on her journey toward an understanding of the mysterious illness that took possession of her body. Gelhaus takes the occasion to reflect on the mind-body problem and the interplay of subjective and objective forces in medical knowledge. *Susanne Rohr* in her contribution "'The image makers': Reality Constitution and the Role of Autism in Siri Hustvedt's *The Blazing World*" analyzes Hustvedt's latest novel as a prime example of the role of art and fiction in constructing reality, and zooms in on the special question of symptoms of autism in one of the characters, Harriet's son Ethan. Rohr claims that by giving a narrative voice to an autistic person, "Hustvedt effectively explores this intersubjective process by installing a narrative self as a curious narrative center within the polyphony of voices that constitute the novel that is unable – or has difficulty – in doing just that: entering into a dialogue with others" (249).

Part IV of the collection explores the dimension of "Vision, Perception, and Power" in Hustvedt's oeuvre. *Carla Schulz-Hoffmann*'s "'What fascinate me are the journeys that begin with looking and only looking': Siri Hustvedt's Visual Imagination" approaches Hustvedt's works from her perspective as an art historian. Examining the role of visual art in both Hustvedt's fictional works – *The*

Blindfold and *What I Loved* – and in her essay collection *Mysteries of the Rectangle*, Schulz-Hoffmann develops a concept of the aesthetic experience of visual art that is centrally hallmarked by intersubjectivity and the potential for narrativity. *Astrid Böger* in "'I look and sometimes I see': The Art of Perception in Siri Hustvedt's Novels" explores the "complex relationship between looking and seeing, remembering and feeling" (281), also including Hustvedt's latest essay collection *Living, Thinking, Looking* in her analysis. Following the author's representations of artistic production and reception from *The Blindfold* to *The Blazing World*, Böger notes "a marked shift toward a more interactive, dialogical process of meaning making via art" (281). In "'Openings that can't be closed': Patterns of Surveillance Culture in Siri Hustvedt's Novels," *Birgit Däwes* employs strategies of surveillance in Velázquez's paintings *La Venus del Espejo*, (or *Rokeby Venus*) in order to analyze "questions of seeing and visual representation, and particularly the connections between observation and power" in *The Blindfold*, *The Enchantment of Lily Dahl*, *The Sorrows of an American*, and *The Blazing World* – novels that "remind us that this 'knowledge' is not inherent in the structures of seeing: on the contrary, we require techniques of decoding, analyzing, and contextualizing information – in short, of interpretation – in order to make meaning" (307). *Anna Thiemann*'s article "Portraits of the (Post-)Feminist Artist: Female Authorship and Authority in Siri Hustvedt's Fiction" constitutes the final essay within this part of the collection. Focusing on "female creativity and identity," she argues that "Hustvedt['s] preoccupation with the figure of the woman artist reflects her strong interest in broader social and political issues like the construction of gender roles and the current state of the women's movement. Her novels evoke and contest established images of female authorship which have served strategic functions in feminist theory and criticism" (312).

Part V concentrates on "Trauma, Memory, and the Ambiguities of Self." This part opens with a contribution by *Jean-Michel Rabaté*, "History and Trauma in *The Sorrows of an American*," describing the historical dimensions of trauma in this novel of loss, mourning, and psychological survival. His essay is followed by *Katharina Donn*'s investigation of structural dimensions of trauma in *The Sorrows of an American*, which she interprets as indicative of a "crisis of knowledge." Donn outlines a literary epistemology of trauma in terms of the material metaphors which pattern this text and highlights the possibility of knowledge in the aftermath of shock and collapse. *Katja Sarkowsky* in "'The wounded psyche is not a broken leg': Illness, Injury, and Writing the Self in Siri Hustvedt's Work" examines the implications of illness and impairment for the narrative construction of self. As she notes, it is "no accident that there is no sense of 'healing' in Hustvedt's fictional and non-fictional work" as "[i]llness, mental and/or physical impairment, in this context most pronouncedly serve to explore the porosity and fragility, but also the necessity of a boundary between self and other" (359). Christopher Schliephake's essay "Embodied Memories, Embodied Meanings: Mind, Matter, and Place in the Works of Siri Hustvedt" analyzes *The Shaking Woman* and *The Sorrows of an American* as exemplifying that "the process of meaning-making in her work – both of the past and of oneself – follows a dialogical principle, combining a take on the past that is embodied and an encounter between the self and the (non-)human world" (374). To delve into the subjective and intersubjective dimensions of memory and narrative in Hustvedt's work, he frames his interpretation with contemporary theories of body memory. In her contribution "'We have different selves over the course of a life, but even all at once': The Multiple Self and Cultural Multiple Personality in Siri Hustvedt's *The Blazing World*," Heike Schwarz bases her analysis of *The Blazing World* on the existence of multiple selves and multiple cultural personalities, claiming that Hustvedt's "fiction negotiates variations of approaches to self-concepts of literary characters and the narrative structure itself, so that especially the multi-voiced *The Blazing World* can be marked as clever variation of the multiple personality genre and its subgenres" (390).

The collection closes with a conversation between Susanne Becker and Siri Hustvedt entitled "Deceiving the reader into the truth," in which they discuss Hustvedt's important themes that have shaped her work and their development in her most recent novel, *The Blazing World*. Their conversation offers insights into Hustvedt's current views of art and literature, with special emphasis on questions of authorship, the aesthetic experience, artistic ambition, and truth in fiction, which reconnect to the preceding sections as well as to the opening essay of this collection. Together, these contributions reflect the various "zones of focused ambiguity" – a term Hustvedt coins in her essay "Borderlands: First, Second, and Third Person Adventures in Crossing Disciplines" – that the author continues to develop in her fictional and non-fictional works.[4] In Hustvedt's *Living, Thinking, Looking*, the term "zone" frequently points toward an intermediate and liminal space, as in a "zone between waking and sleeping" (42), "a middle zone between the bodily senses and intellect" (175), or a "zone between people" (196).[5] Derived from the Greek term for 'girdle,' the word 'zone' traditionally has the connotation of a space safely distinguished from adjacent regions, "comprised between definite limits" (*OED*), circumscribed, separated. Yet Hustvedt's use of 'zone' always carries within it a presence of what lies be-

---

4 Siri Hustvedt. 2013. "Borderlands: First, Second, and Third Person Adventures in Crossing Disciplines." In: Alfred Hornung (ed.). *American Lives*. Heidelberg: Winter. 111–134.
5 Siri Hustvedt. 2012. *Living, Thinking, Looking*. London: Hodder & Stoughton.

yond, its existence often defined by its betweenness and the blurring of boundaries. In this spirit, the essays collected here seek to follow Hustvedt's aesthetics of zoning, embracing ambiguity rather than strict categorization to bring into resonance a polyphony of "plural voices and multiple visions"[6] that intersect, overlap, and transgress boundaries.

We would like to thank the contributors to the volume for their collaboration and support. We also thank the publisher De Gruyter, especially Katja Lehming and Ulrike Krauß, for their helpful and competent cooperation, and the editors of the *Anglia Book Series* for including the volume in the series. Our special thanks are due to Beate Greisel for her careful and reliable help in proofreading and in preparing the manuscript for print.

---

[6] The title of I. V. Hess's book on Søren Kierkegaard, M. M. Bakhtin, and German art historian Aby Warburg in *The Blazing World*.

Literary Creation and Communication

Siri Hustvedt
Why One Story and Not Another?

Why one story and not another? For the fiction writer, any and all stories are possible. Theoretically, there are no restrictions. If I wish to write a story about a child who grows wings and a tail at age thirteen and flies into another world, no one will stop me. I am entirely free, but that is not my question. Why does a story feel right or wrong while I am making it? How do I know that a character must smash another character over the head at this juncture in the narrative? And conversely, why do I know that the paragraph I have just written is false and must be erased and redone? I am not talking about changing sentences to make them more elegant or cutting out a paragraph after reading a text because I realize the story can do without it. Such alterations belong to editing, and, usually, I can explain my decisions. I am asking where fictional stories originate and what guides their creation? Why, as a reader, do some novels feel to me like lies and others feel true? When I read, what do I bring to the text? Are there times when I am simply unable to see what is there? I think these are significant questions that are seldom asked. There is, however, a related question, one universally maligned and ridiculed by writers around the world, a question that dogs every novelist at countless events because someone out there in the audience inevitably asks it. But the dreaded question, regarded as the province of morons, is actually profound. The question is: Where do you get your ideas?

The word "idea" catapults us instantly into philosophy. What does it mean to have an idea? What is an idea? For Plato ideal forms were more real than our world of flux and perceptual sensation. For Plutarch an idea was by its very nature bodiless. Descartes posited thought as the only verifiable aspect of human existence and separated body and mind. Contemporary philosophers and scientists are busily doing their best to smash the Cartesian divide between spirit and matter, but what is the relation between our ideas or thoughts and our feeling, sensing bodies? Where do ideas come from? The mind-body question appears as soon as the person in the back of the room asks me or any other writer on tour where our ideas come from. Are ideas in brain tissue? I have discovered that even when presented in highly lucid language, readers have difficulty grasping the problem. In my book *The Shaking Woman, or, A History of My Nerves* I pose the question again and again from multiple perspectives, and yet I was amazed to find that in interviews about the book, my interlocutors ignored it entirely (Hustvedt 2010). I will try to articulate the problem yet again. As a culture we are so deeply inculcated with the idea that mental faculties – thoughts, ideas, memories, fantasies, and feelings – are different in kind from physical faculties –

walking, running, having stomach aches, farting – that bridging the divide makes little sense to most people, and rather than think about it, they avoid it altogether.

The problem of dualism, that we are two things, intellect and body, not one, was articulated beautifully in 1664 by the natural philosopher Margaret Cavendish, Duchess of Newcastle, whose radical works were either ignored or ridiculed in her own time because she was a woman: "I would ask those that say the brain has neither sense, reason nor self-motion; but that all proceeds from an Immaterial Principle [...] distinct from the body [...] where their Immaterial Ideas reside, in what part or place in the body?" (Cavendish 1664: 185–186). Cavendish's question remains urgent.

Indeed, we all know that a head injury or dementia can make us forget who we are, can change our personalities, our ideas and thoughts. We know that the psychological and the physiological are not unrelated. And yet, how the private inner subjective experience of ideas, thoughts, and memories is connected to the objective outer reality of brain anatomy, neuronal connections, neurochemicals, and hormones remains unanswered. There is no agreed-upon theoretical model for brain-mind function. There are huge amounts of empirical data, and there is a lot of theoretical speculation and guesswork. Some ideas strike me as better than others, but that does not mean we have figured it out. The next time you pick up a newspaper and read about the neural correlates or neural underpinnings or neural representations of fear, joy, sex or anything else under the sun, you can say to yourself, Ah, the words "correlates," "underpinnings," and "representation" are used because the scientists and philosophers are reluctant to say that those brain systems *are* fear, joy, sex or anything else under the sun. The words expose the gap between mind and body rather than close it.

I cannot solve the division for you, but I can say there is a strong return to the body in many disciplines. Some cognitive scientists are abandoning the metaphor that has held sway since the sixties; that our brains are like computers, information processors. The brain is a moist organ inside a body, and the computational metaphor fails to cover many aspects of brain-mind function, our bodily movement, something as simple as how we walk, for example, as well as our emotions and feelings. The writing of Maurice Merleau-Ponty, the French phenomenologist, who emphasized embodiment, has seen a resurgence both in the sciences and the humanities. From this point of view: "Where do you get your ideas?" must involve an embodied self or being. Ideas, too, are embodied.

So how can we think about where the ideas for stories come from? How do we frame the question? It is common to point to writers' biographies, if even a remote connection between writer and novel can be found. Many writers have robbed their own lives, and the lives of their families and friends for material.

Writers frequently place their stories in real places. I have moved between New York City and Minnesota, the Midwestern state where I grew up. The city and my hometown are intimate spaces for me, and when I write, I imagine my characters moving down a familiar street or looking at a cornfield I remember from childhood. I call up known places in my mind and insert my characters into them. Just as conscious autobiographical memory needs a space and ground, loci, the characters in a work of fiction do not float in an empty world. As Mikel Dufrenne points out in *The Phenomenology of Aesthetic Experience*, "the represented world [of the book] also possesses, in its own fashion, the spatiotemporal structure of the perceived world. Space and time here fulfill a dual function. They serve to open up a world and to ordain it objectively by creating a world common to the characters and the readers" (Dufrenne 1973: 171). Writing partakes of this shared spatiotemporal reality as well, even if the story takes place on another planet – some form of recognition must be present.

The art of fiction cannot be reduced to a writer's autobiography. And the geography of fictions, whether real or invented, is the setting for events. And yet, stories must come from somewhere, and they must in one way or another relate to their authors, to their perceptions of the world and their experiences of it. A writer's imagination is not impersonal, is it? And it is somehow connected to memory, isn't it? Homer's *Odyssey* begins with a call to the muse Mnemosyne: "Speak, Memory."

The link between memory and the imagination is very old. The Latin imago for image or picture lies inside the word itself – imagination. In Western philosophy imagination has traditionally referred to the images in our minds that are not immediate perceptions – the mental pictures we carry in our heads. Aristotle insisted on the pictorial character of imagination and that it, unlike direct perception, could be false. He located imagination and memory in the same part of the soul, an idea echoed by Aquinas, which then appeared in various forms for centuries. For Descartes, a dualist, the imagination, *fantasie*, was a middle ground between the bodily senses and the intellect. In *Leviathan* (1651) Hobbes wrote "[…] imagination and memory are but one thing, which for divers considerations has divers names" (Hobbes 2012: 16). Hobbes, a materialist, did not think that thought floated above bodies. Thought was of the body, as it was for Cavendish. Cavendish knew both Hobbes and Descartes, but they refused to engage her directly because she had the wrong body for a philosopher. Her thought differed from Hobbes, but she too was a materialist and proposed a continuum of thought, from reason to fancy, from the conceptual to the imaginative. For Spinoza the lowest level of knowledge was imagination, and it contained memory within it. In *The New Science* (1725), Vico, the philosopher and historian, also regarded *memoria*, *fantasia*, and *ignegno* (invention) as parts of the same mental function, which emerged from the body. Hegel understood consciousness, with its ability to bring the past into the present in memory, as an act of the imagination.

Although parsed in various ways by many thinkers, my point here is broad. Memory and imagination have repeatedly been connected or combined in philosophy, and this makes sense when you think of mental imagery. What are those pictures we have in our heads? I can call forth an image of you at dinner last night or a visual memory of the house where I grew up. But I also have a picture of a character in my most recent novel – I see Harriet Burden working on a sculpture in her studio in Red Hook, Brooklyn. The first two images are from life, the last is from a work of fiction, but I do not think they are *qualitatively* different. In her remarkable book *The Art of Memory*, Frances Yates discusses *Ad Herrenium*, a book written by a scholar for his rhetoric students in 86–82 BC. Yates explains that the practitioner of artificial memory who wishes to remember a speech, moved through a real remembered architecture and sequentially populated the rooms with vivid emotionally potent images, usually human – beautiful, comic, grotesque, or obscene – which helped him remember the words, because, the ancient author points out, "[t]he things we easily remember when they are real we likewise remember when they are figments." Further, he writes, "[f]or the places are very much like wax tablets or papyrus, the images like the letters, the arrangement and disposition of the images like the script and the delivery is like the reading" (qtd. in Yates 1966: 26). The rhetorician uses mental images of places, which he populates with imaginary figures to remember his text.

Artificial memory is a conscious use of our imaginative abilities. Natural memory is also mutable and frequently fictive. We do not retrieve memories from a fixed storehouse in the mind. Our brains are, in fact, not computers that contain intact memories, as in Random-Access Memory. Long before neuroscience came to the conclusion that memory is constructive not reproductive, thinkers such as Wilhelm Wundt, William James, Sigmund Freud, and others argued against the notion of static preserved memories that can be retrieved on demand. Without being conscious of it, our autobiographical, or as scientists often call them, episodic memories are continually altered and recreated by the present in a process called reconsolidation. We do not recall an original memory but rather the last time we took it out for examination.

There is a lot of research on false memory, memory distortion, mis-recognition, and how one event often collapses into another to create a form of hybrid recollection. The same brain systems appear to be activated in both remembering and imagining. Recollecting oneself in the past and casting oneself as a character in the future belong to the same psychobiological processes. People who suffer memory loss from brain damage to the hippocampus are also poor at imagining detailed fictional scenarios. The scientists Daniel Schacter and Donna Rose Addis argue that our flawed, constructive, memory systems are actually adaptive because they are flexible rather than static and used to predict and anticipate what will happen to us through what has already happened to us. They write: "Thus a memory system that simply stored rote records of what happened in the past would not be well suited to simulating future events, which will probably share some similarities with past events while differing in other respects" (Shacter and Addis 2007: 207/776). Imagining oneself in the future is creating a personal fiction, a narrative of *what it might be like...*, which is a close relative to *what if...*, *I hope...*, and *I dread...* .

The writing of fiction clearly partakes of this geography of the potential, the land of play, daydreams, fantasy, and reverie, of wishes and fears. The activity that the psychologist Endel Tulving called time travel, locating the self in the past and imagining it in the future, is a function of reflective self-consciousness, the ability to represent and imagine one's self as another person. There is growing evidence that human beings aren't alone in this – dolphins, elephants, some primates, and birds can recognize themselves in the mirror and learn some forms of language, but our sophisticated linguistic capacities allow for a flowering of artistic and intellectual imaginative play that can't be found among other animals. Nevertheless, physiologically we have much in common with our rat cousins who are alive, alert and aware of their surroundings, who play and mate, and negotiate their environments through learning and memory. It would be interesting to know what mental imagery rats have. I suspect that they do not call up pictures in their minds of a great meal last Sunday or fantasize about one a week from now. And I can say with some confidence that my dog Jack, now dead, who spent many hours in a state of canine torpor, never once had an idea for a novel.

Sometimes a book begins with a feeling. My first novel *The Blindfold* was generated from an uncanny sensation I had felt during and after an encounter with a man who wanted me to write pornography for him. *The Enchantment of Lily Dahl* began with a true story I was told in my hometown about the twin brother of someone I knew. The twin walked into a café, ordered breakfast, ate it, took out a gun and blew his brains out in front of his fellow diners. It was a scene that haunted me. I saw it in my mind over and over. My novel *What I Loved* began with the cinematic mental image of a door opening onto a room. Inside the room was an obese woman lying on a bed, dead. *The Sorrows of an American* began with a recurring image of a girl sitting up in her coffin. The coffin was lying on a table in my grandparents' living room. *The Summer without Men* began with a sentence: "Sometime after he said the word pause, I went mad and landed in the hospital" (Hustvedt 2011a: 1). I found the sentence at once dark and funny and went on to write a comedy.

These anecdotes about beginnings, however, tell us only about consciousness, not unconsciousness. Why that sensation? Why that story about the twins, why those images, and why that sentence? Only the first is autobiographical in any genuine sense, and what I wanted to reproduce was not the incident but the feeling I had had. The twin's suicide was a dramatic story that stuck with me. The mental images seemed to come from nowhere, as did the sentence. This is why writers roll their eyes at the question: Where do you get your ideas? It is because it seems unanswerable. And yet, there are clearly unconscious processes that precede the idea, that are at work before it becomes conscious, work that is done subliminally in a way similar to both remembering and dreaming. Sometimes long after I have finished a book, I realize that I have snatched the voice of one person I know, taken the hairdo of another, and the vulnerability of a third to combine them in a single character. That mingling, however, like the condensations in dreams, had taken place without my knowing it.

I daydream about my characters. I listen to them talk before I go to sleep. When I'm stuck in a book, my effort to discover what should happen in the narrative is very much like trying to remember something that actually happened to me, but which I can't bring to light. I never feel there are a hundred possibilities. I feel there is one true event that must happen, and it must be recalled correctly and put into the book. The right solution is purely a matter of my feeling. It feels right, and I go from there. Once my characters have been born, they direct me. I have sometimes wanted to force them into situations, and they adamantly refuse. This has made me wonder about the connection between novel writing and what used to be called multiple personality disorder, now dissociative identity disorder. Obviously, the two phenomena are not the same. However real my characters may become to me as other selves, I am aware they are my creatures.

In "Evening Over Sussex: Reflections in a Motor Car," Virginia Woolf writes about the spectacle through the window, the colors and forms of the gloaming landscape. She feels the beauty, and she resists it. In a parenthesis, she writes, "[i]t is well known how in circumstances like these the self splits up and one self is eager and dissatisfied and the other stern and philosophical." More selves appear, but at the very end of the essay, she writes, "[o]ff with you, I said to my assembled selves. Your work is done. I dismiss you" (Woolf 1970: 9). The novelist may well have multiple selves, but usually they retire on demand.

Robert Louis Stevenson, a writer who dreamed the doubles "Jekyll and Hyde" and attended closely to the nighttime visits of his brownies, the little people who danced about in the theater of his head, for inspiration, asked the question I posed earlier. Why do some passages, some stories, some books feel wrong? "The trouble with 'Ollala'," he wrote to a friend, "is that it somehow sounds false [...] and I don't know why [...] I admire the style of it myself, more than is perhaps good for me; it is so solidly written. And that brings back (almost with the voice of despair) my unanswerable: Why is it false?" (qtd. in Balfour 1911: 19). I cannot answer for Stevenson. I can say that any number of well-written books feel false to me, that falseness has nothing to do with either good sentences or subject matter. Kafka's Gregor Samsa waking up as an insect and the terrible loneliness of Mary Shelley's monster are just as true as Tolstoy's evocation of Anna Karenina's ostracism or the grief of Wharton's Lily Bart in *The House of Mirth*, for whom the links in her bracelet have come to seem "like manacles chaining her to her fate" (Wharton 1911: 10).

Truth, that is, the kind of truth Stevenson refers to, is located elsewhere. I have written about this kind of fictional truth in an essay that was originally published in the journal *Neuropsychoanalysis* under the title "Three Emotional Stories: Reflections on Memory, the Imagination, Narrative, and the Self." It is republished in my collection of essays, *Living, Thinking, Looking*, without the subtitle, abstract, key words, and peer reviews. In the last line of the lopped off abstract, I write:

> Culling insights from Freud and research in neuroscience and phenomenology, I argue that a core bodily, affective, timeless self is the ground of the narrative, temporal self of autobiographical memory and of fiction and that the secret to creativity lies not in the so-called higher cognitive processes but in the dreamlike reconfigurations of emotional meanings that take place unconsciously. (Hustvedt 2011b: 187)

What does this mean? I cannot reproduce this tightly argued essay here, but I can say that I am interested in what happens underground, before an idea or picture or sentence surfaces. It is now a commonplace to say that most of what the brain does is unconscious, or non-conscious for those who want to avoid sounding Freudian. There are many debates about the exact nature of this subliminal reality, but no one is claiming any longer that it does not exist. Although much of a story may be created unconsciously, the writer's recognition that a story is right is consciously felt. Feelings are by their very nature conscious and serve as guides for our behavior, even when we have no idea why we have the feelings we have. I also stressed that it is important to remember that emotions can never be *unreal* even when they are triggered by fictions.

I used the Russian Formalist term *fabula* in "Three Emotional Stories" to describe what a writer draws upon for a book. The difference between the *fabula* and the *sujet* can be described simply as the difference between *what happens* in a story and *how it is told*. The Cinderella *fabula* is always the same; its *sujet*, on the other hand, has taken myriad forms. The *fabula* of a story feels to me as if it is already there in me, not yet known, but glimpsed as a kind of dream-like memory, part of the subliminal self, a thing that must either be dredged to the surface or unleashed in a great rush. The *sujet*, on the other hand, is often up for grabs. How to tell it? Who should tell it? These are often fully conscious decisions. And yet, it happens that parts of books or poems or entire works are written in trances. The underground pushes upward and appears fully formed to become Coleridge's "Kubla Khan" or Nietzsche's *Thus Spoke Zarathustra*. In his classic work on creativity (1952) that collects the accounts of many brilliant thinkers and artists, Brewster Ghiselin writes in his preface, "[p]roduction by a process of purely conscious calculation seems never to occur [...] automatism is reported by nearly every worker who has much to say about his processes, and no process has been demonstrated to be wholly free from it" (Ghiselin 1954: 15–16).

Countless writers, as well as mathematicians and physicists, have described sudden revelations that came to them in dreams, dream states, or in sudden rushes of inspiration. I have experienced periods of more or less automatic writing in my own work when a book appears to compose itself. It is exciting, and it only occurs in states of physical relaxation and mental openness to whatever comes along. It is a permissive, fearless state, in which one gains access to "stuff" one didn't know was there. The psychoanalyst Ernst Kris, who was interested in the making of art, understood this state as a powerful release of passion while the artist remained under the protection of "the aesthetic illusion" – words that suggest explosive creativity without ego disintegration (Kris 1952). The protection of the aesthetic illusion is no doubt also a way to articulate the vital barrier between the artist's multiple selves and the alters of a traumatized, dissociated patient.

The sudden release of a solution, formula, poem, or part of a novel from subliminal regions of a person, however, is dependent on what is *down there* (to use a metaphor suited to the subterranean), and the bulk of that material, I am convinced, is not produced by an *essential*, fixed self, nor does it come from some elusive quality of "genius." It is the accumulation of years of reading and thinking and living and feeling. It is the result of autobiography in the loosest sense – not as literal facts, but as the creation of a story that appears from a writer's depths and feels emotionally true to her. The story of Mary Shelley's monster expressed her own deep reality. In her preface to the novel she writes that the story poured out of her as in a waking dream. The lonely, vengeful monster is a product of her own emotional complexity, but it is also, and this is essential, the product of her reading of and love for John Milton.

Every good novel is written because it has to be written. The need to tell is compelling, and it is always directed at another, not a real other but an imagined other person. (In my case, the fantasy person is someone who gets all my jokes, references, puns, and has read every single book I have read. I have come to understand that, despite my great longing for this stranger, she or he does not exist.) Nevertheless, every work of fiction inhabits the realm of both "I" and "you" – on what I call the axis of discourse or in the between zone. Even journals and diaries are written at the very least for another self, perhaps the one who returns to the entries years later and is surprised.

That between zone is established long before we learn language in the back and forth gestural, musical, and tactile exchanges between our infant selves and, usually, our mothers. There is even a term used by scientists for the language people use to answer babies – *motherese* – which is not, of course, limited to mothers. This proto-conversation is, however, crucial to human sensory-motor-emotional-cognitive development. Through these early social interactions in combination with genetic temperament, a brain matures and a personality emerges. The rhythms of this back and forth dialogue create expectations in us about the responses of others to us, which undergird who we are and who we are still becoming, despite our total amnesia for that time of life. In *Philosophy in a New Key*, Susanne Langer writes, "there are certain aspects of so-called inner life – physical or mental – which have formal properties similar to those of music – patterns of motion and rest, of tension and release, or agreement and disagreement, proportion, fulfillment, sudden change, etc." (Langer 1979: 228). Langer's description of these aspects of inner life beautifully encapsulates the pulsing realities of narrative art. Meanings in a novel are not limited to dictionary definitions. They are also found in the muscular, sensory, emotional realities of the human body. And it is from these that we recognize the rights and wrongs of fiction. I know when I have hit the right story for myself, when there is no longer any need to change what I have done because the truth of the page is answered by a gut feeling inside me, which I rely upon absolutely.

The relatively new field of epigenetics is illustrative of the inside-outside drama that is part of how a human being becomes herself; our genes are mostly expressed through the environment, and studying that interaction, the two parts of which are not separable, but belong to a single process, is a way to better understand what the human organism is. No one becomes herself in isolation. We are beings embedded in a world. What we learn and master, whether it's riding a bike or reading or running complex machinery or how to solve an equation, the process swiftly becomes unconscious and automatic. We are creatures of perceptual habits and patterns and pay little attention when the world goes along as we expect it to. Those unconscious habits of mind include judgments, prejudices, beliefs, and ideas. There are hundreds of empirical studies on this subject. The unconscious is neither primitive nor unsophisticated; it is a repository of what is so deeply known we don't have to be conscious of it anymore.

Although novels may grow out of this vast underworld, when the book is finished, it is nothing but words. "Art," Susanne Langer wrote, "is the creation of forms symbolic of human feeling" (Langer 1953: 40). When you open a book, what you find inside it is only print. The joys and sorrows of the book's creator, her biography, her personal experiences of emotional truths, her rhythmic sense are there only in so far as they are *represented* by those little black letters on the page. The writer is not there. Her body is absent. And representation, by its very nature, is estranged from what is being represented. In speech and writing we alienate ourselves from ourselves even when we say "I" to indicate the self as speaker.

The reader animates a novel. Without a reader, the words lie inert on the page. The reader *feels* a work's meanings in his body, in the tension of his muscles as a scene develops toward crisis or, in their relaxation, when the same scene dissipates, and the character has survived. The reader brings his own memories, his mental pictures, with their peculiar architecture and landscapes to his reading. He brings his thoughts, as well as prejudices, limitations, and particular emotional tone to the text. Together reader and book form a collaboration of meanings, which have no objective reality, but create yet another between zone, an intersubjective exchange, which sometimes succeeds and sometimes fails. I recall stifling my fury when a well-known novelist sitting across from me at a dinner uttered these words: "Well, everyone knows Dostoyevsky is just no damn good." Recollecting myself in tranquility, I realized that Dostoyevsky is probably not for everyone, even though a part of me thinks his work should be universal. I also realized that this particular writer was so enamored of Nabokov that he had probably adopted his hero's literary views, which, in my opinion, were often egregious.

Such differences are usually understood as a matter of taste. A book that tastes good to you doesn't have the same flavor for me. Literature is not science; there are no experiments that can be run again and again to see if one gets the same results. Books are regularly pronounced good or bad in the newspapers, and this is why, with a couple of exceptions, I have stayed away from reviewing books. Even at its best, it is a superficial form and often inspires pettiness and easy cruelty. I fear my own prejudices as well, my own possible blindness to a great work of art. André Gide is famously credited with rejecting Proust, but Proust's housekeeper, Céleste Albaret, claimed that she and Proust suspected that Gide may never have even opened the manuscript (Albaret 2003: 183). This may be the worst literary mistake, not bothering to read a book because of some vague prejudice, which, like so much in our lives, is often unconscious.

We all have them, I'm afraid: "You mean that giggling girl over there with the low cut sweater and the beautiful breasts is doing her second post-doc at Rockefeller?"

Prejudices against women writers run deep, and yet, all novelists, male and female, are read by women far more than by men. My friend, Ian McKuen, once said, "[w]hen women stop reading, the novel will be dead" (McKuen 2005). I quote the ironic narrator of my novel, *The Summer without Men*, Mia Fredricksen, who has been making jokes about genitals and sexual difference throughout her tale:

> Lots of women read fiction. Most men don't. If a man opens a novel, he likes to have a masculine name on the cover; it's reassuring somehow. You never know what might happen to that external genitalia if you immerse yourself in imaginary doings concocted by someone with the goods on the inside. Moreover, men like to boast about their neglect of fiction: "I don't read fiction, but my wife does." (Hustvedt 2011a: 145–146)

In my experience, the line that follows, "I don't read fiction but my wife does," is: "Would you sign the book to her?" In other words, a novel can taste bad before it is eaten simply because it has been written by a woman. Of course I often wonder what those men are doing at my reading in the first place. Why didn't your wife come? When I published my first novel, an interviewer in Germany praised my text. He said it was brilliant and then added he did not believe I had written it. It was clearly the work of my husband. A young man, a writer himself, once said to me, "you know, you write like a man." He was not referring to the books I had written in the voice of a man, but to all of my work, and this statement was intended as a high compliment. Women are not immune to this prejudice either. A young woman once approached me at an art opening to say, "I never read books by women, but a friend of mine insisted I try one of yours, and I loved it!" I did not feel particularly grateful. A literary editor in New York, Chris Jackson, admitted rather sheepishly last year in a blog that he could not remember the last time he had read a novel by a woman (cf. Jackson 2010).

The work of the human imagination, it seems to me, is about becoming another, looking at the world from another perspective, even if, as in Proust, the writer becomes another Marcel, a kind of second literary self who narrates the story. But, for many of us, it means traveling farther, becoming a person of another sex or class or background or just someone funnier, tougher, and stranger than we are. I have argued that the multiple selves of an author's inner geography are created at the deep levels of her being, which includes the bodily music of her earliest forgotten interactions, as well as all the books she's read, the people she's loved and hated, and her memories, fantasies, hopes, and fears. Can we say then that the process of writing is fundamentally different for a woman than for a man? Is the question, "Why one story and not another?" bound to one's sex?

If we internalize the sexism of the world, and we all do, how can it be escaped? Do women inevitably write differently from men because they have different bodies, menstruate, and can, at least potentially, give birth to children? Is *Frankenstein* a womanly book and *A Portrait of a Lady* a manly one? Margaret Cavendish's works were viewed as so masculine in her time that many refused to believe she had written them. Even Virginia Woolf was unable to see Cavendish's genius. In "A Room of One's Own" she refers to the seventeenth-century writer as "a vision of loneliness and riot [...] as if some giant cucumber had spread itself over the roses and carnations in the garden and choked them to death" (Woolf 1929: 62). Should women writers follow the French feminist Hélène Cixous's famous exhortation in *The Laugh of the Medusa*: "woman must write her self" (Cixous 1976: 875)? She advises women to disrupt syntax itself and all the forms of language that have been created by a phallocentric, logocentric patriarchal world. But what does this really mean? Could I ever get all those great books written by men out of me even if I tried? I doubt it. Would I want to? Haven't I always felt that men and women are a lot more the same than they are different? Am I wrong? Don't I find male characters lurking in me all the time? Should I not write them, too? If I borrow the terms of our culture with its stark divisions between masculine and feminine, do I not have aspects of both? Should I deny my masculinity for my femininity? Can't I be at once feminine and masculine?

Or, more ominously, it is often claimed these days that the female sex is doomed to literary mediocrity for bio-evolutionary reasons. Indeed, everywhere I turn, I run into glib pronouncements such as the following from a book by Brian Boyd called *On the Origin of Stories: Evolution, Cognition, and Fiction*, published in 2009. Boyd tells his reader that because males have more "reproductive variance" than females, they have a stronger competitive drive. What this means is that while few females don't become mothers, some males may be so successful with females, they produce offspring right and left, which deprives other males of reproductive opportunity, hence increasing competition among the guys for the girls. For Boyd, this desire to dominate other males extends to the art of storytelling. "From a tribal storyteller or Homer to Shakespeare or Tolkien," men, Boyd claims, have an edge. They are so intent on winning, in fact, that they are more likely than women to "engage in extreme behaviors," which in turn explains why they are "overrepresented at both extremes – success and genius, as well as failure." "Despite Murasaki, Jane Austen, and J.K. Rowling," Boyd tells us, males outnumber females as classic and even popular storytellers [...] while at the other end of the spectrum, males outnumber females by more than four to one in autism, which corresponds highly with poor performance in social cognition and pretend play. But females, while they do not seek status as urgently as males, also invest more in child-rearing and are the principal tellers of fictional stories, of folk tales and nursery rhymes, to their children. (Boyd 2009: 195)

In other words, women's stories are suitable for nurturing the undeveloped minds of children within the confines of domestic life, but woe to those who venture outside it into the agonistic literary world of bruising masculine competition.

Boyd's breezy sexism is typical of evolutionary approaches to contemporary culture. This is not because Darwin was wrong or evolutionary considerations are unimportant – far from it – but rather because the simplistic yoking of male reproductive variance to the fact that there have been and perhaps still are more men making literature than women is little more than a "just so" story to explain, and I would add, justify, why things are the way they are. Boyd violates one of the primary rules of science, which is never to confuse correlation with cause. His blithe use of autism, the cause of which is unknown, is an indictment in itself. One can only wonder how Boyd explains why there are far more women writers now that women have access to higher education than there were when they did not? Even the most witless of these evolutionary psychologists usually recognize social differences in human societies and what a highly evolved and plastic neocortex (the most recently evolved part of our brains that continually changes in relation to the environment) has made possible in human beings. There are a thousand rebuttals to sloppy thinking of this kind, most of which come from within science itself, but that does not make the Boyds of this world any less numerous.

Bad thinkers, and they are legion, take a theoretical model, whether it's computational theory of mind or crude evolutionism, and squeeze all of life, literature, and the kitchen sink into it. It does not matter if they are scientists or English professors, they ask poor questions because they have assumed far too much already. Assumptions are, after all, unexamined answers. "Why one story and not another?" is at the least a good question. Obviously, being a woman has influenced the stories I tell. I am a daughter, a sister, a wife, and a mother, and these roles have shaped who I am and the geography of that subliminal psychobiological terrain I mine for my fiction, but my stories have also been molded by my quirky nervous system, my ranging intellectual passions, insatiable reading habits, and, Boyd notwithstanding, my rank ambition and iron will to master whatever ideas, be they scientific or literary, that come my way.

The great enemy of thought and creativity is the received idea. The writer who gets his material from the ready-made platitudes of contemporary culture, no matter how famous he is, is doomed to oblivion. And as readers, we must be careful about bringing those same platitudes to the books we read. They can make us blind. The great force of literature lies precisely in its evocation of the particular life and lives of human beings that we are able to experience intimately with the protection of the "aesthetic illusion." In reading a novel, as in writing one, we shift our perspective and enter the world of another person to travel with her or him for the duration of the book. The story's truth or falseness lies in a resonance that is not easily articulated, but it is one that lives between reader and text – and that resonance is at once sensual, rhythmic, emotional, and intellectual. And this is possible because we are not rats, but imaginative beings who can leap out of ourselves and, for a while, at least, become someone else, young or old, sane or mad, woman or man.

Works Cited

Albaret, Céleste. 2003. *Monsieur Proust*. Trans. Barbara Bray. New York: New York Review of Books.
Balfour, Graham. 1911. *The Life of Robert Louis Stevenson*. New York: Charles Scribner's Sons.
Boyd, Brian. 2009. *On the Origin of Stories: Evolution, Cognition, and Fiction*. Cambridge, MA: Harvard University Press.
Cavendish, Margaret. 1664. *Philosophical Letters*. London.
Cixous, Hélène. 1976. "The Laugh of the Medusa." Trans. Keith Cohen and Paula Cohen. *Signs* 1.4: 875–893.
Dufrenne, Mikel. 1973. *The Phenomenology of Aesthetic Experience*. Trans. Edward Casey. Evanston, IL: Northwestern University Press.
Ghiselin, Brewster. 1954. *The Creative Process: Reflections on Invention in the Arts and Sciences*. Berkeley: University of California Press.
Hobbes, Thomas. 2012. *Leviathan*. London: The Folio Society.
Hustvedt, Siri. 2010. *The Shaking Woman, or, A History of My Nerves*. New York: Picador.
Hustvedt, Siri. 2011a. *The Summer without Men*. New York: Picador.
Hustvedt, Siri. 2011b. "Three Emotional Stories: Reflections on Memory, the Imagination, Narrative, and the Self." *Neuropsychoanalysis* 13.2: 187–196.
Jackson, Chris. 2010. "All the Sad Young Literary Women," *The Atlantic* August 20. <http://www.theatlantic.com/entertainment/archive/2010/08/all-the-sad-young-literary-women/61821/> [accessed December 2014].
Kris, Ernst. 1952. *Psychoanalytic Explorations in Art*. New York: International Universities Press.
Langer, Susanne. 1953. *Feeling and Form: A Theory of Art*. New York: Charles Scribners' Sons.
Langer, Susanne. 1979. *Philosophy in a New Key: A Study in the Symbolism of Reason, Rite, and Art*. Cambridge, MA: Harvard University Press.
McKuen, Ian. 2005. "Hello, Would You Like a Free Book?" *The Guardian*, September 20.

Schacter, Daniel and Donna Rose Addis. 2007. "The Cognitive Neuroscience of Constructive Memory: Remembering the Past and Imagining the Future." *Philosophical Transactions of the Royal Society, Biological Sciences* 362.1481: 773–786.
Wharton, Edith. 1911. *House of Mirth*. New York: Charles Scribners' Sons.
Woolf, Virginia. 1929. *A Room of One's Own*. New York: The Fountain Press.
Woolf, Virginia. 1970. *The Death of the Moth, and Other Essays*. San Diego: Harcourt Brace & Co.
Yates, Frances. 1966. *The Art of Memory*. Harmondsworth, Middlesex: Penguin.

Gabriele Rippl
The Rich Zones of Genre Borderlands: Siri Hustvedt's Art of Mingling

1. Introduction: Beyond Postmodernism

This essay investigates Siri Hustvedt's negotiations with genre and genre boundaries in her novels. The blurring of genre boundaries is commonly considered as a typical feature of postmodernist fiction, and Hustvedt's novels have often been discussed within the postmodernist frame. Due to the novelist's indefatigable interest in topics such as the personal, the relational self, and intersubjective bonding, the postmodernist label of her works is becoming, however, increasingly questionable. Debates on American literature have recently announced the emergence of 'post-postmodernism' (Wallace 1993; Robert L. McLaughlin 2004; cf. Rippl 2013 for a detailed discussion) and the return of a 'new realism' (Rebein 2001; cf. also Claviez and Moos 2004). Nicoline Timmer (2010) describes this new aesthetics as one that goes beyond the cerebral character of postmodernist art by stressing ethical responsibility, affect, sincerity, and authenticity, thus embracing a fresh engagement with the real. The recent efforts of American novelists to communicate with the reader allow for communal bonding, emotional intensity, and mutuality, and leave exclusively self-reflexive, self-referential, ironic, metafictional strategies behind:

> [W]e can detect an incentive to move beyond what is perceived as a debilitating way of framing what it means to be human: the postmodern perspective on subjectivity. Most notable in the work of th[e] younger generation of writers is the emphatic expression of feelings and sentiments, a drive towards inter-subjective connection and communication [...]. Their texts perform a complicit and complicated critique on certain aspects of postmodern subjectivity, especially on the perceived solipsistic quality of the subjective postmodern experience world, and envision possible reconfigurations of subjectivity that can no longer be framed, I believe, as 'postmodern.' (Timmer 2010: 13)

Rebelling against the first generation of postmodernists and the sarcasm, cynicism, and irony which permeate their works, this new generation of writers "re-humanize[s] subjectivity" (Timmer 2010: 18 and passim). Recent historical events such as the 9/11 terrorist attacks on the World Trade Center have functioned as turning points in the intellectual debate, "marking a change in how we think of our 'selves,' our identity, and in how we interpret our experience world" (Timmer 2010: 16–17). Likewise, emphatic feelings (and not merely cognition) and a "restructuring of 'affect'" (Timmer 2010: 44) are highly relevant in fiction today, as are "other aspects of subjectivity, most notably the *interpersonal* construction of a sense of self," its sociality and connectivity (Timmer 2010: 22).

This short excursion into recent literary and cultural debates on American literature of the twenty-first century demonstrates that the changes in contemporary aesthetics – which include a concept of the self as relational – are important also for our discussion of Hustvedt's work. Interested in questions of consciousness and the linkage between mind and body, psyche and soma,[1] Hustvedt has declared herself "intellectually and emotionally dissatisfied with the airy postmodern subjects that seem never to put their feet on the ground" (Hustvedt 2013a: 118). She is equally unhappy about what analytical philosophy offers to explain human consciousness, which explains why she has come to privilege a phenomenological approach that bridges the psyche-soma ditch by seeing the personal corporeal perspective as crucial to the human experience and psyche. According to Hustvedt, the complex socio-psycho-biological model of self cannot be discussed within neat divisions and boundaries of disciplines, but needs borderlands as contact zones (cf. Pratt 1992) where boundaries are blurred and identities are hybridized:

> In my discussion of subjectivity, intersubjectivity, and objectivity [...] I have actively worked to blur hard and fast borders. My intention is not to turn all thought to mush, but rather to create zones of focused ambiguity, to insist that 'diverse points of view' when examining the same object are not optional but necessary. For me ambiguity is a rich not an impoverished concept. (Hustvedt 2013a: 132)

One example of Hustvedt's philosophy of mingling is her neurological memoir, *The Shaking Woman, or, A History of My Nerves* (2010), which assembles discourses of neurology, psychoanalysis and life-writing. The manner in which Hustvedt, the critic and intellectual, engages in today's academic debates on subjectivity, intersubjectivity, and objectivity, is also relevant for her art of fiction

---

[1] "In a world of hermetically isolated disciplines in which knowledge accumulates at a spectacular rate, and people know more and more about less and less, interdisciplinary conversation is no longer a luxury but a necessity. [...] The old separation of body and mind, psyche and soma continues to haunt us. This is a root issue, one that travels underground and interferes with our understanding of essential questions. Rampant philosophical naiveté in the so-called hard sciences and total ignorance of the biological body (as opposed to a constructed ideological one) in the humanities has created two deep but narrow ditches stretching ahead to nowhere. Dynamic narratives of subjective experience must modify the objective and mostly static theoretical models of science. In turn, the humanities can no longer afford to pretend that bodies are made entirely of words." (Hustvedt 2013b: 547 and 549)

that blurs boundaries demarcating literary genres from other literary genres and from non-literary ones. In what follows I scrutinize Hustvedt's juxtaposing and mixing of different genres and her nesting and braiding of multiple discourses of personal experience, philosophy, neuroscience and neurobiology, psychology, psychoanalysis and art history in her narrative fiction. Moreover, I ask about the specific functions of her intergeneric, interdisciplinary, and intermedial approach, which plays with the readers' genre expectations and habitual organization of knowledge. In her 2013 article "Borderlands: First, Second, and Third Person Adventures in Crossing Disciplines," Hustvedt states:

> Every theoretical construct, every system of ideas, every intellectual map created to explain us human beings is vulnerable at the site of incision – the place where we sever one thing from another. Without such dissections, there can be no formal thought, no discrete disciplines, no articulations of human experience. [...] For many years now, I have found my mental life parsed in multiple ways for the simple reason that I have been immersed in disciplines, which not only have distinct vocabularies, but may rest on different paradigms and employ different methodologies for understanding the big question I care most about: *What are we?* [...] Rules of knowing – how we can know what we know – lie beneath every edifice we call a discipline, and that knowing turns on perspective, first or third person, as well as notions of what is hard and soft. What is certain is that if we want to do the interdisciplinary dance, we must dislodge ourselves from a fixed place and begin to jump across borders and adopt alien views. (Hustvedt 2013a: 111–112)

While the (supposedly) objective third-person truth of the 'hard' sciences is commonly seen as opposed to the subjective first-person view of artistic truth, it is Hustvedt's project to bring the different discourses together in her novels. By mixing and 'dialogizing' the genre of narrative fiction with those of life-writing, ekphrasis, poetry, and drama, and by including excerpts from articles written in the 'objective' field of the life sciences, psychoanalytical material, and contributions from art historians, Hustvedt's literary texts are the summation of literary, scholarly, and scientific discourses and hence prime examples of genre juxtaposition and genre blending, i.e. of a successful bridging of the divide between the subjective and the objective.

2. Genre Theory: Genre Purity to Genre Hybridity

To discuss Hustvedt's practice of genre blurring, it is necessary to take a look at recent debates in the field of genre theory. The term 'genre' is derived from the biological term *genus*, and refers to a group of literary works that "share significant characteristics in terms of content, form and/or function" (Basseler and Nünning 2011: 12). Generic features and genre conventions help literary scholars to classify works, through which authors can guide the recipients' expectations; they are "a set of cues guiding our reading of texts" (Frow 2006: 4). While 'genre' is a "universal dimension of textuality" (Frow 2006: 2), over time genre theorists have conceptualized this "universal dimension" in many different ways. Plato and Aristotle distinguished three literary types, namely epic, lyric, and dramatic; later, during the Renaissance and Neoclassicism, genre theorists favored generic hierarchies and understood genres as fixed and pure literary classifications. When the novel entered the stage in the late seventeenth/early eighteenth century and writers started to incorporate forms such as the letter and the diary in their texts, a parodying and blending/hybridizing of genres was established, and prescriptive and classificatory approaches to genre became increasingly hard to maintain (cf. Kearns 2008: 202). In the 1980s, scholars began to criticize the strong focus on genre classification and the deductive approaches to literary genres based on *a priori* definitions that went with it. As a result, inductive approaches based on description rather than prescription, on flexible definitions and on genre boundaries as elastic and porous (Friedman 1989: 16–17, 21–23) took over.[2]

Today literary genres are no longer conceived as essential, fixed, and stable 'types' or 'classes,' but as arbitrary modes of classification, as conventions structuring our experience of reality or as cognitive categories.[3] For Michael Kearns genre theory "reflects one of the fundamental realities of human cognition and communication: we understand and refer to phenomena by comparing them to existing categories and if necessary by modifying the categories or creating new ones" (Kearns 2008: 201). As Frow states, "genres actively generate and shape knowledge of the world" (Frow 2006: 2). As "a set of conventional and highly organized constraints on the production and interpretation of meaning," genres create "effects of reality and truth, authority and plausibility, which are central to the different ways the world is understood" (Frow 2006: 10).

This survey has shown that, according to modern genre theory, genres are, first of all, pragmatic constructs that are based on social, socio-cultural, and literary consensus (cf. Vosskamp 2000: 256), and, secondly, only in theory "there is a system of distinct genres and types": in fact "the different kinds of texts actually form a continuum, with permeable and often blurred boundaries between the various categories" (Basseler and Nünning 2011: 13). In the field of genre research, few scholars have worked on blurred boundaries of genres. Alistair Fowler is one of them. He argues for looser genre categories which take into account

---

[2] For an overview of genre theory in the twentieth century, cf. Duff 2000.
[3] For different conceptualizations of genre, cf. Neumann and Nünning 2007: 11–15.

the historical flexibility of genres and differentiates between types of genre changes, among them (a) "aggregation" – an additive process, whereby "several complete short works are grouped in an ordered collection"; Fowler's example is Boccaccio's *Decameron*, which "represents a different genre from that of the tales it orders" (Fowler 1982: 171–172); (b) "inclusion" – "a literary work may enclose another within it. If the inset form then becomes conventionally linked with the matrix, a generic transformation has taken place" (Fowler 1982: 179; Fowler's example is *The Faerie Queen*, which contains "inset triumphal pageants, tapestry poems [...]," 179); and (c) "hybrid" – in the hybrid, the "most obvious form of generic mixture [...], two or more complete repertoires are present in such proportions that no one of them dominates" (Fowler 1982: 183); one of Fowler's examples is the Renaissance sonnet, which often includes an epigram.

Another important scholar is Mikhail Bakhtin, whose analyses of novelistic prose and the resulting concepts of dialogism, polyphony, polyphonic heterogeneity, and heteroglossia have heavily influenced the way critics have discussed the hybridization of genres over the last few decades. In his *Problems of Dostoevsky's Poetics* (1929), Bakhtin characterizes Dostoevsky's poetics as having space for several dialogical voices and consciousnesses where no voice or consciousness dominates the others. Bakhtin's theory of 'dialogical imagination' and his dialogical model of self-consciousness also formed the theoretical basis of Siri Hustvedt's PhD research on Charles Dickens (cf. Marks 2014: 41–45) and inspired her conceptualizations of the relational self, but also her experiments with genre boundaries.

The category of hybrid genres in particular has recently received much attention. According to Christin Galster, hybrid genres are genres that have a mixed character; the term 'hybrid genre' is used

> to designate works of art which transgress genre boundaries by combining characteristic traits and elements of diverse literary and non-literary genres. [...] Although hybrid genres are highly innovative and contribute significantly to the development of novel forms of art, little sustained effort has been made to discuss the impact of generic crossings or to systematise their recent proliferation. (Galster 2008: 227)

Galster suggests reading the history of the novel in terms of hybridity and homogeneity, "with decidedly hybrid beginnings in the seventeenth and eighteenth-centuries (sic), a strong move towards homogenisation in the nineteenth-century (sic), and a similarly strong move towards hybridisation in the late twentieth century" (Galster 2008: 227). Leslie Marmon Silko's *Storyteller* (1981) as well as Adam Thorpe's *Ulverton* (1992) are often used as examples of late twentieth-century genre hybridisation in narrative fiction because they

> combine, transform, and subvert the conventions of several narrative sub-genres; break down the boundaries between fiction, poetry, and drama; import non-literary discourses and text-types; and employ narrative strategies that strive to imitate the organising principles of painting, music, and film. Hybrid narratives can be interspersed with short stories or fairy tales, poetry or drama; they confront the reader with scientific treatises, courtroom testimonies, film scripts, or cooking recipes. By transgressing genre boundaries, hybrid genres aim at distancing themselves from the homogeneous, one-voiced, and 'one-discoursed' worldview conventional narratives seem to suggest, a notion which is closely related to Bakhtin's concept of the dialogic imagination. Moreover, hybrid genres are intricately linked to the notion of hybrid identity, which is fluid, unstable, incessantly in search of and transforming itself. Due to their complex *gestalt*, hybrid genres are best approached with the help of theories of genre, hybridity, intermediality, and intertextuality. (Galster 2008: 227)

Although Galster has developed her list of features describing genre hybridization in connection with Silko and Thorpe, it clearly also applies to Hustvedt's novels. In spite of the fact that all hybrid novels do not conform to systematic genre concepts and neat taxonomies, generic 'mingling' – to use Hustvedt's own term (cf. two quotes below) – has had a long history; after all, hybridization allows for reinvigoration and further development of genres in general. Nevertheless, the blurring of genres has increased in the latter part of the twentieth century and is considered – as Linda Hutcheon also points out – a constitutive feature of postmodernist art practices:

> Postmodernism is a contradictory cultural enterprise, one that is heavily implicated in that which it seeks to contest. It [...] installs and only then subverts the conventions of genre. [...] [G]eneric blurring has been a feature of literature back to the classical epic and the Bible [...], but the simultaneous assertion and crossing of boundaries is more postmodern. (Hutcheon 1989: 55)

The juxtaposition and hybridization of genres can thus be seen as ways of translating "knowing into telling," as the "enabling conditions of possibility of sense-making" (Hutcheon 1989: 69–70). But although postmodernist critics talk about genre hybridization and "praised it as one of [postmodernism's] liberating forces, there are still, after some decades, no systematic approaches to the phenomenon" (Seibel 2007: 137).

3. The Novel as Hybrid: *The Sorrows of an American* (2008) – *The Summer without Men* (2011) – *The Blazing World* (2014)

In 2009, Siri Hustvedt discussed the generic nature of the novel:

> The novel is a chameleon. That is its glory as a genre. It can be an enormous waddling monster or a fast, lean sprite. It can take everything in or leave most things out. It is Tolstoy and Beckett. There are no rules for writing novels. Those who believe there are rules are pedants and poseurs and do not deserve a minute of our time. Modes of writing and various schools come and go: Grub Street, Naturalism, the nouveau roman, magical realism. The novel remains. The modern novel was born a hybrid, to borrow the Russian theorist M. M. Bakhtin's word for the genre's mingling, contradictory voices that shout and murmur from every level and corner of society. (Hustvedt 2009)

The inclusion, juxtaposition, aggregation, hybridization, and mingling of genres is a conspicuous feature in each of Hustvedt's six novels: The short story is an important ingredient in *The Blindfold* (1992), drama plays a major role in *The Enchantment of Lily Dahl* (1996), and poetry figures large in *What I Loved* (2003). But in her three later novels, *The Sorrows of an American* (2008), *The Summer without Men* (2011) and *The Blazing World* (2014), genre hybridization reaches a new level.

In *The Sorrows of an American* Hustvedt discusses, in addition to desire, memory formation, loss, grief, and trauma induced by the 9/11 terrorist attacks. She does so by inserting and including poetry as well as references to and excerpts from biographical, medical, neuro-/psychological and philosophical discourses. The novel engages with the traumatic events suffered by its disoriented characters – an engagement which leads to discontinuity and fragmentation of the narrative genre of the novel. Sonia Blaustein, one of the novel's protagonists, suffers from post-traumatic stress disorder (PTSD), having personally witnessed the fall of the Twin Towers and the death jump of victims. After 9/11 she starts to write lacunary poems characterized by missing stanzas: "There's supposed to be one about September eleventh next, but I haven't been able to write it. I've tried over and over again, but it's too hard. Maybe I'll just have a blank there – a nothing, a big empty spot with only the date" (Hustvedt 2008: 127; cf. also 189). These textual gaps stand for the "unspeakable images" and the "internal crack" they have opened in Sonia (230). In order to deal with personal and collective traumas, Hustvedt opts for a disarranged chronology, introduces various narrative strings and voices, foregoes a chapter structure, and works with repetitions. In addition to Sonia Blaustein's poems, Hustvedt includes lines from John Clare's and Lewis Carroll's poetry (142 and 144) as well as fragmented passages and sentences, ekphrases of drawings and photographs, the descriptions of dreams, newspaper articles (171), letters (e.g. lines from one of Rilke's letters, 219) and excerpts from medical reports, and psychological and psychiatric discourses. The novel also incorporates references to and summaries of the notebook entries of Sonia's uncle, Erik Davidsen, the psychologist/psychiatrist-narrator of the novel. What is more, Hustvedt uses portions of her father's memoir – Lloyd Hustvedt, who died in 2003 – as a fictional memoir of Erik Davidsen's father (Hustvedt 2008: "Acknowledgments," 306). The passages taken from Lloyd Hustvedt's memoir are set in italics to differentiate them from the rest of the text. The different fonts as well as the indentations set these passages apart instead of incorporating them into the novel, hence exposing their alterity. Thus Hustvedt's poetics does not gloss over the sutures between the genres but exhibits them.

This is also the case in *The Summer without Men*, a novel about the poet-narrator Mia Fredricksen, who learns after thirty years of marriage that her husband, a world-renowned neuroscientist, leaves her for a much younger Frenchwoman. After a breakdown and a period in a psychiatric ward, Mia leaves New York to spend the summer in the prairie town of her childhood where her mother lives in an old people's home. Again, Hustvedt incorporates poems in her novel: poems by canonical authors which often express the protagonist's anguish and sorrow in a condensed and deeply emotional way, for instance in the case of Emily Dickinson's poem No. 193 (Hustvedt 2011: 6); there are poems by the poet-narrator, (7, 24, 42); poems by Lewis Carroll (14); John Clare's poem "I am" (31–32); Henry Wadsworth Longfellow's (51) and D. H. Lawrence's poetry (62) as well as Thomas Traherne's (136–137); and also poems written by the pupils of the protagonist's summer poetry workshop (49, 77). In addition, she includes her own line drawings (5, 59, 97, 175); long passages from her protagonist's notebook (22–23) and sex journal (52); letters to and from the protagonist as well as e-mail messages with an 'epistolary dialogue' (24–25, 39–40, 45, 54, 96, 131, 138–139, 140, 144, 153, 173–174); ekphrases of handicrafts created by a friend of the narrator's mother (35–36, 66–67, 162); passages on philosophy and neuroscience (60, 79, 98) and many intermedial references to film (e.g. 17, 181). As in *The Sorrows of an American*, the polyphony of voices and genres is exhibited by setting passages such as the poems apart from the rest of the text.

In her latest novel, *The Blazing World* (2014), this aesthetics of generic juxtaposing and hybridity is showcased even more strongly. Hustvedt's central thematic concern is the suffocating gender roles which straightjacket women, hindering them from developing their creativity. The novel's female protagonist is Harriet Burden, whose brilliant but unsuccessful attempts at gaining recognition for her provocative and daring installations fail in New York's male-dominated, misogynist, vain, and money-driven art world until she conceals her female identity behind three male fronts (i.e. three male artists who pretend to be the creators of her installations). On many occasions Burden refers to Margaret Cavendish, Duchess of Newcastle, as a rich source of inspiration. The title of Hustvedt's novel evokes this seventeenth-century British aristocrat's prose work *The Blazing World* (1666), which is considered the forerunner of science fiction in English. To date, *The Blazing World* is Hustvedt's formally most daring work. Hustvedt's poetics is evident from the novel's cover of the first (hardcover as well as paperback) edition by Simon & Schuster in 2014: It shows torn pieces of red paper (or maybe canvas) which have been reassembled to form the background for the novel's title and genre designation ("a novel"). The individual paper scraps do not hide their fragmented nature and thus figure as a perfect image for Hustvedt's intricate novelistic technique with its scrapbook, collage-like character: The novel consists of a polyphonic spectrum of voices and incorporates a variety of genres which are barely stitched together. The structure is one of a book within a book; the novel does not simply unfold from the start: first there is an "Editor's Introduction," the editor being the fictive professor of aesthetics, I. V. Hess. Hess has gathered Harriet Burden's hundreds of pages of posthumous diaries and notebooks full of ekphrases, references to and discussions of artists, philosophers (phenomenologists in particular), psychologists and neurologists which he carefully edits with many scholarly footnotes. His publication also includes magazine clippings, written statements, edited transcripts, mock interviews with Burden's friends, enemies, family members (her daughter Maisie, a documentary filmmaker, and her son Ethan, an eccentric writer) and gallery owners, all of which are reminiscent of Bakhtin's carnivalesque and polyphonic, multi-perspective novelistic universes.

In his insightful analysis of W.G. Sebald's generically 'unclassifiable' or rather 'multi-classifiable' work, Simon Cooke has recently contended that this work is "also quintessentially intermedial, woven through with photographs and other visual materials so endemically that even so non-descript a term as 'writing' is too inelastic to capture their basic form" (Cooke 2007: 235). This also holds true for Siri Hustvedt's fiction with its plethora of genres and rich literary visuality. In all her novels, Hustvedt uses intermedial strategies such as ekphrasis, a literary mode or genre with roots in Greek antiquity (cf. Rippl 2015). 'Notional ekphrases,' i.e. descriptions of fictional paintings and photographies, are central in Hustvedt's novels, lending them a striking visual quality (cf. Hartmann 2016; Hustvedt 2005; Grønstad 2012). Her novels *The Sorrows of an American* (2008), *The Summer without Men* (2011), and *The Blazing World* (2014) are again highly visual and intermedial (*The Summer without Men*, for instance, includes four line drawings by Hustvedt), and in all three novels Hustvedt makes copious use of ekphrasis. This underlines how important Hustvedt considers visual works of art and visual media in general to be in our life-world and relational identity formations, which she discusses with respect to her protagonists and their involvements with works of art (cf. Marks 2014: 67–129; Zapf 2008).

4. Conclusion

A wide range of reasons for and functions of Hustvedt's genre experiments exist: Firstly, her mingling of genres corresponds to more general features of cultural context of her novels: Genre blurring and the increased employment of intermedial strategies (ekphrases, included drawings, etc.) are recurring characteristics in many contemporary literary texts. Secondly, Hustvedt's genre juxtaposing and mixing are the formal equivalents of her negotiation of the boundaries of the self, i.e. her notion of relational subjectivity and intersubjectivity. As we have seen, for Hustvedt identity is grounded in embodied material existence, and identity formation conceived as a relational process and complex product of conscious and unconscious interconnections with the environment – social, cultural, and biological (cf. Marks 2014: 5). To transfer her relational selves into written form, new modes of literary storytelling are needed, since the associative workings of the human mind and memory which interest Hustvedt cannot be incorporated without the playful and creative adaptation of formal and generic features of the novel. Hustvedt's art of fiction with its genre experimentation is heavily influenced by Bakhtin's concept of the dialogical imagination: She insists "on not compartmentalizing what is shared within one consciousness" and on not delimiting what is linked (Cooke 2007: 241). Hence, Hustvedt's "narrative approach – this weaving together the seemingly heterogeneous and disparate without regard for conventional disciplinary or generic boundaries" (Cooke 2007: 248) can thus be read as the formal expression of the writer's thematic preoccupations. There is, however, one additional and, indeed, important reason for Hustvedt's lack of generic coherence and the fact that the different generic components are barely stitched together: This technique is her literary response to traumatic experience which haunts many of her novels: "The adoption of a coherent generic form is to distance oneself from the inchoate experience of trauma itself; in this, genre is to experience what history is to memory: an intelligible but ultimately distancing and artificial adaptation" (Cooke 2007: 240). Confronting her readers in her hybrid novels with the different forms of knowledge generated by the various mixed genres, she plays with their expectations and allows them to question their habitual organization of knowledge, hence to perceive the (fictional) world in a fresh way that transgresses conventional homogeneous and one-voiced ways of fictional world-making. By keeping the genre boundaries visible Hustvedt simultaneously asserts and crosses them, thus creating relational borderlands, "zones of focused ambiguity."

Works Cited

Bakhtin, Michail. 1981. *The Dialogic Imagination: Four Essays by M. M. Bakhtin*. Ed. Michael Holquist. Trans. Caryl Emerson and Michael Holquist. Austin: University of Texas Press.

Bakhtin, Michail. 1984. *Problems of Dostoevsky's Poetics*. Ed. and trans. Caryl Emerson. Minneapolis: University of Minnesota Press.

Basseler, Michael and Ansgar Nünning (eds.). 2011. *A History of the American Short Story*. Trier: WVT.

Claviez, Thomas and Maria Moos (eds.). 2004. *Neorealism – Between Innovation and Continuation*. Amerikastudien/American Studies 49.1. Heidelberg: Winter.

Cooke, Simon. 2007. "'Always Somewhere Else': Generic 'Unclassifiability' in the Work of W.G. Sebald." In: Marion Gymnich, Birgit Neumann and Ansgar Nünning (eds.). *Gattungstheorie und Gattungsgeschichte*. Trier: WVT. 235–252.

Duff, David (ed.). 2000. *Modern Genre Theory*. Harlow: Longman.

Fowler, Alistair. 1982. *The Kinds of Literature: An Introduction to the Theory of Genres and Modes*. Oxford: Clarendon Press.

Friedman, Norman. 1989. "Recent Short Story Theories: Problems of Definition." In: Susan Lohafer and Jo Ellyn Clarey (eds.). *Short Story Theory at a Crossroads*. Baton Rouge/London: Louisiana State University Press. 13–31.

Frow, John. 2006. *Genre*. The New Critical Idiom. London/New York: Routledge.

Galster, Christin. 2008. "Hybrid Genres." In: David Herman, Manfred Jahn and Marie-Laure Ryan (eds.). *The Routledge Encyclopedia of Narrative Theory*. London/New York: Routledge. 226–227.

Grønstad, Asbjørn. 2012. "Ekphrasis Refigured: Writing Seeing in Siri Hustvedt's *What I Loved*." *Mosaic* 45.3: 33–48.

GXB – Genre Across Borders: An International, Interdisciplinary Network of Reseachers, Theories, and Resources. 2012. <http://genreacrossborders.org> [accessed 22 February 2015].

Hartmann, Johanna. 2016. *Literary Visuality in Siri Hustvedt's Works*. Würzburg: Königshausen & Neumann.

Hustvedt, Siri. 2005. *Mysteries of the Rectangle*. New York: Princeton Architectural Press.

Hustvedt, Siri. 2008. *The Sorrows of an American*. London: Sceptre.

Hustvedt, Siri. 2009. "Playing, Wild Thoughts, and a Novel's Underground." November 20. <http://sirihustvedt.net/2009/11/playing-wild-thoughts-and-a-novel's-underground/> [accessed 17 February 2015].

Hustvedt, Siri. 2011. *The Summer without Men*. London: Hodder & Stoughton.

Hustvedt, Siri. 2013a. "Borderlands: First, Second, and Third Person Adventures." In: Alfred Hornung (ed.). *American Lives*. Heidelberg: Winter. 111–135.

Hustvedt, Siri. 2013b. "Life Writing and Life Sciences – A Path between Ditches?" In: Alfred Hornung (ed.). *American Lives*. Heidelberg: Winter. 547–549.

Hustvedt, Siri. 2014. *The Blazing World*. New York: Simon & Schuster.

Hutcheon, Linda. 1989. "'The Pastime of Past Time': Fiction, History, Historiographic Metafiction." In: Marjorie Perloff (ed.). *Postmodern Genres*. Norman/London: University of Oklahoma Press. 54–74.

Kearns, Michael. 2008. "Genre Theory in Narrative Studies." In: David Herman, Manfred Jahn and Marie-Laure Ryan (eds.). *The Routledge Encyclopedia of Narrative Theory*. London/New York: Routledge. 201–205.

Marks, Christine. 2014. *"I am because you are": Relationality in the Works of Siri Hustvedt*. Heidelberg: Winter.

McLaughlin, Robert L. 2004. "Post-Postmodern Discontent: Contemporary Fiction and the Social World." *Symploke* 12.1–2: 53–68.

Neumann, Birgit and Ansgar Nünning. 2007. "Probleme, Aufgaben und Perspektiven der Gattungstheorie und Gattungsgeschichte." In: Marion Gymnich, Birgit Neumann and Ansgar Nünning (eds.). *Gattungstheorie und Gattungsgeschichte*. Trier: WVT. 1–28.

Pratt, Mary Louise. 1992. *Imperial Eyes: Travel Writing and Transculturation*. London: Routledge.

Rebein, Robert. 2001. *Hicks, Tribes, and Dirty Realists: American Fiction after Postmodernism*. Lexington: The University Press of Kentucky.

Rippl, Gabriele. 2013. "Introduction: Towards a New Monumentalism." In: Gabriele Rippl (ed.). *Anglia: Journal of English Philology*. Special issue *Towards a New Monumentalism? Cultural and Aesthetic Perspectives beyond Postmodernism*, Anglia 131/2+3: 207–217.

Rippl, Gabriele (ed.). 2015. *Handbook of Intermediality*. Berlin/Boston: De Gruyter.

Seibel, Klaudia. 2007. "Mixing Genres: Levels of Contamination and the Formation of Generic Hybrids." In: Marion Gymnich, Birgit Neumann and Ansgar Nünning (eds.). *Gattungstheorie und Gattungsgeschichte*. Trier: WVT. 137–150.

Timmer, Nicoline. 2010. *Do You Feel It Too? The Post-Modern Syndrome in American Fiction at the Turn of the Millenium*. New York: Rodopi.

Vosskamp, Wilhelm. 2000. "Gattungen." In: Helmut Brackert and Jörn Stückrath (eds.). *Literaturwissenschaft: Ein Grundkurs*. Reinbek bei Hamburg: Rowohlt. 253–268.

Wallace, David Foster. 1993. "E Unibus Pluram: Television and U.S. Fiction." *Review of Contemporary Fiction* 13.2: 151–194.

Zapf, Hubert. 2008. "Narrative, Ethics, and Postmodern Art in Siri Hustvedt's *What I Loved*." In: Astrid Erll, Herbert Grabes and Ansgar Nünning (eds.). *Ethics in Culture: The Dissemination of Values through Literature and Other Media*. Berlin/New York: De Gruyter. 171–194.

Diana Tappen-Scheuermann
Reality Bites:
Fractured Narrative and Author-Reader Interaction in Siri Hustvedt's Work

"From this point forth, we shall be leaving the firm foundation of fact and journeying together through the murky marshes of memory into thickets of wildest guesswork" (Rowling 2005: 187). One of the more fictitious aspects in J.K. Rowling's novel *Harry Potter and the Half-Blood Prince* is probably the idea that any wizard can retrieve a memory in its historically accurate form. What Professor Dumbledore considers 'murky' is therefore not so much the unreliability of a subjective memory, but rather the irksome circumstance that he is not in possession of the ones he needs in order to reconstruct Lord Voldemort's – the villain of the Harry Potter series – life story. In the magical world he belongs to, a memory can take shape in a material form mirroring what actually and precisely happened – an idea many people with fewer magical skills seem to share not only in the Harry Potter books. Less fantastical seems to be, however, the idea to lie about what presumably happened. Another professor of Harry Potter tries to conceal the actual event by manipulating his recollections, showing how well aware of a memory's power he is.

In spite of Dumbledore's condescension to such a creative use of memory, Siri Hustvedt – in line here with contemporary neuroscience – doubts that memory is anything *but* fiction: "The public outrage over memoirs that are actually fictions suggests that the contract implied by a work of nonfiction is still in effect, despite the fact that many memoirists seem to be equipped with supernatural abilities for recalling the past" (Hustvedt 2012d: 95). Hustvedt alludes to the controversy over James Frey's memoir *A Million Little Pieces* (2003), which focused on the author's exaggeration or fabrication of his experiences of drug abuse and crime. As a result, readers who felt defrauded having read what was later labeled a semi-fictional novel instead of an autobiographical account were able to claim a refund. The book is now published with 'a note to the reader' in which Frey explains himself narrating his story through a persona: "My mistake, and it is one I deeply regret, is writing about the person I created in my mind to help me cope, and not the person who went through the experience" (Frey 2003: vi). What Frey calls a "mistake" occurs only naturally when writing about the self, because the subject of the text is only a momentary reflection of the self narrating the story.

The indignation about memoirs being more fiction than fact suggests that people still believe that a memoir is merely re-collection (rather than creation), holding an exact record of facts. Mixing fact and fiction – which is rather an involuntary and unconscious necessity than a purposely undertaken act – seems, however, morally wrong.

While in the eye of the public James Frey has defrauded his readership, literary criticism has rehabilitated him as someone who has interpreted the genre according to its appropriate literary relevance:

> As a work gets more autobiographical, more intimate, more confessional, more embarrassing, it breaks into fragments. Our lives aren't prepackaged along narrative lines and, therefore, by its very nature, reality-based art – underprocessed, underproduced – splinters and explodes. (Shields 2010: 27)

Trying to introduce and promote "reality-based" literature, David Shields' *Reality Hunger – A Manifesto* suggests less fictionalising and more reality. Therefore Shields' main thesis is that the novel in its conventional, story-telling form has atrophied, as it does not meet the need for reality which can be diagnosed by looking at cultural products in and outside literature: the rise of the memoir, the appearances of fake memories, or the blurring of genres, e.g. he views the lyric essay as the genre "that gives the writer the best opportunity for rigorous investigation, because its theatre is the world [...] and [it] offers no consoling dream world, no exit door" (Shields 2010: 107). This investigation can also be taken further on to cultural phenomena such as reality TV, sampling, the collage, or plagiarism as, for example, considered recently by Jonathan Lethem in his essay *The Ecstasy of Influence* (2007).

Shields' thoughts on the memoir and on the relationship between fictional and non-fictional writing reverberate with Siri Hustvedt's writing as well as with her own views on autobiographical writing:

> The writing of memoir, then, is not about my real life in some documentary sense. [...] Writing a memoir is a question of organizing remembrances I believe to be true and not invented into a verbal narrative. And that belief is a matter of inner conviction; what feels true now. (Hustvedt 2012d: 105)

Whereas David Shields does not differentiate between an involuntarily blurred memory and one voluntarily invented in order to make the story feel more true to the story-telling persona, Hustvedt denies any intention to defraud the reader, stressing the fact that she has never purposely invented reality or used her fantasy to create an illusion: "[...] I have honoured the pact of nonfiction with the reader – which is simply not to lie knowingly" (2012d: 112). Hustvedt emphasizes the motives of her writing – a process which in particular sets out to be a personal investigation – by which she tries to dissociate herself from Frey. According to her, the fraud then becomes a delusion of oneself; a writing which only serves material or commercial purposes, but is unlikely to be a means of inquiry or necessity.

Shields' idea goes further than Hustvedt's. He suggests the entangling of reality and fiction up to the point where it becomes impossible to distinguish the two. Hence he regards the memoir as a creative and very promising genre. The difference between Hustvedt's and Shields' stances may be due to the difference between an author- and a reader-oriented perspective. Being in the position of the reader, both Hustvedt and Shields alike, have defended Frey's alleged memoir fraud by claiming that writing about oneself in the first person does not imply delivering an exact autobiographical record of one's life. As an author who is eager to cross the boundaries between fiction and non-fiction, Hustvedt denies that her recollections are of a similar quality in terms of truth than Frey's are. Her reaction shows that the literary world is at least in theory not quite in line with Shields' suggestions yet. However, how does Siri Hustvedt's actual body of work compare to the conceptualization of the manifestation of the real in literature?

When James Frey tried to sell his book classified as a novel, it was widely rejected. Only when he labeled it a memoir, stressing its non-fictional nature, he received positive feedback. In a similar vein, criticism of *The Shaking Woman, or, A History of My Nerves* shows how an international readership received the text's ambiguity in terms of its classification. Upon its publication *The Shaking Woman* was not explicitly classified a memoir, although most critics in the English-speaking world reviewed the text as one. As opposed to an autobiography, a memoir connotes a broader definition of biographical writing regarding fictional and nonfictional elements. Furthermore, a memoir rather shows a certain moment or time in life, whereas an autobiography often covers a larger time span. Therefore the memoir is deemed to be a genre closer to fiction than to non-fiction: "The very thing that would seem to be the basis of autobiographical writing – a life over time – is not the ground the memoir can stand on. It has to root itself in the same dilemmas and adventures as poetry and fiction" (Shields 2010: 109). Lacking an appropriate equivalent in matters of genre, German criticism, for example, had to allocate a different genre label to the *The Shaking Woman*. So German reviewers set their own frame of evaluation by choosing a genre with an either non-fictional or fictional emphasis ("Erzählung," von Thadden 2010; "Krankenbericht," Freund 2010; "Erkundungsbuch," Encke 2010). Yet most of the classifications do not consider Hustvedt's incorporation of the real as a unique form of narrative. As a consequence, German criticism seems quite reserved in terms of a positive literary evaluation, uncertain whether to label the book fiction or non-fiction. The rather confused reaction to *The Shaking Woman* as a hybrid form as well as the public outrage over Frey's alleged fraud seem to be symptoms of our time: "It seems to me that we have come to a cultural moment in the United States that is inherently suspicious of fiction and attached to an idea of 'real memory' or 'the true story' that is in itself a fantasy" (Hustvedt 2012d: 108).

Hustvedt's observation above correlates with the recent appearance of the philosophical school of New Realism, which calls into question the postmodern claim that our access to the world is not only limited by our individual perception, but rather is the product of it. New realism suggests that we do not construct reality, but perceive it. [1] According to Markus Gabriel's philosophy, one of the initiators of the movement, everything exists when perceived, but only in a certain 'field of sense.' A field of sense can be a material entity as well as an immaterial one. Gabriel stresses that pieces of literature which blur the boundaries between fiction and non-fiction are in line with new realism because they show that symbolism and imagination are part of human interaction and communication: "Nicht nur die Literatur und die darstellende Kunst unterlaufen immer wieder auf verschiedene Weise den angeblich klar markierten Unterschied zwischen Realität und Fiktion" – *not only literature and the performing art undermine the alleged difference between reality and fiction* (Gabriel 2013: 217). All in all, Gabriel's and Shield's theoretical approaches reflect Hustvedt's views on how the realities of reading and perceiving become entangled, become one: "[...] [I]n my own life as a reader, I, too have felt *I* was the narrator of the novel. [...] Fictions are remembered, too, and they are not stored any differently in the mind from other experiences. They *are* experience" (Hustvedt 2012d: 115).

Unlike Professor Dumbledore's experience with historically accurate and ever-fixed sources of truth, in the human world memories are revised over time: their meaning is constantly judged in different ways. In neuroscience, this phenomenon has been recently studied and is referred to as the

---

[1] This school of thought argues that constructivism – which claims that ontologically everything is based upon our imagination – fails to grasp the complexity of the world. In contrast to metaphysical realism, however, new realism does not claim that the world only exists of the physicality of its objects, but rather that everything exists, *but* the world. In *Warum es die Welt nicht gibt* (2013; *Why the World Doesn't Exist*) Markus Gabriel argues that anything can exist within a certain field of sense, a domain which is constituted by a specific sense. Gabriel suggests that our perception of events is indeed true, but can be at the same time true in a myriad of other ways, as everything exists in an infinite number of fields of sense (cf. Gabriel 2013: 253).

reconsolidation[2] of memory, which means that previously stored memories can be partially destabilized and modified: Memory has been recognized as a "principally dynamic process" (Nader/Hardt 2009: 224) – an experience Siri Hustvedt shares: "We remember, and we tell ourselves a story, but the meanings of what we remember are reconfigured over time" (2012c: 40). "I have stolen 'memories' from photographs [...], I have been forced to accept that what I imagined was a mental picture of my own is, in fact, an image borrowed from an album" (2012d: 105).

Also confronted with the tricky business of reconfiguring memory is Leo Hertzberg, an art historian and professional reviewer of art and the first-person narrator of Hustvedt's third novel *What I Loved*. He struggles with writing his life story in a coherent and self-constituting form, struggling to overcome the ambiguity between his memory fragments and the act of creating a linear narrative. But whenever he reads the written account of his former evaluation of memories, the text does not quite reflect how he recalls the same event at the moment of reading about it.

When reconstructing his recollections, Leo is troubled because he misses important parts of his family's documented history: "The black-and white figures of the photographs have had to stand in place of my memory, and yet I have always felt that their unmarked graves became a part of me. What was unwritten then is inscribed into what I call myself" (Hustvedt 2003: 22). After all, Leo attempts to solve the puzzle of what feels like a fragmented identity by putting together different objects which represent pieces of his life metonymically. He notices that in whatever different arrangement he puts the objects together, the overall interpretation of his life story changes. Unable to create a coherent version and therefore unable to come to a logical and well-rounded interpretation of himself, he remains feeling restless and untrue. The art historian and reviewer is used to interpreting what he sees – and much less to being the creative artist. His attempt to structure his recollections seems to depict the ambiguity and complexity of memoir writing on a fictional level: Leo is severely troubled by the difficulty of seeing clearly. Although he has many possibilities of interpreting his life and the lives of the people he loved, the variability of interpretation haunts him as he misses what in a postmodern world is – when it comes to story-telling – missed most: closure and the reliability of facts. The more he invokes the frag-

---

[2] So far, consolidation has been viewed to be the model to form long-term memory: "Although consolidated memory can be forgotten, LTM is thought of as a state of (relative) permanence and thus stability. The finding that retrieval from LTM [long-term memory] can again induce states of instability requiring additional stabilization (reconsolidation) fundamentally challenged this [consolidation] linear model" (Nader/Hardt 2009: 224).

ments of his memory, the more he appears to be at the mercy of the "ghosts that can't satisfy" (Hustvedt 2003: 364) him:

> Every story we tell about ourselves can only be told in the past tense. It winds backward from where we now stand, no longer the actors in the story but its spectators who have chosen to speak. (Hustvedt 2003: 364)

What I Loved seems to be a threefold allegory for Hustvedt's search to find her identity as a writer: I) On the fictional level, Leo embodies Hustvedt's double position as a reader and writer. Moreover, his attempts to write his memoir show the problems of conventional autobiography which Hustvedt seeks to overcome in her works. II) Siri Hustvedt has described Leo as her male *alter ego*, who became real to her whilst working on the novel: "After a while, I began to hear him. I heard a man" (2006: 102). Thus, she was able to take her consideration of autobiographical accounts to the next level by incorporating traces of her life experience into other characters: "I am convinced that I drew from the experience of listening to the men I have loved, my father and my husband, in particular, but also from others who have been crucial to my intellectual life" (2006: 102). By anticipating a more varied and circumstantial male position through the fictional character Leo, the author, writing from his perspective, could invent stronger female characters in comparison to Hustvedt's preceding novels and create relationships where men and women meet on eye level. A case in point is how the relationship between Leo and Violet Blom, Bill Wechsler's wife, develops when they comfort and support each other after Bill's death. Both of them respect each other compassionately: "I put my arm around her and we sat together for a long time without saying anything" (Hustvedt 2003: 354). Unlike Iris Vegan, the protagonist of her first novel, who cannot help but define herself by the evaluation of the male gaze, the female characters in *What I Loved* can withstand being objectified and act as subjects, realizing what Iris was only trying to achieve by cross-dressing:

> It has never occured to me until now that taking on a masculine position as a survival technique has roots in my own family, that in the suit Iris lives out the duality and uncertainty of my dreams, and that when she reinvents herself as a male character she is finally able to imagine her own rescue. (Hustvedt 2006: 101)

The fact that the heroine reinvents herself by cross-dressing as a rather clichéd male character – "[a]s 'Klaus' she also speaks differently, uses profanity, and adopts a confident swagger she associates with men" (2006: 101) – shows that writing from a male point of view has enabled Hustvedt to see beyond male/female duality. It seems as if this act of liberation was realized, because fiction became reality, at least in the mind of the author or, according to new realism, in one "field of sense."

In Hustvedt's first novel, *The Blindfold* (1992), she played with the borderline between fact and fiction only in a conventional way, for example reversing her first name and giving her mother's name to the character Iris Vegan. She also borrowed other autobiographical material such as place and address of an apartment she used to live in. Thus, *What I Loved* seems to be a more subtle form of incorporating real experiences into the text – if still only on an allegorical level. III) Through the character Violet Blom, Hustvedt introduces the theory of mixing, which is central not only to the novel, but also to the author's overall work:

> I've decided that *mixing* is a key term. It's better than *suggestion*, which is onesided. It explains what people rarely talk about, because we define ourselves as isolated, closed bodies who bump against each other but stay shut. Descartes was wrong. It isn't: I think, therefore I am. It's: I am because you are. (Hustvedt 2003: 91)

Mixing real-life experience and fiction as well as exploring experience through fiction and vice versa shape Hustvedt's work on a poetological level. What Leo does not venture to mix – the fragments of reality and fiction – is realised by the author herself in Hustvedt's fourth novel, *The Sorrows of an American*. The passages in the book from the protagonist's father's memoir are original journal entries from Siri Hustvedt's late father. The novel includes autobiographical material mixing the real with the fictional and "therefore functions as an exploration of identity as well as an attempt to come to terms with the loss of a loved father – both within and beyond the text" (Marks 2010: 185).

In addition to creating a "hybrid form" (Marks 2010: 187) of literature, the text mirrors Hustvedt's complex discourse of self-construction. Erik and Inga, the two protagonists of the novel, share the experience that their identity has become fiction shaped by their gaze upon themselves and the way they are perceived by others: "Every memoir is full of holes. It's obvious that there are stories that can't be told without pain to others or to oneself, that autobiography is fraught with questions of perspective, self-knowledge, repression and outright delusion" (Hustvedt 2008: 8).

As the text suggests, in order to become whole it is necessary to live with the "holes" (Hustvedt 2008: 8) in one's story. Albeit, the urge to create a coherent narrative prevails within the novel's characters, whose well-being depends on the reliability of memory and in how far it remains undisturbed by unexpected or unwanted information. A case in point is Inga's discovering and concealing that she was betrayed by her late husband with the actress Edie Bly. When she finds out about the love affair, she is more troubled by the self-betrayal and how this piece of information adds to her self-perception than by the betrayal itself: "'What's truly odd,' [Inga] said to the darkened street, 'is that I lived another life. Isn't that strange? I mean, now I have to rewrite my own story, redo it from the bottom up'" (Hustvedt 2008: 133). The postmodern concept of fluid identities – "[...] we make our narratives" (Hustvedt 2008: 86) – haunts the characters who seem to have lost the ability to embrace a sheer moment of wholesomeness, being without the need to interpret and evaluate every single event in relation to the self.

Reading the text autobiographically, it is hard not to notice the resemblances between the fictional character Inga and her creator. Besides the obvious matching of facts such as descent (Inga as well as Hustvedt are Norwegian immigrants), marital relations (both are married to a renowned writer), children (both have one daughter), illnesses (both suffer from migraines) and, lastly, bearing witness to 9/11, Hustvedt explores her writing self through Inga.

The fears and insecurities Inga voices also echo within Hustvedt's theoretical writing; for example, the following passage can be read against the backdrop of Hustvedt's essay "Being a Man," which tells of how, in some dreams, she sees herself as male:

> I was never taken as seriously as I wanted to be. I started wishing I were a man. I wished I were ugly. [...] My perceptions of my serious important self and the way I imagined others perceived me were out of wack. (Hustvedt 2008: 131)

Hustvedt uses self-references ostentatively, narrating episodes she knows are known to a fairly informed readership; for instance, the way she met her husband Paul Auster and how Inga met her husband are almost alike: "Inga met Max when she was a graduate student in philosophy at Columbia. He gave a reading at a university, and my sister [Inga] was sitting in the front row" (Hustvedt 2008: 17). Christina Ljungberg regards Hustvedt's and Auster's poetic interferences as mutual, both of their works being "ritual acts of remembrance and passage while, at the same time, their authors authenticate these acts by letting each other perform as 'real' characters within their narratives of identity and selfhood" (Ljungberg 2007: 115). In Inga's chronologically last reflection on her writing career, she holds a comforting idea in regard to her – what she finds questionable – long-lasting impact as a writer: "'One author,' [Inga] quoted, 'seems to be enclosed in another, like the parts in a Chinese puzzle box'" (Hustvedt 2008: 255). The voluntary and involuntary echoes one writer can find within another writer's works are contemporarily dicussed in the humanities and stated as beneficial to both sides: "Any text is woven entirely with citations, references, echoes, cultural languages, which cut across it through and through in a vast stereophony" (Lethem 2007: 68).

However, in line with Hustvedt's idea of a dialogical author-reader relationship it is, of course, the perception of the reader, determining the self-expression of the author by being acknowledged in person, not only in words or ideas which are – according to Lethem[3] – the lasting core of authorship: The reader's face is invisible, and yet, every sentence inscribed on a page represents a bid for contact and a hope for understanding (Hustvedt 2012a: xiii).

Hustvedt's writing circles a lot around herself, dealing with illness, mind/body interrelation, perception, her writing. She places her essay writing within the tradition of the "personal essay" (Hustvedt 2012a: xi) and explains the use of the first person in her latest collection *Living, Thinking, Looking* (2012):

> I *want* to implicate myself. I do not want to hide behind the conventions of an academic paper, because recourse to my own subjective experience can and, I think, does illuminate the problems I hope to untangle. [...] I use my own experiences the way I use the experiences of others – as insights to further an idea. In the following essays I appear and disappear as a character. My presence and absence depends on the argument I am making. (Hustvedt 2012a: xi–xii)

The essays which draw explicitly from Hustvedt's personal life are deemed the "most personal" (Hustvedt 2012a: xiii) ones and are summed up under the heading "Living." Sally Vickers, reviewing the collection for the *Observer*, thinks that in this section "we learn a good deal about the author – all of it fascinating and (old-fashioned word but apt) edifying" (Vickers 2012). Then Vickers characterizes Hustvedt based on her essays:

> She is a lifelong migraine sufferer – both anxiety and joy can trigger the complaint; she also suffers from occasional bouts of insomnia; she knows her Freud and quotes him creatively but in psychoanalytic terms is more in tune with the great child analyst DW Winnicott; and (praise God) she doesn't believe in eschewing maternal instinct and "training" babies to sleep by depriving them of vital attention. (Vickers 2012)

The biographical summary given falls short of what Hustvedt delivers by including herself into the text: to embrace the real angle to diverse subject matters. By using the first person she undermines the effect the third person usually has on the reader: the attempt to conceal subjectivity. Moreover, the ambiguous nature of some of her themes, for example, self-perception, are illustrated on a literal as

---

[3] "As a novelist, I am a cork on the ocean of the story, a leaf on a windy day. Pretty soon I'll be blown away" (Lethem 2007: 68).

well as on a metaphorical level. First of all, in the essay "Outside the Mirror" (2011) Hustvedt points out that our self-image is based on the very few times we actually see ourselves in mirrors and explains further the function of clothing which is supposed to give meaning to ourselves and influence other people's perception. This insight can be used to unmask her own attempt to create a self-image with the reader: For instance, the descriptions of her looks provoke ambiguity in relation to the author's image as she plays with the way she likes to be seen: "I think my body image sometimes lags behind my real body" (Hustvedt 2012e: 53). This can, of course, mean that she is in fact self-conscious, but also that she just wants to appear that way in the eyes of the reader.

Hustvedt's essays dealing with life sciences or visual art are also closely connected to her life experience and are illustrated with personal episodes which highlight the subjective nature of her writing. For example, Hustvedt begins an essay on Annette Messager with recollections on her early childhood: "Dolls and figures and stuffed animals that talked to one another in different voices" (Hustvedt 2012b: 291). Through the interrelations the reader can interact with the author by getting well acquainted with the biographical author as well as with topics such as neuroscience, psychoanalysis, and art.

Nonetheless, Siri Hustvedt is aware of the fact that the use of the first person may place her within the field of the "confessional memoir" (Hustvedt 2012a: xi), where the reader expects to find intimate revelations rather than intellectual discourse. This shows that including the biographical author can still stand for a trivial form of writing. And naturally, the reader can indeed comprehend Hustvedt's essays without knowing anything about the author – but not without getting to know her.

Hustvedt's need as a writer to communicate with the reader in a form which allows the author to intentionally include the biographical self in the text finds its most open form in *The Shaking Woman*. The text is a self-examination, but links to Hustvedt's fictional works are obvious. In fact, *The Shaking Woman* continues Hustvedt's development as a writer dealing with 'the real' as the text is on the one hand an examination of her writing process and on the other hand an exploration of her (wounded) self. The narrator and the author represent the same person, yet the text is no chronological account of facts, but rather the "route to coherence" (Hustvedt 2010: 198) via ambiguity. Reading *The Shaking Woman* against the background of Hustvedt's fictional works, one finds that fictional and non-fictional texts correspond, dealing with the same discourses in an almost literal manner. For example, the fictional model for Hustvedt's theory of memoir writing is the first-person narrator of *What I Loved*, investigating motif and methodology of his writing:

> The story flies over the blanks, filling them in with the hypotaxis of an *and* or an *and then*. I've done it in these pages to stay on a path I know is interrupted by shallow pits and several deep holes. Writing is a way to trace my hunger, and hunger is nothing if not a void. (Hustvedt 2003: 365)

In *The Shaking Woman* Siri Hustvedt reflects on her own writing process, sharing her fictional characters' experiences and needs: Can a story ever be true? There will always be holes in it, the unarticulated breaches in our understanding, which we leap over with an "and" or a "then" or a "later" (Hustvedt 2010: 198). Adding to the unreliability and variability of memory, autobiographical writing requires in addition to writing about oneself the act of reading about oneself or, more precisely, about the former self. As the creative process goes along, the writer is always the first to read about the self mirrored by the text.

Whereas Leo cannot come to terms with his being unable to find coherence ("ambiguity is the route to coherence," Hustvedt 2010: 198) within the double-consciousness of reading and writing the self, Siri Hustvedt finally manages to accept her ambiguity and the fact that the writing self is fluid and therefore always only momentarily reflected by the text.

Furthermore, her "fictional brother," Erik (Hustvedt 2008: 5), already knows the answer – "Health is not a flight into sanity; health tolerates disintegration" (Hustvedt 2008: 265) – Hustvedt looks for in *The Shaking Woman*: "But who owns the self? Is it the 'I'? What does it mean to be integrated and not in pieces?" (Hustvedt 2010: 47). But why did Siri Hustvedt have to ask the question again, although she has answered it already through the voice of her fictional character?

Incorporating herself into the text in the first person and finding a poetic way to investigate her self on an artistic as well as on a biographical level, Hustvedt can finally accept and even embrace *The Shaking Woman* with all her ambiguity. Hustvedt's writing mirrors the attempt to constitute the self through literature on different levels of autobiographical writing. Hence, Siri Hustvedt's writing develops from the conventional use of real life references (*The Blindfold*) to the inclusion of different experiences and voices circling the self (*What I Loved, The Sorrows of an American*) to the point where she continues the same discourses established in her fiction as author and narrator of the text (*The Shaking Woman*). This is why the last sentence of *The Shaking Woman* equates the "I" with the fluid, instable, and imperfect self she has been looking for within her works: "I am the shaking woman" (Hustvedt 2010: 199). At the same time, the reader has to acknowledge that a different understanding of reality is required in order to follow Hustvedt's poetological concept: by mixing imagination and reality on the grounds of a common understanding between author and reader. This way, both will experience something real.

Works Cited

Encke, Julia. 2010. "Krämpfe und Kämpfe." *Frankfurter Allgemeine Sonntagszeitung* January 20. <http://www.faz.net/aktuell/feuilleton/buecher/autoren/siri-hustvedts-neues-buch-kraempfe-und-kaempfe-1912730.html> [accessed 28 May 2015].
Freund, Wieland. 2010. "Krankenbericht: Siri Hustvedt kämpft mit ihren Nerven." *Die Welt* January 17. <http://www.welt.de/kultur/literarischewelt/article5856673/Siri-Hustvedt-kaempft-mit-ihren-Nerven.html> [accessed 28 May 2015].
Frey, James. 2003. *A Million Little Pieces*. London: Doubleday.
Gabriel, Markus. 2013. *Warum es die Welt nicht gibt*. Berlin: Ullstein.
Hustvedt, Siri. 2003. *What I Loved*. London: Sceptre.
Hustvedt, Siri. 2006 [2003]. "Being a Man." *A Plea for Eros*. London: Sceptre. 96–103.
Hustvedt, Siri. 2008. *The Sorrows of an American*. London: Sceptre.
Hustvedt, Siri. 2010. *The Shaking Woman, or, a History of My Nerves*. London: Sceptre.
Hustvedt, Siri. 2012a. "Author's Note." *Living, Thinking, Looking*. New York: Picador. ix–xiii.
Hustvedt, Siri. 2012b [2009]. "Annette Messager: Hers and Mine." *Living, Thinking, Looking*. New York: Picador. 290–297.
Hustvedt, Siri. 2012c [2009]. "Playing, Wild Thoughts, and a Novel's Underground." *Living, Thinking, Looking*. New York: Picador. 37–40.
Hustvedt, Siri. 2012d [2010]. "The Real Story." *Living, Thinking, Looking*. New York: Picador. 93–115.
Hustvedt, Siri. 2012e [2011]. "Outside the Mirror." *Living, Thinking, Looking*. New York: Picador. 52–57.
Lethem, Jonathan. 2007. "The Ecstasy of Influence: A Plagiarism." *Harper's Magazine* 02/2007. <http://harpers.org/archive/2007/02/the-ecstasy-of-influence/> [accessed 28 December 2014].
Ljungberg, Christina. 2007. "Triangular Strategies: Cross-Mapping the Curious Spaces of Siri Hustvedt, Paul Auster and Sophie Calle." In: Lucy Kay et. al. (eds.). *Mapping Liminalities: Thresholds in Cultural and Literary Texts*. Bern: Lang. 111–135.
Marks, Christine. 2010. *Identity Formation at the Beginning of the Twenty-First Century: Intersubjectivity, Art, and Medicine in Siri Hustvedt's Works*. Johannes Gutenberg University Mainz. <http://ubm.opus.hbz-nrw.de/volltexte/2011/2671/> [accessed 28 December 2014].
Nader, Karim and Oliver Hardt. 2009. "A Single Standard for Memory: the Case for Reconsolidation." *Nature Reviews Neuroscience* 10: 224–234.
Rowling, J.K. 2005. *Harry Potter and the Half-Blood Prince*. London: Bloomsbury.
Shields, David. 2010. *Reality Hunger – a Manifesto*. New York: Alfred A. Knopf.
Thadden, Elisabeth von. 2010. "Siri Hustvedt: Warum zittere ich?" *Die Zeit* 05. <http://www.zeit.de/2010/05/L-SM-Hustvedt> [accessed 28 May 2015].
Vickers, Sally. 2012. "Living, Thinking, Looking by Siri Hustvedt – Review." *The Guardian* June 3. <http://www.theguardian.com/books/2012/jun/03/living-thinking-looking-hustvedt-review> [accessed 15 March 2015].

Caroline Rosenthal
"A carnival in hell": Representations of New York City in Siri Hustvedt's Novels

> The film was *Sunrise*, directed by F.W. Murnau in 1927. [...] I can't reconstruct the whole story, but I remember its effect on me and the way the city looked in the movie – a carnival in hell, a grotesque playground; and I believed it.
> – Iris Vegan in *The Blindfold*
> (Hustvedt 1992: 195)

1. Introduction

Siri Hustvedt's oeuvre is firmly wedded to the urban realm of New York City. Her writings draws on the dual symbolic value the city has held in the cultural imaginary of the nation: It has been glorified as an emblem of American diversity, democracy, and freedom – characteristics which Mario Cuomo in his eponymous book has called *The New York Idea* (1994) – and been demonized as signifying hell. The city has been seen as exemplifying the success story of American Exceptionalism, Manifest Destiny, and democracy, but also as a cautionary tale of American failures, of sin, corruption, and degradation. Whether celebrated or shunned, seen as prototypically American or quintessentially un-American, New York City has become a cultural icon and in its "promise of an always unrealized potential" (Brooker 1996: 2) has held a particular appeal for artists. New York, as Thomas Bender puts it in his book by the same title, is "the unfinished city" which resists "metropolitan completion" and refuses a "single logic" (2002: xi). New York is 'The Big Apple' – locus of Edenic promise and perpetual temptation –, it is 'the city that never sleeps' – known for its relentless energies that can be both productive and destructive –, it is 'Gotham' – crazy, carnivalesque, exceptional.

These properties of New York play a fundamental role for recurring themes in Hustvedt's fiction: Doublings, the uncanny, ambiguous sexual identities, and shifting boundaries – both mental and corporeal – abound in her work. New York also influences how Hustvedt designs her characters: All of her protagonists come to New York with high expectations and all experience some kind of disillusionment. New York is portrayed as a place for personal makeovers, reinventions of self, and the Promethean creation of "urban creature[s]" (Hustvedt

2006b: 32). People are not born New Yorkers in Hustvedt's fiction; they become New Yorkers in a reciprocal production of space and subjectivity. Hustvedt draws on her personal experiences as an 'immigrant' to New York and on her resultant status as an outside/inside observer of the urban spectacle. She has described her arrival in New York City in 1978 as the pursuit of a romantic idea:

> I had left small-town, rural life for good, and I had no intention of ever returning [...]. [A]s far as I could tell, adventure lay in the urban wilds of Manhattan, not in the farmland of Minnesota. This was my guiding fiction, and I was determined to make it good. (2006b: 28)

New York became her 'city upon a hill'; she "worshiped the place" (2006b: 29) as "its newness held the promise of my future: dense with the experience I craved – romantic, urban, intellectual" (2006b: 29).

This fascination for New York as a space different from all others, a heterotopia for the full spectrum of human emotions, ethic demeanor, and traits of character, is discernible in Hustvedt's protagonists. Like her, all of them are non-native New Yorkers who came to the city from elsewhere because they were drawn to the particular vigor and urban lifestyle of New York. They crave the city's potential for the reinvention of selves and its intellectual energies, but all of them also run the risk of being destroyed by the inexorable forces of the city.

In this essay, I am going to analyze two of Siri Hustvedt's novels, *The Blindfold* and *What I Loved*, as exemplary for representations of New York City in her work. In both novels, the contradictory sphere of the city mirrors ambivalences in human nature. New York allows people to show hidden elements of the self and to act out dual elements in their personality so that in a reciprocal relationship, urban spaces and subjects make each other in Hustvedt's texts. The two novels under analysis are set in the art and intellectual scene of New York and deal with the shifting boundaries between original and copy, authentic and fake, reality and representation, self and other, inside and outside, psyche and body and their effect on both subjects and spaces. Yet Hustvedt not only uses the space of New York to render repressed and hidden aspects in her figures' psyche, but demonstrates how bodies are informed by spatiality. In *The Blindfold* Iris's corporeality is changed through the embodied practice of flânerie. In *What I Loved* the imprint of urban space on people's minds and bodies is evidenced through the physical presence of Violet Blom and her work on eating disorders.

2. Returned Gazes, Flânerie, and Sexual Ambiguity in *The Blindfold*

Siri Hustvedt's first New York novel, published in 1992, is set in New York between 1978 and 1981. The novel is, however, told a-chronologically and in a postmodern fashion that rejects linearity. The protagonist, Iris Vegan, is the child of Scandinavian immigrants and, just like Hustvedt herself, comes to New York from Minnesota in 1978 to study at Columbia University. These parallels to the author are continued in the choice of names; Iris is a palindrome of Siri, and Vegan is the maiden name of Hustvedt's mother. The alleged autobiographical parallels, just like the aforementioned dates, are part of a postmodern play with representation and reality, fact and fiction, text and extra-textual reality. The name Iris also spells out the importance of seeing as a motif and theme in *The Blindfold* which the very title of the book negates. Seeing, looking, gazing are never neutral acts in Hustvedt's fiction but are always related to power structures, gender hierarchies, personal appropriations, and cultural fashions. Iris's wholeness of self is threatened by a specific male gaze in New York. In the first of the novel's four parts, she is hired by Mr. Morning to describe objects involved in the opaque murder case of a young girl. Hustvedt purports that Iris's vision differs from that of established New Yorkers because she was raised in a different space. Mr. Morning pays her "to see what I cannot see, because you are who you are. [...] You bring your life with you, your nineteenth-century novels, your Minnesota [...]."[1] It is Iris's yet 'un-New Yorkness' that predestines her in Mr. Morning's view to get a hold of the girl's nature via a description of objects connected to her. At the same time, Mr. Morning feeds on Iris: his "gaze had a peculiar strength" (20), Iris relates, and when looking at her he "tak[es] in [her] whole body with his gaze" (11). Iris feels "assaulted" (11) by the possessiveness implied in the gaze and as a "defensive act, a way of protecting [herself]" (11), slips into a new identity by telling Mr. Morning that her name is Iris Davidsen. This game of shifting identities becomes increasingly dangerous for Iris's sanity as in her performances she more and more fails to distinguish between 'true/real' and fake identities.

Throughout the novel the male gaze is described as physically threatening. This becomes even more poignant in the second chapter, set in New York's young hip art and photography scene. It deals with the triangular relationship

---

[1] Hustvedt 1992: 44. All further quotes are taken from this edition as listed in the Works Cited section.

between Iris, her partner Stephen, and his photographer friend George. In his artwork, George combines "an impromptu shot taken in the streets [...] with a studio photo" (44). The results are uncanny photographic pairs in which scenes of the city are used to show what cannot be seen at first sight in people's studio photographs. The city, in other words, enables George to reveal ambiguous and disturbing aspects in allegedly stable selves. Like Teddy Giles in *What I Loved*, George is a ruthless artist who exemplifies the darker aspects of New York, whose voyeurism lacks any kind of empathy, and who feeds on violence and exposure instead. One afternoon, the three friends are sitting on the roof terrace of George's apartment looking "out over the city's other landscape – glistening tar flats, mysterious wiring, rusted pipes, and odd little sheds" (47). The view taken here is one into the city's viscera, into the residual, unglamorous, and odd spaces. It is against this background of the city that they observe a young woman with a seizure collapsing on the sidewalk below them. George incessantly and unsympathetically photographs the scene. When Iris objects to this, he asks her: "You really believe there are subjects that shouldn't be photographed?" (49). As in *What I Loved*, an aesthetics particular to the young and hip art scene of New York is represented as appalling in how it dissolves and negates ethical consideration and emotional empathy. George and Stephen argue that there are no restrictions or taboos to artistic contemplation and curiosity whereas for Iris their "brutal voyeurism" (86) is destructive. Shortly after, George takes studio pictures of Iris in which she experiences the domineering gaze of the camera as both exciting and threatening. George later cuts up one of those studio photos and combines it with the street scene of the woman having a seizure. In a gothic fashion, George mutilates Iris's body as the image detail shows her without limbs. In combination with the street scene of the epileptic woman, Iris's rendition as a fragmented person implies that she is unstable and insane. The picture starts circulating in the art scene of New York and at her university. Iris's image always seems to be there before her and strangers seem to know aspects of Iris unknown to herself so that she accuses George: "You robbed me" (78). The photo becomes Iris's uncanny double, both her and not her. Iris is "the blindfold" because she cannot see herself but in the space of New York is constantly seen and defined by others.

While the novel's third chapter chronicles Iris's mental decline, in the last chapter Iris vigorously attempts to regain control of both her self-representation and her corporeality. She cross-dresses as a man and becomes a flâneur who roams the streets of New York at night. As a historical figure, the *flâneur* is tied to nineteenth-century Paris as evoked in the writings of Charles Baudelaire and their analysis by Walter Benjamin. While Baudelaire used the figure to describe residual spaces and people in the city, Benjamin connected it to the rise of capitalism and looked at how the flâneur aesthetically consumes urban life in order to write about it. Hustvedt, as other contemporary writers, turns the flâneur into "a cultural concept" (Reinicke 2003: par. 3) that in its mobility mirrors urban complexity.² *Flânerie*, the process of walking and observing, becomes a cultural practice with an epistemological function as well as an ontological dimension: It is a search for meaning, a way of making sense of metropolitan space and a specifically urban, New Yorkan, way of life. But flânerie also is a distinctly embodied practice; it is bound to a specific body and requires physical activity.³ In her walks, Iris inscribes herself onto the urban landscape as much as the city starts taking control of her. While initially her nightly strolls in the disguise of a man turn her from a passively looked at object into an actively looking subject, Iris more and more becomes who she pretends to be. As the boundary between illusion and reality shifts, Iris is physically consumed by her imagined persona. Her cross-dressing begins at a Halloween Party for which she dresses up in the suit of her friend's brother. When Iris looks at herself in the mirror, she thinks:

> I was startled by the change in my appearance. It wasn't so much that I looked like a man but that the clothes created an image of sexual doubt. [...] I seemed to be either a masculine woman or an effeminate man, and as I walked through the streets with Ruth I lengthened my stride in imitation of a man's step and pushed my hands deep into the trouser pockets. (123)

What Iris's new look creates is not an unequivocal new entity, but an in-between. Its most fundamental characteristic is ambiguity, which is essential for Hustvedt's work in general. Ambiguity designates a specific kind of contradiction because it cannot be resolved. As in a rabbit-duck-figure, in which the viewer always sees either of the two figures without being able to see them side by side, ambiguity cannot be separated into two parts; rather the contradiction remains an inherent part of the whole. Hustvedt frequently uses ambiguity to defamiliarize our perception and recognition of the world and to unsettle our assumptions about reality. In the case of Iris's cross-dressing, ambiguity is meant to question our assumptions about the allegedly stable opposition of male and female. As Hustvedt emphasizes in her essay "Being a Man," "[...] the wider meanings of femininity and masculinity are [...] ambiguous. *Male* and *female* are words that carry associations so dense, so old, so public, but

---

2 On how the historical figure of the flâneur has been adapted and transformed in contemporary literature, see Brooker 1999 and Tester 1994.
3 For a detailed analysis of flânerie and the figure of the female flâneuse in *The Blindfold*, see Rosenthal 2015. For walking as an embodied practice, see Urry 44–60.

also so private, that drawing a clear line between the two is riddled with difficulty" (2006a: 98). Often, Hustvedt claims, "the body feels like a limitation" (95) because it forces us to be either/or and eclipses the male part in any female body and vice versa. By slipping into the role of a male flâneur, Iris acts out the male aspects of her being and appropriates parts she needs from other people and contexts. The clothes make her "feel different – especially on the street," and excite her (128). Via her flânerie, Iris does not simply reverse the gaze but deconstructs it by dissolving the opposition between male and female.

Hustvedt intensifies Iris's role play as a flâneur/flâneuse by adding an intertextual layer to it, which complicates the separation of fiction and reality. Iris begins working for Professor Rose, who asks her to translate a German novella for him entitled *The Brutal Boy*. Their collective work on the translation blurs various boundaries until the story becomes "a door to another place" (133), a place where identities, power structures, and reality shift. The more Iris turns into Klaus, the novella's protagonist, the better her translation becomes. Professor Rose, who is well-versed in German himself, probably hires Iris for the same reason Mr. Morning did, to extract something from the story that only Iris in her suggestible and ambiguous nature can reveal. Yet, the boundaries shift not only between fiction and reality but also between subjects as Professor Rose and Iris increasingly get caught up in a triangular desire with the fictive character Klaus. In the intertextual novella, Klaus is a boy with sadistic fantasies, a taboo which he at first acts out by simply roaming the forbidden spaces of the city at night, taking in its "chaos of sights and smells and sounds" and by becoming "a tiny voyeur of the city's secrets, hidden witness to street brawls and soliciting prostitutes" (135–136). He then tortures a cat, is caught by a couple who calls him a brutal boy, escapes home and falls into a high fever from which he awakens apparently healed.

Iris begins to impersonate Klaus and roams the streets of New York at night for a whole summer, a practice which physically transforms her. She drastically loses weight and cuts her hair very short resulting in an androgynous appearance. Out in the streets, Iris pretends to be a man who, like the traditional male flâneur, stays uninvolved and observes the urban spectacle for aesthetic contemplation. In the closed interior spaces of bars, however, she reveals her split identity. When a barkeeper asks for her name, she says "[m]y name's Klaus" (165) and when he replies that this is an odd name for a girl, she tells him "[i]t's short for Klausina" (166). Her nightly acquaintances from then on call her Klaus, and the boundaries between Iris and Klaus, reality and fiction, creator and creation blur increasingly. This transformation is intricately related to the carnivalesque space of New York which allows for the constant reinvention of the self. As Iris reflects: "[I]n the city it was easy to change my name, to be someone else. I was just another character, and not even an outlandish one. No one challenged my name or my appearance" (166). On her strolls, Iris, apparently like the traditional flâneur, uses the city as a means of knowledge production. Walking becomes a way of reading the city and of gaining an understanding of human nature. Hustvedt seems to connect the reading of an urban space to writing a story, not unlike Iris who, on her nightly strolls, fills in "[...] the blanks of Klaus Krüger's life (I had given him his author's last name) – working out his narrative very carefully [...]" (169). Yet, while in the modernist context of the traditional flâneur the city was a readable text, in *The Blindfold* it becomes a postmodern labyrinth of signs which confuses rather than clarifies the protagonist's search for meaning and wholeness. Urban and narrative spaces no longer produce aesthetic unity but, on the contrary, perform fragmentation. In a Frankensteinian fashion, Klaus starts devouring Iris. She suddenly has perverse impulses to hurt people and shrinks from this unknown part of her identity. Her nightly strolls turn from liberation to an addictive obsession: "The bars, the streets were a necessity now, a ritual that had to be performed. My life had shrunk [...]" (171). Klaus consumes Iris in a mental and physical sense. She loses her job, runs out of money and increasingly looks emaciated. Iris's nightly strolls end when Professor Rose recognizes her in a bar and they start an affair. In a way, Michael Rose becomes Klaus, the brutal boy, in the end as he tries to rape Iris in her apartment.

3. The Permeable Boundary of Bodies and Spaces in *What I Loved*

While *The Blindfold* largely deals with the public sphere of the city, *What I Loved* depicts a more private, homely space in New York, created through intimate human relationships, into which the uncanny and destructive enters. *What I Loved* is set in SoHo between 1975 and 2000. Situated on the southern tip of Manhattan, SoHo is the district south of Houston Street – hence the acronym SoHo, coined in 1968 – and north of Canal Street. It is a district rich in historical layers: A settlement of freed slaves in the seventeenth century and a farmland up until the mid-nineteenth century, it became a much desired middle class residential area with a building boom that lasted until 1900 and then came to a rapid stop. For the next 60 years, the area was forgotten and abandoned until in the early 1970s when it was discovered by artists and galleries that reinvented and rejuvenated the area creating a stimulating, vibrant urban realm (see Barr 2007). This is when *What I Loved* sets in. By following the lives of two closely related families, the Hertzbergs and the Wechslers, *What I Loved* chronicles how the ethics and aesthetics of SoHo's art scene changed in the last quarter of the twentieth century. Hustvedt uses the art scene of SoHo to trace the rise of the district to a bohemian haven for artists and its decline into a commercialized shopping district. In the late 1990s, through massive gentrification, the art bubble of SoHo burst, turning the district into a ground for shopping boutiques and chain stores. Hustvedt's novel investigates the changing symbolic investment of SoHo and looks at the reciprocal relationship of subject formation and the production of space. While people transform the urban architecture and atmosphere of SoHo, in *What I Loved* they are at the same time substantially informed by the urban landscape surrounding them.

Hustvedt's novel largely takes place in-between three streets in SoHo – Greene, Canal, and Bowery – and creates a proximity and density in the representation of urban space that makes it appear almost private. Hustvedt binds her analysis of the art world largely to two figures, to the art critic Leo Hertzberg, who teaches art history at Columbia University, and to Bill Wechsler, an artist who has a studio on the Bowery, and lives in an apartment in the same building as the Hertzbergs on Greene Street. As mentioned in the introduction, the characters all come from elsewhere and establish a closely knit community in the then bohemian SoHo. The vocabulary used to describe their move resonates with myths of the frontier, of pioneering, of settlement and colonization. Leo and his wife Erica Stein "emigrate" from the Upper West Side of New York when they get married and move to Greene Street.[4] Both want to leave behind their German-Jewish parents' haunting memories of the Holocaust and so they, as Leo remembers retrospectively, "take the long subway ride downtown" where they "staked out new turf among the artists and bohemians further south" (7). Hustvedt's rendition of the Hertzbergs' move semantically resonates with the wagon trains of early settlers who conquered a virgin land, untainted by the old world. SoHo appears like the epitome of the American Dream in this passage, a new Eden, a Mecca, and a better world. A world, which "with its empty streets, low buildings, and young tenants" (8) frees Leo from memories of his "displaced childhood and youth" (8). Hustvedt correlates the make-over of SoHo into a vibrant artistic place with how her characters free themselves from their pasts.

Other characters also seek out SoHo as a place of salvation. The artist William Wechsler grew up in "the New Jersey suburbs" where his father ran a small "cardboard-box business and eventually made a success of it," while his

---

4 Hustvedt 2003: 7. All further quotes are taken from this edition.

mother "volunteered for Jewish charities" (13). From this quintessentially American suburban space with its "green lawns and quiet houses," its "bicycles in driveways" and "two-car garages" (13), Bill, as a teenager, undertakes forays into the diversity of downtown New York. His trips to "the Met, to MoMA, to the Frick, to galleries, and, as he puts it, 'to the streets'" are described as "pilgrimages" (13). New York City becomes Bill's Promised Land not only because of its art but because of its human diversity; Bill spends hours wandering the streets of the city "inhaling the garbage" (13). As a counter-space to the well-ordered but stifling suburban space he grew up in, Bill adores the dirty and darker sides of the metropolis which render the complexity of human nature and existence. Bill, just like Erica and Leo, wants to breathe in diversity, multiplicity, and contradiction. The same holds true for Violet Blom, the third figure in the triangle. Violet grew up "near Dundas, Minnesota, a town with a population of 623" (52), characterized by "alfalfa fields, Holstein cows and stolid characters with names like Harold Lundberg, Gladys Hrbek and Lovey Munkemeyer" (53). As for the Hertzbergs and the Wechslers, New York becomes Violet's sanctuary: from her Midwestern corner she "fled east to graduate school at NYU" (53). Violet is a historian and starts writing her dissertation on hysteria. Through the figure of Violet, Hustvedt makes it very clear that places inscribe themselves into the minds but also bodies of people. Violet's corporeality is marked by the place she grew up in – the "flat landscape under a large sky" (53) – in ways that significantly differ from the other characters. She is comfortable with her body, which in contrast to the ideal of thinness in New York is voluptuous: "Her movements suggested warmth and languor, an unhurried pleasure in her own body" (51). This also has an impact on her mind, because "[u]nlike most intellectuals, Violet didn't distinguish between the cerebral and the physical. Her thoughts seemed to run through her whole being, as if thinking were a sensual experience" (51). Leo says, "[w]hen I spoke to her, I had the feeling that her thoughts had been nourished in wide-open spaces where talk was sparse and silence ruled" (53). Corporeality and the co-building of spaces and bodies is an important aspect in *What I Loved*. Violet's corporeality changes narrative and urban space as in SoHo Bill Wechsler does several paintings of her naked body. Those paintings set in motion the friendship between Bill and Leo and also pattern the triangular desire at the heart of the novel (Rosenthal 2011).

While all characters seek out SoHo as a place of intellectual stimulation and personal salvation, the district's status as a bohemian art capital soon ends, as Leo says: "In the late October of 1983, the SoHo Erica and I had moved to in 1975 was gone. Its mostly vacant streets and quiet dumpiness had been replaced by a new sheen" (69). Galleries turn into clothing stores and massive floods of money completely change the place and its clientele. Urban space becomes trivialized, streamlined, and commercialized so that the diversity and stimulating contradictions disappear. Art is now judged by its marketability only, and this triggers severe changes in the interaction of people in the art world. Leo observes that with the new hype about selling art, the name of the artist becomes more important than the piece of art itself, so that what becomes commodified and sold is not the artwork itself but the artist's reputation. In addition, art loses its function as a counter-discourse outside controlled market forces. As the urban critic Richard Sennett argues in his study *The Conscience of the Eye*, beginning in the late 1980s public urban spaces in America orchestrated either consumption or tourism. Sennett regards this reduction of diversity and of the city as "a stage of life" (1998: xii) critically and instead pleads for appreciating negative aspects of the city – the slums, crime, and dirt – because these spaces are a rich source for creativity. A repression of these sites/sights in his view leads to a dysfunctional and paranoid urban community. In *What I Loved*, with changes in the New York art world, the boundaries between the real and the symbolic, the authentic and the fake begin to shift. The figure who embodies these changes is the young artist Teddy Giles. Teddy uses Bill Wechsler's son Mark for a demonic game in which the differences between representation and reality can no longer be determined. What Teddy and many people involved in his rise to fame lack, like the art critic Henry Hasseborg, is empathy. Leo describes Hasseborg as "an unscrupulous man, but he was also an intelligent man, and in New York that combination could take you far" (47).

Teddy Giles's art is geared to shock and destroy. Just like urban space changes from a stage of life's diversity to a commercialized spectacle, the performative art of Teddy Giles is marked by sensation. In his performances, Giles "cuts things up" (196); he dissects body-replicas of men, women, and children that mimic reality. By breaking artistic and cultural taboos Teddy quickly rises to fame in SoHo because his violent art sticks out and hence sells well. This quality of Teddy's art, and in fact the whole art scene in SoHo in the 1990s, is mirrored in Teddy's persona. Leo describes him as a man "constructed from rumor and hearsay" (287) who creates endlessly changing personas for himself, both male and female. With the art of Teddy Giles – its dismembered bodies and murder-mysteries – the gothic enters the urban realm and the uncanny intrudes into the formerly homely place of New York. When it becomes known that Giles not only simulated the murder of someone but actually committed the crime, the art community is shocked. This, however, only makes the prices for his paintings soar because the currency of SoHo's art scene in the 1990s, Hustvedt claims, is hollow sensationalism. In the depiction of the hyped artist Teddy Giles, she exposes the dark undersides of the American Dream and shows that the myth of the New Eden, of radical newness, of endless rejuvenation ultimately is "regeneration through violence" (Slotkin 1973).

This violent turn in the space of SoHo is not only explored in close observations of the art scene but also in examining correlations between the city's atmosphere – its zeitgeist – and human bodies. While ruminations on art are rooted in the persona of an art historian, reflections on eating disorders in the novel are grounded in the academic work of the historian Violet Blom. The main thesis of Violet's second book, entitled *Locked Bodies: An Exploration of Contemporary Body Images and Eating Disorders*, is that in postmodern times eating disorders arise from the notion that the body, just like urban spaces, has to be perfected and shielded from external influences. Instead of acknowledging that a healthy corporeality depends on the integration of external other elements, in such a view the body/self is "locked" into stasis and regarded as a space in need of fierce protection. But, as Hustvedt puts it in an essay: "The fact is our bodies are not closed but open. We breathe and eat and cry tears. We urinate and defecate, feed our children and enter each other sexually. The world comes into us and goes out of us" (1998: 112). As a historian, Violet looks at body ideals from the Greeks to the present and argues that in our days the body is treated like a garrison. Hustvedt correlates the fear of diversity and the gated communities in New York with how people feel about and treat their bodies. As her figure Violet puts it, in the urban space of New York's 1990s there rules the "idea of the body as extremely vulnerable – one with failing thresholds, one that is under constant threat" (162). Violet sees reflections of this need to control the body and turn it into a fortress due to changes in the urban landscape, as sports facilities, diet centers, and bodybuilding institutions seem to be springing up everywhere. Besides perfecting the body as armor, the specific zeitgeist of the 1990s wants to shield it from all harmful external influences like smoking, sugar, fat, pollutants, germs, and bacteria. However, the attempt to shield the body from all external harm leads to paranoia and diseases. In our time of Aids and nuclear threat, Violet insists, the perfect body has become an "armor – hard, shiny, and impenetrable" (163). This attitude echoes ideals of the contemporary city as clean, aesthetically perfect, and safe. The body as the 'house' of the self is reflected in the design of urban space that, as Sennett argues, out of the fear of exposure creates bland public spaces (1998: xii). For Violet, eating disorders such as anorexia and bulimia are a reaction to this urban lifestyle: "Emaciation in the midst of plenty shows that you are above ordinary desire, obesity that you are protected by stuffing that can ward off all attacks" (163). Urban space becomes a battle field and the body a site of affirmation but also rebellion against cultural norms. Eating disorders affect the body as a private as much as a social space because they expose cultural norms by monstrously exaggerating normative female body shapes. Not only the body, but the city is informed by this duality of order and disorder; both body and city are, as Hooper argues,

> the persistent subjects of a social/civic discourse, of an imaginary obsessed with the fear of the unruly and dangerous elements and the equally obsessive desire to bring them under control: fears of pollution, contagions, disease, things out of place [...]. (Hooper qtd. in Soja 1996: 114–115)

What I Loved explores both sides of this social/civic discourse with respect to urban space; it describes the safe, homely, and stable elements of New York City as well as their dark undersides. The novel does not withdraw into anti-urban or pastoral stereotypes – Leo's son in the novel, for instance, dies not in the city but in a perfectly pastoral setting in a canoeing accident at summer camp – but to the contrary the novel portrays New York as a home in which the uncanny erupts.

4. Conclusion

> [...] when Lola asked me about my life in New York, I regaled her with one story after another [...]. I emphasized the crass, the prurient, the outlandish, I turned the city into a non-stop carnival of poseurs, hucksters, and clowns whose pratfalls and escapades made for higher entertainment.
>
> *The Summer without Men* (Hustvedt 2011: 72–73)

Hustvedt's stories could take place nowhere else but in New York City. Far more than a setting, it is the city's specific urbanity that becomes the engine of narrative in many of her novels. With varying success her characters have to carve out a place for themselves in a city that thrives on newness and the outstanding and whose carnivalesque energies dissolve ethic and aesthetic orders. Hustvedt neither glorifies nor demonizes New York City but portrays it as a contested space of conflicting and conflicted subjectivities. The specificity of representations of New York in Hustvedt's oeuvre, however, lies in how she demonstrates the mutual shaping of urban space and human bodies through images. Changing ways of seeing, of representation and misrepresentation have a major influence on both corporeal and urban spaces. In Hustvedt's fiction images are never unambiguous but reveal as much as they hide and distort as much as they document. Body and city both become contested sites of cultural inscriptions and images, both have material as well as immaterial aspects and oscillate between being real and imagined.

As Violet puts it in *What I Loved*, "bodies are made of ideas as much as of flesh" (162). In almost the same wording, urban theorists regard the city a "slippery notion" because it "slides back and forth between an abstract idea and concrete material" (Shields 1996: 235). In a society depending on images the categories of the real/material and the abstract/representational are increasingly hard to separate. Both city and body are thus unstable entities that rely on exchanges and shifting boundaries and that in fact produce each other. Iris's walks in *The Blindfold* are an embodied practice aimed at knowledge production: Iris wants to "see," to recognize herself, an undertaking that fails because the urban space is so opaque and chaotic that it becomes impossible to gain a coherent notion of self.

Despite their similarities, there are also some decisive differences in how the two discussed novels represent New York. *The Blindfold*, Hustvedt's first New York novel, creates a postmodern space par excellence. As Versluys has put it, the novel's primary goal is

> to construct a postmodern urban 'imaginary.' More precisely, the novel articulates a particular sense of urbanity, if urbanity is taken to be the psychological or individual response to living in a dense, urban setting. It is in sketching the impact of the environment on the mind that the novel achieves its strongest effects. (2003: 100–101)

Yet, it is not only the effect of postmodern urban space on the mind Hustvedt is interested in, but the impact which "a postmodern urban 'imagery'" has on the body as the city informs Iris's psyche as much as her physique. Iris is made by New York as much as she contributes to the carnival in hell in her cross-dressings, transgressions, and border blurring actions. Unlike *What I Loved*, however, there is no comfort, solace, or coherence and no connecting ethics or narrative. In *What I Loved*, in contrast, we have a strong autodiegetic narrator who retrospectively relates events in a time span of 25 years. At the end of the novel, Leo Hertzberg is the last of the characters remaining in SoHo, everybody else is either dead or has moved away. He becomes the lonely old Hopper character that his son Matt portrayed him as (cf. 108 and 366). Nevertheless, his loving memories of what he has lost in his retrospective narrative give an order to random events. It is this empathy, the ability for human emotion and intimate relationships, which is a counterforce to chaos and destruction in *What I Loved*. Despite everything he loses – including his eyesight – Leo does not stop making sense of things; as a chronicler of the events and emotions his narrative rather constructs moral and narrative order (Zapf 2008). This is again reflected in the means and manner of representation which distinctly differ from those of *The Blindfold*. *What I Loved* can be termed a past-postmodern novel that returns to a more realistic form of representation, albeit with a postmodern awareness of the fragility and ambiguity of concepts like the self, the body, space, or representation. *What I Loved* looks at the affective forces which allow people to harness destructive energies and diversity and integrate them into a sense of self and community that makes New York a livable space.

Works Cited

Adey, Peter. 2010. *Mobility*. London: Routledge.
Barr, Alistair. 2007. "SoHo, New York: Mixed Use, Density and the Power of the Myth." *Barrgazetas*. Barr Gazetas Architects London, 2007. <http://www.barrgazetas.com/papers/SoHo.pdf> [accessed 19 December 2014].
Baudelaire, Charles. 1982 [1863]. "The Painter of Modern Life." In: Frascina Francis and Charles Harrison (eds.). *Modern Art and Modernism: A Critical Anthology*. London: Sage. 23–28.
Bender, Thomas. 2002. *The Unfinished City: New York and the Metropolitan Idea*. New York: New Press.
Benjamin, Walter. 2006. *The Writer of Modern Life: Essays on Charles Baudelaire*. Ed. Michael Jennings. Cambridge: Harvard University Press.
Brooker, Peter. 1996. *New York Fictions: Modernity, Postmodernism, the New Modern*. New York: Longman.
Brooker, Peter. 1999. "The Wandering Flâneur, or, Something Lost in Translation." *Miscelánea: A Journal of English and American Studies* 20: 115–130.
Cuomo, Mario. 1994. *The New York Idea: An Experiment in Democracy*. New York: Crown Publishings.
Hustvedt, Siri. 1992. *The Blindfold*. New York: Picador.
Hustvedt, Siri. 1998. *Yonder*. Essays. New York: Henry Holt and Company.
Hustvedt, Siri. 2003. *What I Loved*. London: Sceptre.
Hustvedt, Siri. 2006a. "Being a Man." *A Plea for Eros*. London: Sceptre: 95–105.
Hustvedt, Siri. 2006b. "Yonder." *A Plea for Eros*. London: Sceptre: 1–43.
Hustvedt, Siri. 2011. *The Summer without Men*. New York: Picador.
Reinicke, Gesine. 2003. "Metamorphoses of the Flâneur in New York: Reflections on Aesthetics and Ethics of Urban Perception in William Dean Howells' *A Hazard of New Fortunes*." The3Cities Project, 2000. <www.nottingham.ac.uk/3cities/reinicke.htm> [accessed 25 April 2015].
Rosenthal, Caroline. 2011. "'The Inadequacy of Symbolic Surfaces': Urban Space, Art, and Corporeality in Siri Hustvedt's *What I Loved*." *New York and Toronto Novels after Postmodernism: Explorations of the Urban*. Rochester, NY: Camden House. 73–122.
Rosenthal, Caroline. 2015. "Die Kunst des Gehens: Weibliches Flanieren in Siri Hustvedts *The Blindfold* und Tessa McWatts *Out of My Skin*." In: Georgiana Banita, Judith Ellenbürger and Jörn Glasenapp (eds.). *Eine Frau geht wo: Weibliche Flanerie in Literatur und Film*. Würzburg: Königshausen & Neumann (forthcoming).
Sennett, Richard. 1998. *The Conscience of the Eye: The Design and Social Life of Cities*. New York: Knopf.

Shields, Rob. 1996. "A Guide to Urban Representation and What to Do About It: Alternative Traditions of Urban Theory." In: Anthony D. King (ed.). *Re-Presenting the City: Ethnicity, Capital and Culture in the Twenty-First Century Metropolis*. Houndmills/Basingstoke: Macmillan. 227–251.

Slotkin, Richard. 1973. *Regeneration Through Violence: The Mythology of the American Frontier, 1600–1860*. Middletown, CT: Wesleyan University Press.

Soja, Edward. 1996. *Thirdspace: Journeys to Los Angeles and Other Real-and-Imagined Places*. Oxford: Blackwell.

Tester, Keith (ed.). 1994. *The Flâneur*. New York: Routledge.

Urry, John. 2007. *Mobilities*. Cambridge, UK: Polity.

Versluys, Kristiaan. 2003. "New York as a Maze: Siri Hustvedt's *The Blindfold*." In: Günther H. Lenz, Utz Riese and Jutta Müller (eds.). *Postmodern New York City: Transfiguring Spaces – Raum-Transformationen*. Heidelberg: Winter. 99–108.

Zapf, Hubert. 2008. "Narrative, Ethics, and Postmodern Art in Siri Hustvedt's *What I Loved*." In: Astrid Erll et al. (eds.). *The Dissemination of Values through Literature and Other Media*. Berlin: De Gruyter. 171–194.

Alfred Hornung
The Shaking Woman in the Media: Life Writing and Neuroscience

Concluding the first book-length study of Siri Hustvedt's work, Christine Marks cites the author's remark about her narrators as "alter egos of some kind who embody complex parts of [her]self" to state that "Hustvedt's novels are all self-portraits" (Marks 2014: 215–216). Without doubt, this statement can also be extended to the author's books of essays and most certainly to the autobiographical investigation *The Shaking Woman, or, A History of My Nerves* (2011a). Although the writer does elaborate on the genre differences between memoir and novel, her review of great works by writers such as Rousseau or Proust in the essay "The Real Story" also reveals the blending of the two forms in representing "what it means to be human," which she finds connected to the perennially open questions *"who we are and how we got that way"* (Hustvedt 2012d: 93–115; 2012a: ix; emphasis original). Rather than claiming to obtain the truth through writing, she clearly sees her literary ambitions guided by the principle of "ambiguity," which for her by definition "resists category" (see Hustvedt 2012b: 22–23) and seems to be the only solution to deal with rationally inexplicable situations in life like her shaking incident (Hustvedt 2011a: 198–199). It conforms perfectly to the epigraph Hustvedt chose for *The Shaking Woman*, a poem from Emily Dickinson:

> I felt a Cleaving in my Mind—
> As if my Brain had split—
> I tried to match it—Seam by Seam—
> But could not make it fit.

Ambiguity is the overriding principle which governs Siri Hustvedt's account of the shaking woman. It starts out with Hustvedt's recollection of the news of her father's death, which she received in her home in Brooklyn, of the last conversation on the phone with him, and the preparation of a eulogy the father had asked her during her last visit in Northfield to deliver at his funeral. Laconically she sums up: "When the time came, I didn't weep. I wrote. At the funeral I delivered my speech in a strong voice, without tears" (2011a: 2). Two and a half years later, in 2006, the delivery of a speech in honor of her father at a memorial turns out to be entirely different:

> I was back in my hometown, in Minnesota, standing under a blue May sky on the St. Olaf College campus, just beyond the old building that housed the Norwegian Department, where my father had been a professor for almost forty years. [...] Confident and armed with index cards, I looked out at the fifty or so friends and colleagues of my father's who had gathered around the memorial Norway spruce, launched into my first sentence, and began to shudder violently from the neck down. My arms flapped. My knees knocked. I shook as if I were having a seizure. Weirdly, my voice wasn't affected. It didn't change at all. Astounded by what was happening to me and terrified that I would fall over, I managed to keep my balance and continue, despite the fact that the cards in my hands were flying back and forth in front of me. When the speech ended, the shaking stopped. I looked down at my legs. They had turned a deep red with a bluish cast. (Hustvedt 2011a: 3)

The immediate reactions of her family range from her sister's emotional bonding to her mother's feeling "as if she were looking at an electrocution" (2011a: 4). For Siri Hustvedt the incident actually is the starting point of a retroactive diagnosis of similar occurrences in her life, the recollection of "a history of my nerves" as cast in the subtitle of the book. Yet instead of a continuous chronological reconstruction, this history constitutes itself episodically in relation to personal and professional efforts of finding the causes for these incidents and possibly treating them. The event that Hustvedt immediately recalls occurred twenty-six years earlier in 1982 in an art gallery in Paris which after a moment of "supernatural joy" subsequently resulted in "the violent migraine that lasted for almost a year" during which she tried to find relief in medical treatments for what was eventually diagnosed as *"vascular migraine syndrome"* which also included "eight stuporous days in the neurology ward" (2011a: 4–5). Next the author admits that she had suffered from migraines since her childhood and had "long been curious about my own aching head, my dizziness, my divine lifting feelings, my sparklers and black holes, and my single visual hallucination of a little pink man and a pink ox on the floor of my bedroom" (2011a: 5). This curiosity, which accompanies her writing career, translates itself into substantial readings in psychoanalysis, memoirs of mental illness and the growing fascination with neuroscience and the participation in a discussion group at the New York Psychoanalytic Institute "devoted to a new field: neuropsychoanalysis" in which "neuroscientists, neurologists, psychiatrists, and psychoanalysts sought a common ground that might bring together the insights of analysis with most recent brain research" (2011a: 6). The personal experiences and the search for a cure in a variety of different fields are complemented by teaching a writing class to patients at the Payne Whitney Psychiatric Clinic. The shaking at the memorial on the St. Olaf College campus is actually the turning point when the curiosity about the mysteries of my own nervous system had developed into an overriding passion. Intellectual curiosity about one's own illness is certainly born of a desire for mastery. If I couldn't cure myself, perhaps I could at least begin to understand myself. (2011a: 6)

Hustvedt knows that the split experienced between body and mind is behind a number of neurological and psychiatric illnesses she encountered in psychiatric clinics and it relates to her own experience: "The shaking woman felt like me and not like me at the same time. From the chin up, I was my familiar self. From the neck down, I was a shuddering stranger" (2011a: 7). In her decision "to go in search of the shaking woman" she is fully aware that her "strange seizure must have an emotional component that was somehow connected to [her] father" (2011a: 7). What had been a professional interest behind her fictions, which also appear as fictional examinations of neuropsychoanalytic conditions and forms of behavior credited to the appropriate research in the acknowledgements sections or copious footnotes of the publications, now turns into a major project of research in fictional and autobiographical recollections. Connecting the episodes of her nervous history from childhood to the event in Paris in 1982, which happens to be her honeymoon trip after marrying Paul Auster (Hustvedt 2012c: 25), and to the death of her father constitutes the basis of a narrative investigation via traces of memory, a form of relational life writing between her father and herself.

The shaking fit at the memorial in Minnesota is the final link in a string of seemingly unconnected events, which intensifies Hustvedt's readings about mysteries and motivates her "to write a novel in which I would have to impersonate a psychiatrist and psychoanalyst, a man I came to think of as my imaginary brother, Erik Davidsen" (2011a: 5). The resultant novel *The Sorrows of an American* (2008), which figures as a companion piece to *The Shaking Woman*, incorporates verbatim quotations from her father's memoir. In the Acknowledgements, Hustvedt credits her father and his permission to use these passages, which have allowed her to mingle freely "imaginary stories with real ones" in the novel (2008: 306; see also 2011a: 125). The fictional transformation into "the boy never born to the Hustvedt family" (2011a: 5) accentuates her research efforts: "To be Erik, I threw myself into the convolutions of psychiatric diagnoses and the innumerable mental disorders that afflict human beings" (2011a: 5). The scientific knowledge informing the fictional representation is complemented by the real life experiences of her father captured in his memoir. Hustvedt's cross-gender investigation in *The Sorrows of an American* is followed by the female account of *The Shaking Woman* in which she explores her own brain/mind/body experiences in conjunction with the state of the art in neuropsychoanalysis. The fictional rendition of the male expertise of her imaginary brother based on the father's memoir in the novel turns into the female expertise of a writer who combines the scientific research about her own case history with the narrative knowledge of seeking to understand the shaking woman. Although the personal experiences of shaking clearly guide the narrative, they take up only a small part of the text. Hustvedt attributes ten percent to her personal story and ninety percent to the presentation of science literature (see Rio). The synthesis between these two parts of life writing is achieved by employing the principle of ambiguity, which resists categorization as a prerequisite to arrive at understanding.

The ten percent of Hustvedt's personal story start out from the shaking event at the memorial on the St. Olaf College campus, which then leads to the retrospective concatenation of events that eventually constitute a "history of my nerves" ranging from childhood experiences through lifelong spells of migraine, concrete incidents of shaking, convulsions or seizures in a Parisian art gallery during her honeymoon and on a trip in the Pyrenees (Hustvedt 2011a: 156, 151), or during talks in front of audiences at conferences in Florida and Australia or readings in Europe. Drugs prescribed and taken to prevent the shaking suppress the tremor but still register in Hustvedt's mind:

> While I was on a tour in Germany and Switzerland, I popped propranolol before every reading in the six cities I visited and had no tremor. In the last city, Zurich, I took the pill and read without shaking, but I felt the quiver internally throughout the event, an electric buzz running up and down my limbs. It was like shaking without shaking. (Hustvedt 2011a: 40)

Hustvedt's fight against this feeling in a form of inner dialogue with herself leads to the recollective recognition "that two Siris were present, not one" and that the "duality [... of] a powerful sense of an 'I' and an uncontrollable other," of "the shaking woman as an untamed other self" becomes the study object of the book (Hustvedt 2011a: 40, 47). This principal duality of experience of the 'I' and a double translates into the narrating 'I' and the attempt to account for the patient of the shaking woman. Rather than reproducing the duality of a doctor-patient situation in which a superior expert treats an inferior ignoramus, Hustvedt's history of her nerves sees both positions as poles of an overarching but also synthesizing ambiguity to overcome the assumptions of true-false options. In the ninety percent of her reading, presentation, and discussion of scientific literature she gives a composite account of theories and forms of possible treatment advanced in different disciplines concerned with some aspects of the brain, mind, or body. In a most impressive display of her rich experience as a reader, writer, and patient, Siri Hustvedt covers the ground of an amazing array of disciplines and philosophies from Greek and Roman antiquity to the state of the art in the twenty-first century. For each of the areas of the brain, the mind, and the body she describes and critiques approaches in neurology, psychoanalysis, psychiatry, and new interrelations such as neuropsychoanalysis or neurobiology to evaluate their theories and practices with relation to herself and other patients. In sum *The Shaking Woman* reads like a compendium of studies on hysteria, migraine, conversion disorders, peripheral neuropathy, psychogenic symptoms, mirror neurons, brain scans, MRI, fMRI etc. While the survey of these disciplines also reveals the limits and boundaries of their separate approaches, Hustvedt's synthesizing work rightly asks toward the end of her narrative: "Can brain, psyche, and culture really be distinguished so neatly?" (Hustvedt 2011a: 183) Hustvedt refers to some areas in which cross-border approaches between the humanities and neurosciences are pursued and points to ways in which they could correlate with the philosophies of William James, Edmund Husserl, and Maurice Merleau-Ponty, who have determined her thinking and writing all along (see Marks 2014).

> Without Gallese, Rizzolatti and their colleagues' discovery and the research that followed, my version of synesthesia would probably have remained unidentified in the world of hard science, a *psychological* state without an organic concomitant. Neurobiologists would have regarded it with skepticism (as they did all forms of synesthesia, until it became clear that it could be understood as a function of genetic and neural processes) or they simply would have ignored it as a subject beyond their ken. Without a biologically plausible hypothesis, a study is not possible. The wane of behaviorism in psychology has, no doubt, also played a role. Suddenly, subjective states, at least in some circles, have become a reasonable focus of study. Anglo-American analytical philosophers, writing in the *Journal of Consciousness Studies*, debate endlessly the problem of qualia – each person's phenomenal, personal experience of the world, which cannot (according to some) be reduced to a description of activated neuronal circuits or "information processing." There are scientists in various fields who would disagree with the reductionist formulation "You are a vast assembly of nerve cells." (Hustvedt 2011a: 119–120)

Siri Hustvedt's work has been governed by a synesthetic principle in her essays, fictions, and lectures from the very beginning. The visual arts play a major role in her novels and her creative thinking as expressed in her essays on painting in *Mysteries of the Rectangle* (Hustvedt 2005; see also Reipen 2014). Her belief in writing as a form of creative synesthesia also applies to her scholarship and critical interventions. Six months after her shaking episode in Minnesota, she was invited to give a talk in Columbia University's Program in Narrative Medicine, run by Rita Charon, a physician with a PhD in literature, whose "mission is to bring storytelling back to medical practice" (Hustvedt 2011a: 27). The interest in literature and medicine had been fostered by Hustvedt's and Charon's common PhD supervisor at Columbia University, Steven Marcus. Marcus' work on psychoanalysis and Victorian literature, especially Charles Dickens, encapsulated in his classic study *The Other Victorians*, generated a score of dissertations and eventually an anthology on *Medicine and Western Civilization*, which can be regarded as the basis of the Program of Narrative Medicine (see Marcus 1966, 1984; Rothman, Marcus, Kiceluk 1995). Siri Hustvedt's thesis "Figures of Dust: A Reading of *Our Mutual Friend*" (1986), Maura Spiegel's thesis on "Charles Dickens in the History of Emotions" (1993), and Rita Charon's on *"The Great Beheld Sum of Things": Intersubjective Studies of Henry James, Literary Studies of Medicine* (1999) channel into the ideas of Narrative Medicine and reflect concerns of *The Shaking Woman*. The common link between these different fields of the humanities is the fundamental importance of storytelling. Citing Sigmund Freud's *Studies on Hysteria*, Hustvedt highlights the psychoanalyst's concern "about sounding like a fiction writer" whose case histories read like short stories, which lack "the serious stamp of science." But Freud also admits that the current matters of diagnosis do not yield any results, "whereas a detailed description of mental processes such as we are accustomed to find in the works of imaginative writers enables me, with the use of a few psychological formulas, to obtain at least some kind of insight into the course of that affection" (qtd. in Hustvedt 2011a: 21). In talking about her own shaking fit she uses the methods of "a psychiatrist, a psychoanalyst, and a neurologist – to illustrate" that "[d]isciplinary lenses inevitably inform perception," and it is eventually her "confession about the shakes [which] had a purpose, and everyone seemed to understand it" (Hustvedt 2011a: 28). The confessional mode underlies many autobiographies and uses narrative knowledge, which Rita Charon sees as "a unified set of skills" shared by psychologists and literary scholars and to be used in medical discourses (Charon 2006: 9). Hustvedt quotes from the same page in Charon's book to emphasize the importance of narrative to inform the pursuit of knowledge in all fields:

> Nonnarrative knowledge attempts to illuminate the universal by transcending the particular; narrative knowledge, by looking closely at individual human beings grappling with the conditions of life, attempts to illuminate the universals of the human condition by revealing the particular. (Charon 2006: 9; qtd. in Hustvedt 2011a: 27)

The narrative of the confession seems to be particularly qualified to arrive at knowledge, which accounts for emotions, reactions of the body, and reflections of the mind. It is not surprising that the confessional genre of life writing takes Hustvedt back to Augustine's *Confessions* and connects with his correlation of memory, feelings, and the body (see 2011b: 187). This correlation becomes most evident in the public confession of inexplicable events to a receptive audience. While the speech at the Program in Narrative Medicine at Columbia "in front of psychiatrists, psychoanalysts, and doctoral students in literature" (2011a: 28) went very well, a similar lecture at a literary seminar in Key West, Florida, was accompanied by shaking and a concerned audience, which offered help and advice. One of her former professors at Columbia attending the seminar felt "that it had been like watching a doctor and a patient in the same body" (Hustvedt 2011a: 30). The interrelational constellation of the lecturer and the audience as well as the internal presence of a doctor-patient in the same body contrasts importantly with the cast of professional services in neurology, psychiatry, and medicine. This interrelation also governs the form of autobiography as Hustvedt formulates at the end of *The Shaking Woman*. Summarizing her insights on the shifting boundaries of the conscious self as well as the reconstruction of emotional memories, Hustvedt writes:

> Clearly, a self is much larger than the internal narrator. Around and beneath the island of the self-conscious storyteller is a vast sea of unconsciousness [...]. There is much in us we don't control or will, but that doesn't mean that making a narrative for ourselves is unimportant. In language we represent the passage of time as we sense it – the *was*, the *is*, the *will be*. We abstract and we think and we tell. We order our memories and link them together, and those disparate fragments gain an owner: the "I" of autobiography, who is no one without a "you." For whom do we narrate, after all? Even when alone in our heads, there is a presumed other, the second person of our speech. (2011a: 198)

Autobiography scholars have analyzed this relational structure of the self (Hornung 1990; Eakin 1999), and Christine Marks has made Hustvedt's belief the guiding idea of her study of relationality in the author's works: *"I am because you are."* The autobiographical form hence seems to be most appropriate for Hustvedt to understand "the big question [she] cares most about: *What are we?* [...] What is a person, a self? Is there a self? What is a mind? Is a mind different from a brain?" (2013: 111). If narrative knowledge, as Rita Charon argues, "attempts to illuminate the universals of the human condition by revealing the particular," then Siri Hustvedt represents an exemplary case since she "considers her narrators as 'alter egos of some kind who embody complex parts of myself'" (Marks 2014: 215–216). Her dialogically structured autobiographical narratives hence serve as supreme examples to satisfy her "curiosity about what it means to be human" (Hustvedt 2012a: ix). The internal dialogue of the autobiography includes an external one in form of readers and critics from different fields. The borderland between the different disciplines, between the soft-thinking humanities and the hard-core sciences, becomes a question of different personal pronouns. While for her, the writer's first person always includes the second, the third person conventionally seems to be reserved for the alleged objective voice of critical discourse and science (see Hustvedt 2013: 111–135).

The interrelation of the three pronouns and different disciplines in *The Shaking Woman* is governed by the overarching acceptance and rendition of ambiguity, which resists categories and alone provides knowledge. This also accounts for the public presentation of the book and the person of *The Shaking Woman* on stage and television, which become intersubjective enactments of personal relations relying on narrative episodes and their interpretations in the light of critical theories. In the following I will look at some examples of the public staging of autobiography, the performance of life writing (see Grace/Wasserman 2006; Dünne/Moser 2008).

An increasing number of interviews with Siri Hustvedt conducted by scholars and journalists have appeared in newspapers and journals. In addition, the author generously answers interview questions via e-mail (see e.g. Marks 2014). These one-sided question-and-answer forms of discussion are augmented in scholarly exchanges of ideas published in professional periodicals, such as the interaction between Siri Hustvedt and Vittorio Gallese in an issue of *Neuropsychoanalysis*, in which the Italian neuroscientist and one of the discoverers of mirror neurons responded to the author's article (Hustvedt 2011b; Gallese 2011). Here Hustvedt restates her conviction "that memory and imagination partake of the same mental processes [and] that they are driven by emotion and often take narrative form" (Hustvedt 2011a: 187), a proposition which Gallese supports with reference to embodied simulation theory. Although Hustvedt also stresses the essential dialogical basis of narrative as an interaction of 'I' and 'you,' both articles would nevertheless also qualify as third person objective discourses in scholarship, in spite of their cross-disciplinary intentions. The potential drawback of the print media seems to be overcome in the staged presentation of ideas and the performance of life writing in which the author embodies her ideas in the limelight. Of the number of interviews available in the broadcast media on YouTube, I have selected four to examine the ways in which screened public performances corroborate and intensify the author's assumptions and reconfirm her long-held preference of the "squishy, fuzzy, low" and her "intention not to turn all thought to mush, but rather to create zones of focused ambiguity" (Hustvedt 2013: 129; 132).

The first example is Kim Rio's 14-minute broadcast interview of 2010 (see Rio). It takes place in Siri Hustvedt's study in her home in Brooklyn. The camera focuses on the portrait of the writer sitting at her desk and answering the questions of the unseen interviewer about the genesis of *The Shaking Woman*. In her answers she recapitulates her concerns in writing this memoir and specifies that it is the result of past research on the topic of the history of her nerves. Then she refers to several incidents of conversion disorder in her life, measures to counteract these occurrences by seeking cures in medical treatment, consulting experts of psychiatry and neurology, reading relevant science literature, and giving talks on various aspects of the subject. Countering Hans Olav Brenner's reference to articles on migraine in the *New York Times*, she states her position of accepting her chronic illness as "part of the economy of [her] personality" and regards her writing the book as a way to "take ownership of the shaking person."

More productive for the enactment of Hustvedt's personal history of the shaking woman and the explanation of pertinent theories from different disciplines is the presence of two actors on stage who respectively represent the humanities and the neurosciences. Not only does this scenario allow for a cross-disciplinary encounter, but it also reduplicates the author's internal dialogue in front of cameras and an audience. I want to look at three such broadcasts produced and screened for TV audiences in the United States and in Germany.

On two occasions Siri Hustvedt and the neuroscientist António Damásio meet for a public discussion of the interaction of life writing and life sciences with regard to the writer's shaking incident and her narrative.[1] Hustvedt refers to Damásio several times in *The Shaking Woman* as an example of a neuroscientist whose research crosses disciplinary boundaries. On the one hand "his book *Descartes' Error* [...] gives neurological evidence for what many people know intuitively, that emotion is crucial to reasoning well" (2011a: 89), on the other hand she takes up his research on "the autobiographical self" which Damásio sets off from the core self:

> While the core self pulses away relentlessly, always 'online,' [...] the autobiographical self leads a double life. On the one hand, it can be overt, making up the conscious mind at its grandest and most human; on the other, it can lie dormant, its myriad components waiting their turn to become active. That other life of the autobiographical self takes place off-screen, away from accessible consciousness, and that is where and when the self matures, thanks to the gradual sedimentation and reworking of one's memory. (Damásio 2010: 210)

Hustvedt, in turn, joins her literary understanding with Damásio's neuroscientific explanation:

> We organize the past as explicit autobiographical memory, what António Damásio has called "the autobiographical self"; fragments are linked in a narrative, which in turn shapes our expectations for the future. There can be no autobiographical self without language. (2011a: 58)

---

[1] Here I partially follow my argument in "Life Sciences and Life Writing." Both terms stand for interdisciplinary approaches and different genres to study and represent life in the sciences and in a variety of autobiographical forms (see Hornung 2015: 49–51).

The alignment of Damásio's and her own ideas in the text is enacted on stage. A first conversation takes place on July 2, 2010 in the United States recorded as a YouTube video featured by the Internet forum Big Think. In this unmediated conversation Damásio augments Hustvedt's psychoanalytic and biophysical comments with a neuroscientific platform, which turns on the issue of homeostasis or life regulation. Emphasizing the performance aspect of psychic events, the discussion turns to the operations of the brain in registering human experiences and in allowing the self to reactivate a record of sensory impressions for an autobiographical narrative. Damásio explains the difference between the storage of data in the cerebral cortex at the moment of experience and the recollection of this experience at a later point. Neural networks are responsible for the resultant product in an autobiographical narrative. In trying to account for the shaking incident, Siri Hustvedt relies on the neural networkings because a 'facsimile memory' in Damásio's formulation, such as in a film of the original experience, is impossible.

The second media event happens on the occasion of the international Neuropsychoanalysis Congress in Berlin in October 2011. The philosopher and journalist Gert Scobel conducts a conversation with Hustvedt and Damásio on a stage in front of a live audience. The discussion takes place in English and is broadcast on 3sat on 6 October 2011 with a German voiceover. The broadcast also includes instructive feature films for the TV audience on aspects of "Gefühl, Bewusstsein, Psyche" (Scobel 2011). In the introduction, the host explains the scientific and personal relationship of his discussants and mentions Siri Hustvedt's personal interest in the issues. In the ensuing discussion of *The Shaking Woman* both the life writer and the neuroscientist agree that no definite diagnosis of Hustvedt's psychic suffering has been achieved, nor a solution found at the end of the narrative. Also the attempt of the TV host to bridge the two discourses of life writing and life science in the cross-disciplinary venture does not result in a satisfying solution. Nevertheless, the ambiguity of Hustvedt's autobiographical narrative bolstered by the equally ambiguous findings of the life sciences entails a partially healing effect for the author, which consists in the final acceptance of and identification with her life: "I am the shaking woman" (2011a: 199). Damásio seems to share this position when he acknowledges the creativity of the arts as a special medium of insight also in science. Thus, Damásio argues that the autobiographical self originates in the architecture of the brain whose features are multiply enhanced by the power of imagination. And he eventually likens the resultant narrative to the musical score of an orchestra, which exercises such powerful emotional stimuli that their enthralling effects are shared communally. The discussion concludes with common expressions of hope to bridge the gap between the disciplines and to acknowledge ambiguity as a category of knowledge in all fields.

The third performance of life writing is presented as part of the Brainwave series at the Rubin Museum of Art in New York, which is dedicated to Himalayan Art and Buddhism. The host and producer explains the philosophy of Buddhism to arrive at enlightenment through a marriage of wisdom and compassion, which he sees as the basis of the Brainwave series, namely the exploration of different disciplines to achieve a common language to understand the way the brain functions. The featured speakers on stage, Siri Hustvedt and Hans Breiter, director of the Harvard Laboratory of Neuroimaging and Genetics, seem to be – in the host's introduction – the perfect interlocutors for their program. Both are familiar with each other's work, and Hustvedt mentions at the end of *The Shaking Woman* Hans Breiter's "PowerPoint presentation and lecture on the brain [she] attended in February 2009" (2011a: 192). The program is taped in front of a live audience with the camera focusing alternatively on the writer and the neuroscientist. At the end of the 60-minute dialogue a 30-minute Q-and-A section follows. The host opens the interaction on stage by reading the passage from Rita Charon about the difference between narrative and nonnarrative knowledge as quoted in Hustvedt's book (2011a: 27) and asks both to respond. Hustvedt immediately claims that *The Shaking Woman* encompasses both modes of representation as part of her overall intention to align the different disciplines in her work. Breiter follows suit and mentions his cross-scale research. Writer and scientist also agree on the importance of emotion and the final impossibility to arrive at absolute and objective knowledge since "we are strangers to ourselves." Hans Breiter elaborates on the issue of emotions in relation to free will using the slides of a PowerPoint presentation not always visible on screen. During their dialogue both Hustvedt and Breiter mention colleagues in the audience, some of whom ask questions, thus opening up the dialogue on stage with the audience. Hustvedt appears to be most enthusiastic about answering the questions and is especially intrigued when the issue of neurobiological emotions is raised in conjunction with the origin of ideas and plots. She insists on the importance of reintroducing biology into the humanities discourse, which had been ignored by French postmodernists and sociologists, who were only interested in the social construction of everything. In support of her own position of embodiedness, she refers to phenomenology and her favorite philosophers Husserl and Merleau-Ponty, a position shared by Hans Breiter, who also sees perception as an embodied act including emotions.

In a comparison of the interaction of life writing and neuroscience in the print and broadcast media the representation of the shaking woman seems to gain in the live performance on stage and on the screen. Obviously the rather static focus on Hustvedt's portrait in her study and Hans Olav Brenner's general journalistic questions differ from the informed dialogue situation between the writer and a neuroscientist in the other TV programs. While the program on the Internet forum Big Think does not have a host and leaves the entire interchange of ideas about the subject and author of *The Shaking Woman* to Hustvedt and Damásio, with a more or less static focus of the camera on the two discussants, the German 3sat program figures as part of an educational purpose pursued by Gert Scobel in his series on "Gefühl, Bewusstsein, Psyche" (Scobel 2011). Scobel is on stage and tries to shape the discussion also in relation to the video sequences added later for the broadcast version. He definitely adopts the role of third person in Hustvedt's distinction conventionally reserved for the alleged objective voice of critical discourse and science and does not seem to be inspired by the cross-disciplinary alliance displayed in the interchange of author and neuroscientist. This German version of TV programs with a clear educational mission contrasts with the American Brainwave series at the Rubin Museum of Art in New York, in which the host in his short introduction sets the stage for the 'marriage of wisdom and compassion' derived from the Museum's dedication to Himalayan Art and Buddhism and the TV program's cross-disciplinary mission. His witty remarks create a congenial setting for Siri Hustvedt and Hans Breiter, who – after the introductory question about nonnarrative and narrative knowledge – are left to exchange their ideas from both areas of knowledge, a creative relation of different disciplines and their representatives that eventually also includes the audience. After sixty minutes of Hustvedt's and Breiter's discussion, the host returns to field questions from the audience, and in conclusion he involves the author and the neuroscientist in drawing the winners of special tickets. A harmonious interrelation of different levels of discussion between different participants in the TV show is achieved. It actually corresponds to Siri Hustvedt's achievement as the subject and author of *The Shaking Woman*, in which she combines both narrative and nonnarrative knowledge. Thus the TV appearances corroborate charmingly her cross-disciplinary endeavors and offer her synesthetic position as a new option to life. After all, Hustvedt owns "the shaking woman," but nevertheless subjects her to a critical dialogue in writing and on stage which does not yield a clear result or cure but offers a solution by virtue of ambiguity that she had studied in Charles Dickens' *Our Mutual Friend*, for her an early example of fragmentation and boundary dissolutions, and that she subsequently developed into a creative combination of life writing and life science:

> In my discussion of subjectivity, intersubjectivity, and objectivity, of perspective and perception, of the natural and the social, of the body and metaphor and its role in theory,

of prairie voles and human beings, of reason and emotion, I have actively worked to blur hard and fast borders. My intention is not to turn all thought to mush, but rather to create zones of focused ambiguity, to insist that "diverse points of view" when examining the same object are not optional but necessary. For me ambiguity is a rich not an impoverished concept. (2013: 132)

Works Cited

Brainwave. 2010. "Who is the Shaking Woman?" Rubin Museum of Art on YouTube, 5 March 2010. <https://youtu.be/bv8 A9CerPIM> [accessed 10 January 2015].

Brenner, Hans Olav. 2010. "Interview." Kim Rio on YouTube, 22 January 2012. <https://youtu.be/AQBpBFqeTPE> [accessed 15 January 2015].

Charon, Rita. 1999. *"The Great Beheld Sum of Things": Intersubjective Studies of Henry James, Literary Studies of Medicine*. New York: Columbia University Press.

Charon, Rita. 2006. *Narrative Medicine: Honoring the Stories of Illness*. New York: Oxford University Press.

Damásio, António. 2010. *Self Comes to Mind: Constructing the Conscious Brain*. New York: Pantheon Books.

Dünne, Jörg, and Christian Moser (eds.). 2008. *Automedialität: Subjektkonstitution in Schrift, Bild und neuen Medien*. München: Fink.

Eakin, Paul John. 1999. *How Our Lives Become Stories: Making Selves*. Ithaca, NY: Cornell University Press.

Gallese, Vittorio. 2011. "Embodied Simulation Theory: Imagination and Narrative." *Neuropsychoanalysis* 13.2: 196–200.

Grace, Sherrill, and Jerry Wasserman (eds.). 2006. *Theatre and Autobiography*. Vancouver: Talonbooks.

Hornung, Alfred. 1990. "Social Work and Modern Art: The Autobiographies of Jane Addams and Gertrude Stein." In: Rüdiger Ahrens (ed.). *Anglistentag 1989 Würzburg: Proceedings*. Tübingen: Niemeyer. 207–218.

Hornung, Alfred. 2015. "Life Sciences and Life Writing." *Anglia* 133.1 (Spring): 37–52.

Hustvedt, Siri. 1986. "Figures of Dust: A Reading of *Our Mutual Friend*." Unpubl. PhD Thesis, Columbia University.

Hustvedt, Siri. 2005. *Mysteries of the Rectangle: Essays in Painting*. New York: Princeton Architectural Press.

Hustvedt, Siri. 2008. *The Sorrows of an American*. London: Sceptre.

Hustvedt, Siri. 2011a [2010]. *The Shaking Woman, or, A History of My Nerves*. London: Sceptre.

Hustvedt, Siri. 2011b. "Three Emotional Stories: Reflections on Memory, the Imagination, Narrative, and the Self." *Neuropsychoanalysis* 13.2: 187–196. Also available on YouTube.

Hustvedt, Siri. 2012a. "Author's Note." *Living, Thinking, Looking*. London: Sceptre. ix–xiii.

Hustvedt, Siri. 2012b. "A Search for a Definition." *Living, Thinking, Looking*. London: Sceptre. 22–23.

Hustvedt, Siri. 2012c. "My Strange Head: Notes on Migraine." *Living, Thinking, Looking*. London: Sceptre. 24–38.

Hustvedt, Siri. 2012d. "The Real Story." *Living, Thinking, Looking*. London: Sceptre. 93–115.
Hustvedt, Siri. 2013. "Borderlands: First, Second, and Third Person Adventures in Crossing Disciplines." In: Alfred Hornung (ed.). *American Lives*. Heidelberg: Winter. 111–135.
Hustvedt, Siri and António Damásio. 2010. "A Conversation with António Damásio and Siri Hustvedt." Big Think, 2 July 2010. <http://bigthink.com/videos/a-conversation-with-antonio-damasio-and-siri-hustvedt> [accessed 15 July 2014].
Marcus, Steven. 1966. *The Other Victorians: A Study of Sexuality and Pornography in Mid-Nineteenth-Century England*. New York: Basic Books.
Marks, Christine. 2014. *"I am because you are": Relationality in the Works of Siri Hustvedt*. Heidelberg: Winter.
Reipen, Corinna Sophie. 2014. *Visuality in the Works of Siri Hustvedt*. Frankfurt am Main: Peter Lang.
Rothman, David J., Steven Marcus, and Stephanie A. Kiceluk (eds.). 1995. *Medicine and Western Civilization*. New Brunswick, NJ: Rutgers University Press.
Scobel, Gert. 2011. "Zwischen Psychoanalyse und Neurowissenschaften: Im Gespräch mit Siri Hustvedt und António Damásio." Josef Eisner on YouTube, October 6. <https://youtu.be/akUC-h9JUBA> [accessed 30 June 2014].
Spiegel, Maura. 1993. "Charles Dickens in the History of Emotions." Unpubl. PhD Thesis, Columbia University.

Psychoanalysis and Philosophy

Lucien Mélèse
~~The~~ No Truth about Siri

Foreword

When a psychoanalyst writes about a novel or an essay, he must not be considered as representing psychoanalysis.

He is only proceeding inside a 'transitional' space created by the writer to address the reader. This being so, the reader (psychoanalyst or not) is not given the opportunity to modify the game setting or the rules. This intermediary space – signs on a page, eyes to read – could more rightly be called 'transitory,' implying a compulsory need to re-enact 'writing,' putting signs on page after page, in the hope that 'reading' will occur again.

But in fact, this re-enactment finds no ending on its own.

"Starter"

Dear Siri,
You asked me to take part in a book 'about' your work; however, knowing me, you know this means writing 'to' you. Here I go!

In order to give me freedom in my search for ideas, let us consider from now on that the sign 'SIRI' designates the abstract subject of your works – and of my writings – and that I shall refer to you in the third person.

I*
Nothing other than my own dream, starting in November 2010 in Tangier, Morocco.

Reading *The Shaking Woman:* I had brought this book with me (the French translation) because of my nearly half-a-century experience in 'epilepsy,' as a practicing psychoanalyst. At that moment, as I sat reading in a splendid park, overlooking two seas, something happened to me.

Something I didn't expect, that made me start to write to her immediately. Indeed, I found this book written 'for me,' as Paul Valéry says of books one feels to be almost written 'by me' (Not to compare talents, of course!).

Afterwards, I read everything she had written and published in French, and later in English, too. I also went back to Paul Auster's books, and enjoyed reading his new ones. I was fascinated by *The Sorrows of an American*, which I read three times. This and several other books of hers became companions and references in my seminars (in Paris and Brussels). I had the opportunity to tell Siri in person that *Sorrows* was, for me, one of the best books ever written, as it describes and delves into psychoanalysis as I imagine it should be.

Fictional works, essays, and other texts by 'Siri' I read as 'fragments of a dream,' in some kind of shared 'transitional space,' neither mine nor hers (or belonging to another, as I define the other of body, of sex, and of time). 'Siri' compels those different bodies to share this transitional space with her.

As a dream, did I say, but also as a 'Panic Journal,' – remember the god Pan, swift escape and wild eroticism, paradox of 'homogeneous otherness.'

Here are parts of my first letter (written in French, my translation):

Madam,
As I read "a history of (your) nerves," so elegant and rich, I was delighted as a reader, and stimulated as a researcher; in my own work, (psychoanalyst), though reading is not separated from practice nor from self-analysis. [...]

"A History of my Fears" could be the effect of that reading.

(October 2010) I dream of a difficult situation, a frightened small boy, whom I try to notice behind M. (my second wife), hiding him partly.

(September) a few days before, housed by friends, I see their grandson, named Vito (vital, living), playing. I cannot hold back my tears as I imagine and see T.

(July 16) T. is killed in a car accident, in South America, the father being partly responsible. T. was a "solar" child, aged 10, always open to everyone, playful and creative. He was the first grandchild of M., who had always been anxious about the "borderline" father, her son. [...]

(M. and I were by then to be separated, in a very hostile atmosphere, which made me be more absent than I should have been).

The ashes were brought back to France to our village, while in the church (requested by the South-American mother) I was overwhelmed with emotion, and turning aside, I sobbed for long minutes. Then I felt an arm, a breast: it was a friend of the mother, I did not know her, "there she was," that's all.

After the October dream, I acknowledged, talking with my analyst, that the young boy was myself, hidden behind M.'s grief. I was 8 when WW II ended, Vito's age, by that time my mother was constantly ill [...] as a result of horror and fear. We were refugees in the Pyrenees, both protected and threatened; at the worst period (spring 1944), my elder brothers hid on mountain farms, and I was sent to stay with some women who belonged to the Resistance in Bordeaux, with false papers. In September 1942, an aunt and her four children were deported to Auschwitz; later, in July 1944, just before the liberation of Paris, my mother's parents...

I have no conscious remembrance of terror, but I can *reconstruct* that in winter '42 I was severely ill with whooping cough, I remained unconscious for several days. When I woke up I didn't know where I was, or how much time had passed. As another "proof," photos taken with cousins at the end of '41, all of us smiling, and other photos of us taken at the end of '42, our faces gloomy, wry, with an absent expression. We were not supposed to "know" the tragedy, our parents' silence; adults underestimate the ability of children for empathy and foresight. (Today, in 2014, I have finally come to realize that in the autumn of '44, after a minor accident, I had to receive tetanus serum. Luckily enough! Since afterwards I had a moderate tetanus attack and had to spend a week alone in a darkened room, with episodic "tetanic" fits at the least intrusion of light or sound. I was therefore supposed to be unaware of the last July deportation. Proof that post-traumatic work is infinite.)

In this psychoanalytic session I found again the terrified child, frozen and paralyzed. Unable to feel empathy for this mother burdened with mourning, cold and out of reach despite her "normal" kindness, but also subject to violence (I understood later she had three generations of tragedy to cope with). This very day I understood that my mother was unable to look at me without seeing ghosts (ghosts became my main analytic research). I had assumed she was depressed, not taking into account her real traumatic experiences. Thirty years later, on a photo where she looks at my two-year old son, she stares to the side with a frantic gaze. Almost all her life she took refuge in migraines – and so did my first wife.

I endured multiple psychosomatic "acting-ins" until I started psychoanalysis, but I had to identify unaided my own migraines as signals of unconscious survivor's guilt [...]: having survived the war, that gigantic murderous orgasm; and having survived the sorrows of my mother, and her murderous but unconscious eyes. (She said about my father, a kind of anxious and somewhat hysterical chap, full of energy and resources: "nothing will put him down," as a reproach, not as recognition of a resource).

My refuge was an armor, although my skin suffered and all my senses were awakened almost too much, as you, S.H., describe it so well. My ability to perceive the inner state of others became useful later in my practice, but for a long time I remained inhibited with women, of course.

You can guess that Jacques Lacan's intuition was good when he sent me to work with "epileptics." From 1966 on this has been very fruitful. [...]

From this session on, that is, with a delay of about 70 years, I stopped being that unknowing terrified child, refusing emotional sharing and fleeing under the bombs (which I experienced close by in Bordeaux, living very near the submarine base under bombing).[...] My gratitude for having me write this letter! Maybe it will find its way to your memory box. [...].

As I go back to Siri's first novel, *The Blindfold*, I am astounded by the accuracy of her quasi-clinical description of 'migraine,' feelings, delusions, and hallucinations, and generally pain, suffering and anxiety, all of it bound up with intimacy and humor. Psychiatric-psychoanalytic literature is far from achieving this effect. In fact I hear, see, feel, and almost smell her progression along the pages.

In vivid contrast to this, I remembered the attitude of one of my analysts, quite renowned under his non-Jewish alias. One night, I had a gigantic dream, many episodes of going through the Auschwitz Camp, toward the "HÔTEL DES ÂMES MORTES," the Dead Souls Hotel. He remained silent, then said "well, we shall stop this analysis now!" Yet another 'expulsion,' this time by an analyst overwhelmed by his own history, reduced to silence. Gathering myself up from the couch, I again found myself alone, having to cope with the history 'before' the Camp, this camp that had caused my mother to pace up and down within her dreams and nightmares, trying to find her parents, so long that she wore out her knees' cartilages.

Alone, I was to explore hidden deaths in both parental lineages, going back at least three generations (later becoming the 'young dead woman' complex: a lost woman in both branches; a fiancée for my father and an aunt for my mother aged five, whose suicide was of course concealed – both named Gaby (Gabriela/Gabrielle), which makes a bond, unconscious and thus stronger). And all this buried under the Nazi madness, but neither blurred nor erased.

For me, the creative results of encountering Siri's writing did not stop at exploring horror. Art, and the practice of my 'art,' were enriched too. Here is an excerpt from another letter:

> ... I finished reading (partly in English) all your published work, except *Mysteries of the Rectangle*, which I shall read tomorrow. Always a pleasure, and an enormous stimulus which helps me prepare my seminars for the coming years (Paris, Brussels, and maybe Rabat). (I also found pleasure and stimulus in *Timbuktu*, *Invisible*, and especially *Man in the Dark*, you know the author[1]...)
>
> The following story might interest you, and explains why my first letter was written from Tangier.
>
> Around 1970, I started the psychoanalysis of a young woman; she came from Morocco, was very beautiful and especially active as a student in psychology and sociology – so exciting in that rich period – and also, or mainly, as an ardent militant against the royal dictatorship; her husband was a comrade of Ben Barka, and was also condemned to death. They had a baby girl, and were divorcing or divorced.
>
> She came from a very modest, even poor family, with an illiterate mother, a passionate, severe and non-religious father, and many children, all well-educated and having attained high social positions. During Mo.'s very regular analysis, five or six years, there were of course many painful or dramatic episodes; in the end, she left and went back to Morocco. She started as a psychotherapist in Rabat and Tangier, married a second time and brought up her girl Y. (who, now aged 41, is a world-famous photographer). From time to time Mo. invited me to exhibitions of her paintings and sculptures in Paris (talented). Later she asked me to see one of her daughters-in-law for severe physical and mental illnesses (she tells me I helped).
>
> Then, about 1982, she phoned me in a situation of great emergency, arriving in Paris for medical care following a third or fourth miscarriage: she didn't succeed in having another child. I went to her clinic and we had sessions every day by her bed for a week or so. We went back through her analysis, and one day I said "I have a good image of your father, but I just can't see your mother!"; she instantly replied "but I have no mother!" To my surprise she explained that with so many children her mother had no time for her; so her real mother was her goat, which she suckled and played with all days long. I then asked – not knowing what I was saying – "how long does a goat bear the foetus?"

---

[1] The author mentioned here is Paul Auster.

"five and half months," she replied; "and when do you lose your babies?" "at five and a half months"!!! Well, it was too late for that time, but her next baby was born at term: her son Ch., now 28 or 29, who runs a big stud-farm with great success, and sells horses the world over.

End of this episode. A few years ago she wrote me again, wanting to meet me (in Paris: they have an apartment), and she then explained that she had created a (most remarkable) NGO in Tangier, for lost children, persecuted or errant women, and later female students. It functions, of course, in very liberal and creative ways, and has great success (and little money; her rich husband helps a lot). For this, she even acquired "la Légion d'honneur," given by Chirac!!! (and no money from the King, but she is rather influential on the liberal – even leftist – side).

Two years ago (2009) she invited my wife and me to visit her (and Morocco), and we were very impressed by her firm and subtle strategy as director of those numerous houses, workshops, pension, restaurant, educational garden, and more.

PS: Mo. wrote her own story, at length and with family history, too, gave me the manuscript 30 years ago, and forgot it. I found it not long ago, gave it back to her, and she chose to hand it to my elder daughter (who was then scouting for film locations in Tangier: houses, brothels...). So her book might become a film some day...!

As I went on reading *The Blindfold*, the strange pleasure of familiarity, or rather uncanny 'intimacy,' with this kind of 'Bildungsroman' was growing. I expressed this in a letter written a few months ago:

This summer I felt so close to you that I could not avoid writing. Of course, you may read this or discard it, but just before my 77th birthday I give myself the pleasure of "talking" to you.

Re-rereading *What I Loved*, in this fine late summer in the Luxembourg Gardens, I found this man Leo unbelievably close to "myself," just as if you, the writer, had been to some extent "my own."

I had to go to California in July, my elder brother seeming to be close to death; I stayed in Oakland for 12 days, until he was out of (immediate) danger. Then I could travel in France with "a friend" (see below).

But with so much time lost in planes, hotels, and hospitals, I managed to read in English, first *Mr. Vertigo* by Paul Auster (crossing through slang and idiomatic phrases!) and *Fault Lines* by Nancy Huston (for the third time). But *Tout ce que j'aimais* in French, by Siri H., or maybe "written by me" in some dream I had unknowingly!

Your description of the delicate interweaving relations between some level of American (occidental) culture not so long ago, and history, tragedy, war, and exile, is a masterpiece of invention. I shall cite again sentences and remarks (after *The Shaking Woman* and *The Sorrows of an American*) in my ongoing seminar (Paris and Brussels), still about Crisis and Trauma. Mainly their effects on subsequent generations: my own, the first, and my Armenian (French) friend's, the third. Hatred uncontrolled, destruction and false "normality."

You insist on hunger, be it "portrayed" by anorexia or obesity: showing that beyond all pertinent mother-child questions, it remains the history of extreme poverty, wars, and panics, insisting silently through generations. Hunger also for love, respect, and consideration.

You have divided the feeling of "indignity" between the two friends, Leo, more introspective, and Bill, more creative, at a heavy cost. But both are running desperately after such tragic events ("Mutti!"). Quite a dull and sterile future for these friends, this generation born around 1930/1940, unable to overcome the mass destruction, in spite of their culture, intelligence, and psychoanalysis (question: does this refer to strictly Oedipal and ahistorical psychoanalysis?). The death of "Matt" denotes, in my opinion, the fall into nothingness. Furthermore "Mark" is a terrifying example of non-humanity inside a human body (or "corpse," if he represents death in action). Your tragedy finds some kind of redemption in *The Sorrows*, where the multiple paths of unknown pasts can be explored anew.

Indeed, fiction adds to reality, the "as if..." propels the reader (or spectator) into another world, with a renewed experience of "common circumstances." You succeed wonderfully at this. (The episode of Matt's death is, as you can guess, especially touching for me, as I wrote to you about the death of the 10-year-old grandson of my ex-wife).

You created, through "Mark," the kind of "bland personality" that seems to me related to "the last stage of capitalism," i.e. general equivalence: "anything is worth something" = nothing IS, exists as sacred and irreplaceable. (I suspect some kinds of psychoanalysis to be accomplices to this tragic decadence, for instance orthodox or Lacanian practices, where "structure" is just another name for incurable predestination!).

In some way, my own story appears in your novel, some kind of "late bursting of love" – alas for a young woman, with all the frustrations of chastity, required after a long approach, and then a short passionate encounter. A strong relationship persists, stronger than anything I felt up to now (unless memory tricks me, or maybe I am becoming more sensitive and demanding). This new story in my late life is both sad and exhilarating, sad but in no way depressing. Maybe a "brief encounter" is the fate of my age and I am reading for the second time *Winter Chronicles*.

Age to take into account: I suggested to a friend filmmaker, who already has filmed a dozen psychoanalysts,[2] to film my old friend Judith Dupont. You know her even if you don't remember: she is the niece of Alice Balint, the literary heir of Ferenczi whom she knew as a child in Budapest – she was born Dormandy-Szekely-Kovacs. We owe her the complete works of Ferenczi, his complete correspondence with Freud, his Clinical Journal and many other discoveries. Now aged 88, she stays as active and intense as ever (and still practices).

These past few days I have been driven to read *The Blindfold* again, after four years of lingering over most of what Siri has written, and hearing her in person several times, in various places and on the web. This book was a refreshing plunge into surprises and intensity, crowded with ideas almost line after line. To start with, the vivid and lengthy description of a grand-mal fit; making the reader feel it both from the outside and the inside. The long chapter on migraine, that I always considered a close cousin to epilepsy, drives me into delusions – the blotting out of images and memories – as though the experience had been my own. Thinking of *The Tempest* by Giorgione, the forgotten "man on the

---

2 Daniel Friedman, *"Être Psy"*, collection, éd Montparnasse, Paris.

left" of the picture brings to mind the two later books, *The Shaking Woman* and *The Sorrows of an American*, books I always regarded as a pair.

In *The Shaking Woman*, Siri tries to think of, and present, the occurrence of the 'seizure' after her father's death. Two and a half years after his death, while giving a lecture, she is 'seized' by complex movements, irrepressible, her arms thrust up in the air. This occurs without affects or 'aura.' She had dreamed of her father extending his arms. Starting from this, she engages in lengthy, learned research, consulting friends, psychiatrists, neurologists, neuropsychologists. The book is written like a spiral, repeating themes in different ways, along with her various meetings, her associations and elaborations, memories, frozen affects, weird perceptions. Other traumatic situations return to her, sometimes denied, like a car accident, yet still present as a recurring nightmare. She also mentions sexual aggression, and the death of a close friend, which gives way to a dream she analyzes brilliantly. She is then provided with some chemistry, which impedes the onset of the seizure, which emerges in latent form in situations of lectures or teaching.

As time passes, she starts accepting 'depression,' and is willing to revisit the circumstances of the first crisis,[3] to add to this her hyperesthesia, her migraines, the "voices" she heard (and points out that several members of her family share this symptom). Also her excessive sensitivity to the feelings of others. Throughout this research, she presents remarkable scientific and philosophic constructions; however, did the psychoanalysts she met at that time really appreciate the intensity and value of underlying conflicts?

She brings back her infant convulsions, and the "oceanic feeling" accompanying her migraines, ecstasy mingled with pain (Hustvedt 2010: 160). From the most regressed of those states comes again the moment of agony, when her father was in such inexpressible communion with her: "*I was my father*," she writes; questioning her mother contributes little more (2010: 125; emphasis original).

The last sentence, "I am the shaking woman" (2010: 199), open to self-appropriation of family history and dramas, is addressed to an 'ideal analyst' who shall appear in the parallel book *The Sorrows of an American*. In this book she is present in a double persona, the psychoanalyst and his sister, as a 'hetero-biography' in which she transmits to the reader the 'ghost of her fear,' this word being rare both in the novel and in *The Shaking Woman*.

---

[3] I insist on the word 'Crisis', as my own research extends far beyond the sole domain of epilepsy (cf. Mélèse 2012).

(So powerful is this ghost that it aroused my own ghosts, still frozen after over 50 years of analysis, pertaining to the maternal link, melancholy, war terrors, and the great extermination called "Shoah," as I have written above, October 2010).

We note the remarkable power of the writer, regaining both sides of her genealogy by 'infinite writing.' This book 'exhibits' her 'crisis' but leaves out 'shame.' Shame of an impossible grief, or mourning of her father's "crime," as can be read in his War Journal, citing the Japanese officer sitting wounded, raising his arms to surrender, and whom he shot by reflex, obeying his American officer's order.[4]

Can we think that there has been a lack of 'maternal' or equivalent protection, so that the father's 'psychic body' (as D.W. Winnicott says) can be 'introjected' by his daughter, producing enigmatic and complex 'psyche/soma' consequences? Or a lack of informed and subjective accounts, between 1945 and 1955, in the world of our writer?

"Shame! Where is thy blush?" says Hamlet to Gertrude (Shakespeare 2008 [1603]: 98). Here, Hamlet is appropriate, since his father, "Hamlet" also, goes on talking to him. "*I was my father*," says SIRI, echoing his last moments (Hustvedt 2010: 125; emphasis original).

Pertaining to 'shame,' I don't imply some personal affect, but shame that is carried by the whole clan (family, group) – from "Put your arms up," in 1945, to the daughter's 'crisis' (Let us not forget that the word 'arm' also means 'weapon').

II*

All my life, my activities and research have been some kind of jumble, my way to mix or combine various tones of thought (or was it a mess?), with no other aim than to rush to the surprise of the next idea.

"But where do you want to go?" – to which I answer: "please, *you* tell me!"

Isn't this the trade-off involved in the creative process, to obtain from the other's looking, thinking, and reading a bit of truth, or at least some knowledge about what I am looking for?

---

4 2015: this is a most remarkable 'trouble' in memory, the kind S.H. describes so often! Not only did the Japanese officer NOT raise his arms (he stayed in prayer) but the father did NOT shoot him, being witness (as described in his memoirs) and thus somehow 'accomplice.' But this melting of my memory and imagination helps me guess that *maybe* in her 'crisis' S.H. in some way 'performs' the *missing gesture, "raising the arms"*, as an unconscious cathartic method. Open question.

It is in this process that I met 'SIRI.' For me, her texts were like soft, strong fabrics, whose fibres provided a secure nest. The great variety of her interests and competencies was a complement to my patchwork style of reflection. 'Eclecticism' is not an insulting word to me: in Greek it means the choice of the best in different theories or practices.

A different story has to be told every day – or night: Sheherazade did this to survive the murderous hatred of her 'lover.' In the same way, I need to pursue day after day, whether I like it or not, my task of listening as a psychoanalyst, and of writing. No glory to be expected, the only aim is to survive my greatest inner enemy.

There is a creative effect in 'binding together' fragments, pieces of my findings in so many diverse fields. The emotions I experience as I read 'SIRI' give me the perception of a 'body' holding the whole. It is essential to me that 'SIRI's' immense erudition is never on the academic side, but always poetically linked to the reader; she always creates and protects the area between the 'spectator' and the work of art. Therein lies the ambiguity of writing about 'SIRI' in the abstract sense, while feeling at the same time so intimately linked to someone I know so little – an ambiguity paralleling my relation to the English language.

My mother spoke a fluent but old-fashioned English, learned from her English governess. The circumstances were dramatic. In 1908 she was six, her brother seven, a sister four years old. A young maternal aunt, Gabrielle, used to look after them. One morning she was not there, and the parents arrived later dressed in black.[5] Of course, not a word was said, and a very long silence persisted about her suicide, so that today I can only guess the reasons for it (was she in love with a brother-in-law who seduced her, was she pregnant?). The family home was extended to reunite the cousins, and a nurse was hired – old-fashioned, rigid and brutal.

The story of 'English' goes on during the war, listening to Radio-London, blurred, of course (did my attraction for non-tonal music begin then?). Later, when I was 10, my English teacher at school was a charming and attractive woman (while my mother, although only 44, was ruined by bereavement and depression). In 1950 my father was invited as a visiting professor to the French department of a Toronto university (he spoke very little English, but he learned fast). I arrived as a very average teenager, but was lucky enough to obtain an A in English two years later. My elder brother, then a postdoctoral student in Baltimore, later married and settled in the US (he is now in California).

I very often think, or find a better word or phrase, in English, but you can see that I am no longer perfectly bilingual!

---

5 As my uncle writes in his memoirs.

I started sending letters to 'SIRI' in French, and went on in English; and the 'SIRI-PAUL story' (through their books) provides me with some kind of anchor within my perhaps overly nomadic life, since I come from a 'no man's land' called WWII, haunted by the destiny of Jews in occupied and officially pro-Nazi France. 'No-Jews-land' it was; and during the most dangerous period, for me, also 'no-name-land': I was hidden with a borrowed name by two women in the Resistance, in Bordeaux, where the infamous 'préfet' Papon succeeded in deporting about 1,500 Jews – a fate I escaped. (After the war he pursued a brilliant and murderous (colonial wars) career, and was ultimately condemned only in 1998!).

From 'no-man's-land' to 'no-mad's-land'? I also escaped from several careers: medicine, music, cinema, pure science and research in biophysics; and afterwards 'fell' into psychoanalysis. And within this field, I kept 'escaping' from one group to another, and I submitted to seven or eight different analysts. Likewise for love affairs and families, on the way to loneliness...?

Isn't this what we call in French *la course du lièvre*, the hare's flight when chased after: the strategy of changing direction and pace often and in an instant? (Or maybe *"the heir's flight,"* when heirloom occurs to be too heavy to cope with!)

But like a beautiful 'affair' happening to me in my old age, I can dedicate some gratitude to 'SIRI's' works, in parallel with my ever ongoing analysis (no age for this), bringing me to a more secure ground and environment. An anchor, this 'SIRI-PAUL' chimera, as these 'young' (for me) people have come to know how to combine, to 'brew' their own exiles, no lighter than mine (except for Nazism) with everyday life, past and future.

Not a brief, but a 'long encounter' was the meeting with SIRI through her texts. They drove me to feel different, to modify my own perceptive field, leaning more towards poiesis and aesthesis, creation and sensibility, in 'private' life as well as in this very curious adventure of 'privacy' called psychoanalytic practice.

III*

While reading the book *Kinderzimmer*[6] I had a dream, for once clear and complete.

---

[6] A very moving novel, or "docu-fiction" (the author is a historian) about a woman in the Resistance, deported to Ravensbrück while pregnant. She will discover the ward for newborns and babies, where of course most of them die. We are inside this woman as she learns, and above all feels, the effects of meaningless cruelty and destructive organization. Her baby dies, she adopts the child of another woman, who is dead also. Both will succeed in surviving the atrocious ordeals until freedom. Only several decades later is she able to reveal the truth to her "son," who denies it at first. Actual survivors, and the real nurse still alive, did confirm the authenticity of this story (cf. Goby 2013).

I was in my mother's family house (still in existence in 1998) with all of us children of the three surviving branches – but for the deportees. No parents nor grandparents, and all of us rather young, 20 to 30. There was a ceremony in the main living room, maybe a little boring, so we moved here and there, and I remember looking at my cell phone and trying to light it. A number of texts were being read, such a number that I remember saying "we must meet again tomorrow to finish reading." By this time I had gone to the entrance, maybe to phone someone, and there I discovered a usually closed door, but now wide open unto a brightly lit apartment with a very large window in the rear. A woman says, "it is the next house"... I didn't know there was one (in the dream).

Waking up I instantly thought of my father's death (July 1978), or rather about the fact that I, the youngest child, was left alone to organize his cremation. Our mother fled to the USA with my elder brother, the second one left for holidays, and I had to ask a friend to take my three children to the Riviera. My (first) wife was nowhere I can remember... I did organize what had to be done, from the hospital morgue to the urn in Père-Lachaise. But I also took to the road, southward, before the corpse was cremated (our father's option). I always considered that through this choice (cremation), father discharged us of the impossible burden of the seven people (including four children) gassed and burned in Auschwitz – along with millions of others. In short, none of us was present and there was no ceremony, the absence of which I try to remedy in the dream. Nor was there any from 1945 until my mother's death (the last senior) in January 1998; when her urn was (also) brought into the parlour, where a large part of the family was present, I read a lengthy homage, in which I talked about this long life of traumas, starting long before WWII. Thus did this dream (that I had at the end of 2013) achieve an unachievable ceremony, now 'lit up,' and 'open unto a new house,' and some kind of 'unknown woman,' too.

Why so many personal notes? To testify that survival is a long road, with no more ending than psychoanalysis itself. And art, or other creative paths, demand perseverance, as shown by the unending writing to which 'SIRI' is committed. Unsubdued 'SIRI,' to whom I pay homage by describing an 'artistic' event that could concern and arouse both of us.

IV*

A / HANTAÏ, Paris exhibition, 2013

To start with, a surprise about his first paintings: where did they come from, where do they go, awkwardly? Then this stiff world bursts out, and we might perceive in the newer works Ernst, Matta, Miro... abstract beauty is appreciated without shadows.

However, in the next room, *Peintures D'Ecritures et a Petites Touches* ("writing painting by small touches"), I sit exhausted, thoughtless for minutes; later awakened by one picture – 'small touches' indeed, regular, crowded one upon the next, white with little shades, all alike and lined up. Suddenly I 'see' the recent massacre in Damas, and so many others in photos, be it Buchenwald or... I can stand again, full of sensations and inner images.

Next come large monochrome 'wounds' tightened in the canvas, like shrouds first empty, then swollen with heavy presence. Hantaï calls them 'paunches.' The shroud has shrunk, full of nameless fragments (in French *panse/pansement*) or bandages. Next room, big full 'bodies,' but torn to pieces as a small child could have done before he talks – all this held together firmly by the frame.

The next canvases make me feel as if the environment itself had been broken in new shapeless splinters, the space being filled up with them. And farther, regular tiling as if to protect or add strength.

Taking strength from this torn environment? The author will tear to pieces his older paintings, in order to reuse them ("Destruction as the Cause of Becoming," an article first published in 1912 by Sabina Spielrein, whom I admire and cherish; cf. Spielrein 1994).

(It so happens that Hantaï, born into a German family, 'magyarized' his name to protest against Hitlerism. He took a stand against Nazism, and had to hide. He then married a Jewish woman, who by incredible chance survived the biggest of all exterminations in one country (over 400,000 murdered in a few weeks in Hungary and the Camps, just before the arrival of the Russian Army)).

Far from simplistic psychology, I have in this exhibition a feeling of 'survival,' and hidden ordeals, but becoming more and more present. Heart-breaking beauty, 'haunted' silence. (In French, which Hantaï spoke, since he lived in France, Hantaï and *hanté* ['haunted'] sound alike).

B / back to *The Shaking Woman*

According to my theoretical requirements, I made a thorough commentary of this book for my psychoanalytic seminars – not suitable for this text. Call it a kind of Midrash, in which small details are a good means to provoke a 'crisis' within the text, or, in clinical situations, within a patient.

When I was *herem*, i.e. excommunicated from society (1940/44), most of the time I immersed myself in books about 'Indians,' identifying not with the cowboys, but with the Indians, sharing their frights, fights, and flights for survival.

I still own *The Adventures of Sajo and her Beaver People* [7]: How to survive along the River. Next came a time for heroes, found in *The Iliad* and the *Odyssey*. At age seven, I read these books in a village that hid over 2,000 Jewish people.[8] A village from which had 'disappeared' my cousin Bernard, aged 17, who joined the 1rst Army of the French Resistance. As usual, I was not supposed to learn of that heroic action.

Now and all other times is what I wander about, thinking with my body, where the most remote times and the present are fighting. When or if 'another body' is lacking, books may be a barrier to the vital collapse.

Coda

And SIRI's books acted for me as both a new and an almost ever-known 'interior person.'

Epilogue

Writing: why suffer this never-ending burden? Moreover, for those who underwent (long or multiple) psychoanalysis, what is there left to find – or perhaps to conceal? Something else – or the same thing, to hide or to expose?

Not being a 'professional' writer (the pieces of fiction or poetry I 'had to write' were never published outside small, intimate, or strictly professional circles), my only writing consists of clinical notes, or wider explorations of this insufficiently investigated field called 'Crisis.' I was at first immersed in it through epileptic patients, but not long afterwards it became clear to me how much myself had been implicated in that very specific and queer space. This field, I repeat, was not at all, or hardly at all, explored by psychoanalysts. Therefore, as I went on and on with epileptic (and other 'psychosomatic' or 'borderline') patients, I felt supported in my own elaboration by Siri Hustvedt, one of my stimulating encounters – and no doubt a major one.

I have carried the burden of this unceasing reading/writing activity (soon half a century, and longer for poetry!), specific in style or tone. Benevolent readers call it 'poetic,' reticent readers, the wide majority (not only 'academic') call it

---

7 Nelson édit. 1938.
8 Le Chambon sur Lignon was awarded the Medal of the Just; see *Weapons of the Spirit*, film by Pierre Sauvage.

enigmatic or useless, asking, at best, "where are you going, and what do you aim for?" to which my only answer is "you tell me"! Writing is on the same level as art, and no one dares ask the artist "what does it mean?" to which he would receive the same answer.

Now it happens that, meeting 'SIRI' through her serious opus *The Shaking Woman*, at the end of 2010, in personally tragic circumstances, I end this paper in the very same place, in this splendid domain above Tanger, and in a much lighter mood, finishing a much more vivid and enigmatic book (in English, if I may call such all those different idioms so well adapted to each figure of the plot).

The structure of *The Blazing World*, in tone both grave and comical, brings to mind numerous musical structures, the nearest for me being *Archipels* by André Boucourechliev (from 1967 onwards): more or less developed elements, offered to the interpreters (piano, two pianos, quartet, harpsichord, orchestra), for them to select freely, combine, and order those short pieces of written music. A grand achievement.

In this book one can dream of shuffling the cards of chapters, in order to bring them together according to themes, dates, persons, or what else...? Such pleasure can be taken in 'the art of fugue' (as each interpreter follows a different order) unto the last piece, an unfinished triple fugue for four voices. This 'foliated' structure can be found in the finale of the Jupiter symphony – quadruple fugue with four voices also; and later in the gigantic finale of the Hammerklavier sonata, then lightened by simple, lyrical themes.

Charm is not absent from those 'enormous' works, and so does 'SIRI's' last book end, with a surprising, light, and witty 'countersubject,' about that 'pharma-Siri' joking with her 'self' all through the book. 'Enormous' is the key word of a film by J.L. Godard, *Je vous salue, Marie* (Hail Mary) where the first part, told by his wife A.M. Miéville, tells of a young anorexic girl, ending on an 'enormous hunger,' and the second part wanders about the visit of Gabriel sent by 'the Father' to the grown-up girl. Did 'Harry' know this film?

No ending to this infinite rereading!

Tanger – Paris, August 2014
(over-read by Mrs Agnès Jacob)

Works Cited

Goby, Valentine. 2013. *Kinderzimmer*. Paris: Actes Sud.
Hustvedt, Siri. 1992. *The Blindfold*. New York: Norton.
Hustvedt, Siri. 2008. *The Sorrows of an American*. New York: Holt.
Hustvedt, Siri. 2010. *The Shaking Woman, or, A History of My Nerves*. London: Sceptre.
Hustvedt, Siri. 2014. *The Blazing World*. New York: Simon & Schuster.
Mélèse, Lucien. 2012. "Critical Transference in a Case of Severe Epilepsy." *The American Journal of Psychoanalysis* 72.3: 223–241.
Shakespeare, William. 2008 [1603]. *Hamlet*. Basingstoke: Macmillan.
Spielrein, Sabina. 1994. "Destruction as the Cause of Coming Into Being." *Journal of Analytical Psychology* 39.2: 155–186.
Je vous salue, Marie. 1985. Dir. Jean-Luc Godard. Sara Films.
Weapons of the Spirit. 1987. Dir. Pierre Sauvage. Pierre Sauvage Productions.

Françoise Davoine
Siri's Timequakes

I wish to pay tribute to Siri Hustvedt, whom I encountered on a wandering and wondering path, between her book *The Shaking Woman* and mine, *Mother Folly*, which she supported in its process of being published in the US.[1] 'Folly' is a common ground for us, located during the Middle Ages, in *l'espace de la merveille*, the space and time of the wondrous. The wonder is, as soon as I read *The Shaking Woman*, I began to wonder about her father's war, completely unaware. I do the same with descendants of veterans, who unexpectedly bring me diaries from WWI or II which had been discarded in a drawer or in an attic. I treasure those testimonies, which lay in exile in an outlandish space and time. They play a major part in the healing of madness and trauma when I, the analyst, am able to connect with this common lore. However, it takes time.

Afterwards I found *The Sorrows of an American*. It was right there, the memoir of an American soldier during the Pacific War and his childhood during the Great Depression. Printed in italics it stood out, as a core, around which the different stories were woven, or rather sewn like a quilt. It struck me as a major book for the psychoanalytical healing of trauma and psychosis, which tends toward the inscription of silenced historical and social catastrophes. At the end of the novel, the elderly psychoanalyst Magda, who is perhaps my age, assumes psychoanalysis is a work that "can turn ghosts into ancestors" (Hustvedt 2008: 296).

This age-old work of trauma therapy, as old as war itself, was traditionally performed by ceremonies – poetry, songs, theater, storytelling – and became literature, such as the Mahabharata, Homeric epics, Greek tragedies and comedies, Nô theater, the Feast of Fools, Don Quixote, Shakespeare, Molière, or Tristram Shandy – to mention only my favorites. While not every book has this healing power, Siri Hustvedt's *The Sorrows of an American* does. Her novel indeed turns Lars Davidsen, the American father whose sorrows are being told, from a ghost into an ancestor.

The narrative's time span encompasses a space "in between two deaths." The expression is from Lacan's *Seminar on the Ethics of Psychoanalysis* (Lacan 1992: ch. 21). It refers to the space between the real death and its inscription – let us say on a grave, through a story, or in history. Ceremonies are held in the frame of that in-between, to turn ghosts into ancestors and things into symbols,

---

[1] I would like to thank Dyani Gaudillière for her thoughtful revision of my English.

with the help of spirits and gods. "One could almost say that man is a ceremonial animal," states Wittgenstein in his *Remarks on Frazer's Golden Bough* (Wittgenstein 1995: 129). He cannot help showing what cannot be said, thanks to animistic rituals. Still, jokes the French psychoanalyst, "we no longer have any idea about who the gods are, [...] except when we are willing to go to other regions of the globe and do anthropology, [...] the question is, what do we put at that place, in the light of psychoanalysis?" (Lacan 1992: 259–260). We could add that this applies especially when psychoanalysis addresses what cannot be said, but cannot help being shown, even extravagantly, through surviving images. In the novel, indeed, the main character in charge of this task is a psychoanalyst, Lars Davidsen's son Erik, with the help of his sister, Inga.

The story begins on a snowy day, four days after their father's funeral, and it ends on a snowy day in New York almost one year later, with the resuscitation of a child, Eggy, from a coma. Meanwhile, the burial of the urn takes place in June, when their hometown's earth is unfrozen in Minnesota. Then in October, another burial is publicly inscribed, which had been kept a secret by their father – as if the father's rest could be achieved only after a secret promise he swore when he was 15 was revealed not only to his children, but also to the reader. To keep one's word is at the root of the social link, especially in the wake of chaos and destruction of all laws, well on its way at that time. But the symbolic efficiency of such a promise empowers the social link only when it is not only mentioned but inscribed.

The novel opens with the discovery of a mysterious short letter dated June 1937 in the father's papers, sent by an unknown Lisa, evoking an enigmatic promise they have sworn to each other on the Bible, and a deceased "she" who "is in heaven" (Hustvedt 2008: 5). From that moment, I started to consider this father as a genuine *therapon* (Nagy 1979: 292–293). In the *Iliad*, this means not only the second in combat, but also the ritual double who performs funeral duties after the death of his comrade. This last task is not only ritualistic, but also political. The decision to leave corpses unburied, abandoned to the dogs, has been against the laws of war since antiquity, as shown by the supplication of Priam to Achilles to retrieve his son Hector's body. More extensively, it has become a tool for the genocide of Jews, Armenians, Cambodians, Bosniacs, Tutsis, and *desaparecidos* in the hands of recent totalitarianisms across the planet. Let us call this pervasive and insistent mechanism "perversion," which transforms people's souls and bodies into things, destroys their symbolic treasures, and changes children's playgrounds into murderous places.

As a historian, the father resists annihilation by collecting archives of the Norwegian past, which have threatened to disappear along with immigration. This duty is obviously transmitted to his "twin" children. Even if they are not the same age, they accomplish the parallel task to fend off perversion, in his and her own domains. In her other novels, Siri Hustvedt also presents heroes who feel and deny that they have been used as puppets and exploited under the guise of artistic creation. With a special craft she highlights the trembling edge between an awareness of the attack impressed upon the body, and a complacent discourse, which denies the truth. Inga, Erik's sister, wrestles against the media appropriators of her husband's literary identity; Erik, the brother, against the intrusions of a stalker photographer who threatens him and his tenants – a young mother, Miranda, and Eggy, her daughter. Both eventually put perversion at bay.

I like books that do not leave the reader in charge of the end. Here, compromising letters are retrieved from the blackmail, the little girl comes out safe after a fall, and silent matters find their address, carried by uncanny dolls, able to cross the looking glass on the bridge of the secret promise after mirrors have been shattered by lies.

From the start I had imagined a baby conceived in shame, and looked for it throughout the book. At the end, the recluse Lisa tells the story: "The labor pains were bad, but after it was over, it wasn't me no more. I was looking on. Saw the blood, the little thing, saw it all from afar. Just like when it was made. Was just like I had nothing to do with it" (Hustvedt 2008: 245).

Trauma is linked both to one's exposure to death and to the betrayal of one's own people (Shay 1995: 27). Lisa's solitude resonates with a previous loneliness. Nobody ever mentioned to her that she escaped a fire when she was two, and her mother died with an infant sibling. In that context, the 15-year-old Lars acts as a genuine *therapon* when he rushes to the site of her cries, cuts the umbilical cord, buries the little corpse, and promises not to tell, to be true to her.

The promise not to tell lays the foundation of the book. If the father's legacy is to be transmitted to his children, the Catch 22 is how to tell a promise not to tell, without treachery. The vivid answer to this logical impasse is given by Lisa's decision to address the surviving images of the kept promise to Lars' children as their heritage. An underground method of survival for the psyche is passed on when it is attacked by perverse mechanisms such as bullying, erasure of tracks, stalking, blackmail, fake scenarios, fascination for horror, torture, and predation.

Let us say now that madness and traumatic episodes are a fight against perversion in order to put time into motion. For time stops when speech is no longer reliable, and people may be treated as things.

As an analyst, I find myself haunted – like Lars, his son Erik, but also like Uncle Toby in *Tristram Shandy* – by the erasure of tracks, in war and also in peacetime, like the disappearance of gestures and ways of life in the country, or in the mountains where I spent my childhood. As I mentioned, I am often asked to read the diaries and letters written during the war, lost and found by grandchildren who don't know what to do with that "rubbish." Stories of hell, of buddies, of errants, like their uncle David or my uncle Emile, who fought in Narvick in the Alpine troops, came back to France after that purloined victory in far away Norway at the beginning of WWII, joined the Resistance in the Alps, was deported in Mauthausen, used as a guinea pig by Nazi doctors, came back to the hotel Lutetia in Paris where my father fetched him, sent back all his medals, and died without saying a word of what had happened.

The novel speaks for all the *desaparecidos* and disquieted souls who linger in an arrested time. As I am writing this, Jean Max Gaudillière and I are coming back from the invitation of the *Abuelas* in Buenos Aires. Their "Center of Attention for the Right to Identity" has already retrieved 109 of their grandchildren, hijacked as babies during the *Processo*, and given to *appropriadores* after the murder of their mothers under the guise of a fake adoption. This Nazi practice in Argentina, where Mengele and others took refuge, had already caused the abduction of 100,000 Polish babies the same way as in Europe during WWII. Linked to the policy of the *Lebensborn* association in Norway, it is recalled by the mother, Lars' wife, when she mentions, after the war, the "ostracized [...] children of German soldiers and Norwegian women [called] [...] German brats" (Hustvedt 2008: 194).

Beyond the central role of their veteran father, keeper of the promise in the wake of WWII, the narrator, keeper of the soul in the current triumph of reification, is like Musil's *The Man without Qualities*, torn between brother and sister, both threatened by the appropriation of their identities. Terror is alternately defused and denied. The heroes cannot help feeling hints of distrust or fear through non-verbal, physical language games, which inform them while they doubt their true impressions, and rationalize them into normality for the sake of generosity.

This oscillation between "Knowing and Not Knowing" is analyzed by Dori Laub and Nanette Auerhahn in cases of extreme trauma among Holocaust survivors and their children (Laub and Auerhahn 1993). In another text, "Art and Trauma," Dori Laub addresses the so-called artistic voyeurism triggered by the fascination for atrocities (Laub and Podell 1995). Siri Hustvedt's other novels also present heroes who know and don't know that they have been used as dolls or puppets under the guise of artistic creation. By the way, the second part of *Don Quixote* reacts to the same kind of defacement, after Cervantes discovered that the first part of his world-famous bestseller has been counterfeited in an anonymous forgery, sponsored by some envious authors of the time (cf. Davoine and Gaudillière 2013).

Still there is a way of knowledge, constantly at work in the book, which does not lie.

When one has seen one's own death impending at the hands of unknown agents, as a newborn, a soldier, a mad person, or as anybody, unusual bodily and psychic reactions occur. Later on, delusions and uncanny feelings warn you of the danger, so you do not lower your guard. Bodily loss of sphincter control, a racing heart rate, roaring headaches, withdrawal, tremors, auditory exclusion, blurred vision, or slow motion time are symptoms of survival in the solitude facing an imminent life threat (cf. Grossman 2004: 55).

In his book *On Combat*, Dave Grossman spoke to firemen who went up the towers of the World Trade Center, to soldiers who came back from the front, and to policemen who faced murderers. They all mention such shameful reactions never told to anybody, as well as the guilt to have survived – as does Lars, the narrator's father, in the novel. To have watched the shooting of a Japanese enemy in a position of prayer erases for him all reflection on his own terror, shuts down the possibility for a witness at that moment of truth, and leads to withdrawal. The fact that you have survived, as an infant or as a soldier, erases your agony: what has happened never happened, don't think about the past.

When soldiers come back from war nowadays, they are rarely asked about their experiences, but instead they are asked about the suspicion: how many babies have you killed? When babies come back alive from an intensive care unit, the question is rarely asked about their exceptional knowledge, in that case for the sake of love. Sometimes, truth is more important than love, say the *Abuelas* of the *Plazza di Mayo*, when the families who took their grandchildren from their murdered mothers still argue that they "love them." In Siri's Jamaican story of Maroon slaves, a fetus speaks the truth from the womb and says "Me a man," when a soldier asks the question of his gender, on the verge of opening his mother's belly. Then, "the sword in the soldier's hand mashed up, and the Englishman fell down dead" (Hustvedt 2008: 222).

What kind of a psychoanalyst is Siri Hustvedt's "analyst in fiction" (Hustvedt 2012: 152–165)? Free from rigid orthodoxy, he is able to learn from "the association of practices" between different cultures; a practice Wittgenstein encourages in his *Remarks on Frazer's Golden Bough* through the model of association of ideas (Wittgenstein 1993: 143). "The worry doctor," as the little girl Eggy calls "the shrink upstairs," has worked in a psychiatric hospital, has treated many veterans, and knows how to stand by their side from his father's experience. Back with his patients in his private practice, he uses his own dreams and tells his patients about his impressions triggered by the session. In return, he has to face the question from Mr. R, "what do you know?" (Hustvedt 2008: 82). When trauma is at stake, the question asked to the analyst, says Dori Laub, is "Who are you?" to pretend to be a witness of a story without a witness. For "[t]rauma isn't part of a story; it is outside the story. It is what we refuse to make part of our story" (Hustvedt 2008: 52). The disclosure of some of the analyst's "irrational reactions" to the uncanny outside story in the session is a way to validate the patient's powerful sense of observation, although it is not easy (Blank 1985: 90).

Still, the "trauma fashion" may be used abusively as a causality to justify all kinds of manipulations. The analyst Erik struggles with the limits of psychoanalysis in such a case when he finally fails to face Ms. L's hate, "whose anger is a drug against feeling frozen out." Her identification to the label "abused child" (Hustvedt 2008: 235) justifies a power game, rather than the quest for truth.

Madness and traumatic revivals explore a different field than the endless control of the other. They aim to create 'otherness.' The analyst can stay by the side of Mr. T, even when he goes back to the hospital, haunted by the "voices of the dead." Erik's definition of psychosis – "They're looking for the bones of the world" (Hustvedt 2008: 184) – allows him to be a co-researcher in their investigation.

This 'psychoanalyst in fiction' reminds me of William Rivers, a historical psychoanalyst, put into fiction by Pat Barker in her *Trilogy* (Barker 1991–1995). Rivers was at first a famous anthropologist in the Salomon Islands and a neurologist, who later became a psychoanalyst for the British traumatized soldiers coming back from the trenches in France and Belgium during WWI. As he was reading Freud, book in one hand, he was forced to invent another method for transference in order to join the traumatized soldiers into the no man's land where the haunting exploded dead comrades lingered. He used himself, or more precisely, the cut out unconscious on his side,[2] manifested in an irrepressible tottering since childhood, which occurred at some precise moments in the sessions, and intermediately greeted the patient soldier as his *therapon* in a brief exchange of their places.

A newborn knowledge of truth speaks all through the book and speaks strangely to me. A precocious agony is described in "[t]he story of Inga's birth and near demise" (Hustvedt 2008: 163). While I am writing now, long after I read *The Shaking Woman*, I realize that on some occasions, invisible banal tremors seize me from head to foot, which I master in an effort not to show them, each time a patient tells me about a cut out experience of death. I have never paid attention to some familiar oddities, which Jean Max notices nevertheless with some irritation, for example when he speaks to me and I answer several

---

2 The "cut out" unconscious in psychoanalysis refers to a dimension of the unconscious that is not tied to repression and inscribed by repressed signifiers but is 'impressed into the body.' In that case, Freud speaks of an unconscious which is not repressed.

hours later. This could be called dissociation, a shut-down of sounds. Now I realize that, like the fetus in the Jamaican tale, I stood as a witness when the Nazis put my mother in jail at the beginning of her pregnancy, in a crowded cell next to the torture chamber. From inside her womb, I must have known about tremors, heart skyrocketing, withdrawal, and so on, of which she never spoke except that she would not be here had she been Jewish – probably her cell and train companions' fate. When she was released, before my delivery, all her hair had turned white.

When I read *The Shaking Woman*, I did not know Siri Hustvedt's work, and I was unaware that this book would take me through a new journey. In 2010, Jennifer Allen, a critic living in Berlin whom we did not know either at that time, had sent us a letter to mention quotations from our book *History beyond Trauma* in *The Shaking Woman*. Soon after, we flew to Boston for a conference on trauma, at the invitation of the Massachusetts Institute of Psychoanalysis. In the Harvard Coop, we bought the little yellow and green book, which I could not stop reading. I was struck by its proximity to our own bearings.

Our next conference was also on trauma, in the Miami Veterans Hospital. There, I found the answer to my question in another green and yellow book: *The Sorrows of an American*. In the discussion after my talk, I could not help mentioning my new readings and launched myself into an unexpected confession on the "Sorrows of a French Resistant" coupled with a little delusion when I was around eight. I had persuaded my school friends Monday after Monday that I had a lover in a blue uniform, who took me for rides every weekend. Although I half believed it, I got short on ideas after a while and stopped, keeping that crazy love to myself ever since, even unbeknownst to my very Lacanian psychoanalyst.

When I was around 60 and stayed in the Alps for winter vacations in the valley near my birth place, I suddenly asked my very old father: "But what did I do during the meetings of the Resistance leaders in our kitchen?" I had been told as a normal fact, as banal as an incarcerated pregnant mother in wartime, that they were meeting there until 1945 when I was two years old.

To my surprise, he answered casually, lifting years of silence:

You were very quiet with a book, a Don Quixote coloring book. Two men came by. A tall and a short one. They were suspects to the others for they wore blue uniforms. I was the only one to know that they were spies for another resistance network, in Pétain's administration. The shorter one loved you so much, he always took you on his lap. He must have had a child of your age. One day, we were rounded up, I was told to hide quickly by a guy who told me, 'you are right, he is with us, he has been caught.' When I last saw him, it was at the station between two SS soldiers. His face was like raw meat. He looked at me, I looked at him, I was the last one he saw for they shot him soon after. Every day I see his eyes. His name is Vitek, he was Jewish.

Recently, I discovered his name in a book brought by a patient, about a network called *L'Arche de Noé*, the Noah Arch, connected with the English Intelligence Service (cf. Fourcade 1968: 643).

After I delivered that love story and was already regretting this sudden exposure, a young girl came to me during the pause. While I was standing with a coffee and doughnut, she told me her parents knew Vitek's wife. She had emigrated to the US after her husband had died in the war. Yes, they had a boy my age. I was stunned, thunderstruck. Did not think of asking her phone number, went back to the table for the next talk, looked for her afterward. She had disappeared. I know only her first name: Deborah.

The impulse to make public this quixotic story had been triggered by *The Sorrows of an American*. "The trauma speaks to trauma and only to trauma," says Jean Max. My soldier in the blue uniform was my Dulcinea. Of course one could object, "but Dulcinea is a lady!"

La Dame lointaine des Pensées, the Faraway Lady of the Thoughts... for me is a man.

During the European long Middle Age, the Theater of the Fools, among whom stood Don Quixote and his *therapon* Sancho Pança, laughed out abusive leaders making bubbles of themselves, thanks to Carnival inversions. They put the world upside down, and gender too.

No wonder then, my favorite character in the book is Burton, the sweating quixotic fellow, who fights for the honor of his blackmailed Dulcinea, Inga. He ends the novel as in a Carnival ritual, disguised as a huge woman: "both mad and feminine [...] in my false bosoms and preponderant behind, in my big, fat, uninhibited woman-ness roving the city streets" (Hustvedt 2008: 291). Here is, I thought, my dear "Mother Folly," the main character of fifteenth century French sotties, at the end of the Great Plague and the Hundred Years' War. She also takes the floor "as a woman," in Erasmus' *Praise of Folly*. Likewise, Burton's woman-ness unmasks the almighty journalist, oozing with hatred and envy.

Now, do we have a gender problem here? I had no difficulty identifying with Erik, "the renegade psychoanalyst" in Brooklyn, from a rural culture (Hustvedt 2008: 9). Still, this culture trusts, whatever happens, the Green Man to come back.[3] This confidence permeates his style of psychic healing through unnoticed

---

[3] The Green Man is a very ancient divinity of irrepressible life. He is dressed with leaves, and

thresholds carefully crafted in the novel, "to fend off the ugly truths of chaos, death and decay" (Hustvedt 2008: 18). The two vectors of psychotherapy, the old storytelling and more recent psychoanalysis, are dispatched between the masculine and feminine gender. Well, I always had a male imaginary companion as far as I remember, perhaps the surviving images of the youths meeting in our kitchen, among whom many were killed.

This familiarity with death from a young age may perhaps, later on, attract other children's sadism toward the stranger coming from beyond the rainbow. Inga is a bullied child, for she has a knowledge which escapes the control of her peers. A visceral memory, a resonance "of yore," says Burton. We call this resonance with un-symbolized matters 'cut out impressions,' and use them as a link with spaced patients, powerful against attacks on linking and on thinking they have to face, resulting, says Bion, in "thoughts without a thinker" (Bion 1997: 27).

There are many thoughts in the novel looking for a thinker. They proceed from what we call a 'cut out unconscious,' not inscribed by signifiers, but impressed into bodily sensations, "following the scent leading to blood," as says the chorus of the Erynies, in Eschyles' Euménides (v.247). Leading to ancient sorrows too. *The Sorrows of an American* follows that path, on which wander people, like the knight, with a sad countenance: "All his life, my father freely distributed his tenderness to the downtrodden, the misshapen, the sorry, and the sad" (Hustvedt 2008: 38).

This unconscious does not know time either. But as it is not repressed – for no signifiers exist there, no Otherness, except a ruthless other for whom there is no other – it imposes an arrested time on everyday life. The novel makes clear that stoppage of time by juxtaposing moments of catastrophes – both in the little story of the heroes and the contemporary History. They are separated by blank lines, which give the reader a space to breathe and to build his or her own patchwork from cut out pieces of worn out fabrics on her side.

The father's first traumatic revival happens as he hears the choir in the college church sing "O day full of Grace," which triggers the flashback of the kneeling Japanese officer on the verge of being shot in prayer. "I began to tremble," writes the young man of 24. "Traumatic memory arrives like a blast in the brain [...] a roar of terror" (Hustvedt 2008: 136), writes his daughter who is connected to his experience, as an infant, by two weeks spent in the wake of immi-

---

from his mouth disgorges vegetation. One can see him carved on the vaults and capitals of churches and cathedrals all over Europe (cf. Anderson 1990).

nent death, and later by the apocalyptic day of 9/11, when "[w]e were running. I thought we were going to die" (Hustvedt 2008: 137).

After reading *The Shaking Woman*, I was looking for this outlandish shaking, overflowing as a tidal wave, from the father in the Pacific to his daughter in the US, through an abolition of time and space distance. In December 2001, soon after 9/11, Erik acknowledges, "I believed that in my own analysis [...] I had been able to articulate the distance I felt from my father [...] the gulf between us [...] I realized that I was deluded" (Hustvedt 2008: 70–71). Their connection happens thanks to a 'time quake.'

'Time quake' is a neologism dear to Jean Max, created by Kurt Vonnegut (Vonnegut 1997). It deals with such a proximity and immediacy at "the crossroad between the little story and the big History where delusion happens," said one of my first delusional patients. The insignificant and unseen witness of this momentum is precisely the fool, Burton, the analyst's buddy, "a fat, waddling, red-faced person who had little luck with girls [...] [for] he was humid to the core, a peripatetic swamp of a man" (Hustvedt 2008: 71). He stands for the power of the powerless against the appropriation of their identity during war and peace traumas.

The link between the healing of war traumas and psychosis by psychoanalysis is made clear in the book by a question put to Erik during a dinner at his sister's, "do you follow the orthodox Freudian line?" He answers, "[a] lot has happened in psychoanalysis since Freud" (Hustvedt 2008: 104), and I would add since Lacan too. Erik's criticism of structural diagnosis is clear: "I've come to think of consciousness as a continuum of states from awake cogitation to daydreaming to the altered consciousness of hallucinations and dreams" (Hustvedt 2008: 105). His statement echoes Harry Stack Sullivan's claim that "the difference between the well and the disordered is wholly one of degree and not one of kind" (Sullivan 1974: 271). In other terms, ghosts may intervene without warning at critical moments for anybody. For instance, when Inga evokes her dead husband and father, her hands begin to shake. When I tell stories about psychotic transference in order to argue that one may get out of psychosis, a question is regularly asked: "But what you say applies also to neurotics and even normal people." Of course. We speak of moments, of 'time quakes,' when the other fades away; besides, one is never mad or traumatized 24 hours a day.

Another passage of the book confirms this proximity of war traumas and psychosis. The soldier's return greeted by betrayals, revenges, "Dear John letters," and the deadly worries of his home front, often its incomprehension, which makes him "homesick at home" (Hustvedt 2008: 107). The next paragraph tells about Mr. T's admission to the psychiatric hospital. Haunted by "killer words" and voices from the dead, he is seen by a doctor in a hurry who labels him with "thought disorders." His analyst knows that "his paternal grandparents had survived the Nazi death camps, but his father had never spoken of it." Returning to his old notes, Erik reads the first words this patient had ever spoken to him: "The ground is screaming" (Hustvedt 2008: 109). *Griten las piedras del campo*, "the stones are screaming in the country," is a powerful love song, a healing song too, sung by Mexican Mariachis.

When human speech is not available, the animist world speaks. But also, when one is told to shut up, voices happen as a witness of traumatic experiences. By claiming that their voices are helpful and teach them "an unclaimed experience" (Caruth 1996), the Hearing Voices Network compares itself to the liberation from enslavement, the conquest of identity rights. The history of Maroon slaves in Miranda's Jamaican family, in the novel, traces an "underground railroad," a path of freedom from psychic enslavement.

The second half of the book takes place mainly in the protagonists' home town in Minnesota for their father's funeral urn burial in June. This sacred space and time opens with a memory told in the present tense, resonating like a thunderclap. The two children discover their father's uniform and medals in an old trunk. Their joy, "Look, Pappa, look!" is greeted by a palpable wrath: "Put it back, he barks at us, Right now!" (Hustvedt 2008: 155). This order shuts down the subject of a traumatic past, which will reappear throughout the text of the memoir. Still its full return from exile is the book itself. Athapascan Indians in the Northern Territories describe myths in the making by the sharing of childhood secrets, first to an elder after he has dreamt about that child and is able to weave the childhood secret with the visions of his dream, then to a wider circle, enlarging throughout life.

Minnesota is revisited during the funeral in the graveyard. The ritual allows the inscription, both on a grave and into a story, of two disappeared persons: the mysterious Lisa who lives as a recluse with her niece, Lorelei, and the vanished uncle David. In that sacred moment, time stops again: "My life [, says Erik,] had suddenly slowed down. [...] my perception of time had been skewed" (Hustvedt 2008: 175). This spectral time allows the children to proceed beyond their father's innumerable archives of a dying world, and to cross, as on a Nô Theater stage, the bridge toward and from the beyond. From there, unwritten truths may come back as characters dressed with ancient garments, who will dance, sing, and tell, for instance, about the unspeakable betrayals which murdered them.

A theater of dolls made by the recluse Lisa and her niece performs the traumas erased by the lies of her own people, and her delivery at night, in 1937, outside in the dirt, of the stillborn infant. No wonder if the babies of shame, soon to be delivered in Norway for the sake of the Aryan race, had been remembered by their mother, just after the first mention of the strange dolls, in June, at the time of the funeral (cf. Hustvedt 2008: 194). Surviving another genocide in Cambodia, the moviemaker and writer Rithy Pahn recently invented clay figures for his film *L'image manquante*, in order to perform the "annihilation" which escapes words, "the raw truth" which cannot be told. Like Lisa's dolls, the clay figures answer the question, "which comes first? The doll or the story? – The story of course…" The dolls and the clay figures show a story out of history, for the first time when one considers, as writes Rithy Panh, that Cambodian mass murders were supported by some French intelligentsia (Pahn 2011). "'We found the wrong story,' Inga said […]. 'We were looking for one story and ran into another.' […] 'The dolls were testimonies of some sort'" (Hustvedt 2008: 200–201).

Coming back from their father's burial, the psychoanalyst confesses to his sister that he misses his patients, in particular those in the hospital, for they "might be raving or mute or even violent, but there is an existential urgency to them that's invigorating" (Hustvedt 2008: 202). Yet, nowadays, "patients are […] officially referred to as *customers*" (Hustvedt 2008: 202). The dolls will soon protest against the hypocritical marketing of the soul, and enter the scene again to show the truth, during Inga and Erik's second visit to Minnesota in the fall, at Lisa's request. Meanwhile the effects of the inscription process are already on their way. The analyst feels invigorated, and his thoughts while walking in the streets of New York follow a new beat, "a reverie with rhythm" (Hustvedt 2008: 208). On the road!

A cathartic dream appears to Erik with three big detonations at the crossroad of the big History of wars – his father's trenches of 1945, 9/11, the Iraq War – and the little history of his lineage, actually articulated in a 'timequake,' by

> [t]hree detonations. Three men of three generations – himself, his father and grandfather – together in a house that was going to pieces, a house I had inherited – the white little farm in the prairie – a house that shuddered and shook.

As Erik accepts his legacy after the dream, he says "I quake" (Hustvedt 1998: 232). Be the subject of that quake of time and, as such, be ready to receive the true story of the mysterious promise. By entering the arrested time, both brother and sister may follow Lisa's second visit to their father in the autumn of 1941, just before the deflagration of Pearl Harbor.

Lisa greets them lying in her bed which is staged like a space in between two deaths. "I knew the old lady was going to confess," says Eric. "She was enjoying the scene, that it was a production. She had planned it, hairdo and all; perhaps even her sickbed was a charade. For a dying woman, she struck me as unusually robust" (Hustvedt 2008: 244). Nevertheless, the ceremonial space is set, the dolls are unveiled through three dioramas: a squatting doll whose mouth has been stitched, a boy in overalls with a knife, cutting the umbilical cord, and a male pressing a spade into the dirt.

The burial "of yore," as says Burton the fool, can be accomplished only when the truth is finally told: the stillborn baby is not their father's, but another man's, a "nobody." Old Lisa can at last say, "The labor pains was bad, real bad, but after it was over, it wasn't me no more. [...] Was just like I had nothin' to do with it" (Hustvedt 2008: 245). At the same time, she "delivers" that she has found her mother's and sibling's graves. Then her niece tucks her into her bed, "tight enough," like a baby. The regeneration of otherness and speech has been performed thanks to the seed planted by their father, while he was burying the "little thing." "[H]e kept his word," so that his descendant may rely and create on that foundation (Hustvedt 2008: 248).

At that point, the psychoanalyst pays a visit to the dead, *nekuia* in ancient Greek, and can be together now with his father and grandfather who "was also a man steeped in regional lore, and he passed on the tales he had heard" (Hustvedt 2008: 256). This is true to the author herself and to the psychoanalyst who, in such 'timequakes,' has to be steeped in the art of storytelling.

Works Cited

Anderson, William. 1990. *Green Man: The Archetype of Our Oneness with the Earth.* Photography by Clive Hucks. London/San Francisco: Harper & Collins.
Barker, Pat. 1991. *Regeneration.* London: Viking.
Bion, Wilfred. 1997. *Taming Wild Thoughts.* London: Karnac.
Blank, Arthur, Stephen Sonnenberg and John Talbott. 1985. *The Trauma of War: Stress and Recovery in Viet Nam Veterans.* Washington: The American Psychiatric Press.
Caruth, Cathy. 1996. *Unclaimed Experience, Trauma, Narrative, and History.* Baltimore: The Johns Hopkins University Press.
Davoine, Françoise and Jean Max Gaudillière. 2004. *History beyond Trauma.* New York: Other Press.
Davoine, Françoise and Jean Max Gaudillière. 2013. *A bon entendeur, salut! Face à la perversion, le retour de Don Quichotte.* Paris: Stock.
Fourcade, Marie-Madeleine. 1968. *L'Arche de Noé. Réseau "Alliance," 1940–1045.* Paris: Plon.
Grossman, Dave. 2004. *On Combat: The Psychology and Physiology of Deadly Conflict in War and in Peace.* Warrior Science Publications.
Hustvedt, Siri. 2008. *The Sorrows of an American.* New York: Picador.
Hustvedt, Siri. 2009. *The Shaking Woman, or, A History of My Nerves.* New York: Picador.
Hustvedt, Siri. 2012. *Living, Thinking, Looking.* New York: Picador.
Lacan, Jacques. 1992. *The Ethics of Psychoanalysis (1959–1960).* Trans. Dennis Porter. New York: Norton.

Laub, Dori and Nanette Auerhahn. 1993. "Knowing and not Knowing: Forms of Traumatic Memory." *International Journal of Psycho-Analysis* 74: 287–302.
Laub, Dori and Daniel Podell. 1995. "Art and Trauma." *International Journal of Psycho-Analysis* 76: 991–1005.
Nagy, Gregory. 1979. *The Best of the Achaeans*. Baltimore: The Johns Hopkins University Press.
Pahn, Rithy. 2011. *L'annihilation*. Paris: Grasset.
Pahn, Rithy. 2013. *L'image manquante*. Paris: Grasset. et Film. CDP/ARTE. France/Bophana Production.
Shay, Jonathan. 1995. *Achilles in Viet Nam*. New York: A Touchstone Book.
Sullivan, Harry Stack. 1974. *Schizophrenia as a Human Process*. New York: Norton.
Vonnegut, Kurt. 1997. *Timequake*. New York: Berkley Books.
Wittgenstein, Ludwig. 1993. *Philosophical Occasions: 1912–1951*. Cambridge: Hackett.

Jason Tougaw
The Self Is a Moving Target:
The Neuroscience of Siri Hustvedt's Artists

> [...] there is a coherent foundational process, or "self representation," that does not observe in the conventional sense but is observed or at least strongly "intermeshed" with various higher perceptual processes. In other words, the self-schema provides input into many sensory analyzers, and it is also strongly influenced by the primal emotional circuits [...] These interactions may constitute affective consciousness.
> – Jaak Panksepp (1999: 309)

Ekphrasis – the literary descripton of visual art – would appear to have little to do with theoretical neuroscience. But in Siri Hustvedt's novels, she represents painting and other visual arts to ask many of the same questions about the meaning of selfhood that animate her interest in neuroscience, psychology, and the philosophy of mind. All of Hustvedt's novels portray artists interested in representing the self – with varying degrees of villainy – and her descriptions of their work belong to the venerable history of ekphrasis: Achilles' shield in Homer's *The Iliad*, the frescoes in Cervantes' *Don Quixote*, the Grecian urn in Keats, the masterpiece in Zola, Dorian Gray's portrait in Wilde, Icarus falling in Auden, *The Goldfinch* in Donna Tartt. Unlike most of these fictional artworks, Hustvedt's tend to be contiguous with forms of "self representation" our brains engage in.

It's rare enough for a writer to employ ekphrasis so routinely and even rarer for a novelist to describe entire collections or exhibitions of visual art, as Hustvedt does in several of her novels. In Siri Hustvedt's novels, ekphrasis is central to the development of mystery plots whose resolutions require more than the solving of crimes or the revelation of secrets. They require characters to confront Hustvedt's primary preoccupations – with the relations between minds, bodies, identities, and felt, unfelt, and barely felt subjective experience. Visual art – and especially portraits – is one of Hustvedt's vehicles for dramatizing thorny questions about what it feels like to be human. When her artists are villains, it is because they abuse their power to fix or exploit identity through representation. Neuropsychologist Jaak Panksepp (a colleague and friend of Hustvedt's) describes "affective consciousness" – the feeling of having a self – as a product of an organism's experience of the full range of emotions, felt and unfelt, "intermeshed" (or mixed) with "higher perceptual processes" and "strongly influenced by the primal emotional circuits" (1999: 309). Hustvedt's artists tend to invite brainy characters struggling with primal emotions to sit for them. Their portraits tend to reveal the flux of experience that makes identity. They also tend to provoke identity crises, rooted in the subjects' discomfort with what is revealed in the portraits. What is revealed has everything to with proposals about the physiology of self in the work of neuroscientists – for example, Panksepp's argument about relationships between "primal emotions" and cognition, Damásio's theory about consciousness arising from the brain's mapping of the body's basic functions, or Solms' demonstration of how the psychoanalytic and neurological minds may be reconciled. In Hustvedt, ekphrasis becomes a vehicle for exploring the interpersonal implications of hypotheses like the ones they propose.

Hustvedt nestles a joke into *The Blazing World* (2014) that hints at the connection between art and neuroscience. Her artist-protagonist Harriet Burden places Hustvedt at the end of a lengthy list of writers and thinkers who have theorized the relationship between mind, body, and self: "[...] and an obscure novelist and essayist, Siri Hustvedt, whose position Burden calls a 'moving target'" (254). The joke signals Hustvedt's stance. She is insistent on the inconsistencies that define her dramatization of identity. Hustvedt's writing is about moving targets, about the framing and reframing that makes selfhood intelligible. Her writing – fiction and nonfiction – invites readers to step into the various frames, to try on points of view. If there is a crime in Hustvedt's fiction, it is nearly always tied to a criminal who clings too rabidly to a philosophical position, refusing or unable to be influenced by other points of view. These crimes nearly always involve works of art, and they tend to yoke questions about mind and body, representation, and barely felt experience. Collectively, the crimes and misdemeanors of Hustvedt's artist characters become an index of the philosophical positions she dramatizes.

Hustvedt's joke works through a form of double ventriloquism. The joke appears in an essay attributed to art critic Richard Brickman, a persona adopted by Harriet Burden, who publishes philosophical essays in academic journals using the pseudonym. In other words, the joke is a product of mixing personae. Siri Hustvedt is Richard Brickman, who is Harriet Burden, philosophizing about the relationship of the work of Siri Hustvedt to a lineage of philosophers and neuroscientists making arguments about the mind, body, and self. Brickman's tone is downright severe; Burden's position is playful, in the sense that she is playing a trick on her academic audience, but her remark is earnest. To get the joke, you have to be in on the levels of ventriloquism that mix the points of view. Hustvedt's position is a moving target because her method is to dramatize gaps and questions in response to a history of arguments and propositions. Taking too firm a position would make her like one of her artist criminals.[1]

---

[1] A firm position would also make Hustvedt an author of didactic fiction, designed to instruct

One way to trace the "moving target" of Hustvedt's position is to examine the portrait artists who reappear in all of Hustvedt's six published novels. A significant number of these artists are in the business of exploiting others through portraiture – almost a kind of soul stealing, whereby the artists capture some unnerving image of their subjects, an image that reveals some degree of instability in their identities. Hustvedt is interested in revealing these instabilities, but her narratives condemn their exploitation, which generally involves a fixing of unstable moments, through which a marginal aspect of the subject's identity becomes a public replacement for the person who posed for the portrait.

As Christine Marks argues in her book *"I am because you are": Relationality in the Works of Siri Hustvedt* (2014), "Hustvedt's work exhibits the inevitable interrelatedness of the human experience while advocating self-other relations based on dialogical intersubjectivity" (2). Marks identifies a lineage of modern thinkers whose theories about "self-other relations" reverberate through Hustvedt's fiction like moving targets, including Hegel, Lacan, Winnicott, and Merleau-Ponty. Marks's choice of verbs captures key qualities of Hustvedt's narrative style. In her novels, she exhibits ideas about the self that she explores in her essays, where she advocates what Marks calls "a philosophy of mixing" – articulated explicitly by the character Violet in *What I Loved*: "mixing is the way of the world. The world passes through us – food, books, pictures, other people" (88). Exhibition is a recurring theme in the novels. Hustvedt's artists capture and exhibit portraits of her other characters, who respond with varying degrees of discomfort to finding images of themselves fixed, framed, and displayed for others. The discomfort arises from a tension that emerges from portraiture. Artist and subject mix in the process of creating images, but the subjects end up feeling exploited through the artists' denials of the mixing. The denials leave the subjects feeling exposed during moments when the world is passing through them.

In Hustvedt's first novel, *The Blindfold* (1992), the artist, a photographer named George, seduces Iris (famously, an anagram for *Siri*), into posing for him. Unnerved by the results, Iris accuses George of stealing her soul:

---

rather than to catalyze the kinds of subjective experience she writes about. David Brooks's *The Social Animal: The Hidden Sources of Love, Character, and Achievement* is a useful foil for Hustvedt's fiction. The "hidden sources" in Brooks's fictional thought experiment lie in the unconscious work of the mind-brain. Unlike Hustvedt, Brooks's position is a stable target – the unconscious is the creative, social force of cognitive neuroscience, not the roiling menace of psychoanalysis – and his prose plodding.

> "You robbed me." I didn't know what the words meant, but they seemed to identify an amorphous truth.
> He looked at me squarely. "You came here. I photographed you. You came because you wanted to come."
> I stopped breathing. He was right. (78)

Iris is not sure why the print upsets her, but she knows she does not want it exhibited. The evidence is in her body. When Iris stops breathing, Hustvedt invites readers to imagine the interruption of her breath – to imagine George's power over Iris's autonomic nervous system. Her embodied experience becomes the evidence of his violation *and* her complicity. Iris wanted to be fixed, and George manipulated her. The only resolution to their debate is to acknowledge both truths. Nonetheless, George is the villain. He uses the portrait to instigate social controversy and to hurt her so he can witness her in a state of pain. Outright manipulation trumps a little unconscious desire for objectification. In his "dialogic intersubjective" relationships, George wields power through his position as witness and distributor, the one who controls who mixes with whom and how.

1. The Artists

Most of Hustvedt's artists are portraitists of one kind or another. They work in a range of media; some are obsessive, others nearly deranged, some malicious, some ruthless, others merely eccentric. They share a devotion to visual representation that overshadows decorum. They flout conventional attitudes about privacy, devote themselves to craft at the expense of intimate relationships, and they document what others don't want to see. While they are all interested in challenging cultural and aesthetic convention, their ethical stances – about the relationship between art and life or the portrait and the person – vary enormously. Their ethical positions become legible through their attitudes about framing. They all know that visual composition is powerful because it endows images with meaning. They all enjoy the power to manipulate the meanings of images. They all know that a portrait is a creative distortion. Their portraits frame the "dialogical intersubjectivity" (2014: 2) Christine Marks traces in Hustvedt's fiction. Portraits frame the mixing of artist, subject, and viewer. Reading about Hustvedt's portraits is almost like climbing into this frame to muck around with the materials that shape the encounters they engender. She judges her portraitists according to their ethical relationship to the mixing they provoke.

The artists who exploit portraiture's power to fix their subjects – including *The Blindfold*'s George, *What I Loved*'s Teddy Giles, *The Sorrows of an American*'s

Jeffrey Lane, and *The Blazing World*'s Rune – are outright villains. Those who experiment with visual forms that foreground unseen or unrepresentable qualities of their subjects' experience – including *The Enchantment of Lily Dahl*'s Edward Shapiro, *What I Loved*'s Bill Wechsler, *The Summer without Men*'s Abigail, and *The Blazing World*'s Harriet Burden – are difficult people who struggle with success at forming mutually rewarding social relationships. *The Enchantment of Lily Dahl*'s Martin Petersen is in a category of his own. Deranged by his obsession with the image's power to distort reality, Petersen's work becomes evidence of crime and mental instability, yet his collages and life-size doll project share many of the aesthetic hallmarks of Hustvedt's other artists, especially the emphasis on the ironic relationship between the artist's materials and the subject's experience.

Portraits represent living bodies inhabiting physical space – in Hustvedt, apartments and streets, mostly – but they also represent the immaterial experience of those living bodies and the relationship between artist and subject. In that sense, portraiture is a vehicle for exploring elements of selfhood uncannily similar to the ones that comprise the theory of self and consciousness proposed by António R. Damásio, with whom Hustvedt has engaged in an ongoing public dialogue about their shared preoccupations. Damásio's theory of consciousness hinges on the dynamic relationship between "organisms" and "objects," a relationship that produces the mental "images" that comprise subjective experience (1999: 11). Damásio's model shares a great deal with Panksepp's. Both identify what Damásio calls "primordial feelings" (echoing Panksepp) as a foundation for both self and consciousness. In Damásio's words, these are "the elementary feelings of existence that spring spontaneously" from our brains' constant mapping of the changing states of our bodies (2010: 24). Damásio acknowledges what philosophers call an "explanatory gap" concerning bodies and the feelings that animate them. Hustvedt's artists explore or exploit this gap. In a sense, her novels are about the ethics of visual representation focused on how the artist's tools – paint, camera, plastic, clay – make new objects from selves. Damásio's argument suggests that objectification is fundamental to consciousness. We become who we are through our relationships with the objects in our worlds. As Christine Marks observes, Merleau-Ponty conceptualized self and other as "a union which transcends the distinction between subject and object and allows for intersubjective harmony" (2014: 57). That's the ideal, but as Marks acknowledges, it can go wrong. If relations are not reciprocal, the result can be "cleavage," "loss of subjectivity," and even "annihilation." In Hustvedt's fiction, the relationship between artists and their subjects is fraught with the ethics of reciprocity implied in Merleau-Ponty's philosophy of the self. The artists document objectification, and her novels dramatize the ethical questions that ensue: What does the new object – the portrait – do to its subject? Does it foster union or catalyze annihilation? Might it transform the psyche of the subject? Is it the artist's responsibility to care?

Hustvedt doesn't answer these questions in her novels. Instead, she dramatizes the ethics of visual representation – which she explores in more concrete terms in her essays. In *The Blindfold* (1992), George persuades Iris to pose. She objects to the photograph, taken while she danced around his apartment in a frenzy, because it seems to represent her as "a face without reason" (63). The photograph circulates around New York City with a kind of talismanic force, gaining a social life of its own as its subject goes into a kind of peripatetic hiding. In *The Enchantment of Lily Dahl* (1996), two portraitists propel the eponymous heroine's confrontations with reality, perception, and illusion. Edward Shapiro, a New York artist visiting the small town where Lily was raised, becomes her lover – and drives her to jealousy when he paints her elderly neighbor while local misfit Martin Petersen builds a life-size doll of Lily. In *What I Loved* (2003), Bill Wechsler's paintings propel plot. The novel opens with narrator Leo Hertzberg's description of a portrait of a woman lying on the floor, haunted by the shadow of the artist and the foot and ankle of a woman apparently walking out of the frame. The second painting is a portrait of Mark, as the two-year-old son of Wechsler's friends and neighbors. When Mark becomes a teenager with a severe case of empathy disorder, he befriends *enfant terrible* artist Teddy Giles, who steals the portrait and exhibits it – torn and slashed – as his own work of metacommentary on the art world. In *The Sorrows of an American* (2008), protagonist Erik Davidsen develops a case of unrequited love for a neighbor whose estranged husband, Jeffrey Lane, is a controversial photographer. Lane photographs his daughter and her mother secretly, breaks into Davidsen's apartment, and photographs him in a state of uncontrolled rage – exhibiting the portrait without his permission. In *The Summer without Men* (2011), the elderly Abigail bewilders the novel's heroine and narrator, Mia Fredericksen, with her sinister "amusements" – works of needlepoint planted with secret buttons that open upon sinister worlds that seem to represent her community's history of sexual violence. In *The Blazing World* (2014), Harriet Burden, a giant, loquacious autodidact of an artist, hires successively three men to exhibit her works as their own, including her various versions of her "metamorphs" – three dimensional portraits of humanity's abject or liminal experience. In the end, the art scammer is scammed by her more ruthless peer, Rune, who taunts her with a video of her dead husband and seduces her into revealing a video portrait of her own antics, whereby the two artists don masks and play a sadomasochistic game. If there is an ethical undercurrent shared by these novels, it goes something like this: Human beings will represent the world and objectify each other in the process.

We should be careful about the process and the results. But the dynamics of objectification vary with relationships, so there is no singular ethical stance to guide us. It is all in the details – and the relations.

If *The Blindfold* inaugurates Hustvedt's use of portraits to propel plot, *The Blazing World*, her latest novel, complicates the narrative role of the portrait in too many ways to trace. Early in *The Blindfold*, Iris and George witness a woman undone by an epileptic seizure on a city street. George swears and fumbles in a failed attempt to get a shot of the suffering woman. Afterwards, he and Iris argue about the ethics of portraiture after she annoys him by suggesting "maybe it was for the best":

> "Why?" said Stephen. He sounded annoyed.
> "Well, because it would be terrible for her if she knew, and it seems so invasive, recording a person's suffering."
> "You really believe that there are subjects that shouldn't be photographed?" George said. He spoke evenly and softly.
> "Maybe I do," I said, thinking aloud. (49)

Maybe. George interprets Iris's uncertainty as weakness. But he cannot see what he cannot see. An epileptic seizure represents the kind of experience – primordial feelings – that haunts a portrait. It is powerful and disabling, but it is also inarticulate. It marks a person, but that person cannot remember what happened. Put another way, the phenomenology of experience holds a spectral relationship to the portrait (a relationship Oscar Wilde dramatizes ingeniously in *The Portrait of Dorian Gray*).

When Iris poses for George, the scene is a staged re-enactment of the seizure episode, with Iris cast in the part of the epileptic:

> It doesn't matter, I said to myself. Maybe that thought was the break, the change I willed in myself without knowing why. The pace quickened. I heard myself laugh. We found a rhythm. George moved from side to side. He squatted, stood, knelt, and I moved with him. He laughed, and I danced, carefully at first, aware of my arms and legs, my waist and hips, seeing myself as in a mirror, but then I forgot myself and moved faster and faster. I gyrated and spun like a lunatic for George, who shouted encouragements and took what seemed like hundreds of pictures, stopping only to put more film in the camera. My feet pounded the floor. I made noise, slapping my thighs, beating a chair with my hands, and hooting with an exuberance that made me dizzy. My heart raced. I don't know how long it went on, but I remember panting from the effort, feeling the sweat in my hair and under my arms, and finally bending over in exhaustion. I looked at George. He grinned. He was sitting on the floor with his camera in his lap. I knelt down and crawled toward him, looking at his lean arms and beautiful mouth. I lifted my right arm and extended my hand toward his face, but something in his expression stopped me. I have what I

want, it seemed to say. Don't come any closer. I dropped my arm and sat back, still breathing hard. (54–55)

Iris performs like one of Charcot's nineteenth-century hysterics, willed by a man into a frenzy of feeling whose physicality and irrationality contrast starkly with her ordinary behavior and identity. She hears herself laugh; she slaps her thighs; she hoots; becomes dizzy and sweats. George grins, because he has gotten what he wanted: an image that seems to capture the interstices of Iris Vegan's composed public identity. His mistake is that he believes the performance is more real than Iris's public self, that unconscious or physical expression are more revealing than public behavior governed by social decorum.

In Hustvedt's fictional worlds, it is usually a mistake to believe in one form of experience at the expense of another. When Iris sees the photo George selects and prints, she is startled by the way it forces her to confront herself:

At first I didn't recognize myself. The person in the picture seemed to bear no resemblance to me, and for an instant I thought George had made a mistake, had given me the wrong photo, but then I saw myself, and I had a peculiar sensation of recovery, of remembering a forgotten event, something unpleasant and disorienting. I tried to catch it, but it was like a fragment of a dream that surfaces for a moment during the day, brought forth by a sight or sound, and then retreats – as quickly as it came – into unconsciousness. I put the picture down on the table but picked it up again. (62)

What does it mean that light projected onto paper, or paint, or plastics, or words can represent fragments of experience that "surfaces for a moment [...] then retreats – as quickly as it came"? How should we respond when forgotten experience or alien aspects of our identities are fixed or objectified in art? These are questions that remain alive throughout all Hustvedt's fiction.

If George's photograph suggests these questions indirectly, Harriet Burden addresses them directly in her work. She makes portraits in the form of three-dimensional metamorphs, whose bodies come in a variety of temperatures. She describes them as "the creatures that lived in my memory, not only actual persons, but those borrowed from my vast collection of books. I don't mean just characters but ideas, voices, shapes, figures, articulated thoughts, unarticulated feelings" (2014: 30). Burden extends and blurs the portrait, plays with its capacity to represent something like what Damásio calls "primordial feelings" (2010: 11). Her metamorphs suggest that aspects of self that cannot be seen can nonetheless be manipulated through portraiture, because what you do see makes you think about what you cannot.

Hustvedt endows Harriet Burden with many of her own philosophical positions – particularly the identity mixing that is so central to both her fiction and nonfiction. "We are all a ménage," Harriet states (2014: 230). As the two artists initiate their collaboration, she elaborates:

> And, Harry asked, where does it begin? The thoughts, words, joys, and fears of other people enter us and become ours. They live in us from the start. Moral panic, the multiple-personality epidemic, and recovered-memory mania ran wild in the eighties and early nineties as a wave of suggestion passed from one person to another, a kind of mass hypnosis or spreading unconscious permission that allowed countless people to suddenly become a man, a Pandora's box. Therapists reported on patients with dozens of personalities. Whole populations housed inside a single body – men, women, and children coming out as alters. What did it mean? And then when the name of the illness was changed to Dissociative Identity Disorder and skepticism reasserted itself, the numbers of people diagnosed with the illness diminished to a few cases here and there. What Harry wanted to know was: Were we just one person or were we all many? (326–337)

But Harry is a mess. She allows herself to be duped by a sociopathic charlatan with a shallow interest in philosophy and a fixation with provoking a limited range of feelings in his work – mainly shock, terror, and envy. She may be a mess because she cannot resist provoking the populations housed in her body into savage warfare. She cannot resist making herself an experiment.

Burden's metamorphs are experimental portraits in three dimensions. They free their subjects of conventional frames. Her multiple narrators describe them from their own points of view, generally documenting their ambivalence to the uncanny creatures. She exhibits them in a show entitled *The Suffocation Rooms* under the name Phineas Q. Eldridge, one of her lodgers – a drag queen and performance artist whose experiments with mutable identity meld well with her ethos. In Eldridge's words,

> When I arrived at the lodge, Harry was tending to her own characters, a group of stuffed figures – cold, coolish, warm, and hot. I became fond of her "metamorphs" (as Harry called them), even though a good number of them were injured or deformed. I take that back. I liked the hurt metamorphs most, the ones with missing legs and arms, with braces and slings, humps, or rashes painted on them. They did not look real, but they felt more human than a lot of humans I know, and Harry was gentle with her homemade critters. (117–118)

Burden "tends" her metamorphs – like you would an infant or a farm animal. Eldridge calls them "homemade critters." The metamorphs are humanoid, designed to call attention to the fact that a human is an organism, a species of mammal. Their injuries and deformities are reminders that there is no norm or absolute when it comes to human bodies. They do not look like "real" humans, because a portrait is not a real human. But to Eldridge they "*felt* more human than *a lot* of humans" (italics mine). Notice the wily slip from "real" to "human" here. Eldridge uses the two words like synonyms, but there is always a subtle difference in meaning between words that mean almost the same thing. Burden's metamorphs challenge the idea that we can access another person's reality. Instead, they emphasize feeling. It is more important that her critters feel human. Eldridge's "a lot" is a subtle addition to what amounts to a kind of code for reading the metamorphs. A lot of humans do not feel real to him, but this means that others do. Burden's critters land somewhere between those who feel real to him and those who do not. They disturb binary responses between art and subject. Some art feels more human than humans; some humans feel more human than others; some humans feel less human than art.

The Suffocation Rooms consists of a series of rooms, each a little warmer than the last, amplifying the metamorphs' peculiar range of body temperatures. Burden has placed critters made from beeswax in boxes, "trying to get out," and populated the rooms with other metamorphs, who grow larger as visitors walk from one room to the next (125). In Eldridge's words, "The metamorphs were big, goofy-looking, lumpy things, who sat at their tables in all seven rooms" (125). The seventh room is the warmest and most startling:

> Because she did want the person to look like an alien in some 1950s sci-fi film, the model became more and more realistic: skinny, eerily transparent (liver, heart, stomach, and intestines just barely visible), hermaphroditic (small breast buds and not-yet-grown penis), frizzy red human hair. The creature is strangely beautiful, and when you see him/her in the seventh room out of the box, standing on a stool to look out the window, or rather into the mirror, you can't help feeling touched somehow. The really large (by now) metamorphs have finally noticed that the personage is out and have turned their heads to look at it. (125)

The rooms and the body temperatures replace the conventional frames of portraitures – moving targets replacing fixed ones. *The Suffocation Rooms* involves portraits within portraits. The figure in the box works like a stand-in for all portraits and their subjects, while the metamorphs looking on become portraits of the art's audience. In that sense, viewers are asked to consider their own identities in the act of relating to portraiture, a collective and dynamic act that makes everybody involved both a subject and an object.

The key difference between Burden's art and Rune's lies in their approaches to objectification. Rune makes portraits of himself with the intent to objectify everybody involved, including himself. As Burden's starving poet lover Bruno observes, "I thought he looked like a goddamn male model with his rippling abdomen, popping biceps, films of him scratching his ass, picking his nose" (160). As the objectifier, though, he gets to be the last remaining subject in a world of objects. Burden's collaboration with him is a challenge – to herself as much as to him. She's determined to convince him that identity is dynamic, relational, messy, hard to see, lost in feelings, recursive. Early in their relationship, Burden buys one of Rune's video portraits, which Bruno describes in one of the sections he narrates:

> I'm not sure Harry really liked the thing she bought by Rune – the video screen with faces cut to bits and put back together again, a movie mishmash of glamour and gore. It was multiple – which meant "not that expensive." One afternoon, I parked myself in front of the screen and gave it a yeoman's try. Let me be fair, I said, and not loaded with prejudice just because the artist is an asshole. T.S. Eliot was no paragon, was he? Are these bloody mugs and sliced cheeks any good? Am I interested? Do I care? To be honest, the darned thing stumped me. I told Harry it made me feel lonely, and she laughed, but the she said it made her lonely, too. It's not about communion. (162)

It's not about communion. When there is a problem with a portrait in Hustvedt's work, this is it. Communion is the art of mixing, an antidote to the exploitive potential of portraiture. The climax of Burden's relationship involves a private game in which the two artists don masks and engage in some gender-switching role playing – embodied portraits of characters that represent their commingled fantasy lives. Burden loses. She cannot help becoming Rune's object, and in the end he steals her work and discredits her as a lunatic. If *The Blazing World* is a critique of the art world, its thesis is that too often the art world is interested only in objects and objectification.

2. Dorian Gray's Grandchildren

When Dorian Gray examines his reflection in Basil Hallward's portrait, seeing his own moral and corporeal decay displaced onto the canvas, ekphrasis – a device that ordinarily freezes time – acquires the momentum of narrative. Dorian Gray's painting reverses portraiture's tendency to fix its subjects:

> Hour by hour, and week by week, the thing upon the canvas was growing old. It might escape the hideousness of sin, but the hideousness of age was in store for it. The cheeks would become hollow or flaccid. Yellow crow's feet would creep round the fading eyes and make them horrible. The hair would lose its brightness, the mouth would gape or droop, would be foolish or gross, as the mouths of old men are. There would be the wrinkled throat, the cold, blue-veined hands, the twisted body. (Wilde 1989: 99)

Still beatific, Dorian Gray resists narrative time and maintains his perfection on the surface, but the portrait accumulates his experience and is marked by the sins he displaces. Ordinarily, portraiture captures a moment of subjectivity while narrative chronicles an indeterminate series of passing moments and feelings. Wilde requires the supernatural to transform conventional portraiture into a form that can represent the flux of identity. Hustvedt's artists require only the magic of aesthetic innovation. Wilde places Dorian Gray before the canvas to read the image of his disintegrating body. Like Iris Vegan, an artist seems to have robbed his soul, but unlike Iris's, Dorian's portrait does not circulate. Comparatively, this turns out to be worse. With Hustvedt's novels as a clue, it is easy to see that Dorian prevents himself from mixing, communing, or relating. He is alone with a portrait that documents the hideous evolution of his primordial feelings.

In his book *Portraiture* (2004), art historian Richard Brilliant surveys an intellectual history of the portrait – a history that focuses on paradoxes and tensions created when the flux of identity is represented in static forms. Sounding a little like Hustvedt, Brilliant observes that "[i]f identity is a flexible concept, then defining the relationship between the original and his portrait is surely problematic" (59). Hustvedt's portrait artists tend to revel in the flexibility of identity – and to various degrees they seek power through manipulating that flexibility by exercising control over the relationship between subject and viewer. The trick is to deliver the viewer with a moment of flux and to fix the subject in that moment. A viewer may wonder about the life that surrounds the subject, but the captured moment dominates.

Brilliant describes portraiture "as a method of packaging individuals in neat containers of personhood" (83), but he acknowledges that the particular method is never simple and the packages rarely neat:

> Historically, portrait artists have often sought to discover some central core of personhood as the proper object of their representation. They have done so not because they doubted its existence, as did Klee, but because they wanted to capture, unmistakably, the special quality or qualities of their subject. That invisible core of self was always hard to grasp and even harder to portray, so various solutions were invented that would extend the metaphorical nature of the portrait in a manner consistent with the subject's own behaviour or patterns of self-representation. This mode of portrayal has, as its ruling principle, the presentation of the individual in some special, personal capacity, however extreme that might appear. (67)

Each of Hustvedt's portrait artists deals with the difficulties of grasping "the invisible core self" with particular techniques, using various means to shape "the metaphorical nature of the portrait" in a way that fulfills a set of drives that reveal cracks or gaps in his own flexible identity – though Hustvedt does not provide a sustained representation of the artists' mental lives, thereby making it impossible to do much other than conjecture about what the cracks and gaps mean.

In her book *Portraits and Persons*, philosopher Cynthia Vreeland describes portraiture in similar terms:

> [I]n portraiture, both artist and viewer confront the perennial philosophical problem of the mind's relation to the body. The portrait artist is an alchemist who seeks to make inert physical material 'live' and show us a person, an actual individual whose physical embodiment reveals psychological awareness, consciousness, and an inner emotional life. (2010: 1)

In Hustvedt's novels, the alchemists are powerful, because they possess a unique control over what is revealed – or concocted – with regard to the relationship between "physical embodiment" and "psychological awareness, consciousness, and an inner emotional life." Building on this idea, Vreeland argues that "since antiquity, portraits have been valued because they facilitate contact with important persons who are lost to us" (2010: 72–73). Hustvedt's artists are postmodern. They are not in the business of painting important personages, but they do associate loss with portraiture. The subject of a portrait will never be as she was when it was painted.

Bill's portrait of Violet in *What I Loved* illustrates the problem of time in portraiture by including multiple figures:

> Bill's painting hung alone on a wall. It was a large picture, about six feet high and eight feet long, that showed a young woman lying on the floor in an empty room. She was propped up on one elbow, and she seemed to be looking at something beyond the edge of the painting. Brilliant light streamed into the room from that side of the canvas and illuminated her face and chest. Her right hand was resting on her pubic bone, and when I moved closer, I saw that she was holding a little taxi in that hand – a miniature version of the ubiquitous yellow cab that moves up and down the streets of New York.
>
> It took me about a minute to understand that there were actually three people in the painting. Far to my right, on the dark side of the canvas, I noticed that a woman was leaving the picture. Only her foot and ankle could be seen inside the frame, but the loafer she was wearing had been rendered with excruciating care, and once I had seen it, I kept looking back at it. The invisible woman became as important as the one who dominated the canvas. The third person was only a shadow. For a moment I mistook the shadow for my own, but then I understood that the artist had included it in the work. The beautiful woman, who was wearing only a man's T-shirt, was being looked at by someone outside the painting, a spectator who seemed to be standing just where I was standing when I noticed the darkness that fell over her belly and her thighs. (2003: 4)

The woman leaving the frame and the artist's shadow suggest a narrative – and therefore time. The light streaming through the windows and the miniature taxi suggest a larger milieu for that narrative. The viewer – in this case the novel's narrator – draws attention to the fact that identity implies relationship: "The invisible woman became as important as the one who dominated the canvas." Why? Because she is a sign of Violet's relational identity.

Of course, there is a lot the viewer cannot know. His relation to the figures on the canvas involves a fantasy of relating to its subjects. The painter distorts identity through technique; the viewer grasps for it by looking. What happens to the subject of the portrait? That is the question that Hustvedt dramatizes with all her fictional portraits. The answers vary. They are a moving target that depends on the ethical stance of the artist, the social and psychological position of the subject, and both their relationships to a history of ideas about mind and body – a history that is like a canvas for Hustvedt's narratives. Hustvedt's representation of characters is focalized by this history of ideas; she puts her own audiences in the position of investing emotionally in the lives of characters who embody its insights and gaps. Theoretical problems become narrative ones, urgent and embodied in fictional lives.

A second portrait animates *What I Loved*, a portrait of Mark as a toddler, painted by Bill and later acquired by the villain-artist Teddy Giles: "The little boy was laughing madly as he held a lamp shade on top of his head like a hat, and he was naked except for a paper diaper so heavy with urine and feces that it had sunk low on his hips" (2003: 289). Cryptically, Teddy Giles informs Leo that he has bought the painting "and may use it" (290). Leo is disturbed:

> I knew as well as anyone that paintings circulate – move from owner to owner, languish in dark rooms, reappear, are sold and resold, stolen, destroyed, restored for better or for worse. A painting may resurface anywhere, and yet the sight of that canvas in this place appalled me. (290)

Paintings circulate. They "languish in dark rooms" like Dorian Gray's. They reappear, are stolen and destroyed, like Iris's photograph. Why is Leo appalled? Partly because Mark has grown into a problem – a liar who seems to lack empathy, like Teddy Giles. When Teddy repurposes the portrait, he works in a tradition of shock art very much like Rune's:

> Teddy Giles used the painting of Mark in his new exhibition. The scandal revolved around the fact that the valuable canvas had been destroyed. A figure of a murdered woman, missing one arm and a leg, had been pushed through Bill's painting of his son. Her head protrude through one side of the canvas, choking her at the neck. The rest of her maimed body stuck out on the other side. The force of the piece relied on the fact that an original work of art, owned by Giles, was now as mutilated as the mannequin. (299)

In the art world, the scandal is about the destruction of a valuable work of art. In the novel, it is about the artist's willful exploitation of the flux of identity. His dark reading of relationality equates it with mutilation. If identity is not fixed, there is no self to value. That is the nihilistic reading shared by Hustvedt's villains.

Christine Marks emphasizes the "ambivalence of the other's presence" in Hustvedt's "conceptualization of vision and visual art" (2014: 68). Marks links this ambivalence to Hustvedt's deconstruction of "epistemological certainties attributed to the scopic field" (68). Hustvedt's villains have a way of asserting their own vision as a reflection – or successful manipulation – of the realities they represent. They deny or mock the ambivalence of their subjects. As Marks argues, Hustvedt "highlights how the perception of other people, as a well as the perception of visual art, reflects identity constellations governed by either intersubjective exchange or subject-object domination. [. . .] Looking at somebody else, the individual sees part of herself reflected through the eyes of the other. The look can be both an instrument of subjection and a mediator of affirmation" (69). When a Teddy Giles or a Rune insists on stamping an image with an imprimatur of definitiveness or ownership, he yokes the perception of art and people, he makes art "an instrument of subjection." When they do, it is up to the subjects to find new, more reciprocal frames to occupy.

3. Hustvedt's Frames

Siri Hustvedt has at least one thing in common with Harriet Burden: "The woman was chin-deep in the neuroscience of perception, and for some reason those unreadable papers with their abstracts and discussions justified her second life as a scam artist" (2014: 159). Hustvedt's villain-artists are reductionists, an accusation often lobbed at scientists. They believe they fix identity – or rob souls. That reductionism is key to Hustvedt's use of portraiture as a means for exploring the questions about identity and embodiment that drive her involvement with neuroscience. She draws explicit connections between art and neuroscience throughout her essay collection *Living, Thinking, Looking* (2012). In an essay entitled "Embodied Visions: What Does It Mean to Look at a Work of Art?" she makes her position with regard to neuroscience clear:

> Despite the scientific zeal to atomize experience, to break it down into comprehensible bits and pieces, this approach often results in a frozen view of reality. In recent years, parts of the scientific community have been influenced by the phenomenology of Husserl, and,

more important, by Merleau-Ponty, to challenge a paralyzed, purely third-person view of perception. (2012: 348)

Hustvedt's aim, in the multiple genres she writes, goads neuroscience into accounting for first-person subjectivity. Her term "paralyzed" could be adapted to describe the portraits of her more nefarious artists, the ones who atomize or freeze the experience of their subjects.

Unlike Burden, Siri Hustvedt does not mask herself with pseudonyms when she publishes articles in peer-reviewed science journals – a highly unusual practice for a contemporary novelist – or engages in public discussion with world-renowned neuroscientists and philosophers like Antonio Damásio, Jaak Panksepp, and Ned Block. Instead, she creates new frames for her ideas about relationships between mind, body, self, and art. To date, Hustvedt has published three collections of essays. She has also published three articles in three peer-reviewed neuroscience journals: "Three Emotional Stories" in *Neuropsychoanalysis*, "Philosophy Matters in Brain Matters" in *Seizure*, and "I Wept for Four Years and When I Stopped I Was Blind" in *Clinical Neurophysiology*. She published a book-length essay, *The Shaking Woman, or, A History of My Nerves*, documenting her own neurological anomalies. She has lectured at numerous conferences devoted to neuroscience and philosophy, she has made public appearances in dialogue with neuroscientists like Damásio and Panksepp, and she engaged in debate with philosopher turned cognitive scientist Ned Block in *The New York Times*. In her essays and lectures, Hustvedt translates her narrative preoccupations into arguments – and in the process creates new relations between art and science. She also establishes new contexts for the ideas she explores in fiction, creating for herself an unprecedented position as a novelist who makes direct contributions to debates in theoretical neuroscience.

Hustvedt articulates her roving investigations of these questions in terms of frames in *The Shaking Woman*:

> Who are we, anyway? What do I actually know about myself? My symptom has taken me from the Greeks to the present day, in and out of theories and thoughts that are built on various ways of seeing the world. What is body and what is mind? Is each of us a singular being or a plural one? How do we remember things and how do we forget them? Tracking my pathology turns out to be an adventure in the history of experience and perception. How do we read a symptom or an illness? How do we frame what we observe? What is inside the frame and what falls outside it? (2010: 69)

If the self is a moving target in Hustvedt's work, she inventories some of its movements in her extended essay on her own convulsions and migraines. To know herself, Hustvedt traces the history of medicine, neuroscientific theory, philosophy, and the representation of gender. The implication is that the self cannot be contained within a single frame.

In an essay published in the journal *Neuropsychoanalysis*, Hustvedt rehearses yet another set of frames – disciplinary ones. She proposes a hypothetical novelist, psychoanalyst, and neuroscientist and ventriloquizes their respective explanations of the relationship between memory and imagination. For the novelist, "The story does all the work"; "the novel develops an internal logic of its own, guided by my feelings"; for the psychoanalyst, memories, fantasies, and dreams "exist in a dialogical atmosphere and an abstract conceptual framework. [...] What is created between the analyst and patient is not necessarily a story that represents historical fact, but one that reconstructs a past into a narrative that makes sense of troubling emotions"; for the neuroscientist, "subjective memory and creative acts [are] objective categories, which she or he hopes will unveil the neurobiological realities of a self that remembers and imagines" (2011: 188). If we want to understand phenomena as complex as imagination, memory, creativity, or self, we need multiple frames to do it.

At the end of "Three Emotional Stories," Hustvedt makes an elegant argument about her craft: "Writing fiction, creating an imaginary world, is, it seems, rather like remembering what never happened" (195). Publishing memories of what never happened is a potentially powerful thing to do. That is where ethics come in. By making a career of mixing genres and disciplines, she refuses the methodological or epistemological assumptions that tend to be associated with the novelist, the psychoanalyst, or the neuroscientist. As Marks argues, "Hustvedt [...] promotes a responsibility of the artist in the way in which he or she represents the object" (2014: 100). Quoting Hustvedt, she observes that "[a] good photographer thus does not simply objectify and control her subject, but 'recognizes all that remains unseen'" (101). If Hustvedt's position is a moving target, it is because she emulates that good photographer. She dramatizes "all that remains unseen" in her novels, but she also engages with contemporary neuroscience and neuroscientists in order to encourage them into recognizing the vitality of the unseen in their methods. When the object is the brain, it quickly becomes the self too. So Hustvedt delivers lessons in Merleau-Ponty to the world of neuroscience (and the reading public).

Hustvedt's friend and sometimes collaborator Antonio Damásio argues that the feelings of selfhood involve a kind of constant vacillation and mixing of the "self-as-subject" and "self-as-object." Of course, *mixing* is Hustvedt's term, but it is an apt description of the concept. The self-as-object is "the material me," a "*dynamic collection of integrated neural processes, centered on the representation of the living body, that finds expression in a dynamic collection of integrated mental processes*" (Damásio 2010: 9; emphasis original). The self-as-subject is

> a more elusive presence, far less collected in mental or biological terms than the me, more dispersed, often dissolved in the stream of consciousness, at times so annoyingly subtle that it is there but almost not there. The self-as-knower is more difficult to capture than the plain me, unquestionably. But that does not diminish its significance for consciousness. The self-as-subject-and-knower is not only a very real presence but a turning point in biological evolution. We can imagine that the self-as-subject-and-knower is stacked, so to speak, on top of the self-as-object, as a new layer of neural processes giving rise to yet another layer of mental processing. There is no dichotomy between self-as-object and self-as-knower; there is, rather, a continuity and a progression. The self-as-knower is grounded on the self-as-object. (79)

In the world of Hustvedt's novels, an ethical portrait is one that provides an aesthetic home for the subject-object dynamic that makes the relational self.

Ironically, the self-as-subject becomes 'there' through its relations – which inevitably involves objectification, as we see in the relationships that ensue from the portraits Hustvedt's artists create. In the opening of her essay entitled "Outside the Mirror," Hustvedt describes herself in terms that recall the frenzied dance Iris does for George in order to illustrate the role of the witness in the making of identity:

> It is a peculiar truth that I see far less of myself than other people do. I can see my fingers typing when I look down at them. I can examine my shoes, the details of a shirt cuff, or admire a pair of new tights on my legs while I am sitting down, but the mirror is the only place where I am whole to myself. Only then do I see my body as others see it. But does my mirror-self really represent my persona in the world? Is that woman who gives herself the once-over, who checks for parsley in incisors to avoid a green smile, who leans close to study new wrinkles or the red blotches that sometimes appear on her rapidly aging countenance a reasonable approximation of what others see? I do not witness myself as I talk and gesture emphatically to make absolutely sure my point has been made. I do not see myself as I stride down the street, dance, or stumble, nor do I know what I look like when I laugh, grimace, cry, or sneer. (2012: 52)

Hustvedt sees herself in the frame and wonders, "does my mirror-self really represent my persona in the world?" She makes an object of herself, but it is not the object others make of her. She studies new wrinkles and red blotches on her face, like Dorian Gray gazing at his portrait. She can never witness the dancing, stumbling, laughing, or grimacing others see. If, like Dorian Gray, she were to sit for a portrait, she would see the inexorable flux of her identity fixed at a particular moment, as seen from the particular point of view of the artist. She would see a portrait that objectifies her, but also one that gives aesthetic form to her relationship with the artist and viewers' relationships with the portrait. She would see a fixed representation haunted by the elusive and dense relations that make identity.

4. Final Frame

> "I have come home to die, but dying is not so simple in this our twenty-first-century world. It takes a team."
>
> – Harriet Burden, *The Blazing World*

Sweet Autumn Pinkney, the new age metaphysical dualist, has the last word in *The Blazing World* – and her last word frames Hustvedt's preoccupation with mixing in a voice that is unlike any other to appear in her fiction:

> Auras are like magnets. They pick up all kinds of crap, and mine was getting mucky from the vibrations and negative energies. I was running my hands through my hair all the time and washing up, washing up. Sometimes I'd go outside and walk and let the wind from the water blow over me and clean me. (Hustvedt 2014: 97)

The gesture is not ironic. Harriet is dying, and Sweet Autumn Pinkney's arrival – new age philosophies and all – provides the solace she cannot seem to find from anybody else on the team that marshals her death. With Sweet Autumn Pinkney, Hustvedt adds yet another frame to her exploration of self. If the novelist finds it in story, the psychoanalyst in memory, and the neurobiologist in physiology, Sweet Autumn Pinkney finds it everywhere. She uses new age language to express an idea that suffuses Hustvedt's fiction, from *The Blindfold* to *The Blazing World:* Identity is relational, but its relations can be dangerous. Her artists are measured by their ethical responses to the danger. In the hands of a George or a Teddy Giles or a Rune, subjects become objects with little recourse to the dynamic relationship between objectivity and subjectivity necessary for a person to thrive. In the hands of a Harriet Burden, we all become subjects on the verge of abjection. But in the hands of a Sweet Autumn Pinkney, we are magnets. In each case, it takes a team – not just to die, but to live. Relationships constitute identity. How they do it has everything to do with the ethics of those involved. In Siri Hustvedt's works, portraits are vehicles for exploring the dynamics of objectification involved in being human, and frames become symbols for the ethical choices confronted by an artist attuned to those dynamics.

Works Cited

Brilliant, Richard. 2004 [1992]. *Portraiture.* Cambridge, MA: Harvard University Press. Kindle file.

Brooks, David. 2011. *The Social Animal: The Hidden Sources of Love, Character, and Achievement.* New York: Random House.

Damásio, Antonio R. 1999. *The Feeling of What Happens: Body and Emotion in the Making of Consciousness*. New York: Houghton Mifflin Harcourt.
Damásio, Antonio R. 2010. *Self Comes to Mind: Constructing the Conscious Brain*. New York: Pantheon.
Hustvedt, Siri. 1993. *The Blindfold*. New York: Poseidon Press.
Hustvedt, Siri. 2003. *What I Loved*. New York: Hodder and Stoughton.
Hustvedt, Siri. 2010. *The Shaking Woman, or, A History of My Nerves*. New York: Picador.
Hustvedt, Siri. 2011. "Three Emotional Stories." *Neuropsychoanalysis* 13.2: 187–196.
Hustvedt, Siri. 2012. *Living, Thinking, Looking: Essays*. New York: Picador.
Hustvedt, Siri. 2014. *The Blazing World*. New York: Simon and Schuster.
Marks, Christine. 2014. *"I am because you are": Relationality in the Works of Siri Hustvedt*. Heidelberg: Winter.
Panksepp, Jaak. 1999. *Affective Neuroscience: The Foundation of Human and Animal Emotions*. Oxford/New York: Oxford University Press.
Vreeland, Cynthia. 2010. *Portraits and Persons*. Oxford, UK: Oxford University Press.
Wilde, Oscar. 1989. *The Picture of Dorian Gray*. In: J. B. Foreman (ed.). *The Complete Works of Oscar Wilde*. New York: Harper & Row.

Klaus Lösch and Heike Paul
Dimensions of Tacit Knowledge and the Art(s) of Explication in Siri Hustvedt's Work

1. Introduction

Siri Hustvedt's fictional and non-fictional works circle around the themes of (female) subjectivity and creativity as they are of central relevance to art and aesthetic experience, psychoanalysis, history, and memory. Exploring these broad and complex topics, Hustvedt eclectically engages with texts from a large (and rather male-dominated) canon of Western philosophy and literature in order to point out argumentative fault lines, ambiguities, and (gender) biases along the way and to create new stories in the interstices opened up by these maneuvers. Her (re)formulations of old but still pertinent questions relate to notions of the (autonomous) self, the workings of the psyche, the problem of intersubjectivity, and the role of the imagination. This essay seeks to identify dimensions of tacit knowledge in Hustvedt's writings in order to analyze her work in the wider multidisciplinary framework of critical approaches to knowledge production, and, in turn, to probe the gender-specific aspect of tacit knowledge which appears to be often neglected in recent scholarship. We will single out three different texts in order to focus on three different ways in which the tacit dimension (to use the title of Michael Polanyi's well-known work [1966]) of knowing is 'presentified' in her writings.[1] 'Presentifying' here means to make the tacit/implicit partially explicit and thus to make it tentatively accessible (but not easily graspable or comprehensible) in language; the concept of the tacit dimension of knowing thus allows for the discussion of divergent topics and effects of such implicitness. First, in her non-fictional account *The Shaking Woman, or, A History of My Nerves* (2009), which may be classified as life writing and has been called a "neuro-memoir" (Boyers 2014) and in some of her personal essays collected in *Living, Thinking, Looking* (2012), Siri Hustvedt looks at conceptualizations of subjectivity and the embodied subject specifically in terms of 'saneness' vs. pathol-

---

[1] The Erlanger research program on "presence and tacit knowledge" funded by the German research foundation is the institutional context for this essay. The program is dedicated to analyses of (culturally specific) phenomena of presence and their interdependency with forms of tacit knowledge. The latter is understood in light of a repertoire of theories and perspectives in the sociology of knowledge and the philosophy of knowledge ranging from Gilbert Ryle, Karl Mannheim, and Michael Polanyi to Alexis Shotwell and Alva Noë.

ogy and describes how this normative dichotomy is defined in the fields of psychoanalysis, philosophy, and neuroscience. It is particularly the realm of the latter she encounters in her own medical treatment of a mysterious, iterative condition that she refers to as "shaking." The inexplicability of that condition and the longing to find some clues how best to deal with it prompt her to delve into an essayistic appraisal of those explanations that are (more or less) tentatively offered by various 'experts,' while she is well aware of the long patriarchal psychiatric/medical history that has labeled women pathological, i.e. 'hysterical' and of the often implicitly gendered relationship of the female patient to the male doctor and to medical authority at large which has been experienced mostly as disempowering by the patients. Second, in her novel *The Sorrows of an American* (2008) Hustvedt probes, through the perspective of the psychoanalyst-protagonist, Erik Davidsen, into the analogies between the "talking cure," as Freud has described psychoanalytical therapy, and fictional works that also try to make sense of a past by employing narrative patterns that create coherence (re-membering) and causality – but with a certain twist as Hustvedt puts it: "writing fiction is like remembering what never happened" (Hustvedt 2012: 175). Both narrative procedures hinge on forms of explication and poiesis and provide articulations of processes of remembering – and mourning. Hustvedt's textual method closely relates the imaginative work of the human psyche to questions of explication as therapy and as art and *vice versa*. The second part of this essay thus looks more closely at *The Sorrows of an American*, and finds its poetological model invested in psychoanalysis and in art. By drawing on the works of German-Jewish-American psychoanalyst Hans W. Loewald, who is evoked in Hustvedt's novel, our reading will explore the affinities of psychoanalysis as a "therapeutic art" (Loewald 1980: 353) and literary forms of artistic expression in their respective dealing with the implicit dimension of knowledge by following a series of leads in the novel. Although the gender aspect is not prominent in the novel, psychoanalysis, the foundational theory of (the production of) gender difference, is. Third, Hustvedt's most recent novel to date, *The Blazing World* (2014) creates a multi-layered narrative in order to analyze the mechanisms of gender bias which again can be described as a kind of tacit knowledge that we find the protagonist, Harriet Burden, literally burdened with. The protagonist's masquerade in impersonating male artists uncovers this tacit bias that is so ubiquitous and widely accepted. Even the revelation of her own (i.e. female) authorship of three very different art shows meets with stubborn disbelief in the male-dominated art world. This kind of tacit understanding that resists all contrary evidence points to the agnotological dimension of knowledge production and to what has been referred to as "epistemologies of ignorance," addressed in an analogous context (with regard to race, not gender) by Shannon Sullivan and Nancy Tuana. Such a production of ignorance can be aligned with notions of habitus and cultural capital in the art world and thus would call for a consideration of intersectionality which Hustvedt somewhat falls short of for lack of a thorough critique of white privilege.

In each of these texts, Hustvedt engages with different forms and effects of knowledge production and their investment in matters that are partially or at times unspeakable and non-verifiable. Her concern is, we want to suggest, the tacit dimension of knowing that is an essential part of everyday practices of meaning construction as well as quite a central concern in the realm of creative expression and aesthetic experience. This multi-faceted dimension should not and can not, contrary to what various recent imaging procedures seem to suggest, be reduced to a cognitive mapping that allows for an allocation of its origin and its processing in the human brain (or elsewhere). By way of concluding, we will draw together our findings and make a few suggestions how the various aspects of the tacit might be analyzed in other texts by Hustvedt and other authors.

2. Against Positivism?: *The Shaking Woman* and the Sciences

> "I decided to go in search of the shaking woman."
> (Hustvedt 2009: 7)

In a first step, we will explore tacit knowledge with regard to its presence in Hustvedt's work on psychoanalysis, (creative) writing, and neuroscience. Thus, we will situate Hustvedt's work in the context of the sociology and philosophy of knowledge, where we see her sharing a similar concern like the one which propelled Michael Polanyi's work on the tacit dimension: a distrust of (neo-)positivism as it is currently also at work in the popular neuro-scientific 'fad' and its approach to the human body, brain, and being. Polanyi, himself a scientist by training, half a century ago spoke to the powers of human perception, experience, and skill as somehow tacit (tacitly acquired and tacitly performed) and for the most part unduly neglected by the 'hard' natural sciences and their respective reductionisms. His turn to this tacit knowledge was also a turn from physics to philosophy. In her books, Hustvedt, as a writer of fiction, engages with the neuro-sciences and their promise of curative progress regarding matters of medicinal diagnosis and treatment in quite personal a context: not as expert-scientist, but as object-patient. Yet she also wonders how this progress can actually be measured and verified and how it may be defined vis-à-vis the work of the imagination. Hustvedt's work is concerned with understanding subjectivity and autonomy in their full complexity, and this means human existence in its intertwined conscious and unconscious aspects. Both Polanyi and Hustvedt share an interest in 'alternative' forms of knowledge and knowing, in what we know 'otherwise,' as Alexis Shotwell refers to it in the title of her book (2011), i.e. in those forms of knowing that transcend our cognitive grasp.

Michael Polanyi, the eminent scholar of "tacit knowing," has suggested that "we know more than we can tell" (1969: 159), and that much of what we know we cannot say. In making a strong case for the centrality of the tacit dimension in any form of knowledge production, Polanyi, a physical chemist and philosopher, critically engaged with positivistic notions of knowledge acquisition that he saw as the dominant paradigm particularly in the natural sciences. Against the backdrop of a particular brand of Anglo-Saxon scientific positivism that he sought to criticize and to demystify, he elevated the tacit dimension, provided by the "tacit powers of the mind" (1969: 19), to the status of "the dominant principle of all knowledge" (1969: 13). According to him, it is impossible to achieve objective knowledge or any kind of knowledge that would come detached from personal experience, as Sen emphasizes in his foreword to Polanyi's *Tacit Dimension:* "the process of formalizing all knowledge to the exclusion of any tacit knowledge is self-defeating" (Sen 2009: xi), he wrote. More recently, Jens Loenhoff und Lois Wacquant – following Polanyi's trajectory – have articulated similar concerns. Whereas the latter develops his idea of a "carnal sociology" and a "sociology of flesh and blood" as a critique of an "excessively cerebral and passive notion of knowledge" (Wacquant 2014: 186), the former describes a re-focusing in the study of (tacit) knowledge: "Discourses about tacit knowledge focus on the body and its senso-motoric faculties because they break with intellectualist or mentalist positions and oppose the dogma of the Cartesian cogito" (Loenhoff 2015: 26).

When we study Siri Hustvedt's fictional and non-fictional work, we can detect similar interests and arguments. Hustvedt has repeatedly compared notions of knowledge production in different fields and disciplines in order to point to the shortcomings and blind spots of each of them. For one thing, as a writer, she has critically discussed the role and relevance of neuroscience. Even as she is, according to Christine Marks, "combining scientific inquiry with a writer's imagination" (Marks 2014: 7), she does not settle for the explanatory mode provided. Polanyi never appears as a reference in her texts, yet, she enlists pragmatist and phenomenological philosophers, such as William James and Maurice Merleau-Ponty, alongside Freud, to engage with neuroscientific models of (inter)subjectivity, and thus shifts the argumentative base, once again, from propositional knowledge production to forms of unconscious knowing, embodiment of knowledge, "involuntary memory" (Hustvedt 2012: 191), and the "subliminal self" (2012: 193).

In her essay "Three Emotional Stories," first published in 2010 and reprinted in the collection *Living, Thinking, Looking*, Hustvedt pits forms of world making as they are conceptualized in psychoanalytical, narrative, and neurological discourse against each other, valorizing the distinct knowledges of the mind and the body and describing how they appear to be intricately connected. Her argument departs from the premise that "[t]he novelist, the psychoanalyst, and the neuroscientist inevitably regard memory and imagination from different perspectives" (2012: 177): "Emotions, memory, imagination, story – all vital to our subjective mental landscapes, central to literature and psychoanalysis and, much more recently, hot topics in the neurosciences" (2012: 175). And she summarizes her position:

> We have not solved the mystery of the mind's eye, or what is now framed as a brain/mind problem. [...] Suffice it to say that our inner subjective experience of mental images, thoughts, memories, and fantasies bears no resemblance to the objective realities of brain regions, synaptic connections, neurochemicals, and hormones, however closely they are connected. (2012: 177)

Not the problem of imaging or conceptualization is crucial here, but the distinction between the 'implicit' and 'explicit.' Thus, "[f]ictions are born of the same faculty that transmutes experience into the narratives we remember explicitly but which are formed unconsciously" (2012: 195). Stumbling over the definition of creativity in neuroscience research as "the production of something novel and useful within a given social context" (2012: 194) prompts her to wonder: "Useful? Was Emily Dickinson's work considered useful? Within her given social context, her radical, blazingly innovative poems had no place. Are they useful now? This research definition must be creativity understood in the corporate terms of late capitalism" (2012: 194). Her comment emancipates creativity from an utilitaristic perspective that is centered on 'novelty' and 'usefulness' and that re-inscribes a narrative of progress into art. Contrary to that view, Hustvedt emphasizes her concern with the implicit and inexplicable dimension of creativity that may not be easily described nor grasped nor contained in prefabricated cultural scripts.

The account of the author's illnesses (migraines and 'shaking') – often addressed in her fictional work as well, e. g. her first novel *The Blindfold* (1992), is at the center of the non-fiction work *The Shaking Woman*. It chronicles how she undergoes various treatments to arrive at a diagnosis for the mysterious symptom referred to as "shaking." She experienced these fits at her father's funeral for the first time and has to cope with that condition repeatedly in situations of public speaking and physical exertion ever since. She is given prescription drugs in order to suppress the symptoms and to make her 'function' in social and professional contexts but does not get a medical explanation and thus keeps looking for answers. Being sent from pillar to post, i.e. from doctor to doctor (psychologists, psychiatrists, psychoanalysts, neurologists) and having been told (by two female doctors) that she is not hysterical – because, for one thing, at 53, she is called ostensibly too old for that – but having been diagnosed with "classical migraine, occasionally morphing into status migrainosis" (Hustvedt 2009: 174), she undergoes one final procedure in order to rule out epilepsy as a possible reason for her fits. This high-tech examination – which is reported toward the end of the book – is a key scene in the text. Hustvedt meticulously describes the procedure, how her head is taped, how the earplugs fuel her anxiety, and how she is slid into the long tube of the machine:

> I feel I have been immobilized at an extraterrestrial rock concert, the rhythms of which arrive as incessant whacks to my head. I try counting the beats. Three long blasts of sound, then six shorter taps. I can assimilate this pattern, but after that a speed hammer arrives. The concert has turned into a robot on amphetamines using me as his drum. I find it hard to remain still. The sounds slam into my head, but I also feel them in my torso, my arms, and my legs. My face convulses involuntarily, and I emerge dazed after my half hour of encapsulation. (2009: 176)

It is quite ironic that the MRI of her brain does not reveal any specific diagnosis, least of all alterations that may account for a history of epilepsy, yet it triggers the symptoms it set out to explain and provokes a serious headache:

> As I leave the building, I am aware of the haze lowering in my head. My vision has changed. Outside, the sunlight hurts. The dizziness arrives, and the nausea. Then sharp pain and the stupefying exhaustion that slows my every step. The MRI has triggered a migraine. The test to search for scars in my brain that would support a diagnosis of epilepsy has knocked that poor organ into familiar territory – the land of Headache. (2009: 176)

In search for visible evidence to explain and account for her symptom of shaking, the medical procedure has activated the realm of implicit corporeal patterns that cause renewed physical pain, one may conclude. Approaching Hustvedt's text from the perspective of knowledge production points to an inaccessible and thus inexplicable dimension of body-knowledge/-experience that defies and counteracts the physical screening of high-tech medicine and other attempts of applying the specific rationality of academic medicine. And that leaves the narrator in a somewhat aporetic situation: "Am I back at the beginning again? I now have a psychoanalyst-psychiatrist and a neurologist treating me, but neither of them can tell me who the shaking woman is" (2009: 186). What is needed here, it seems, is a holistic form of approach, an interpretation that heeds the explicit and the implicit dimension of knowing. The question "who is the shaking woman?" suggests that it is not her but someone else, that she 'knows' about that shaking woman but has dissociated herself from her. There is a sense of intrapersonal alterity involved, one may argue, that is presentified in the seizures of her body (Lösch and Paul 2013: 152). This alterity is known otherwise, as it were, but cannot be articulated in language; neither can it be suppressed for good, nor can it be done away with or contained. The traditional notion that autobiographical discourse in the end is able to produce a coherent self, even if it is a self that "does not necessarily precede its constitution in narrative" (Eakin 1999: 100), seems no option here since the narrative fails to heal the rift. There is no recipe for make-over or redemption, there is nothing to be done but to accept otherness as being as deep-seated as any notion of the self. Thus it does not only shake the body but also assumptions about subjectivity and wholeness themselves echoing Julia Kristeva's reworking of Freud in *Strangers to Ourselves* (1994). In a Waldenfelsian twist in Hustvedt's chronicle, alterity becomes constitutive of (and stays foreign to) an intimate self-perception and 'knowing,' and while the tacit dimension of being and not being a self at the same time is not open to direct verbalization, the text tries to render this experience of being simultaneously self and other as explicit as it can manage. It is the acceptance of this intimately experienced 'otherness' that concludes and ends Hustvedt's 'career' as a patient and thus the last sentence articulates her 'living' owning the alterity of the shaking woman: "I am the shaking woman" (Hustvedt 2009: 199). This matter-of-fact statement is part claim and part confession yet it does not bring about resolution or a sense of closure but stays tentatively performative, so to speak. The ambiguity and non-finality of this last sentence is anticipated by the epigraph to the book, a stanza from a Dickinson poem:

> I felt a cleaving in my mind –
> As if my brain had split –
> I tried to match it – Seam by Seam –
> But could not make them fit. (Dickinson 1960: 439)

Again, it is a sense of intrapersonal alterity that is evoked in the poem as it is in Hustvedt's book, but Dickinson's lines could also be read as resisting any pathological diagnosis by insisting on the "as if." This refusal anticipates Hustvedt's own resistance to a reductive pathologization of her symptoms.

3. The Art of Explication: 'Turning Ghosts into Ancestors' in *The Sorrows of an American*

"I think we all have ghosts inside us, and it's better when they speak than when they don't."

(Hustvedt 2008: 1)

"In one of his essays," Martha said, "Hans Loewald wrote, 'The work of psychoanalysis can turn ghosts into ancestors.'"

(Hustvedt 2008: 296)

These two quotations, one from the first page and the other from one of the last pages of *The Sorrows of an American* (2008) frame a painful process of presentifying the tacit, of making ghosts speak, so to say. The ghosts in Hustvedt's novel come in many forms and guises and often seem quite difficult to tell apart. For one thing, the narrator's father, whose death opens the novel, appears to be one such ghost who has bequeathed upon his children an unresolved mystery from his youth as well as his memories from a war he could never forget; second, it is the narrator's sister Inga's deceased husband, a well-known cult author, who appears as a ghostly presence in terms of his interactions with another woman while married to Inga; third, there is the ghostly presence of an artist who seems mentally instable and who is stalking his former girlfriend and her (and his) daughter who happen to live in the narrator's building. The narrator thus also gets into his line of 'vision.' In addition, the reader encounters those ghostly presences through the people who are patients in the narrator's psychoanalytical practice. Lastly, there is the presence of 9/11: Inga's daughter and Erik's niece, Sonia, has witnessed the events of that day while at her school in Manhattan and suffers from post-traumatic stress disorder. Coming to terms with the ghosts of the past is the central task all characters are confronted with. These 'ghosts' are connected to people who have 'died,' and to family secrets that supposedly have died with them but whose effects are very much present. They are also part of collective trauma and suffering: in relationships, in the family, in the city, in the nation. The novel, however, is, of course, not a classical ghost story, nor is it a postmodern spin on the gothic genre of the kind that we have seen in recent decades; rather it can be described as a neo-realist/mildly postmodern novel of manners that strongly relies on narration as the key to explication of tacit ghostly matters. It is the art of explication and art as explication, we can infer, that is at the center of the novel – of this novel and of fiction as such, as it is suggested, while at the same time, explication is also central to psychoanalytic analysis. Freud famously noted his surprise and concern (as is well known and as Hustvedt points out elsewhere) that his case studies should resemble fictional stories and that his writing style should be quite metaphorical: "It still strikes me myself as strange that the case histories I write should read like short stories and that, as one might say, they lack the serious stamp of science" (Freud 1999: II, 160).[2] The psychoanalyst Hans W. Loewald early on emphasized the resemblance of art and psychoanalysis, thus following up on Freud's dictum (cf. Loewald 1980: 352–371). While observing the various claims to its scientific quality that refute those who consider psychoanalysis to be non-scientific or unscientific, there is "much emphasis on psychoanalysis as a basic science" (Loewald 1980: 352). He proceeds to argue against the sharp distinction between science and art – and for the likeness of psychoanalysis and art. Loewald, in fact, refers to "psychoanalysis as an art" or as a "therapeutic art" (1980: 353) that re-unites, so to speak, 'reality' and 'fantasy' in the "re-enactment" of past experiences involving patient and analyst as co-authors of a new piece/drama (that may at times include Shakespearian twists or moments of Greek tragedy) and with that analogy he again draws attention to the contingency of the common distinction between psychoanalysis and art with respect to the activity of fabrication or, in Latin, *fingere*. Narrative and speech "function as a symbolic expression of action" (Loewald 1980: 366) in both cases. Rendering the novel a form of explication of the formerly implicit or hidden also raises questions of authorship when we turn once more to Loewald's suggestive model: "the fantasy character of the transference neurosis has been referred to as the make-believe aspect of the psychoanalytic situation. In the promotion and development of the transference neurosis, analyst and patient conspire in the creation of an illusion, a play" (1980: 354). From another angle and yet in a similar vein, Shoshana Felman has rejected the polarization that, from the perspective of psychoanalysis, literature is merely considered the "object" of analysis, a condition "in which literature is submitted to the authority, to the prestige of psychoanalysis. While literature is considered as a body of *language* – to *be interpreted* – psychoanalysis is considered as a body of *knowledge*, whose competence is called upon to *interpret*" (Felman 1982: 5). In addition, even contradistinction to that, Felman argues that "in much the same way as literature falls within the realm of psychoanalysis […], psychoanalysis itself falls within the realm of literature, and its specific logic and rhetoric" (1982: 6–7). She suggests therefore to view psychoanalysis and literature as inextricably bound to each other, as "'enfolded within' each other" (1982: 9), and she contends that

---

[2] On Freud and literature, cf. Jean-Michel Rey's "Freud's Writing on Writing" (1982) and Peter-André Alt and Thomas Anz's *Sigmund Freud und das Wissen der Literatur* (2008).

each is concerned with the unconscious, the unthought, of the other and thus with modes of explication.

It is this complicated relationship between psychoanalysis and literature, i.e. the art of writing, that Hustvedt is interested in and that she pursues. In this novel and in other (con)texts Hustvedt makes a claim for the connection of fiction writing to psychoanalytical treatment as both invested in processes of a difficult and painful presentification of things known tacitly, a presentification that can have different functions such as putting into words emotional discomfort and pain or breaking a ban or entering an intersubjective realm of communication and shared feeling and thus creating empathy. *The Sorrows of an American* is about this painful process of presentification and explication and, prior to that, about those things that haunt its characters: the traumatic quality of often seemingly banal experiences, the awkward combination of ordinariness and intensity, of things manifest and latent: the 'every-day gothic,' so to speak. The 'every-day gothic' is a phrase we have coined in order to signify on various levels of experience as they are topics in Hustvedt's novel: the uncanny echoes of family secret(s), the inexplicable presence and tacit knowledge of the past, individual or shared, and the presence of loss and mourning (the dead, failed relationships, one's own loneliness); it may also be a symptom of the displacement of traumatic memories, of passing them on to subsequent generations and onto other realms of individual and collective experiences.[3]

Erik Davidsen, the protagonist whom Hustvedt elsewhere has introduced as "a man I came to think of as my imaginary brother" (Hustvedt 2009: 5), is mourning his father's death as well as the end of his marriage. In going through his father's things in his home, he finds the latter's archive that consists of a complicated "filing system" (Hustvedt 2008: 2) in the shape of "an elaborate code of letters, numbers, and colors devised to allow for a descending hierarchy within a single category" (2008: 2–3). Stunned by this systematic approach at ordering one's existence, he describes his father's records and the material dimension of his life:

> My father had catalogued every tool that had ever hung in the garage, every receipt for the six used cars he had owned in his lifetime, every lawnmower, and every home appliance – the extensive documentation of a long and exceptionally frugal history. (2008: 3)

---

[3] In a larger project, we use 'every-day gothic' as a phrase that aptly describes one dimension/phenomenon in contemporary North American literature and that we see at work not only in the works of Siri Hustvedt but also in the fiction of Stewart O'Nan, Michael Ondaatje, Alice Munroe, Anna Lee Walters to name but a few authors. For a reading of Walters' novel *Ghost Singer*, see Paul 2012.

Much of those tracks are simply dumped into "large black garbage bags" (Hustvedt 2008: 3) along with "innumerable inventories of things that no longer existed" (2008: 3). Erik and his sister keep the letters, among them a mysterious one, and "eleven boxes of papers" (2008: 5) to sort through. It is these impressions of the father's meticulous and seemingly all-encompassing archive, its elaborateness and its futility that open the novel. And yet, the father also seems to speak from the archive, as the novel integrates parts of his memoirs (apparently the memoirs of Hustvedt's 'real' father or a re-telling) into the texture of the novel in order to create a dialogic and a transgenerational narrative. Still, the narrative has to remain incomplete for various reasons:

> Every memoir is full of holes. It's obvious that there are stories that can't be told without pain to others or to oneself, that autobiography is fraught with questions of perspective, self-knowledge, repression, and outright delusion (2008: 8).

And "[m]uch had been hidden" (2008: 8). To some extent, the novel offers the method of psychoanalysis as its poetological model. The power of explication, of finding out, of putting into words, of turning 'hidden' knowledge into narrative, ghosts into ancestors, obviously has its limits – both limits the speaker may impose on him- or herself and limits that are imposed on her/him. These limits – tacit and overt kinds of censorship – can take many forms. In the novel, the plot is propelled by the logic of supplying "a missing piece" (Hustvedt 2008: 237) – for the story of the father as well as for all the other enigmas. This emphasizes that re-membering means re-collection and production. The end of the novel nicely, perhaps a little too nicely, unravels all the mysteries: Erik finds temporary relief and happiness with an analyst-colleague and lets go of and overcomes his fixation on his tenant; Inga can remain assured of her husband's fidelity; and her daughter also finds relief from her post 9/11-nightmares. This sense of 'total' closure is thwarted only by a long stream of consciousness sequence that ties together the various plotlines and memories:

> The wars are raging. Men and women are raging. My father sleeps in a hole on the beach as the rocket fire booms above him. *Our brave young men and women in uniform fighting for freedom.* A loghouse goes up in flames. A little girl is rescued from a burning house. *We cleaned up them graves nice, didn't we?* The towers are burning. *Bad people burn up. No they don't.* My father cuts down trees. My grandfather cries out in his sleep and his small son shakes him awake. [...] The road isn't long enough. A Japanese officer falls over in the long grass. Sarah jumps, falls. Eggy falls. Sonia watches from the window. People are jumping, falling. They're on fire. The buildings fall. [...] We hear voices. I hear my father saying my mother's name. [...] I stand and watch the snow, and it is all happening at once. It cannot last, I say, this feeling cannot last, but it doesn't matter. It is here now. (Hustvedt 2008: 304)

Erik's experience of profound and 'messy' presence palimpsestically enfolds diachronic and synchronic references of trauma and suffering and contrasts sharply with his father's orderly archive with which the novel began. As in the case of *The Shaking Woman*, we are left with a sense of an entanglement of implicit and explicit knowledge and with fragmented subjectivity in language: "That is the strangeness of language: it crosses the boundaries of the body, is at once inside and outside, and it sometimes happens that we don't notice the threshold has been crossed" (Hustvedt 2008: 16–17).

Reading Hustvedt with Loewald, i.e. picking up her clue as to how she sees their work connected and interrelated, we encounter the power of explication that is captured in the notion of psychoanalytic treatment as "the talking cure," a process that may partially explicate what is hidden and part of the "unthought known" (Bollas 1987). In Loewald's psychoanalytical therapy as well as in Hustvedt's poetics, explication turns out to be an art, a form of creation, poiesis rather than rehearsal or mimesis. Both share an investment in "interiority" even as "the relation of interiority conveyed by the inter-implication of literature and psychoanalysis is by no means a simple one" (Felman 1982: 9), the novel, like the therapy, practices the art of explication. As readers, we spend more than one sitting figuring out the narrative – the one we read and the one we create. Erik is the psychoanalyst-protagonist in the novel who listens to and co-produces (in Loewald's and Bollas's sense) his patients' stories. And the writer? In the words of Max, Inga's husband and the only (white, dead, male) author in the book: "crippled and crazy, we hobble toward the finish line, pen in hand" (Hustvedt 2008: 45). The pen is a phallic symbol of male creativity, as second-wave feminists have repeatedly pointed out (Gilbert and Gubar 1979: 19); and it is specifically this male conceptualization of creativity that is at stake – and undermined – in Hustvedt's most recent novel to date.

4. The Masquerade of Masculinity: Tacit Knowledge and Implicit (Gender) Bias

"I am erased."
(Hustvedt 2014: 140)

While *Sorrows* operates with a male protagonist and also a male sense of authorship, our third and last example, Hustvedt's most recent novel, *The Blazing World*, published in 2014, dramatizes the "commonsensical" gendered and male-centered expectations with regard to the artistic subject. In fact, it takes up the unfinished business of second wave feminism and its shift from representational critique to a critique of the mechanisms of gender difference and gender normativity in the fields of creativity and knowledge production. In that sense, the plot of *The Blazing World* engages with Freud's dictum that "[w]hen you meet a human being, the first distinction you make is 'male or female?' and you are accustomed to make the distinction with unhesitating certainty" (Freud 1999: XXII, 113) and calls into question the distinction as well as the certainty with which it is pronounced. At the same time, the novel points to the tacit dimension of knowing that guarantees this kind of certainty and that may override perceived contingencies in favour of consistency with internalized schemata of gender specific attributions. Thus, the tacit knowledge works in the affirmative mode with gendered symbolizations and interpretive conventions since it continually disambiguates and reduces complex phenomena into selective perceptions.

In the novel, it is Harriet Burden, a largely unrecognized artist and the middle-aged widow of a highly successful art dealer, who uses male personae as cover for her art exhibitions three times in a row, in a series she calls "*Maskings*," and with three different "poster boys" creating "gender trouble" for herself and others. In doing so Burden follows in the footsteps of those women writers who for centuries have fronted male pseudonyms in order to be published (and read) in a patriarchal system, while her story points as well to the long history of male appropriation of female creativity in the arts. After the final performance, Burden reveals her masquerade in order to shock her audience and to orchestrate a great teaching moment of gender sensibility in the art world (reviewer Clare McHugh in the *Wall Street Journal* has referred to Hustvedt's text not unkindly as "a didactic novel" [McHugh 2014]). Burden thus instigates an inversion of the "detective story of psychoanalysis" (Garber 1992: 205) and invokes "a scene of gender 'discovery'" (Garber 1992: 205) that is quite unexpected by her audience. As it turns out, her subversive project of masquerade is all too successful, as it were, in its impersonating, the "masculine enhancement effect" (Hustvedt 2014: 252), as Burden herself calls it in the novel, is too powerful, and not all of the 'poster boys' are willing to admit that the credit goes to her. Whereas number one and two of her male stand-ins, Anton Tish and Phineas Q. Eldridge, still play by the rules, her rules, it is Rune, the third 'cover,' a celebrated artist in his own right, who contradicts Burden's revelation by claiming her work as his own, and eventually, in a final performance, spectacularly killing himself in front of a camera. Much is revealed about the various layers of their relationship (including Rune's affair with Burden's husband), and it is this last leg in Burden's attempted spectacular orchestration and ultimate proof of implicit but ubiquitous gender bias in the art world that reveals the shortcomings of her scheme and the problematic quality of her own fixation (in psychoanalytical terms) that unfolds into an increasingly all-consuming revenge fantasy which, in turn, victimizes others as well as herself. So, at one point she appropriately wonders: "What am I doing? Maybe I am the mad scientist" (Hustvedt 2014: 216).

While we learn much of the plot already on the first pages of the book in the frame narrative, through the voice of the editor of Burden's notebooks, just exactly how this plot unfolds is the subject of the next 350 pages told in postmodern fashion through various framing devices, shifts in narrative voice, multiple focalizations, the incorporation of different text types, a plethora of intertextual references, a complex cast of characters, and a great deal of ambiguity with regard to the protagonist's identity. In this essay, we obviously cannot do justice to all of the formal and thematic aspects of the novel but we will focus on the relation of tacit knowledge and implicit gender bias as it is simultaneously disclosed and subdued in the enactment of the gender masquerade. Reading Hustvedt in view of critical discussions of implicit bias brings to light the intricacies of Burden's success and failure on the one hand and shows the limits of Hustvedt's project to make explicit what remains implicit in everyday social interaction on the other hand.

The concept of gender as masquerade and as 'cover' has been a prominent topos in the 1990s feminist and gender studies discussions: among the most prominent publications (some of which appeared in the wake of the re-discovery of Joan Riviere's 1929 essay "Womanliness as Masquerade") are those by Marjorie Garber, Mary Anne Doane, Naomi Schor, Emily Apter, all of whose essays have been collected by Liliane Weissberg in the German-language volume *Weiblichkeit als Maskerade* (1994) and are also referenced in Elfi Bettinger's and Julika Funk's *Maskeraden: Geschlechterdifferenz in der literarischen Inszenierung* (1995). To take up the connection of gender and masquerade as a central theme in a 2014 novel thus has led critics to consider Hustvedt's book a mildly old-fashioned feminist text. Already in the mid-1990s, Emily Apter has asked whether masquerade may be seen as "the fetish of feminism" (Apter 1991: 201) as it affirms the enigma of femininity historically formulated by Sigmund Freud. On the contrary, masquerade has been considered a subversive intervention that may dismantle the absence of authenticity in commonsensical, i.e. ideological constructions of gender difference and identity:

> Diese [doppelte] Perspektive auf Maskerade hat jedoch zwei nicht immer kompatible strukturelle Konsequenzen: Maskerade einerseits dasjenige, was sich hinter der Maske verbirgt, erst mit den Attributen der Eigentlichkeit und des Essentiellen auszustatten, andererseits wird die Verhüllung zum einzig Zugänglichen und Sichtbaren, das Uneigentliche wird zum Modus der (Re-)Präsentation. (Funk 1995: 19)[4]

---

[4] "This [double] perspective on masquerade has two structural consequences that may be at

In Hustvedt's novel, the masquerade-plot is used to reveal the various kinds of social and cultural capital that get accrued differently (or not at all) by men and women in the art world and that leads to different gradations of recognition that are attributed in a highly asymmetrical way. Ultimately, it is the modesty that Joan Riviere in her classic text sees behind the masquerade of womanliness that Burden abhors and wholeheartedly rejects. Riviere writes:

> Womanliness therefore could be assumed and worn as a mask, both to hide the possession of masculinity and to avert the reprisals expected if she was found to possess it – much as a thief will turn out his pockets and ask to be searched to prove that he has not the stolen goods. (Riviere 2010 [1929]: 77)

Burden's experiment uses masculinity as a mask to gain entrance into an elitist art world and to gain attention and recognition by the representatives of that market and yet she "takes her beliefs about the advantages of having both an X and a Y chromosome to a destructive extreme" (McHugh 2014), that is, she is adamant about inverting the patriarchal gender hierarchy. Thus, it is exactly that "higher purpose" of her project, revealing (and possibly overcoming) the art world's misogyny, that is increasingly called into question by Burden's fixation on her morally superior victim status. That narrative of victimization is based on gender alone at the expense of other markers of difference that are used to fabricate symbolic and social hierarchies. Thus, her project is jeopardized (from the start, one might add) by her disavowal of white privilege – after all, in her second project it is also a queer, non-white artist, whom she uses for her own purposes. No wonder, the novel has been sharply criticized by Terry Castle and others for its half-hearted engagement with hegemonic normativity that keeps leading back to heterosexuality, heteronormativity, white privilege and to all kinds of binary oppositions whose power effects remain untouched by the critique of gender bias alone (cf. Castle 2015). Castle argues that the novel is blind to its own tacit normativity with regard to race and sexuality, a critique that brings to mind the critique of mainstream second wave feminists by women of color.

Burden's project of revelation through explication of implicit bias seems to fail for various reasons, but we should refrain from mistaking Burden's failure as Hustvedt's failure. Rather we may infer that it is Hustvedt's ploy to point to

---

odds with each other: masquerade, on the one hand, as the strategy that bestows on what hides behind the mask attributes of the authentic and the essential; on the other hand, masquerade becomes the only accessible and visible form; the inauthentic becomes the mode of (re)presentation" (our translation).

the limits of revisionism when it comes to knowledge that is so deeply anchored in the implicit dimension and that pre-determines our perceptions (harking back to Freud's contention) and whose effects in terms of social differentiation are invested with such an enormous amount of social and cultural capital that it cannot be simply dissolved by artistic hoax or other eye-opening performances. Agnotological scholarship has shown that the power of ignorance, specifically in view of particular ideological investments and hegemonic norms, cannot be underestimated (cf. Proctor and Schiebinger 2008; Sullivan and Tuana 2007). In analogy to Alexis Shotwell's study of implicit racial bias as "racism without words" (2015: 175) i.e. a perceptive mode on the basis of tacit knowledge that gets actualized subliminally, Hustvedt's novel attempts to bring to the fore the 'sexism without words' as it is practiced in Harriet Burden's well-educated and rather exclusive and elitist circles. Yet, Burden falters exactly because, in the final analysis, she herself is stuck to some of the cultural scripts and cultural mechanisms producing inequality and hierarchy she seeks to dismantle. The tacit "knowing in the bones" (Shotwell 2011: 125) of the individual gendered subject (here: Harriet's) can only partially be presentified and made accessible intersubjectively; thus, the understanding and recognition she seeks clashes with societal norms and collectively shared tacit presuppositions that are taken for granted (and that have to stay implicit if they are to do their ideological work). Yet, tacit knowledge as an effect of such individual and collective denial works both ways: in the same way in which Burden's demasking of gendered privilege meets with disbelief and defense reactions on the part of her audience, Burden herself is apparently confusing her individual narrative of victimization with a larger kind of structural sexism thus claiming a kind of totality for her own project. Even as feminist solidarity aims at valorizing individual suffering as collectively shared, Burden's perspective appears to be quite limited.

5. Conclusion

"Knowledge does not always accumulate; it also gets lost."

(Hustvedt 2009: 72)

"We are intricately and intimately connected with others and with the world, and most of these connections happen alongside, beneath, and in other spheres than the words we say and the propositions we formulate."

(Shotwell 2011: ix)

Tacit knowledge can take different forms, fulfil various functions, and bring about diverse effects. Siri Hustvedt's writings are concerned with these various dimensions in nuanced ways: *The Shaking Woman* presents a critical interrogation of knowledge production and what 'gets lost' in the process within and among disciplines. The text takes issue with the dangers of a neo-positivism in the medical field and points to the tacit aspects of human experience that remain enigmatic ('alien'?) and are hardly 'measurable' or explicable in the rational framework of professional medicine. *The Sorrows of an American* pursues the tacit as closely related to the unconscious and thus evokes an analogy between psychoanalysis and art/literature as two discourses of explication and presentification: both rely on language and both are concerned with interiority and a special kind of genealogy of knowledge. In *The Blazing World*, it is the implicit gender bias as part of a tacit cultural imaginary that does its (cultural) work without being wholly accessible for explication and thus for revisionist critique. This most recent text seems to confirm agnotological suspicions that there is a hidden logic to what we do not and 'cannot' know.

Tacit knowledge as a kind of umbrella term is a useful concept for an interpretation of Siri Hustvedt's writings and the various ways the implicit is played out. In one way or another, her works are concerned with this tacit dimension and the question of its explicability and presentification. The tacit may bring forth pathologies, trigger extreme physical responses, store negative experiences, affirm dominant ideologies, and stabilize symbolic and social order; at the same time, it may also be the origin/touchstone of protest and resistance. Stringing together the multiple aspects of the tacit in Hustvedt's work has been at the center of this essay. Beyond the three readings in the present paper, further instances could be identified and pursued in other works by Hustvedt to demonstrate her interest in and her grasp on the tacit: *The Blindfold*, *The Enchantment of Lily Dahl*, or *What I Loved*. In addition, Hustvedt's fictional and non-fictional work and its exploration of the tacit should be contextualized and compared with similar figurations in contemporary American literature. Of course, there are other forms, functions, and effects of implicitness that are dealt with in the narrative mode. Katharina Gerund (2015), for example, has recently analyzed the implicit dimension in the cultural script of sisterhood in popular US literature, while Stephen Koetzing (2015) has tackled the role of tacit knowledge in the works of Philip Roth and Paul Harding (two male colleagues of Hustvedt) and their representations of old age and impending death. Over all, there is still very little scholarship on tacit knowledge in literary texts, yet, approaching literature and its functions in the light of tacit knowledge will certainly prove to be fruitful for literary studies as well as cultural critique.

Works Cited

Adloff, Frank, Katharina Gerund and David Kaldewey (eds.). 2015. *Revealing Tacit Knowledge: Embodiment and Explication*. Bielefeld: transcript.
Alt, Peter-André and Thomas Anz (eds.). 2008. *Sigmund Freud und das Wissen der Literatur*. Berlin: De Gruyter.
Apter, Emily. 1991. *Feminizing the Fetish: Psychoanalysis and Narrative Obsession in Turn-of-the-Century France*. Ithaca: Cornell University Press.
Bettinger, Elfi and Julika Funk (eds.). 1995. *Maskeraden: Geschlechterdifferenz in der literarischen Inszenierung*. Berlin: Schmidt.
Bollas, Christopher. 1987. *The Shadow of the Object: Psychoanalysis of the Unthought Known*. New York: Columbia University Press.
Boyers, Robert. 2014. "'The Blazing World': An Exchange." *The New York Review of Books*, September 25.
 <http://www.nybooks.com/articles/archives/2014/sep/25/blazing-world-exchange/> [accessed 21 July 2015].
Butler, Judith. 2005. *Giving an Account of Oneself*. New York: Fordham University Press.
Castle, Terry. 2015. "The Woman in the Gallery." *The New York Review of Books*, August 14.
 <http://www.nybooks.com/articles/archives/2014/aug/14/siri-hustvedt-woman-gallery/> [accessed 21 July 2015].
Dickinson, Emily. 1960. "I Felt a Cleaving in My Mind." In: Thomas Herbert Johnson (ed.). *The Complete Poems of Emily Dickinson*. Boston: Little & Brown. 439–440.
Eakin, Paul. 1999. *How Our Lives Become Stories: Making Selves*. Ithaca: Cornell University Press.
Felman, Shoshana. 1982. "To Open the Questions." In: Shoshana Felman (ed.). *Literature and Psychoanalysis: The Question of Reading: Otherwise*. Baltimore: Johns Hopkins University Press. 5–10.
Freud, Sigmund. 1999. *The Standard Edition of the Complete Psychological Works of Sigmund Freud*. 24 vols. Trans. and ed. James Strachey. London: Vintage.
Funk, Julika. 1995. "Die schillernde Schönheit der Maskerade: Einleitende Überlegungen zu einer Debatte." In: Elfi Bettinger and Julika Funk (eds.). *Maskeraden: Geschlechterdifferenz in der literarischen Inszenierung*. Berlin: Schmidt. 15–28.
Garber, Marjorie. 1992. *Vested Interests: Cross Dressing and Cultural Anxiety*. New York: Routledge.
Gerund, Katharina. 2015. "Wie Schwestern? Freundschaft in Ann Brashares' *Sisterhood*-Reihe." In: Ulrike Schneider, Helga Völkening and Daniel Vorpahl (eds.). *Zwischen Ideal und Ambivalenz: Geschwisterbeziehungen in ihren soziokulturellen Kontexten*. Frankfurt am Main: Peter Lang. 319–338.
Gilbert, Sandra and Susan Gubar. 1979. *The Madwoman in the Attic*. New Haven: Yale University Press.
Hustvedt, Siri. 2008. *The Sorrows of an American*. New York: Henry Holt.
Hustvedt, Siri. 2009. *The Shaking Woman, or, A History of My Nerves*. New York: Henry Holt.
Hustvedt, Siri. 2012. *Living, Thinking, Looking*. New York: Picador.
Hustvedt, Siri. 2014. *The Blazing World*. New York: Simon & Schuster.
James, William. 2002 [1902]. *The Varieties of Religious Experience: A Study in Human Nature*. London: Routledge.

Koetzing, Stephen. 2015. "The End of Life and the Limits of Explication: Metaphors and Time in *Everyman* and *Tinkers*." In: Frank Adloff, Katharina Gerund and David Kaldewey (eds.). *Revealing Tacit Knowledge: Embodiment and Explication.* Bielefeld: transcript. 224–243.

Kristeva, Julia. 1994. *Strangers to Ourselves.* New York: Columbia University Press.

Loenhoff, Jens. 2015. "Tacit Knowledge: Shared and Embodied." In: Frank Adloff, Katharina Gerund and David Kaldewey (eds.). *Revealing Tacit Knowledge: Embodiment and Explication.* Bielefeld: transcript. 21–40.

Loewald, Hans W. 1980. *Papers on Psychoanalysis.* New Haven: Yale University Press.

Lösch, Klaus and Heike Paul. 2013. "Präsenz, implizites Wissen und Fremdheit aus kulturwissenschaftlicher Perspektive." In: Christoph Ernst and Heike Paul (eds.). *Präsenz und implizites Wissen: Zur Interdependenz zweier Schlüsselbegriffe der Kultur- und Sozialwissenschaften.* Bielefeld: transcript. 151–183.

Mannheim, Karl. 1982. *Structures of Thinking.* Eds. David Kettler, Volker Meja and Nico Stehr. London: Routledge and Kegan Paul.

Marks, Christine. 2014. *"I Am Because You Are": Relationality in the Works of Siri Hustvedt.* Heidelberg: Winter.

McHugh, Clare. 2014. "Vengeance by Deception." *The Wall Street Journal,* Eastern Edition March 15. http://www.wsj.com/articles/ SB10001424052702303795904579431460059821576 [accessed 26 February 2015].

Merleau-Ponty, Maurice. 2007. *The Merleau Ponty-Reader.* Eds. Ted Toadvine and Leonard Lawlor. Boston: Northwestern University Press.

Noe, Alva. 2012. *Varieties of Presence.* Cambridge: Harvard University Press.

Paul, Heike. 2012. "Das Unheimliche und die Präsenz: Fremdheit in der US-amerikanischen Gegenwartsliteratur und -kultur." In: Simone Broders, Susanne Gruß and Stefanie Waldow (eds.). *Phänomene der Fremdheit.* Würzburg: Königshausen & Neumann. 95–116.

Polanyi, Michael. 1966. *The Tacit Dimension.* Chicago: University of Chicago Press.

Polanyi, Michael. 1969. *Knowing and Being: Essays.* Ed. Marjorie Grene. Chicago: University of Chicago Press.

Proctor, Robert N. and Londa Schiebinger (eds.). 2008. *Agnotology: The Making and Unmaking of Ignorance.* Stanford: Stanford University Press.

Rey, Jean-Michel. "Freud's Writing on Writing." In: Shoshana Felman (ed.). *Literature and Psychoanalysis: The Question of Reading: Otherwise.* Baltimore: Johns Hopkins University Press. 301–328.

Riviere, Joan. 2010 [1929]. "Womanliness as Masquerade." *Hurly-Burly* 3: 75–84.

Ryle, Gilbert. 1949. *The Concept of Mind.* Chicago: University of Chicago Press.

Sen, Amartya. 2009. "Foreword." In: Michael Polanyi. *The Tacit Dimension.* Chicago: University of Chicago Press. vii–xvi.

Shotwell, Alexis. 2011. *Knowing Otherwise: Race, Gender, and Implicit Understanding.* University Park: Pennsylvania State University Press.

Shotwell, Alexis. 2015. "Racial Formation, Implicit Understanding, and Problems with Implicit Association Tests." In: Frank Adloff, Katharina Gerund and David Kaldewey (eds.). *Revealing Tacit Knowledge: Embodiment and Explication.* Bielefeld: transcript. 169–184.

Sullivan, Shannon and Nancy Tuana (eds.). 2007. *Race and Epistemologies of Ignorance.* Albany: State University of New York Press.

Wacquant, Lois. 2015 "For a Sociology of Flesh and Blood." In: Frank Adloff, Katharina Gerund and David Kaldewey (eds.). *Revealing Tacit Knowledge: Embodiment and Explication*. Bielefeld: transcript. 185–194.

Waldenfels, Bernhard. 2006. *Grundmotive einer Phänomenologie des Fremden*. Frankfurt am Main: Suhrkamp.

Weissberg, Liliane (ed.). 1994. *Weiblichkeit als Maskerade*. Frankfurt am Main: Fischer.

Mark C. Taylor
Wounding Words

> ...my whole huge literary work had just one idea: to wound from behind.
> Søren Kierkegaard, *Journals and Papers* (no. 6016)
>
> I am afraid of writing [...] because when I write I am always moving toward the unarticulated, the dangerous, the place where the walls don't hold. I don't know what's there, but I am pulled toward it. Is the wounded self the writing self? Is the writing self the wounded self? The wound is static, a given. The writing self is multiple and elastic and it circles the wound. Over time, I have become more aware of the fact that I must try not to cover that speechless, hurt core, that I must fight my dread of the mess and violence that are also there. I have to write the fear. The writing self is restless and searching, and it listens for voices.
> Siri Hustvedt, *A Plea for Eros*

Ghosts

Søren Kierkegaard is the most literary philosopher in the history of western philosophy; Siri Hustvedt is the most philosophical novelist now writing. Perhaps this is not an accident because SH grew up in Northfield, Minnesota, where her father taught linguistics at St. Olaf College for many years. Her parents, like many before them, immigrated from Scandinavia and settled on the Midwestern plains. For Norwegians, unlike Danes, the attraction of this often desolate territory could not have been the flat land but must have been the light. Northern light is different, its angle and tone lend land as well as life a different cast that often has a melancholy hue. The family's ties to Norway remained strong; SH and her three sisters speak Norwegian, and during her youth she spent several years in Bergen, where her *mormor* lived.

The Hustvedts' neighbors in Northfield were Edna and Howard Hong, who, for many years, were the premier translators of Kierkegaard's writings. Their monumental translation and critical notes of his collected works remain one of the most impressive scholarly accomplishments in recent memory. But the Hongs' lifelong dedication to SK was not limited to publication – they also established the Kierkegaard Library at Saint Olaf, where they assembled a collection of primary and secondary works that rivals the Søren Kierkegaard Research Center at the University of Copenhagen. The Howard and Edna Hong Kierkegaard Library is an invaluable resource for students and scholars from all over the world. I visited the library many years ago. One of my most prized possessions is a twenty-volume first edition of Kierkegaard's *Papirer*, which the Hongs generously sold to me at cost and carefully wrapped in newspaper to protect the fragile bindings when I carried the books home. For SH and her three sisters, the Hongs were not world-renowned Kierkegaard scholars but friendly neighbors whose land was both joined to and separated from their property by the stream where the Hustvedt girls played. Such experiences create memories that take a lifetime to fathom.

On May 11, 2013, the organizers of the national celebration of Kierkegaard's two-hundredth birthday in Copenhagen invited a philosopher (Slavoj Žižek) and a writer (Siri Hustvedt) to present keynote addresses. SH began her lecture, entitled "Kierkegaard's Pseudonyms and the Truths of Fiction," by declaring "I will say 'I' to Kierkegaard's pseudonymous brood. I will not adopt the authoritative, objective, third person, professional voice, in which most academic prose is written." A bold move: speaking in the first person to perform the impossibility of speaking in the first person. This savvy stylistic gesture is carefully calculated to remain true to the intention and spirit of SK's pseudonymous authorship by criticizing the supposed objectivity and detachment of traditional academic scholarship. The lecture, however, turns out to be as much about SH's own writing as about SK's work; indeed, it is impossible to appreciate SH's writing without understanding the multiple ways in which the ghost of SK haunts her work. Her defiance of scholarly convention is understandably shadowed by anxiety.

> I will stay securely in the personal *discours*. And yet, it is not without anxiety that I step into the shows of *"hiin Enkelte,"* that single individual. I am a reader, surely, but am I the reader, the beloved reader? Am I Mr. X, or the bird S.K. sees diving to retrieve his book? Am I the one to be deceived into truth with a capital T? No, but I will take on my "I," to whom the poetized personalities may say "you," as one side of an intimate dialogical relation. After all, the crowd, *Maengden*, is not a reader. Every book is read one person at a time. The question "who is speaking?" in the pseudonymous texts is surely mirrored by the question "who is reading?" (Hustvedt 2013)

And who is writing? While every book is read one person at a time, not all books are written one person at a time because writers are haunted by ghosts both known and unknown. Where does SK end and SH begin? Is SH a belated pseudonym for SK?

Lines designed to separate begin to blur until they become little more than trickling streams marking boundaries and defining properties that no longer seem proper or secure. As the lecture unfolds, SH, like SK, weaves together fact and fiction, philosophy and autobiography until it is impossible to tell where one ends and the other begins. Who is speaking? Who is being spoken to? Is my voice ever my own? Can communication ever be direct? Is there an "I"? Am I one, or is "my" name legion?

Midway through the lecture SH interrupts her discussion of SK with "Autobiographical Fragments or *Smuler*."

> 1. My mother told me that her father, my *morfar*, read *only* Kierkegaard and church history. Not until I was grown up did I wonder if he read them as oppositional texts. He died of heart disease in 1943 during the Nazi occupation of Norway. I was never able to ask him.
> 2. When I was nine, my Sunday school class studied the Abraham and Isaac story. The teacher's moral: to love God more than anyone or anything. "Even more than your parents?" I asked her. "Even more than your parents," she said solemnly. The story was not abstract. I had felt God in my moments of euphoria and what I called "lifting feelings," not to speak of the repeated powerful sensations I had of a menacing felt presence at the bottom of the stairs, a devil, an angel – the auras of an undiagnosed child migraineur. I lay awake night after night terrified God would command me to kill my parents. Now I am able to read my fear through an apt Freudian reversal, that the paternal figure of the law, God, might unleash my repressed hostility toward my own mysterious father, whom I also loved terribly, but at the time, all I felt was sleepless horror, *frykt og baeven*, in the face of a monstrous, incomprehensible deity.
> 3. Behind my childhood house outside Northfield, Minnesota ran a stream. Across Heath Creek and up a steep embankment lay another house that belonged to Edna and Howard Hong who, for as long as I can remember, were translating Kierkegaard's writings, volume after volume, for the English Princeton edition I now own. Every time I visited, I saw Søren Kierkegaard as a tall pile of papers on Edna's desk. I remember conjuring a gloomy, gray, ghostly saint of a man, probably because I saw gravestones in a *kirkegård* in my mind.
> 4. When I was twelve I heard voices and thought I might be insane. (Hustvedt 2013)

Voices haunting voices. Voices of others, who pose an Either/Or. Ghosts either silence the writer or give her a voice that is never her own.

Secrets

SK's life was brief – merely 42 years (1813–1855). Between 1842 and 1855, he wrote obsessively and excessively: twenty volumes of papers he was confident would be published after his death; countless articles in the popular press attacking the university, church and Danish society; collections of edifying discourses, which were explicitly religious works; and, most important, a series of pseudonymous writings.[1] Though Denmark is a small country and Copenha-

---

[1] I might say of Kierkegaard what Jacques Derrida said of Hegel: "We will never be finished with the reading or rereading of [Kierkegaard], and, in a certain way, I do nothing other than attempt to explain myself on this point. In effect, I believe that [Kierkegaard's] text is necessarily fissured; that it is something more and other than the circular closure of its representation" (Jacques Derrida 1981). Though it took years for Derrida to realize it, Kierkegaard is the nec-

gen was a very small town during SK's lifetime, his identity as the author of the pseudonymous writings remained a secret until he published *Concluding Unscientific Postscript* in 1846. In "A First and Last Declaration," issued as a postscript to the *Postscript* under the pseudonym Johannes Climacus (J.C.), SK, writing in "his own" name insists,

> [s]o in the pseudonymous works there is not a single word that is mine, I have no opinion about these works except as third person, no knowledge of their meaning except as a reader, not the remotest private relation to them, since such a thing is impossible in the case of a doubly reflected communication. One single word of mine uttered personally in my name would be an instance of presumptuous self-forgetfulness, and dialectically viewed it would incur with one word the guilt of annihilating the pseudonyms. (Kierkegaard: 551)

During the years SK was writing the pseudonymous works, he went to extraordinary lengths to disguise his identity by assuming the persona of a carefree man-about-town, who had no job and seemingly endless free time. Throughout his life he lived in the center of Copenhagen near the Royal Theater. During the years he was writing most intensely, he assumed his disguise by going to theater to mingle with the crowd, rushing home to write, returning at intermission to mix with theatergoers, rushing home to write again, and, finally, returning when the crowd was leaving. Secrecy was at the heart of his strategy as a writer.

SK's first pseudonymous work, *Either/Or*, published in 1842, begins with the question of secrecy. To protect his identity as the author, Howard and Edna Hong explain, he went so far as to transcribe the final manuscript in different styles of handwriting, "lest the secret be detected and divulged by someone at the printing house" (Hong and Hong: I.). Parodying Hegelian philosophy, whose foundational principle captured in the dialectical term "both-and" through which all opposites are supposed to be reconciled, Victor Eremita, the pseudonymous editor of the two-volume work, writes,

> [i]t may at times have occurred to you, dear reader, to doubt somewhat the accuracy of that familiar philosophical thesis that the outer is the inner and the inner is the outer. Perhaps you yourself have concealed a secret that in its joy or in its pain you felt was too intimate to share with others. (Kierkegaard: I, 1)

---

essay fissure in Hegel's text. Two of my first books were on Kierkegaard: *Kierkegaard's Pseudonymous Authorship: A Study of Time and Self*, 1975, and *Journeys to Selfhood: Hegel and Kierkegaard*, 1980. Everything I have written has been written directly or more often indirectly in Kierkegaard's shadow. In view of some of SH's linguistic twists, it is helpful to note that in Danish *kierkegaard* means cemetery – *kirke*, church + *gaard*, yard.

Eremita proceeds to spin a fanciful tale of discovering the manuscript in a hidden compartment of a writing desk. On his daily strolls through the city, he spied a secretary with many drawers in a secondhand furniture store, and developed an irrational obsession with the writing desk that led him to buy it even though he had no use for it. When a coachman arrived early one morning to take him on a trip, Eremita discovered he had no money and, in a fit of panic, grabbed a hatchet and smashed the secretary in the vain hope of finding some cash. (NB: The word "secretary" derives from the Latin word *secretus*. Secretaries, who can be trusted, keep secrets no matter how terrible they might be.) "Whether my blow struck precisely this spot or the vibration through the entire structure of the desk was the occasion," Emerita muses,

> I do not know, but this I do know – a secret door that I had never noticed before sprung open. The door closed off a compartment that I obviously had not discovered. Here, to my great amazement, I found a mass of papers, the papers that constitute the contents of the present publication. (Kierkegaard: I, 6.)

Writing, we will see, remains cryptic even when it betrays secrets.

The manuscript Emerita discovers consists of papers written by two different authors, whom he dubs A and B. There was also an additional manuscript, "The Diary of a Seducer," which A claims he did not write but did edit. Suspicious of A's claim not to have written the diary, Emerita observes, "[t]his is an old literary device to which I would not have much to object if it did not further complicate my own position, since one author becomes enclosed within the other like the boxes in a Chinese puzzle" (Kierkegaard: I, 9). Authors within authors within authors. Who is writing? Who is being written? Why all the disguises? Why all the masks? Why this endless game of hide-and-seek? Perhaps because, as SH notes Oscar Wilde suggests, "[m]an is least himself when he talks in his own person. Give him a mask, and he will tell you the truth" (Hustvedt 2014: 114). But what, then, is truth?

Over the course of the next four years, SK published books at an astonishing rate and pseudonyms proliferated, creating a puzzle that became more and more intriguing. In the confession at the end of *Concluding Unscientific Postscript* as well as his ostensibly autobiographical *The Point of View of My Work as an Author: A Report to History* (1848), he explains that he crafted his pseudonymous authorship to fulfill what he understood to be his religious mission of "reintroducing Christianity into Christendom." The synthesis of Hegelian philosophy, the Danish Lutheran state church, and modern mass media and society transformed individuals into ciphers of the crowd, who are unable or unwilling to make independent decisions. SK's pseudonymous authorship is designed to address each person individually by representing a different perspective or point of view constituting a particular existential possibility that an individual might realize through his or her free decisions. While differing in many ways, the pseudonyms represent variations of three distinct forms of life: aesthetic, ethical, and religious. Since these pseudonymous works deal with ideal abstractions rather than the concrete reality of individual lives, SK describes these writings as poetic or aesthetic. The poet describes alternative forms of life that provide the occasion for the reader's self-reflection, self-clarification, and self-transforming decision. Johannes Climacus, the pseudonymous author of *Concluding Unscientific Postscript*, insists that rather than the objective correspondence between subject and object or word and thing, truth is personal and must be lived. In his famous dictum: "truth is subjectivity." Truth, in other words, involves the translation of abstract possibilities into concrete individual lives through the responsible decisions of free individuals. From the point of view of SK, who might, after all, be nothing more than another pseudonym of an unknowable author, the progression from the aesthetic through the ethical, to the religious stage on life's way, leads a person from less to more authentic forms of life. In a manner reminiscent of Hegel's dialectic of spirit, later stages displace but do not replace earlier stages – previous stages are displaced but taken up into later stages. Since traces of the aesthetic and ethical stages remain in religious life, the singular individual is not really one but actually many selves. For his existential therapy to be effective, SK believes, he must personally withdraw from his works in order to allow each reader to turn his or her attention back on himself or herself. In the first part of *Stages On Life's Way*, the only work in which SK presents all three stages in one volume, edited by Hilarius Bookbinder, William Afham prefaces his recollection, "In Vino Veritas," with an epigram from Lichtenberg: "Such works are mirrors: when a monkey peers into them, no Apostle can be seen looking out" (Kierkegaard: 26). Every pseudonym indirectly says to the individual reader:

> Take time to think about the life you are living. You will be for eternity what you become through your decisions during your life time. Time is short and each moment might be the last. Here are some possibilities for you to consider. Now it's your move.

Traum(a)deutung

But there is silence, too, at once unspeakably terrible and ineffably beautiful, demonic and divine. It is hidden in a sealed box where the True Self may be protected, but where it longs for the other and for otherness. The unwritten mother lives in the box with the father's unspeakable secret. "I am the silent letter," SK wrote to his friend Boesen, "which no one can pronounce and which does not say anything to anyone." But he circled the silence and the wound with torrents of words, with multi-tongued reflection, and I for one am grateful for those worlds within worlds within worlds. (Hustvedt 2013)

Pseudonyms are not the only ones who have secrets – sometimes "real" authors do as well. While SK claimed to have withdrawn from the pseudonymous writings, these works are nonetheless profoundly, even if indirectly, autobiographical. The pseudonyms are multiple masks that simultaneously conceal and reveal an interiority that sets writing in motion. Before (the) beginning, SK repeatedly insisted he had a secret he could not betray – a secret he used to tease readers by sometimes calling it "a thorn in the flesh," and other times "an earthquake." In his *Journals*, written in his own name – but how can you trust an ironic trickster like SK? – he repeatedly returns to this secret. "After my death," he writes,

> no one will find among my papers a single explanation as to what really filled my life (that is my consolation); no one will find the words that explain everything and which often made what the world would call a bagatelle [or trifle] into an event of tremendous importance to me, and what I look upon as something insignificant when I take away the secret gloss which explains all. (Kierkegaard: V, 84)

For more than two hundred years, commentators have taken the bait by trying to figure out what SK's secret was. The most common focus of these analyses is SK's father, Michael Pederson Kierkegaard, who was born into a poor farming family, and, desperate to escape oppressive poverty, cursed God on the desolate Jutland heath. When his uncle, who was a successful merchant, invited Michael to Copenhagen to work for him, his life changed dramatically. Years later, after inheriting the business and becoming wealthy, he suddenly retired at a relatively young age and became immersed in the Protestant pietism that was sweeping Europe at the time. Preoccupied with his personal sin and human corruption, Michael subjected Søren to an extraordinarily severe religious upbringing in the hope that the chosen son's virtue would redeem the guilty father's sins. From this point of view, Søren is Isaac and Michael is Abraham, who offers his son to God. While many commentators support this interpretation of SK's secret, it seems unlikely that his father's childhood curse could have such drastic lifelong consequences.

A more likely possibility concerns SK's mother, or, more precisely, the relationship between his father and his mother. In 1794, Michael married Kirstine Royen, the sister of his business partner, Mads Royen; two years later she died, leaving Michael childless. On April 27, 1797, before the year of mourning had expired, Michael married Ane Sørendsdatter Lund, who had been Kirstine's maid, and less than five months later, the couple's first child, Maren Kirstine, was born. Though Michael remained ambivalent about his relationship to Ane, the marriage survived and they had six more children, the youngest of whom was Søren Aabye, born May 5, 1813. The more likely transgression that obsessed the father and transformed the life of the son was Michael's violation of Ane. Søren was obsessed with his father, who is a constant presence throughout his *Journals* and haunts the pseudonymous works. The mother, however, is absent – totally absent – Ane does not appear once in the twenty volumes of *Journals*. And yet, behind, beneath, before the presence of the father, there is the absence of the mother, and this absence might be what all writing and literature are *about*. Commenting on SK's pseudonymous brood of boys, SH writes,

> A 'Mysterious Family' then – with its distant surrogate father, absent mother, and slew of fertile boys spawning paragraphs. And famously or infamously in the journals: no mother of Søren either. She does not exist in his words. She is the unarticulated, the hole, gap, silence in the productivity. (Hustvedt 2013)

Michael and Ane had no maid – apparently Michael thought a woman beneath his social standing had no need for a servant; Ane, it seems, was already his domestic. But is her silence a sign of her absence? What role did Ane play in the economy of the Kierkegaard household? What secrets did she harbor? What secrets did she tell her precocious son? None of the children left any direct testimony, so it is impossible to know for sure. Since Ane was always something of a stranger who did not fit into the Kierkegaard household, she might not have been domesticated as Michael presumed. Never completely at home in the house of the father, Ane remained *uhyggelig*, and as such is endlessly fascinating. The fascination of the uncanny – *uhyggelig/unheimlich* – is its ambiguity. A symptom or trace of something or nothing that is simultaneously present and absent, the uncanny is both attractive and repulsive.

The Danish word for secret is *hemmelighed*, which, like its German equivalent, carries the trace of home, *hjem* (home). A secret is separate, cut off, private; something that is inside or interior, as if restricted to and by the family hearth. There is, however, something strange about *hemmelighed* – the word *hemmelighedsfuld* means both mysterious and uncanny. The other Danish word that designates "uncanny" is *uhyggelig*. *Hyggelig* is an extremely important word in Danish language and culture that has no precise equivalent in English. *U-hyggelig* suggests something that cannot be domesticated, and, thus, disrupts whatever seems to be *hyggelig*.

The implications of these associations can be clarified by considering Freud's discussion of their German equivalents in his famous essay, "The Uncanny." The German word for secret is *geheim*, which, like the Danish *hemmelighed*, is associated with the home – *das Heim*. Freud notes that *geheim* and *Heim* bear an unexpected relationship to the uncanny – *unheimlich*. After a long etymological excursus in which he explores the interplay of *unheimlich*, *Heim* and *geheim*, he summarizes his conclusion: "Schelling says something that throws quite a new light on the concept of the uncanny, one which we had certainly not awaited. According to him, everything is uncanny that ought to have remained hidden and secret, yet comes to light" (Freud 1965). To explain the importance of Schelling's insight, Freud presents an extended analysis of E. T. A. Hoffmann's children's story, "The Sand-Man."

> To conclude this collection of examples, which is certainly not complete, I will relate an instance taken from psycho-analytic experience; if it does not rest upon mere coincidence, it furnishes a beautiful confirmation of our theory of the uncanny. It often happens that neurotic men declare that they feel there is something uncanny about the female genital organs. This *unheimlich* place, however, is the entrance to the former *Heim* of all human beings, to the place where each one of us lived once upon a time and in the beginning. There is a humorous saying that "Love is home-sickness," and whenever a man dreams of a place or a country and says to himself, while he is still dreaming: "this place is familiar to me, I've been here before," we may interpret the place as being his mother's genitals or her body. In this case too, then, the *unheimlich* is what was once *heimisch*, familiar; the prefix "*un*" is the token of repression. (Freud 1965)

From a psychoanalytic perspective, the secret of secrets is the mother who "is" not, or is not present, though she is not absent. Might her impossible presence/unbearable absence be the secret that secrets the texts of SK and SH?

Even this secret, however, does not betray writing – it is necessary to dig deeper, go even farther back. In the beginning there is loss, which is always traumatic. This trauma is the ever-elusive origin of both the self and writing. SK always insisted that his "whole huge literary work had just one idea: to wound from behind." (Kierkegaard: no. 6107). The writer's wounding words, however, are themselves always already wounded by an originary loss that traumatizes the subject. The loss that gives birth to the "I" is the loss of what I never possess – when it (*es*, *ca*, id) is there, the "I" is not, and when the "I" is there it (*es*, *ca*, id) is not. The traces of this nonabsent absence of what is never present are *eros* and *thanatos*, which forever circumscribe the void I cannot fill. In an appropriately inconspicuous footnote in *The Interpretation of Dreams*, Freud makes a remarkable confession: "There is at least one spot in every dream at which it is unplumable – a navel, as it were, that is its point of contact with the unknown" (Freud 1965: 143). This point of contact with the unknowable marks and remarks the trauma that renders all consciousness and every text cryptic. When *Traumdeutung* becomes *Traum(a)deutung*, every text must be read and reread as the *Nachträglichkeit* of the null point, which is, "degree zero" that renders writing possible but leaves every text incomplete. Through a pseudonym, who is a psychoanalyst, SH writes, "[t]rauma doesn't appear in words, but in a roar of terror, sometimes with images. Words create the anatomy of a story, but within that story there are openings that cannot be closed" (Hustvedt 2008: 85). The same opening that allows writing to begin makes it impossible to end. Writing is a repetition compulsion that reinfects the wound it is trying to heal by ceaselessly seeking to recover what is always slipping away.

A final detail that might or might not be important. In a rarely noted comment, Freud associates the uncanny with "secret powers" that might be a symptom of epilepsy. Throughout his life, SK suffered what appear to have been seizures. In the autumn of 1855, he was returning to his flat after withdrawing from the bank the last of the inheritance. Having never had to work for a living and with no prospect of gainful employment, he had no idea what he was going to do. It turned out that he did not have to worry because before he got home, he suffered a seizure and was rushed to Frederik's Hospital, where he died forty days later. SK's death has been the subject of much debate but its cause has never been determined. In her Copenhagen lecture, SH joins others who speculate that SK's death might have been the result of an epileptic seizure.

> SK's body pained him. He felt crippled, aggrieved, and grotesquely anxious about it. If seizures were the cause, this is hardly strange. The hallucinatory auras that may precede them, the distinct feeling of being struck down by a great external force, the subsequent loss of bodily control, even consciousness, and the depressions that often follow are wrenching. And for many epileptics over the centuries there has been shame, secrecy, and ostracism. (Hustvedt 2013)

Having studied neuroscience and run a writing program in a psychiatric ward, SH understands the neurology of hallucinations and religious visions. Rejecting any mind/body dualism without subscribing to any simplistic reductionism, she suggests that SK's experiences and sense of calling were undoubtedly inseparable from physiological processes. SH, like SK, realizes that there is a fine line between religious vision and madness. "When is prophesy nervous madness?" she asks.

> Every person's profound emotional history affects her or his philosophical *outlook* or, in SK's case, *Inblikk* – in-look or insight. Feeling plays a far greater role in the ideas we adopt than the long Western philosophical tradition that hails reason over emotion has ever been able to admit and, furthermore, even when scholars busily work to undermine that split tradition – to denounce Cartesian dualism or humanism or the Enlightenment subject, or what-have-you, they usually *do it* in a *dispassionate*, abstract, objective mode in a voice from nowhere. As I wrote in my book *The Shaking Woman, or, a History of My Nerves*, people gravitate to certain ideas for reasons that are far from objective. (Hustvedt 2013)

SK's story is, in many ways, SH's story; just as SK assumes the mask of the pseudonyms to probe the truth of subjectivity, so SH creates characters in her novels through which she explores the multiple selves she and her readers knowingly and unknowingly harbor.

Ghost Stories

SH is haunted by ghosts who tell their stories through stories that appear to be her own. Like Kierkegaard, she – or is it her pseudonym? – is obsessed with the possibility of her father's youthful transgression on the barren Minnesota plains. This secret, and there might be others but how can anyone know, creates a trauma that is the absent origin of her wounded words. Echoing SK's pseudonymous authorship, SH's novels mingle fact and fiction, history and fable until it is impossible to distinguish one from the other. Like SK, SH had what she understood to be religious visions from the time she was a child, and as an adult began to suffer seizures, which seem to bear some resemblance to epilepsy. She tells the story of these afflictions, which are also a gift, in her apparently nonfiction book *The Shaking Woman, or, A History of My Nerves*. Her father, I have noted, taught linguistics at St. Olaf College in the heart of New World Scandinavia. Haunting experiences became undeniable during the last week of her father's life. After spending the day at her father's bedside with her mother, SH reports she returned to her childhood home

> and crawled into the narrow, too short bed I had slept in as a child and pulled the covers over me. As I lay there, thinking of my father, I felt the oxygen line in my nostrils and its discomfort, the heaviness of my lame leg, from which the tumor had been removed years before, the pressure in my tightened lungs, and a sudden panicked helplessness that I could not move from the bed on my own but would have to call for help. For however long it lasted, only minutes, *I was my father*. The sensation was both overwhelming and awful. I felt the proximity of death, its inexorable pull, and I had to struggle to leap back into my own body, to find myself again. (Hustvedt 2010: 25)

But the self to which one returns after having journeyed elsewhere is never the same as the self one seemed to have been.

Though the father's absence was at times an overwhelming non-presence, for SH, as for SK, the deeper, more primordial absence of the mother proves to be even more disturbing. Birth is always traumatic but when the original separation is doubled by separation after birth, the wound is compounded and leaves scars that never heal. In a revealing 2004 essay in *A Plea for Eros* entitled "Extracts from a Story of the Wounded Self," SH recalls an early memory of her mother asking "[h]ow is it possible for a person to be as sad as I am?"

> My mother was miserable because I was born too early. My lungs were undeveloped and the doctor told my parents that I might die. For two weeks, I lay in an incubator while my mother and father waited for my fate to be decided. In those days, the nurses didn't touch or massage babies left in incubators. I was separated from my mother in the first days of my life, and I now think that experience marks the beginning of a particular personality. When I suffered convulsions on the day of my christening party, I scared my mother yet again. [...] We can't remember our infancies, but they live in our bodies, and had I not been frail at birth, I would have been someone else, and I would have had other thoughts. When I look back, I can't remember a time when I didn't carry around in me a sensation of being wounded. (Hustvedt 2006: 195–196)

Wounded selves – and who has not been wounded? – write words that wound from behind.

If life begins with loss, everyone is always already wounded from behind. The lingering trace of this originary loss creates an ever-present anxiety of personal fragmentation. A dream that once again is "about" the mother.

> *It is night, and I am lying in bed. Above me I notice a large drill thrust into the wall. No one is holding it; it begins to turn on its own, and as it turns, I see that long, thin cracks are forming in the wall. The cracks get larger and then the wall begins to break open. I am overwhelmed with terror and throw myself against the wall to try to keep the fragments together, to stop the wall from collapsing. I'm screaming. I wake my mother.* (Hustvedt 2006: 196)

This dream revived SH's childhood memory of a trip to Chicago with her mother and sister during which she saw a woman suffering an epileptic seizure. *Traumdeutung as Traum(a)deutung.* Wounded words are thrust against the wall to fill the cracks and keep the self from falling to pieces. But words fail, always fail, because "trauma isn't part of a story; it is outside story. It is what we refuse to make part of our story" (Hustvedt 2008: 52).

From father to mother and back to father. Two and a half years after her father's death, SH gave a talk in his honor at St. Olaf College. She recalls that while writing the text, she had "a strong sensation of hearing my father's voice" (Hustvedt 2010: 3). What followed is most arresting. In *The Shaking Woman*, SH reports that when she began her talk in the building housing the Norwegian Department, where her father was a professor for almost forty years, she "began to shudder violently from the neck down. My arms flapped. My knees knocked. I shook as if I were having a seizure. Weirdly, my voice wasn't affected. It didn't change at all. [...] When the speech ended, the shaking stopped" (Hustvedt 2010: 3). This was the first but not the last time SH suffered such a seizure. Whenever it occurs, it seems as if she is literally falling to pieces. "*From the chin up, I was my familiar self. From the neck down, I was a shuddering stranger*" (Hustvedt 2010, 7. Emphasis mine). "[A] grim sense that two Siris were present, not one" (Hustvedt 2010: 40). Is the split subject, the fragmented self abnormal or normal? Am I – is the I – one or many?

In retrospect, it appears that there had been precursors to the "first" seizure. Recalling an experience she had forgotten or repressed, SH writes, "[o]nce before, during the summer of 1982, I'd felt as if some superior power picked me up and tossed me about as if I were a doll." Rather than anxiety or terror, SH felt euphoria but the high was short-lived and immediately gave way to a "violent migraine that lasted for almost a year" (Hustvedt 2010: 4). When the seizures became violent, SH began her long journey "through the worlds of neurology, psychiatry, and psychoanalysis" (Hustvedt 2010: 5). Though she had been studying the mind-body problem for years, the seizure during her father's memorial service changed the stakes of her work. She decided

> to write a novel in which I would have to impersonate a psychiatrist and psychoanalyst, a man I came to think of as my imaginary brother, Erik Davidsen. Brought up in Minnesota by parents very much like mine, he was the boy never born into the Hustvedt family. (Hustvedt 2010: 5)

That book became *The Sorrows of an American*.

Unknowable Keys

"How is it possible for a person to be as sad as I am?" A frightful question for a mother to ask a child, especially when the child feels she is responsible for her mother's sadness. Where do one person's sorrows end and another's begin? Where do one generation's sorrows end and another's begin? In an essay entitled "The Analyst in Fiction: Reflections on a More or Less Hidden Being," SH comments on *The Sorrows of an American*.

> Writing as Erik, I felt an underground music that determined the rhythms of the book's form. I knew I was writing a verbal fugue, point and counterpoint, themes chasing themes, and variations on them that kept returning: telling and not telling, listening and deafness, parents and children, the past and the present, one generation's sorrows living on in the generations that follow it. (Hustvedt 2012: 165)

Point and counterpoint: father/daughter, mother/daughter, brother/sister, Erik/Inga, Siri/Siri.

The last book SH's father wrote was a memoir that tells not only his own story but also the story of his parents and their immigration from Norway. During their final conversations, SH asked her father for permission to include excerpts from his memoir in the novel she was beginning to imagine. *The Sorrows of an American* weaves together what appear to be excerpts from the dead father's memoir with the daughter's fictive text. Erik, the psychoanalyst, and Inga, the philosophy student and writer, are pseudonyms for two Siris who write the text. The story begins with a desk that harbors a secret. SH assumes the persona of a man, Erik, who is the narrator and begins the story:

> My sister called it "the year of secrets," but when I look back on it now, I've come to understand that it was a time not of what was there, but of what wasn't. A patient of mine once said, "there are ghosts walking around inside me, but they don't always talk. Sometimes they have nothing to say." [...] I think we all have ghosts inside us, and it's better when they speak than when they don't. After my father died, I couldn't talk to him in person any more, but I didn't stop having conversations in my head. I didn't stop seeing him in my dreams or stop hearing his words. And yet it was what my father hadn't said that took over my life for a while – what he hadn't told us. It turned out that he wasn't the only person who had kept secrets. On January sixth, four days after his funeral, Inga and I came across the letter in his study. (Hustvedt 2008: 1)

Absence – what is unsaid and, perhaps, unsayable – always sets the story in motion.

Inga, like SH, is a shaking woman, who suffers seizures and whose hands tremble violently when she lectures in public. Opening a file drawer, Inga and Erik discover a letter dated June 27, 1937, addressed to their father from an unknown woman. "Dear Lars, I know you will never ever say nothing about what happened. We swore it on the BIBLE. It can't matter now she's in heaven or to the ones here on earth. I believe in your promise, Lisa" (Hustvedt 2008: 4–5). Fearing the worst but knowing their father left the letter for them to discover, Inga and Erik become obsessed with finding the mysterious Lisa and solving the mystery of the father's secret.

Inga received her Ph.D. in philosophy from Columbia University, where she wrote her dissertation on Kierkegaard's *Either/Or*. At the time of her father's death she was working on a book unlike any she had previously written. It was a book of stories of philosophers that was intended to demonstrate the inseparability of feelings and ideas by focusing on Pascal's carriage accident, Descartes's phantoms, Wittgenstein's mystical visions and last, but most important, "Kierkegaard's discovery of his father's secret." "Kierkegaard," Inga explains, sensed something in his gloomy, strict, religious father, and when his father was dying, he discovered it. He called it 'the great earthquake, the terrible upheaval,' which forced on him 'a new and infallible interpretation of all phenomena.' (Hustvedt 2008: 55)

The secret of SK's "real" father is inherited by the father of SH's pseudonym, Inga. "Kierkegaard," Inga continues,

> never recorded what his father's secret was. We may never know about our own father. I've had all kinds of fantasies about it, making up stories in my mind, thinking that they saw a woman die or found a corpse in the woods. I've even thought of murder, that they saw something terrible.... Pappa would never have stayed silent about a crime would he? I can't believe that. (Hustvedt 2008: 56)

Questions linger because the most important secrets can never be told, or can only be told by not telling.

As stories within stories proliferate and enfold, Inga and Erik become personae for a self that is incurably divided. Like Alma and Elizabeth in another Scandinavian masterpiece, Ingmar Bergman's *Persona*, their images fade into each other and incessantly alternate until one becomes two.

> Alma stops, sees herself for a brief moment, this is Alma, this is Elisabeth and herself. She can no longer distinguish, nor does it matter. Elisabeth laughs, shortly, coarsely.
> – Try to listen. (*Whispers Alma.*) Please. Can't you hear what I'm saying?
> – Try to answer now.
> Elisabeth lifts her face from her hands. It is naked, sweating. She nods slowly.
> – Nothing, nothing, no, nothing.
> – Nothing (*Ingenting*).
> – It'll be alright. That's how it must be. (Bergman 1966)

The "Nothing" that Elisabeth and/or Alma (it is impossible to be sure who is who) recalls SK's *Angest*. Commenting on the innocence that is always already lost, SK, through his pseudonym Vigilius Haufniesis explains,

> [i]n this strife [of innocence] there is peace and repose, but there is simultaneously something other (*noget Andet*) that is not contention and strife, for there is indeed nothing against which to strive. What, then, is it? Nothing (*Intet*). But what effect does nothing have? It begets dread. (Kierkegaard: 41)

This passage appears in *The Concept of Dread*, whose extended subtitle is *A simple psychological deliberation oriented in the direction of the dogmatic problem of original sin*. The Danish word that is translated "original sin" is *Arvesynden*, which should be rendered "inherited sin." Vigilius Haufniensis distinguishes *Angest* (dread or anxiety), which is apprehension of indeterminate possibility that is inseparable from freedom, from fear, which has determinate object and is, therefore, manageable. For the "melancholy Dane," psychic inheritance was more than an abstract theological, philosophical, or psychological issue. The sins of the father are visited upon sons and daughters in the form of dread, which can become overwhelming. From generation to generation, psychic debt (*die Schuld*) is compounded and guilt (*die Schuld*) increases. When Inga's daughter Sonia informs her that she has decided that she will also attend Columbia, her mother admits that she senses that she too "had silent ghosts inside her, and she guarded them carefully" (Hustvedt 2008: 65). (SH's daughter is named Sophie but did not, like her mother and father, attend Columbia.)[2]

SH makes no secret of her rewriting of SK. As *The Sorrows of an American* draws to a close, brother and sister leave the family farmhouse for the final time and drive to the airport. Inga reflects, "Maybe you've kept a secret in your heart that you felt in all its joy or pain was too precious to share with someone else." "What are you saying?" Erik asks. Inga explains, "I'm quoting Kierkegaard, the preface to *Either/Or*. He's making a philosophical point about the internal and the external" (Hustvedt 2008: 252). She then proceeds to recount Victor Emerita's story of smashing the secretary and discovering the manuscript that became *Either/Or*.

> "Bear with me," she said curtly. "I've always felt that the secretary is standing in for a living body, a person giving up secrets under duress, like Kierkegaard's brooding, guilty father before he died. After he injures the chest, Emerita says that he begs its forgiveness and then goes away to the country. He leaves the broken, hurt piece of furniture behind, but he takes the documents, its hidden contents, its *inner voice*, with him."
> "We all have secret drawers."
> "Exactly," she said. "And most of the time they're never found." (Hustvedt 2008: 253)

---

[2] SH received her Ph.D. in English at Columbia in 1986. In her dissertation, entitled "Charles Dickens – Figures of Dust: A Reading of *Our Mutual Friend*," she explores the relationship of language and identity through a consideration of the metaphors of fragmentation. Her argument draws on the writings of Kierkegaard, Emil Benveniste, Mikhail Bakhtin, Sigmund Freud, Jacques Lacan, Paul Ricoeur and Julia Kristeva. (See http://en.wikipedia.org/wiki/Siri_Hustvedt.) Another ghost? Sophia is the name of the wife of one of the writers who has been most influential for Paul Auster – Nathaniel Hawthorne.

SH's Pseudonymous Authorship

"Erik, I know you sometimes think I don't get to the point, but I started my little story about Max [her dead husband] with *Either/Or* for a reason. 'One author,'" she quoted, "'seems to be enclosed within another, like the parts in a Chinese puzzle box.'" I stood there in the doorway, looking at my husband as he gestured those words, and wondered, 'Which I and which you? There are too many.'" (Hustvedt 2008: 255)

The Blazing World is a novel about naming whose title is improper because it has been stolen, though the theft is confessed. The original version, published in 1666 by an English author, Margaret Cavendish, Duchess of Newcastle, is a satirical novel about a utopian kingdom that is one of the first works of science fiction written by a woman. The work was republished in 1668 under the title *Observations upon Experimental Philosophy*, which might well have been the title of SH's work. Though "the duchess sometimes wore men's clothes, vests and cavalier hats" (Hustvedt 2014: 208), she published in her own name at a time when most women writers wrote anonymously or under male pseudonyms. SH's novel centers around Harriet Burden, aka Harry, who, after the death of her husband, a well-known art dealer named Felix Lord, begins creating her own art. In an extended philosophical-artistic experiment, she co-opts three male artists to show her work under their names. Between 1999 and 2003 she mounts three major exhibitions, with the title *Maskings*, that are ostensibly the work of three men: Anton Tish, Phineas Q. Eldridge, and Rune Larsen, whose name recalls both the proto-Norse alphabets inscribed on Rune stones that can still be found in Scandinavia, and a popular Norwegian journalist and TV personality, who wrote for the *Bergens Arbeiderblad* around the time SH spent a year with her grandmother in Bergen. Harriet/Harry intended this complex work "to uncover the complex workings of human perception and how unconscious ideas about gender, race, and celebrity influence a viewer's understanding of a given work of art" (Hustvedt 2014: 102).

SH organizes *The Blazing World* around excerpts from 24 notebooks that Harriet/Harry's daughter, Maisie, found in her mother's Nantucket cottage at the time of her death. Each fragment is labeled with a single letter of the alphabet; the two missing letters are I and O, or so it seems. The work also includes recollections and interviews with family members, friends, fellow artists and critics. SH once again assumes a male persona by making I. V. Hess both the editor of the work and the narrator of the novel. Hess claims to be an art professor who is writing a book entitled *Plural Voices and Multiple Visions* in which he considers the works of Søren Kierkegaard, M. M. Bakhtin and Aby Warburg. In his "Editor's Introduction," Hess explains that he was drawn to the project by Harriet/Harry's description of her work as *"poeticized personalities,"* a phrase, he notes, she borrows from Kierkegaard. The book opens with a quotation from a letter about the *Maskings* project written by Richard Brickman to the editor of an art journal. Hess reports that *Maskings* was an artistic project designed as a psychological experiment to make a political point. "Burden insisted," he writes,

> that the pseudonym she adopted changed the character of the art she made. In other words, the man she used as a mask played a role in the *kind* of art she produced: 'Each artist mask became for Burden a 'poetized personality,' a visual elaboration of a 'hermaphroditic self,' which cannot be said to belong to either her or to the mask, but to a 'mingled reality created between them.' (Hustvedt 2014: 2)

When Peter Wentworth, the editor of the journal, checked out Brickman's credentials, he found that Brickman had received his Ph.D. in philosophy from Emory University and was an assistant professor at St. Olaf College in Northfield, Minnesota. However, when he followed up by contacting both institutions about Brickman, he discovered, predictably, that neither school had ever heard of him. With suspicion aroused, Hess concludes his or her introduction with a postscript in which he admits that the notebooks "provide further information on Harriet Burden's relationship with Rune and reveal that Richard Brickman is, as I had guessed, a pseudonym for Burden herself" (Hustvedt 2014: 11).

Why are there 24 rather than 26 notebooks? And why are the missing letters I and O? The letter "I" is, of course, the first person pronoun, but also can designate the number 1. With pseudonyms proliferating like nested Russian dolls and every proper name improper, no one speaks in the first person – in other words, always in other words, the "I" is always missing. This issue is not merely aesthetic, it is also psychological and, more important, philosophical. SH's work is, like SK's, "philosophical art and artistic philosophy." Throughout much, though certainly not all, the history of western philosophy, the self has been considered to be unified: I = 1. "As for O," Hess observes, "it is [also] a number as well as a letter, a nullity, an opening, a void" (Hustvedt 2014: 10). The question SH relentlessly, sometimes obsessively, probes is not merely "Who am I?" but "What is the 'I'"? Am I, is the "I" one or many? Present or absent? Knowable or unknowable? If the "I" is missing, the I = O. And if the "I" is always already missing, who writes? How could no one write about anything? Perhaps by writing "about" nothing, writing "around" the void, "writing degree zero" through an endless series of pseudonyms.[3]

---

3 See Barthes, Roland. 2012. *Writing Degree Zero*. Trans. Annette Lavers. New York: Hill and Wang.

I. V. Hess is SH's Victor Emerita, the editor who explains how the published manuscript was formed from scattered papers that seem to be as much a collection of philosophical fragments as a coherent narrative. *The Blazing World*, like *The Sorrows of an American*, is also, if Hess is to be believed, a ghost story. Hess explains that *The Blazing World* was not his first choice for the book's title. In notebook R, he/she reports that three words appear repeatedly: *revenant* (ghost), *revisit*, and *repetition*. "[A]fter twenty pages on ghosts and dreaming, there is a blank space followed by the words *Monsters at Home*" (Hustvedt 2014: 10). This was the initial title of the book but, after reading all the notebooks, Hess changed his/her mind and gave the book the same title Burden had given the last art work she completed before her difficult death from ovarian cancer. This decision was the result of his conclusion that Margaret Cavendish is, in fact, Harriet Burden's alter ego. Just as Harriet/Harry created a Bakhtinian dialogical theater through her pseudonyms, so the Duchess of Newcastle "created a world of interlocutors in her writings. As with Cavendish," Hess suggests,

> I believe that Burden cannot be understood unless the dialogical quality of her thought is taken into consideration. All of Burden's notebooks may be read as forms of dialogue. She continually shifts from the first person to the second and then to the third. Some passages are written as arguments between two versions of herself. One voice makes a statement. Another disputes it. Her notebooks became the ground where her conflicted anger and divided intellect could do battle on the page. (Hustvedt 2014: 6)

The *revenants* are many – some named, others unnamed, some real, others fake: Vermeer, Velazquez, Louise Bourgeois, Eliza Heywood, Lawrence Sterne, John Milton, Emily Dickinson, Ezra Pound, Franz Kafka, René Descartes, G. [not S.] Kierkegaard, G. W. F. Hegel, Maurice Merleau-Ponty, Mikhail Bakhtin, Edmund Husserl, Martin Heidegger, Paul Ricoeur, Sigmund Freud, Émil Benveniste, Roman Jakobson, Roland Barthes, Guy Debord, Jean Baudrillard, Donald Winnicott, William James, Mary Douglas, Victor Turner, Simone de Beauvoir, Anne Fausto-Sterling, Toril Moi, Elizabeth Wilson, Julia Kristeva, Judith Butler, Jacques Lacan, Ray Kurtzweil, Daniel Dennett, David Chalmers, Colin McGinn, Dan Zahavi, Jacques Derrida. There are others – many others. When the full text of "Brinkman's" letter, originally published in *The Open Eye: An Interdisciplinary Journal of Art and Perception Studies*, finally appears more than halfway through the novel, it reveals a surprise:

> The letter takes a further turn into theories of the self. Again, Burden seems to be aware of the philosophical and scientific debates on the nature of the self, and her letter escorts the reader on a convoluted path from Homer to the Stoics to Vico, leaping forward to W.T.H. Myers's subliminal self, to Janet, Freud, and James, to Edmund Husserl's phenomenology of time con-

sciousness and intersubjectivity and then to contemporary infant research, as well as neuroscience findings about primordial selves, and locationist hypotheses which focus on the hypothalamus and periaqueductal gray areas of the brain, as well as a Finnish scholar, Pauli Pylkko, who advances a notion of "aconceptual mind," an obscure novelist and essayist Siri Hustvedt, whose position Burden calls "a moving target." As far as I can tell, Burden attempts to undermine all conceptual borders, which, I believe, define human experience itself. I cannot say that her wild romp into the more peculiar aspects of continental philosophy convinced me. The woman flirts with the irrational. (Hustvedt 2014: 255. Emphasis mine)

Richard Brickman is Harriet Burden is Harry Burden is Anton Tish is Phineas Q. Eldridge is Rune Larsen is SK is SH is Siri Hustvedt. A flirt, indeed, and not only a flirt, but, as Harriet/Harry has confessed, also a liminal figure of a "trickster." Neither inside nor outside, this nor that, here nor there, present nor absent, one nor many, but forever *entre-deux*, always betwixt and between. No wonder Harriet/Harry claims "Siri Hustvedt" is "a moving target."

The pseudonyms under which Harriet/Harry "publishes" her/his work are the names of "real" people: Anton Tish (whose name is an anagram of "shit")[4] – an "enfant terrible," who is nothing more than a "little boy with a few fresh acne scars"; Phineas Q. Eldridge, who changed his name from John Whittier when he came out – "a performance artist; he performs in 'half drag,' half man, half woman, half white, half black, cut straight down the middle, and the two parts of him have conversations on stage;" and Rune Larsen, a cross between the performance artist Orlan and Jeff Koons, who "never gave up on irony" (Hustvedt 2014: 57, 59, 60). Rune established his reputation with a 1997 blockbuster show with the Koonsian title "The Banality of Glamour," which is a knock-off of the performance artist Orlan's work except that Rune, unlike Orlan, does not put himself on the operating table. Rune's friend Oswald Case comments on Rune's work,

> using facial morphing technology to incrementally alter his features in video sequence of himself waking up, walking in streets, and attending an opening at night wearing a T-shirt that says *Artificial Man*. Simultaneous films of plastic-surgery patients under the knife (both cosmetic and reconstructive) mixed with images of prosthetic and robotic hands, arms, legs, as well as crucifixes and crosses. *Art, Artificial, Art Man, Man Art, Man-*

---

4 Like all of SH's works, *The Blazing* World is deeply informed by Freud's writing. Psychoanalytic theory collapses high into low by interpreting and other aspects of culture as the symptom of the sublimation of base instincts. The identification of art with excess, waste, and impurity was the cornerstone of Georges Bataille's theory of art. Bataille's work was all the rage at Columbia University during the years SH and her pseudonym Inga were pursuing their doctoral degrees.

art, *Artman*, *Cross*, *Crosses*, and *Crucifix*. Brisk business in bricks. *Art Assembly* publishes article 'Rune: Constructing the Non-Self.' (Hustvedt 2014: 173–174)

In his last work, *Houdini Smash*, Rune pushes subjectivity beyond the human to the post-human, where the boundary separating mind, body, and machine seems to disappear. In an article entitled "Rune's Ego Machine: Harbinger of the New Aesthetics," published in *Visibility: A Magazine of the Arts*, Timothy Hardwick writes that Rune draws on the work of computer scientist and science fiction writer Vernon Vinge, who coined the term "singularity," and Ray Kurtzweil, computer scientist, director of engineering at Google, awarded the National Medal of Technology and Innovation, which is the nation's highest honor in technology, by President Clinton in 1999, and author of *The Singularity is Near: Why Humans Transcend Biology* (2006), to support his assertion that "AI is the cutting edge in art, whether people know it or not. It will revolutionize artistic practice by providing artists with tools or works that are animate and intelligent" (Hustvedt 2014: 303). Rune, unlike Vinge, Kurtzweil and their Silicon epigones, who founded Singularity University, sees a dark side to these technological developments. "The artist will no longer control his art. It will function independently of the designer, and therefore create exciting and dangerous new zones of interaction" (Hustvedt 2014: 303). But has the artist ever really controlled her art?

Sometimes names are destiny – Rune's name is almost homophonic with "ruin," and his story does not end well. Harriet/Harry makes a deal with Rune – she will show her work *Beneath*, under his name. A thoroughly postmodern artist, Rune is convinced that everything has been done before and, therefore, unconcerned about originality and willingly agrees to play the role Harriet/Harry assigns him. But midway through the game, Rune changes the rules and Harriet/Harry loses control of the work she had thought was her own. Harriet/Harry and Rune become engaged in a life-and-death struggle when she accuses him of literally and figuratively stealing her art by claiming it as his own. In a fragment from Notebook O, which the reader had been told was missing but now appears (you can never trust a trickster), Harriet/Harry writes,

> I sat in silence, still as a stone. Harry the [Rune?] stone. He talked about how well it had gone, *Beneath*, how much better than he had expected. He was surprised by its success, really surprised, and he moved his hands to my shoulders and gripped them hard. He said, But then, really think what would have happened if your name had been on it? You are right, Harry. It would have been nothing. (Hustvedt 2014: 279)

Rune Larson creates Harry/Harriet Burden as much as Harriet/Harry Burden creates Rune Larson. The artist, in other words, creates the work, which, in turn, creates the artist.

Strange loops remain ellipses that might become an ellipsis but never a circle. In the postmodern, posthuman world there no longer are any secrets – interiority and depth seem to disappear in a play of surfaces that knows no end. Rune/Harriet/Harry/SH knows the stakes of the game she/he/they is/are playing. Through the pseudonym of Oswald Case, Rune/Harriet/Harry/SH writes,

> Rune was a fabulist. He reinvented himself again and again ceaselessly until the end. In this respect, he was a man of our time, a creature of the media and of virtual realities, an avatar walking the earth, a digitized being. No one knew him. His comment about his autobiography as a "fake" is at once deep and shallow. And that is the point. There can be no depth in our world, no personality, no true story, only images without substance projected anywhere and everywhere instantaneously. Soon we will have communication devices implanted directly into our brains. The distinctions between reality and image are fading. People live in their screens. Social media are replacing social life. (Hustvedt 2014: 177)

Staged as an elaborate con game, *Beneath* lies. In the postmodern, posthuman world, not only has interiority disappeared, but nothing lies beneath. *Beneath* is a work of art that is "about" nothing, "about" a void whose opening is simultaneously the impossibility and possibility of wounding words.

With the ground disappearing beneath his feet, the only thing left for Rune to do is die – Harriet/Harry must kill him off. His death, however, cannot be the end of the story. Rune dies in an apparent suicide staged as performance art. But questions linger: Was his death really planned or was it an accident, an artistic work that got out of control? When Rune dies, obituaries confirm the premise of Harry/Harriet's experiment by attributing *Beneath* to him without ever mentioning her. The artist/writer vanishes into her work/pseudonym.

By killing off Rune, Harriet/Harry stages her own death – she withdraws and assumes, in the words of Margaret Cavendish, "the Kierkegaardian position." Bruno Kleinfeld, Harriet/Harry's second husband, reports, "she/he" quoted Margaret Cavendish regularly, that colorful lady philosopher, whose most fervent hope was that she would find readers after she was dead. The Duchess of Newcastle had dreamed of a glorious posthumous life" (Hustvedt 2014: 295). With cancer ravaging her body, Harry/Harriet returns to a work she had abandoned to take up her experiment. "The Blazing World" was a sculpture of a huge reclining pregnant Margaret Cavendish.

> This woman had worlds inside her. When you looked into her bald, see-through cranium, you saw little people, hoards of busy wax Lilliputians going about their business. They ran and jumped. They danced and sang. They sat at miniature desks facing computers, typewriters, or pages. When you looked closely, you could see that they were making musical scores, drawings, mathematical formulas, poems, and stories. (Hustvedt 2014: 295)

Stories, always stories and more stories. The last words from Harriet/Harry's notebooks are:

> I am multitudes.
> This earth a spot, a grain, an atom.[5]
> I am made of the dead.
> Even my thoughts are not my own anymore. (Hustvedt 2014: 340)

Siri's Pharmacy

Why do we write? Why do we read? What is writing? Who is reading? Many ghosts haunt SH's writing but one *revenant* returns more than any other – SK. In the first excerpt from her notebooks included in *The Blazing World*, Harry/Harriet writes,

> I wanted my own indirect communications à la Kierkegaard, whose masks clashed and fought, works in which the ironies were thick and thin and nearly invisible. Where would I find a Victor Eremita, an A and a B, a Judge William, a Johannes de Silentio, a Constantin Constantius, a Vigilius Haufniensis, a Nicholas Notabene, a Hilarius Bookbinder, an Inter et Inter, a Johannes Climacus, and an Anti-Climacus all my own? (Hustvedt 2014: 34)

In a footnote I. V. Hess, who, we have seen in Harry/Harriet's Victor Emerita, notes that in Notebook K, Burden devotes seventy-five pages to Kierkegaard's pseudonyms and his "indirect communications." Gradually, an answer to her own question emerges: she would find a multitude of pseudonymous selves in her own imagination.

> Hadn't S.K., under his pseudonym Notabene, written a series of prefaces that were followed by no text? What if I invented an artist who was all art criticism, all catalog copy, and no work? How many artists, after all, had been catapulted into importance by drivel written by all those hacks who had taken the linguistic turn? Ah, *écriture!* The artist would have to be a young man, an *enfant terrible* whose emptiness generates page after page of text. Oh, the fun of it! (Hustvedt 2014: 34)

"[T]he linguistic turn […] Ah, *écriture!*" Who is the *enfant terrible* and what is *écriture?* Nota Bene: prefaces to prefaces, postscripts to postscripts. Always a supplement or a supplement to the supplement, never the text proper. *Hors Livre*... *Hors d'oeuvre*... Foreplay. Gender/genre bending: Johannes the Seducer becomes SH the Seductress.

---

5 John Milton, *Paradise Lost*, Book VIII, 17–18.

Immediately after the comment about the *"enfant terrible* whose emptiness generates page after page," Harriet/Harry parodies Jacques Derrida.

> *The aporia in the work of X is achieved through the process of auto-induction into absence. The implied, hence invisible, autoerotic acts with a sexual origin facilitate an abysmal collapse, the phantasms of rupture and the withdrawal of the object of desire.* (Hustvedt 2014: 34)

Though not mentioned in the "body" of the "text," two works by Derrida are relevant in this context – one "about" Kierkegaard's notion of the secret, which he wrote at my urging, *The Gift of Death*, and the other "about" *inter alia*, Hegel. *Dissemination* begins with a preface, entitled "*Hors Livre, Hors d'Oeuvre*," devoted to Hegel's *Phenomenology of Spirit*, which is itself a preface to his system, and is followed by a substantial text, "Plato's Pharmacy." Derrida's prefaces to prefaces are mirror images of SK's postscripts to postscripts. Questions, like those who pose them, proliferate: What is a pharmacy? Who is a pharmacist?

Telephonics. *The Blazing World* ends with an unusual postscript by a most unlikely character. Sweet Autumn Pinkney is a flakey New Ager who was Anton Tish's studio assistant. Having played virtually no role in the novel, she appears at the end of the story as if she had just landed from another planet. In her written transcript, Autumn recounts hearing the televoices of a man saying "Harry," as she was passing the Siri Pharmacy on Atlantic Avenue in Brooklyn. Who is speaking and who is being spoken to? SH confesses that she sees angels and hears voices she can neither control nor silence. Is SH speaking through her pseudonym Autumn, or is Autumn ventriloquizing SH? Are these voices signs that refer to something real or are they signifiers floating through the ether like parasites that create the noise disrupting lines of communication? What is a *pharmakon*? Autumn takes the voice to be a meaningful sign whose referent is the voice of her spiritual master, Peter Deunov, who has moved to a higher planetary system called Sirius. Deunov (1864–1944) was a "real" historical figure who founded a school of esoteric Christianity. Born in Bulgaria, Deunov immigrated to the United States, where he studied theology at Drew Theological Seminary and the Boston University School of Theology. He returned to Bulgaria and in 1922 founded the School of the Universal White Brotherhood, where, as if to mimic the unlikely couple of Hegel and Madam Blavatsky, he taught a synthesis of phrenology, theosophy and mystical Christianity. Autumn's spiritual master instructs her to find Harriet/Harry and help her reach higher levels of consciousness by assisting her transition to the other side.

More names that might or might not be proper; is Sirius serious, or is the unconcluding postscript an elaborate joke? Is the higher planetary system that transmits voices to earth really SiriusXM? SH, who is fluent in French and knows her theory, surely realizes that in French *parasite* can mean interference, static or noise.[6] The baffling hall of mirrors created in *The Blazing World* provokes endless reflection and makes it impossible to be sure about anything or to know who is who. For five days Autumn, accompanied by her dog Kali (Kali is the Hindu goddess, who is the consort of Shiva, the lord of death) and the hospice doctor Gupta (Sanjay, perhaps?) cares for Harriet/Harry.[7] Family members are disturbed by the presence of this uncanny stranger, but Harriet/Harry welcomes Autumn into her home at the most critical moment of her life.

While *The Sorrows of an American* begins with the death of the father, *The Blazing World* ends with the death of the mother. Eight months after Harriet/Harry's death, her son, Ethan, invites Autumn to return to the studio to see her final work, which turned out to be the sculpture of Margaret Cavendish. In a twist that by now is predictable this work of art turns out to be a self-portrait – Harriet/Harry Burden is Margaret Cavendish, and a description of *The Blazing World* is the work's last chapter. Viewing the work, Autumn is blessed with yet another sign that brings a vision.

> It was a sign, maybe it was coming from Harry. I could feel something important happening to me and then I saw a woman squatting on the floor, not a real person, but a great big statue with no hair. And she had lots of people inside her head, but also numbers, letters, and she was raining numbers and letters and little people from her private parts, her vagina, anyway, and I felt a big grin come over my face, and I walked over to her to get a close look. There's a lot of art I don't understand. To be honest, it's kind of boring to me, but this was different. I got down on my hands and knees and started looking around at the tiny ones, and I had the sacred feeling. I told Ethan I had it. I opened up my arms and said, "Wow," and then I saw her. "Look," I said. "Look, it's Harry. Can I touch her?" They didn't know that Harry had put herself into the art, so it was exciting. I pointed at the little person, and Ethan and Maisie got down on their knees. They saw right away. Maisie said, "It's Mother, all right." (Hustvedt 2014: 356)

Writing, which begins with loss, lack, and absence, is always "about" the void. Before the beginning is trauma, birth trauma, which is the death/disappearance of the mother. This is what "Derrida," writing under the name Harriet/Harry Burden describes as "an abysmal collapse, the phantasms of rupture and the withdrawal of the object of desire" (Hustvedt 2014: 34). But the trauma of death makes the trauma of birth possible.

---

6 See Serres, Michael. 2007. *The Parasite*. Minneapolis: University of Minnesota Press.
7 All of this is beginning to spin out of control. I no longer am sure whether or not it is significant that "God" is an anagram of "dog."

"The Music of Chance?" I write these words in the darkness before dawn on the day of the winter solstice; twenty-five years ago today, my mother died during the longest night of the year.

For Autumn, Harry/Harriet's bodily death makes it possible to be reborn in another world where her consciousness will expand. Harry/Harriet/SH lives on after death through the multiple masks she/they has/have created. Pausing before leaving the studio the final time, Autumn recalls,

> I turned around to take one last look at Harry's artworks, and then I saw their auras blazing out all around them. I took a big breath and held it for a few seconds. They weren't people, after all. They were just things a person had made. For the first time, I really had the understanding of why the master taught that there were artists on the higher plane living on Sirius. It was because they had given their spirits and energies into what they made. [...] I closed my eyes. I opened them again, and I just stood there smiling because the colors were still there – reds and oranges and yellows and greens and blues and violets – blazing hot and bright in that big room where Harry used to work, and I knew for certain that each and every one of those wild, nutty, sad things Harry had made was alive with the spirit. For a second there, I could almost hear them breathing. (Hustvedt 2014: 357)

The Blazing World animates the blazing world.

But who *is* "Siri" and what is she selling in her pharmacy? Is she real or fake? Is the pharmacy real of fake? It is impossible to be sure. After all, there is a real Siri Pharmacy near the home of the real Siri – 23 Flatbush Avenue Extension, Brooklyn, NY 11201 (718–596–7397). Is Siri a person who asks difficult questions that cannot be answered, or an avatar, a digitized being whose automated voice on the telephone provides all the answers? A clue, perhaps, a clue: All serious writing/art is autobiographical even if there is no self for it to be "about." There is no simple answer to the question of Siri's identity because the self is not simple but is multiple. Writing in what appears to be her own name, SH admits,

> [t]he strangeness of a duality in myself remains, a powerful sense of an 'I' and an uncontrollable other. The shaking woman is certainly not anyone with a *name*. She is a speechless alien who appears only during my speeches [...] But who owns the self? Is it the 'I'? What does it mean to be integrated and not in pieces? What is subjectivity? Is it a singular property or a plural one? (Hustvedt 2010: 47)

If I am not one but many, no name is proper and every name is a pseudonym for the "I" that is always missing. The shaking woman confesses,

> [w]hen I am writing well, I often lose all sense of composition; the sentences come as if I hadn't willed them, as if they were manufactured by another being. This is not my day-to-day mode of writing, which includes grinding, painful periods of starts and stops. But the

sense that I have been taken over happens several times during the course of a book usually in the latter stages. I don't write; I am written. (Hustvedt 2010: 72)

Televoices, perhaps from the planet Sirius?
Derrida begins "Plato's Pharmacy" with a secret:

> A text is not a text unless it hides from the first comer, from the first glance, the law of its composition and the rules of its game. A text remains, moreover, forever imperceptible. Its law and its rules are not, however, harbored in the inaccessibility of a secret; it is simply that they can never be booked, in the *present*, into anything that could rigorously be called a perception. (Derrida 1981: 63)

Since texts are as complicated as the people who write them, nothing is straightforward, and it is always necessary to read against the grain. Sirius' texts inevitably undo what they are fashioned to do, unsay what they are designed to say. The secret of writing is that failure is success because, as Derrida insists, what is never present cannot be represented but forever slips away, leaving a wound that never heals. Plato was always suspicious of writing because he thought it engendered forgetting. His point is more telling today than when he voiced it – scriptural technologies weaken memory by outsourcing it to machines that no one controls.

There is, however, another forgetting that forgets an Other that is never known. Freud labels this abyssal forgetting "repression." The wound that never heals is the trace of the primal repression that gives birth to the "I." Writing is always duplicitous. On the one hand, narratives are constructed to heal fragmented selves and lend life meaning by filling gaps, covering holes and avoiding the void. Whether fictional stories, historical narratives, or autobiographical memories, writing is an imaginative construction that struggles to create unity through gestures of exclusion, omission, and repression. But all stories turn out to be ghost stories because the repressed inevitably returns to expose the void left by trauma. Harriet/Harry admits to her friend Rachel Briefman, "*I don't know if I should tell you. No, I can tell you. Maybe I shouldn't. I will. There's something in me, Rachel, something I don't understand. I felt it when I wanted to kill Anton. I'm not kidding. I hated him when he was sitting there in my apartment. I was afraid of myself. What is that? It's old, Rachel. It's like a memory in me, but it's not. I feel it, and it's been coming up. With Dr. F., I mean. It's something horrible in me*" (Hustvedt 2014: 110. My emphasis).[8] "It's old [...]. It's like a memory

---

[8] Harriet/Harry's psychoanalyst is named Dr. Fertig, which SH abbreviates Dr. F, which, of course, suggests Freud.

in me, but it's not." A memory that cannot be re(-)membered leaves the self forever faulty.

On the one hand, but, on the other. Writing betrays the self by revealing the very void it is designed to conceal. Words "I" once thought were my own are always already wounded, rend(er)ing all communication indirect. It is not I – not the "I" – who is speaking because an other – many others – is/are speaking through me. This other can only be part of the story by not being part of the story. It is forever *hors livre, hors d'oeuvre*. Another memoir, which might or might not be fiction, Paul Auster's *The Invention of Solitude*, also begins with the death of the father and never stops circling around his absence.

> Never before have I been so aware of the rift between thinking and writing. For the past few days, in fact, I have begun to feel that the story I am trying to tell is somehow incompatible with language, that the degree to which it resists language is an exact measure of how closely I have come to saying something important, and that when the moment arrives for me to say the one truly important thing (assuming it exists), I will not be able to say it.
>
> There has been a wound, and I realize now that it is very deep. Instead of healing me as I thought it would, the act of writing has kept this wound open. (Auster 1982: 32.)

The wound stays open because trauma cannot be narrated. "Trauma isn't part of a story; it is outside the story" (Hustvedt 2008: 52) – forever *hors d'oeuvre*.

Writing is the *pharmakon* – a drug that is also a poison, a gift that is at the same time *ein Gift* (poison). In her attempt to close gaps, fill holes and cover the void, the writer "leads astray" by creating the illusion that the self is unified and the world comprehensible. But the hand that writes the prescription is at the same time the hand that inflicts the wound that cures by not curing. *Écriture* is a repetition compulsion that sometimes knowingly but more often unknowingly inscribes and reinscribes the trauma that can be neither remembered nor forgotten: "phantasms of rupture" in the wake of "the withdrawal of the object of desire." What if the cure is the acceptance of the impossibility of cure? What if trauma opens "the space of literature"? What if "the gift of death" is life? What if the writer's fix is a *pharmakon*?

> If the *pharmakon* [which or who is also a trickster] is "ambivalent," it is because it constitutes the medium in which opposites are opposed, the movement and the play that link them among themselves, reverses them or makes one side cross over into the other (soul/body, good/evil, inside/outside, memory/forgetfulness, speech/writing, etc.) [...]. The *pharmakon*, without being anything itself, always exceeds them [i.e., clear and distinct philosophical concepts]. It keeps itself forever in reserve even though it has no fundamental nor ultimate locality. We will watch it infinitely promise itself and endlessly vanish through concealed doorways that shine like mirrors and open onto a labyrinth. It is this store of deep background that we are calling the *pharmacy*. (Derrida : 127–28)

This is Siri's pharmacy where, through the prescriptions SH writes, the self might find itself by losing the oneness of the "I" in the manyness of pseudonyms.

> Don't turn away.
> Keep looking at the bandaged place.
> That's where the light enters you.
> Rumi (*Sorrows of an American*.)

Works Cited

Auster, Paul. 1982. *The Invention of Solitude*. New York: Sun Press.
Barthes, Roland. 2012. *Writing Degree Zero*. Trans. Annette Lavers. New York: Hill and Wang.
Derrida, Jacques. 1981. *Positions*. Trans. Alan Bass. Chicago: University of Chicago Press.
Derrida, Jacques. 1981. *Disseminations*. Trans. Barbara Johnson. Chicago: University of Chicago Press.
Freud, Sigmund. 2003. "The Uncanny". Trans. David McLimbock. London: Penguin Classics.
Freud, Sigmund. 1965. *The Interpretation of Dreams*. Trans. James Strachey. New York: Avon Books.
Hong, Howard V. and Edna H. Hong. "Introduction." Kierkegaard, Søren. 1987 *Either/Or*. Trans. Hong & Hong. Princeton, NJ: Princeton University Press.
Hustvedt, Siri. 2006. *A Plea for Eros: Essays*. London: Sceptre.
Hustvedt, Siri. 2008. *The Sorrows of an American*. New York: Henry Holt and Company.
Hustvedt, Siri. 2010. *The Shaking Woman, or, A History of My Nerves*. London: Sceptre.
Hustvedt, Siri. 2012. *Living, Thinking, Looking*. London: Picador.
Hustvedt, Siri. 2013. "Kierkegaard's Pseudonyms and the Truths of Fiction." Lecture Copenhagen. 11 May 2013.
Hustvedt, Siri. 2014. *The Blazing World*. New York: Simon & Schuster.
Kierkegaard, Søren. 1941. *Concluding Unscientific Postscript*. Trans. D. F. Swenson and W. Lowrie. Princeton: Princeton University Press.
Kierkegaard, Søren. 1987. *Either/Or*. Trans. Hong & Hong. Princeton, NJ: Princeton University Press
Kierkegaard, Søren. 1967. *Søren Kierkegaards Journals and Papers*. Trans. Howard and Edna Hong. Bloomington: Indiana University Press.
Milton, John. *Paradise Lost*. Book VIII.
Persona. 1966. Dir. Ingmar Bergman. MGM.
Serres, Michel. 2007. *The Parasite*. Minneapolis: University of Minnesota Press.
Taylor, Mark. 1975. *Kierkegaard's Pseudonymous Authorship: A Study of Time and Self*. Princeton: Princeton University Press.
Taylor, Mark. 1980. *Journeys to Selfhood: Hegel and Kierkegaard*. Berkeley: University of California Press.

Medicine and Narrative

Rita Charon
The Great Glazed Tank of Art: From the Real to the Imaginary with Siri Hustvedt

I have had the odd and powerful experience of assisting at the surgeries of Siri Hustvedt. I don't mean operations done on her but by her. It is as if I have stood at her elbow, meekly handing her the instruments, as she performs risky and life-saving interventions, interventions that have taken place in the operating theaters of medicine over the past several years.

A novelist and essayist of the stature and range of Siri Hustvedt typically addresses groups of scholars, writers, and trainees anxious for her creative and intellectual guidance. The majority of the essays in this book treat matters of literary theory, aesthetic theory, creative influences, and the like. Some of the essays address psychoanalytic theory, neuro-cognitive aspects of mind/body influences, or the relationships between creativity and mood disorders.

But when I play scrub nurse to Dr. Hustvedt, our theater is a hospital conference room filled with doctors and nurses. Or a graduate seminar devoted to intersubjectivity in the doctor/patient relationship. Or a book launch in what appears to be a typical bookstore locale but is, as it turns out, a clinical consultation. Time and time over, Siri Hustvedt has granted to those of us who perform the often unduly technical aspects of health care the wherewithal to travel into realms undreamed of. These are the realms of the imagination.

Four instances bear description in detail. The first took place years ago in the Irving Center for Clinical Research conference room of the Columbia University Medical Center around a solemn board room table that fits 40. Dr. Hustvedt was there to teach Henry James's novella, "The Turn of the Screw." Her learners were internists, psychiatrists, social workers, pediatricians, nurses, and neuroscientists. We were reading James as a means to appreciate ambiguity, to build our tolerance for uncertainty, to wean ourselves away, even for the time it takes to read and reread the novella, from the insistence on conclusion. Prior to this session, this group had been reading contemporary fiction in the spirit of an informal book club. The participants had become, over the course of months, quite good close readers. I remember being happy that they were game to devote a semester to reading novels and tales of Henry James. We started with *Washington Square*. I followed that with the short story "The Middle Years," the story that ends with the writer Dencombe's deathbed words, "We work in the dark – we do what we can – we give what we have. Our doubt is our passion and our passion is our task. The rest is the madness of art," a credo of sorts for all physicians (James 1909: XVI, 105). And then, because Siri's and my paths crossed and she expressed an interest in reading James with this group, I invited her to come teach "The Turn of the Screw," James's famous ghost story where an impressionable governess either imagines or faces visitors from nether realms.

My group didn't know what hit them. We went where courage is needed to go in reading that tale, and Siri lent us the necessary courage. Maybe the governess is not *merely* hysterical. Maybe the children Miles and Flora *are* under the spell of the apparitions Peter Quint and Miss Jessel, who maybe *do*, unusually, exist. Maybe there *is* evil in the world. Maybe there is something beyond that which is available to the logical sectors of our minds. Maybe at the edges of the self, where they overlap with the edges of other selves, even absent or dead ones, strange shadowy things happen. (In "The Middle Years," Dencombe rereads his own novel: "He dived once more into his story and was drawn down, as by a siren's hand, to where, in the dim underworld of fiction, the great glazed tank of art, strange silent subjects float," James 1909: XVI, 81.)

Courage is not a visible or measureable thing, much less one that can be transferred easily from one to another. But when a great teacher teaches a great text, readers undergo an experience, much like the experience of beholding a great work of art that John Dewey describes in *Art as Experience* (Dewey 1980). To surrender to the power of a text like "The Turn of the Screw" demands a reckless trust, an at least provisional regard for one's author and one's text, and a willingness to change by virtue of the contact. Such trust, Siri knows, comes not only from within the self but from the intersubjective contact with another, mediated by a trained guide. This is perhaps the center of the psychoanalytic process, in which the analysand makes contact with his or her "othered" self, with the guidance of the analyst. It is perhaps the center of the process of close reading, the reader making contact with the text or, spookily, with its author, with the guidance of the teacher.

As we clinicians read this ghost story with Siri, we recognized the implications of its metaphorical harmonics. Here is the protagonist governess's description of Bly, the house that appears haunted:

> [I]t was a big ugly antique but convenient house, embodying a few features of a building still older, half-displaced and half-utilised, in which I had the fancy of our being almost as lost as a handful of passengers in a great drifting ship. Well, I was strangely at the helm! (James 1909: XII, 163–164)

Whatever the helm, whatever the rooms abandoned, whatever the age of the edifice, whatever the sectors of self thereby invoked, we readers could respond to the invitation of our teacher to enter that house and to welcome other readers around the table as fellow passengers on this great drifting ship of experience. The edges of self, so rarely exposed in medical practice, became immediately felt for those who accepted Siri's invitation.

My group was never the same after that. We went on from that semester of James to reading all of Proust over the course of a year and then continued to take up challenging fiction. It was as if Siri's operation opened something up in us clinician-readers. She put a stent, if you will, into a clogged artery to the imagination. This renowned visiting professor, leading the seminar with a blend of eminence and intimacy, let flow into our brains/minds/selves the circulatory nourishment to expand dormant homes of creativity. Or to see it another way, when we perform a nuclear medicine scan on a patient with a tumor, in order to identify exactly what substance is in that tumor, we inject a radio-isotope, say octreotide, that would be taken up by a particular type of tumor cells. If the tumor absorbs the isotope, its tissues glow. The report of such a scan, with a glowing result, might read: "The nodule is octreotide-avid." Siri's intervention made us imagination-avid.

The dimensional, candid, concrete thing that Siri lent to the members of my group was language. Siri lent us words through which to partake of James's story, for she knows that without language, one cannot harbor thoughts. She cites Mark Solms in *The Shaking Woman*, who makes the even more tantalizing point: "For someone to reflect consciously on visual experience, he or she has to recode the visual experiences into words" (Solms 2002: 82, qtd. in Hustvedt 2010: 53). We readers were not exactly having visual experience in reading James; we were *imagining* visual experiences. Each of us around that solemn boardroom table was host to a visualization of the governess, of Miles and Flora, of Bly, and of the unhatted and now dead Quint. Once we created the pictures we "saw" as we read this story, we could then marshal words with which to describe them, and it was the invitation to speak those words that our teacher extended.

This seminar happened a long time ago, yet I can still summon the picture of Siri sitting at the narrow end of that table in the deep of the room. I can summon the vision of her striking presence there among white-coated tired-looking clinicians at the end of a day in practice. Siri's bearings, her command of the room, her ivory quality seemed to us a visitation from something both fragile and timeless. It was as if she, in person, *came* from the pages of fiction, something certainly not as pedestrianly real as the rest of us, stethoscopes stuffed in pockets, beepers making their always unwelcome sounds, trapped in the material, so rarely freeing ourselves into the imaginary, as we were being invited to do by Siri.

Another of Siri's "operations" at Columbia more directly opened doors into clinical creativity. When Siri told me about her experience of shaking at the memorial of her father, and then the work she subsequently did in cognitive neurosciences and their interplay with psychoanalytic theory, of her participation in the high-level neuropsychoanalytic discussion group at New York Hospital, and of teaching writing to patients in Payne Whitney psychiatric hospital, I invited her to give Narrative Medicine Rounds at Columbia. A monthly lecture/presentation on matters that brave the boundary between medical practice and narrative matters (that such a boundary persists is another story), my Rounds seemed a good place to bring such questions about mind/brain/body phenomena to the attention of clinicians. It seemed to me to be a chance to counter the dismissive characterization of some bodily symptoms as "psychosomatic" (it's all in your head) and to propose a muscular – or at least brainy or at least meaningful – connection between what the body feels and what the mind/self might know, even if unthought (Bollas 1987).

Siri stood at the podium in Columbia's Faculty Club, natural light behind her, rows of attentive clinicians, students, scholars, writers who had come out to hear the novelist, literary critic, and student of the mind speak. She told us the story of having given a eulogy for her father at a memorial marking his death. She described herself standing, much as she was in front of us then, at the graveside podium to address rows of family and friends and intellectual colleagues of her father. She described the unexplainable shuddering that befell her then, how she could not control her limbs from shaking and flapping to the point that she was not sure she could remain standing. She held on to the little podium, itself shaky on the lawn, and mustered herself through her speech about her father. And then she wondered aloud with us what had happened – was it to her body? Was it to her emotions? Was it her father's ghost-like visitation? Whence had he come?

Then we heard the fruits of her having thought hard about this episode. She had consulted texts on seizure disorder, which she herself was thought to have. She reread her Freud and Breuer. She located new veins of breaking research in neuroscience, made possible by more and more accurate localization images of the brain's function. I remember how seamless seemed the connections among these disparate and usually conflicting bodies of thought. It was as if Siri's mind was capacious enough to contain antinomous ways of thinking without exploding or imploding. The psychoanalytic *can* exist side-by-side with the EEG. The literary sensibilities of this Columbia University PhD in English *could* deepen the implications of these edgy provisional "findings" from early fMRI studies of what the brain does when in the throes of certain emotions. Few other brains in the world, I am convinced, could have had the receptor sites necessary to hold in stillness all these thoughts at once, a stillness needed so that they could exist in the shadow of one another. This is what, I have come to think,

Siri's brain is like. This explains the power of her teaching literature for my physician-colleagues. It is her willing surrender to the destabilizing unpredictable results of risky thought, thought that does not respect disciplinary boundaries, thought that lets itself wander, lost passenger on a great drifting ship of knowledge and experience, in the dark, in doubt, toward art.

I didn't realize until I read the Acknowledgements in Siri's subsequently published *The Shaking Woman, or, A History of My Nerves* that our Narrative Medicine Rounds ignited her idea to write the book. Am I ever glad we invited her to come! For the book has opened up gates for scholars and practitioners in disparate disciplines, often constitutionally suspicious of one another, to wander together through mysterious and consequential forms of human experience.

Upon publication of *The Shaking Woman*, Siri and I appeared together at a Brooklyn book store's launch of the book. I had come prepared to ask her a few questions about the book and its ideas, and was even more eager to simply hear her talk about her book. Over the course of the hour, we talked about Siri's view of the legacy of Freud as a creative writer. We wondered whether the "self" represented in *The Shaking Woman* book is the unified self to which Siri gained access through the writing, or if her experience at least stands as evidence that there *is* unity to be had over time. I asked Siri to talk about the genre of the book – mixing diction from *DSM-IV* (*Diagnostic and Statistical Manual of Mental Disorders*, the clinical guide for psychiatric diagnosticians) with descriptions of intimate scenes in her family. She reminded us that the *DSM* does not tell stories, and that her book was in part an effort to redress that lack. She talked at length about how the writing of the book opened up questions regarding not just her own experience but about theories of representing illnesses and the power of naming them.

We took questions from the audience, and some people stayed after the formal part of the talk to ask questions individually. I was floored that most of the questions were not about literary matters or psychoanalytic matters but about individual persons' symptoms and illnesses. Some of the persons who had come to hear Siri talk about this book were themselves suffering from neurological or psychiatric diseases, and they approached Siri as they would a diagnostician or medical advisor. One woman told at length about her refractory seizure disorder, how she had to decide whether or not to submit to the neurosurgery that had been recommended. Another told of mysterious and undiagnosable problems with visual acuity. Siri had opened a clearing for others who shared her brand of uncertainty, others who had experienced symptoms on those borderlands between things. A sadness filled me to hear these questions, to realize how few places ill persons can go with grave worries, with radical doubt, in search of answers or at least of being heard. These conversations convinced me of the urgency of what Siri is doing in this realm of her work. Her work provides a vehicle to approach the tenor of mortality. Her erudition alongside her willingness to expose elements of her own illness make it possible for others who are ill to follow her model and to speak, to give voice to the unbearable.

Some weeks later, Siri graciously accepted my invitation to visit my graduate seminar in the Master of Science in Narrative Medicine program at Columbia, a seminar entitled "Giving and Receiving Accounts of Self." Between sessions on Dostoevsky's *Notes from the Underground* and W.G. Sebald's *Austerlitz*, we read *The Shaking Woman, or, A History of My Nerves*. The following quotations are edited from notes taken during the class:

> M_____ welcomes Siri, says that what she loves most about the book is that it goes beyond illness and inquires further. It expands the field from "me" to "me plus you." Siri begins by saying that she feels like her fantasy readers have come to life and are sitting in the room. She talks about the process of writing her book, says that over the course of completing *The Shaking Woman*, of making her argument, things happened that were integrated. The third person alien becomes by the end of the book first person reality.

Some of these graduate students were physicians – one an emergency room doctor, one an endocrinologist, another an obstetrician. One student was planning to begin nursing school the following year. One was a recent college graduate English major, becoming involved in trauma recovery research. Another was a graduate student in the creative writing MFA program who found narrative medicine's boundary-crossing between writing and health freeing. They expanded their own understanding of their commitments to their inter-disciplinary work by virtue of the recognition (We are her ideal readers?) that Siri conferred on them.

> T_____ says that in medical training one's curiosity gets driven out of you. You can't help a patient if you don't understand, name, or treat. She says that in obstetrics there is an entire taxonomy of unexplained phenomena. "We don't know why." Siri says, "The mantle of medical expertise is complicated because patients want you to have it."

These themes of knowing and unknowing, of mystery about the body, about the power and lure of expertise circulated around the seminar, for Siri had permitted or even privileged a tolerance for doubt, an acceptance of the limits of knowledge, at least about the body. As the session drew to a close, my students clustered around Siri, not to ask her questions about illness, as had our audience in the bookstore. Instead, they were seeking reassurance from her that the world could accept boundary-crossing and that appreciating mystery did not consign one to being considered a crank.

The intellectual risks Siri has taken and the power of her literary teaching contribute additional insights into her pluripotent oeuvre in fiction. That body of work itself crosses formidable boundaries into futurism, possible worlds, the all-too real worlds of misogyny, mental states of psychiatric illness, tests of loyalty, and demands of passion. Perhaps keeping in mind the agility and vision of Siri Hustvedt, the teacher who recognizes her learners, the medical connoisseur who enables the ill to speak, and the wielder of the scalpel of the imagination, might add to our collective appreciation for what, in fact, she does with words.

Works Cited

Bollas, Christopher. 1987. *The Shadow of the Object: Psychoanalysis of the Unthought Known*. New York: Columbia University Press.

Dewey, John. 1980. *Art as Experience*. New York: Perigree/Penguin.

Hustvedt, Siri. 2010. *The Shaking Woman, or, A History of My Nerves*. New York: Henry Holt and Company.

James, Henry. 1909. "The Turn of the Screw." In: *The Novels and Tales of Henry James: New York Edition*, Vol. 12. New York: Charles Scribner's Sons. 145–309.

James, Henry. 1909. "The Middle Years." In: *The Novels and Tales of Henry James: New York Edition*, Volume 16. New York: Charles Scribner's Sons. 75–106.

Solms, Mark. 2002. *The Brain and the Inner World*. New York: Other Press.

Carmen Birkle
"No self is an island": Doctor-Patient Relationships in Siri Hustvedt's Work

1. Introduction

With the publication of the autobiographical narrative *The Shaking Woman, or, A History of My Nerves* (2010), Siri Hustvedt reveals her own search for possible cures for the inexplicable shaking that seized her two and a half years after her father's death when she gave a talk in honor of her father on the St. Olaf College campus in Minnesota where he had taught. This was only the beginning of a long series of shakings. In *The Shaking Woman*, she traces her odyssey of doctors' visits, the theories they propose about what is wrong with her health, and the final realization: "I am the shaking woman" (199). In the very first pages of the book, Hustvedt relates her shaking to her history with migraines and to the various (semi-) autobiographical novels she has published over the years in which she is both doctor and patient in order to understand her own physical and psychological condition. On the one hand, she is the young student and patient Iris Vegan, who also calls herself Iris Davidsen, in *The Blindfold* (1992), and who is at the mercy of "Dr. Fish." On the other hand, she becomes the imaginary brother, psychiatrist and psychoanalyst, Erik Davidsen, in *The Sorrows of an American* (2008). In addition, in *What I Loved* (2003), Hustvedt chooses the doctoral student Violet as one of the protagonists who is working on a dissertation in psychology on women hysterics and their medical treatment in nineteenth-century France. Here, too, she identifies with Leo Hertzberg, the first-person narrator who is gradually going blind.[1] In *The Summer without Men* (2011), the protagonist Mia Fredricksen cracks up after her husband temporarily leaves her for another woman, and she "went mad and landed in the hospital" (1). In her most recent novel, *The Blazing World* (2014), multiple perspectives, among them the protagonist's, portray Harriet Burden's struggle for artistic recognition and her eventual death by cancer.

The practice of shifting sides in the encounter of doctors and patients and representing these encounters in narrative offers insights into Hustvedt's percep-

---

[1] This essay will not discuss *The Enchantment of Lily Dahl* (1996) because doctor-patient relationships are of no significance in Hustvedt's second novel.

tion of the medical profession and, at the same time, allows her to situate herself and her illness within the medical discourse as a form of therapy: "Intellectual curiosity about one's own illness is certainly born of a desire for mastery. If I couldn't cure myself, perhaps I could at least begin to understand myself" (Hustvedt 2010: 6).

Illness, patients, doctors, hospitals – these are key terms in Siri Hustvedt's writing. In this paper, I will focus on the representation of doctor-patient relationships, which shed light on Hustvedt's critical perspective toward medical practice and reveal the (often) failed communication between both sides, the powers at work in these relationships, and, ultimately, Hustvedt's passionate desire to understand what is happening in these inter-human encounters. Questions of power, perception, and perspective as well as of context, code, and communication will be taken into consideration in my analysis.

2. Doctors and Patients and Their Relationships

As the title of my essay already indicates, illness and health are relational issues that are often shaped by a relationship that is multi-dimensional on many levels. Illness is a state of being which is expected to be temporary and transitory, and should be left behind as soon as possible. In contrast, "health is a state of complete physical, mental and social well-being and not merely the absence of disease or infirmity" (qtd. in Bein 2013: 7), according to the World Health Organization. The desire to be healthy again or to at least understand the nature of one's illness drives people toward consulting with a doctor of their choice, who is expected to diagnose and treat the illness and, ultimately, to remove it through a cure. Therefore, Siri Hustvedt, as Christine Marks argues, "finds intersubjectivity to be the basis for a healthy development" (2014: 2), and not just between doctors and patients.

Furthermore, illness is a rather vague term that depends on cultural definitions in their respective contexts. It, too, is a relational term that cannot exist and does not make sense without its binary opposition, but between those binaries, multiple statuses of illness and health reveal how subjective most of their facets are. Similarly, an individual cannot just subsist on individualism, even though this is the major credo of American society. As Marks points out, Siri Hustvedt in her work "scrutinizes the detrimental effects of American society's failure to promote relational identity formation" (2014: 2).

Identity is always at stake when Hustvedt's characters grapple with illness, look for relief with doctors, and actually face or simply talk to their medical other. In the encounter of the self with representatives of the medical profession a power play is at work that is based on the assumed knowledge of the medical authority over the perceived ignorance of the ill self. The mechanisms of power in such an encounter are obviously not exclusive to but do play an important role in Hustvedt's work. Similarly, the translation of feelings and thoughts, of facts and ideas into language, that is, into a medical narrative, is not just particular to Hustvedt's work either. Both power and narrative are significant features in any doctor-patient relationship. The self's expectation in a best-case scenario is to hear from the knowledgeable doctor either that nothing is wrong, thus illness is not present, or that there is a simple treatment and/or medication that will restore health and order in a minimum of time. Thus, the doctor is expected to understand and heal the rupture that a possible illness has caused in a person's life in order to "create continuity after an unexpected disruption to life" (Becker 1997: 4); that is, to transform chaos into order again and to come to terms with the experience that "the life course" is not "predictable, knowable, and continuous" (Becker 1997: 7). Moreover, as Deborah Lupton points out,

> illness [is] a potential state of social 'deviance'; that is, a failure to conform to societal expectations and norms in some way. Illness is considered an unnatural state of the human body, causing both physical and social dysfunction, and therefore must be alleviated as soon as possible. (2012: 4)

The doctor's task is to motivate, support, and enhance this process toward the restoration of social balance. However, doctor and patient may not agree on how this is best achieved (Segal 2005). Therefore, depending on the respective values, the doctor-patient relationship may be "characterized by conflict and the clash of differing interests and priorities" (Lupton 2012: 6).

Additionally, a doctor-patient relationship is very much characterized by perspective and, in fiction, the ways in which this perspective is represented. Does the reader of fiction perceive the encounter from the patient's or the doctor's perspective? Is the perceiver the/a focal character? Is the perspective omniscient, first-person, or figural or hetero- or homodiegetic? What kind of perception is rendered? Is it visual or auditive, pictorial or verbal, transmitted in person or via phone, computer, or other technical devices? Who encodes and who decodes the message? What are some of the extra-narrative features that shape the transmission and interpretation process? Does the encounter take place at the patient's home or at the doctor's office? Do patient and doctor speak the same social code, that is, are they of a similar social background? Do the participants in this encounter know each other outside of the professional relationship? Do they have the same ethnic background? How is language used to represent this encounter?

This relational interaction is what Hustvedt herself describes as "the problem of the between" (2012e: 196),[2] which she understands as "a geographical metaphor – *the between* is a road to wellness and realism" (197; emphasis original). In psychoanalysis, which is where most of Hustvedt's doctor-patient encounters are situated, Sigmund Freud offers the term "Tummelplatz," which Hustvedt reads as a "field of 'struggle' or, more dramatically, as 'a battlefield' between doctor and patient" (197). Without being able to delve deeply into Hustvedt's recovery and discussion of Freud's studies on psychoanalysis, it is worth noting some of the points she raises as significant also for her own work.

First, a doctor, and not just the psychoanalyst, "may well find herself playing somebody else – mother, father, sister, brother [...]" (2012e: 199) – depending on the patient's disposition and needs. In spite of this "case of mistaken identity" (199) – whether the patient is aware of it (conscious) or not – the doctor has to take this transference into consideration and also has to be aware of his or her own potential fall into the same trap since, as Hustvedt argues, "transference is human, and it moves in both directions" (199). Second, a recognition that may or may not derive from psychoanalysis is that while Hustvedt emphasizes "identity as grounded in embodied, material existence" (Marks 2014: 5), she also increasingly stresses "ambiguity over clear binaries and absolutes [...] to undo epistemological certainties [...]" (5). A third aspect is the idea that the physical/material body "constitutes a medium of exchange between inside and outside, of communication between self and other" (10).

Obviously, illnesses such as Iris Vegan's debilitating migraines in *The Blindfold* or Harriet Burden's stage-four ovarian cancer and her slow dying process in *The Blazing World* bring the body very much to the foreground of attention. A doctor-patient relationship always also contains an actual material presence of gendered bodies that engage in representational processes that are culturally but also individually determined and, at least to some extent, remain unknown and unknowable to the respective other (see Lupton 2012: 139). As is generally true for Hustvedt's characters, a "sense of mystery pervades Hustvedt's fictional work, as she foregrounds elements of unknowability and ambiguity in her characters' interpersonal relations" (Marks 2014: 61). This mystery also – almost by definition – grants the other "his or her own private space – a space to be respected and unharmed. Self and other consequently enter into an ethical relationship" (60). The body of both patient and doctor is as much part of the

---

[2] In her essay "Yonder," Hustvedt talks about 'yonder,' that is, according to her father, "'between here and there.' [...] a new space – a middle region that was neither here nor there – a place that simply didn't exist for me until it was given a name" (1).

world and enters into a dialogical relationship as the mind does, as Marks points out with reference to Maurice Merleau-Ponty's concept of embodied intersubjectivity (53–54).

However, although patients expect doctors to reflect on them and to return an image of a healthy person or, at least, give them more information about themselves, they will never know and see what the other, in this case the doctor, knows and sees (Berger 2008). The doctor simply is not the patient's mirror (image) and does not restore the kind of wholeness the patient expects. The gaze, after all, is multiple, and, as Hustvedt proclaims, "the mirror is the only place where I am whole to myself. Only then do I see my body as others see it" (2012c: 52). In spite of the mirror image's material wholeness, all it reflects is outside or surface reality whereas the inside of the mind is invisible to the naked eye. Therefore, Jacques Lacan and other critics have spoken of "misrecognition" or a "méconnaissance [...] of the self as unified" (Marks 2014: 77). This twofold limitation of one's own vision enhances the relevance for the self of what the other sees and knows; thus, the other, just like the mirror image, is meant "to fill the hole of the self" (76).

This relationship, which gives the other a prominent place in the self's identity formation, is ultimately about power mechanisms (Furst 1998) and the prerogative of interpretation, about who is seen as ill, about mind-body dualism versus embodied cognition, about the values and norms in anamnesis or illness experience, etc. Observing or 'looking at' is essential for the profession and role of the doctor, 'being looked at' and subjected to the gaze a characteristic experience of a patient, although s/he is not without the opportunity to return and resist the gaze and attain access to medical techniques of visualization and their use and interpretation. A doctor's *look* at (or even inside) a patient has a diagnostic function and is legitimized as such, but it has a side effect of producing a certain *view* of that patient as a subject, or even contributing to the subjectivization of that patient. The doctor's vision in this encounter is, among many things, shaped by the illness narrative that is jointly created in this doctor-patient exchange (Balint 1957).

When doctors and patients meet, it is within a cultural setting (Engelhardt 1996: 20) evoking historically contingent scripts and roles. It is commonly assumed that a clear-cut, if only analytical and context-specific, separation between the sick person and the aiding professional, whose health is of no interest whatsoever, is possible. Hierarchies of knowledge, medical anthropologies, professional ethics, issues of trust and cooperation etc. will influence their encounter on the personal and on a more abstract level, and their (visual) perception of each other is inevitably coded by preconceptions that reflect and reproduce social structures of dominance. While most analyses focus on the doctors and their gaze on patients, patients' positions, perspectives, and knowledges are equally situated and essential in medical encounters, in particular in the cases presented in Hustvedt's fiction. Shifting the gaze implies a change of perspective from the observer to the observed and results in the rise to prominence of the return gaze (Stoeckle 1987; see also Berger 2008 and Mohr 1997) that seems to be at work above all in *The Sorrows of an American.*

Patients and doctors are as myriad in Hustvedt's fiction as they are in actual life (Helman 2002; Posen 2007). Their encounters are highly complex and subject to personal, institutional, socio-cultural, and historical conditions and changes. In Hustvedt's novels, they depend on gender as well as on space and time and medical progress and knowledge. How readers and writers view these encounters and how characters are made to carry them out are similarly dependent on context and are manifest in verbal communication and practices of looking. Thus, the subjective experience of illness and each participant's subjectivity in the encounter are of utmost importance for an analysis (Fischer 1996: 127) of Hustvedt's work.

3. Doctors and Patients on the Fictional Battlefield

The Blindfold (1992): The Power of Language, or, The Mantra of Migraines

"[M]igraine is a mysterious disease," as neurologist Joost Haan (2013) points out in his essay on "Migraine and Metaphor." He continues,

> [t]he most typical part of migraine – the aura – cannot be perceived by others [...]. As a consequence, a diagnosis of migraine is solely and completely based on the narrative of the patient. Migraine depends on language, but linguistic signs are arbitrary. The relation of words with reality is problematic [...]. (126)

In this quotation, Haan establishes a binary opposition between the outside and inside and the invincible surface of the boundaries of the body. No one can look into the inside of someone's head, and the only possibility to translate a migraineur's painful experience to the outside is through language. However, Haan views this translation process as inherently faulty and arbitrary and, thus, considers language as inadequate to express pain. In an assumed case, a doctor would have to rely completely on the patient's narrative, which, too, for Haan, seems to be doubtful and problematic. On the one hand, this linguistic inexpressiveness renders a doctor's diagnosis of a patient's illness difficult; on the other hand, it leaves room for interpretation and an inscription of the doctor's ideas onto the patient.

When the graduate student Iris Vegan in Hustvedt's debut novel *The Blindfold* is hospitalized because of her migraines, she is at the end of her tether, having suffered for seven months from severe migraines that have left her debilitated and unable to either study or work. (For an analysis of *The Blindfold* as an illness narrative, see also the contribution by Britta Bein in this volume) Right at the beginning of part three of the novel, the reader learns that all other treatments have failed and that no medication has worked. Iris has internalized society's perception of migraines as a form of hysteria that women bring onto themselves: "As a migraineur, I had low status. Admittedly, I was a bad case [...] but what I had was still a headache, and headaches had little clout on the neurology ward" (Hustvedt 1992: 91). The nurses immediately classify her as the doctor's property; "'She's one of Dr. Fish's'" (91) and, from Iris's point of view, "seemed suspicious" (91). She experiences guilt: "It was clear to me that I had made the headache, created the monster myself, and just because I couldn't get rid of the damned thing didn't mean I wasn't to blame" (91). She has trouble speaking because of the strong sedative medication, an indication that her own narrative is not of interest to the doctor.

Iris believes that because she does not get better, Dr. Fish[3] is no longer interested in her because he "was a man who liked successes" (92). "He liked them so much," as she continues, "that before I landed in the hospital, he told me that I was improving when I was not, and now I was so conspicuously unimproved, he shunned me" (92). This behavior is a first indication that Dr. Fish, too, believes in the inadequacy of the patient's narrative, that he replaces Iris's attempts to voice her pain with his own conviction with which he tries to triumph over Iris's illness. Dr. Fish is in control of language; however, Iris's body still resists. Dr. Fish uses a tape recorder in his interrogations. Yet, here, too, it is not the patient's narrative that is recorded but his own voice: "Had he actually recorded his patients' speech, this approach might have been harmless, but as it was, the only voice on those tapes was Dr. Fish's" (92). He literally erases Iris's story, makes her speechless, and turns her into a case with a number and date: "'Iris Vegan. Case number 63912. Tuesday, September 2, 1980'" (92). He frequently interrupts her and records his diagnosis, expressed in one-sentence

---

[3] Hustvedt describes a similar doctor in *The Shaking Woman*: "[...] the Headache Czar himself, Dr. C., a man who mostly ignored me and seemed irritated that I didn't cooperate and get well [...]" (2010: 4).

medical lines that seem to summarize Iris's own story and completely erase her experience, her words, and her pain. As she continues, his frequent interruptions cause her to lose track of her own story. She reads his behavior as a "ferocious editing" (93) that reveals that the doctor-patient relationship is based on the power over language, interpretation, and healing. Again, Iris feels that she is guilty of not being able to tell the right story. She puts pressure onto herself because she believes that "if only I could articulate my illness in all its aspects, I might give a trained ear the clue that would make me well, but my words were always inadequate" (93) and, ultimately, irrelevant to Dr. Fish.

The representation of Iris's story is a perfect example of the need for what Rita Charon and others have called "narrative medicine." As Charon explains,

> [a]long with their growing scientific expertise, doctors need the expertise to listen to their patients, to understand as best they can the ordeal of illness, to honor the meanings of their patients' narratives of illness, and to be moved by what they behold so that they can act on their patients' behalf. (2008: 3)

Dr. Fish certainly does not possess narrative knowledge: he does not see Iris in "a singular and meaningful situation" (Charon 2008: 9), but wants to press her into his pattern of cases. What Iris reads as an "editing" of her story, Susan Wells describes as the "medical interview" that "is inherently discontinuous since the patient experiences the symptom as a history, while the doctor attempts to localize it within a segmented body" (2001: 35).

While both doctor and patient have their own separate agenda, their common goal is the patient's health, thus, Iris's well-being and Dr. Fish's triumph. Obviously for Iris, the relevance of health is so that she begins to identify with her doctor's statements in spite of her own knowledge to the contrary. As she admits, "[t]he truth is that I participated in the deception" (94). She attempts to become what he sees in her; her self silences itself, and she begins to perform for him: "Concealing illness from a physician is absurd, but I couldn't bear to be seen for what I was – a person going to pieces" (94).

With her self-admission to Dr. Fish's hospital when her headaches become unbearable, she gives up any pretense of fitting into the category of a healthy person. Dr. Fish assumes control over her body as well as mind since she is sedated most of the time. The story she subsequently tells is one of becoming one with the hospital world. Her "senses were oddly acute"; "[e]very sound on the ward vibrate[s] through" her body; "nerves [are] as resonant as a tuning fork" (95). Her own perception of inside and outside begins to blur. Her vision of her roommates, Mrs. O. and Mrs. M., distinguishes between the powerful and mentally sane Mrs. M., who bluntly tells her that "'[t]here's nothing really wrong with you, is there? It's all in your head'" (96), and the rather quiet but not less disturbing Mrs. O. Whether labeled psychosomatic or neurasthenic, Iris's illness, from Mrs. M.'s perspective, which Iris seems to have internalized, is considered insignificant, self-caused, and, most importantly, could be cured by herself if she only wanted to. Mrs. M. turns into Iris's superego and, thus, into the voice of society that is in control and has power over Iris's perception of herself.

Since Iris's ego, that is, her own rational perception of her own self, is disturbed, super-ego and id take over. Mrs. O., with whom Iris in a way identifies, is small and silent, just like Iris feels. Iris, who is, from her own point of view, a person falling to pieces, describes Mrs. O. in very similar terms. "What remained was a fragmented being, a person shattered into a thousand pieces, but those bits of Mrs. O. inhabited the room like a crowd of invisible demons" (97). "[...] Mrs. O. wasn't one person, she was many people" (100). The deconstruction of her own self into, in Sigmund Freud's terminology, the superego, the ego, and the id, helps Iris to turn away from being appropriated by Dr. Fish or any other doctor since they cannot lay their hands on all fragments at once. Mrs. O. has a reputation of being unpredictable, of resisting the incorporation by doctors. When a young doctor approaches her with the belittling and, usually, disinterested question "'[a]nd how are we doing today'" (99), she seems to have shocked the doctor with an unexpected response or action because he immediately leaves the room. What is most interesting, however, is Iris's reaction:

> When I leaned over to look at Mrs. O., she was smiling broadly, and it was then that she reminded me of someone I knew or had known. I tried to dredge up the lost face and name, but they resisted me. This uncanny sense of familiarity subsided very quickly though it left a residue, a doubt that stayed with me. What had spawned that moment of recognition? Was it really something in her expression or was it something inside me? In any case, I began to watch Mrs. O. more closely. (99)

Mrs. O. reaches Iris's interior as no one else does. This attempt at unification is even physically staged when she gets into bed with Iris. Mrs. O.'s approaches can be read as the attempt of the id to reunite with the ego, but Iris is not ready yet: "Perhaps it was that she had come too close, that my bed had lost its boundaries, and that once that invisible threshold had been crossed, I no longer felt safe. She would be back, I knew it" (105). Mutual recognition seems to trigger these events; boundaries break down between Mrs. O. and Iris, and eventually Mrs. O. is in bed with Iris "in a suffocating embrace," kissing her (105). Iris reads this kiss as an intrusion into her own private self, which, however, might be nothing but a reunification with one of her own fragments, which she cannot yet undergo and to which she immediately reacts with renewed and even worse migraine attacks.

Subsequently, Iris increasingly turns toward her inner body; any attempts to communicate with her by her mother or her doctors are without effect. Her body tries to reestablish the boundaries that it has lost. Just like Leo in *What I Loved*, as we will see, Iris begins to reconnect with what is inside her, to rejoin body and mind even if her mind envisions it in terms of imprisonment; it gives her "a sense that I was shut inside a body that was going its own way" (107). She hears Mrs. O.'s sounds but "the noise seemed to be coming from within my own head" (108). Ultimately, a vision of Mrs. O. has taken root in Iris, accepting her first name, Eleanor, for Iris herself (111–112): "She's calling me," and Iris responds: "'I'm here!'" (112). Significantly, in this scene, her boyfriend Stephen visits her, but his significance is reduced to Iris telling him to leave, rejecting his prior power over her. After this turning point in their relationship, which seems to have reunited Iris with her id, Mrs. O. for Iris loses her familiarity and then completely disappears. After a final attack of nausea, Iris begins to gradually reconnect to life outside of her body: "'It's snowing,' I said. 'Of course it is,' said Mrs. M. 'It's been snowing for days'" (115). It seems as if at least ego and id have overcome the "self-shattering, [...] dangerous destabilization of any sense of personal identity" (Jameson 2010: 422), which goes together with a renewed sense of (self-) control and power.

Ultimately, Iris's struggle with her own fragmentation is an attempt at preventing the final medical takeover by Dr. Fish. The story she tells him becomes a case which he reads in his own way. Like in reader-response theory, Dr. Fish creates his own narrative by reading Iris's story. In the encounter between Dr. Fish and Iris, the patient's own pathography and the doctor's case narrative seem to be almost mutually exclusive, but also reveal the differences in approach, relevance, and purpose. As Hunter explains,

> [h]owever valuable pathography may be, its focus is on the patient rather than the disease. The case, by contrast, serves an essential diagnostic purpose, and for this purpose its narrowness makes sense. It orders the messy and confusing details of experience and filters out clinical "irrelevancies." (1981: 154)

However, the difference is that Iris is not a text that only comes to life in the process of being read but needs to claim her own story in order to survive as a human being. What Caroline Rosenthal points out about *What I Loved* can equally be applied to *The Blindfold* and Iris's situation:

> A 'mixing' of identities is vital in order to unravel the unseen and hidden in the self and to incorporate the Other. Mixing is a way of feeling empathy, but only [...] if the self is rooted in contexts of love and human understanding that allow the individual to establish a notion of self and belonging. (2011: 117)

Empathy is what Iris feels for Mrs. O. and does not see expressed in her doctor; empathy makes us willing to open up for the other in the self; lacking empathy on her doctor's side causes her to lose any sense of self.

What I Loved (2003): Conflicting Intersubjectivity

In Siri Hustvedt's fiction, self and other are never separate entities, but are intimately interwoven with each other, as Christine Marks (2009, 2014) and Hubert Zapf (2008) have pointed out in their respective studies. Marks analyzes the 2003 novel *What I Loved* with reference to doctor-patient relationships that obviously are affected by this close connection. As Marks argues, *What I Loved* "traces the relation between hysterics and their physicians as an example of a self which has become overmixed with its environment, in which the distinction between inside and outside has become blurred to the point of dissolution" (2009: 1). While part of my own analysis of the novel will be related to the nineteenth-century doctor-patient relationship, I will as well include a very short scene in which the novel's first-person narrator, the art historian and professor at Columbia University, Leo Hertzberg, learns from his ophthalmologist that nothing can be done against his slowly fading eyesight. I will argue that Leo's fading vision is the attempt to protect himself against the further onslaught of images and other-identities that destroy his attempt at reconciliation with who or whatever he himself is, with his inner self, an identity of his own that has not been allowed to develop in its own right. Through the constant incorporation of the outside into the inside, of the other into the self, the self is in danger of "self-effacement" (Zapf 2008: 179). Therefore, I read nineteenth-century hysteria and Leo's eventual blindness as two opposite ways of struggling with self-other and, thus, patient-doctor relationships.

The novel *What I Loved* is told from Leo's perspective at a moment when he is almost completely blind. He can still type on his old type-writer instead of using a computer because the former renders it easier for him to find the right letters. As Hubert Zapf has noted, "it seems […] that this external limitation of his vision allows him to see all the more sharply with his inner eye: Leo is capable of visualizing the past in minute detail" (2008: 178). Being able to see others means that "we're missing from our own picture" (Hustvedt 2003: 255); we are never in that picture and, therefore, never see ourselves as part of the outer landscape. If we are what we see, then we are simply not visible or we identify with the other. This troubling misrecognition of who we are seems to be solved the moment the self is left without exterior images and is thrown onto itself to recreate a vision that can include itself.

Leo's encounter with his ophthalmologist is presented from Leo's point of view without direct speech and in a way that makes clear that Leo has simply accepted the fact of his growing blindness. The doctor comes across as almost brutally honest telling him that nothing can be done because of a specific kind of degeneration. Leo's reaction is similarly matter-of-fact-like: "[...] I nodded, thanked him, and stood up to leave" (356). Leo's interpretation of the doctor's facial expression, "he frowned at me" (356), instills in the doctor the term "perverse" applied to Leo's behavior. This unspoken accusation motivates Leo to explain that "[he] had been lucky with [his] health so far, and [he] wasn't surprised by illnesses that had no cure" (356). Since the two parts of the explanation are joined by the conjunctive "and," there does not seem to be a logical connection. But this response is puzzling. Having been lucky with health would let the reader expect a more drastic and questioning reaction, but it seems that the second part reveals that Leo has expected all along that some incurable disease might affect him. This implication would point to Leo's fatalistic attitude toward life, perhaps ever since his son's death. The doctor's final response is even more surprising: "He said that was un-American, and I [Leo] agreed" (356).

This indirectly rendered communication between doctor and patient exposes the categories the doctor has in mind about patients, and these categories are embedded in and contextualized by national stereotypes. As the doctor implies, a true American would not have taken this information as stoically as Leo has done but would have questioned and rebelled against this diagnosis and the impossibility of treatment. Leo's agreement might have surprised the doctor even more. But Leo no longer lives in a world in which national characteristics or belonging play any role. He no longer needs to behave in ways that are expected of him. He still interacts but refuses to let anyone or anything touch him on the inside. He lives within himself, within his "inner sanctum" (Hustvedt 2003: 48), and within his novel, and, for that, he does not need to physically see anymore.[4]

Although his interest in Violet, Bill's second wife, triggers the writing of the novel, Leo withdraws completely into the fictional world of his "post-traumatic

---

[4] Leo's reaction is similar to what Siri Hustvedt describes as her coming to terms with her migraines: "Chronic headaches are my fate, and I have adopted a position of philosophical resignation. I am aware that such a view is resoundingly un-American. Our culture does not encourage anyone to accept adversity. [...] And yet, the very moment I stopped thinking of my condition as the 'enemy,' I made a turn and began to get better. I wasn't cured, wasn't forever well, but I was better. Metaphors matter" (2012b: 24). Similarly, as Hustvedt explains, "what we see is a combination of sensory information coming in from the outside, which has been *dynamically* translated or decoded in our brains through both our expectations of what it is we are looking at and our human ability to create coherent images. We don't just digest the world; we make it" (2012b: 35; emphasis original).

narrative" which displays "a search for orientation and meaning which brings about extreme fragility, experience of loss, and self-exposure, but also a transformative potential" (2008: 181–182), as Zapf explains. In narrative, Leo no longer needs the physical concreteness of the "face-to-face-encounter with the Other" but "can find a specifically instructive, because complex, medium of (self-)exploration" (Zapf 2008: 172). While stories may "allow the imaginative transcendence of the individual self towards other selves" (173), they may also re-join the self to its own desires and emotions and bring about self-recognition. This does not mean that Leo is no longer interested in the other but he wants to satisfy his urge for understanding and, thus, enhance his appreciation of intersubjectivity. What this reading of the doctor-patient scene and the relevance of vision unfolds is "the dialogical interdependence between self and other" but also "the irreducible difference and alterity of the other [...]" (173). What Leo explores without eyesight is the "dynamical network of relationships" (174); to do so, he needs to shut out the exterior world because he has experienced "the dangers of 'mixing'" (184), like Violet, that is, "the danger of losing oneself in the other [...]" (184), and this is exactly what the nineteenth-century inmates of the French hospital La Salpêtrière had to go through. While Leo resists the melting of self and other, the hysterics seem to embrace it.

The female hysterics Jean Martin Charcot treated at La Salpêtrière have been the subject of numerous studies, analyses, and research so that there is no need here to repeat this information. It is, however, important to understand that Hustvedt's form of representation of these women in *What I Loved* is shaped by the character Violet's perception. According to Christine Marks, "Violet points out how strongly the hysterics' symptoms were related to the expectations of their doctors" (2009: 1). Their relationship seems to take on the form of "a performance of transgression" (1) that turns the hysteric into the object and the production of the medical gaze. The doctors seem to project onto these women's bodies their own visions of and about hysteria and, thus, see what they want to see. When Violet talks about the hysterics' desire to explode boundaries (Hustvedt 2003: 81), she refers to the opening up of the self – the hysteric – toward the other – the doctor. Hustvedt assumes that the description of a unity of self that all human beings suffer at birth leads to a perpetual desire to regain this unity, to dissolve the separation into self and other, even at the cost of losing the core of one's own identity. In the case of the hysterics, "the desire to explode the boundaries of the self [...] is bound to end in a disaster, since identity requires limits – crossable limits, yet limits nevertheless" (Marks 2009: 2).[5]

---

5 Violet also discusses anorexia and the anorexic young women as doing the opposite of the

The hysterics become accessible in *What I Loved* through Bill's artistic representation of Violet's research. In his installations, he emphasizes the power and violence of their situation and their attempt at making themselves heard. A small blond doll with eyes that are screwed shut and a mouth that seems to scream in agony but does not produce any sound is an example of the pain as well as the impossibility of making themselves understood except by their doctors. The doctors surrounding this female patient in the background, ready with pen and paper to record whatever the hysteric does, do not see the suffering; they consider her the medical object whose behavior and body yield scientific information and results. The "ten shadowy male figures in black and white" (Hustvedt 2003: 72) possess power over the reading of the female body. Their interpretation cannot be contested by the silent women. The doll hysteric, like others in Bill's artwork, is "muted by the discourse of medical classification" (Marks 2009: 3). Hysteria signifies outside of language, but language – as the doctor's pen and paper indicate – is the only medium through which the medical institution communicates. Without a voice, the bodies of hysterics become empty paper to be written on. These stories, therefore, can never be their own, but appear to have also been written onto their skins, as Bill's art shows. This dermagraphism, that is, the writing on naked skin, not only turns these women into objects but also into art objects, however, expressive only of the artists – here the doctors at La Salpêtriére – and not of the object. Bill's "installation focuses on the topography of the female body mapped out by the clinical observer. Art and medicine are conflated in the body of the woman [...]" (Marks 2009: 3). As Marks convincingly argues, in a perversion of the Pygmalion myth, the doctors turn "their Galateas from living beings into statues. Rather than creating life, they create art" and deny "the living interior of the patient, reducing her to the surface" (3). Inscribing a text onto the hysteric's body also implies the taking possession of her as property. The doctor as the owner of her body experiences pleasure in "mastering the patient's body" (3). Eroticism is certainly one of the effects of this act. Photography as a means of perpetuating the status quo of both doctors and patients is just an enhanced means of the other's intrusion into the self's body via the surface skin, the other's power over the self, the other's annihilation of the self that is unable to defend itself against this violent appropriation. The only defense, as Violet in the novel points out, is cross-dressing. The inmate Augustine one days walks out of the hospital disguised as a man. She

---

hysterics as a reaction to the feeling of overmixing, namely shutting themselves up against the outside world and, thus, also against food, disregarding the fact that "a healthy corporeality depends on the integration of 'other' elements" (Rosenthal 2011: 109).

liberates herself from objectification, possession, and dissolution by the male and medical gaze.

The Sorrows of an American (2008): Mirror Neurons and the Uncanny

In both *The Blindfold* and *What I Loved* all doctors are male, and the patients are of both sexes. In contrast to Leo, who in *What I Loved* is much more resigned to his increasing blindness and actually embraces this development as an advantage in his exploration of himself, Iris in *The Blindfold* fights her migraines not only because of the pain they cause but also because of the threat to her identity, that is, the loss of who she believes to be. As a graduate student at Columbia University in New York City, it is an essential part of her life to read, which is, however, made impossible by her physical status. In these two novels, the doctor-patient relationship is seen from the point of view of the respective patient, thus from the subjective perspective of the one who is suffering.

In *The Sorrows of an American*, the first-person narrator Dr. Erik Davidsen is a psychoanalyst. In the novel, he tries to come to terms with the death of his father as well as with his father's seeming secrets of the past. At the same time, Erik is very unsure about his situation in life and is looking for a stable and perhaps even lasting relationship. When young Eggy, the daughter of his new renter Miranda, asks him whether he is "'a worry doctor'" (Hustvedt 2009: 27), he agrees and explains: "'I went to school to become a doctor, and I help people with their worries and other problems'" (27). The service that he wants to offer as a doctor is the seemingly simple act of listening to his patients' stories.

While very few sessions of psychotherapy are actually presented, those are highly significant. In contrast to all other characters in the novel the patients are anonymous; they are labeled, for example, Mr. R., immediately evoking Mrs. O. and Mrs. M. from *The Blindfold*.

> In order to prove his professional distance from his patients, Erik never uses their full names, instead referring to them by abbreviations when he tells curious stories about Ms. L, Mr. T, Mr. R, Ms. W, Mr. J, Mrs. B or Mr. B. The use of pseudonyms or abbreviations has apparently been a common convention since the beginning of psychoanalysis as practiced by Josef Breuer and Sigmund Freud. (Reipen 2014: 193)

As medical cases, their identity is protected; as fictional patients, they become almost nameless, just examples of cases Erik has to deal with. While Erik as a doctor attempts to keep the boundaries between himself and his patients, he cannot avoid reacting emotionally to them or drawing analogies to his own life. He is angry at Mr. R. for being late (81–82) and compares his own frustrated waiting to Mr. R. as a child who was constantly waiting for his parents to come home after their long workdays. Erik implies that Mr. R. has internalized his parents' behavior, turns being late into a position of power, and, thus, turns the one who is waiting into a dependent person. By voicing his point of view, Erik explains his own behavior to Mr. R. With this insight into his own patterns of behavior, Mr. R. for the first time becomes aware of his surroundings such as a small rug on the wall that has been hanging there for a long time. Like Iris, who recognizes the snow for the first time after Mrs. O.'s disappearance, Mr. R. has obviously made a significant step in the understanding of and reconciliation with his own self.

Similarly, in the case of Ms. L., Erik begins to suspect that she does not distinguish "between fact and fiction" (86). Erik explains his task as "not reconstructing the 'facts' of a case history but listening for patterns, strains of feeling, and associations that may move us out of painful repetitions and into an articulated understanding" (86). Understanding, of course, can be very different on the doctor's and on the patient's sides. Erik is unable to keep his emotional distance when Ms. L. throws her tantrums. He presents her almost like a hysteric who wants to become one with him in a process of transference: "It was difficult to keep my balance, but worse, she sometimes had a hard time separating the two of us, and her confusion began to cause me acute discomfort" (87). The struggle that Erik undergoes with his patients is that between self and other. In order to keep his own integrity of self, he needs to fight his patients' attempts to get closer to him, to assault his self, and thus to burden him with their problems. As a psychoanalyst, he needs to stay calm, distant, and emotionless. But he, like his patients, brings his own social, cultural, and personal background into the analysis. He understands this mutuality after Ms. L. has left: "Before I stood up, I understood that my vision of Ms. L. in the cold had also been an image of myself" (89).

Like Iris, Ms. L. watches herself in the stories she tells Erik. His analysis of her "dissociated vision" (109) turns into his own recognition of being manipulated by her: "It was as if I, not she, were the rag doll [thrown against the wall]" (109). Like in Iris when she observes Mrs. O., Erik's distance and boundaries begin to loosen up and blur; the self and the other begin to fight about power and position: "The words *I hate you* came to *my* mind, and I felt the pronoun slide between us. *You hate me.* What did I mean?" (109–110; emphasis original). In *The Blindfold* and *What I Loved*, the doctors control the conversation with their patients, at least from the patients' point of view, but Erik risks being controlled by his patients, in particular by Ms. L. She makes seductive gestures toward him so that Erik feels "disoriented. Ms. L.'s delusions, paranoia and what I feared were lies affected me like a man lost in a poisonous fog as he desperately searches for a way out" (110).

In contrast to patients' expectations of the superior control of psychotherapists, Erik's self-rendering of his vulnerability sheds a new light on psychotherapy and reveals that, of course, the doctor is subject to contexts, personal experiences, gender expectations, etc. To carry this to an extreme, as Erik's sister Inga explains, "'we're all blind, all dependent on preordained representations, on what we think we'll see. [...] We don't experience the world. We experience our expectations of the world'" (130–131). Consequently, there is no objective encounter between doctor and patient; there is only an exchange of subjective points of view, which are, however, divided into the one that is privileged because educated and professional and the one that is unprivileged because ill and personal. The difference lies in quantity not quality and the doctor's awareness of his own subjectivity. While the patient expects the doctor's objectivity, the doctor is painfully aware of his own shortcomings as Erik's colleague Magda admits: "'It took me some time to acknowledge material in myself I had kept safely buried'" (138).

Erik meets Magda to talk about Ms. L. Their conversation turns into his own therapeutic session in which he is trying to understand himself, to understand what Ms. L. does to him, to find in him "'something hidden, something I can't get to'" (138). Magda explains to Erik his own fragility because of his father's death. Her choice of words is similar to those Iris uses when she feels she is going to pieces:

> "Erik, we all go to pieces with our patients at one time or another. We all go to pieces now and then even without a patient to help us along. Your grief makes you more fragile. You know I've always thought of wholeness and integration as necessary myths. We're fragmented beings who cement ourselves together, but there are always cracks. Living with the cracks is part of being, well, reasonably healthy." (139)

After this conversation, Erik leaves Magda and has a new outlook on life: "[...] I felt restored [...]." (140)

All of Erik's sessions with patients trigger associations in him of his own life, his childhood, and, in particular, of his father. When the elderly Mrs. W. talks about her relationship to her parents, as much as she can remember, not only are the utterances of doctor and patient occasionally indistinguishable, but Erik's memory of his own father comes alive: "For some reason, I thought about my father in the yard, sawing boards. Then an image of a barbed-wire fence came to my mind" (147). The ensuing conversation implies that Mrs. W.'s father might have recognized his own pedophilic tendencies and, therefore, stopped hugging his daughter. Mrs. W. simply felt the loss of parental love, but Erik explains: "'[...] your father was protecting you. [...] From his feelings. You were growing up. There was an attraction, and he put up a fence'" (148). Erik's empathy for his patients makes it impossible for him to separate his self from the(ir) other. When tears run down Mrs. W.'s cheeks, Erik "felt an incalculable sadness for all of us" (148). His patients are never a separate entity and ultimately intermingle with him, his own past, feelings, and desires.

While Erik as an analyst becomes a "'container'" for his patients, "a vessel, a place to put your mess" (183), he, too, needs his patients: "I missed work. Work was my skeleton, my musculature. Without it, I felt like a jellyfish. The forms of things – the outlines. We can't live without them" (183). In other words, patients are metaphorically but also literally his bones and muscles without which he would not be able to survive for long. Since he cannot see himself, he is not in his own picture when he talks to his patients; he projects his unknown onto them to better observe himself.

What Hustvedt describes in *The Sorrows of an American* as a patient's reaction to Erik's gestures of scratching his own nose – "'Don't touch my nose, you shit'" (183) – not only makes Erik understand his own entanglement with whoever is opposite – "After that, I learned how precarious it all is – where we begin and end, our bodies, our words, inside and outside" (183–184) – but is explained as "mirror neurons" (Marks 2014: 210–212). In his encounter with his old friend Burton, Erik hears about them for the first time: "'[B]rain research on empathy. Terribly, terribly interesting. Mirror neurons, you know'" (143). Although Erik does not immediately react to this announcement, in his own practical work he does reflect on this idea. Marks points out: "The discovery of mirror neurons thus demonstrated that human beings mirror each other's actions in their brains" (2014: 211).

One of the consequences of this almost physical connection between self and other is Hustvedt's conclusion that there is nothing like an objective psychoanalyst: "The analyst as a *neutral* figure has long struck me as a flawed idea, but then so does the notion of *objectivity* in the sciences. Is it possible to drain any person of subjectivity [...]?" (Hustvedt 2012d: 157; emphasis original). The analyst cannot take on a "disembodied third-person view [...]" (158). Erik is constantly struggling with how close he can get to his patients. His colleague Magda defines the struggle as one "'between empathy and distance. Too close, and you can be of no help. Without compassion, there's no alliance between you and the patient'" (2009: 215). Erik learns the hard way that his personal situation in life is always a factor in his work as psychoanalyst, and frequently a disturbing one that causes anxiety attacks and mood disorders in himself. He is afraid that the encounters with his patients trigger in him the recognition that "beneath the self I had believed in was another person" (228), a person whom he does not know, cannot understand, and is afraid of; an other to his self, occasionally surfacing in his patients' reactions to him, in his patients' mirroring of the inexplicable other within him (235). He may be afraid of Freud's uncanny, which is "the other as the repressed, rejected, and ignored part of the self [...]" (Birkle 2004: 22). The uncanny is often the unknown that, however, eventually comes to the surface.

His other indeed emerges in the photographs Jeffrey Lane, Eggy's father and Miranda's former lover, has taken of him and exhibits at a show. It is one of his patients again, Mrs. W., who tells him about the contrast between the photograph and the actual person: "'I don't know you. You sit here and listen'" (Hustvedt 2009: 258). As Erik understands, "she had seen a picture that embodied her fear" (258) "of losing control, of madness [...]" (258). The picture Jeffrey Lane exhibits of Erik is the one taken when Erik surprised Lane breaking into his house. Lane entitles it *Head Doctor Goes Insane* and shows Erik semi-naked, angry like "a rabid dog" (263) with bulging eyes and shining teeth, wielding a hammer, thus representing a deep-seated anger that may reveal more than Erik's fury about Lane's transgression of physical private boundaries. This revelatory photograph, in spite of a court order to veil the face, continues to haunt Erik and Mrs. W. and shapes their sessions so that their lives for these brief moments intermingle.

Hustvedt's own life connects with Erik's and his patients'. As she explains, "[w]riting the sessions between my narrator and the people he treats came from places in me both known and unknown" (2012d: 163). She makes Erik aware that "he is not neutral, knows that psychotherapy happens in the land of Between, that wilderness between you and me" (163–164), that is, transference and counter-transference are constantly at work. The uncanny lies as much in the doctor as in the patient.

The photograph taken of Erik by definition assumes that what is represented is real, but what becomes very obvious in Mrs. W.'s and Erik's own reactions is that "even the *photographic image* is shaped by an intersubjective meeting between the subjective perspective of the photographer and the narrator's way of seeing" (Reipen 2014: 62; emphasis original). Mrs. W. – because she tells her story of seeing Erik's photograph's public display – affects Erik's reaction to it. Both Erik and Mrs. W. experience what Susan Sontag explains as violation: "To photograph people is to violate them, by seeing them as they never see themselves, by having knowledge of them they can never have; it turns people into objects that can be symbolically possessed" (2008: 14). Jeffrey Lane has not only "appropriate[d] the thing photographed" (Sontag 2008: 4) but has even manipulated it so that it looks like it was taken outside on the street. Despite Lane's deliberate changes, viewers take it for real, as Mrs. W. does, and even

Erik has to admit that there is a truth to it that goes far below his surface identity. The photograph becomes relevant for my reading only through its intrusion into Erik's relationship with his patient Mrs. W., who returns the medical gaze and subjects the doctor to her own analysis. It gives this relationship a whole new direction of simultaneous distance and closeness and makes Erik see himself in a new and disturbing way. The fact that it is entitled *Head Doctor Goes Insane* once more reverses the role between the psychoanalyst Erik and his patients. One may even go as far as saying that Jeffrey Lane becomes the doctor who looks deep into his patient Erik's inside. Jeffrey also assaults Erik's profession "by accusing Erik of not being the reliable psychoanalyst he pretends to be" (Reipen 2014: 227). The photograph continues to haunt Erik, and he has to admit that it reflects "[h]idden fury made apparent" (Hustvedt 2009: 265) on the part of the photographer-doctor and the photographed patient.

The Summer without Men (2011): Magical Thinking and the Absence of Meaning

As my analysis of Hustvedt's novels has shown so far, doctor-patient encounters are not only omnipresent but also structurally relevant to the movements of plot that are ultimately linked to characters' identity formation and the recognition of the self-other entanglement, that is, the intersubjectivity without which human beings would not be human. This recognition is by no means an easy process and hardly leads to a moment of know-it-all, but gives insight into the multi-leveledness of human identity that forms on the levels of the conscious as well as unconscious and, to a large extent, remains rationally inexplicable and unknowable.

When Mia Fredricksen collapses and has to be hospitalized after her husband of thirty years announces that he needs a "pause" in their relationship, she goes mad, as she sees it, because the most important other in her life is absent. The doctor's subsequent diagnosis gives her crack-up the label "Brief Psychotic Disorder, also known as Brief Reactive Psychosis, which means that you are genuinely crazy but not for long" (Hustvedt 2011: 1). This is an external definition for her to hold on to. But she realizes that she herself needs to give it "a name"; "I need to call it something, not nothing" (212). Mia's healing process is signified in the transformation of namelessness into name, of nobody into somebody. In contrast to *The Sorrows of an American*, Mia's psychological and emotional state is presented from the patient's point of view, and, for the first time, her psychotherapist, Dr. S., is a woman, who discusses with Mia the meaning of this absence, which has also taken away her meaning in/of life. The doctors Mia has to deal with only have initials as last names as if she wanted to protect their identity. The story is told from hindsight with Mia critically and rationally reflecting on what happened to her. Like Erik, she recognizes a part in her that she has never known. It is the part of the madwoman which Mia talks about in third person because she does not want to associate with her: "I don't like to remember the madwoman. She shamed me. For a long time, I was reluctant to look at what she had written in a black-and-white notebook during her stay on the ward. [...] I was afraid of her, you see" (2). Mia's self feels hurt by what is outside of her, her husband in particular, and, therefore, withdraws into herself. Like Iris in *The Blindfold*, Mia becomes sane again when she is ready to let the outside world in, to open up the boundaries between self and other. As she points out,

> [i]nsanity is a state of profound self-absorption. An extreme effort is required just to keep track of one's self, and the turn toward wellness happens the moment a bit of the world is allowed back in, when a person or thing passes through the gate. (12)

For Mia, the disruption of her relationship to her husband shatters her self-knowledge, but she re-emerges and tells her own "story of healing and recovery" (Marks 2014: 173). Mia's process of recovery takes shape in writing because it reminds her of the fact "that body and mind are inseparable" (212). Both the five elderly women and the seven young girls to whom she teaches poetry help her come to terms with the inside and outside world. Teaching creative writing also makes her aware of the "dialogical nature of writing" (213), which she puts into practice by addressing her story to the imagined reader and teaching her students poetry. Mia's pathography is the story of her illness, which, of course, needs to be listened to by her doctors, but, first of all, the readers become psychoanalysts of sorts since they are addressed although they do not have the necessary medical knowledge and education. However, as Hunter points out, "pathography cannot substitute for case narrative" (1981: 154). But pathography does give insight into how the subject attempts to heal through representation (in words and/or images).

Mia's conversations by telephone with her doctor are short and interspersed in the narrative. They serve Mia to process what she has experienced. Her own narrative on the one hand, and her strange e-mail conversation with Mr. Nobody as well as the reading of old Abigail's subtexts in the form of hidden images beneath the obvious stitched images, on the other hand, are complements to the doctor's analysis. Mr. Nobody is Mia's harshest critic, in particular when it comes to Mia's poetry: "'Your poetry's cracked,' my anonymous tormentor had written. 'Nobody can understand it. Nobody wants twisted shit like that. Who do you think you are?!#* Mr. Nobody'" (Hustvedt 2011: 64). This harsh and unconditional criticism reminds readers of Mia's own comments about the writing that she did when still in hospital. Although these are actual e-mails written to her, as she tells her readers, Mr. Nobody comes across as a second voice within Mia, the other in Mia who cannot accept the breakdown and tries to prevent her recovery. Mia tells herself: "Everyone hates you. You're nothing. No wonder he [her husband] left you" (66). Mia clings to life whereas Mr. Nobody tends to negate it. The play upon "nobody" reveals the opposite of what is actually expressed. On a second level, "nobody" does read Mia's poetry, and "nobody" wants and understands it. "Nobody" is part of Mia, which is also why she continues her e-mail correspondence with "nobody" so that Mia's destructive side gradually begins to serve as another therapist and as someone who challenges her (out of her) meaninglessness (see Bein 2013: 13).

Mia becomes well aware of such a hidden self whose rage serves as therapy in her encounter with Abigail, one of her mother's friends. Abigail's hidden image of an almost naked woman in high heels using a huge vacuum cleaner to "sucking up a miniature town below" (Hustvedt 2011: 42) does not need much of a feminist to be recognized as female rage at society, at being relegated and reduced to housework and sexuality. As Abigail admits, "'I was spitting mad at the time. Made me feel better'" (43). Writing, stitching, talking – these are means to promote recovery from wounds caused by men. Therefore, the summer needs to be without men to make the healing process possible.

Dr. S., Mia's psychotherapist, is responsible for the talking cure via the medium of the telephone. While conversation is possible, and changes in emphasis, sound, and tone can be taken into consideration, the visual aspect is missing in their encounter, which gives language much more importance. Mia makes sure that the reader knows that Dr. S. has given her consent to this form of counseling, that is, "telephone sessions once a week except during August, when she took her usual vacation" (4). Dr. S. is portrayed as the distanced psychotherapist who has her own life with which her patients do not interfere. In contrast to *The Sorrows of an American*, *The Summer without Men* does not give us insights into "the physician's thoughts and feelings about the medical encounter" (Hunter 1981: 163). Readers encounter Dr. S. through Mia's narrative.

Dr. S. explains Boris's, Mia's husband's, side of the story to Mia, calms Mia about the difficult nights she has when the marriage break-up or "pause" looms large in her mind. She makes clear to Mia that what she is going through is simply part of life and that she has to acknowledge and work through her feelings:

> Blowing up is not the same as breaking down and, as we've said before, even breaking down can have its purpose, its meanings. You held yourself together for a long time, but

tolerating cracks is part of being well and alive. I think you're doing that. You don't seem so afraid of yourself. (Hustvedt 2011: 19)[6]

Mia's response shows her full agreement and the invigorating effects of Dr. S.'s words: "'I love you, Dr. S.' 'I'm glad to hear that'" (19), Dr. S. responds. Dr. S.'s task is to explain but not judge situations and make Mia understand that "magical thinking," that is, whishing "our worlds into being" does not work. "That was *her* magic" (100; emphasis original).

Rage is an important reaction to her husband's cutting off of the marriage bond through which Mia is thrown onto herself without a male authority that gives meaning to her life. As Britta Bein argues, Boris's absence leaves "behind only the presence of Mia, the woman who is rendered meaningless without his presence" (2013: 4–5). From a feminist point of view, rage has to be considered a necessary step toward recovery. Rage implies power, as Mia experiences in one of her dreams, in which she experiences a powerful storm, and that is subject to discussion with Dr. S.: "'It was like listening to my own rage, but rage with real power, big, masculine, godlike, magisterial, paternal bangs in the heavens, the kind of thundering rage that makes the lackeys hop to, a baritone roar shaking the sky. I could almost feel the town move'" (Hustvedt 2011: 60). Dr. S. immediately connects this manifest masculine rage as power to Mia's latent feelings about her father and then her husband:

> "Is it perhaps that you felt your father's emotions had power in the family, power over your mother, your sister, and you, and you were always stepping around his feelings, trying not to upset him. And you've felt the same thing in your marriage, perhaps reproduced the same story and all the while you've gotten angrier and angrier." (61)

Although Mia immediately affirms Dr. S.'s insights, the reader might be struck by the suggestive tone of these rhetorical questions that do not give Mia the possibility of figuring out her own her childhood and marriage dependence.

Although Audre Lorde, an African American feminist, poet, and essayist, speaks about racism in her essay "The Uses of Anger" (1981), it can be applied to Mia's situation with reference to the relationship between father and daughter and husband and wife: "Most women have not developed tools for facing anger constructively" (1984a: 130). For Lorde, anger means "survival" (1984a: 132); for her, anger "is loaded with information and energy" (1984a: 127). In her essay "Eye to Eye" (1983), Lorde concludes: "Anger, used, does not destroy" (1984b:

---

6 Hustvedt reads D. W. Winnicott as arguing the following: "I understand him to mean that health can tolerate some disintegration" (Hustvedt 2010: 80).

152). It is this creative potential of anger that Mia lives through in her dream, but is at first only able to recognize as masculine, thus, as not applicable to herself. Dr. S. transforms the dream into empowerment through which Mia can turn her experience of weakness and total helplessness into one of power, self-confidence, and strength, that is, Dr. S. helps Mia to cope with her emotions and to transform them into healthy strategies. Dr. S. accompanies Mia's process of "the subjective experience of illness, the individual interpretation of it, and the patient's [Mia's] subsequent behavior" (Bein 2013: 7).

Mia's positive reaction to Dr. S. signals on the one hand her acceptance of what the doctor tells her, and reveals Mia's gradual process of recovery on the other hand. Dr. S. gives Mia the feeling that everything that is happening is part of a regular healing process. Her fears, her dreams, and her tears are necessary to finally reconnect to herself again. Like Iris, Mia has to split into an ego and an id, the id being Mr. Nobody, and rejoins the two with the help of the superego Dr. S. Like Iris's Dr. Fish, Dr. S. does not directly interfere, does not judge, but in contrast to Dr. Fish, she shows empathy and a willingness to respond to Mia's own story. Iris feels let down and manipulated by Dr. Fish whereas Dr. S. successfully supports Mia's process of recovery.

The Blazing World (2014): Multiple Perspectives and Death by Cancer

Siri Hustvedt's most recent novel *The Blazing World* is the fragmented story of the artist Harriet Burden's life and contains very few actual encounters of doctors and patients until Burden herself becomes ill and is about to die. The book has a fictional editor who claims to have pieced together Burden's story by editing her own notebooks and adding comments by people who knew the artist when she was still alive. The story that is told is Harriet Burden's use of three men to act as front for her own creative work in order to show, above all, the anti-female bias in the art world. It is also about how perception works, that is, how perception is subject to context and never objective or devoid of influence. This subjectivity, of course, also holds true for the doctor-patient encounter and its visual and verbal exchange.

Harriet Burden is in therapy with Dr. F., whose name is actually Adam Fertig, as Rachel Briefman, another psychotherapist and Harriet's friend, reveals. Harriet reveals to Rachel that in her therapeutic sessions she and Dr. F. talk about "'something horrible inside [her]'" (Hustvedt 2014: 110), which she cannot put her finger on and cannot label it. But it haunts her, and she is afraid of the uncanny. Although Rachel is a friend and not her psychotherapist, their meetings turn out to be like therapy. Harriet confides in Rachel, who in turn tries to make sense of Harriet's fear by relating it to the stories of some of her patients. Rachel, like Erik in *The Sorrows of an American*, is not the distant listener but continues to read Harriet in her dreams. As she is well aware,

> [o]f course, the dream is more about me than about Harry [...]. Almost every day I sit with people, and I listen to them. Sometimes, with particular patients, I worry that I don't really hear them. They are all trying to make sense of their stories [...]. (113)

As in *The Sorrows of an American* and *The Summer without Men*, Harriet's conversations with Dr. F. are never presented at any length but are interspersed in the description of experiences. When Harriet is deceived by a lover, Dr. F. tells her: "I don't think you understood how angry you were," to which she adds her thoughts: "No, I did not understand how angry I was" (140). This short exchange reveals that in psychotherapy the therapist helps the patient to reconnect to his/her feelings of anger and rage in particularly hurtful situations – as in Iris, Erik, the hysterics, and Mia. This, however, assumes a very trusting and intimate relationship between doctor and patient, which, for the doctor, is meant to be work that entails no involvement with the patients. These, however, cannot distinguish between telling their stories to a friend or to their therapist and, therefore, are disappointed when they feel the therapist's distance. As Harriet tells Dr. F., "I want you to see *me*" (151; emphasis original).

In an actual physical encounter with a doctor, Harriet learns that she has stage-four ovarian cancer and will die soon. Again, the reader views the doctor from the patient's perspective and can follow the attempt at representing the shock and incredulity when learning about her cancer diagnosis. In that moment, Harriet remembers small insignificant details of the doctor's mouth and teeth, the photograph on his desk, and the price sticker on the back. She does not remember his exacts words but only the effect they have on her, which she describes as "breathless paralysis" (331). She remembers that he insists that there is no cure, that surgery would probably not be effective, but still wants her to check into the hospital to undergo immediate surgery. The reader follows her disbelief and, like her, has to accept the seeming contradiction. From hindsight, too, she comments on the way in which Dr. P. communicates with her in an impersonal way:

> They do not protect you. Dr. P. did not shake his head sadly. He did not meet my eyes. I suppose that's how they do it. They do it all the time, after all. I am one of thousands. This was his method, delivering information for me to process. (331)

She is able to voice a form of ghetto humor when she asks about stage five: "Sure there is, I said. When you hit stage five, you're dead. That's what you're telling me, right? I'm dead" (332). She realizes that he does not like what she says. What follows is a description of her perception and judgment of surgery and subsequent chemotherapy.

In the representation of the doctor-patient relationship, presented from the patient's perspective, the two worlds clash, that is, the doctor's attempt at distance and insistence on facts and the patient's desire for human empathy. Even her desperate humor clashes with the doctor's stoic outlook. Harriet's feelings of despair, disbelief, and terror make the world look very different to her; she all of a sudden is aware of the impending loss of "city and sky and pavement, the swift and slow-moving pedestrians, and the color of things. It will vanish with you, every color, even the ones that have never had names but are perceived plainly enough. Incalculable losses" (332). The doctor and subsequent medical treatment, including surgery, turn her into an object or, as she cries out, she feels "gutted like a fish" (332). For her, medicine has become a hell that she will not survive. Twelve days between the announcement and surgery have passed, and all that is left to her is to "pray for the magic of remission" (333).

Harriet is surrounded by doctors, Dr. P., whom she calls "robotic" (333), Dr. R., a woman and "somewhat kinder" (333), and her psychotherapist, Dr. F., to whom she talks about her fears. Talking is one way of dealing with her situation, and the kind of language she uses falls into the categories of apocalypse and war. She describes her "abdominal disaster area" as her "very own corporeal ground zero, debulked, but not divested of horrors" (333). She feels "attacked from within" by cells that have become "killer legions" (333). Ground zero immediately evokes images of the towers collapsing into each other, of debris and death. In contrast to the planes attacking from the outside, the enemy comes from within her body, which "eat[s] itself alive" (333). As these different word fields indicate, Harriet is desperate to find words that adequately describe the horror and pain she feels. The absence of life, the self-cannibalism of a body eating itself can only shed glimpses on what she must go through. For her, there is only the dichotomy of "the good body, the fertile body" (333) versus her bad and infertile body, "the dying beast" (337), as she later says when she has come home to die. It is the moment when even the "shrink," Dr. F., allows his voice to express a tone of sadness, of "sorrow" and of "love" (338). It is a form of comfort for her: "I am grateful for that strange form of intimacy, for the one-way telling. He has known me better than anyone. Strange, but true" (338). And he comes to visit the day she dies.

The Blazing World is Hustvedt's only novel in which the patient's perspective on herself and her relationship to doctors is one perspective out of several, and it is the only one in which the patient eventually dies. The fragmentation of and multiplied narrative perspective makes the narration of Harriet's death possible. The most prominent form of doctor – excluding the cancer treatment – in the novel is that of the psychotherapist. Like Iris Vegan and Mia Fredricksen, Harriet Burden has a doctor to whom she talks about herself; like Erik Davidsen, Rachel Briefman (not Harriet's doctor but a psychotherapist, nevertheless) gives insight into patients' and Harriet's minds. Psychotherapy, for all characters, is essential in two ways: first, to come to terms with traumatic or at least painful experiences in life; second, to explore their own identities and understand the multiple levels on which a human being operates, whether it is the self and other or the ego and the id. Even Dr. Erik Davidsen needs his colleague Magda to help him deal with both his patients and his personal inexplicability. However, for Harriet, in the face of death, psychotherapy no longer holds, and she is subject to the medical and technological machinery that reduces her to her physical body, and this body to a battlefield from which she cannot emerge alive.

4. Conclusion

Jean-François Lyotard's hypothesis that "no self is an island; each exists in a fabric of relations that is now more complex and mobile than ever before" (1984: 15) can be seen as a leitmotif in Siri Hustvedt's work. It is particularly adequate when looking at how she presents doctor-patient relationships in her fiction. By definition, the participants in this relationship cannot exist one without the other. Moreover, identity, the self, and self-consciousness can only be understood in their relationship to the other and in the recognition by the other. Hustvedt refers to Hegel's concept of self-consciousness which, according to Hegel, "'exists in itself and for itself, in that, and by the fact that it exists for another self-consciousness; that is so to say only being acknowledged or 'recognized'" (qtd. in Hustvedt 2010: 93). Self and other depend on each other, mirror each other, as in the mirror neurons discovered in 1995 in macaque monkeys (see Hustvedt 2010: 93), and exist through mutual engagement and recognition. This can pathologically result in transference, transitivism (Carl Wernicke; see Hustvedt 2010: 121) or in the projection of aspects of the self onto a *Doppelgänger*, that is, the "threshold between the 'I' and the 'you' begins to merge or collapses entirely" (Hustvedt 2010: 121), as seems to be the case with Iris and Mrs. O.

In addition to this mutuality of existence, from the patient's perspective, the doctor is an authority whose knowledge and expertise promises healing and, thereby, a solution to the patient's problem. Because of the doctor's intimate knowledge of the patient's body and mind, he/she is invested with power both to help and to disappoint since magical thinking is hardly a psychotherapist's priority. Both a physician and a psychoanalyst, as Iris's case and Erik's behavior show, can do much damage if handling their cases in the wrong way. Furthermore, the patients' expectations, as Harriet Burden reveals, of the doctors' empathy with or even personal interest in their patients can hardly be fulfilled since distance is required for an adequate diagnosis. Personal involvement, which, however, can hardly be avoided in human encounters, brings in each participant's personal stories into the relationship and, in this way, renders it indissolubly complex and, occasionally, conflicting.

Yet, as narrative medicine and Hustvedt's characters propose, case studies and narrative knowledge have to be joined in an efficient encounter leading to successful diagnosis, treatment, and eventual healing. As Rita Charon points out:

> Nonnarrative knowledge attempts to illuminate the universal by transcending the particular; narrative knowledge, by looking closely at individual human beings grappling with the conditions of life, attempts to illuminate the universals of the human condition by revealing the particular. (2008: 9)

Not only is narrative knowledge different from doctor to doctor, but, as Hustvedt explains in *The Shaking Woman*, "[d]isciplinary lenses inevitably inform perception" (2010: 28). The language that is used by doctors and patients can lead to (mis)understanding, reflect power hierarchies, and emphasize gender differences.

Siri Hustvedt's preference for the exploration of psychological or psychologically induced illnesses results from her interest in human identity as well as in the intricate relationship of body and mind. Her representation of psychotherapy is very much based on Sigmund Freud and Josef Breuer's deliberations on and experiments with hysteria as well as on Freud's ideas on repression, the ego and the id, the conscious and the unconscious, and the uncanny. While there are ways of making the id and the unconscious emerge to the surface to be rationally grasped, for example through "the analytic process, the talking cure, which allow the speaking subject, the I, to own the experience" (61), memories can be repressed and may remain forever hidden, unknown, inexplicable. That is what Hustvedt's characters – sometimes painfully – experience, but that is also what may motivate them to proceed with their explorations. Sometimes, however, as Hustvedt explains in *The Shaking Woman*, "I have a vague sense that there are hidden recesses of my personality that I am reluctant to penetrate" (19). "The respective first-person narrator," as Corinna Reipen concludes, "uses narrative as a way of organizing experience in order to arrive at a form of selfhood" (2014: 233) and thus to overcome the absence of meaning.

Through her novels, her essays, and her autobiography *The Shaking Woman*, Siri Hustvedt becomes her own doctor and writes about her own psychological and physiological illnesses so that her narratives become illness narratives in which she is doctor and patient at the same time. The multiple perspectives she uses on illness and the doctor-patient relationship shed light on a number of factors playing into these encounters. By analyzing herself, she attempts to find explanations for her conditions, in particular in *The Shaking Woman*; she desperately wants a diagnosis, a label to put on an illness: "Doctors need diagnoses, names for groups of symptoms, and so do patients" (Hustvedt 2010: 186). When Hustvedt at a seminar lectures on different medical disciplines – psychiatry, psychoanalysis, neurology – and their disciplinary differences of perception, she begins to shake again, but continues to speak. Afterwards, a friend and former professor at Columbia University tells her "that it had been like watching a doctor and a patient in the same body" (30). Hustvedt herself divides these two beings into "the narrating, interpreting woman," who is the doctor, and "the shaking woman" (54) as the patient. All her novels "show a drive towards intersubjective connection and communication" (Reipen 2014: 237). As Reipen points out, "Hustvedt's work trains our capacity for empathy and teaches us how to see the other in ourselves" (238). However, no matter how desperately patients try to become their own healers based on the privileged understanding of their own narratives, a doctor's distance is necessary to turn the personal story into a case that in alignment with other cases may lead to adequate treatment. Individual narrative and trans-individual case history need to merge in empathy.

Works Cited

Balint, Michael. 1957. *The Doctor, His Patient and the Illness*. London: Pitman Medical.

Becker, Gay. 1997. *Disrupted Lives: How People Create Meaning in a Chaotic World*. Berkeley: University of California Press.

Bein, Britta. 2013. "Present Women/Absent Men in Siri Hustvedt's *The Summer without Men*." *Copas* 14.1: 1–19. <http://copas.uni-regensburg.de/article/view/160/207> [accessed 8 March 2015].

Berger, John. 2008 [1972]. *Ways of Seeing*. Harmondsworth: Penguin.

Birkle, Carmen. 2004. *Migration – Miscegenation – Transculturation: Writing Multicultural America into the Twentieth Century*. Heidelberg: Winter.

Charon, Rita. 2008 [2006]. *Narrative Medicine: Honoring the Stories of Illness*. Oxford: Oxford University Press.

Engelhardt, Dietrich von. 1996. "Die Arzt-Patient-Beziehung – gestern, heute, morgen." In: E. Lang and K. Arnold (eds.). *Die Arzt-Patient-Beziehung im Wandel*. Stuttgart: Enke. 19–48.

Fischer, Gisela. 1996. "Die Arzt-Patient-Beziehung: Kernstück einer 'Reform von innen.'" In: E. Lang and K. Arnold (eds.). *Die Arzt-Patient-Beziehung im Wandel*. Stuttgart: Enke. 123–129.

Freud, Sigmund. 1993 [1919]. "Das Unheimliche." In: *Der Moses des Michelangelo: Schriften über Kunst und Künstler*. Frankfurt: Fischer. 135–172.

Freud, Sigmund. 1997 [1923]. "Das Ich und das Es." In: *Das Ich und das Es: Metapsychologische Schriften*. Frankfurt: Fischer. 253–295.

Furst, Lilian R. 1998. *Between Doctors and Patients: The Changing Balance of Power*. Charlottesville: University Press of Virginia.

Haan, Joost. 2013 "Migraine and Metaphor." In: J. Bogousslavsky and S. Dieguez (eds.). *Literary Medicine: Brain Disease and Doctors in Novels, Theater, and Film. Frontiers of Neurology and Neuroscience* Vol. 31. Basel: Karger. 126–136. DOI: 10.1159/000343255.

Helman, Cecil (ed.). 2002. *Doctors and Patients: An Anthology*. Abingdon: Radcliffe.

Hunter, Kathryn Montgomery. 1981. *Doctors' Stories: The Narrative Structure of Medical Knowledge*. Princeton, NJ: Princeton University Press.

Hustvedt, Siri. 1992. *The Blindfold*. New York: Norton.

Hustvedt, Siri. 2003. *What I Loved*. London: Sceptre.

Hustvedt, Siri. 2006a. *A Plea for Eros*. New York: Picador.

Hustvedt, Siri. 2006b [1998]. "Yonder." In: *A Plea for Eros*. New York: Picador. 1–43.

Hustvedt, Siri. 2009 [2008]. *The Sorrows of an American*. London: Sceptre.

Hustvedt, Siri. 2010. *The Shaking Woman, or, A History of My Nerves*. London: Sceptre.

Hustvedt, Siri. 2011. *Summer without Men*. London: Sceptre.

Hustvedt, Siri. 2012a. *Living, Thinking, Looking: Essays*. New York: Picador.

Hustvedt, Siri. 2012b [2007]. "My Strange Head: Notes on Migraine." In: *Living, Thinking, Looking: Essays*. New York: Picador. 24–36.

Hustvedt, Siri. 2012c [2011]. "Outside the Mirror." *Living, Thinking, Looking: Essays*. New York: Picador. 52–57.

Hustvedt, Siri. 2012d [2010]. "The Analyst in Fiction: Reflections on a More or Less Hidden Being." In: *Living, Thinking, Looking: Essays*. New York: Picador. 152–165.

Hustvedt, Siri. 2012e [2011–2012]. "Freud's Playground." In: *Living, Thinking, Looking: Essays*. New York: Picador. 196–219.

Hustvedt, Siri. 2014. *The Blazing World*. New York: Simon & Schuster.

Jameson, Alise. 2010. "Pleasure and Peril: Dynamic Forces of Power and Desire in Siri Hustvedt's *The Blindfold*." *Studies in the Novel* 42.4: 421–442. EBSCO [accessed 8 March 2015].

Lorde, Audre. 1984a [1981]. "The Uses of Anger: Women Responding to Racism." In: *Sister Outsider: Essays and Speeches*. Trumansburg, NY: Crossing Press. 124–133.

Lorde, Audre. 1984b [1983]. "Eye to Eye: Black Women, Hatred, and Anger." In: *Sister Outsider: Essays and Speeches*. Trumansburg, NY: Crossing Press. 145–175.

Lupton, Deborah. 2012 [1994]. *Medicine as Culture: Illness, Disease and the Body*. Los Angeles: Sage.

Lyotard, Jean François. 1984 [1979]. *The Postmodern Condition*. Trans. Geoff Bennington and Brian Massumi. Minneapolis: University of Minnesota Press.

Marks, Christine. 2009. "Hysteria, Doctor-Patient Relationships, and Identity Boundaries in Siri Hustvedt's *What I Loved*." *Literature and Medicine: Women in the Medical Profession, Part I*. In: Carmen Birkle (ed.). Special Issue of *Gender Forum* 25: 4 pages. <http://www.genderforum.org/index.php?id=220> [accessed 8 March 2015].

Marks, Christine 2014. *"I Am because You Are": Relationality in the Works of Siri Hustvedt*. Heidelberg: Winter.

Posen, Solomon. 2005. *The Doctor in Literature: Satisfaction or Resentment?* Abingdon: Radcliffe.

Posen, Solomon. 2007. *The Doctor in Literature: Private Life*. Abingdon: Radcliffe.

Reipen, Corinna. 2014. *Visuality in the Works of Siri Hustvedt*. Frankfurt: Lang.

Rosenthal, Caroline. 2011. *New York and Toronto Novels after Postmodernism: Explorations of the Urban*. Rochester, NY: Camden House.

Segal, Judy Z. 2005. *Health and the Rhetoric of Medicine*. Carbondale: Southern Illinois University Press.

Sontag, Susan. 2008 [1977]. *On Photography*. New York: Penguin.

Stoeckle, John D. (ed.). 1987. *Encounters between Patients and Doctors: An Anthology*. Cambridge, MA: MIT Press.

Wells, Susan. 2001. *Out of the Dead House: Nineteenth-Century Women Physicians and the Writing of Medicine*. Madison: University of Wisconsin Press.

World Health Organization (WHO). 1948. *Preamble to the Constitution of the World Health Organization as Adopted by the International Health Conference*. New York. <http://www.who.int/about/definition/en/print.html> [accessed 1 May 2015].

Zapf, Hubert. 2008. "Narrative, Ethics, and Postmodern Art in Siri Hustvedt's *What I Loved*." In: Astrid Erll, Herbert Grabes and Ansgar Nünning (eds.). *Ethics in Culture: The Dissemination of Values through Literature and Other Media*. Berlin: De Gruyter. 171–194.

Britta Bein
Mysterious Illness and the Acceptance of Ambiguity

> "I felt that if only I could articulate my illness in all its aspects, I might give a trained ear the clue that would make me well, but my words were always inadequate."
>
> (Hustvedt 1992: 93)

> "Again, I am writing myself elsewhere."
>
> (Hustvedt 2011: 210)

In her work *Narrative Medicine* (2006), Rita Charon argues that narrative is always part of the medical setting. When patients tell about their symptoms, they reveal something about their understanding of who they are, as "in the destabilizing times of illness, [...] questions of self and worth naturally emerge" (78). Understanding the patient's idea of his or her self is crucial for a doctor's treatment of an illness because it provides information about the patient's perception of and respective dealing with the illness, which can have an effect on the healing process. While Charon's focus lies on how to improve medical practice, narrative can also play a part in an ill person's life that goes beyond its clearly biomedical use. This is particularly important for incurable illnesses that call for coping strategies outside of the realm of classical biomedical treatment.

When there is no diagnosis or, even worse, no successful treatment possible, the search for the illness's meaning gains special urgency, shifting the focus from the impossible elimination of the illness to a possible coping with it. In line with Charon and others, I argue that narrative form helps a patient make meaning of illness. The best form for an analysis of narrative is the written form, which is one reason why I am using two works of literature in my investigation of narrative strategies to cope with incurable illnesses.

Another reason why literature serves such an analysis well is that it has a lot in common with illness, which becomes apparent in the German Lexicon *Literatur und Medizin* by Jagow and Steger, which tells us that like illness, literature relies on crisis. It usually involves a conflict leading to a climax, the turning point of the story that triggers a decision between a positive ending (traditionally a comedy) or a negative one (the tragedy; Tebben 2005: 460–461). Illness also has such a critical moment. Medically speaking, a crisis is "the crucial turn in the course of a life threatening illness or within a psychic process" (458, my translation). It marks the turn of the illness towards recovery or death (458), which naturally has an impact on the sufferer's self-understanding. In a similar vein, the literary crisis usually takes the form of the protagonist's identity crisis (461). The resulting search for meaning by the literary character takes place in the context of the story and is influenced by the perspective taken. In other words, the same conflict can be solved in different ways, and a piece of literature depicts only one (or a few) of these possible solutions. The same is true for the interpretation of illness. While the doctor can make a diagnosis, it is still the patient who has to make something of it – and that is an individual task that can vary from one patient to another (Engelhardt 2005: 159–160). Thus, like literature, illness can be 'read' in different ways. David Morris clarifies this by pointing out in his 1998 work *Illness and Culture in the Postmodern Age* that

> illness constitutes a 'social text': something at least partly created by the densely interwoven network of experiences and interpretations we bring to it. Illnesses, like texts, are amenable to various traditions of reading, both medical and nonmedical. [...] Yet, illness is unique among social texts. It touches each of us. [...] It is a text we cannot put down or put off. One day it will likely kill us. (6)

In order for an illness to be read, it first has to be told. There are of course several ways of telling about an illness, depending, among others, on the teller's perspective (e.g. from a theoretical medical distance, an engaged doctor's encounter with a patient's illness, or a suffering patient's point of view), the illness's form (as e.g. the symptoms of an everyday cold affect a patient's telling differently than, for instance, an episode of hallucinatory migraine) and also the form of narration (e.g. the written or spoken form or even body language, or other wordless physical symptoms). These factors are crucial to the way an illness can be read, since they help understand that the way an illness is expressed cannot be separated from something one might want to call 'the illness itself.' Such a concept, however, cannot be grasped in any other way than through language, or as Chris Weedon formulates in her 1987 work *Feminist Practice and Poststructuralist Theory*, "it is language which enables us to think, speak and give meaning to the world around us. Meaning and consciousness do not exist outside language" (Weedon 1987: 32). This way, like any other experience, the meaning of an illness is constructed in its linguistic expression.

In a postmodern sense, however, the narrator of an illness is not the single instance giving meaning to it. Rather, the process of making meaning is bound to existing discourses within which the telling takes place. As Weedon explains, there are usually many discourses that play a role in the meaning-making of a narration, but among them there is always a dominant discourse expressing the prevailing ideas and values in a society (35). Such a dominant discourse, also called a 'grand narrative,' constructs meaning that a society holds to be true.

To Morris, biomedicine is an example for that. While he stresses that biomedicine is of course of crucial importance to the treatment of most illnesses, he demands an end of denying the culturally constructed aspects of illness. Applying a postmodern view to illness, Morris declares that biomedicine is yet another 'grand narrative' that makes us view illness as something that can easily be done away with through the expertise of medical science (1998: 11). This 'grand narrative,' the most common way to read illness in the Western world, makes us believe in biomedicine so firmly that it becomes more difficult for us to deal with serious illness or death these days. Deborah Lupton formulates in her work *Medicine as Culture* (1994):

> There is a set of expectations surrounding health and the body prevailing in western societies: we expect to feel well, without pain or disability, long after middle-age, we expect all children to survive birth and infancy, all women to give birth with no complications, all surgery and medical treatment to be successful. And for the majority of individuals, these expectations are indeed met, serving to reinforce them even more strongly. (1994: 1)

Indeed, our expectations to get well again or not to fall ill in the first place are met quite often, but what about the cases when they are not? What about the illnesses that are not curable, difficult to treat, or hard to diagnose? Illnesses with such characteristics can be called 'mysterious,' as, like a mystery, they are constituted by unanswered or even unanswerable questions for meaning. I call an illness 'mysterious' if it *feels* mysterious to the person suffering from it. I argue that this is particularly the case when 'classical biomedicine' fails to cure the patient, or to be more precise, when it fails to meet the patient's expectations of being cured. The patient is forced to find other ways of making meaning of the illness that enable him or her to live with it.

This is where the other discourses come into play, which Weedon acknowledges to be capable of influencing a narration, yet being marginalized by the dominant discourse of the 'grand narrative' (1987: 35). Postmodernism helps to bring these other discourses into focus, this way forming feasible strategies to cope with 'mysterious illness.' Realizing that the truth of biomedicine is only constructed takes away power from this 'grand narrative.' As Jean-François Lyotard concludes in "The Postmodern Condition," postmodernism acknowledges that there are many co-existing discourses with different truths, which fosters the toleration of diversity and heterogeneity (cf. Lyotard 2004). Such a view can be considered problematic, as it makes it impossible to find the truth, leaving us in doubt and disorientation instead. At the same time, it reduces our obligation to be definite, which helps us live with the contradictions and uncertainties life has in store for us. Mysterious illnesses are a good example to prove that universal truth is only an illusion because they do not allow for one answer that helps all, but instead requires each patient to search for his or her personal narrative that makes life possible through the acceptance of ambiguity. Since illnesses are ambiguous in their possible meanings, their treatment cannot be a clear matter either.

This is what Iris Vegan has to learn, the protagonist of *The Blindfold*, one of the novels I want to analyze in my investigation of possible strategies to cope with 'mysterious illnesses.' Iris is the narrator of the first novel of US-American author Siri Hustvedt, whom I consider a representative of the noticeable trend in contemporary literature to deal with illness. *The Blindfold* was published in 1992; her novel *The Summer without Men*, the other novel that is part of my analysis, was released in 2011. In both works, the narrators are subject to what I call 'mysterious illnesses': Iris Vegan suffers from a serious kind of migraine with hallucinatory side effects, and Mia Fredricksen in *The Summer without Men* experiences a severe nervous breakdown. The illnesses Hustvedt's characters have to face are not fatal, but they are mysterious to them because they disrupt their lives with frightening symptoms that, despite existing scientific knowledge about them, turn out incurable by biomedical means. However, doctors are the first they turn to for help, which speaks for Iris's and Mia's initial expectations to be healed in traditionally biomedical ways. In *The Blindfold*, the young literature student Iris Vegan formulates these expectations as she is on her way to the office of Dr. Fish, a famous doctor in the field of neurology, specializing in headaches and migraines. Equipped with a stack of index cards carrying the chronological details about her migraines, Iris is positive that "if only I could articulate my illness in all its aspects, I might give a trained ear the clue that would make me well" (Hustvedt 1992: 93). Iris's hopes to be cured are directed at a medical expert, a "trained ear." Already at this point she feels a strong need to express herself, wanting to tell her version of truth concerning her illness. What is more, she wishes to "articulate her illness in all its aspects," to incorporate different views from various contexts into the bigger picture of her illness. This approach of narrative diversity, she hopes, will bring her health back. However, the "trained ear" she expects to make sense of her story and to figure from her story what kind of medical treatment will cure her, is not willing to listen. Instead, Dr. Fish filters out the medical data from her story by recording his own synopsis of what she has said on tape. Iris feels that the doctor's method does not only ignore the narrative aspects of her story that seem so crucially important to her, but that it even *adds* to her illness by directly harming her: "Had he actually recorded his patients' speech, this approach might have been harmless, but as it was, the only voice on those tapes was Dr. Fish's" (Hustvedt 1992: 92). Dr.

Fish's behavior is 'harmful,' since his ignorance lowers the chance of successful treatment, as he fails to understand what exactly Iris is suffering from. What is more, Iris immediately develops physical and behavioral symptoms, noting that "[t]his ferocious editing had a peculiar effect on me. [...] I mumbled, coughed, forgot words, and lost track of what I was saying" (93). Iris is kept from telling her story, and even made to believe that her story is irrelevant to her recovery. Dr. Fish's approach takes away the bit of self-agency she felt to have and instead fills her with self-blame. In her desperate need for relief of pain (Dr. Fish is the seventh expert she is consulting), she depends on him and thus locates the blame for her persisting illness in herself: [M]y words were always inadequate" (93), she concludes after so many medical sessions of trying to report on her illness. She begins to feel guilty for not improving, which is further intensified by Dr. Fish's loss of interest in her case, for he is "a man who liked successes" (92).

> It goes as far as him telling her she "was improving though I was not" (92), which even leads Iris to "participate [...] in the deception" (94), acting as if she really felt better at first, and later, in the hospital, she "didn't demand further attention, because I was guilty" (91).

This episode is a good example in *The Blindfold* of how harmful it can be if the doctor does not take into consideration the *story* of the illness as it is presented by the patient. In addition to the failure of his prescribed treatment to reduce Iris's migraine symptoms, Dr. Fish's behavior also changes his patient's idea of self in a harmful way, as it causes her to blame herself for being and staying ill. This is clearly connected to the suppression of her story that is brought about by the power of the expert standing above the patient depending on him. In addition, this effect is intensified by Iris's general belief in the healing powers of biomedicine that is so typical of the Western world. These two parts constitute the 'grand narrative' of biomedicine referred to by Morris. In Iris's case, however, the boundaries of what biomedicine can do are reached, and it is cases like these that call for alternative ways of approaching illness, as Morris suggests (1998: 15).

Had Iris insisted and had Dr. Fish been open to her story, he might have been able to give his patient some advice other than which drugs to consume. Instead, he has her committed to hospital, forcing her to struggle through a time of almost self-annihilating illness only to find that nothing and no-one can help her other than Iris herself. In the hospital, her condition at first becomes worse than ever before, triggering the most disturbing scenes of the already unsettling novel. It is not coincidental that the novel's events are arranged in a non-chronological order that creates a feeling of confusion in the reader which is likely to mirror what Iris feels like. In the hospital scenes, the lines between reality and imagination blur so intensely that Iris loses her sense of self and feels like being on the verge of madness. This self-alienation is personified by Mrs. O., "the looney" in the bed next to her (Hustvedt 1992: 96) who does not know who she is anymore and terrorizes the ward at night, escaping the straps that tie her to the hospital bed. Although Mrs. O. bothers her increasingly, Iris repeatedly feels as if she were a part of herself. Parallel to the old lady's behavior, Iris's condition worsens to the unbearable, until one day Mrs. O. calls out to Iris. The medical staff and other patients consider their communicative exchange crazy, but for Iris, it is the key scene that brings her back to life. The next day, Mrs. O. has disappeared, leaving the strong impression of having been only Iris's invention (Iris herself suspects that). That morning, Iris symbolically gets rid of her internalized self-guilt triggered by Dr. Fish, by vomiting violently into the toilet, feeling as if "my bowels fell out of me" (115). Then, she takes a look in the mirror, addressing herself rather factually: "'You're a ridiculous person, Iris'" (115). These words seem to take off the dramatically perceived reality of her maddening hospital experience by "ridiculing" its seriousness. Moreover, the self-address puts into words that Iris is indeed a "person" who, no matter how "ridiculous," is a subject with boundaries, no longer blurring beyond recognition into other imaginary or non-imaginary characters. Her newly gained degree of self-control becomes visible immediately, as Iris, returning to her bed from the bathroom, "clutch[es] the back of my gown so that it wouldn't fly open" (115), something she might not have cared about during her episode of self-loss and pain. Taking a seat on the bed's edge, she gains a new perspective and suddenly recognizes the world outside her window for the first time in weeks. She has come back to herself and back to the world, but she had to make a detour through her own disturbing fantasies first. They are a fiction she needed after her 'factual' attempt has failed with Dr. Fish. Both approaches are attempts of self-narration, but while her first report in the doctor's office cannot help Iris to make sense of her illness, the episode in the neurological ward, despite its confusing and disturbing quality, eventually leads to a kind of insight that opens a new way to recovery in the form of a vague notion instead of a clearly articulated, factual report. She does put this notion into words, though, naming what she sees outside the window: "'It's snowing,' I said" (115), describing, so it seems, not only the weather outside, but also the view she now has on her ill self: not an entirely clear one, but one that allows her to make out something behind the flakes, and, perhaps even more importantly, the flakes themselves. She now seems able to name the blur that has distracted her from herself, no longer being lost in it, but looking at it from a certain distance, distinguishing between inside and outside again.

Paradoxically, it is not narrative coherence but a confusing fictitious story with a "fragmented" protagonist (97) that helps Iris understand her confusing condition expressed in the symptoms of her migraine. As Charon puts it, "sickness does not travel in straight lines, and we who care for sick people have to be equipped for a circuitous journey if we want to be of help" (2008: 67). Dr. Fish has failed to do so, and thus also failed to cure Iris with the means of pharmacology. It must be noted, though, that Iris's unconscious self-help does not manage to cure her either. The migraine returns in intervals, and she still suffers from hallucinations when they occur. However, she is out of the hospital, no longer a hopeless case, because she has found a way to cope with her disease. This does not make her healthy, but it allows her to deal with her illness in a more self-respecting way that helps her regain a *feeling* of self-worth that she has almost lost for good among the ignorant hospital staff. In a narrative as circuitous as described by Charon, Iris recalls at a later point in the novel how she "checked [her] self out" of the hospital (1992: 179). While she still feels "sick as a dog" that she can hardly communicate with the lady handing over the hospital bill to her in the lobby (180), she is still able to articulate what she herself has decided: "'I'm signing out,' I told the woman" (179), expressing a regained notion of self-agency that she had lost in the course of Dr. Fish's ignorant dealing with her story.

In a similar, though perhaps more advanced way, Mia Fredricksen, the protagonist of Hustvedt's novel *The Summer without Men*, manages to reestablish her self-respect after a sickening episode in her life. When her husband of thirty years leaves her for a "pause" of their marriage, a declaredly temporal affair with a much younger colleague, she breaks down and finds herself in a psychiatric ward with what is later diagnosed as "Brief Psychotic Disorder" (Hustvedt 2011: 1). Again, it is an illness that cannot be treated easily. Rather, the doctors have to *hope* that the condition is "brief" as its title suggests, for Mia informs her readers that "[i]f it goes on for more than one month, you need another label" (1). This rather ironic remark on the novel's very first page indicates Mia's skepticism about the biomedical approach to her suffering. Although the doctors can provide her with a diagnosis, it remains only a name for something Mia still has to make sense of. Moreover, Mia's statement hints at the coping strategy that she develops in the course of the novel, which is colored with wit and self-reflection. As a poet, Mia naturally launches into writing, already in her acute 'madness,' during which she feels genuinely alienated from herself, referring to herself in the third person as a "madwoman" (2).

Her symptoms do not appear arbitrary when considering what she has lost. Over the years, her husband Boris has become an integral part of her life, so much that she felt they would one day "become the same person" (118). Now

Boris has opted for a pause of their marriage, and Mia judges this as a particularly "cruel crack of hope," because "he said *pause*, not *stop*, to keep the narrative open, in case he changed his mind" (3). With Boris gone, Mia is "lost to myself" (2). So far, her husband has given her life meaning; it was Mia's 'grand narrative' of marriage that Boris seemed to have been the author of, for he is in power of deciding when the narrative is over – or rather, interrupted. Mia was never asked to provide meaning for herself – thus the temporary self-alienation in the form of the diagnosed disorder.

Similarly to Iris Vegan in *The Blindfold*, Hustvedt's protagonist in *The Summer without Men* is not cured by biomedicine, and she also does not seem impressed by its achievements. Soberly summarizing her time in the hospital, Mia states that "[t]hey kept me locked up for a week and a half, and then they let me go" (2). Yet, she does not consider herself cured. In fact, she remains the patient of a psychotherapist for the rest of the summer, which indicates her ongoing illness. To Mia, it is an illness of meaninglessness deriving from the absence of her husband Boris. Absence generally plays a crucial role in postmodern texts, where it is often referred to as a void or gap, which the literary character tries to fill with meaning in an oftentimes desperately obsessive way. To Mia, the absence of her husband deprives Mia of her source of meaning, her stability in life, her identification figure as a wife, mother and sexual subject. Boris is a Lacanian phallic symbol, an ultimate meaning-giver, to Mia, which according to Julia Kristeva's critique of Jacques Lacan's theory stands for the patriarchic oppression of women (Moi 1988: 163). Her immediate reaction to his leaving is a nervous breakdown, epitomizing how her world breaks apart without the traditionally male set of rules Boris has stood for. Without male power in her life (as there are no other men present during the summer either), she is threatened to drown in meaninglessness.[1]

Since postmodernism not only treats the problem of meaninglessness but also, from a more optimistic point of view, allows for the co-existence of many meanings, Mia learns that her illness can be interpreted in different ways. For instance, her illness can be seen as an expression of her dependence on her husband just as well as a chance for a new beginning and a change of herself, or even as a stereotypically female reaction. Either view on her illness, as meaningless or full of meanings, naturally calls for strategies to find meaning or to deal

---

[1] I elaborate on the problem of absence and meaninglessness in *The Summer without Men* in detail and with more extensive reference to Lacanian theory in my article "Present Women/Absent Men in Siri Hustvedt's *The Summer without Men* (2011)." *Current Objectives of Postgraduate American Studies (COPAS)* 14.1 (2013).

with the ambiguity of the illness. For Mia, this takes the shape of her own written narrative, her project of finding out which story is the right one for her.

Mia's narrative is of an unusual quality. While we as readers naturally expect a novel to spring from someone's imagination, it is rather surprising to find a narrator who not only explicitly claims authorship of the novel, but also presents herself as being very aware of the fictional nature of her story – and even of herself as being a creation of fantasy. Ironically, she reminds the reader (and herself) that

> the pen, [...] Dear Reader, is now in my hand, and I am claiming the advantage, taking it for myself, for you will notice that the written word hides the body of the one who writes. For all you know, I might be a MAN in disguise. [...] I, your own personal narrator, might be wearing a pseudonymous mask. (2011: 178–179)

This quote from the novel's last pages expresses how aware Mia has become of her agency as a writer, something that stands in stark contrast to her aforementioned feeling of meaninglessness expressed in her self-alienation as a "madwoman" in the hospital at the beginning of the book (2). Now, she knows that she has power over the story she is telling, including the right to lie. Repeatedly addressing the reader, she makes this newly learned position clear and at the same time shows the pleasure she takes in this style of writing.

It is not only the ambiguity of the imagination that is so useful to Mia, but also the concomitant self-irony that has a positive effect on her health, as she explains in one of her increasingly frequent e-mail conversations with her husband Boris. Having broken up with his affair, Boris informs Mia that he wants her back, which she comments with a vicious joke:

> M.F.: [...] Seeing the error of his ways, Spouse penetrates his Folly (ha, ha, ha) and has revelation. Worn Old Wife looks better from Uptown.
> B.I.: Can we dispense with the bitter irony?
> M.F.: How on earth do you think I would have made it through this without it? I would have stayed mad. (170)

These two and many other examples in the book show how Mia grows more and more aware of the narrative techniques that serve to foster her recovery. Throughout the novel, the reader can trace a positive development from maddening self-doubt to a strong (and nevertheless self-ironical) self-confidence, which runs parallel to the development of her illness and her marital crisis. As the end of the novel approaches, Mia has realized that she feels much better, and her husband is about to come back to her. In her last reference to the reader, she declares that "[t]here are tragedies and there are comedies, aren't there? [...] A comedy depends on stopping the story at exactly the right moment" (214). And then she ends it, with her husband ringing the bell. She does not make his personal appearance part of her story of recovery.

In fact, by keeping her husband's (and all other men's) personal appearance out of her story, she expresses a new awareness of herself as a woman.[2] The many women she meets during her summer stay away from home have an effect on her self-definition as a woman. Mirroring her own past as a young girl or mother, and inspiring her to think about her future as a woman after menopause and a self-expressing artist, these women become part of her story, showing her how she can write her own life without the necessity of an ever-present man in power. In the end, the initially sickening absence of men turns into a source of recovery and self-definition.

It is important to note that this different point of view does not cause Mia to turn against men in general, nor against her husband in particular. She is open to meet him again, but she will not let him take sole control over the status of their relationship again. Protecting herself from being sickened again by his will in such a harmful way, she now decides when and how she allows Boris to come back to her life. In the end of the novel, her narrative does not allow him to enter the 'stage.' Instead, she "keep[s] the narrative open" (3). This way, Mia has gained power, she has become independent of her husband to a degree that would keep her from going crazy again, which renders her self-narrative not only a coping strategy, but also a remedy and a kind of preventive measure. It suits Mia's illness well, which was caused by an interruption in the narrative of her life, and has now asked her to fill this gap of meaning with her own narrative of a different but equally open kind. This way, she gives credit to the many meanings 'hiding' behind her symptoms, instead of trying to eliminate them for the sake of stability and coherence.

In both novels, Hustvedt's protagonists suffer from mysterious illnesses that cannot be cured with the help of biomedicine alone. Their experiences with doctors that are not open to the complicated circumstances of their illnesses lead them to look for their own coping strategies. In both cases, the solution is narration. Since their symptoms are of a strongly self-alienating kind, their sense of identity is affected, which automatically calls for a re-definition of self that exceeds the medical realm. Their disturbing conditions are existential crises that can be seen as expressions of a de-unified world in which the grand narratives, such as that of biomedicine, no longer hold universal truth. Consequently, their

---

[2] Also see my aforementioned article "Present Women/Absent Men" for a more detailed discussion of the roles women and men play in the novel.

alternative strategies of making meaning of their ill selves take the form of personal narrative.

Following Charon's account that the self relies on narration, and that the medical setting is one where self-narration is very likely to occur if the medical staff only lets the patients speak, Iris's and Mia's self-narrations appear necessary for their recovery. In their state of chaos and confusion, narration could be expected to make sense in the form of a coherent story, but instead, their attempts to establish coherence initially fail and even make their conditions temporarily worse. It becomes apparent that the narrative must suit the illness in order to take effect. In both novels, the patients learn to deal with ambiguity, providing a discontinuous or highly self-ironic story with an open ending that leaves much room for speculation. It is not only the reader who is left wondering, but the tellers themselves acknowledge that life is neither predictable nor unified by a grand narrative, and yet they gain some agency through their conscious choice of how to tell their stories. Embracing ambiguity can mean to open up possibilities, to become more positive about one's own inner fears and contradictions. These may indeed cause crises of different kinds, but these crises, as we have learned, can also be a chance for a change, a decision between a good or bad ending – or perhaps a little bit of both.

Works Cited

Bein, Britta. 2013. "Present Women/Absent Men in Siri Hustvedt's *The Summer without Men* (2011)." *Current Objectives of Postgraduate American Studies (COPAS)* 14.1. 1–19.

Charon, Rita. 2008. *Narrative Medicine: Honoring the Stories of Illness*. Oxford: Oxford University Press.

Engelhardt, Dietrich von. 2005. "Coping." In: Bettina von Jagow and Florian Steger (eds.). *Literatur und Medizin: Ein Lexikon*. Göttingen: Vandenhoeck & Ruprecht. 159–163.

Hustvedt, Siri. 1992. *The Blindfold*. New York: Picador.

Hustvedt, Siri. 2011. *The Summer without Men*. London: Sceptre.

Lupton, Deborah. 1994. *Medicine as Culture: Illness, Disease and the Body in Western Societies*. London: Sage.

Kristeva, Julia. 1980. "Motherhood According to Giovanni Bellini." In: Leon S. Roudiez (ed.). *Desire in Language: A Semiotic Approach to Literature and Art*. New York: Columbia University Press. 237–270.

Kristeva, Julia. 2002. "Revolution in Poetic Language." In: Kelly Oliver (ed.). *The Portable Kristeva*. New York: Columbia University Press. 27–92.

Lacan, Jacques. 2001 [1949]. "The Mirror Stage as Formative of the Function of the I as Revealed in Psychoanalytic Experience." *Écrits: A Selection*. Trans. Alan Sheridan. London: Routledge. 1–8.

Lacan, Jacques. 2001 [1955–56]. "On a Question Preliminary to any Possible Treatment of Psychosis." *Écrits: A Selection*. Trans. Alan Sheridan. London: Routledge. 179–225.

Lacan, Jacques. 2001 [1958]. "The Signification of the Phallus." *Écrits: A Selection*. Trans. Alan Sheridan. London: Routledge. 281–291.
Lupton, Deborah. 1994. *Medicine and Culture: Illness, Disease and the Body in Western Societies*. London: Sage.
Lyotard, Jean-François. 2004. "From The Postmodern Condition: A Report on Knowledge." In: Michael Drolet (ed.). *The Postmodernism Reader: Foundational Texts*. London: Routledge. 123–146.
Moi, Toril. 1988. *Sexual/Textual Politics: Feminist Literary Theory*. London: Routledge.
Morris, David B. 1998. *Illness and Culture in the Postmodern Age*. Berkeley: University of California Press.
Paccaud-Huguet, Josiane. 2006. "Psychoanalysis after Freud." In: Patricia Waugh (ed.). *Modern Literary Theory and Criticism: An Oxford Guide*. Oxford: Oxford University Press. 280–297.
Tebben, Karin. 2005. "Krise." In: Bettina von Jagow and Florian Steger (eds.). *Literatur und Medizin: Ein Lexikon*. Göttingen: Vandenhoeck & Ruprecht. 458–463.
Weedon, Chris. 1987. *Feminist Practice and Poststructuralist Theory*. Oxford: Basil Blackwell.

Petra Gelhaus
In Search of a Diagnosis: Siri Hustvedt's *The Shaking Woman*

"To ask for an explanation is to explain the obscure by the more obscure."
Maurice Merleau-Ponty

1. Introduction

Siri Hustvedt's *The Shaking Woman, or, A History of My Nerves* is a book that is not easily categorized – and it is about difficulties with the tension between categorization, explanation, and understanding. On the one hand, it is an autobiographical report about an illness of the author, a nosography. On the other hand, it is a more general deliberation about the mind-body problem and the disease-illness problem, a work with philosophical, historical, and scientific impact. It could qualify as popular science, but this would not do justice to its depth and originality. At the same time, it is skilful and elegant prose, a narrative of high format that probably does not allow too many conclusions about the private aspects of the author's person, about the "facts" behind the presented narrator. If one dares to draw such conclusions, they founded more in the omissions, the order and structure of the narrative, and the metaphors, than on plain confession or explanation. Nevertheless, it is an extraordinarily personal piece of work.

Siri Hustvedt got a mysterious and frightening attack of seizures when talking at a memorial event for her father who died two years before. Her whole body from the neck down shook vigorously, but all the same she felt calm and controlled and managed to finish the speech as planned with an unaffected voice. "Whatever was happening to my arms, legs, and torso, my mind was all right, and I spoke calmly" (Hustvedt 2010: 11).

Later, when she talks publicly about this experience and its possible meanings, this happens again, not always, but sometimes. Not surprisingly, she gets frightened of these experiences and wants to prevent such attacks and get an explanation for them. What is surprising (and wise) is the fact that she does not avoid occasions that could trigger her seizures. When the audience witnessing such a scene comments that she is "brave," she feels misunderstood – she does not feel brave. "But above all, what I felt was fear," at least after the event (Hustvedt 2010: 30).

What does she fear? The loss of control? The loss of respect from the audience? That the symptoms may be a part of something even worse, a life-threatening condition? All this may be a part of it, but the fear that fills the whole book lies in the inexplicability of what happens to her. She, Siri Hustvedt, the talker, feels like her usual self, and yet her body stops being a loyal part of her. This is conceivable to others more than to herself: they want to rush to help her, to hold her, to make the seizures stop, while Siri Hustvedt herself is disturbed, but unaffected in her self-perception. The others perceive her as one person who in a strange way unites a shaking body and an intellectual mind that focuses nonetheless on her original task. The admiration of her being "brave" might attribute a superior power of will to her that prohibits the failing body to disturb her in her talk. But that is not what she feels. She experiences no inner conflict, no fight of one part of herself against the other, no conflicting impulses that she overcomes by strength of will. "Indeed, I had been two people that day – a reasonable orator and a woman in the middle of a personal earthquake" (Hustvedt 2010: 30). She feels like her normal self.[1] "The problem was, I hadn't *felt* emotional" (Hustvedt 2010: 7). Some alien has taken over her body, which is of course frightening, but as a person she is not altered – not in the acute situation. "It appeared that some unknown force had suddenly taken over my body and decided I needed a good, sustained jolting" (Hustvedt 2010: 4).

As the author elaborates herself, her experience resembles most the invasion of a demon or an ill-minded will that steals her usually obedient body. At another time and place, this explanation of what happened would have fit widespread explanation models, and exorcism would have been regarded as a promising cure. In secular modern times, a scientific, non-metaphysical explanation would be much more welcome. Furthermore, the disturbing phenomenon took place in the author's *body*, so a medical explanation is what usually would be regarded as an adequate and sufficient way to give meaning to the happenings in our days, and Siri Hustvedt gives the impression that such an explanation would satisfy also her. The reader might wonder why this is the case, and if a more or less mechanistic explanation had the potential to reduce fear and alienation from the own body. The demonic description seems to be nearest to the subjective experience; the problem is that we lack belief in demons, so we would not accept the validity of the explanation in spite of phenomenological adequacy. Does a medical explanation have the potential to imply the subjective experience the author describes, given that such a description is available? Or does it just disqualify subjective perceptions and replace them with explanations on the basis of objective facts?

---

[1] Certainly, there is an inner conflict involved that is reason for all considerations, but the immediate sensation is that of a normal person, and a split shaking woman.

As a matter of fact, medicine traditionally has room for both, the objective and the subjective. The traditional exemplary case in medicine is that a person feels that something is wrong with her body and goes to the doctor for examination, explanation, and – if available – therapy (Nordenfelt 2013). The scientific paradigm rules the diagnostic and therapeutic procedures and the range of acceptable explanations – the objective or third-person perspective is influential. The first-person experience, however, is the point of beginning, the question that is asked to the expert is a necessarily subjective one. Disease is (according to many medical epistemologists, among them Nordenfelt, Gert/Culver/Clouser and myself) impossible to define without a personal as well as without a normative element (Nordenfelt 1995; Gert et al. 2006; Gelhaus 2007, 2012). The phenomenon of disease paradigmatically implies a state of illness which usually is defined as the subjective and normative side of disease (Boorse 1975). This implied state of illness, of not-well-being, is usually perceived as something alien that comes from outside and befalls the healthy (normal) organism. Therefore, an explanation in terms of medical science indeed has the potential to fulfil the same function as the phenomenologically obvious demonist explanation: to explain who the alien is that suddenly took over Siri Hustvedt's body, and the more so if the diagnostic considerations are imbedded in first person experiences and their possible meanings, i.e., reflected in a narrative way (Ahlzen et al. 2010).

2. Diagnosis

"Diagnosis" means from the ancient Greek roots "identify thoroughly." It relates relevant medical knowledge about a certain problem to the individual person who suffers from it. At the same time, it gives a name to the problem and explains it "thoroughly," that is in medical terms. Nowadays, diagnosis is more often used as a label for a problem, it distances it from the person who suffers from it and looks upon it from an objectivist perspective. Many medical professionals even forget that the crucial point in setting a diagnosis is to attribute a disease entity to a special and unique person. Nevertheless, if one has a problem that is manifested in somatic symptoms, getting a diagnosis can be helpful and calming. The mere act of naming the problem makes it more concrete, and possibly easier to handle. At the same time it demonstrates that there are other people with the same problem, and one is no longer isolated with it: "Many people experience relief when they discover that a trait that has always been with them has a name, belongs to a legitimate scientific category, and is part of a greater taxonomy of illnesses and syndrome" (Hustvedt 2010: 120). Finally, the diagnosis often offers a causal explanation and therefore a possibility to solve the problem rationally. Small wonder that Siri Hustvedt engaged in the project of finding a medical diagnosis that could explain her condition.

The usual diagnostic process begins with an assiduous history-taking that is focused on the actual problem but also addresses other former diseases, social and personal backgrounds, and possible hereditary aspects. The questions a doctor asks are guided by differential diagnostic hypotheses. During the course of her memoir, Hustvedt addresses all stations that medical diagnostics would cover, though not necessarily in the same order a merely medical case report would choose. The book, after all, is not as one-dimensional as *only* a search for a diagnosis, but the longing for a diagnosis fills the book even more than the longing for a cure or for a way of coping with the problem.

One crucial crossroad in the diagnostic procedure is the question if the symptoms have a somatic or a psychiatric background. As the symptoms are seizures (which appear only in certain circumstances), both answers are possible: some kind of epileptic or psychogenic explanation lies at hand. Siri Hustvedt follows these tracks with imaginary consultations of a neurologist and a psychoanalyst, and describes which explanation models these experts would probably use. She does not actually address those experts at first, though, because she has bad experiences with neurologists when she was treated for severe migraine, and because she is afraid of things she might discover together with a psychoanalyst. The imaginary experts, however, illustrate the explanation models the author considers. The neurological explanation however seems to have little attraction. Too clear seems the psychological link to the father's death, an only neurologically triggered epileptic seizure would be a too simple, too reductionist explanation. Much more attractive is a psychogenic seizure, because it involves more levels of explanations, though the symptoms from the perspective of an external observer are the same. The author describes and goes through many states of minds and neurologic disturbances that shed some light on what happens to her. In the main, the most acceptable explanation seems to be hysterical seizures. This is, as the author points out with much knowledge and scrutinized understanding, no valid diagnosis according to current psychiatric manuals, partly because of the unfortunate name-giving that relates to the female uterus, which does not mirror modern theories. Nevertheless, the phenomena are still known and now called dissociative states (DSM-5: American Psychiatric Association 2013: 291–307). Siri Hustvedt analyzes many different kinds of dissociative symptoms and explains which aspects of them seem important and somehow relevant to her, e.g. posttraumatic stress syndrome, automatic writing, anosognosia (lacking disease insight), synaesthesia (the stimulation of one cognitive or sensory pathway also evokes experiences in other pathways). The author does not make the mistake of medical beginners to identify with every disease she reads about; rather she uses the examples of extraordinary states of minds which seem to have something in common with her own. This travel is difficult because a big part of the problem is that she does not feel what she thinks she should feel: no "real" adequate grief for her father, no "real" worry for her shaking body. Though she perfectly understands her state and can without bigger problems categorize it medically, however strange her symptoms are, she is unable to grasp them in a thoroughly satisfactory way. Though, actually from the beginning of the book, she is prepared to give a plausible personal meaning to the phenomenon, she needs many detours in order to get nearer to some blind spots. These blind spots are neither physiological and can be overcome by neurological explanations nor mental and can be overcome by psychological explanations. The irritating blind spots are in-between and refer to the mind-body problem and the difficulties of dualism. This problem has been much discussed in philosophy during many centuries, and it would be unfair to lay all the blame on Descartes, which is often done (e.g. *Descartes' Error*, Damásio 2000). He, however, in his wonderfully clear and lucid "*Discours de la méthode pour bien conduire sa raison*" (Descartes 1637), implemented not only the scientific method of radical doubt (Descartes 1961, chapter 2: 18–19), but also extreme subjectivism as the ultimate proof of existence: *I* can clearly question everything, and never be sure that things exist, but '*I*' cannot doubt about that there is something that exerts all these considerations. "*Je pense, donc je suis.*" – my doubting is the ultimate proof for that something exists, not nothing (Descartes 1961, chapter 4: 31). The way out of solipsism, however, leads over a theodicy which is not quite as waterproof (Descartes 1961, chapter 4: 33–37). Moreover, with the extreme starting point of one's own mind/soul, it is not only hard to prove the existence of the outer world, but also a bodily existence of the self. As a matter of fact, the world – and the body – have a different way of being: a mechanical one (Gelhaus 2009). Descartes is one of the early thinkers who locate the thinking existence in the brain, and he had a special interest in the pituitary gland that he assumed to be closely related to the immaterial soul, but he had no good explanation how the "I" and "my automatic body" can interact. Descartes' dualism is most well-known and illustrative, but the mind-body-problem is older and not consensually solved in the "philosophy of mind" until today.

What makes *The Shaking Woman* so interesting philosophically is that it is hinting at the mind-body problem from a clearly personal subjective perspective (like Descartes), while using results and theories from science, psychology, and history of medicine in order to come nearer to the required knowledge (like Descartes). Does Siri Hustvedt succeed better?

3. The Objective and the Subjective

In addition to practical consequences for her life as a lecturer, it seems most irritating for the author that she is split by her shaking experiences. She feels her normal self, controlled and rational, and has yet no access to her shaking body. It seems as if her body is no longer part of her. Thus, in the first place, it is not suffering which is her problem, but rather "not-suffering," that is *la belle indifférence* in confrontation with an obvious and disturbing affliction (Hustvedt 2010: 25). She feels complete without her body, though she obviously is not. An important part of her problem is that her subjective experience does not really extend to her shaking body. Objectively, her body belongs to her all the time, and as a reflected experience, this splitting and alienating of the body is frightening and causes suffering. For Siri Hustvedt, the division of the body into "Leib" and "Körper," into "lived body" and "objectified body" (Husserl 1950–1952) becomes a personal experience by her seizures. And paradoxically enough, she loses her lived body by maintaining her usual, normal self.

Modern medicine is often criticized of focusing too much on science and the objective world, and neglecting the subjective reality and personal meaning of disease. Thereby, medicine is not only using its possibilities in an ineffective way, it also leaves the patient alone in his suffering and aggravates it instead of consoling and getting the patient back into community (Parsons 1967). In matters of medical diagnosis – originally meant to relate the individual person to a general disease category – forgotten subjectivity is counter-productive. It re-enforces clashes in meaning: the medical "objective" interpretation of the phenomena loses its potential to communicate with the individual interpretation, and creates conflicts instead of opening for broader understanding (Cassell 1982).

In Siri Hustvedt's case, it is not medicine that initiates the exclusion of the subjective. Rather, the alienation is presented as an original symptom of illness. The Swedish philosopher Fredrik Svenaeus describes with reference to Heidegger a specific aspect in illness that adds to individual suffering and objective loss of function: an "unhomelike being-in-the-world" (Svenaeus 2001: 99) that replaces the self-evident trust in one's health that Gadamer presents (Gadamer 1993). In health, one easily forgets one's body. Disease, as an intruder, makes aware of the disobeying body and disturbs the natural integrity of body and mind. This also happens to Siri Hustvedt, but she lacks the genuine perception of illness; rather, in the acute situation, she seems to feel some *"belle indifférence"* (Hustvedt 2010: 24–27, 84).

From the book's very beginning, the author's hypothesis is that her lack of perceived grief over her father's death might have caused the seizures. On an intellectual level, a personal meaning of the event lies at hand. However, this hypothesis does not help her to get rid of the seizures, to feel what she thinks would be adequate about her father, or to find a way to cope with the phenomenon. She engages in the project to understand herself better: "Intellectual curiosity about one's own illness is certainly born of a desire for mastery. If I couldn't cure myself, I could at least begin to understand myself" (Hustvedt 2010: 6). Siri Hustvedt decides to "go in search of the shaking woman" (Hustvedt 2010: 7), and she does this in a nearly "obsessively" intellectual way. On first view, this seems strange: how can she regain a lost part of subjectivity by engaging in a big rational project, using all objective and theoretical sources she can find? At a closer look, this strategy is not as obsolete as it seems. If we do not have access to subjective experience, we use the experience of others in order to get knowledge about it. The American philosopher Thomas Nagel describes impressively that objectivity is a gradual abstraction. You can imagine a much distanced perspective from outer space that is blind for all subjective meanings and perceptions, but this perspective has no higher degree of truth than more subjective perspectives. An absolute objectivity, a standpoint without a standpoint, is impossible according to Nagel; thus his book title *The View from Nowhere* (Nagel 1986). If this is true, every objective statement, every proven observation, every scientific theory, implies a perspective and thus certain subjectivity, however hard it tries to avoid that. So paradoxically, it seems methodologically possible to use intellectual and objective information in order to get access to different subjective contents. However, it is helpful in this case not to use just a single explanation model, but as many explanation models as possible, in order to get access to many perspectives, that is, many different subjective traces in the objective, shareable theories. The cores of subjectivity might help to approach by intellectual means the lost shaking-woman-experience.

4. Narrativity and the Paradox

Another way of approaching subjective experience is literature. Narrating stories implies taking positions through imagination and presenting inner and outer states. Small wonder that initiatives to re-invent the subjective aspect of sickness to medical education make use of reading (and sometimes writing) fiction. Siri Hustvedt is deeply familiar not only, of course, with writing fictional stories, but also with the project of the medical humanities. As a matter of fact, the second time she was affected by her mysterious seizures, she was presenting a lecture in a series of talks about narrative medicine organized by Rita Charon, one of its leading activists (Charon 2006). In addition, she has given writing courses for psychiatric patients in order to give them a chance to express and work with their experiences, be it pathogenic experiences, or experiences with their disease. In short, no one could be more expert in using narration in order to illuminate subjective aspects of disease than Siri Hustvedt. However, she is not using fiction in order to present the shaking woman's subjectivity. It might be interesting to speculate about her reasons insofar as it could show more general aspects of the possibilities and limitations of narrative medicine.

After all, Siri Hustvedt indeed offers a complex narration: a very personal one that begins with her father's death, the first shaking event two years later, and a complicated overview of possible theoretical explanation models interwoven with memories of different episodes in her life, structured not by chronology but the order of the tested explanations –none of which seems to be sufficient or satisfying. However, it is a search for the shaking woman from the outside, for the lived body that the author is excluded from. Siri Hustvedt imagines different possible therapists and what they might have to say and offer, but she never uses the fictive experiences of the "woman in a personal earthquake" (Hustvedt 2010: 30). Instead, she engages in different kinds of neurological neglects where people are blind for certain experiences as she, apparently, is for the subjective shaking (and grieving) woman. On the other hand, she deliberates a lot about dissociative, hysterical, and posttraumatic states and emphasizes the lacking *distance* that the affected persons have with regard to their attacks. Does she lack distance? The reader wonders rather how much analytic distance and overview she has. Is it the shaking woman that lacks distance, and is that part of the reason why it is difficult for the author to imagine her?

Thus one reason for not using fiction in order to get nearer to the shaking woman may be that Siri Hustvedt simply cannot, because this is precisely a major aspect of her affliction. Maybe a more intellectualizing and analyzing method is the only possibility. On the other hand, the reason might go deeper than that. As the author points out herself, the search for the shaking woman is a project of mastery. She has lost control about a part of herself, if only in certain circumstances, and she assumes implicitly that understanding herself might increase her self-control. Imagining a story gives much control to an author to scrutinize certain aspects she is interested in. Certainly she can imagine a protagonist that is far from herself and indulge in speculating with much more freedom than a fact-oriented argumentation allows. Nevertheless it is the author that governs the presentation – exclusively the author. The author chooses from the complexity of the whole and presents her meaning to an (imaginative) readership. This is precisely why reading has the potential of learning about others' meanings, even on a subjective level. The reader gets in contact with a subjectivity governed and presented (mastered?) by the author. If, however, Siri Hustvedt lacks mastery over the shaking woman, a fictive presentation by her might turn out to be either shallow or very far from the point. Being the author of it might be too difficult even for such a skillful and imaginative author – or it might be simply the wrong way. If I want to come into contact with another individual, I need to listen rather than to speak. But the shaking woman does not communicate in words. If Siri Hustvedt wants to learn more about the shaking woman, it is perhaps wise that she tries to scrutinize *other*'s ideas, namely medical theories and case reports about a state like hers, instead of speculating about her own feelings that she lacks access to. But why does she focus on diagnostic considerations? She is familiar with and quotes the works of Alexander R. Luria and Oliver Sacks, two neurologists who prefer narrative case reports over abstract reports in order to get to a deeper knowledge about the personal meaning of the neurological dysfunctions they describe. But she mainly chooses cases with neglects or similar affections, and their common trait is that the patient is unaware of the core problem. Usually, the narrative method allows a deeper understanding of a pathological state, because neurological descriptions are confronted with personal meanings. In these special cases, the narrative method reveals less than usual, only an existential concern. When the patients lack awareness of the defect, it is difficult to find out more about the meaning they attribute to the disease. They do not realize what happens, therefore Luria cannot really know why it happens in the phenomenological sense, and so it is also difficult for Siri Hustvedt and her readers to develop an understanding of the phenomenological level of these complaints.

In the search of a lost 'first-person perspective,' the 'third person perspective' may help a bit further on the way. In the personal development of a child, individuation depends necessarily on the meeting with another person, a 'you,' most often the mother. It is the premise for getting the idea of an objectivity outside of the self (von Uexkuell 2011). In the search of the lost shaking woman, however, the contact with the "second-person perspective" is rudimental.

> Clearly, a self is much larger than the internal narrator. [...] We abstract and we think and we tell. We order our memories and link them together, and those disparate fragments get an owner: the 'I' of autobiography, who is no one without a 'you.' For whom do we narrate, after all? Even when alone in our heads, there is a presumed other, the second person of our speech. (Hustvedt 2010: 198)

The 'you' is implicit, but it is a non-responding 'you.' And this may be a shortcoming, not only in the personal travel, but in narrative medicine as a whole. The explicit or implicit goal is to get in contact with the other (in Siri Hustvedt's case a split part of herself), and the method is using the literary presentation of an author. "Reading is the closest we come to being another person" (Hustvedt 2010: 148). The author, of course, is another person than the reader. If she writes a narrative about herself, the reader gets into contact with her self-representation. This is a sort of communication, but a complicated one, difficult to analyze, and therefore useful in order to interpret it in many different ways. It may be a good training in order to speculate about many different persons, but it is not really interactive, and therefore it is no real mutual meeting of two individuals, an 'I' and a 'you.' It may elucidate subjectivity versus objectivity, but it has no potential to create a 'we.' If understanding another's subjectivity implies inner states of the other, the 'first person plural perspective' is a necessary step in it. It allows amalgamating the 'I' and the 'you' without melting one into the other or forgetting about the separations and differences. It opens a shared floor for understanding without threatening the individuality.

This form of individual development may also apply analogously to the integration of neglected or denied parts of the self. Merleau-Ponty describes how an amputated limb can still be a part in self-representation (Merleau-Ponty 1945). On the other hand even a mechanical tool may be integrated into the 'self,' as eye-glasses or a stick (Carel 2011). A way of understanding the inarticulate shaking woman may lead from an imagined 'you' (perhaps with the help of different third-person-perspectives) via a 'we' – rational Siri Hustvedt *and* the woman in a personal earthquake – to an integrated 'I.' The way out of a paradox is to find a level on which the apparently contradicting parts can be synthesized.

5. Conclusion

Siri Hustvedt finishes her book with a lucid summary of the results of her journey. In the end, she gets the opinion of real, not only imagined experts – a psychiatrist and a neurologist; she undergoes an MRI that shows nothing pathological. Medicine does not solve her problem of understanding:

> While helpful, cutting the inside of a person (the neurological and the psychological) off from what is outside him (other people, language, the world) is artificial. The difference revealed by these incisions are a matter of focus, how to see and interpret an illness or symptom. Even if my tremor were hysterical, a form of dissociation, a personal metaphor for the unspeakable or for mourning or for an emotional conflict with my father that I have repressed, which then appeared as a psychogenic seizure, I doubt it would have taken that particular form if I didn't have a neurological predisposition to it [...]. On the other hand, let us say that somewhere in my brain, undetected by the MRI, or somewhere in my unexplored cervical spine area, there is a *lesion* that could be designated as the *cause* for the shaking. I still don't believe I would have started shuddering if I had not been speaking

about my father [...]. I would not have shaken that day if there had not been some strong, if hidden emotional catalyst. (Hustvedt 2010: 186–187)

Perhaps a painter or a poet could succeed somehow, but Siri Hustvedt is too intelligent an author in order to solve her personal body-mind-problem. The coherence she creates as autobiographic author cannot eliminate the paradox, and she sees no rational way to deal with that:

> The logician says 'To tolerate contradiction is to be indifferent to the truth.' Those particular philosophers like to play games of true and false. It is one or the other, never both. But ambiguity is inherently contradictory and insoluble [...]. I chase it with words even though it won't be captured, and, every once in a while, I imagine I have come close to it. (Hustvedt 2010: 199)

The last sentences of her book sound like a surrender:

> In May of 2006, I stood outside under a cloudless blue sky and started to speak about my father, who had been dead for over two years. As soon as I opened my mouth, I began to shake violently. I shook that day, and I shook again on other days. I am the shaking woman. (Hustvedt 2010: 199)

Several of Siri Hustvedt's readers I have talked to are disconcerted by this end; they take the surrender as a defeat and feel compassion and the impulse to encourage her not to give up. I felt the same at first reading. After more reflection, I came to understand the same lines not as surrender, but as a hopeful seed for a different kind of nameless understanding. The mastery project is given up, after stretching it to the extremes. But the last sentence is not "I don't understand the shaking woman," or "I will never understand her," or "This is hopeless, I have failed." The last sentence is "I *am* the shaking woman." After the long travel, Siri Hustvedt is not happy or healed, but she accepts being one person, both an intellectual master of language, and at times a trembling and speechless being that is overwhelmed. It sounds exhausted and disillusioned, but the split that chased her through the whole book is overcome. She can do without a diagnosis – a name – for a split part of herself.

Works Cited

Ahlzen, Rolf, Martyn Evans, Pekka Louhiala and Raimo Puustinen (eds.). 2010. *Diagnosis. Medical Humanities Companion 2.* Oxford/New York: Radcliffe Publishing.

American Psychiatric Association. 2013. *Diagnostic and Statistical Manual of Mental Disorders.* 5th ed. Washington DC/London: American Psychiatric Publishing.

Boorse, Christopher. 1975. "On the Distinction Between Disease and Illness." *Philosophy and Public Affairs* 5: 49–68.

Carel, Havi. 2011. "Phenomenology and its Application in Medicine." *Theoretical Medicine and Bioethics* 32: 33–46.

Cassell, E .J. 1982. "The Nature of Suffering and the Goals of Medicine." *The New England Journal of Medicine* 306.11: 639–645.

Charon, Rita. 2006. *Narrative Medicine: Honoring the Stories of Illness*. Oxford: Oxford University Press.

Damásio, António. 2000. *Descartes' Error: Emotion, Reason and the Human Brain*. New York: Harper Collins.

Descartes, René. 1961 [1637]. *Abhandlung über die Methode des richtigen Vernunftgebrauchs*. Stuttgart [Leiden]: Reclam.

Gadamer, Hans-Georg. 1993. *Über die Verborgenheit der Gesundheit*. Frankfurt am Main: Suhrkamp.

Gelhaus, Petra. 2007. "'Theoretischer' und normativer Krankheitsbegriff." *Erwägen-Wissen-Ethik* 18.1: 107–109.

Gelhaus, Petra. 2009. "Der Mensch als Gen-Maschine: Reichweite und Geschichte einer Metapher." *Zeitschrift für Semiotik* 31 (3–4): 397–410.

Gelhaus, Petra. 2012. "Moralische Implikationen des Krankheitsbegriffs: Eine Skizze." In: Andreas Frewer and Markus Rothhaar (eds.). *Das Gesunde, das Kranke und die Medizinethik. Moralische Implikationen des Krankheitsbegriffs*. Stuttgart: Franz Steiner Verlag. 133–147.

Gert, Bernard, Charles M. Culver and K. Danner Clouser. 2006. *Bioethics: A Systematic Approach*. 2nd ed. New York/Oxford: University Press.

Husserl, Edmund. 1950–1952. *Ideen zu einer reinen Phänomenologie und phänomenologischen Philosophie*. Den Haag: Martinus Nijhof.

Hustvedt, Siri. 2010. *The Shaking Woman, or, A History of My Nerves*. London: Hodder and Stoughton Ltd.

Merleau-Ponty, Maurice. 1945. *Phénomenologie de la Perception*. Paris: Gallimard.

Nagel, Thomas. 1986. *A View from Nowhere*. New York/Oxford: Oxford University Press.

Nordenfelt, Lennart. 1995. *On the Nature of Health: An Action-Theoretic Approach*. 2nd ed. Dordrecht/Boston/London: Kluwer.

Nordenfelt, Lennart. 2013. "Ill Health or Illness: A Reply to Hofmann." *Health Care Analysis* 21: 298–305.

Parsons, Talcott. 1967. "Definition von Gesundheit und Krankheit im Lichte der Wertbegriffe und der sozialen Struktur Amerikas." In: Alexander Mitscherlich et al. (eds.). *Der Kranke in der modernen Gesellschaft*. Köln/Berlin: Kiepenheuer & Witsch. 57–87.

Svenaeus, Fredrik. 2001. *The Hermeneutics of Medicine and the Phenomenology of Health: Steps towards a Philosophy of Medical Practice*. Dordrecht: Kluwer.

Uexküll, Thure von. 2011. *Psychosomatische Medizin. Theoretische Modelle und klinische Praxis*. München/Jena: Urban & Fischer (Elsevier).

Susanne Rohr
"The image makers":
Reality Constitution and the Role of Autism in Siri Hustvedt's *The Blazing World*

In her latest novel, *The Blazing World* (2014), Siri Hustvedt brings the topics that she has explored widely over the last decades into a powerful dialogue: visual art, science, and philosophy. In examining visual art in ekphrastic writing,[1] the novel examines processes of perception, the structures of memory and imagination, and the female perspective in all of these. "We are the image makers," Hustvedt posits in the essay "Embodied Visions," and this distinctly human faculty to represent "ourselves to ourselves" (2010: 22) is one of the main concerns of the novel, yet it is enlarged by the dialectical moment of intersubjectivity. Thus, the novel is indeed about representing ourselves to ourselves, but also to others, and about reappropriating the others' interpretations again by making them part of our self-knowledge.

My thesis here is that Hustvedt effectively explores this intersubjective process by installing a narrative self as a curious narrative center within the polyphony of voices that constitute the novel that is unable – or has difficulty – in doing just that: entering into a dialogue with others. I am referring to Ethan Lord, the son of the novel's artist-protagonist Harriet Burden, who is said to "'fall [...] into the high autistic spectrum somewhere'" (2014: 92). That is, whenever Ethan's voice enters the polyphony, the communicative exchange is somewhat slowed down so that the structures that govern the dialogic process are exposed and the pragmatist underpinning of the novel, as I see it, becomes visible. By introducing autism into the fictional reality of her novel and granting the autistic personality a vital role in it, Hustvedt seems to share the distinct interest that American culture at large has in this mental illness and its physiological reality, and that has grown exponentially over the last years. The preoccupation with autism, particularly with Asperger's syndrome, has become so pronounced that Paul Hellker and Melanie Yergeau believe that "[p]ublic awareness and public discourse about autism are approaching critical mass" (2011: 485), and Jennifer C. Sarrett even talks about an "autism 'epidemic'" (2011: 142). Fittingly, an

---

[1] Referring to Hustvedt's writing among others, Asbjørn Grønstad even diagnoses a distinct form of literature, "ocular literature," which "is one that engages acutely and powerfully with the domain of visual culture, that blends into it and thereby reveals the extent to which the novel also can be considered a visual medium" (2012: 41).

"Autism Awareness Month" was introduced some years ago. This fascination with autism, in particular with forms of Asperger's syndrome or so-called "high functioning autism," which Ethan seems to display, can surely be explained in a multitude of ways. In my view, high functioning autism seems to represent America's cultural condition, one that increasingly is steering away from direct interpersonal contact towards mediated exchange via technological means that in their ever growing sophistication necessitate a high level of technical competency. This kind of exchange is precisely that in which persons with high functioning autism excel, and in this way they seem to represent a new kind of "normalcy."[2]

Nevertheless, the function that autism has in this novel is somewhat more complex, as I now will elaborate. *The Blazing World*, Hustvedt's sixth novel, explores the structures of reality constitution, thereby unfolding a distinctly feminist perspective as it is also concerned with the topic of the muted female artist. After all, when we meet her, protagonist Harriet Burden is an embittered middle-aged woman, tired of having been overlooked in her creative talent and intellectual accomplishments for so long, who collects lists in her notebook of "contemporary visual artists, novelists, philosophers, and scientists, in which no woman's name appeared" (2014: 5).

The novel is set in New York at the close of the twentieth century and describes Harriet Burden's desperate struggle to finally be acknowledged as the artist that she is. Harriet, or Harry to her friends, an eminently learned individual, has been ignored, or even snubbed, by the art world for her creative work and was only noticed because she is the wife of powerful art dealer Felix Lord, the mother of his two children, and the hostess of his famous dinner parties. Harry, after her husband's death, decides to use her inheritance to finally launch her career as an artist. She moves to Brooklyn and transforms a deserted industrial building into the "Red Hook" lodge, a studio and a shelter for somewhat stranded or disturbed fellow artists. Along the way, she meets the second and last love of her life, Bruno Kleinfeld.

In her struggle for recognition Harry develops the plan not to exhibit her art under her own name, but to use three male personas to do so. She calls the whole project *Maskings*. In this scheme, the attention she would then finally get would expose the sexist bias of the art scene by demonstrating that "[a]ll intellectual and artistic endeavor, even jokes, ironies, and parodies, fare better in the mind of the crowd when the crowd knows that somewhere behind the great

---

[2] Cf. my publication "Screening Madness in American Culture" (2015a) where I develop the argument in more detail.

work or the great spoof it can locate a cock and a pair of balls" (2014: 1). With her first two shows the experiment seems to be successfully executed. Harry's first surrogate, the young and inexperienced Anton Tish, is indeed hailed as a rising star in the art scene for the exhibition *The History of Western Art*, but he is deeply disturbed by his sudden fame and, after making a melodramatic scene at Red Hook, retreats into remote corners of the world to recover. Her second substitute, Phineas Q. Eldridge, a performance artist and one of her lodgers, is a more mature personality and is able to professionally handle the attention that he receives due to the exhibition, but the show *The Suffocation Rooms* is only a moderate success. The whole plan, however, explodes in her face as Harry's third surrogate, the narcissistic superstar Rune, betrays her. After the third and last show, *Beneath*, that opens to almost hysterical success in New York, Rune denies Harry's involvement in the show and claims the triumph all for himself. He relegates her to the traditional position of a muse at best, and in a well-known patriarchal gesture declares her to be insane. Refusing to be used by her and using her instead, he teaches her a cruel lesson: (male) power depends largely on the willingness to be conniving, selfish, and ruthless. What completes Harry's undoing is the fact that the opinions of those who dominate the art world, the art critics, simply follow Rune's perspective, despite her protests. The novel ends with Harriet Burden losing yet another more dramatic battle: the fight against her ovarian cancer.

1. 'Maskings 4'

The novel is composed as a compilation of around 20 different voices and discourses, constituting, as Harriet Burden titled one of her own texts, a "Missive from the Realm of Fictional Being" (Hustvedt 2014: 2). It is presented as a scholarly work, edited by one I. V. Hess, professor of aesthetics, who takes an interest in Burden's *Maskings* and, two years after Harriet Burden's death, wants to do justice to Harriet Burden and her art by compiling letters, statements, interviews, and essays by her friends and family, but also by art critics, art dealers, journalists and bystanders, all expressing their views on the artist and their memories of her or her work. However, a significant part of the text consists of Harriet Burden's own voice, her diaries, each one labeled with a letter of the alphabet. The editor, whose gender is not revealed, states that Harriet Burden's daughter, Maisie Lord, felt sure that her mother "had left a number of 'clues' inside the journals, not only to her pseudonymous project but also to what she called 'the secrets of my mother's personality'" (2014: 3). Thus from the start, the well-known (by now probably a bit too well-known) literary game is set into motion: the reader is invited to look for these clues and to construct his or her own image of Harriet Burden and her project from the multitude of voices. Fittingly, each entry starts with the visual representation of a piece of a jigsaw puzzle that divides the caption from the text that follows, inviting the reader to compose her picture with the pieces provided. It goes without saying that the reader is held in constant insecurity as to the reliability of the sources, particularly the entries of the diaries, as the editor mentions that in these Burden calls herself a "trickster" a number of times[3] and suspects s/he may have been "teased" by Burden (10). As with all life writing, the question remains: can the author(s) be trusted?

The reader's attempt to make sense of it all and construct a narrative out of the various elements thus mirrors the editor's own situation, who states in the introduction s/he had felt compelled to "try to construct a story of sorts out of the diverse material" (7) and create "a reasonable order" (10). Accordingly, the introduction functions as a kind of *mise en abyme* for the entire text's structure and sets the intersubjective dialogue in motion. What is more, the text that seeks to evoke the personality and work of the artist Harriet Burden and that, with the artist a trickster and gone, revolves around an empty middle, posthumously constitutes the very last artwork of Harriet Burden, which I would like to call 'Maskings 4,' with the editor and the reader acting as her surrogates producing the last expression of her blazing creativity. Our ensuing artifact, that is the reader's subjective evocation of the artist and her work, will then affirm Harry's understanding that taking on a particular persona in the creative process will inevitably affect the outcome. Yet taking on another persona, or, as the editor calls it by quoting Kierkegaard, becoming various "poetized personalities" (3), also changes the person who is wearing the mask. As her daughter Maisie retells Burden's insight: "When you take on a male persona, something happens" (187). As such, Burden's many diary entries at various stages during her *Maskings* trilogy also represent her different "poetized personalities," and in interacting with those, the reader not only witnesses "arguments between two versions of herself" (6), but also enters into a dialogue with dissimilar versions of the artist and her art that will inevitably influence the reader's own artwork created in 'Maskings 4.' When we as readers enter this dialogue and become the artist's fourth surrogate, we become deeply involved in Burden's project. For wearing a mask, as Burden herself notes, is "not a disguise but a means of revelation" (58).

---

[3] One such instance can be found in one of the notebook entries dealing with Rune. Burden writes "I will borrow a trickster self. Look at me, a Prometheus. I am myself a myth about myself. Who I am has nothing to do with it" (Hustvedt 2014: 203).

But there is still another way of interpreting the status of Burden's entire project that only comes into being because she is holding back her own identity, refraining from showing herself in showing her work. After the first exhibition in the *Maskings* trilogy and still wearing the mask of young, effeminate and slightly hysterical Anton Tish, she brings up Anna O. in one of her notebook entries. Anna O. – her given name being Bertha Pappenheim – was a famous patient of Josef Breuer's, a gifted woman, feminist activist, writer, and one of the documented patients in Breuer and Freud's 1895 *Studies in Hysteria*. Not surprisingly, Burden feels attracted to Pappenheim as well as to Margaret Cavendish as all three of them are strong and courageous women who have had trouble getting full recognition during their lifetime and were denigrated for sexist reasons. They were all silenced by classic patriarchal gestures, or at least there were attempts to silence them: Pappenheim was treated by Breuer for her 'hysterical' symptoms and then abandoned by him, Cavendish was mocked as a "mad [...] woman" (Hustvedt 2014: 208), and Burden is labeled by an art critic as "*eccentric, paranoid, belligerent, hysterical, and even violent*" (9; emphasis original).

If we stay in the realm of psychoanalysis for a moment, Burden's reluctance to show herself and her work under her own name may well be related to some kind of *Urszene* or original narcissistic wound to which Burden returns time and again in her diary entries. In this scene Harry as a child wanted to pay her father a surprise visit in his office. When she got there, her father greeted her with the words "Harriet, what are you doing here? You should not be here" (142). The paternal verdict "You should not be here" haunts Harriet Burden for the rest of her life, as does his rejection of her creative work. She is also injured by the knowledge that her father initially did not want her and the fact that by calling her "Harry" he showed that he obviously would have preferred a son. The whole *Maskings* trilogy can then be read as a reenactment of the original narcissistic wound: You should not be here – and Harriet obeys and is not. As such, the whole project can be understood as the expression, and acting out, of a neurotic symptom.

When Burden writes about Pappenheim, she brings up a scene between Breuer and his patient after which Breuer is said to have abandoned her. In this encounter, Anna O. complained of abdominal pain and told Breuer "Now comes Dr. B.'s child" (Hustvedt 2014: 64). Harriet Burden then muses "[i]t is the thing they have made together. Look at it. [...] It will out. Where is the borderland between memory and hallucination? We make images spontaneously. They will out" (64–65). While this obviously refers to the first *Maskings* exhibition, we can also extend it to the reader's activity. For if we as readers act as Burden's surrogates in bringing out 'Maskings 4,' we indeed "make images spontaneously" when taking our place in the neurotic reenactment of the initial drama.

In the process of making sense of it all, the reader is also invited to enter the interplay of references and cross-references pervading the text. For after the "Introduction" the editor retreats behind the edited material, only making his or her own work visible in scholarly footnotes that comment on Harriet Burden's enormously learned commentaries on all fields of philosophy and the sciences, thus making sure that the distinct (and in its ostentation sometimes tiresome) intellectuality of the participants in the interplay is not lost to the reader. And of course, the game demands that some of the footnotes refer to sources existing outside the fictional universe while others are hoax entries. Building up a tight intertextual network throughout the text, there are also references to elements from other novels by Hustvedt, such as the mention of William Wechsler, a character in Hustvedt's *What I Loved*, as one of the artists whom Harriet Burden likes (4). But above all, the text bristles with discussions of countless theories and theorists from all fields of learned discourse. One of these is the writing and person of Margaret Cavendish, the Duchess of Newcastle (1623–1673), who was mentioned previously and to whom Harriet Burden in her diaries refers very often. Being female, Cavendish in her time had been ridiculed for her ambitions in scientific and creative work, just like Burden herself. The editor in the introduction thus calls the Duchess Burden's "alter ego" (6),[4] and Cavendish and her utopian novel *The Blazing World* function not only as the artist's alter ego and archive for the title of Hustvedt's book, but also as an important connector to Burden's final triumph. After her death, we learn in the editor's introduction, Harriet Burden's work finally gets the attention the artist has longed for all her life (7). In her last artwork, a large female figure to which Harriet Burden refers as the "blazing mother Margaret" (339) gives birth to a number of little figures, one of them being Harriet Burden herself. Through Margaret Cavendish's extravagance and courage, that is, Harriet Burden finally brings herself out into the world as the artist she is.

2. The Odd One Out

As I mentioned earlier, in this concerto of voices that constitute Hustvedt's *The Blazing World*, one is particularly prominent. This voice belongs to Harriet Burden's son Ethan Lord, who is frequently referred to as being a "catalogue of odd-

---

[4] In this text that is thick with masquerade and pseudonyms of all kinds, other alter egos besides Margaret Cavendish appear as well. One is for instance young Anton Tish, Burden's first mask, whom she impersonates in her friend Rachel's apartment as a girl – "as a form of revenge," according to Rachel (111).

ities," "very smart" (92) and even a "boy-genius" (189), as having "a different pattern of mind" (215) and an eidetic memory (285) but as otherwise lacking in social and emotional skills. He reports of himself that he "did not want anyone to touch him" (269) after his father's death. As all of these characteristics may also describe autistic personalities, it is not surprising that, as previously mentioned, Ethan is thought of as "fall[ing] into the high autistic spectrum somewhere" (92). He is also a writer of bizarre stories and admits to Sweet Autumn Pinkney, a kind and esoteric young woman who accompanies Harriet Burden in her dying process, that the fictional worlds that Harry had made up in the bedtime stories she had told her children inspired him to become a writer. He is also the one who carries on his mother's project. In a story entitled "Less Than Me" he writes about a woman who loses her "me-ness," her essence (319) and decides to build the "Thing" that is to serve as a "monument to her lost self" (320). In the end, however, the "Thing" represents not the woman's essence but that of her neighbor who may or may not exist and about whom the woman has begun to fantasize. Although Ethan would not admit it, Harriet Burden realizes that the "Thing" bears resemblance to her own artworks (320), and convincingly so, as her *Maskings* trilogy can certainly be read as "a monument to her lost self," or rather to her forbidden self. When Burden's lost diary O is found after her death, a vital one describing her devastating encounters with her third surrogate and later antagonist Rune, Ethan, who does not get carried away in emotional situations, notices and comments upon the aesthetic quality of Harriet's writing, while his sister Maisie is upset by the emotional power of what she reads (285).

His own written contributions to the assemblage that constitutes *The Blazing World* are curiously different from all the others, and one might well read them as expressing an autistic or quasi-autistic personality. The first one, "A Compendium of Thirteen: Characters, a Non Sequitur, a Confession, a Riddle, and Memories for H.B." (53–56) is a sequence of thirteen entries, the first letters of which when read consecutively form the acronym HARRIET BURDEN. The first and last entries refer to the fictional world of Harriet Burden's influential bedtime stories, thus framing the middle elements in which Ethan renders his own thoughts, creating a bond between mother and son in their respective creative expression. Ethan calls his thirteen bits and pieces in the title "Memories for H.B.," not "of H.B.," thereby expressing that he wants to offer her a gift by returning to her the traces she has left in his own thinking. This entry shows how deeply Ethan Lord has understood the dynamics of memory and identity formation.

An autistic personality's construction of and interaction with reality is believed to follow individual patterns. Harriet Burden relates how she would defend her child against his father who asked her "Do you think the child is normal?" She would answer him "He just has a different pattern of mind" (215), and in "A Compendium of Thirteen," Ethan himself reflects upon the phenomenon when he writes in entry 6, presumably addressing his mother: "Everything has a pattern or a rhythm that can be discerned through close examination,[5] but whether those repetitions exist outside the mind is an open question. You and I did not see the same patterns" (54), and in relation to his sister Maisie: "Different patterns of mind" (56).

His next contribution, "An Alphabet Toward Several Meanings of Art and Generation" (135–136), is an elaborate equation trying to describe the relationship between artist, artwork, and observer. Without explicitly mentioning his mother and her project, it attempts to explain what happens when the original producer of an artwork vanishes and another artist claims proprietorship. If Harriet Burden has understood that taking on another persona in the creative process will inevitably alter the created product, Ethan here in his abstract reasoning goes a step further when he asks if the created product itself, the artwork, will change when another artist is brought into connection with it. Bringing this text into dialogue with Ethan's story "Less Than Me," he seems to ask: will the "me-ness" or essence of the artist that enters the artwork and of which it is an expression remain in it after a change of origin, or will the "me-ness" of the new originator be projected onto the object by the observer? The latter will be the case, as Ethan concludes, and with this he understands the tragic failure of Burden's *Maskings* trilogy. With the original artist vanished, her art will not speak for her as it will not be connected to her by the observer. And without an observer, the artwork "has no significance in itself" (136). Thus by retreating behind her three male stand-ins, Harriet, contrary to her intentions, does not make the value of her work visible in the exhibitions, as this is impossible without connection to its origin, but on the contrary mutes her own creative expression efficiently, thereby obeying the paternal verdict. To put it differently, by denying her artworks their origin, Harriet Burden withholds her gift and disrupts the dialogue with her audience, thus impairing the intersubjective exchange. Hustvedt expresses the concomitant view in a scholarly article that she wrote in 2010:

> art is always a gift made for another – not a specific other but a generalized other person who is asked to read or listen or look. Art necessarily establishes a relation between the artist and an imaginary reader, viewer, or listener; it is inherently dialogical. (2010: 28)

---

[5] I cannot help but notice that Gertrude Stein has expressed the very same opinion in her portraits, where her repetitions, or, as she would have it, insistences try to bring out the rhythm of a particular personality.

Ethan's text consequently ends with the sign A taking on a new meaning: A, formerly the variable for artist, is now "the sign of ABSENCE" (136). As I mentioned earlier, in the passages written by Ethan Lord the reading process slows down considerably, right to the point where, as in "An Alphabet," it halts altogether, as the reader is forced to write down the equation with its variables in order to better follow the explanation given. In these important moments the narrative structure of *The Blazing World* gains a self-reflexive quality that highlights the readers' process of making sense in the process of putting together the novel's fictional universe. Given the potentially different "patterns of mind" of autistic personalities, it is an effective narrative move for unfolding the self-reflexive quality via Ethan Lord. His contributions exhibit the characteristics typically ascribed to autistic persons: above all the need to continually look for and establish rules and routines, as a person with autism has difficulty falling back on a canon of pre-established standards. As Ethan himself puts it, they "do not see the same patterns" as their fellow human beings. Thus, in highlighting this process of pattern formation, *The Blazing World* reflects upon its own mode of being: it is an invitation to put together the patterns of Harriet Burden's *Maskings* trilogy and to come up with the reader's own version of it, or 'Maskings 4' as I have called it.

What is more, by placing a quasi-autistic personality in the narrative center of the novel, Hustvedt seizes a development in American culture at large that has become palpable over the last decade: autism and particularly Asperger's syndrome seem to hold center stage when it comes to the artistic exploration of mental illness, and the topic is more or less omnipresent in the contemporary arts. There are certainly different ways to explain this intense interest in autism, and I would suggest that the autistic personality has come to be understood as the embodiment of the present *conditio humana*. As I have argued elsewhere,[6] in this view the autistic personality comes to constitute the paradigmatic 'normal' individual in times of dramatic change, brought about by processes of globalization and cosmopolitanism. These lead to unsettling normlessness and the breakdown of social values. The resulting indeterminateness and uncertainty create chaos that leave the contemporary individual displaced and driven at the same time by the persistent necessity to make fast choices and decisions and to find rules instead of simply following or applying them. The pressure to adjust to the normal chaos is complemented by high technological competence. In the practice of social relations, the individual of globalized modernity, much like the

---

6 Cf. my publication "Screening Madness in American Culture" (2015a), where I unfold the argument in more detail, following Ulrich Beck's individualization thesis.

autistic personality, is forced to continuously renegotiate the conditions of social co-operation as few are prescribed per se in contemporary culture.

The artistic personality, seen this way, epitomizes the contemporary individual's exhausting task of continuously establishing rules and patterns to organize reality. By integrating such a voice into her novel with Ethan's contributions, Hustvedt has installed significant self-reflexive centerpieces. If his curious "Compendium of Thirteen" shows how deeply Ethan Lord has understood the dynamics of memory and identity formation, his "Alphabet Toward Several Meanings of Art" in its abstraction beautifully explains the failure of Harriet Burden's project. And Ethan Lord's third contribution, as I understand it, even constitutes the narrative core of the novel.

3. Messages from the Underground

"A Dispatch from Elsewhere" (265–270) functions, like the editor's introduction, as another moment of *mise en abyme* in the novel. While the introduction describes the process of making sense as regulative intervention, as a sorting, screening, selecting, composing, and explaining of material, Ethan here reflects on another moment in the operation. He explains to the reader that making sense implies creative action, creatively guessing connections that would provide meaningful links between seemingly disparate elements. In this contribution, Ethan describes a dream he had had and then his process of interpreting it. As such, it is truly a dispatch from elsewhere, strictly speaking a dispatch from his unconscious. Freud recognized that the mechanisms of dream work operate just like poetic language, with condensation and displacement acting very much like the poetic functions metaphor and metonymy. Freud realized that dreams have to be interpreted like a poetic text, with the interpreter performing hermeneutical efforts in a close reading.

Ethan thus follows Freud's example and, after reporting his dream text, enters into a systematic step-by-step interpretation. However, Ethan creates a distance from his dream text and his interpretative activity as a whole as he retreats behind a third person perspective. As a matter of fact, this entry is the only one in the whole novel in which a heterodiegetic narrative strategy with internal focalization is established, allowing for a fairly ironic distance from the workings of the own mind, as for instance the subtitle "E isolates the dream elements to propose possible soulful interpretations" indicates. It is here, in this solitary yet dialogic process, that the project of *The Blazing World* becomes obvious. In a scholarly text from 2011, Hustvedt holds that "having a narrator, external and voiced or internal and silent, is a way of keeping company with one's self. In language, the self is always touched by otherness, if only because it is represented" (2011: 193). *The Blazing World* combines many voices that keep each other company, touching each other. Ethan's text, the only one told through a third-person perspective, illuminates and reflects upon all the activities that constitute the process of making sense and thereby creates reality, whether it be a fictional one or not.

It is at this point that I locate the pragmatist fundament informing the novel. For pragmatists, in this case the founder of the movement Charles S. Peirce, understood that reality is the product of both communal, intersubjective and individual, subjective activities. According to Peirce, it all starts with the individual trying to make sense of what he or she sees, and this is done by guessing – more or less wildly. Peirce calls these processes of guessing, which have the internal structure of a logical inference, abductions.[7] Abductions perform the most crucial function: in every conscious moment they transform one class of signs – sensory impressions, the percepts – into another class of signs, perceptual judgments, thereby creating meaning. To put it differently, abduction transforms images into texts, and these texts, our perceptual judgments, are our prime interpretations of reality. Peirce writes: "Abduction is the process of forming an explanatory hypothesis. It is the only logical operation which introduces any new idea" (1931–1958: 5.171).[8] As such, abduction is our gateway to creativity, since there is always the possibility of interpreting percepts *differently*, in lesser or greater proximity to culturally preformed patterns. It thus does not come as a surprise that Peirce calls perceptual judgments "hypotheses" about reality. Peirce gives the following description of the everyday role of abductions:

> Looking out my window this lovely spring morning I see an azalea in full bloom. No, no! I do not see that; though that is the only way I can describe what I see. *That* is a proposition, a sentence, a fact; but what I perceive is not proposition, sentence, fact, but only an image, which I make intelligible in part by means of a statement of fact. This statement is abstract; but what I see is concrete. I perform an abduction when I so much as express in a sentence anything I see. The truth is that the whole fabric of our knowledge is one matted felt of pure hypothesis confirmed and refined by induction. Not the smallest advance can be made in

---

[7] I have published extensively on the topics of pragmatism and the logic of abduction. For the most recent publications cf. for instance my "'Amazing Mazes': The Locus of the Subject in Charles S. Peirce's Pragmatist Epistemology" (2013) or "Madness as a Liminal State in the American Short Story: Edgar Allan Poe's Ratiocination and Charles Sanders Peirce's Logic of Abduction" (2015b).

[8] References to Charles Sanders Peirce's *Collected Papers* are generally made in the form of decimal quotation, i.e. indicating volume and paragraph. Thus, a reference like the above "5.171" would refer to Volume V, § 171.

knowledge beyond the stage of vacant staring, without making an abduction at every step. (Ms 692, qtd. in Sebeok/Umiker-Sebeok 1983: 16)

Guessing or making abductions at every step thus constitutes our interminable activity in the process of making sense of what we perceive. Thus, faced with the particularly challenging task of interpreting a dream, as Ethan is, or just having to come to terms with what we perceive in everyday situations, we are always forced to solve riddles, to make sense of what we see and thereby create reality. Otherwise, our interaction with our perceptions would never leave the realm of "vacant staring," as Peirce puts it. In this view, reality is not the source of cognitive processes but rather its result. These results that we have created individually – yet in reference to a specific cultural context – form our understanding of ourselves, of reality, and they determine our beliefs and habits which in turn determine our actions and interactions with others. The results of these subjective guesses then enter the process of intersubjective exchange whereby a given culture negotiates what it holds to be real. Here is Peirce on the pragmatist understanding of reality:

> The real, then, is that which, sooner or later, information and reasoning would finally result in, and which is therefore independent of the vagaries of me and you. Thus, the very origin of the conception of reality shows that this conception essentially involves the notion of a COMMUNITY, without definite limits, and capable of a definite increase of knowledge. (1931–1958: 5.311)

I understand the multi-voiced project of *The Blazing World* as a reflection on these subjective and intersubjective activities whereby reality is created, on the creative act of making sense of perceptions, on guessing connections between singular elements, on bringing all of these together into various narratives of reality, on comparing these narratives and finally coming up with one particular version of the real.

Ethan Lord's dream text and dream interpretations illustrate with particular clarity one crucial moment in this process, the moment of producing creative hypotheses. What better exemplification of abductive guesses than the attempt to make sense of your own unconscious narratives? Yet what Ethan Lord recognizes with some dissatisfaction in the end is that "interpretation is always multiple" and that "associations can lead a person down many paths" (Hustvedt 2014: 270). And this is exactly what we, as readers, also have to realize when we emerge out of the text as part of our own subjective artwork 'Maskings 4,' in a process that Hustvedt herself calls the "excursion into you that is also I" (2010: 38).

Works Cited

Cavendish, Margaret. 1668 [1666]. *Observations upon Experimental Philosophy: To Which is Added, The Description of a New Blazing World*. 2nd ed. London: A. Maxwell.

Grønstad, Asbjørn. 2012. "Ekphrasis Refigured: Writing Seeing in Siri Hustvedt's *What I Loved*." *Mosaic* 45.3: 33–48.

Hellker, Paul and Melanie Yergeau. 2011. "Autism and Rhetoric." *College English* 73.5: 485–497.

Hustvedt, Siri. 2010. "Embodied Visions: What Does It Mean to Look at a Work of Art?" *The Yale Review* 98.4: 22–38.

Hustvedt, Siri. 2011. "Three Emotional Stories: Reflections on Memory, the Imagination, Narrative, and the Self." *Neuropsychoanalysis* 13.2: 187–196.

Hustvedt, Siri. 2014. *The Blazing World*. New York: Simon & Schuster.

Peirce, Charles Sanders. 1931–1958. *Collected Papers of Charles Sanders Peirce*. Eds. Charles Hartshorne, Paul Weiss and Arthur W. Burks. 8 vols. Cambridge: Harvard University Press.

Rohr, Susanne. 2013. "'Amazing Mazes': The Locus of the Subject in Charles S. Peirce's Pragmatist Epistemology." *Amerikastudien /American Studies* 58.2: 199–212.

Rohr, Susanne. 2015a. "Screening Madness in American Culture." *Journal of Medical Humanities* 36.3: 231–240.

Rohr, Susanne. 2015b. "Madness as a Liminal State in the American Short Story: Edgar Allan Poe's Ratiocination and Charles Sanders Peirce's Logic of Abduction." In: Jochen Achilles and Ina Bergmann (eds.). *Liminality and the Short Story: Boundary Crossings in American, Canadian, and British Writing*. New York: Routledge. 175–185.

Sarrett, Jennifer C. 2011. "Trapped Children: Popular Images of Children with Autism in the 1960s and 2000s." *Journal of Medical Humanities* 32.2: 141–153.

Sebeok, Thomas A., and Jean Umiker-Sebeok. 1983. "'You Know My Method': A Juxtaposition of Charles S. Peirce and Sherlock Holmes." In: Umberto Eco and Thomas A. Sebeok (eds.). *The Sign of Three: Dupin, Holmes, Peirce*. Bloomington: Indiana University Press. 11–54.

Vision, Perception, and Power

Carla Schulz-Hoffmann
"What fascinate me are the journeys that begin with looking and only looking": Siri Hustvedt's Visual Imagination

It was the lively memory of my first reading of *The Blindfold* in the 1990s, and subsequently of later works, that motivated me to ask Siri Hustvedt in 2012 to contribute to the catalogue of my farewell exhibition at the Bayerische Staatsgemäldesammlungen *Frauen. Picasso, Beckmann, de Kooning* (Schulz-Hoffmann 2012), an invitation which she spontaneously accepted. Already the title of her essay, "A Woman Looking at Men Looking at Women" (Hustvedt 2012: 188), indicates a pictorially inspired method, which was also a guideline for my own project. For in choosing this overarching topic, my aim was not primarily the presentation of strictly art historical models of explanation, and even less the attempt to elucidate the relationship of the artists to their partners, lovers, or muses, through the medium of paintings. What was central to my conception was rather a double perspective of artistic reception, as far as it involves the relation between the gaze of the artist and the gaze of the person looking at the artwork. Can the perception and interpretation of the one be fused into a unified whole with that of the other? Simplifying matters, one could say that the individual gaze of artist and viewer, which is shaped by their respective coordinates of biography, subjective characteristics, sociocultural environment etc., accumulates a wealth of possible fragments of reality and perception, but that they can never be fully congruent. What is essential is whether an artwork triggers a reaction in its observers – positive or negative is not significant here –, whether they can connect it to their horizon of experience and that way make it graspable for themselves.

"For one road to reality is by way of pictures. I don't believe there's any better road" (Canetti 1982: 113). This is how, in the second part of his biography, Elias Canetti laconically describes the existential significance of art, not without, however, failing to add that it entails interaction. After all, only the viewer's gaze has a capacity to find the questions that affect his or her reality in a painting: "That is why pictures slumber for generations: no one can see them with the experience that awakes them" (Canetti 1982: 113). Marcel Duchamp described much the same phenomenon when he articulated his now legendary theory that "it is the spectator who makes the pictures" (Duchamp 1994: 83). It is the resolutely contemporary, but to a certain extent always subjective gaze that seeks engagement with a work of art. What questions does it raise? Does it still have the power to unsettle or annoy us – or does it belong to that far-away Olympus of automatic, unquestioning acceptance? Does it still touch a nerve, even today? Is it provocative, or just hopelessly outdated?

In the center stands the artwork in its optical presence and density. And even though, as in the case of Picasso's, Beckmann's, and de Kooning's pictures of females (Schulz-Hoffmann 2012), the artists' biographies, the general social, historical, and political as well as artistic developments by which they were influenced, are of course taken into consideration as a basis and corrective, the starting-point of any such critical-creative process remains the artwork itself. It is the invitation to the viewer to enter an open dialogue.

> But art is not possible without intersubjective human experience because art is always a gift made for another, not a specific other, but a generalized other person who is asked to read or to listen to or to look at. Art necessarily establishes a relation between the artist and an imaginary reader, viewer, or listener; it is inherently dialogical. Therefore, *all visual art implies a spectator*, even when that other is part of the self, the viewing self. (Hustvedt 2010: 34)

It was precisely this immediate, insistent approach which has captured me right from the start in Hustvedt's view on artworks.

The following thoughts attempt to describe more precisely the ways in which Hustvedt deals with visual art in her essays about single artworks or artists, which are interconnected like a string of small, precious pearls, but especially also in some of her novels. I am not relying thereby on stringent art historical models or theories but am rather interested in the epistemic question of elucidating the specific perspective of the author on works of visual art, and to relate it to her work as a writer.[1]

What is important, first of all, is that Siri Hustvedt explicitly talks about *pictures* – i.e., about two-dimensional works –, that genre within the visual arts which is limited to its own immanent space. Pictures, according to the classic formula, represent a view through a window into another world imagined by the artist. In contrast, sculptures or installations are part of the real spatial environment.

> A painting allows my eyes to focus on a space delimited by an absolute perimeter and ponder a still, silent, and odorless image. This is a highly restricted, contemplative form of look-

---

[1] For this, see some excellent literary analyses of Siri Hustvedt's works, in which these questions are thematized as well, among others Christine Marks, or Hubert Zapf (Marks 2014; Zapf 2008).

ing that is in many ways much easier than absorbing the myriad sights of daily life. (Hustvedt 2005: xvi)

This objective immobility of pictures corresponds to the perception by the viewer, which is necessarily not complete with a single look but unfolds as a process: "[M]y own experience with a picture can't mirror that simultaneity. My engagement with a painting takes place in time" (Hustvedt 2005: xvi).

1. "Visual art exists only to be seen"

At first sight, many of Siri Hustvedt's observations about visual art may strike one as almost banal in their pointedness and apparent self-evidence. They often simply seem to repeat truisms, such as, when she pithily states:

> Visual art exists only to be seen. It is the silent encounter between the viewer, 'I,' and the object, 'it.' That 'it,' however, is the material trace of another human consciousness. The artist, who is missing from the scene, has nevertheless left us a work, an act of pure will, which has no practical purpose. The painting carries within it the residue of an 'I' or a 'you.' In art, the meeting between viewer and thing implies intersubjectivity. (Hustvedt 2005: xix)

But it is the rigorous application of this postulate of 'intersubjectivity,' of an open discourse between the artwork as an individual utterance of the artist and the responding viewer, and, most importantly, of the commitment to the emotionality of perception, that constitutes the enriching contribution of Siri Hustvedt for the contemporary debate about visual arts.

It is not so much the – doubtlessly legitimate – wish to underpin this procedure scientifically with knowledge gained from neurobiological research than the directness of her vision that opens stunning new perspectives on artworks. Thus she remarks somewhat smugly but with a core of truth:

> Most art historians are similarly queasy about emotion and instead write about form, color, influences, or historical context. Feeling, however, is not only unavoidable, it is crucial to understanding a work of art. Indeed, an artwork becomes senseless without it. (Hustvedt 2012: 190)

To an extent, this statement applies without doubt for any form of artistic work. In her introduction to the essay collection *Mysteries of the Rectangle* (Hustvedt 2005), however, the author encapsulates a central distinction in the perception of literature, music, and film on the one hand, and painting on the other hand. While the former have to rely on the successive experience of reading, hearing, or looking, painting is

> there all at once [...]. Hours may pass but a painting will not gain or lose any part of itself. It has no beginning, no middle, and no end. I love painting because in its immutable stillness it seems to exist outside time in a way no other art can. (Hustvedt 2005: xv)

This may be the reason why Siri Hustvedt in her writings assigns such an unusually prominent role to visual art. The degree of compositional complexity thereby increases from the art essays to the novels. While in the former case, the dialogue occurs exclusively between viewer/author and work, an additional level is created in the novels, that of the (inter-)acting protagonists. For the reader, the *recipient*, both forms of texts develop their own appeal, one through its focusing on two partners, the other through the interplay between a multiplicity of different *participants* – the co-actors in the novel itself and those who are reading it.

2. "Painting is there all at once"

Let me start with a few examples to understand Siri Hustvedt's specific way of engaging with *one* artwork. Her starting-point for every analysis is the open contemplation of the work, which claims all senses. This apparently obvious assumption, which on closer inspection turns out to present an obstacle that is hard to overcome, to her is a basic condition for any adequate approach to visual art. The trust in the appropriateness of my first, uninhibited vision, of my spontaneous response – such is her creed – offers the sole viable point of entry into any further dialogue. I must be aware that "the experience of looking at visual art always involves a form of mirroring, which may be, but is not necessarily, conscious" (Hustvedt 2010: 22).

By accepting that my physical and psychic perception initially precedes the rational deciphering of formal features, I gain a basis without which a satisfactory engagement with art would be prevented.

> I look at Picasso's *Weeping Woman,* and before I have time to analyze what I am seeing, to speak of color or form or gesture or style, I have registered the face, hand, and part of a torso on the canvas and have an immediate emotional response to the image. The picture upsets me. (Hustvedt 2012: 191)

At the same time, she is aware that her gaze is guided to a degree by the artist.

> I am looking at a work – at "Painter's Forms." And this looking is a little like having someone else's dream. Because the objects of still life are ordinary – a sausage, a melon, a bowl, a boot – their translation into paint intensifies them. They are dignified by the metamorphosis we call art. (Hustvedt 2005: 59)

Yet she reacts to this dream of the artist, which pre-establishes in the picture a specific form and atmosphere, on premises that are completely her own: She dreams the dream of the artist anew under the conditions of her own biography, her history, her character, and her singular subjectivity.

"Our temperaments in tandem with our personal stories as we grow as human beings will affect our responses to a painting and become part of the dialogue" (Hustvedt 2010: 40). Hustvedt manages to draw especially beautiful analogies in this dialogic contemplation in view of *still* works, which depict little activity, and underline the objective stasis of the representation in their motifs. This applies to still lifes, for example, but also to the paintings by Vermeer that seem to be resting in themselves, or even to the cycle *October 18, 1977* by Gerhard Richter, which conveys the impression of frozen *memory*. Giorgio Morandi's still lifes demand concentrated attention from the viewer, a readiness to get fully involved in them. To the passing gaze, the countless small treasures, which are always similar in repertoire, mainly modest in format, reduced in color, and completely unagitated, may appear unambitious, almost bland. Nothing happens which one could hold onto, and yet, if one opens oneself to them, one is gripped by their plain, completely unassuming presence. The absence of what makes up our ordinary lives – speed, variegation, profusion of things and sounds – captures us in its spell.

> He may have found his path to freedom, but that path was one of restraint, patience, repression, and suggestion. His canvases are controlled and masterly. Looking at the actual paintings is important, because the light that seems to come out of them reproduces very poorly. These canvases reveal themselves slowly and reward the spectator who bothers to look long and hard. In the end, they create a surprising tension between thought and the senses. (Hustvedt 2005: 132)

Incomparably floating and yet precisely to the point is likewise Siri Hustvedt's text about Vermeer's *Woman with a Pearl Necklace.*

Already her realization why she happened to choose precisely this among the works of Vermeer illustrates how strongly she trusts in a first intuitive judgment, which is not yet logically founded, "[w]hile I was looking at the painting, I realized that I had picked it because of its empty center, a quality that distinguished it from other related works" (Hustvedt 2005: 15). And as if in passing she subsequently describes the incomparable calm, which distinguishes this pic-

Figure 1: Giorgio Morandi, *Still Life*, 1916, Oil on canvas, The Museum of Modern Art, New York.

"What fascinate me are the journeys that begin with looking and only looking" — 271

Figure 2: Jan (Johannes) Vermeer, *Woman with a Pearl Necklace*, c. 1662–1665, Oil on canvas, Gemäldegalerie, Staatliche Museen zu Berlin, Germany.

ture to a degree which lends it its aura. "In fact, the painting is stillness itself – a woman alone and motionless in a room. I am looking in at her solitude, and she cannot see me" (Hustvedt 2005: 14). By immersing ourselves fully into this depiction, meditatively melting with it, as it were, we become conscious of the enchantment of a kind of *supra-real* essence of pure *Being-as-Itself*, in which myriad small moments of our existence converge.

> In Vermeer, the gulf between the symbol and the real is closed. *Woman with a Pearl Necklace* is a work of reflection at its most sublime. The viewer reflects on the woman who also reflects and is reflected, and through this mirroring of wonder, Vermeer elevates not only his creature – the woman in the painting – but all of us who look at her, because looking at her and the memory of looking at her become nothing less than an affirmation of the strangeness and beauty of simply being alive. (Hustvedt 2005: 25)

In contrast to this beauty of stillness, of *Being-With-Oneself* as a quintessence of life, the *Baader-Meinhof-Zyklus* by Gerhard Richter conveys the tragic, frozen omnipresence of the past. The fifteen-part work cycle, which was created ten years after the death of three leading RAF terrorists in the Stammheim Prison, is based on press and police photos from different years. The dull gray motifs that are blurred in varying degrees converge in their *colorlessness* into a total cosmos, whose timeless intensity is hard to resist. Siri describes this unusual quality, which turns the cycle into a contemporary form of history painting, from the intensity of her emotional response.

> Standing in that room, I felt that with these paintings Richter broke through an invisible barrier, and after I had left it, I became more convinced that I was right. There is something oddly liberating about looking at those pictures of the dead, as if the artist had discovered an extraordinary balance between perception and memory, recognition and blindness, photo-document and apparition. The corpse, after all, is human erasure. It means becoming nobody. (Hustvedt 2005: 160–165)

3. "It's the story part"

Hustvedt's narratives, which frequently circle around art, also consistently go beyond it by offering the opportunity to interlink viewer/author, artist, work *and* acting persons with each other. In fact, they are the foil against which the complex interplay between the single actors as well as the inextricable interfusion of the different spaces they *inhabit* can alone develop.

Already in *The Blindfold*, a book which made Siri Hustvedt famous almost overnight in 1993, crucial aspects of this tight-meshed web of relationships are formulated. The name of the heroine, "Iris," is itself programmatic. It refers, on the one hand, unmistakably to the author (Siri in reverse reading) and on the other hand to the seeing eye, its "iris." It is the *vision of the author*, which is mirrored in manifold ways in the narrated events, and which reflects its subjective perception in the image of others (the artist as well as those who are confronted with his or her work in the story) and thereby merges with it.

Both mysterious and fascinating strong characters accompany the impoverished student Iris through a labyrinthine New York, which seems mutated into a disturbing parallel world. Is it her own *Night Visions*, which she encounters in Mr. Morning, the photographer George, or the mentally deranged, threatening Mrs. O.? Or in her teacher and secret lover Professor Rose, whom she assists in the translation of a German novella, whose mentally fragile protagonist Klaus temporarily becomes her alter ego? But doesn't the art critic Paris, her presumed friend, who in fact only uses her like a parasite for his own purposes, also bear traces of her? All of this is right and wrong at the same time, for all these characters contribute countless facets to possible combinations of her self. What emerges are manifold kaleidoscopes, which, as soon as one has formed them into a unified image, collapse into new formations.

Characteristic of this is the great portrait photograph of Iris which George is taking in a session. She is disturbed about the disparate result, which strikes her as at the same time familiar and alien. Drifting phantomlike through strange places in New York, the picture causes confusion. Nothing in it appears to be based on reliable facts, nothing corresponds to a graspable reality. It gains a life of its own far beyond the limits of the comprehensible, and at the same time aligns itself in a mysterious way with every other being, the objectively represented *Iris* as well as all the others that it encounters.[2]

---

[2] A similar experience is related by Mabel in *The Enchantment of Lily Dahl*: "'The portrait's bothering me, Lily.' [...] 'when I look at it, I feel upset. I'm well aware that no one's going to care one way or the other about the identity of the old lady in the Edward Shapiro's painting, and yet I feel that I'm being pulled into a crisis a part of me willed and another part resists. [...] 'I'm not sure he even knows what he's doing, but there's something in him that's aggressive, not his manner, you understand, but the work – he strikes the heart.' Mabel swallowed. 'He painted his wife. Did you know that?'" (Hustvedt 1997: 208–209).
Christine Marks concludes: "This dangerous exchangeability of reality and fiction, of the inner and the outer, finds its most powerful manifestation in the photograph George takes of Iris" (Marks 2014: 90).

4. "A feeling of vertigo"

The rigorously exhibited subjectivity of perception of every individual person in every phase of life and, especially, the unfathomable interconnection of countless single moments, which are fused in the creation as well as the contemplation of an artwork, evokes models of the philosophy of life as they were formulated by Henri Bergson and later became formative of the ideas of Futurism.[3] Exemplary cases of this are the portraits which Umberto Boccioni, the leading figure of futurism, made of his mother, such as *Volumi orizzontali*.

Movement here shifts from the linear idea of a sequence from A to B, as it was experimentally explored in the photographs of Muybridge or in early film, into a dynamic process. The interior kinesis of the character is transferred to the ambience, forming a unity with it. Movement is understood as co-temporality, as endless simultaneity. This idea of the picture corresponded, in the view of the futurists, to the incessantly changing modern life. More rigorously than his friends, however, Boccioni conceives of 'dynamism' and 'simultaneity' as co-temporality of all physical *and* psychic aspects, which are connected in his perception with the represented subject.

The "elan vital" (Bergson), the wholeness of rational and non-rational, creative and dynamic elements, the fusion of reason with intuition, instinct with sensuousness, went hand in hand with a radical rejection of positivism and materialism. Bergson distinguishes between 'intellect' as a form of thinking characteristic of the natural sciences, and 'intuition' as a form of thinking rooted in lived experience, and summarizes: "But it is to the very inwardness of life that intuition leads us, – by intuition I mean instinct that has become disinterested, self-conscious, capable of reflecting upon its object and of enlarging it indefinitely" (Bergson 1922: 186).

Siri Hustvedt finds a fitting example for this subjectivity of perception in *The Blindfold*. Being asked about Giorgione's *The Tempest*, Iris describes the composition in minute detail including the background. One is left with the impression that she possesses a photographic memory, but then is all the more surprised she does not mention the young knight on the left margin of the picture, who is characterized as an observer of the scene, and in fact believes he does not exist. Only

---

[3] Bergson was influential in recent times for Gilles Deleuze and Maurice Merleau-Ponty among others, who in turn were important for the theoretical framework of Siri Hustvedt's thought and writing.

"What fascinate me are the journeys that begin with looking and only looking" — 275

Figure 3: Umberto Boccioni, *Volumi orizzontali*, 1912, Oil on canvas, Bayerische Staatsgemäldesammlungen München.

a reproduction of the painting can convince her of her error.[4] How could this happen to Iris, why this selective perception? Her friend, the art historian Paris, offers her an explanation which is equally astonishing and insightful: "'You became the man,' Paris said. 'You stepped into his shoes and promptly deleted him from the painting. He's a spectator, too, almost a double of the person viewing the picture. For you he was expendable. You saw him but didn't see

---

4 Siri Hustvedt here draws on a personal experience from a seminar: "I gave this extraordinary gaffe to the heroine of my first novel, *The Blindfold*" (Hustvedt 2005: 5).

Figure 4: Giorgione, *The Tempest*, c. 1503–1504, Oil on canvas, Accademia Venice.

him'" (Hustvedt 1993: 152). Yes, she *had to overlook* the knight on the left margin of the picture to build up as close as possible a contact with the main figure on the painting, to feel with her in all the fibers of her self, to be able to completely empathize with her.

> I do not see myself when I look at a painting. I see the imaginary person in the canvas. I have not disappeared from myself. I am aware of my feelings – my awe, irritation, distress, and admiration – but for the time being, the painted person fills up my perception. She is of

me while I look and, later, she is of me when I remember her. In memory [...]. (Hustvedt 2012: 190)

Siri Hustvedt is always concerned with this double role of the observer, who perceives an artwork with all senses individually and at the same time shares the reflection of another, the artist, about a certain theme. Art "is activated both by a cultural mythos that has decidedly religious undertones and by a real, even transforming, relation between the viewer and the thing viewed" (Hustvedt 2005: 4). This symbiotic relationship involves an element of voyeurism, which turns the viewer into an accomplice:

> *The Tempest*, it seems to me, is about voyeurism itself, and it isn't static, but reveals a game of glances in an imaginary place. Bewildered, the spectator, who is always 'I,' is drawn into the mysterious otherness of the nude woman. [...] The drama of looking depicted in *The Tempest* is a reflective one. I, as spectator, am made conscious of my status as voyeur, which in turn binds me to the man in the foreground. (Hustvedt 2005: 7–8)

In the figure of the artist Bill Wechsler in *What I Loved* (Hustvedt 2003), Siri Hustvedt carries this mutual collapsing of subject and object to an extreme. "'They're all self-portraits,' he said. 'While I was working with Violet, I realized that I was mapping out a territory in myself I hadn't seen before, or maybe a territory between her and me'" (Hustvedt 2003: 15).

She draws on ideas here which Willem de Kooning has formulated especially in connection with his pictures of women. The only certainty, according to de Kooning's conviction, is a reality, and therefore also an art, that undergoes permanent alterations. This is what constitutes its disturbing force as well as its intoxicating beauty, which does not want fixed images, avoids any stasis, and instead celebrates the one glimpse of an eye which can change everything:

> When I'm falling, I am doing all right. And when I am slipping, I say, 'Hey, this is very interesting.' It is when I am standing upright that bothers me. I'm not doing so good. I'm stiff, you know [...]. As a matter of fact, I'm really slipping most of the time into that glimpse. That is a wonderful sensation, I realize right now, to slip into this glimpse. I'm like a slipping glimpser. (De Kooning 1994: 53)

De Kooning wants to capture these fleeting moments in pictures which retain an utmost degree of movement in the stroke of the brush, the technique, the dissolving colors, displaying his permanently changing emotional disposition in the act of painting itself.

When looking from here once more at the protagonists in *What I Loved*, it is somewhat amusing to discover that Bill, who has so much in common with de Kooning in his theoretical comments, seems to be light years away from him in his art. In contrast, the observer, in this case the author, vicariously assumes the role of the artist. She is the one who assimilates into her perception the floating quality, the constant changeability suggested by de Kooning's paintings, and makes it her own principle. "But with paintings, when you look hard and keep looking, every once in a while you may begin to suffer a feeling of vertigo, and that is a sign that the world may be turning upside down" (Hustvedt 2012: 200).

This feeling of "falling out of the world," according to Hustvedt, can occur as a shock-like experience at the first viewing of a picture. In *The Enchantment of Lily Dahl,* Mabel, the older friend and mentor of Iris, reacts to a portrait that the artist Ed Shapiro shows her by fainting.

> "I don't understand it," she said slowly. "It's the painting, of course. It happened once before many years ago when I was a student, with a reproduction, if you can imagine that. The professor passed around that famous Grünewald painting of the dead Christ. I took one look at it and keeled over." (Hustvedt 1997: 113–114)

In an extreme form, Hustvedt here exemplifies the powerful effect that art can exercise when, like Mabel, one opens oneself to it in a completely unprotected way. But the irritation, which it simultaneously provokes in its co-actors as well as its readers, again produces still other perspectives and asks new questions. How would I react? Is there, in the multiplicity of roles which I encounter here, a role for myself, and which reactions would be appropriate for me? Both astonished and relieved, I realize that *all* the indicated facets could potentially define my own perception – provided that I dare to assume this *unprotected gaze.* This tricky game with a multitude of different angles, observer-positions, and their manifold interfaces, which Hustvedt performs, takes its origin in the apparently so simple concentration on *looking at something* with all one's senses: "What fascinate me are the journeys that begin with looking and only looking" (Hustvedt 2005: xxi). But this special form of looking also requires an unusual *discipline,* which some find suspect: the obligation to engage in an unrestricted participation in the process of seeing!

Works Cited

Bergson, Henri. 1922 [1912]. *Creative Evolution.* Trans. Arthur Mitchell. London: Macmillan.
Canetti, Elias. 1982. *The Torch in My Ear.* London: Granta Books.
Duchamp, Marcel. 1994. Cited in Michael Crichton, *Jasper Johns.* New York: Harry N. Abrams.
Hustvedt, Siri. 1993. *The Blindfold.* London: Hodder and Stoughton.
Hustvedt, Siri. 1997. *The Enchantment of Lily Dahl.* London: Hodder and Stoughton.
Hustvedt, Siri. 2003. *What I Loved.* London: Hodder and Stoughton.

"What fascinate me are the journeys that begin with looking and only looking" —— 279

Hustvedt, Siri. 2005. *Mysteries of the Rectangle: Essays on Painting*. Princeton: Princeton Architectural Press.
Hustvedt, Siri. 2010. *Embodied Visions: What Does it Mean to Look at a Work of Art?* Berlin/München: Deutscher Kunstverlag.
Hustvedt, Siri. 2012. "A Woman Looking at Men Looking at Women." In: Carla Schulz-Hoffmann (ed.). *Women: Picasso, Beckmann, de Kooning*, exh. cat. Pinakothek der Moderne (München, 2012). Ostfildern: Hatje Cantz. 188–201.
Kooning, Willem de. 1994. Cited in Richard Shiff, "Water and Lipstick: De Kooning in Transition." In: *Willem de Kooning: Paintings*, exh. cat. National Gallery of Art, Washington, D.C.; The Metropolitan Museum of Modern Art, New York; Tate Gallery, London. 33–73.
Marks, Christine. 2014. *"I am because you are": Relationality in the Works of Siri Hustvedt*. Heidelberg: Winter.
Peña Aguado, María Isabel. 2010. "The Schelling Lecture on the Arts and Humanities / Internationale Schelling-Vorlesung 2010." In: Siri Hustvedt. *Embodied Visions: What Does it Mean to Look at a Work of Art?* Berlin/München: Deutscher Kunstverlag. 6–15.
Schulz-Hoffmann, Carla. 2012. "Women: Pablo Picasso, Max Beckmann, Willem de Kooning. An Introduction." In: Carla Schulz-Hoffmann (ed.). *Women: Picasso, Beckmann, de Kooning*, exh. cat. Pinakothek der Moderne (München, 2012). Ostfildern: Hatje Cantz. 11–29.
Schulz-Hoffmann, Carla (ed.). 2012. *Women: Picasso, Beckmann, de Kooning*, exh. cat. Pinakothek der Moderne (München, 2012). Ostfildern: Hatje Cantz.
Zapf, Hubert. 2008. "Narrative, Ethics, and Postmodern Art in Siri Hustvedt's *What I Loved*". In: Astrid Erll, Herbert Grabes, Ansgar Nünning (eds.). *Ethics in Culture: The Dissemination of Values through Literature and Other Media*. Berlin: De Gruyter. 171–194.

Illustrations

Umberto Boccioni
   Volumi orrizzontali, 1912
   Oil on canvas
   95 × 95,5 cm
   Bayerische Staatsgemäldesammlungen München
   © bpk / Bayerische Staatsgemäldesammlungen
Giorgione
   The Tempest, c. 1503–1504
   Oil on canvas
   32¼ × 28¾ in.
   Accademia, Venice
   Museo dell'Opera Metropolitana, Siena, Italy
   © Scala, Florence – courtesy of the Ministero Beni e Att. Culturali
Giorgio Morandi
   Still Life, 1916
   Oil on canvas

32½ × 22⅝ in.
The Museum of Modern Art, New York
© Artists Rights Society, New York
© Digital Image, The Museum of Modern Art, New York / Scala, Florence
Jan (Johannes) Vermeer
Woman with a Pearl Necklace, c. 1662–1665
Oil on canvas
21½ × 17½ in.
Gemäldegalerie, Staatliche Museen zu Berlin, Germany
Photo: Joerg P. Anders
© Bildarchiv Preußischer Kulturbesitz, Berlin

Additional References

Willem de Kooning
Woman II, 1952
Oil, enamel and charcoal on canvas
59 × 43 in.
The Museum of Modern Art, New York, Gift of Blanchette Hooker Rockefeller, 1995
© The Willem de Kooning Foundation, New York / VG Bild-Kunst, Bonn
© Digital Image, The Museum of Modern Art, New York / Scala, Florence

Gerhard Richter
Confrontation 2 (Gegenüberstellung 2), from the series *October 18, 1977*, 1988
Oil on canvas
44 × 40¼ in.
The Museum of Modern Art, New York
© Gerhard Richter
© Digital Image, The Museum of Modern Art, New York / Scala, Art Resource

Gerhard Richter
Hanged (Erhängte), from the series *October 18, 1977*, 1988
Oil on canvas
79 × 55 in.
The Museum of Modern Art, New York
© Gerhard Richter
© Digital Image, The Museum of Modern Art, New York / Scala, Art Resource

Gerhard Richter
Dead I (Tote I), from the series *October 18, 1977*, 1988
Oil on canvas
24½ × 28¾ in.
The Museum of Modern Art, New York
© Gerhard Richter
© Digital Image, The Museum of Modern Art, New York / Scala, Art Resource

Astrid Böger
"I look and sometimes I see": The Art of Perception in Siri Hustvedt's Novels

Few authors have tackled the complex relationship between looking and seeing, remembering and feeling as consistently as Siri Hustvedt has, both in her fictional and her non-fictional works published to date. Here, my aim is to create some fruitful resonances between her earlier works with a focus on *The Blindfold* (1993) and *What I Loved* (2003), as well as her more recent ones including the essay collection *Living, Thinking, Looking* (2012) and finally her latest novel *The Blazing World*, published in 2014. In particular, Hustvedt's engagement with visual art in her novels will be explored as a multi-layered and open-ended process, at the same time profoundly subjective and dialogical. More specifically, aesthetic experience has a major influence on how her protagonists move around in the world even as they try to lead meaningful lives against considerable odds. Aesthetics, in other words, is closely tied up with ethics in Hustvedt's œuvre (cf. Zapf 2008: 187–188). Throughout her fictional and non-fictional works alike, visual art thus serves as a privileged site for negotiating the self in relation to others, as has previously been argued by Christine Marks, among others (cf. Marks 2014: 67–129). For instance, the self-perception of the central protagonist of *The Blindfold* is seriously challenged when an uncanny photo portrait made by a friend of hers develops a life of its own and haunts her throughout much of the narrative. Moreover, while close personal friendships can certainly develop around the shared appreciation of art, as is the case in *What I Loved*, they are likewise compromised when its perception becomes distorted or when concrete artworks are used, in the same book, like a weapon to hurt others. On the other hand, visual art can also become an arena to explore different versions or perhaps rather embodiments of one's self, as can be seen in Hustvedt's latest novel *The Blazing World*, where the protagonist Harriet Burden takes on the persona of three different male artists, *inter alia*, in order to finally earn the critical appreciation she had been denied as a female artist for most of her creative life. Generally speaking, while art has always taken center stage in Hustvedt's novels, there has of late been a marked shift toward a more interactive, dialogical process of meaning making via art which is not limited to the world inhabited by the protagonists but which extends to ours as well.

1. Looking but not Seeing: *The Blindfold*

In the opening paragraph of Siri Hustvedt's first novel *The Blindfold*, the problematic relationship between seeing, recognition, and affect is established by introducing the perceptual as well as emotional predicament of the female protagonist Iris Vegan as follows:

> Sometimes even now I think I see him in the street or standing in a window or bent over a book in a coffee shop. And in that instant, before I understand that it's someone else, my lungs tighten and I lose my breath. (1993: 9)

Among other things, what is remarkable about this opening is the palpable tension between the protagonist, whose account is rendered in the first person singular, and a male other she (falsely) perceives in anonymous scenarios across New York City, the urban setting of all the novels considered here. Even though the moment of (mis)recognition is limited to a brief instant in each case, the physical and emotional repercussions are nonetheless strongly registered. Interestingly, the relationship between the I-narrator and the other referred to as "he" is negotiated through sight alone, which is also suggested by the "I" homonymously invoking the "eye" of the perceiving subject. Arguing strongly in favor of the first person singular when attempting to render subjective experience, Hustvedt commented on the intimate connection between perception and perspective in a keynote lecture delivered in 2012 at the annual conference of the German Association for American Studies as follows:

> We all bodily inhabit the first person, and it's a phenomenological truth that what you see depends upon where you are. Personal perception is crucial to experience, and fortunately, we are not plants, but mobile beings exploring our world. We can literally move around other people and objects and get multiple perspectives on them. And this very dynamism assumes an openness to the world of others and things that changes what we do and what we are. (2013: 118)

Relying on insights from European phenomenology and American pragmatism, Hustvedt argues that there is no objective, but only subjective experience primarily based on "varying perspectives" or *points of view*, as well as sensations and feelings (2013: 113). As a consequence, perception is always embodied experience, as already expounded by Maurice Merleau-Ponty in *Phenomenology of Perception*, clearly an important inspiration for Hustvedt. Being both highly subjective and embodied, perception is always a form of self-perception as well. What is more, it is by definition limited and forever changing, therefore fraught with uncertainty and potential for error. Indeed, the problem of (mis)recognition haunts

Hustvedt's entire fictional œuvre, often compromising the heroine's sense of self or even her bodily integrity, as seen in the opening of *The Blindfold* above.

The novel's protagonist is a graduate student of literature whose very name suggests the delicacy of a flower while also referring to the central organ of seeing. What is more, Iris is introduced as someone who struggles to form a coherent perspective on her precarious existence as she is pulled back and forth between various males who dominate and, more often than not, obstruct her self-perception. These include a mysterious urban recluse who calls himself Mr. Morning and pays her to write and tape detailed descriptions of objects left by a female murder victim. Next, there is Stephen, her sometime boyfriend, and George, his artist friend and likely lover, who hide the real nature of their relationship from Iris, thereby purposefully keeping her in the dark. Moreover, a physician by the name of Dr. Fish is consulted, though to little avail, when Iris is incapacitated by (literally) blinding migraines. And finally, Prof. Michael Rose, her literature professor at Columbia University, eventually becomes her lover before things get out of control following an erotic encounter involving the titular blindfolding incident. Significantly, Iris's relationship to each of the male characters just named is primarily cast in visual terms, frequently taking the form of voyeurism. What is more, vision appears throughout as embodied vision and is thus prone to failure or blindness, be it voluntary (as in the blindfolding scene) or due to illness (such as migraine).

Even though there are obviously plenty of mysterious men complicating Iris's life, there is arguably nothing more destructive to her sense of self than the photographic portrait George makes of her. Iris later simply refers to it as "that damned photograph" (1993: 41) when it begins to haunt her by unpredictably appearing all over the city, threatening to spin her entire life out of control. Iris's first encounter with the photograph is described as follows:

> I opened the clasp and pulled out the large photograph. Despite my anxieties about the afternoon I had spent with George, I wasn't prepared for what I saw. At first I didn't even recognize myself. The person in the picture seemed to bear no resemblance to me, and for an instant I thought George had made a mistake, had given me the wrong photo, but then I saw myself, and I had a peculiar sensation of recovery, of remembering a forgotten event, something unpleasant and disorienting. I tried to catch it, but it was like the fragment of a dream that surfaces for a moment during the day, brought forth by a sight or sound, and then retreats – as quickly as it came – into unconsciousness. I put the picture down on the table but picked it up again. (1993: 62)

Remarkably, even before Iris looks at it for the first time, she clearly has certain expectations of George's portrait of her. However, these are not merely frustrated; as a matter of fact, Iris does not identify with the image at all, not even recognizing herself at first. Only gradually does she begin to see herself in it or, rather, "something unpleasant and disorienting" that does not fit her ordinary sense of self but belongs to the realm of negative and repressed emotional content ("like the fragment of a dream") instead. Evidently, George's photograph captured a version of Iris that she is not ready to face and that threatens her very being, as becomes apparent in Iris's closer scrutiny of the image:

> It wasn't a full-body shot. I was cut off below my breasts, and my extended arms were severed at the elbows. Photographs are cropped in all sorts of ways, and the results are seldom disturbing. The viewer fills in the missing pieces, but this picture was different. The convention didn't seem to work, and I had the awful impression that the parts of me that weren't in the photo were really absent. I didn't understand it at the time, but I've thought about it so often since, I've come to believe that this effect was created by the fact that what appeared of me inside the photograph was also fragmented. A long piece of hair was swept across my right cheek and part of my mouth, slicing my face in two. A dark shadow beneath my uplifted chin made my head appear to float away from my body. My whole face lacked clarity, in part because the light was obscure, but also because the expression I had was nonsensical, an inward leer or grimace that signified no definite emotion or even sensation. It was a face without reason, and I hated it. I am not that, I thought, and let the photograph fall from my hands to the table. (Hustvedt 1993: 62–63)

What at first appears as classical ekphrasis, consisting of "the verbal representation of visual representation" (Heffernan qtd. in Rippl 2014: 151), turns out to be a rather different kind of rendition, namely of Iris's painstaking and ultimately failed attempt to connect the image with her own bodily awareness. For as hard as she tries to recognize herself in the photo, she only perceives fragments of her physical self in it, such as severed limbs, "a long piece of hair," which is, perhaps the most disturbing detail of all, "slicing my face in two." The sense of fragmentation that Iris experiences when faced with George's photo of her has been read as a reflection of her precarious inner life, as maintained by Corinna Sophie Reipen when she writes, "Iris identifies herself as being fragmented on the inside and on the outside" (Reipen 2014: 100; cf. also Rohr 2003). This reading is indeed supported by the account of Iris's regarding the image above. After all, when she notes that "I was cut off below my breasts," she elides the fact that she is merely looking at a distorted representation of her body, and not her actual self, a transgression of boundaries – ultimately that between art and life – which appears throughout the book, threatening Iris's mental and physical integrity. Indeed, her "identity is as fragmented as George's photographic portrait of her" which, according to Reipen, simultaneously marks *The Blindfold* as a postmodern novel (cf. Reipen 2014: 106–107).

Not only does the image – and, by extension, Iris herself – appear fragmented, however; what is more, it can be considered as a representation of the 'male gaze' as initially theorized by Laura Mulvey (1975; cf. also Reipen 2014: 101). Indeed, there is a metonymic relationship between the camera and George, the voyeuristic male subject behind it, whose presence is obfuscated in the account above but who nonetheless exerts full control over the photographic act itself, as well as the image resulting from it, turning Iris into a mere object and, at least from her perspective, into his passive victim in the process. This process clearly poses a threat to Iris's already precarious sense of self. As Marks notes, "George's photograph of Iris gains control over and disrupts her identity" (Marks 2014: 92). After being thus transfixed by the photograph, Iris finally experiences an emotional reaction which allows her to reject and then part with it ("I hated it. I am not that," Hustvedt 1993: 63) and thereby to reclaim her selfhood, if only momentarily. In the course of the narrative, however, the haunting image continues to threaten Iris's sense of self and compromises her most intimate relations, for instance when Stephen seems far more attached to the photograph than to the person in it. As Iris notes, "suddenly I had the feeling that for Stephen I had become invisible. An unexpected turn had been taken, and I had dropped out of sight" (Hustvedt 1993: 64). Again confronted with the photo, Iris experiences loss of vision due to the onset of a migraine attack (67), and while later she manages to "describe the picture with some accuracy" and "name its parts," she is "unable really to see it" (71). As a matter of fact, there is no point in the narrative when Iris fully regains control over her own image and, hence, her self-perception. Instead, her vision remains unstable until the end.

2. Looking Back in *What I Loved*

Hustvedt's third novel *What I Loved*, published in 2003, builds on some of the core themes of *The Blindfold* including the intertwining of art and life, prompting Hubert Zapf to call it "to a great extent a novel about art, about its past and present forms, and particularly about its relation to life and the human culture that produces, consumes, and recycles it" (2008: 187). Hence, the scope of *What I Loved* is considerably larger than that of the earlier book, and it seems in many ways a more mature work as a result. Its protagonists are accomplished artists and academics in their middle age living in the same SoHo building and engaging in various couplings over the course of the narrative spanning several decades. Visual art again occupies center stage and serves as a catalyst setting in motion a whole string of events eventually veering in the direction of tragedy. The book opens with the close description of an enigmatic painting the narrator, art historian Leon Hertzberg, acquired decades earlier from an artist named William ("Bill") Wechsler, marking the beginning of their close friendship at the heart of the narrative constituting Leo's memories of the people he loved:

> I first saw the painting [...] twenty-five years ago in a gallery on Prince Street in SoHo. [...] Most of the canvases in the group show were thin minimalist works that didn't interest me. Bill's painting hung alone on a wall. It was a large picture, about six feet high and eight feet long, that showed a young woman lying on the floor in an empty room. She was propped up on one elbow, and she seemed to be looking at something beyond the edge of the painting. Brilliant light streamed into the room from that side of the canvas and illuminated her face and chest. Her right hand was resting on her pubic bone, and when I moved closer, I saw that she was holding a little taxi in that hand – a miniature version of the ubiquitous yellow cab that moves up and down the streets of New York. (Hustvedt 2003: 4)

Befitting Leo's professional background, the passage mostly consists of an ekphrastic description of the oversized painting immediately attracting his attention in a gallery show of contemporary art in downtown New York. Significantly, what Leo recognizes in the painting depends on his viewpoint, which he changes in order to take in the detail of the realistically rendered miniature taxi, in turn locating the painting in the spatio-temporal urban environment of New York City in the early 1980s. Being representational rather than abstract, the painting could hardly be more different from the others in the show done in the minimalist style *en vogue* then, which holds so little interest for Leo that he does not even pay attention to them. Rather, the following paragraph continues his painstaking process of studying and trying to decipher the painted portrait; and the longer this process takes, the more he enters the picture, so to speak, thereby increasing the conundrum it poses:

> It took me about a minute to understand that there were actually three people in the painting. Far to my right, on the dark side of the canvas, I noticed that a woman was leaving the picture. Only her foot and ankle could be seen inside the frame, but the loafer she was wearing had been rendered with excruciating care, and once I had seen it, I kept looking back at it. The invisible woman became as important as the one who dominated the canvas. The third person was only a shadow. For a moment I mistook the shadow for my own, but then I understood that the artist had included it in the work. The beautiful woman, who was wearing only a man's T-shirt, was being looked at by someone outside the painting, a spectator who seemed to be standing just where I was standing when I noticed the darkness that fell over her belly and her thighs. (Hustvedt 2003: 4)

Leaving ekphrastic description behind, the passage traces the slow process of putting together the individual parts of the picture including the "invisible woman" who, Leo is surprised to realize, is "as important as the one who dominated the canvas." Not only does his perception of the painting become increasingly subjective; what is more, Leo for an instant mistakes a painted shadow for his own, thereby projecting himself into the picture, an effect that is strongly reinforced when he eventually realizes that he stands in the position of the invisible spectator – which is likely to be also that of the painter – looking at the semi-nude woman facing him. The painting's mystery is further increased by its title, "Self-Portrait," which appears as a misnomer at first but actually points to its transgressive aesthetic power, by calling into question various boundaries such as that between the visible and the invisible, the viewer and the viewed, and above all else the one between life and art.

As in the case of the eerie photograph in *The Blindfold*, the mysterious power of the painting extends into the protagonists' lives soon after Leo buys it from Bill. Unlike in the earlier novel, however, it is for the most part a welcome presence leading at least in one instance to a fulfilling act of love-making inspiring Leo to turn his wife into an aesthetic object to be appreciated even as she straddles him in front of the painting: "I loved that view of my wife" (5). And yet, the central themes of hidden realities, distorted perception and the general instability of human relations have been implemented from the beginning, in the form of an arresting painting that is not merely open to interpretation but in fact depends so much on what viewers see in it that its meaning changes considerably over time, as do the relationships of the people represented in it – or seeing themselves in it as the case may be. The painting is thus representative of some core aesthetic notions expressed throughout the book and elsewhere in Hustvedt's œuvre. Interestingly, it also serves as a form of meta-commentary on art including literature and its perception. As Caroline Rosenthal argues: "Like a palimpsest, the painting from the beginning seems to include all the different layers of the plot and all the figurative constellations of the novel" (Rosenthal 2011: 75).

The art in *What I Loved* has variously been said to mark the transition from postmodernism to post-postmodernism (cf. Timmer 2010: 95; qtd. in Reipen 2014: 233), or in any case "the period after postmodernism" (Zapf 2008: 171). According to Zapf, this would entail "a new attention to the relationships of texts to concrete, biographically embedded subjects and to the wider context of the intersubjective life-world" (171). What is more, the book was completed in the wake of September 11, 2001, and as such partakes of what Ulla Haselstein and others have identified as a new "pathos of authenticity" (Haselstein, Gross, Snyder-Körber 2010) typical of many American novels published since then. And indeed, there is more than enough evidence supporting both claims, beginning with the perishing of Leo's paternal family in the Holocaust of Auschwitz-Birkenau, which he remembers in connection with his father's death from a stroke and the tragic loss of his only son due to an accident (Hustvedt 2003: 232–233). While these traumatic experiences weigh heavily upon Leo's memory and more generally confirm the notion of a renewed ethical engagement in post-9/11 literature, in *What I Loved* the ethical fault lines mainly run along "the horizon of postmodern art, as represented by the New York art scene of the later twentieth century," as Zapf notes (2008: 171).

Bill Wechsler's art reflects the *zeitgeist* of that art scene (Reipen 2014: 171), even though he is only a reluctant member who openly resents its fast-increasing commodification. Thus, his works roughly spanning three decades might be placed under the general rubric of postmodern conceptual art, with a progressive development from two-dimensional forms such as painting and collages to three-dimensional sculpture, before Bill finally turns to video art with a project he is unable to finish titled *Icarus*, about the everyday lives of children in New York City, which Leo interprets as Bill's way of dealing with his "fallen son" Mark (Hustvedt 2003: 242). As a matter of fact, all of Bill's artworks are based, in one way or another, on his personal life without being autobiographical (for lack of a better term) in any narrow sense. Thus, an early series of paintings, *Missing Men* invokes his remote father after he died, and the installation *Hansel and Gretel* recalls Bill's telling the well-known fairy tale to his young son over and over again, eventually knowing it by heart. The latter work provides a good example of the novel's particular 'aesthetic ethics' filtered through the perspective of Leo, who regularly visits Bill's studio and describes what he sees in detail as he gradually comes to understand the individual works. Upon looking at the *Hansel and Gretel* pieces for the third time, and after discussing her research on eating disorders with Bill's wife Violet, he thus comments, "I suddenly realized that the fairy tale Bill had chosen was also about food. The whole story turned on the problem of eating, of not eating, and of being eaten" (83). Surpassing the circumscribed terrain of traditional fairy tales by creating images of bodily violence reminiscent of Goya, Bill's art expresses what Hal Foster identified as "the return of the real" in avant-garde art. As Leo notes: "In Bill's witch, the fairy tale's literal horror came true. The woman was a cannibal" (Hustvedt 2003: 83). Bill Wechsler's hard-to-digest art thus makes visible certain violent strands in mainstream culture otherwise hidden from view. What is more, it turns viewers into active participants in the meaning-making process, ultimately transcending the boundaries between the artwork, the person who created it, and the one looking at it.

In her 2010 essay "Embodied Visions: What Does It Mean to Look at a Work of Art," Siri Hustvedt elaborates on the aesthetic experience of looking at art as an activity that "always involves a form of mirroring, which may be but is not necessarily conscious," a "back and forth dialectic between spectator and artwork" (338–339). The dynamic interplay of necessity also includes the artist, "a living, breathing human being with an embodied self that functions both consciously and unconsciously within a larger world of meanings" (340–341). Art, then, negotiates between the subjective, embodied experience of both artist and spectator, who in turn participate in "language and culture, which shape our beliefs about how things are" (344). Art's meaning, therefore, is always subjective but simultaneously transcends individual experience; it is, above all, open-ended and, in Hustvedt's apt phrase, "created at every level of our experience" (344). Based on her reading of theories of perception informed by neuroscience, philosophy and pragmatism, she comes to the conclusion that "viewers are not merely passive reflectors of the out-there, but embodied creative seers" (348). Embodied vision can therefore be considered to be a form of world-making (cf. 348), which is at the same time its larger, ethical purpose; it is also what lies at the heart of Hustvedt's fictional universe.

3. Looking Up: *The Blazing World*

In 2014, Hustvedt's latest novel, *The Blazing World*, appeared to considerable critical acclaim. Structured rather differently from her previous ones, the book consists of a collage-like array of diverse texts including interviews as well as diaries, reviews, and notebooks by a varied cast of about twenty characters which, considered in their entirety, present the posthumous puzzle of the life of Harriet Burden assembled and edited by a professor of aesthetics named I. V. Hess. What gradually emerges is a polyvocal web of perspectives requiring a great effort on the part of the reader (and ideally, multiple readings) in order to get the collective picture – or rather, the mosaic – of Harriet, better known to her friends and family as "Harry."

Harriet was a prolific artist all her life, but having been married to a highly successful Manhattan art dealer named Felix Lord, her work has gone nearly unnoticed by the art world or, worse, taken as the mere pastime of the bored wife of a well-to-do art expert. Only in her mid-fifties, after Felix suddenly dies followed by her intense mourning, does Harriet leave behind her privileged life in Manhattan in exchange for a gritty artist loft in Brooklyn, which she shares with "human strays" (Hustvedt 2014: 21), as her daughter Maisie calls the changing group of poets, artists, and at least one schizophrenic intermittently living with her. Harriet now turns to making so-called 'metamorphs' or sculpted figurines of varying size giving embodied expression to "the creatures that lived in my memory" (30), beginning "with a life-size effigy of Felix" (29). Still feeling bitter about being underappreciated by the art world, however, Harriet decides on an experiment and creates, over the course of five years (1998–2003), a series of so-called *Maskings* or installations respectively titled "The History of Western Art," "The Suffocation

Rooms," and "Beneath," for which she uses three real-life, male artists' personas to 'mask' her own identity, which does remain undisclosed at first. According to Hess (quoting, in turn, the art critic Richard Brickman, another persona Burden takes on to explain her approach), *Maskings* was

> meant not only to expose the antifeminist bias of the art world, but to uncover the complex workings of human perception and how unconscious ideas about gender, race, and celebrity influence a viewer's understanding of a given work of art. (1–2)

Moreover, according to Harriet's life-long friend Rachel Briefman, she wanted "to investigate the complex dynamics of perception itself, how we all create what we see, in order to force people to examine their own modes of looking, and to dismantle their smug assumptions" (104). In the simpler words of Maisie Lord, "[s]he was trying to figure out why people see what they see" (86).

Whereas in *What I Loved* the expertise of creating art and meditating on its larger meaning was conveniently split between the creative force of nature named Bill Wechsler and his close friend, the art historian Leo Hertzberg, Harriet Burden – who likes to refer to herself as "Harriet Unbound" (30) – is the first artist in Hustvedt's fictional universe who is driven by a forceful fury both creative and intellectual, which is often intimidating to others or simply beyond their grasp. Putting *Maskings* in the context of Harriet's earlier work, art critic Rosemary Lerner writes, "the masks must be considered as furthering what she did best – creating works of focused ambiguity" (71). There is a close connection to the aesthetics of Wechsler, whose work Harriet greatly admires (Hustvedt 2014: 131), in that both are aiming for the dissolution of various boundaries such as that between what is seen and what is invisible, the self vs. other, and art vs. life. But in her work, another important boundary is specifically targeted and frequently transgressed, namely that between the male and female. As Brickman/Burden explains in a letter to the editor of an art journal featuring Burden's work in 2003 (i.e. shortly after her experiment was made public):

> Burden insists on ambiguity as a philosophical position, and furiously denies hard binary oppositions, even on the biological level of human sexuality [...]. She staunchly maintains that adopting the masks allowed her greater fluidity as an artist, and ability to locate herself elsewhere, to alter her gestures, and to live out "a liberating duplicity and ambiguity." Each artist mask became for Burden a "poeticized personality," a visual elaboration on a "hermaphroditic self," which cannot be said to belong to either her or the mask, but to a "mingled reality created between them." (254–255)

In the end, however, even though *Maskings* turns out to be a roaring success, it is doubtful that Burden's larger mission – compromised by the public scandal following her 'coming out' as the creative genius behind the shows, as well as her falling-out with Rune, the artist behind the third installation, "Beneath" – is equally fulfilled. Considering her need to feel acknowledged, it is ironic, to say the least, that, "to be really seen, Harry had to be invisible" (130), as her fellow artist Phineas Q. Eldridge, the 'mask' of "The Suffocation Rooms," aptly puts it.

In the final phase of her life, stricken with terminal cancer, but still full of fury and unwilling to die, Harriet turns to the work of a Margaret Cavendish, a little known seventeenth-century intellectual whom Harriet's boyfriend Bruno Kleinfeld refers to as a "colorful lady philosopher, whose most fervent hope was that she would find readers after she was dead" (Hustvedt 2014: 295). Like Harriet, Cavendish was underappreciated in her time; what is more, she, too, combined imaginative work, notably a utopian novel titled *The Blazing World* published in 1666, with her pursuit of natural philosophy, thereby defying established norms and expectations, in particular regarding women. Nearing her end, Harriet acknowledges her strong identification with Cavendish (whom she fondly refers to as "Mad Madge" at times): "I am back to my blazing mother Margaret" (328). Harriet had previously worked on an oversized figure provisionally titled *The Blazing World Mother*, but abandoned working on it, according to Bruno, "because this monster had never satisfied her."(314) In her final weeks, however, she takes it up again and completes the impressive sculpture, which is unlike anything she had previously done: "This woman had worlds inside her," as Bruno admiringly acknowledges (295).

In the book's final part, Harriet's prolonged death struggle is rendered at great length with intensely moving parting scenes involving the people around her. Her – and their – misery is greatly assuaged when the New Age healer Sweet Autumn Pinkney arrives on the scene after being mysteriously called to help Harriet in her suffering. Sometime after Harriet's eventual passing, Sweet Autumn is invited by Harriet's son Ethan to look at the artwork the deceased has left behind, including *The Blazing World Mother*, while still in the studio about to be cleared. Even though Sweet Autumn freely admits that she understands little about art, she is immediately struck by what she sees – or rather, feels: "I felt that funny lifting feeling I get sometimes, as if I'm getting pulled up toward the ceiling. It was a sign, maybe it was coming from Harry. I could feel something important was happening to me" (356). In an ironic twist of fate, true appreciation for Harriet Burden's creative genius comes from someone who knows next to nothing about art. What is more, unburdened by formal training or aesthetic preferences, Sweet Autumn allows herself to be truly moved by the piece: "I got down on my hands and knees and started looking around at the tiny ones [i.e. the small figurines falling out of the Blazing Mother's vagina in great numbers], and I had the sacred feeling." She then recognizes among the figures a small version of Harriet, who "had put herself into the art," (356) thereby ensuring her survival in the world of art. The book ends with an epiphany, as related by Sweet Autumn:

> While I was down on my knees looking at the figure of Harry, it started to glow. I swear. It glowed purple. I was seeing its energy. [...] I turned around to take one last look at Harry's artworks, and then I saw their auras blazing out all around them.

Harriet Burden's art thus finally comes alive in an act of creative embodied seeing, "blazing hot and bright" (357) for anyone open to the experience.

4. Conclusion

As argued throughout, seeing and perception are truly at the core of Siri Hustvedt's fictional as well as her non-fictional oeuvre published to date, allowing for an extraordinarily rich spectrum of embodied visual experiences challenging readers to 'enter into the picture.' Intriguingly, whereas the first novel *The Blindfold* presents the perception of art as a dangerous force field more often than not threatening its protagonist's sense of self, in her later novels Hustvedt treats art as a rather more complex arena in which her protagonists meet and mix, and eventually have to part, only to find memories of a shared past prompted by the artworks that stay. In *The Blazing World*, finally, another major turn has been taken, in that art in this novel has a genuinely transformative power. Not only does it enable its creators and viewers to transgress numerous boundaries toward more fully realized selfhood; what is more, it offers readers the rare opportunity to collaborate in the making of art, via the process of assembling a narrative that, like the final creation of its protagonist, has worlds inside it.

Works Cited

Foster, Hal. 1996. *The Return of the Real: The Avant-Garde at the End of the Century.* Cambridge, MA/London: MIT Press.
Haselstein, Ulla, Andrew Gross and Maryann Snyder-Körber (eds.). 2010. *The Pathos of Authenticity: American Passions of the Real.* Heidelberg: Winter.
Heffernan, James A. W. 1991. "Ekphrasis and Representation." *New Literary History* 22: 297–316.
Hustvedt, Siri. 1993. *The Blindfold.* London: Hodder & Stoughton.
Hustvedt, Siri. 2003. *What I Loved.* London: Hodder & Stoughton.
Hustvedt, Siri. 2012. "Embodied Visions: What Does It Mean to Look at a Work of Art?" *Living, Thinking, Looking.* London: Hodder & Stoughton. 336–354.

Hustvedt, Siri. 2013. "Borderlands: First, Second, and Third Person Adventures in Crossing Disciplines." In: Alfred Hornung (ed.). *American Lives*. Heidelberg: Winter. 111–135.

Hustvedt, Siri. 2014. *The Blazing World*. New York: Simon & Schuster.

Marks, Christine. 2014. *"I am because you are": Relationality in the Works of Siri Hustvedt*. Heidelberg: Winter.

Merleau-Ponty, Maurice. 1962. *Phenomenology of Perception*. Trans. Colin Smith. London: Routledge & Kegan Paul.

Mulvey, Laura. 1975. "Visual Pleasure and Narrative Cinema." *Screen* 16.3: 6–18.

Reipen, Corinna Sophie. 2014. *Visuality in the Works of Siri Hustvedt*. Frankfurt am Main: Peter Lang.

Rippl, Gabriele. 2014. "Intermedialität: Text/Bild-Verhältnisse." In: Claudia Benthien and Brigitte Weingart (eds.). *Handbuch Literatur & Visuelle Kultur*. Berlin: De Gruyter. 139–158.

Rohr, Susanne. 2003. "On 'The Perils of Going Astray': Female Figures in the City." In: Günter H. Lenz and Utz Riese (eds.). *Postmodern New York City: Transfiguring Spaces – Raum-Transformationen*. Heidelberg: Winter. 89–97.

Rosenthal, Caroline. 2011. *New York and Toronto Novels After Postmodernism: Explorations of the Urban*. Rochester, NY: Camden House.

Timmer, Nicoline. 2010. *Do You Feel It Too? The Post-Postmodern Syndrome in American Fiction at the Turn of the Millennium*. Amsterdam/New York: Rodopi.

Zapf, Hubert. 2008. "Narrative, Ethics, and Postmodern Art in Siri Hustvedt's *What I Loved*." In: Astrid Erll, Hubert Grabes and Ansgar Nünning (eds.). *Ethics in Culture: The Dissemination of Values through Literature and Other Media*. Berlin: De Gruyter. 171–194.

Birgit Däwes
"Openings that can't be closed": Patterns of Surveillance Culture in Siri Hustvedt's Novels

> "To look and not see: an old problem. It usually means a lack of understanding, an inability to divine the meaning of something in the world around us."
> – Siri Hustvedt, "Notes on Seeing" (2012: 223)

1. Introduction: Framing Surveillance

In a 1648 painting by Diego Rodríguez de Silva y Velázquez, entitled *La Venus del Espejo*, or *Rokeby Venus*, we see the artist's only female nude reclining on a bed with her back to the viewer. A winged figure, Venus's son Cupid, is holding up a mirror that shows the woman's face – however blurry – and redirects her gaze at the viewer (fig. 1).[1]

Besides the provoking depiction of nudity at the time of the Counter-Reformation in Catholic Spain and a representational playfulness that is characteristic of Velázquez's art (and best exemplified by his famous *Las Meninas* of 1656), this painting resonates with a number of visual and psychological features that can also be applied in remarkably fitting ways to Siri Hustvedt's literary work. From the celebrated debut of *The Blindfold* (1992) to her most recent *The Blazing World* (2014), Hustvedt's novels have been centrally concerned with questions of seeing and visual representation, and particularly with the connections between observation and power.[2] Using Velázquez as a visual preface in the following not only allows for a framing and structuring of particular narrative patterns and motifs in Hustvedt's literary work, but it also invites a historicized and diversified reading of a phenomenon that has been widely perceived as radically present- or future-related: our contemporary involvement with practices of surveillance.

In the twenty-first century, there is no doubt that surveillance – defined by David Lyon as "any collection and processing of personal data, whether identi-

---
[1] The painting is owned by the National Gallery, London. For details, see "Toilet" and "Rokeby."
[2] It is surprising that a recent study on *Visuality in the Works of Siri Hustvedt* does address issues of voyeurism and stalking (cf. Reipen 2014: 72, 216) but places its focus on paintings, visual art, and images while leaving out both *The Enchantment of Lily Dahl* and an analysis of the link between seeing and power, especially as they are manifested in practices of surveillance.

Figure 1: Diego Velázquez, *Rokeby Venus*, c. 1647–1651. 122 cm × 177 cm (48 in × 49.7 in). National Gallery, London.

fiable or not, for the purposes of influencing or managing those whose data have been garnered" (2001: 2) – has come to play a major role in contemporary western societies. This role has become increasingly complex over the past two decades: On the one hand, as symbolized by the widely circulated screenshot of Mohamed Atta, who was filmed at the passenger security checkpoint while boarding his plane in Portland, Maine, in the early morning of September 11, 2001, surveillance has been closely intertwined with the discourse of security governance that also propelled the passing of the USA PATRIOT Act in 2001 and the proliferation of CCTV cameras in public spaces in Europe. Gathering data, this discourse asserts, ensures public safety and helps to prevent crime, acts of terror, or even acts of war. On the other hand, as Edward Snowden's disclosures about the extent, technologies, and specific operational tactics of governmental intelligence agencies (including the United States' National Security Agency and the British Government Communications Headquarters) demonstrated in 2013, the discursive pairing of surveillance and security is disrupted by a counter-discourse of privacy and civil rights, which inquires more critically into the connections between seeing and (governmental) power. This latter concern is far from new, of course – it has been thematized in surveillance dystopias such as George Orwell's *1984* (1949) or Ray Bradbury's *Fahrenheit 451* (1953), Francis Ford Coppola's film *The Conversation* (1973), or Foucault's famous 1975 use of the panopticon as an architectural model for the shift of a modern "anatomy of power" (Foucault 1995: 215) from physical violence to psychological control.³ What is new, however, is a number of recent trends that dissolve the nexus between surveillance and governance and indicate what Kevin Haggerty calls a "paradigm shift" in surveillance studies (2006: 24).

Whereas Foucault's panoptic model, which has dominated the research landscape for the past forty years, emphasizes the linear top-down monitoring of subordinate individuals as a governmental strategy for power, the twenty-first century's developments of online social media such as Facebook (cf. Allmer et al. 2014), of multilateral "big data" corporations such as Google (cf. van Dijck 2014), of facial recognition software (cf. Gates 2011), and of personalized advertisement and diverse customer control strategies in a digitalized consumer culture (cf. Zurawski 2014) call for new understandings of the ways in which surveillance works today. "No central watchtower dominates the social landscape," David Lyon writes in 2001,

> and few people feel constrained, let alone controlled, by surveillance regimes. Most of the time, most people comply cheerfully with requests to show their identification, or acknowledge that they divulge personal data to companies, believing that the benefits are greater than the costs [...]. (7)

In this altered, less tangible set-up, the representation of classic scenarios of panopticism and dystopian depictions of totalitarian surveillance regimes, as in Margaret Atwood's *The Handmaid's Tale* or Suzanne Collins's *The Hunger Games* trilogy, or in NSA novels by Tom Clancy, M. E. Harrigan, or Brad Thor, seem to call attention away from, rather than provide reliable diagnoses of, recent shifts in power structures. Siri Hustvedt's work, I argue here, reflects these

---

3 Michel Foucault uses Jeremy Bentham's architectural model of the panopticon as an illustration of how state power has shifted. In the panopticon, designed in 1791 for prisons, schools, or hospitals, individual cells are arranged in a circular structure around a central observatory; vesting authority in an administrative structure rather than in individual wardens, as power becomes inseparable from the technology of seeing. The "perfect disciplinary apparatus," in Foucault's words, "would make it possible for a single gaze to see everything constantly. A central point would be both the source of light illuminating everything and a locus of convergence for everything that must be known: a perfect eye that nothing would escape and a center towards which all gazes would be turned" (Foucault 1995: 173). Foucault sees this new tactics of power at the heart of modernity: through panopticism, the state refrains from exercising power physically, "like a faceless gaze that transformed the whole social body into a field of perception" (214).

new developments much more accurately than the more conspicuous candidates of a "literature of surveillance" possibly can by their flashy displays of cameras, spies, and agencies. As Christine Marks writes,

> Hustvedt's works [...] make an innovative contribution to the contemporary debate over the dynamics of vision and subjectivity. Although vision, especially through the medium of photography, is shown to have power over characters' identities, this power can also be used to affirm the subject rather than objectifying it. (2014: 71)

Visuality is always linked to both individual agency and intersubjective relations, both of which are the core elements of understanding contemporary surveillance societies. The intricately intertwined patterns of seeing, visual representation, knowledge, and control in Hustvedt's novels thus not only provide fresh perspectives on the foundations of surveillance studies, but they can help us to rethink the theoretical paradigms of contemporary surveillance culture on a micro-level – and thus as "a form of knowledge which is always mediated through personal perspectives" (Zapf 2008: 173).

2. Naked Definitions, Visualizing Mirrors, and Lines of Sight

According to art historian Lynda Nead, Diego Velázquez's *Rokeby Venus* "is one of the world's greatest and most famous pictures" (2002: 43). For the purpose of structuring this paper, I would like to highlight four of its features that are particularly relevant to a reading of visuality and of the traces of surveillance culture in Siri Hustvedt's work: (1) the vulnerable boundaries between private and public spaces, (2) the overlapping of different lines of sight, (3) a mirror that raises questions of representation and authenticity, and (4) a more or less subtle meta-artistic reflection on creative and epistemological processes at large. Guiding my analysis of Hustvedt's narratives, these features illustrate and differentiate the intricate connections between seeing and control and expand the critical framework beyond reductive dichotomies.

(1) First of all, the situation of Velázquez's painting is clearly a private one, restricted to the domestic and intimate setting of the bedroom. Unlike many conventional nudes in art history (Prater 2002: 20), this one is turning her back toward the viewer, suggesting a non-consensual intrusion into the private sphere.[4]

---

4 The scene also illustrates the thin line between voyeurism and surveillance: while the former

In the *Oxford English Dictionary*, privacy is defined as "the state or condition of being alone, undisturbed, or free from public attention, as a matter of choice or right; seclusion; freedom from interference or intrusion" ("Privacy"). Just as much as this state is compromised in the painting,[5] several of Siri Hustvedt's novels deal with violations of the boundary between private and public spaces. In *The Blindfold*, protagonist and first-person narrator Iris Vegan[6] meets George, a photographer who is not held back by ethical considerations when opportunities arise to take unusual pictures in the cityscape of New York. In one scene, he uses the vulnerability of a woman having a seizure in the street to take her picture; and one of the pictures he shows to Iris has apparently also not been taken with the consent of the depicted subject:

> [It] was a shot that had been taken through a window covered with a grate. Through the diamond-shaped bars, one glimpsed a tiny room with an unmade bed, an old stuffed chair, and a remarkable hairy rug, but what had obviously intrigued George was a poster hanging on the wall. The image of a young woman in a bathing suit was obscured by the grate – her face couldn't be seen at all, but her well-shaped torso was perfectly visible. (Hustvedt 1992: 45)

Their discussion of any moral implications is clearly oppositional (Hustvedt 1992: 49), but Iris soon succumbs to what Monika Taddicken terms the "privacy paradox," a phenomenon that describes the concerns people express about issues of their privacy (often in connection to using the internet) while their behavior is largely contradictory to such concerns (Taddicken 2014: 248). Because of a "buoyant mood" (Hustvedt 1992: 53), Iris agrees to having her picture taken by George and dances for him in his apartment. When she sees the outcome a few days later, she is severely shocked by, and alienated from, her own represen-

---

is defined by the *Oxford English Dictionary* as the activity of "a person whose sexual desires are stimulated or satisfied by covert observation of the sex organs or sexual activities of others" ("Voyeur"), surveillance has come to be understood, according to Stephen Miller, as "the monitoring and regimenting of an object, an institution, an area, a group, or a person" (1999: 2). As both social media and surveillance games demonstrate (cf. Mäkinen and Koskela 2014), these differences (largely of scale and purpose) are increasingly difficult to distinguish in contemporary culture.

5 More recent definitions describe privacy as "a dynamic process of negotiating personal boundaries" (Steeves 2009: 193) or as "the right to self-determine which information is made accessible to whom and when" (Taddicken 2014: 249), both of which equally apply to both Velázquez's *Venus* and many of Hustvedt's protagonists.

6 While all of Hustvedt's novels rely on a certain autobiographical impetus, this novel's protagonist mirrors the autobiographical relationality most clearly through her name: Iris is, of course, Siri spelled backwards; and Vegan was Hustvedt's mother's maiden name.

tation: the picture is fragmented and cut off, the distribution of light and shadows seems wrong, and "the expression I had was nonsensical, an inward leer or grimace that signified no definite emotion or even sensation. It was a face without reason, and I hated it" (Hustvedt 1992: 63). As Christine Marks summarizes, this effect works like an inverse version of the Lacanian mirror stage: "[t]he presence of the photograph seems to produce an absence within Iris's inner core; she feels that with the advent of the picture she loses presence" (2014: 91). Iris is all the more disturbed when she realizes over the next few weeks that many of her friends and acquaintances have apparently seen the picture, and she learns that George has given it to an art dealer for an exhibition without requesting her permission. In addition to permeating the thin line between voyeurism and surveillance, this scene also documents the risk in contributing to other people's (or corporations') collection of data (here in the form of visual images), and the loss of control that is involved when these data are publicly accessed.

This kind of situation is rendered even more radically – yet without an involvement of the privacy paradox – in *The Sorrows of an American* (2008): Erik Davidsen, autodiegetic narrator and divorced Brooklyn-based psychoanalyst from Minnesota, finds out that his tenant Miranda and her daughter Eglantine are being followed by an anonymous photographer: at first, he finds simple, mimetic Polaroids on the steps of their house (Hustvedt 2008: 28), but these are soon replaced by photographs that have been digitally manipulated: "I recognized Miranda's face at once, but the black-and-white photograph had been altered. The irises and pupils in Miranda's eyes were missing. I looked into the blank spaces and suffered an uncanny feeling of recognition, then lost it" (35). It is not until after he receives another series of pictures, this time of a walk he had taken with Miranda and Eggy, in which the child "had been wiped out – all that remained of her was a small white silhouette on the sidewalk" (74), that Miranda discloses the photographer's identity as Jeffrey Lane, Eggy's father, who is psychologically unstable with occasional violent tendencies. Echoing the debates about surveillance that were triggered by the USA PATRIOT Act and the war on terror after September 11, 2001,[7] Lane's artistic assault on the private sphere culminates in a nocturnal encounter, when Erik wakes up to the sounds of an intruder in his home. He arms himself with a hammer for self-defense, then realizes that he is facing Jeffrey Lane, who "had the gall to stop and photograph me" (112) before leaving. A few months later, both Miranda and one of his pa-

---

[7] The novel is also both an explicit and an allegorical response to the terrorist attacks of 9/11 (cf. Däwes 2011: 362–363), a theme taken up again in *The Blazing World* (Hustvedt 2014: 172–173).

tients tell him that they saw his picture in an exhibition by Lane, and when Erik goes to see it, his reaction to the image – which is offensively entitled "*Head Doctor Goes Insane*" – is similar to Iris's in *The Blindfold:* "I wasn't sure who I was looking at. Anger had contorted my face to such a degree that I was almost unrecognizable" (Hustvedt 2008: 263). Again, the photograph has been altered in several ways: the setting is now no longer the violated domestic space of Erik's house but a street, and most crucially, Jeffrey Lane has pasted himself into the picture as an injured casualty, thus reversing the roles of perpetrator and victim and drastically raising the level of violence originally involved. Even though Erik's threat to take legal action persuades the gallery "to have a black square put over the face of *Head Doctor Goes Insane*" (264), the damage has been done: "The photograph lived on [...] in Ms. W.'s head, as well as in mine" (246).

In explorations both of voyeurism, stalking, and surveillance, as well as of the more complicit "privacy paradox," these passages from *The Blindfold* and *The Sorrows of an American* illustrate the outdatedness of Foucault's panoptic model for contemporary intersections of seeing and power while simultaneously highlighting the precariousness of the boundary between private and public spaces. Especially in contexts of image distribution and representational authority, we are warned not to take visual transgressions too lightly.

(2) In the panoptic model, which continues to dominate the debate on surveillance practices today, the gaze is both linear and unilateral, and contained within a specific architectural setting. In contemporary society, by contrast, Kevin Haggerty sees a "multiplication of the sites of surveillance" which emerge "in unpredictable configurations and combinations, while undermining the neat distinction between watchers and watched through a proliferation of criss-crossing, overlapping and intersecting scrutiny" (Haggerty 2006: 29). This development can be visualized by the multilateral lines of sight in Velázquez's painting: Cupid is looking at the frame within the frame from the left, and Venus is doing the same from the right: both are looking towards the center of the painting and thus directing viewers' attention to the object of their gaze. The reflection of Venus, then, placed slightly above the geometrical center of the painting, is looking outward and thus directly at the viewer. By returning the gaze, the object of observation not only resists any potential patterns of (patriarchal) visual control, but it responds to the practice of surveillance in unexpected ways. Instead of a panoptic hierarchy of observer and observed, in which the latter is given neither visual participation nor agency, this scene illustrates a structure of "interveillance" (Jansson 2014: 145), which denotes

> a cultural condition where identity creation, expressivity, and mediated peer-to-peer monitoring come together. In late modern societies, interveillance, and the media applied, have become a routinized means (amongst others) for maintaining a sense of ontological security. (Jansson 2014: 146)

Along the same lines, Siri Hustvedt's novels feature a number of interveillant situations: both *The Blindfold* and *The Enchantment of Lily Dahl* (1996), for instance, begin with routine observations of neighbors through windows. In the earlier of the two novels, Iris Vegan finds pleasure in spying without being detected:

> I watched the neighbors from my bed. Through my barred window, across the narrow airshaft, I looked into the apartment opposite mine and saw the two men who lived there wander from one room to another, half dressed in the sultry weather. On a day in July, not long before I met Mr. Morning, one of the men came naked to the window. It was dusk and he stood there for a long time, his body lit from behind by a yellow lamp. I hid in the darkness of my bedroom and he never knew I was there. (Hustvedt 1992: 9)

This situation is the same in *Lily Dahl*, when the protagonist admits to her habit of observing Edward Shapiro, an artist living across the street (this time in Webster, Minnesota): "She had been watching him for three weeks. Every morning since the beginning of May, she had gone to the window to look at him. It was always early, just before dawn, and as far as she knew he had never seen her" (Hustvedt 1996: 1). Whereas Iris Vegan's neighbors never notice the intrusion into their privacy, Edward Shapiro suddenly looks back: "before [Lily] understood what was happening, he walked to his window, jerked it open and leaned out into the rain" (2). In addition to crossing and reversing the lines of sight, *Lily Dahl* also adds a purpose to surveillance that is usually left out from classic panoptic models: "Both watching others and exposing oneself," Haggerty writes, "can, at times, be pleasant entertainment activities and are themselves occasionally part of larger processes of identity formation" (2006: 28). This becomes particularly apparent in the next encounter between Lily and Edward, when a pair of used shoes inspires her to enact an erotic performance at her window. Instead of stabilizing identity, however, her performance conjures up the construction of alterity through "an image of herself as someone else" (Hustvedt 1996: 38); and eventually the inauthenticity of her "borrowed gestures" becomes the very source "of the pleasure" (39). This scene not only nicely illustrates once again the "privacy paradox" in contemporary surveillance society, but it also changes the hierarchical model of surveillant situations: in the balance of the gazes, with

Lily and Edward "look[ing] at each other for what seemed like a long time" (40), identity and alterity are blurred in a balanced visual exchange.[8]

Furthermore, interveillance is not restricted to the bilateral role reversal between observer and observed (which eventually triggers their love affair), but the novel extends the visual direction into a whole network of intersecting gazes. Martin Petersen, a childhood friend with a few psychological problems, regularly "stares" at Lily "as if it were his job to look at her" (Hustvedt 1996: 8), and when the latter leaves her boyfriend Hank Farmer, a mysterious nightly visitor appears at night in front of her building, "watching and waiting" (94) (before he turns out to be Hank himself). This interlacing of different visual directions reframes the phenomenon of surveillance in a more complex dynamic of subjectivity and relationality – opening its epistemological framework to possibilities of interaction and multilateral exchange.

(3) The central object of the *Rokeby Venus* is the mirror, both in a literal and a figurative way. This mirror frames Venus's face, but something seems wrong about it: the proportions of the head in the mirror appear to be at odds with a realistic refraction of its original. If "there is," as Andreas Prater confirms, "every reason to believe that Velázquez was aware of the fundamental laws of optics" (2002: 24), then this cannot be a simple mistake of perspective or measure:

> The problem is that the vantage point from which the scene is represented (as well as the vantage point of the viewer, were they to differ) is different from the vantage point of Venus. Therefore, if we see Venus's face nicely framed inside the mirror, she must see something quite different. (Bertamini et al. 2003: 595)[9]

Observers, however, tend to incorrectly assume "that Venus is also seeing herself in the mirror in the same location," a psychological reflex that Bertamini et al. call the "Venus effect" (593). The mirror's angle, however, suggests that the reflected face is looking directly at the viewer, as if in a straight response to an illegitimate glance. In addition to the issues of privacy and of intersecting gazes as discussed above, this effect pinpoints representation itself: the mirror – usually a

---

8 Gianna Zocco phrases this similarly: "Lily's experience at the window points to a conception of art in which the dichotomies defining both parameters of the metafictional window-scenario complement each other, i.e., in which objectivity/subjectivity and *mimesis/poiesis* are mutually dependent" (Zocco 2013: 6). See also Marks 2014: 112.
9 Other art historians have argued that the mirror's angle necessitates a representation of Venus's lower body (cf. Prater 2002: 24–25), leaving her face entirely out of the picture.

loyal reflector of reality – becomes an unreliable archive, a communicational device, and a comment on the polysemy of visual knowledge.

The Venus effect also befalls Lily Dahl, who, according to Susanne Wegener, is frequently deceived by "referential fallacy" (2005: 52): a misperception of the relationship between a culturally coded referent and its object, or, in other words, a discrepancy in "the possible states of the world supposedly corresponding to the content of a sign-function" (Eco, qtd. in Wegener 2005: 52). To begin with, Lily constantly moves between reality and simulation in her pose of "a party girl crashing a strip show" (Hustvedt 1996: 38), her fantasies of being Marilyn Monroe (25) or Cinderella (30), or her role as an actress in Shakespeare's *Midsummer Night's Dream*. This also includes her role as an investigator, since *The Enchantment of Lily Dahl* is not only a novel of cultural initiation (Wegener 2005: 54), but also a postmodern detective novel. Yet just as the mirror in the *Rokeby Venus* suggests two different versions of 'reality,' the detective plot in Hustvedt's novel also operates on referential fallacy. Atmospherically interwoven with the murder of Helen Bodler, a local farmer's wife who disappeared in 1932, a case of mystery and (failed) surveillance revolves around Martin Petersen's gradual exposure as a psychopath. Martin, who "has been spying on [Lily] for a long time" (Hustvedt 1996: 233) and who owns an archive of "articles about John Wayne Gacy [and] Jack the Ripper" (127), hands her a newspaper clipping about Becky Runevold, a teenager killed by her father. According to Martin, she "looks like you when you were a little girl" (129). Lily is quick to deny any lines of comparison, but Martin's comments and behavior are increasingly meta-representational ("Do you ever feel that nothing's real?" [64]), and soon similar cases of referential analogy occur. Several people around town claim to have seen Lily in different places while she was elsewhere: "Either there was a virus on the march in Webster that caused hallucinations or everybody was seeing the same thing and thinking it was something else" (167). When a police report also records "[a] man carrying an injured woman" (168), Lily decides to investigate the case herself. Together with her neighbor Mabel, she decides to switch roles and spy on Martin, until they see "a long, dark bundle he was carrying in his arms" (217): they "recognized the limp form of a person [...], the girl's head uncovered, her small, beautiful face" bearing a "strong resemblance" to Lily (218, 220). Firmly convinced that Martin has committed a murder, Lily eventually confronts him, only to find out that he has been carrying around a doll that he made himself: a simulation of Lily which he claims he "suffocated" (238) in order to reunite reality and representation: "Pictures are fakes, the play is a fake. But maybe, if you push them onto the real thing – they can open each other up" (64). In terms of the visual analogy to the *Rokeby Venus*, the artistic mirror in which Lily had been hoping to see the solution of a crime literally displays but her own face.

(4) As Andreas Prater diagnoses more generally, "[p]aintings featuring mirror images often address the subject of painting itself, and, as such, are self-referential because they portray their task – the mimesis of the visible – by means of precisely this object, the 'mirror'" (2002: 86). Siri Hustvedt's work adds another layer to this visual self-referentiality by narrating visual art – and especially art (both historical and fictitious) that is in itself self-reflexive and questions mimetic approaches to reality. From Iris Vegan's flawed memorization of Giorgione's *The Tempest* in *The Blindfold* and Edward Shapiro's town portraits in *The Enchantment of Lily Dahl*, and from Bill Wechsler's *Self-Portrait* in *What I Loved* to Harriet Burden's *Suffocation Rooms* in *The Blazing World*, narratively represented works of art play central roles in all of her novels, especially so in *What I Loved*.[10]

Her latest piece, *The Blazing World*, is arguably the most meta-representational among these: The story of Harriet "Harry" Burden, a New York artist who uses male covers to gain more recognition and continuously reflects on art in her writing, is layered into a compilation of different kinds of text, including (for the most part) passages from Harriet's notebooks, but also interviews, essays, art reviews, and letters from friends and relatives. Prefaced by the editor, a professor of aesthetics named I. V. Hess, the novel cloaks itself in the traditional topos of documentary authenticity – only to dismantle such topoi in the relativities and uncertainties of its multiple perspectives. In *The Blazing World*, all lines from Velázquez's painting converge: the issue of privacy is most explicitly addressed through the publication of Harriet's personal notes and her balancing act between pseudonyms and authentic recognition; the plurality of diverse, even contradictory (visual) perspectives is translated into the narrative genre of an anthology, and questions of representation are extensively pondered – especially in fundamental revisions of the relationship between signifier and signified. In this context, reminiscent of Martin's Lily-doll, Harriet also primarily produces life-sized figures (often of her late husband) she calls "metamorphs" (Hustvedt 2014: 143) or "odd bodies of all kinds that frightened the children" (13): dolls of different sizes which she sometimes heats up electrically: "I began with a life-size effigy of Felix; it was an idea of him, not a likeness [...], man as canvas, but I added short white hair on the top of his head. When I plugged him in, his soft body ran a fever" (30). The disturbing effect on the spectators

---

10 See also Hustvedt's many essays on art, such as *Mysteries of the Rectangle: Essays on Painting* (2005) and *Living, Thinking, Looking* (2012).

illustrates that the line between original and replica is permeable; the effect of crossing it – as in Velázquez's mirror – unsettles our reliance on representation as such. This metafictional impetus of poststructuralist semiotics is also explicitly referenced in the text: One of the installations in the novel stages the actual death of its artist, Rune, and whereas some reviewers discard it as "a snuff film" (324), art critic Timothy Hardwick defends it as "a spectacle of simulacra" (324). Quoting Baudrillard's famous dictum that "*[t]here is no more fiction*" (324; emphasis original), Hardwick summarizes: "The real and the imaginary, animate and inanimate, artist and product, have entered the zone of the hyperreal, the zone in which these antiquated distinctions will soon be wholly erased" (324). Even though Burden is reported to have expressed her opposition to Baudrillard in a review, "dumping on the Baudrillard craze, demolishing his simulacra argument" (24), these words can be taken as programmatic for the novel at large, and, I believe, as indicative of one of the core philosophical problems of twenty-first-century surveillance culture.

In a quest for new models to aptly describe surveillance effects in contemporary society, William Bogard emphasizes that we are facing a "new semiotic of control" (34), which is "founded not on truth relations between a sign and the reality it purports to represent, but on the radical indeterminacy of those relations" (2012: 34). Surveillance increasingly relies on virtual realities or on simulation as a strategy of power, or, in Dieter Kammerer's words, "representations of surveillance are essential to the functioning of surveillance in general" (2012: 99). This effect is a strategic one: the proliferation of particularly iconic images of surveillance, especially in popular culture (including, for instance, Showtime's successful serial *Homeland* or FX's *The Americans*)[11] suggests that threats to privacy or public safety are identifiable, curbed, and thus containable. If the CIA or NSA are the agents behind data collection and information control, the spotlight moves away from corporations and digital applications we use every day. Thus, the "imaginary of surveillant control" (Bogard 1996: 4) not only stabilizes the system, but it distracts us from other sites of ideological power, and from the underlying narrative matrix of normative order. Similarly, Velázquez's mirror, Lily Dahl's misleading detective story, and I. V. Hess's process of ordering textual

---

11 *Homeland*, a serial about a CIA agent spying on a returning prisoner of war, was first broadcast in 2011 and is, according to Leslie Goffe, "one of the most watched TV shows in America" as well as "President Obama's favorite TV show" (Goffe 2013: n. pag.). It is at the time of writing in its fourth season. *The Americans* (2013), on the other hand, takes up the Cold War again and is set in Washington D.C. during the 1980s. It is, according to critic Graeme Virtue (2014), "a lo-fi spy story that values interpersonal skills over hi-tech gadgets," and its third season began in January 2015.

and visual fragments into a coherent narrative suggest closure in the epistemological move from seeing to knowing, yet instead of identifying the referents clearly, they merely "substitut[e] the signs of the real for the real" (Baudrillard 1981: 2) and imitate the operational principle of surveillance culture today.

3. Toward an Ethics of Seeing

While Diego Velázquez's painting and Siri Hustvedt's novels might seem, at first glance, to provide much less appropriate tropes for contemporary surveillance culture than television series such as *Homeland* or *The Americans*, their deep structures of visual representation hold a number of surprisingly topical effects. If one of surveillance culture's most fundamental tacit agreements holds that seeing and collecting data is causally connected to knowledge, paintings such as *The Rokeby Venus* and novels such as *The Blindfold, The Enchantment of Lily Dahl*, and *The Blazing World* clearly teach us otherwise. Not only do activities of spying not necessarily lead to the desired results, but the signifiers that can be perceived – whether they refer to actual signifieds or merely back to themselves – invite multiple, sometimes contradictory, readings. As Erik Davidsen puts it in *The Sorrows of an American*, "[w]ords create the anatomy of a story, but within that story there are openings that can't be closed" (Hustvedt 2008: 85). Narrative knowledge, in other words, is subjective, relative, and never fixed – and in analogy to the raw material of words, seeing is a highly unreliable process, particularly so in the context of surveillance. Whereas Foucault argues that through the panopticon, "an obscure art of light and the visible was secretly preparing a new knowledge of man" (1995: 171), Hustvedt's novels remind us that this "knowledge" is not inherent in the structures of seeing: on the contrary, we require techniques of decoding, analyzing, and contextualizing information – in short, of interpretation – in order to make meaning. The "openings that can't be closed" remain a constitutive part within this process.

Velázquez's painting also contains such an opening: If the angles in Velázquez's painting can be assumed to be correct, the *Rokeby Venus* does not look at herself in the mirror, but her gaze is directed instead at a point beyond the painting, where the viewer is standing or sitting to meet the gaze. The site of reception is thus implicated in the visual situation, which not only complicates the principle of mimesis diegetically, but which celebrates precisely the "opening" or factor of uncertainty: the indeterminate and polyvalent co-producer of meaning in the space beyond the work of art. Hustvedt's narratives work with the same effect: "By moving the spectator into the field of the painting through a transgression of the frame," Christine Marks writes, "Hustvedt stresses the interplay between the work and the recipient, and dissolves notions of a bodiless and ideal gaze" (Marks 2014: 129).[12]

Finally, these layers of self-reflexiveness and reception-oriented metafiction are crucial to her novels, but they are not ends in themselves. As Hubert Zapf summarizes, recent fiction more generally seeks

> to explore new forms of narration in which neither pure self-referentiality nor referential certainties are the focus and productive principle of texts, but a constant and complex mediation between signifier and signified, subject and experience, text and life, aesthetics and ethics. (Zapf 2008: 171)

This return of ethical questions to the postmodern stage, for which Hustvedt's work is a prime example, is one of the most pressing concerns in our understanding of contemporary surveillance society.

Whereas David Lyon and others see disciplines such as "history, sociology, criminology, and organization studies" as well as "geography, law, international relations, computer science and psychoanalysis, ethics and marketing" (2001: 6) as the core contributors of research perspectives on surveillance, both Velázquez and Hustvedt demonstrate the relevance of art and literature in exploring the deeper layers of seeing, representation, and knowledge. As the twenty-first century compels us to find new metaphors for the post-panoptic scenery of our future, and to develop a new ethics of seeing, watching, and making sense, we are well advised not to close the openings that visual art and fiction create.

Works Cited

Allmer, Thomas, Christian Fuchs, Verena Kreilinger, and Sebastian Sevignani. 2014. "Social Networking Sites in the Surveillance Society: Critical Perspectives and Empirical Findings." In: André Jansson and Miyase Christensen (eds.). *Media, Surveillance and Identity: Social Perspectives*. New York: Peter Lang. 49–70.

Baudrillard, Jean. 1981. *Simulacra and Simulations*. Ann Arbor: University of Michigan Press.

Bertamini, Marco, Richard Latto and Alice Spooner. 2003. "The Venus Effect: People's Understanding of Mirror Reflections in Paintings." *Perception* 32.5: 593–599.

Bogard, William. 1996. *The Simulation of Surveillance: Hypercontrol in Telematic Societies*. Cambridge: Cambridge University Press.

Bogard, William. 2012. "Simulation and Post-Panopticism." In: Kirstie Ball, Kevin D. Haggerty, and David Lyon (eds.). *Routledge Handbook of Surveillance Studies*. New York: Routledge. 30–37.

---

[12] This responds to one of the central weaknesses that Kevin Haggerty sees in surveillance research today: the agents of surveillance are mostly neglected, and the panoptic model in particular "provides no sustained account of the role or importance of the watchers" (2006: 33).

Däwes, Birgit. 2011. *Ground Zero Fiction: History, Memory, and Representation in the American 9/11 Novel*. Heidelberg: Winter.
Dijck, José van. 2014. "Datafication, Dataism and Dataveillance: Big Data between Scientific Paradigm and Ideology." *Surveillance & Society* 12.2: 197–208. <http://library.queensu.ca/ojs/index.php/surveillance-and-society/article/view/datafication> [accessed 23 March 2015].
Flieger, Jerry Aline. 1997. "Postmodern Perspective: The Paranoid Eye." *New Literary History* 28.1: 87–109.
Foucault, Michel. 1995 [1975]. *Discipline and Punish: The Birth of the Prison*. Trans. Alan Sheridan. New York: Vintage.
Gasta, Chad M. 2006. "The Politics of Painting: Velázquez and Diplomacy in the Court of Philip IV." *Letras Hispanas* 3.2: 1–20.
Gates, Kelly. 2011. *Our Biometric Future: Facial Recognition Technology and the Culture of Surveillance*. New York: New York University Press.
Goffe, Leslie. 2013. "The Homeland Phenomenon." *Middle East* 440: 54–56. <http://connection.ebscohost.com/c/articles/85635604/homeland-phenomenon> [accessed 23 March 2015].
Haggerty, Kevin. 2006. "Tear Down the Walls: On Demolishing the Panopticon." In: David Lyon (ed.). *Theorizing Surveillance: The Panopticon and Beyond*. Portland, OR: Willan Publishing. 23–45.
Hustvedt, Siri. 1992. *The Blindfold*. London: Hodder & Stoughton.
Hustvedt, Siri. 1996. *The Enchantment of Lily Dahl*. New York: Henry Holt.
Hustvedt, Siri. 2008. *The Sorrows of an American*. New York: Henry Holt.
Hustvedt, Siri. 2012. *Living, Thinking, Looking*. New York: Henry Holt.
Hustvedt, Siri. 2014. *The Blazing World*. London: Hodder & Stoughton.
Jansson, André. 2014. "Textures of Interveillance: A Socio-Material Approach to the Appropriation of Transmedia Technologies in Domestic Life." In: Miyase Christensen and André Jansson (eds.). *Media, Surveillance and Identity: Social Perspectives*. Frankfurt am Main: Peter Lang. 145–152.
Kammerer, Dietmar. 2012. "Surveillance in Literature, Film, and Television." In: Kirstie Ball, Kevin D. Haggerty, and David Lyon (eds.). *Routledge Handbook of Surveillance Studies*. New York: Routledge. 99–106.
Lyon, David. 2001. *Surveillance Society: Monitoring Everyday Life*. Philadelphia: Open University Press.
Lyon, David, Kevin D. Haggerty and Kirstie Ball. 2012. "Introducing Surveillance Studies." In: Kirstie Ball, Kevin D. Haggerty, and David Lyon (eds.). *Routledge Handbook of Surveillance Studies*. New York: Routledge. 1–11.
Mäkinen, Liisa A., and Hille Koskela. 2014. "Surveillance as a Reality Game." In: Miyase Christensen and André Jansson (eds.). *Media, Surveillance and Identity: Social Perspectives*. Frankfurt am Main: Peter Lang. 183–200.
Marks, Christine. 2014. *"I am because you are": Relationality in the Works of Siri Hustvedt*. Heidelberg: Winter.
Miller, Stephen Paul. 1999. *The Seventies Now: Culture as Surveillance*. Durham: Duke University Press.
Mulvey, Laura. 1975. "Visual Pleasure and Narrative Cinema." *Screen* 153.3: 6–18.
Nead, Lynda. 2002. *The Female Nude: Art, Obscenity, and Sexuality*. New York: Routledge.

OED = *The Oxford English Dictionary*. September 2014. 3rd ed. online. Oxford: Oxford University Press. <http://www.oed.com/> [accessed 12 November 2014].

Prater, Andreas. 2002. *Venus at her Mirror*. München: Prestel.

Reipen, Corinna Sophie. 2014. *Visuality in the Works of Siri Hustvedt*. Frankfurt am Main: Peter Lang.

Renzi, Kristen. 2013. "Safety in Objects: Discourses of Violence and Value – *The Rokeby Venus* and *Rhythm 0*." *SubStance* 42.1: 120–145.

"Rokeby Venus." 2010. In: Lilian H. Zirpolo (ed.). *Historical Dictionary of Baroque Art and Architecture*. Lanham, MD: Scarecrow Press. 449–450.

Steeves, Valerie M. 2009. "Reclaiming the Social Value of Privacy." In: Ian Kerr, Valerie M. Steeves, and Carole Lucock (eds.). *Lessons from the Identity Trail: Anonymity, Privacy, and Identity in a Networked Society*. Oxford: Oxford University Press. 191–208.

Taddicken, Monika. 2014. "The 'Privacy Paradox' in the Social Web: The Impact of Privacy Concerns, Individual Characteristics, and the Perceived Social Relevance on Different Forms of Self-Disclosure." *Journal of Computer-Mediated Communication* 19: 248–273.

"The Toilet of Venus." 2014. *The National Gallery*. <http://www.nationalgallery.org.uk/paintings/diego-velazquez-the-toilet-of-venus-the-rokeby-venus> [accessed 26 November 2014].

Virtue, Graeme. 2014. "Have you been watching… *The Americans?*" *The Guardian* April 18. <http://www.theguardian.com/tv-and-radio/tvandradioblog/2014/apr/18/the-americans-kgb-agents-washington-1980s> [accessed 2 November 2014].

Wegener, Susanne. 2005. "Die 'kulturelle Initiation' der Lily Dahl: Identität und Zeichen in Siri Hustvedts *The Enchantment of Lily Dahl*." *Philologie im Netz* 32. <http://web.fu-berlin.de/phin/phin32/p32 t4.htm> [accessed 16 December 2014].

Zapf, Hubert. 2008. "Narrative, Ethics, and Postmodern Art in Siri Hustvedt's *What I Loved*." In: Astrid Erll, Herbert Grabes, and Ansgar Nünning (eds.). *Ethics in Culture: The Dissemination of Values through Literature and Other Media*. Berlin: De Gruyter. 171–194.

Zocco, Gianna. 2013. "The Art of Watching: The Literary Motif of the Window and its Potential for Metafiction in Contemporary Literature." *TRANS*- 16: 2–11.

Zurawski, Nils. 2014. "Consuming Surveillance: Mediating Control Practices Through Consumer Culture and Everyday Life." In: André Jansson and Miyase Christensen (eds.). *Media, Surveillance and Identity: Social Perspectives*. New York: Peter Lang. 32–48.

Anna Thiemann
Portraits of the (Post-)Feminist Artist: Female Authorship and Authority in Siri Hustvedt's Fiction

Many of Siri Hustvedt's essays and interviews revolve around the social status of the woman artist, which she regards as symptomatic of the "widespread, corrosive presence" of sexism in today's society (Hustvedt 2013). As a writer, Hustvedt has been personally affected by what she calls "sexual stereotyping" in the art world (Freeman 2011: n. pag.). In her contribution to the essay collection *Fifty Shades of Feminism* (2013), she remembers that even after her first major successes, male publishers kept adopting a paternalistic and condescending attitude towards her writing. Moreover, at least one journalist assumed that her first novel, *The Blindfold* (1993), was actually written by her husband, Paul Auster. Occasional doubts about Hustvedt's authorship have not stopped other readers from classifying her novels as 'women's fiction,' that is, supposedly confessional works that have a female target audience (Hustvedt 2013). According to Hustvedt, the main problem behind these 'misreadings' is that women writers are still considered unable to move beyond their own experience while male authors are assumed to address the big and allegedly universal questions of human existence. Or, to use her own words, "[i]t takes the authority of a male voice to write from the centre of culture. [...] As women, we're just barking from the margins" (qtd. in Elkin 2013).

It is certainly no coincidence that women artists are equally prominent in Hustvedt's fictional oeuvre. All of her four last novels, *What I Loved* (2003), *The Sorrows of an American* (2008), *The Summer without Men* (2011), and *The Blazing World* (2014), focus on female poets or visual artists who struggle against gender prejudices. Yet, it would be reductive and false to read these characters as a mere embodiment of the author and her personal experience. Such narrow biographical readings would only perpetuate the sexist discourse that Hustvedt attacks so vehemently in her writing. It is true that she privileges first-person narration and that certain aspects of her works are loosely based on her or her family's and friends' experiences (Freeman 2011). But these personal memories are not represented for their own sake, nor are they used as a means for personal introspection. In a 2008 interview, Hustvedt points out that she is "not interested in confessional literature at all even if I write about pretty personal stuff sometimes. My writing serves a greater purpose; it is never only about myself" (Hoch 2008; my translation).

In this paper, I will argue that Hustvedt's preoccupation with the figure of the woman artist reflects her strong interest in broader social and political issues like the construction of gender roles and the current state of the women's movement. Her novels evoke and contest established images of female authorship which have served strategic functions in feminist theory and criticism. By renegotiating these "*allegories of authorship*" (Felski 2003: 59; emphasis original) in her works, Hustvedt participates in debates about the *raison d'être* of feminism in the twenty-first century, the so-called postfeminist age. Before turning to Hustvedt's novels, I will provide a brief overview of past and current perspectives on female authorship and the literary texts that feature prominently in feminist arguments about female creativity and identity. These literary predecessors are important intertexts[1] that will guide my reading of Hustvedt's works.

Scholars often note that "the struggles of feminism have been primarily a struggle for authorship" (Burke 1995: 145). After all, key goals of the women's movement such as attaining a public and political voice as well as self-empowerment and self-representation are inextricably bound up with the right to be an author. Women's struggle for authorship and equality became the main focus of modern feminist literary criticism, which developed in the 1970s and 1980s. At a time when French theorists announced the "death of the author" (Barthes), feminist scholars sought to recover a distinctly female literary tradition and turned their attention to the life and works of nineteenth-century writers who had been denied the status of author and agent. For not only, so the argument went, were Victorian women culturally destined to become dutiful wives and mothers rather than 'serious' writers. They were also turned into frail, passive objects of the male (artist's) gaze. "Kill[ing women] into art" (Gilbert and Gubar 1984: 25) became a metaphor for misogynist strategies that were most blatantly illustrated by Edgar Allan Poe's artistic obsession with dead beautiful women. Poe's tale "The Oval Portrait" (1842) in particular revealed the mechanisms of a male-dominated art world which created fixed images of angelic women while quite literally, in this case, killing its 'natural' counterpart (Bronfen 1992: 59–75).

The founding text of modern feminist literary theory, Sandra Gilbert and Susan Gubar's *The Madwoman in the Attic: The Woman Writer and the Nineteenth-Century Literary Imagination* (1979), explored women's "parallel confinements in texts, houses, and maternal female bodies" (Gilbert and Gubar 1984:

---

1 I follow Michael Riffaterre's definition of this term. He argues that "[a]n intertext is one or more texts which the reader must know in order to understand a work of literature in terms of its overall significance (as opposed to the discrete meanings of its successive words, phrases, and sentences)" (Riffaterre 1990: 56).

89) and the devastating effects of patriarchal culture, which apparently manifested itself not only in female maladies like hysteria and anorexia but also in women's writing. In Gilbert and Gubar's argument, female literary production such as Charlotte Brontë's *Jane Eyre* (1847) and Charlotte Perkins Gilman's "The Yellow Wallpaper" (1892) came to be seen as an expression of women's social and psychological condition and as an implicit comment on the difficulties of female authorship. Gilman's story in particular was interpreted as a "paradigmatic tale which (like *Jane Eyre*) seems to tell *the* story that all literary women would tell if they could speak their 'speechless woe'" (Gilbert and Gubar 1984: 89; emphasis original). Condemned to stay in the former nursery of an old mansion to cure her postpartum depression, Gilman's narrator struggles to write a diary against her husband's will and eventually descends into madness. Pursuing a biographical approach, Gilbert and Gubar argue that "the madwoman in literature by women [...] is usually in some sense the *author's* double, an image of her own anxiety and rage" (Gilbert and Gubar 1984: 78; emphasis original). In their reading, the female writer emerges as an oppressed and silenced being whose "self-definition is complicated by all those patriarchal definitions that intervene between herself and herself" (Gilbert and Gubar 1984: 17). As a consequence, she suffers from an "'anxiety of authorship' – a radical fear that she cannot create, that [...] the act of writing will isolate and destroy her" (Gilbert and Gubar 1984: 49).

Gilbert and Gubar's notion of a distinctly female imagination struck a chord with second wave theorists and activists who promoted identity politics and consciousness-raising in order to overcome patriarchal oppression that hampered women's self-determination. Yet, not all feminist scholars were in line with *The Madwoman in the Attic*, and the work has received sustained criticism since its publication. In her review of Gilbert and Gubar's work, Mary Jacobus criticizes the authors' "Story of the Woman Writer" (Jacobus 1981: 517) as a repressive and "reductive" (Jacobus 1981: 518) myth that over-emphasizes female victimization and relies on universalist notions of femininity, which were increasingly contested in feminist circles. Poststructuralist feminists in particular saw no point in discovering the 'essence' of female identity and creativity. French theorists of *écriture feminine* envisioned a subversive 'feminine' (but not gender-specific) writing that destabilizes phallocentric notions of fixed truths, categories, and identities (Cixous 1976). Along similar lines, Judith Butler deconstructed the link between sex and gender and insisted that they were culturally constructed categories that depend on discursive reiteration and performance (Butler 1990).

Discussing the implications of poststructuralist feminism for theories of authorship, Rita Felski explains that the female writer "was now reimagined as a kind of drag artist, endlessly trying different genders, behaviors, and personalities" (Felski 2003: 77). Hence, the allegory of the "madwoman in the attic" was effectively challenged by the image of "masquerading women" who are able to "perform both masculinity and femininity in their writing" (Felski 2003: 177). Modernist and postmodernist texts like Virginia Woolf's *Orlando* (1928), Angela Carter's *Nights at the Circus* (1984), and Jeanette Winterson's *Written on the Body* (1992) were hailed as perfect illustrations of these subversive practices. In addition to displaying gender ambiguity on the level of content and form, these novels are a rich source of self-reflexive comments on "the freedom that lies behind the mask, within dissimulation, the freedom to juggle with being, and indeed, with the language which is vital to our being" (Carter 2012: 119). Some feminist critics regarded these texts as bridges between theory and practice and held them up as models of subversive gender politics. Others, however, were appalled at the "unworldliness" (Felski 2003: 78) of such claims, pointing out that gender difference and inequality are "not likely to disappear because a few texts will it so" (Burke 1995: 149).

Instead of another grand theory of female authorship, early twenty-first century critics have opted for less dogmatic approaches that avoid one-sided narratives of repression and resistance (Felski 2003: 89). Many of these scholars revisit Gilbert and Gubar's eponymous woman writer and the nineteenth-century literary imagination. More recent revisionist accounts of Victorian women's writing like Marianne Noble's *The Masochistic Pleasures of Sentimental Literature* (2000) argue that

> [f]emale sentimental authors were not simply victims who were silenced or forced to function as mouthpieces of patriarchal ideology, nor simply crusaders for truth and justice. They were authors eager to empower themselves and ambitious to explore and put into words their thoughts on a range of subjects not confined to tender love, regional portraiture, and womanly desires for kindness and compassion. They had selfish desires, violent fantasies, contradictory ambitions, and competing identifications – as did men. (Noble 2000: 5)

The idea that sentimentality offers an opportunity for agency and self-empowerment is not new, but Noble's study is the first to allow the writers (and readers) of sentimental fiction to include a complex sexuality by acknowledging their "longings for intimacy, ecstasy [and] reconnection to the body" (Noble 2000: 146). Noble's argument about Victorian literature resonates with postfeminist renegotiations of traditional feminist ideologies, the current trend against "victim feminism" and a new interest in "sexuality as an expression of female agency and determination" (Genz and Brabon 2009: 14, 12).

Siri Hustvedt is highly aware of these developments, and her fictional and non-fictional work participates in the contemporary debate about femininity and the current state of feminism by revisiting and revising established allegories of female authorship and authority.[2] Especially her novels enter into a dialog with traditional feminist perspectives on female creativity and identity by playing with voices and perspectives and reimagining the woman artist as a highly complex and ambivalent figure. On the level of form, Hustvedt's fictional oeuvre exemplifies the concept of "masquerading women" since she uses both male and female narrators in her novels. The most obvious illustration of the author's ability to invent multiple selves is her latest novel, *The Blazing World*, which consists of an artist's autobiographical and philosophical notebooks, personal statements by her friends and family, interviews, articles and reviews, which are meant to unravel the mysteries of the protagonist's life and work. But this does not mean that Hustvedt's fiction denies the importance of gender difference and inequality. Quite the contrary, her novels, which are set in the second half of the twentieth and the early twenty-first century, are deeply concerned with the social construction of gender roles and the unequal distribution of power and authority. Hustvedt approaches these issues by concentrating on the figure of the female artist because it allows her to expose not only the persisting problem of gender discrimination but also the inadequacies of traditional feminist approaches to female (and male) identity. In the following, I will substantiate my argument by taking a closer look at selected novels in which art and creativity take center stage. After a detailed discussion of *What I Loved* and its perspective on feminism and femininity, I will analyze how these issues are addressed in her most recent novels, *The Summer without Men* and *The Blazing World*.[3]

What I Loved revolves around two couples – Leo Hertzberg, an art historian and the male narrator of the story, and his wife Erica Stein, a literature professor, on the one hand, and William Wechsler, an artist, and his wife Lucille Alcott, a poet, on the other – who become close friends in the 1970s and end up living in the same apartment building. Both women get pregnant around the same time, and both couples eventually separate for different reasons. Bill falls in love with

---

[2] For a detailed analysis of Hustvedt's non-fictional works on (post-)feminism and female authorship, see my article on "Shaking Patterns of Diagnosis: Siri Hustvedt and Charlotte Perkins Gilman" (2013).

[3] I am not going to discuss *The Sorrows of an American* because it does not quite fit into my argument. The novel features a black graphic designer and her mixed-race photographer ex-boyfriend, but art and female creativity are arguably not the main focus of the story. This is not to say that Hustvedt's fourth novel does not offer any new insights into these issues—quite the contrary. Yet, it also opens up new contexts and questions about the specificities of black female authorship and Hustvedt's ethnic ventriloquism, which are unfortunately beyond the scope of this essay.

Violet Blom, a feminist historian, and Erica decides to leave New York and her husband after their eleven-year-old son, Matthew, died in a canoe accident. The plot of *What I Loved* is foreshadowed in one of Bill's early paintings, the portrait of a woman which the narrator describes at the beginning of the novel. At closer inspection, the image depicts not one but three people: two women, one of which is leaving the picture so that "[o]nly her foot and ankle could be seen inside the frame" (Hustvedt 2003: 4), and the shadow of a third person. The women are later revealed to be Violet and Lucille, and the shadow is said to represent the artist and the narrator, who are outside the frame looking at them. Thus, the image alludes not only to Lucille's 'exit' from her marriage and Violet's perseverance but also to the fact that, at the end of the novel, both men will have fallen in love with or at least felt attracted to the women who are portrayed in it. Yet, the picture is more than a metafictional ploy to be discovered by the careful reader. The painting is also central to Hustvedt's renegotiation of feminist ideology – and so are the women who are in it. Through Lucille and Violet, the author explores and challenges the main assumptions and arguments of modern feminist criticism, whose historical development happens to coincide with the setting of the novel.

At first sight, Lucille seems to be the spitting image of Gilbert and Gubar's powerless madwoman in the attic who feels uncomfortable in her role as a woman and a writer. When Leo describes the above-mentioned painting, he refers to Lucille as the "invisible woman" (Hustvedt 2003: 4), and he later presents her as a stiff and elusive character. Bill gives the impression that his wife suffers from an "illness," that she is "frail, a woman who needed protection from something he had chosen not to talk about" (Hustvedt 2003: 16). Later, the artist reveals that early on in their relationship, Lucille cut her wrists in a half-hearted suicide attempt. In a scene that is reminiscent of Poe's misogynist aesthetics, Bill recalls that he was curiously attracted to the "beautiful, bleeding girl" (Hustvedt 2003: 100) and that Lucille's parents blamed him for their daughter's mental derangement. However, the real reasons for Lucille's auto-aggressive behavior remain obscure.

Like Charlotte Perkins Gilman's protagonist, Lucille is apparently destined to fail as both a wife and an artist. In contrast to Violet, she has poor domestic skills and Bill's second wife thinks that she is an "unnatural" (Hustvedt 2003: 294) mother who obsesses over her poems but does not care about her child. Lucille's success as a writer is equally limited. Although she produces "sheaf[s]" (Hustvedt 2003: 40) of poems, only a few get published. Moreover, she finds it hard to accept praise for her artistic productions or to present them in public. The narrator, who takes an interest in her work, remarks that her poems are "[i]nevitably [...] autobiographical" (Hustvedt 2003: 40) and quotes a few lines from a piece that seems to reflect the author's anxiety, her physical and mental entrapment: "A woman sits by the window. She thinks / And while she thinks, she despairs / She despairs because she is who she is / And nobody else" (Hustvedt 2003: 19). Lucille's failure as an artist is amplified by her husband's successful career. Recalling the couples' first meeting, the narrator remembers that next to her artist husband, who used to radiate "extravagant potency" (Hustvedt 2003: 27), "she looked very small and very self-conscious" (Hustvedt 2003: 18). Her work is moreover in sharp contrast to that of another male artist in the novel, the sculptor and performance artist Teddy Giles. Giles owes his fame to his impersonations and revolting installations which feature massacred bodies and bloody instruments of torture. One critic describes his art as "a spectacle of shifting identities" (Hustvedt 2003: 338), which include the "psychopathic killer" (Hustvedt 2003: 338) and a character called "She-Monster" (Hustvedt 2003: 209). It thus seems that, in contrast to Lucille, Giles is not limited by strict aesthetic rules and his cultural identity.

It is impossible to miss the parallels between *What I Loved* and Gilbert and Gubar's famous argument about male invention and female self-analysis. Yet, Hustvedt does more than transpose their story of the Victorian woman writer to the 1970s. She undermines Gilbert and Gubar's theory of female identity and creativity and contests its validity in both a twentieth- and a nineteenth-century context. Reading *What I Loved* as a novel about patriarchal oppression would be too reductive and miss the complexity of Hustvedt's work, which effectively challenges the traditional feminist narrative of male villainy and female victimhood. Lucille's painter-husband may have had a few Poesque moments in his life, but he has outgrown his misogynist views to become a feminist artist. Even though he fell for Lucille when she was young, beautiful and most vulnerable, he now admits that his fascination for her "craziness" and deliberate self-mutilation was "awful," explaining apologetically that he was "twenty years old and a total idiot" (Hustvedt 2003: 100). Bill's mature art is inspired by feminist politics and challenges the sexist idealization of frail, beautiful women. The above-mentioned portrait of Violet, for instance, is part of a series that depicts her with various body shapes and accessories. The thinnest version of Violet "was lying on a mattress in her underwear looking down at her body with an expression that seemed to be at once autoerotic and self-critical. She was gripping a large fountain pen in her hand, about twice the size of a normal pen" (Hustvedt 2003: 10–11). Like the series as a whole, this particular painting seeks to confront and undermine gender stereotypes by constructing the image of a self-aware and independent woman writer who enjoys herself and her art.

Perhaps the most spectacular move in Hustvedt's novel is its subversive depiction of male inventiveness and ingenuity. For not only does it become apparent that most of Bill's works are autobiographical – "the fascinating and mysterious genius" (Hustvedt 2003: 86) even painted his son in a dirty diaper (Hustvedt 2003: 293). It also turns out that Teddy Giles, the most "celebrated, mythical" (Hustvedt 2003: 338) artist in the novel, blurs the boundaries between life and art. In the third and final part of the novel, it is revealed that the most outrageous rumor about Giles, the 'myth' that he brutally murdered a homeless boy, is actually true. Thus, in hindsight it seems that his signature performance as a psychopathic killer was not really an act, and his gory installations are eventually viewed as an expression of his morbid personality: "Giles's arrest turned the perception of his work inside out. What had been seen as a clever commentary on the horror genre began to look like the sadistic fantasies of a murderer" (Hustvedt 2003: 342).

Hustvedt's renegotiation of masculinity goes beyond novel conceptions of male creativity. After all, Bill's belief in gender equality affects not only his work but also his private life. As indicated above, he is apparently used to 'dealing' with dirty diapers, and he genuinely admires his wife's literary achievements. He clearly supports Lucille's career, and her inability to accept her husband's praise is incomprehensible (Hustvedt 2003: 16). Towards the end of the novel, Violet maintains that Lucille is "all boarded up and shut down like a condemned house" (Hustvedt 2003: 353), thus suggesting that it is not the outside world, her imprisonment in the architecture of patriarchy that makes it so difficult for Lucille to be a successful artist and a lovable wife and mother but her emotional detachment.

It is certainly no coincidence that Lucille is eventually 'replaced' by Violet, a woman who writes passionate love letters and feminist books rather than gloomy poetry. In contrast to Bill's first wife, Violet feels at ease with her body and offers a more optimistic perspective on women's position in society. As a historian in women's studies with an interest in individual life stories, she embodies a new generation of feminist scholars who try to move away from facile cultural readings and reductive arguments about women's victimization. Her research serves as a link between the Victorian and the present age, and it explicitly revises Gilbert and Gubar's core assumptions. At the beginning of the novel, Violet is working on hysteria in *fin-de-siècle* France, and she later embarks on a project that focuses on the current spread of teenage anorexia. In Gilbert and Gubar's reading, hysteria was a result of patriarchal socialization, which acted as a barrier to women's self-fulfillment. By contrast, Violet's historical case studies suggest that hysteria was "a permissible way out" (Hustvedt 2003: 54), a means to escape abusive men and domestic confinements. Violet is particularly interested in the story of Augustine, a domestic servant who started to suffer from fits and hallucinations after her master had raped her. Augustine's mother had no choice but to take her to the Salpêtrière, where she became a 'celebrity' patient of Jean-Martin Charcot until she escaped from the hospital "dressed as a man" (Hustvedt 2003: 73). Another patient who fascinates Violet is Blanche Wittmann, the "Queen of Hysterics" (Hustvedt 2003: 275) who feigned symptoms because she adored Charcot. After the neurologist's death, she "never had another hysterical attack" (Hustvedt 2003: 275) and stayed at the Salpêtrière to become a radiology technician. In contrast to Gilbert and Gubar, Violet highlights women's agency, their ability to actively shape their lives and to challenge patriarchal gender norms. Her case studies moreover imply that gender relations are not reducible to a static hierarchy. Blanche's case in particular refutes the notion that all men are natural oppressors who force their female victims into inferior social positions and are thus unworthy of their love and loyalty. That things are more complicated and open to change is also evident in Violet's revisionist reading of the current increase of anorexia among teenagers, which Gilbert and Gubar present as evidence for the longevity of traditional ideals of femininity (Gilbert and Gubar 1984: 54). Violet's case studies on the other hand reveal that anorexia nervosa is not a gender-specific phenomenon, and she argues that this epidemic phenomenon results from the current upheaval of social structures and gender relations rather than their firm fixation (Hustvedt 2003: 163).

At the end of *What I Loved*, the narrator takes stock of the people that mattered most in his life. He keeps memorabilia in his desk drawer which remind him of Erica, Matthew, Bill and his son Mark, and Violet. The only main character missing is Lucille, the anxious and elusive poet:

> I have no object for Lucille in my drawer. It would have been easy to save some scrap of her, but I never did. [...] The idea of Lucille was strong, but I don't know what that idea was except maybe evasion itself, which is best expressed by nothing. (Hustvedt 2003: 365)

Yet, Lucille's 'absence' does not mean that she, or her 'idea,' is inconsequential to Hustvedt's postfeminist plot. As Violet's predecessor, she represents the beginnings of feminist interrogations of female authorship and identity, which were shaped by critics like Gilbert and Gubar. *What I Loved* may be critical of their reductive interpretation of women's agency and creativity, but the novel still acknowledges that contemporary women's studies and feminist criticism would not exist without their groundbreaking work of the 1970s and 80s. After all, the narrator of the novel states early on in his description of Violet's portrait that the "invisible woman became as important as the one who dominated the canvas" (Hustvedt 2003: 4).

Hustvedt's most recent works revisit many of the above-mentioned issues and cast a new light on female identity and creativity. Her fifth novel, *The Summ-*

er without Men, zooms in on the life of a female poet who seems to be the exact opposite of the anxious woman writer in *What I Loved*. In contrast to Lucille, Mia is a successful artist who has published six volumes of poetry and is a newly awakened feminist entering into cross-generational "alliance[s]" (Hustvedt 2011: 59). The only thing the two women seem to have in common is that their husbands leave them – although only temporarily in Mia's case – for a younger love interest. Mia's success and perseverance indicate that she embodies a new type of woman (writer) that is more representative of the current postfeminist generation.

Similar to *What I Loved*, Hustvedt's fifth novel revisits the historical development of second wave feminism by entering into an intertextual dialog with Gilbert and Gubar's *The Madwoman in the Attic* and the literary texts that inspired their argument. *The Summer without Men* contains direct references to Jane Austen's *Emma* and *Persuasion*, Charlotte Brontë's *Jane Eyre*, and Emily Dickinson's poetry, which feature prominently in Gilbert and Gubar's work. Yet, neither of these intertexts seems to be as important as "The Yellow Wallpaper." Gilman's short story is not explicitly mentioned in Hustvedt's work, but *The Summer without Men* is apparently a subversive retelling of this "paradigmatic tale." Like Gilman's narrator, Hustvedt's woman writer turns into a "madwoman" (Hustvedt 2011: 2), yet the novel is about her recovery and self-empowerment rather than her mental deterioration. After a short stay in a psychiatric ward, Mia leaves New York to figure out her life and teach a poetry class in Bonden, her Minnesota hometown. Besides, Hustvedt's heroine has a mental breakdown because her husband leaves her, not because he smothers her. Thus, she enjoys a freedom and cherishes her husband in a way that would be inconceivable for Gilbert and Gubar's madwoman in the attic.

Hustvedt's choice of setting is remarkably similar to – and different from – that in "The Yellow Wallpaper." Gilman's protagonists "secure ancestral halls for the summer," a "colonial mansion," which is located "three miles from the village" (Gilman 1997: 254). Mia, on the other hand, spends the summer of 2009 in "a small house at the edge of the town not far from [her] mother's apartment" (Hustvedt 2011: 4). Moving into the deserted family home, she sets herself up in the "husband's study" (Hustvedt 2011: 7), where she later starts writing a "sex journal" (Hustvedt 2011: 44) about her premarital escapades. Yet, even though Hustvedt confronts Gilbert and Gubar's story of the mad woman writer head on, she does not turn a blind eye on the pressing issue of gender inequality. Early on in the novel, Mia reminisces that, as a young wife and mother, she did not have a room of her own: "I had been a scribbler of the stolen interval. I had worked at the kitchen table in the early days" (Hustvedt 2011: 6). But rather than putting all the blame on "paternal power" (Hustvedt 2011: 51), she admits with hindsight that she "hadn't fought for [herself] or, rather, [she] hadn't fought in the right way" (Hustvedt 2011: 6).

Hustvedt's fifth novel follows *What I Loved* in refusing to present women as defenseless victims of patriarchal oppression. Perhaps the best example of female resistance is Abigail, a close friend of Mia's mother. As a young woman, she loved both women and men, got married and divorced, and eventually started a "double life" as a creator of "conventional and subversive" art (Hustvedt 2011: 161). Abigail makes embroidered pillows, quilts, and other domestic handicrafts with secret pockets that reveal subversive messages, images of raging housewives and white-haired female onanists. These artworks illustrate Hustvedt's interest in women's self-empowerment and the problem of ongoing gender discrimination. Shortly before Abigail dies, she tells Mia that they share the same rigid personality, thus encouraging the poet narrator to continue her secret resistance against gender discrimination. Yet, the old woman's programmatic announcement conjures images of domestic confinement: "'[...] Mia,' she said. We're two peas in a pod.' I was flattered even though I was forced to see us round and green in a pod on a kitchen counter" (Hustvedt 2011: 162). The narrator's hesitant and ambivalent response indicates that the feminist project needs to be not only continued but also adapted to new contexts and developments.

Fittingly, the novel turns its attention to a more recent theory of female authorship, the poststructuralist notion of "masquerading women." Mia imitates the style of both male and female authors in her writing,[4] and towards the end of the novel, she insists that "the written word hides the body of the one who writes." She even dares her reader to imagine that, notwithstanding her "feminist prattle," she might in fact be "a MAN in disguise" (Hustvedt 2011: 151). Yet, this (potential) playful subversion of gender roles is apparently restricted to the world of 'fiction' since the narrator continues to grapple with gender discrimination in her 'real (narrated) life.' Despite this excursion into the field of liberating poststructuralist identity politics, the novel stands out for its interest in gender inequality, which is more pronounced than in *What I Loved*. Besides, *The Summer without Men* goes one step further in revising Gilbert and Gubert's image of the woman writer by putting her in the limelight and giving her a postfeminist 'makeover.'

> Hustvedt's renegotiation of feminist criticism continues in her latest novel, *The Blazing World*, which turns Gilbert and Gubar's argument (and the character constellation of *What I Loved*) on its head and deals more extensively with poststructuralist theories of fe-

---

4 She offers two versions of her return to Bonden in the style of Daniel Defoe and Emily Brontë (Hustvedt 2011: 75).

male authorship. Hustvedt's sixth novel opens with the observation that [a]ll intellectual and artistic endeavors, even jokes, ironies, and parodies, fare better in the mind of the crowd when the crowd knows that somewhere behind the great work of art or great spoof it can locate a cock and a pair of balls. (Hustvedt 2014: 1)

This quote by Harriet (a.k.a. Harry) Burden, the protagonist of the novel, expresses the artist's fury at the lack of *recognition* she has received throughout her life, which is the main driving force behind *Maskings*, her most ambitious art project. Yet, the citation is more than a trenchant summary of the novel's central issues. It is also self-referential, a hint to the reader how *The Blazing World* is to be understood: as a parody, a highly ironic and humorous work about the plights of the female/feminist artist.

Much of the novel's humor derives from its hyperbolic reversal of gender roles, which serves to dismantle Gilbert and Gubar's argument about male and female creativity. The only poet in the novel is male and he suffers from a pronounced anxiety of authorship, which forces him to give up on his masterpiece, his "darling work of great verse, the one of Whitmanian proportions, [his] own American Commedia" (Hustvedt 2014: 157). Just like Gilbert and Gubar's madwoman in the attic, Bruno Kleinfeld does not trust in his abilities as a writer and even fears that his work will annihilate him: "Sometimes he can't see it anymore. He is under the poem, and it is threatening to crush him" (Hustvedt 2014: 73). After working on the same epic poem for twenty-five years, he decides to write a memoir instead, which is aptly titled *Confessions of a Minor Poet*.

As Harriet's lover, Bruno stands in the shadow of an affluent and highly intelligent artist who is likewise a twisted character from the history of Western feminism. Hustvedt's heroine is a parody of a poststructuralist feminist who "furiously denies hard binary oppositions, even on the biological level of human sexuality" (Hustvedt 2014: 254) and ironically ends up dying from ovarian cancer. Harriet's "oblique" and "arcane" (Hustvedt 2014: 77) ways of thinking and writing are reminiscent of Derridean arguments, which, as Richard Rorty reminds us, present themselves "obliquely, with the help of as many foreign words and as much allusiveness and *name-dropping* as possible" (Rorty 2001: 123). In an article that was most likely written by Harriet herself (although the author's official name is Richard Brickman), her writing is characterized as follows:

> Its style, at once peculiar and various, includes circumlocutions, elaborate tangents, extravagant quotations, as well as terse philosophical sentences and argumentative leaps which distance it from every standard readers have come to expect from an academic journal. (Hustvedt 2014: 250)

Harriet's obsession with convoluted and over-intellectual arguments is curiously at odds with her political agenda, her aspiration to change the world by revealing the socially constructed nature of gender roles and dismantling the system of sexist discrimination. Even more puzzling, Harriet seems to be aware that nobody understands her (Hustvedt 2014: 151), but she refuses to rethink her political strategies even when Bruno warns her that her philosophies will isolate her and "bury [her] alive" (Hustvedt 2014: 318).

What makes *The Blazing World* particularly interesting for my argument is Harriet's appropriation of poststructuralist theories of authorship. After an unsuccessful career as a female artist, she decides to "take artistic excursions behind other names" (Hustvedt 2014: 34), to use male masks, or rather bodies, in order to reveal the sexist bias of the New York art establishment. She persuades three male artists to present her new art under their name, but her project fails – not least because her third "puppet" (Hustvedt 2014: 69) claims that *he* is the mastermind behind their project. The motives behind Rune's betrayal are not quite clear, but it is suggested that it has something to do with jealousy and sexual obsession since he had a love affair with Harriet's deceased husband, the art dealer Felix Lord.

The reasons for Harriet's inability to prove her authorship are highly complex, and lack of evidence is only one of them. In her second experiment, for instance, the case seems to be settled early on when journalists insist that the exhibition is an expression of the artist's queer identity (Hustvedt 2014: 196–199). Besides, she obviously has not reckoned with difficulties resulting from her collaborators' (let alone her own) ambivalent motives and desires. What these unexpected complications have in common is that they reveal the naivety of Harriet's project and beliefs, the fact that she turns a blind eye not only on the complexities of human life but also on her own flaws and deficiencies. Harriet is apparently well-read in literature, science, and philosophy, but she does not realize that her eclectic theoretical constructs, the foundation of her worldview, self-conception, and political agenda, are full of inconsistencies and simplifications. On the one hand, she rejects

> conventional ways of dividing up the world – black/white, male/female, gay/straight, abnormal/normal – none of these boundaries convinced her. These were impositions, defining categories that failed to recognize the muddle that is us, us human beings. "Reductionism!" She used to shout this every now and then. (Hustvedt 2014: 122)

Yet, on the other hand, she likes to present herself as the defenseless victim of a "monolith of adversarial forces [...] [a]n enemy with a masculine, not a feminine face, [which] squatted the likes of Harry away like a mosquito" (Hustvedt 2014: 104). Accordingly, she also falls prey to the fatal misconception that only female artists struggle against reductive biographical readings of their works (Hustvedt 2014: 132), a claim that is all the more astonishing since she is the first to suggest to Bruno that his (limited) imagination may be better suited for writing an autobiography. Unsurprisingly, the novel reveals that these simplistic and incompatible positions and theories offer a poor basis for a 'product oriented' art project like *Maskings*, let alone a means to bring about social change.

Among the three novels I analyzed in this essay, *The Blazing World* is perhaps the least optimistic. The political project of Hustvedt's "feminist warrior" (Hustvedt 2014: 158) goes disastrously wrong, and she dies before the novel's end. Yet, this is not to say that *The Blazing World* allows for no hope in a better future. Before Harriet makes her exit, she makes her granddaughter promise that she will pursue her dreams: "'Fight for yourself. Don't let anybody push you around. You hear me?'" (Hustvedt 2014: 353). This rather straight-forward and practical advice contrasts sharply to the way in which Harriet has handled her life. Hiding behind masks, extreme positions, and illogical theories, her (surprisingly non-misandrist) last words seem to suggest, is not a promising strategy when it comes to fighting for one's rights.

Siri Hustvedt's *Künstlerromane* are postfeminist in the sense that they distance themselves from established feminist ideologies, yet without questioning the need for feminist interventions in a world that is still far from achieving gender equality. Her novels take issue with particular kinds of feminism, especially those that reduce women (artists) to victims of patriarchal oppression or believe in the redeeming power of subversive masquerade and poststructuralist theories of identity. By embedding these concepts of female authorship and femininity into a complex web of human interaction, she reveals their unworldliness and calls for a more nuanced and pragmatic approach to feminist issues that acknowledges women's (and men's) freedoms and constraints and their ambivalent desires and identifications.

Works Cited

Barthes, Roland. 2001. "The Death of the Author." Trans. Stephen Heath. In: Vincent B. Leitch et al. (eds.). *The Norton Anthology of Theory and Criticism*. New York: Norton. 1466–1475.

Bronfen, Elisabeth. 1992. *Over Her Dead Body: Death, Femininity and the Aesthetics*. Manchester: Manchester University Press.

Burke, Seán. 1995. "Feminism and the Authorial Subject." *Authorship: From Plato to the Postmodern, a Reader*. Edinburgh: Edinburgh University Press. 143–150.

Butler, Judith. 1990. *Gender Trouble: Feminism and the Subversion of Identity*. New York: Routledge.

Carter, Angela. 2012. *Nights at the Circus.* New York: Random House.
Cixous, Hélène. 1976. "The Laugh of the Medusa." Trans. Keith Cohen and Paula Cohan. *Signs* 1.4: 875–893.
Elkin, Lauren. 2013. "Barking From the Margins: On Écriture Feminine." *The White Review* 8. <http://www.thewhitereview.org/features/barking-from-the-margins-on-ecriture-feminine/> [accessed 15 December 2014].
Felski, Rita. 2003. *Literature After Feminism.* Chicago: University of Chicago Press.
Freeman, Hadley. 2011. "Siri Hustvedt: My Life and Other Fiction." Interview with Hadley Freeman. *The Guardian* March 25. <http://www.theguardian.com/lifeandstyle/2011/mar/25/siri-hustvedt-life-fiction> [accessed 10 December 2014].
Genz, Stephanie and Benjamin A. Brabon. 2009. *Postfeminism: Cultural Texts and Theories.* Edinburgh: Edinburgh University Press.
Gilbert, Sandra M. and Susan Gubar. 1984. *The Madwoman in the Attic: The Woman Writer and the Nineteenth-Century Literary Imagination.* 2nd ed. New Haven: Yale University Press.
Gilman, Charlotte Perkins. 1997. "The Yellow Wallpaper." In: James Nagel and Tom Quirk (eds.). *The Portable American Realism Reader.* New York: Penguin. 254–269.
Hoch, Jenny. 2008. "Autorin Siri Hustvedt: 'Ich benutze mich selbst.'" *Spiegel Online* April 14. <http://www.spiegel.de/kultur/literatur/autorin-siri-hustvedt-ich-benutze-mich-selbst-a-546633.html> [accessed 10 February 2013].
Hustvedt, Siri. 2003. *What I Loved: A Novel.* New York: Picador.
Hustvedt, Siri. 2009. *The Sorrows of an American.* London: Sceptre.
Hustvedt, Siri. 2011. *The Summer without Men.* New York: Picador.
Hustvedt, Siri. 2013. "Underground Sexism: What Was That You Just Said?" In: Lisa Appignanesi, Rachel Holmes and Susie Orbach (eds.), *Fifty Shades of Feminism.* London: Hachette Digital. N. p.
Hustvedt, Siri. 2014. *The Blazing World.* New York: Simon & Schuster.
Jacobus, Mary. 1981. "Review of *The Madwoman in the Attic.*" *Signs* 6.3: 517–523.
Noble, Marianne. 2000. *The Masochistic Pleasures of Sentimental Literature.* Princeton: Princeton University Press.
Riffaterre, Michael. 1990. "Compulsory Reader Response: The Intertextual Drive." In: Michael Worton and Judith Still (eds.), *Intertextuality: Theories and Practices.* Manchester: Manchester University Press. 56–76.
Rorty, Richard. 2001. "Philosophy as a Kind of Writing: An Essay on Derrida." In: Martin McQuillan (ed.), *Deconstruction: A Reader.* New York: Routledge. 121–125.
Thiemann, Anna. 2013. "Shaking Patterns of Diagnosis: Siri Hustvedt and Charlotte Perkins Gilman." In: Carmen Birkle and Johanna Heil (eds.), *Communicating Disease: Cultural Representations of American Medicine.* Heidelberg: Winter. 365–386.

Trauma, Memory, and the Ambiguities of Self

Jean-Michel Rabaté
History and Trauma in Siri Hustvedt's *The Sorrows of an American*

I will start with a personal illustration of the still vexed issue of trauma and post-traumatic stress disorder. It is a vignette that was provided by Siri Hustvedt, who is always ready to share and analyze her own symptoms, as she did brilliantly in *The Shaking Woman*, with its ironical subtitle deftly evoking Freud's Schreber case, "*Or, A History of My Nerves.*" Hustvedt has written about the emotional impact left on her by an automobile accident in which she was caught ten years before. The car crash that destroyed the car in which she was sitting next to her husband and daughter took place in 2002. Ten years later, attempting to document the double process of traumatic repetition and attendant dissociation and forgetting, she published "Reliving the Crash" in *The New York Times* of February 18, 2012. Here is a passage from this lively and thoughtful piece.

> My husband is speaking to me from the driver's seat, but I cannot answer him. All I know is that I do not want to move. I feel at once serene and distant. I have this thought: *If I'm going to die, this is not such a bad way to go.* [emphasis original] [...] Although it was terrible, I am oddly grateful for the experience because it offered me an insight into the strange realities of emotional trauma. Although I recall those nighttime flashbacks, I still am unable to remember the smash-up itself. [...] According to the Diagnostic and Statistical Manual of Mental Disorders, or DSM, acute stress disorder, like PTSD, begins with an "extreme traumatic stressor," followed by intrusive memories or nightmares of that event. Further, the person must show dissociative symptoms – numbing, detachment, depersonalization or emotional unresponsiveness. [...] After the accident, I was clearly in a dissociated state – weirdly detached from myself – and although I left the hospital without an injury that could be seen on a CT scan, both my memory and my sense of self had been altered by the shock. My amnesia for the accident and the flashbacks that followed, belong to my psychological state, but they are also, of course, part of my physiological state that involved changes in my brain. This is obvious, and yet this truth has led to a lot of confusion, not only about PTSD, but all mental illnesses. [...] It is not known why some people develop traumatic symptoms and others don't. My husband, daughter, and the family dog were all in the car with me, and I was the only one who came down with acute stress disorder. Then again, I took the brunt of the shock. The van hit the side of the vehicle where I was sitting. Apparently, children of people who suffered from PTSD have a greater chance of developing the illness, but why they do remains mysterious. There is no PTSD without emotional trauma, but some of us may be temperamentally more disposed to become ill with it than others.
> My late father, who fought in New Guinea and the Philippines during the Second World War, had repeated flashbacks at night after he returned to civilian life, and once while he was awake – the intrusive memory seemed to have been triggered by a hymn he was listening to in chapel. As the horrible images unfolded before him, he began to shake uncontrollably, and he

> *found himself back in the Philippines witnessing what he believed was the unwarranted killing of a Japanese officer.* [my emphasis]
>
> As an infant I had febrile convulsions. In 1981 I had a brief seizure that threw me against a wall, followed by a yearlong migraine. In 2006 I developed a mysterious seizure disorder that manifests itself in violent shaking, which I now control with medicine. The shaking symptoms first appeared when I gave a speech in memory of my father, but I also once had a seizure while climbing a mountain, which was probably caused by hyperventilation.
>
> *It is tempting to link my shaking and my flashbacks to my father's. The question is how? If there is a genetic susceptibility to PTSD, it remains unknown, but both strong emotion – a psychological state – and a lack of oxygen – a physiological one – are known to cause seizures.* [my emphasis]
>
> PTSD is a relatively new term, but emotional trauma has been cataloged in various ways and gone by many names over time – soldier's heart, railway spine, shell shock, battle fatigue, hysterical neurosis and the one I think is most apt, physioneurosis. [...] Luckily, my flashbacks disappeared, but I am still often anxious when I ride in a car. My muscles become tense. I feel a constriction in my lungs, and I avoid looking ahead into the traffic. A bump in the road, a sudden stop, a loud noise – all of these make me gasp in fear. I am not entirely free of the "physioneurosis" that began with a car accident almost 10 years ago. (Hustvedt 2012b)

I wanted to quote this article because it contains a reference to her 2008 novel *The Sorrow of an American*. The two sections that I italicized contain a whole problematic subsequently deployed by Hustvedt in her fiction and essays: What was it that caused her father's trauma? Could there be a link between the father's trauma and her own symptoms? A tentative answer to these questions may have been given by the novel, even if the narrator is a man, a psychiatrist who wants to understand his own father's war trauma. But before discussing the role played by trauma in the novel and the interpretations it receives, it is useful to sketch a brief history of the term and of the debates its current visibility has given rise to.

The term finds its roots in Freudian concepts, and one of the most outspoken advocates of trauma studies, Cathy Caruth, systematically goes back to Freud. One sees this in her eloquent book, *Unclaimed Experience: Trauma, Narrative and History*. Caruth's point of departure is Freud's notion of a 'traumatic neurosis' because it can be applied to history, especially to the history of Jewish religion. Freud introduced a loaded analogy between patients who have suffered a shock from a wound or after an accident, and what happened to the Jewish people as it elaborated its religion. In most cases, for victims of a trauma, it is only later, after a period of 'latency' or 'incubation,' that they develop symptoms that repeat the initial traumatic situation (Freud 1967: 84; Caruth 1996: 16–17). Most of the time, moreover, victims of the trauma are not fully conscious of what happened. Although at first they have the impression that their emotions are under control, it is only later that symptoms appear. This pattern of deferral entailing a structural delay is akin to Freud's principle of *Nachträglichkeit*; such a structure is taken as a fundamental hermeneutic paradigm by Caruth. According to her, there is something like an 'unclaimed experience,' hence historical narratives cannot follow the experiential model defined by the sequence of events witnessed by observers and later consigned in chronicles. There is no immediate understanding when trauma is concerned. This structure finds obvious applications in the field of Holocaust studies.

Following Caruth's lead, Giorgio Agamben has taken Primo Levi's memoirs of Auschwitz as the starting point for an original meditation on the unspeakable in history. (Agamben 1999) As Levi has argued, the true witnesses were not the survivors, they were those who had abandoned all hope in the camps, those who were called the *Muselmänner*. All died because they had gone too deep into the horror.

However, critics have objected to the fetishization of the unspeakable. Thus Ruth Leys has attacked Cathy Caruth for what she sees as a misreading of Freud on the concept of trauma, and aims at showing that there are at least two models of trauma for Freud, one in which he believes in the reality of the event, the other in which it may just be a simulation (Leys 2000). And then Thomas Trezise published a virulent attack on Agamben's account of Auschwitz in *Witnessing Witnessing: On the Reception of Holocaust Survivor Testimony*. (Trezise 2013) In this book, Trezise debunks the myth of an unspeakable event that could not be inscribed in subjective consciousness or collective memory. He attacks the rhetoric of pathos and awe deployed by Adorno and Agamben mostly by pointing to a dangerous consequence of these theories: if one can merely repeat the trauma, this prevents victims from giving any testimony about their experiences, whereas most victims insist upon their ability (or wish) to provide a true account of their condition.

This is the dialogical framework from which trauma studies have grown. Trauma studies include memoirs of abuse, rape, murder and stories about extreme situations. In *Trauma: Explorations in Memory* and in *Unclaimed Experience: Trauma, Narrative and History*, Caruth starts from Freud's *Beyond the Pleasure Principle* to sketch a theory of the impossibility of registering or figuring certain events that can be called traumatic. The events being by definition "excessive," they cannot be inscribed either in the memory or consciousness. This is why they have to be repeated compulsively, literally and mutely. Caruth's examples are taken from Marguerite Duras (*Hiroshima mon amour*), Lacan, and Kleist. They all insist on missed experiences and on the inability to inscribe the trauma in a linear and coherent narrative.

A formidable refutation has been launched by Ruth Leys. Whereas Caruth was inspired by Paul de Man's mixture of materialist literality in the repetition of the trauma, and of rhetorical strategies of indirection that all kept a performative agency, Leys, who was influenced by Mikkel Borch-Jakobsen's deconstructive reading of Lacan and Freud, attacked both the physician Bessel van der Kolk and the critic Caruth. Both van der Kolk and Caruth believe that the symptoms of traumas are literal and veridical repetitions of events that have happened. They happened but implied some kind of excess, thus they were not fully registered. The consequence is that the Freudian concepts of repression cannot be applied to a traumatic experience (Leys 2000: 230). The "wound" of the trauma (its etymology, in fact) has been so deep that it has affected the very organs of perception and memory. Leys compares this thesis with the abundant medical and legal literature that was produced about Post-Traumatic Stress Disorder since the 1980s. The term of PTSD became an official term in the *Diagnostic and Statistical Manual of Mental Disorders (DSM) III* in 1980. However, the two more recent versions of the *DSM* were more cautious in attributing a literal and truthful nature to traumatic phenomena. The growing number of persons suffering from recurrent memories, flashbacks, hallucinations, recurrent nightmares generated by traumatic injuries or experiences produced a monstrous archive that is hard to interpret.

Freud, who was aware of the phenomenon, ended up thinking that it testified to the existence of a death-drive that should be posited beyond the pleasure principle. However, if the traumatic suffering is real, can we be assured that the cause is always a real event? This interrogation takes us back to the interrogations of Freud as he was changing his views about the reality of the seduction of hysterical daughters in the hands of perverse fathers in 1897.

Thus Leys points out simplifications of the evidence in Kolk, and more damagingly, a contradiction in Caruth's thesis. For Caruth, victims of trauma can only repeat them because they have no possibility of narrating them to themselves. They are literally happening over and over again. "The truth of the trauma [is] the failure of representation," (1996: 253) she neatly summarizes. For instance, Caruth interprets Claude Lanzmann's film *Shoah* not as a representation destined to make people understand the Holocaust, the transportation toward death camps, but as a way of transmitting the trauma as such, in its incomprehensible horror. She calls the "pathos of the literal" this combination of scientism about overwhelmed neuro-transmitters and a performative literary theory of the contagion of the unspeakable.

Leys criticizes the way Caruth reads Freud; according to her critical re-reading, Caruth tendentiously selected passages about the temporal aspect of the "traumatic neurosis" but avoided anything that resembled the castration model of the trauma brought forward by Freud elsewhere. In the book I quoted, Caruth's point of departure was the story of Tancred who killed Clorinda twice, once because he did not recognize her in combat, the second time after she has been metamorphosed into a tree. The analogy is flawed, Leys argues. She points out that Tancred was conscious of the horrible deed he had accomplished after unwittingly killing his fiancée in battle. Moreover once Tancred saw that Clorinda has been changed into a tree, he stated that she spoke of her wound. This wound was another cause for trauma, but the beautiful Clorinda cannot both speak and not speak.

More damaging then was Thomas Trezise's refutation of Agamben's application of the same paradigm of trauma to discuss the quandary of Holocaust survivors. Agamben exploits some of Primo Levi's hesitations about his own role. Levi felt that he was inadequate as a witness, and left that role to those who could not fulfill it by definition since they were the glassy-eyed vanquished, the haggard mute shadows, those who had abandoned any hope. Trezise's question is whether the way survivors have witnessed historical events can lead to disclose a truth, whether the silenced speech of survivors brings about a reconstruction of the crime. If, as Agamben avers after Primo Levi, the only true witnesses of the Shoah are catatonic "Muselmänner," who believe that they will never return to the world of the living, abandon any hope, are barely human, and are readily thrown into the ovens, this passivity does not leave a chance to those who try to narrate their experiences.

Trezise provides examples of witnesses who wanted to be witnessing, those for whom it was crucial to convey to the outside the extent of the horror. He mentions Charlotte Delbo's *Auschwitz and After*, and one can think of Robert Antelme's *The Human Species*, books presenting the survivors of the camps engaged in a frenzy of talk as soon they were able to do so. For them, this was the only way to attempt an eradication of the roots of the horror. One might want to refuse the paradox of an unspeakable account of the unspeakable, and request a new responsibility in the narrative of trauma.

In my book *Cambridge Introduction to Literature and Psychoanalysis* (2014: 188–196), to give flesh to this debate, I opposed Marguerite Duras's novel of "ravishment," *The Ravishing of Lol Stein*, which ends with a trauma so total that the heroine remains a psychotic, and Robert Antelme's memoir of Auschwitz, *The Human Race*. I had noted the fact that Duras and Antelme had been married for a while. If Antelme's book contradicts the idea that survivors were mute witnesses whose trauma left them unable to assimilate or be conscious of what happened, his first wife (they separated soon after his return from the camps) bore witness to the horror he had experienced by introducing characters like Lol Stein who remain eternally marked by the scar of the trauma – they are engulfed by psychosis and catatonic silence.

The question is whether such witnesses carry a message of which they are unaware, a message pathetically and obliquely transmitted to awed readers only. As Trezise argues, Caruth mixes up consciousness and assimilation. There is a difference between a linear narrative and an ethical decision to be a witness to something that borders the unspeakable but that can find a logical ordering via a later narrative. Perhaps because Antelme was a Communist militant (although he was excluded from the Communist Party soon after the Liberation), and not a Jew like Primo Levi, his experience of the trauma caused by the Shoah was different. However, the events he narrates still carry the generic name of "Auschwitz." Antelme insists, much as Trezise implies, that there is a need to use narrative to testify and thus overcome the trauma. The main difference between his testimony and that of his ex-wife Marguerite Duras was that he experienced the traumatic event directly; she recreated it, and made it echo creatively in her novels and films. However, there is a transmission of trauma, as has often been observed with children of Holocaust survivors. This transgenerational genealogy also impacted Siri Hustvedt's relationship with her father's war trauma.

Let us note at this point that when Freud sketched parallels between traumatic neurosis and Jewish history, he was aware that his own writing was caught up in the *Nachträglichkeit* affecting historical phenomena. This important admission is neither mentioned by Caruth nor by Leys. The English translation of the Moses book minimizes the crucial role played by deferred temporality in Freud's mythical history. Here is the English version:

> As an afterthought we observe that – in spite of the fundamental difference in the two cases, the problem of the traumatic neurosis and that of Jewish monotheism – there is a correspondence in one point. It is the feature which one might term *latency*. (Freud 1967: 84)

The German original states it as follows:

> *Nachträglich muss es uns auffallen, dass trotz der fundamentalen Verschiedenheit der beiden Fälle zwischen dem Problem der traumatischen Neurose und dem des jüdischen Monotheismus doch in einem Punkt eine Übereinstimmung besteht.* (Freud 1969: 516)

Indeed this is how Freud introduces the concept of latency into his Jewish historiography, by insisting upon the fact that the same or a similar delay marks individual trauma, the invention of monotheism, and his own narrative, even as this narrative aims at finding a solution to what caused the *Nachträglichkeit* in the first place.

In a radical gesture, Freud has "denied" (*absprechen*) its greatest prophet to the community of the Jews. His decision entails a progression that evokes a novel much more than a history book. The first chapter "Moses an Egyptian" is followed by a second chapter, "If Moses was an Egyptian...," and the third chapter, "Moses, His People, and Monotheistic Religion." The narrative of the repetition of the murder of the father must be repeated twice. The difficulty of writing a psychoanalytic history when concealment and forgetting have impacted all records can be solved by an old and imaginative recourse to the dialectics of fiction. The logics of the Greek *pseudos* (the lie, but also any creative mask or departure from truth) provides a bridge between unspeakable facts and the need to bring some testimony today, and I will find a similar "solution" in Hustvedt's work, and it runs through her novels, her essays and her memoirs.

Let us see where Siri Hustvedt's recent novel stands on the issue of the reality and unspeakability of traumas. On the one hand, the plot of *The Sorrows of an American* seems to side with Duras and Caruth. Erik Davidsen, the hero of the novel, is a middle-aged and divorced male psychiatrist/psychoanalyst who works at the Payne Whitney Psychiatric Clinic in New York, and who, at some point, meditates on trauma and history:

> History is made by amnesia. In the American Civil War, they called it soldier's heart, and over time it changed its name to shell shock, then war neurosis. Now it's PTSD, post-traumatic stress disorder, the most antiseptic of the terms for what can happen to people who witness the unspeakable. During World War I, in the barracks of field hospitals French and British doctors saw them coming in droves – men blind, deaf, shaking, paralyzed, aphasic, catatonic, hallucinating, plagued by recurring nightmares and insomnia, seeing and re-seeing what no one should see, or feeling nothing at all. [...] Trauma isn't part of a story; it is outside the story. It is what we refuse to make part of the story. (Hustvedt 2008: 51–52)

This opinion falls in line with Caruth's thesis, quite clearly.

Erik Davidsen keeps returning to the notes his father took during WWII. The main source of the trauma the father experienced was when he saw his friends shoot a Japanese officer to death who was trying to surrender himself, or perhaps had begun praying. Was he asking for mercy? At any rate, he was killed without mercy by the Americans, even though he posed no threat. This image of the shot supplicant never leaves Lars Davidsen's memory. It haunts him until he superimposes it onto older memories of ancient family dramas. His son Erik meditates on this predicament:

> I knew that my research was confirming what I had always felt was true in my patients: their memories of war, rape, near-fatal accidents, and collapsing buildings aren't like other memories. They are kept separate in the mind. I remembered the images from PET scans of PTSD patients and the colored highlights showing increased blood flow to the

right side of the brain and to the limbic and paralimbic areas, the old brain in evolutionary terms, and decreased flow to the let cortical areas, the language sites. Trauma does not appear in words, but in a roar of terror, sometimes with images. Words create the anatomy of a story, but within that story there are openings that cannot be closed. (Hustvedt 2008: 85)

A later section is devoted to the father's return to civil life after the war, starting college again with the G.I. Bill. One of his notes narrates how listening to the Lutheran hymn "O Day Full of Grace" triggered in him unstoppable shaking:

> To Don's alarm, I began to tremble. I lied and said it was a touch of malaria. This was my only daytime flashback, but I lived in fear that more might come. I read these sentences to myself many times, trying to penetrate their meaning. [...] Traumatic memory arrives like a blast in the brain. (Hustvedt 2008: 136–137)

The son compares this experience with that of traumatized survivors of 9/11: "They came to us later with their wounds of indelible memory, the images that were burned into them and then released again and again in a hormonal surge, the brain flood that accompanies a return to unbearable reality" (Hustvedt 2008: 137).

On the other hand, after a while, it seems that the narrative of the novel gains a Freudian dynamism of its own. As Inga admits at some point: "We were looking for one story and ran into another" (Hustvedt 2008: 200), which is a perfect exemplification of how ramified networks of verbal knots, in the sense of Freud's famous theory of the *Knotenpunkte* in *The Interpretation of Dreams*, generate new narratives.

In the novel there are other important traumatic events in the past, like the 1924 fire that destroyed the family farm, but it may not matter whether this is the true source or cause of the original trauma. A painful family secret is uncovered when we learn that Erik's father had helped Lisa Odland, then his girlfriend, to give birth one night. Lars may not have known, as Lisa did, that the stillborn child was not his. Lars then buried the corpse and avoided mentioning the disturbing incident again, which was henceforth buried in his unconscious.

Such a secret is not necessarily a locked crypt, a hidden ghost in the closet, but it is also presented as the most precious possession. Inga, Erik's sister who is a philosopher, quotes Kierkegaard to him: "Maybe you've kept a secret in your heart that you felt in all its joy or pain was too precious to share with someone else" (Hustvedt 2008: 252). Knowing that "[s]ecrets define people" (201), Inga sums up the basic dialogical set-up of Kierkegaard's *Either/Or*. Obviously, this is valid for Hustvedt who seems to agree with Kierkegaard device of using proliferating masks, gender-bending projections and the calculated use of fictional alter egos.

A counter-example is provided by the character of the crazy and narcissistic artist Jeffrey Lane, a one-time rival for Erik in the affections of Miranda, his Jamaican lodger who obsesses him with her beauty and sexuality. Lane seems to believe that everything is a simulacrum, in which he repeats in a sort of parody the postmodern philosophy of Baudrillard or Virilio. All this section of the novel, presenting the photographs taken by Lane and showing Erik in an unflattering light, should be linked with Hustvedt's forceful rejection of this dated postmodernism, as when she discusses a show organized by Paul Virilio in Paris in which images of 9/11 were used to argue that reality has ceased to exist in our technological age. I have seen this show at the Foundation Cartier, and in spite of all the brilliance of Virilio's impassioned rhetorics, I can only agree with Hustvedt that the result felt sickening: "The alarm in Virilio's writings is palpable; his voice is pitched high. (I venture to say that had he been a woman his fate as a thinker would have been far more uncertain.)" (2012a: 263). The parable works perfectly when Lane is brutally forced to confront reality: his six-year-old daughter he has had with the estranged Miranda falls from his window when she is in his distracted care. Erik and Miranda will not have an affair, even though he helps her overcome a different trauma, the murder of her uncle Richard. However, he will be instrumental in bringing her and Lane back together as a more or less "normal" family, since they will be reunited, we can guess, by the miracle of the child's survival after her coma. Thus stories have their own logics, and one trauma can be cured by a narrative generated by another trauma. The little girls have played tying up Erik, and he muses: "Telling always binds one thing to another" (276).

The last section of the novel brings about a partial resolution to the issue of trauma: Miranda and Lane, reunited in their grief, wait until young Eggy wakes up from her coma. The final ending is uncertain: we are not sure whether Erik will let his relationship with Laura dominate or whether he will continue living alone. No matter what, the ending follows a Freudian paradigm: it affirms that talking, like writing, can lift the trauma. Writing can transform the unspeakable wound into a metaphorical scar – a true "scar-letter."

The theoretical key can be found in Hustvedt's essay on "The Real Story," in which she juxtaposes fiction with memoirs. Hustvedt rejects the idea that writers are "professional liars" (Hustvedt 2012a: 95). A good novel does not lie, even if some of the "facts" it has taken as a point of departure can be altered, transposed or distorted. Rousseau's *Confessions* may have changed some basic data in his biography, yet what stands out nevertheless is that he was able to provide "emotional truth": "His appeal is to the truth of sentiments, to *emotional truth*" (Hustvedt 2012a: 103). And then Hustvedt quotes William James's *The Principles of Psychology*: "There is no such thing as mental retention, the persistence of an idea from month to month or year to year in some mental pigeon-hole from which it can be drawn when wanted. What persists is a tendency to connection" (qtd. in Hustvedt 2012a: 104), which is not far from the principle laid out by E. M. Forster of the need to 'Only connect.' This principle has to do with history in the sense defined by Freud, since Hustvedt quotes Vico, for whom memory is the same as imagination (106).

Hustvedt explains that her own imagination was stirred when she hit upon the idea of inventing her main character, Erik Davidsen, as if he was an "imaginary brother" (Hustvedt 2012a: 163). This brother had to be a psychoanalyst. She invented a fictional therapist obsessed with his father's war trauma in order to overcome the grief that she had felt at her own father's death. Writing as one's imaginary twin who happens to be male and in a position of authority facing medical knowledge is in no way a manner of deferring to a male-centered ideology of the scientific domination of the psyche. It is rather a bold exploration of otherness. Hustvedt's "Other" is not the radical Other of Lacan or Levinas, but a fantasmatic other who is needed to entangle a web of secrets. It is much more a heuristic otherness, and it extends the limits of the self. Thus one of the main points about Lars's war trauma is that it was not caused by a wound, an accident, or a near-death experience, but by his empathy and guilt at the shooting of an unarmed enemy. The compassion for an unjustly murdered enemy puts a face on the anonymous reality of warfare – this one Japanese haunts Lars's dreams because it embodies a certain sense of ethics and responsibility for a mass slaughter of immense proportions, a Juggernaut machine in which he has been only a tiny cog.

We guess that the "shaking woman" found a point of traumatic origin in the shaken (and at times shaking) father. What has been transmitted has not just been their wound but the lethal wound done to another. The umbilicus, Freud's *Nabel*, of dreams will remain opaque, but there lies the chance of an address to the other person, the *Nebenmensch*, who thus becomes, just as I do, a *Nabelmensch*. We are all wounded by the trauma of birth, of separation, of sexuality – such a trauma will be buried in a dark forest, the forest of all myth, like the stillborn baby whose death still underpins Lars's subsequent actions. Writing the novel thus took the function of a therapy, but as Hustvedt notes, one cannot "psychoanalyze" oneself:

> Obviously, writing fictional versions of psychoanalytical sessions is not the same as being in analysis. There is no *real other* in a novel, only imagined others. But writing novels is nevertheless a form of open listening to those imagined others, one that draws on memories, transmuted by both fantasies and fears. (Hustvedt 2012a: 165)

In conclusion, then, Hustvedt would reject the thesis of an unspeakable trauma that would remain inaccessible to words; she also rejects the opposite view, the postmodern thesis that there are only virtual copies that destroy any original. For her, there is a real event at the root of the trauma, and it can be spoken, but it cannot be said fully. Without quoting Lacan on this point, Hustvedt confirms the most basic Lacanian insight: truth can only be brought to us through language, hence "half-said" (*mi-dire*) in a structure of fiction.[1] Therefore the part that has to be left unsaid, the other half of the half "well-said," should not be taken for trauma. This extra pathos is unnecessary since the "holes" of any narrative derive entirely from the structural condition of language. This is what Hustvedt explains that she follows a certain music when she writes, runs after "wild thoughts," thoughts that, as Bion always claimed, had no thinker, and are also determined by the recursive temporal logics of *Nachträglichkeit:*

> There are always things that are left unsaid – significant holes. I was aware that I was writing about memory. Freud's notion of *Nachträglichkeit* haunted the book. We remember, and we tell ourselves a story, but the meanings of what we remember are reconfigured over time. Memory and imagination cannot be separated. (Hustvedt 2012a: 40)

As Beckett would repeat: "Imagination dead, Imagine!"

Works Cited

Agamben, Giorgio. 1999. *Remnants of Auschwitz: The Witness and the Archive.* Trans. Daniel Heller-Roazen. New York: Zone Books.
Caruth, Cathy. 1996. *Unclaimed Experience: Trauma, Narrative, and History.* Baltimore: Johns Hopkins.
Freud, Sigmund. 1967. *Moses and Monotheism.* New York: Random House.
Freud, Sigmund. 1969. *Studienausgabe, IX, Fragen der Gesellschaft, Ursprünge der Religion.* Frankfurt: S. Fischer.
Hustvedt, Siri. 2008. *The Sorrows of an American.* New York: Picador.
Hustvedt, Siri. 2012a. *Living, Thinking, Looking.* New York: Picador.
Hustvedt, Siri. 2012b. "Reliving the Crash." *New York Times*, February 18. <www.opinionator.blogs.nytimes.com/2012/02/18/reliving-the-crash> [last accessed 14 January 2015].
Lacan, Jacques. 1990. *Television.* Trans. Denis Hollier, Rosalind Krauss and Annette Michelson. New York: Norton.
Leys, Ruth. 2000. *Trauma: A Genealogy.* Chicago: Chicago University Press.
Rabaté, Jean-Michel. 2014. *The Cambridge Introduction to Literature and Psychoanalysis.* Cambridge: Cambridge University Press.

---

1 I am quoting the beginning of Lacan's Television address: "I always speak the truth. Not the whole truth, because there's no way, to say it all." (Lacan 1990: 3).

Trezise, Thomas. 2013. *Witnessing Witnessing: On the Reception of Holocaust Survivor Testimony.* New York: Fordham University Press.

Katharina Donn
Crisis of Knowledge:
Trauma in *The Sorrows of an American*

In a 2010 essay, Siri Hustvedt reflects on a literary quandary that is vital for *The Sorrows of an American*, and her poetics in general. The essay, entitled "The Analyst in Fiction: Reflections on a More or Less Hidden Being," explores the parallels between two representatives of critical reflection which, according to Hustvedt, share similar roots: the literary critic and the psychoanalyst. Hustvedt argues that both invest themselves in the process of finding order in chaos, whilst still tolerating ambivalence. Their perception uncovers, as she puts it, "the strange underground of the unconscious struggling to find an articulate narrative that makes emotional sense" (Hustvedt 2010: 224). This interdisciplinary approach to fiction features in *The Sorrows of an American*, which, after all, is told through the perspective of a psychoanalyst; but it also positions Hustvedt's fictional writing in the centre of a conceptual knot which entwines metaphor and artistic creativity with the affectivity of an embodied mind on the one hand, and the reflective stance of a clinically trained professional on the other.

Trauma, the pathology of collapse, becomes a troubled testing ground for a literary epistemology which reflects on the limits and potentials of factuality, metaphor, and language. Hustvedt stages subjective shock and analytical method as a field of mutual disturbance. Her novel therefore represents a fascinating twist on the genre of trauma fiction. From within the inner turmoil and violent undercurrents of human existence, *The Sorrows of an American* develops a literary epistemology which originates in the pathology of trauma itself. It is the aim of this essay to take this as a starting point towards defining in more detail a similar interest that is currently emerging within trauma studies. As Robert Eaglestone argues when he states that

> if we are to respond to traumatic events, it must be not only to analyse the ways that these atrocities outrage the principles and virtues by which we live, but also the ways that they disrupt even how these principles and virtues come to be understood (Eaglestone 2014: 19).

Trauma affects the most basic conditions of human existence. Siri Hustvedt's novel is one response to this challenge.

In a first step, this essay defines trauma in *The Sorrows of an American* as a challenge to practices of knowing via a close reading of the various manifestations of trauma. The haunting memories which disturb the protagonists' dreams are a force that motivates the text, but simultaneously they are its object of analysis. This is a precarious balance, because trauma, as Rothberg points out, does not make for a comfortable "object of knowledge" (Rothberg 2000: 103). The shock of trauma dissociates meaning from rational as well as narrative frames, and relies on the affective embodiment of human existence to provide the more unstable knowledge of shock. Its most forceful impact is to uncover a disturbing undercurrent in human reality which eludes habitual categories of knowing that might allow to structure information according to truth or falsehood, reality or unreality, past or present. Thus moving beyond the tendency in trauma studies to emphasize ethics, gender, or identity (e.g. Deborah Horvitz, 2000; Stef Craps, 2005; Robert Hughes, 2010), *The Sorrows of an American* turns trauma into a crisis of knowledge.

What emerges through this crisis of knowledge is the potential of literary, imaginative modes to establish innovative forms of knowing. In the second and most important argumentative step, I take this as a basis to evaluate specifically literary forms of knowledge in the text by tracing the patterns of conceptual metaphors which structure the novel. My focal point, therefore, is the synthetic and synesthetic form of knowledge that the literary text develops. This goes beyond notions such as "learning from fiction" (Novitz 1987: 119), which Novitz understands in terms of factual beliefs and cognitive skills of, for instance, empathy or flexibility. Stephen Everson rather deduces a wide range of epistemic states from ancient epistemology and argues for a "natural" epistemology which is part of psychology or cognitive science (Everson 1990: 6). This multidimensional approach is crucial in a novel which is told through the perspective of a psychological analyst, and which entwines the embodied human mind with the metaphoric language of imaginative literature.

This is also the reason why the focus here is on the novel *The Sorrows of an American*, and not primarily on Hustvedt's essays. The imaginative mode (even though her novel plays with the borderlines of autobiography and fiction itself) makes the novel a space for developing a multi-dimensional knowledge not without, but beyond the rational. While the impact of trauma with its disturbing flashbacks and haunting memories undermines the epistemological categories of a purely empirical, diagnostic approach from the start, the symbolic complexity of a literary text can offer a way out of this paralyzing state of shock. Thus, the traumatic collapse re-defines the relation between clinical analysis, medical knowledge, and narrative fiction. What this novel of pathological crisis explores, therefore, are the challenges involved in the relation between literature and the sciences that the medical humanities have recently started to uncover.

1. Knowledge in Crisis: Traumatic Symptoms in *The Sorrows of an American*

Trauma is a pathology of collapse, mental and physical, and challenges the boundaries of human existence. Its almost paradigmatic status has made it a complex conceptual "trauma knot" (Luckhurst 2010: 194), touching on the humanities, medicine, the arts, and ethics. This convergence, however, also reflects one central challenge of trauma: Overwhelming in its shock impact, trauma becomes dissociated from networks of memory and cognitive structures, to become an insistent, yet absent presence in the mind. While traumatization in this novel entails the typical symptoms of nightmares or personality disorders, I will focus not on the individual pathology but on the ways in which trauma becomes a crisis of understanding itself. Trauma in *The Sorrows of an American* causes numbing and expression at the same time, and it is this ambivalence that uncovers the epistemological impact of shock.

In clinical terms, trauma is defined as an event, either experienced or witnessed, that involves the occurrence of death or an immediate threat to one's psychological or physical integrity, and leaves the victim in a condition of intense helplessness and distress, often suffering intrusive and uncontrollable recollections of the event (American Psychiatric Association 2013: 271). In contrast to this diagnostic picture, psychoanalyst Dori Laub sees a "record yet to be made" (Laub 1992: 57) in trauma, emphasizing the hauntingly elusive nature of traumatic memories which, from this psychoanalytical point of view, can be uncovered in the tentative and mutual dialogue between speaker and listener. There is a narrative quality to this dialogue that becomes even more pronounced when considering a seminal literary perspective on trauma; the unspeakable shock, as critics like Cathy Caruth or Robert Eaglestone (Caruth 1996; Eaglestone 2014) point out, wrenches experience and language apart and makes trauma a case in point for a language beyond direct reference.

Trauma is ubiquitous in *The Sorrows of an American*. The "ghost[s] walking around inside" (Hustvedt 2008: 1) have many causes and guises, but all these inner disturbances trigger changes in the ways in which reality is perceived and understood. For each affected character, trauma thus transforms into a doubled pathology: it impacts their minds and bodies, but it is also an object of reflection which challenges the connection between experience, expression, and truth. Accordingly, the traumata in *The Sorrows of an American* develop an epistemological spectrum between metaphorical meaning and analytical reason. This forms a network which relates trauma to the metaphoric referentiality of literature, to a form of visual art that plays with notions of reality and documentary truth, and to the troubled factuality of memoir.

Erik, the narrator and psychoanalytical voice of Hustvedt's novel, embodies the liminal status of psychoanalysis between clinical diagnosis and narrative. Whether in his dialogues with patients or in his own, inward struggle with the death of his father, Erik consciously relies on the synthesis of cognition and affect to order mental turmoil. On the one hand, this doubled approach inheres in psychoanalysis as such. In his essay entitled "Erinnern, Wiederholen, und Durcharbeiten"[1] (Freud 1914), Freud argues for a post-traumatic, therapeutic process that relies on affect and traumatic re-enactment to bring the traumatic experience onto the surface of consciousness. Only then can it be tackled by cognition, which, in Erik's case, means facing the fact that there will always be gaps in what he knows about his father. On the other hand, though, Hustvedt places her narrator into a contemporaneity in which this narrative, dialogical approach to trauma is further challenged by the emergence of neuroscience (Hustvedt 2008: 5). It is interesting to observe how Hustvedt, rather than mimicking the neurological or psychoanalytical method, instead awards the pivotal place to memories fused with imagination. It is the "blazing image in my mind" (Hustvedt 2008: 32), the sudden intrusion of a dreamlike reality, that becomes a central trope in a novel that explores new practices of knowledge after trauma.

The plot of *The Sorrows of an American* revolves around Erik's recently deceased father, who left his children a memoir with enigmatic gaps. The fact that this memoir is actually a reproduction of Hustvedt's father's writing is telling here, as it inscribes the notion and expectation of authenticity into this text. However, events in the novel make it clear this allegedly direct pathway into another person's mind and suffering has multiple layers, in which the very factual knowledge of survival – which firewood will serve you best (Hustvedt 2008: 7), or how to catch gophers (Hustvedt 2008: 12) – allows the underlying traumata of the Great Depression and war to emerge through unsaid gaps in between the lines.

For Erik and Inga, the most tantalizing of these gaps is the story of Lisa Odland. The note they find in his papers, "it can't matter now that she's in heaven or to the ones here on earth" (Hustvedt 2008: 4) implies a troubling story that might potentially explain the absences in the memoir. Just as the claims of the

---

1 In his essay "Erinnern, Wiederholen und Durcharbeiten" (1914), Freud develops a tripartite therapeutic model: Repetitions of a traumatic memory in the sense of enactment or transference function as a trigger for actual remembering in the work of remembrance; in so, the resistance which causes the pathological repression is made conscious and the corresponding drives can then be 'worked through.'

memoir genre to give a coherent story generally fail, though, Erik's and Inga's quest for the missing knowledge that might give their father's accounts a deeper meaning is illusory. They find Lisa, and learn her story of a stillborn birth and a dead baby buried in the ground close to their father's farm. "But it doesn't *explain* much about Pappa, does it?" (Hustvedt 2008: 233; emphasis original), Inga notes at the end, and this is exactly the point here. The factual knowledge of Lisa's history of trauma alone cannot provide the intimate understanding the family craves. Nevertheless, the character of Lisa Odland does introduce the required trajectory to the emotionality of their father's life as well. She manufactures dolls with stories of loss, injury, and death, and these materializations of hidden pain are the actual instances of truth that Erik and Inga find. Neither factual nor linked to any specific person, these dolls embody the traumatic suffering which is tangible between the lines of their father's "memoir full of holes" (Hustvedt 2008: 8).

Lisa Odland, therefore, is one instance in the novel where the affective embodiment of pain is translated into artistic expression, and replaces factual truth claims. Miranda, illustrator, artist, and Erik's elusive object of desire, as well as her ex-partner Jeffrey Lane are two other characters who play with similar notions. Miranda's trauma is cultural instead of personal. Her grotesque drawings of nightmarish figures channel the history of colonial oppression and slavery. The gaping mouths, sharp teeth, and distorted figures of her pictures are part of an alternate reality where the habitual world re-emerges in an uncannily estranged form. Traumatic history, thus, does not obey historiographical claims but the embodied emotionality and disguises of the dream.

Lane's photographic art revolves around similarly reversed categories of reality and truth. His work is haunted by his parents' violent death in a car crash. The compulsiveness of this "documenting maniac" (Hustvedt 2008: 74), however, is a performance as much as it might be a psychological symptom. He negates the documentary claims of photography by manipulating the pictures he takes, so that reality infinitely regresses behind his distorted simulacra. It is fitting, of course, that he quotes postmodern theories of virtuality (Hustvedt 2008: 204), but even more to the point is the realization that any truth claim of his photographs can emerge through personal association and the representation of corporeality alone. Both Miranda and Erik are troubled when they find themselves to be embodiments of affective states, be it anger, vulnerability, or personal intimacy in his exhibition. As the documentary potential of photography fails, this individualized and emotional response points to a different, traumatic reality underneath the surface.

References to literary culture add another dimension to this, and it is interesting to observe how the topic of trauma literature in *The Sorrows of an Amer-*

ican enacts the haunting nature of trauma. On the novel's surface, this is represented by Sonia, Erik's teenage niece, who is suffering from intrusive nightmares after witnessing people falling to their deaths from the World Trade Towers outside the windows of her high school on September 11, 2001. Her compulsive orderliness is a symptom of her disturbed mind, and a strategy to keep her troubled emotions at bay. However, Sonia also writes poems, belatedly and exclamatory, which convey the inherent connection between traumatic numbing and embodied memory, between "locked throats and streaming bowels" (Hustvedt 2008: 178). These poems are framed by two more elusive presences, and need to be read in relation to one of Erik's patients, Mr. T., and her father, the author Max Blaustein. Blaustein haunts the novel as an authority in touching the dark undercurrents of human existence with stories that, as his widow Inga puts it, "scraped on some darkness in people" (Hustvedt 2008: 19). It is Mr. T., though, who truly embodies the implosive force that trauma has on literature. In a stark contrast to Hustvedt's own vision of narrative as a strategy of order (Hustvedt 2010: 225), Mr. T., the son of Holocaust survivors, embodies a nightmare of words. When he is fearing the "texts coming through, beating me hard up there" (Hustvedt 2008: 89), language for him attains a threatening materiality. The "killer words" (Hustvedt 2008: 89) he fears are those of the dead, but their forcefulness is ambivalent. It simultaneously exhibits the compulsion to express and the failure of language, and is thus the most striking instance of traumatized language in the novel.

Trauma, therefore, generates a crisis of knowledge and exposes the limits of habitual categories of what is factual and real. It introduces corporeality, affect, and the alternate world of dreams into the equation and calls for a form of cognition that is open to what lies beyond the purely rational in the conventional sense of the word. Imaginative texts can be a strategy of renewed order to some extent, as Marks points out when she observes that *The Sorrows of an American* "confronts the ghosts of the past and strives to re-establish a sense of completeness in the aftermath of death" (Marks 2014: 203). On another level, though, the synthesizing voice of psychoanalysis, in between medical study and narrative exploration, provides a space in which an innovative literary epistemology of trauma that is based on ambivalence and collapse can be developed.

Trauma, therefore, holds a liminal epistemological status that challenges Foucault's "clinical gaze" and its more contemporary counterparts that Jeffrey Lanes plays with, the narrativity of psychoanalytical analysis, and the language of literary metaphor alike. Trauma distorts the ways in which we know and perceive the world. It offers, in Caruth's words, an "active resistance to the platitudes of knowledge" (Caruth 1995: 155), but this is a deconstructive move in the most literal sense of the word. Whilst imploding the most basic habitual categories such as real or unreal, true or false, it also opens up the possibility of a new, emergent form of knowledge. When it comes to defining this, however, Cathy Caruth focuses on the enigmatic referential status of a traumatic unspeakability, which is increasingly controversial in trauma studies and falls a little short in terms of Siri Hustvedt's fiction of analysis as well. Thus, this essay suggests an epistemology of trauma based on what Eaglestone calls a "post-deconstructive understanding of language" (Eaglestone 2014: 20). *The Sorrows of an American* develops a language and patterns of metaphor which create meaning because they are multidimensional and intertwine the materiality of human embodiment with an intuitive, flexible form of cognition.

2. Between Materiality and Innovative Meaning: Patterns of Metaphor in *The Sorrows of an American*

These multidimensional metaphors combine the corporeality of trauma with imaginative flexibility, and thus take trauma beyond paralysis. In a novel with as eclectic a mix of characters as *The Sorrows of an American*, this has implications for the limits and potentials of various cultures of knowledge as well. The conceptual metaphors which structure the text introduce a literary epistemology that synthesizes and transgresses the established disciplines of research that the characters here represent. Considering that psychoanalysis, as a discipline, is positioned in between clinical diagnosis and narration, this seems only apt. Trauma thus becomes not only a crisis of knowledge for individual minds but a broader challenge.

The Sorrows of an American responds to this by staging the encounter of various such cultures within the fields of psychoanalysis, neuroscience, the history of medicine, and philosophy. The culminating point of this is a dinner party which assembles an expert in medical history and dream theories, a psychoanalyst, a philosopher, an artist, and a professor of art history and English. Traumatic nightmares thus become the subject of scholarly discussion as much as a troubling experience in this novel, and this entwinement of experience with analysis is crucial for the question of knowledge here. The characters draw back on their habitual academic categories in their attempts to discover hidden meanings via embodied intuition, rational analysis, or artistic experiment. Hustvedt's knowledge cultures, though, are no fixed entities. The symbolic dimensions of knowledge as in literature or philosophy embrace the medico-scientific desire for epistemic security, while the analyst's objectifying gaze equally seeps through the imaginative, metaphoric patterns which structure *The Sorrows of an American*. Trauma, the point at which "knowing and not-knowing" (Caruth 1996: 2–3) intersect, redefines the relation between the various truth claims represented here. This is voiced by Inga, the narrator Erik's sister, when she observes that "[i]t's as if my sadness soaked the architecture. I can tell you a story about it, and I wouldn't be lying, but would that reconstruction of events be real or true?" (Hustvedt 2008: 45) The different ways to gain knowledge about reality, whether intuitive, metaphoric or empirical, all revolve around this realization that notions of the real story, objective facts, or pure factuality do not hold any more. If and in which ways central categories of meaning can be re-established in a post-traumatic condition that takes knowledge beyond the purely rational therefore constitutes the central question of the novel.

That all these knowledge cultures come into contact with the more elusive epistemologies of art, but also more generally of embodiment, affect, empathy, and intuition, is one response to the traumatic crisis of understanding that defines the novel. Musselman has rightly pointed out that trauma is an "embodied epistemology" (Musselman 2006: 3), but its potential is more than just the materialization of scientific method, as she suggests. In the aftermath of traumatic collapse, the encounter between art and science becomes mutually transformative. The traumata in the novel thus become troubled starting points for innovations in meaning and the ways in which we can know the world.

Through patterns of metaphor and corporeality, *The Sorrows of an American* develops a post-rational, literary form of knowledge. It emphasizes the perspectivity of knowledge but also acknowledges the epistemological potential of emotion and corporeal sensitivity. What makes this so noticeable, though, is that this physicality is inherently interconnected with conceptual metaphoric patterns surrounding the fall, the scar, as well as another central network revolving around manifestations of the 'fugue.' These interconnect language, embodiment and knowledge. Both the referentiality of language to experience and the meaning and knowledge that can be obtained about it are therefore rooted in the materialized metaphors of literary language.

Cathy Caruth structures her 1996 monograph on trauma around the metaphors of 'departure,' 'awakening,' 'falling,' or 'burning.' This approach is interesting for two reasons: it emphasizes the typical tropes which imaginative trauma literature shares with Freudian or Lacanian psychoanalysis, thus uncovering not only the common topics, but also the commonalities in expression used by both. Even if she does not explicitly state this, this also means that Caruth's analysis relies on patterns which can be read literally as well as figuratively. These two dimensions – for instance, the actual, embodied fall suffered by some trauma victims and the metaphoric fall from security which trauma entails – point to the potential of metaphor that this essay explores.

Such conceptual metaphors in *The Sorrows of an American* include the fall as well, but also revolve around dreaming, scarring and hiding. All of these share three dimensions: Firstly, they are objects of analysis for the philosophers, dream theorists, and doctors who people this novel; secondly, they underline the embodied materiality of human existence; and thirdly, they function on a figurative level when they become markers of the alternate reality of dark undercurrents and unspoken trauma in the novel as a whole. Not part of language alone, these metaphors materialize the impact of trauma whilst simultaneously providing an imaginative meta-level on which to develop responses to the traumatic collapse. They are therefore part of an epistemology that interconnects embodiment with literary language and makes known the parts of human existence that are beyond the grasp of the factual, but also too material to be treated as purely emotional.

These metaphoric constellations are patterns of meaning which live off Ricoeur's "semantic clash" (Ricœur 1986: 214) of metaphor that is always also the creation of new meaning, and a distorted, de-mechanized, and embodied perception. However, this does not entail an undifferentiated unity of science and literature, or the vagueness of an "irrational epistemology of literature" (Porush 1993: 38). Hustvedt's text rather shows how a literary approach can transform knowledge in relational and metadiscursive ways. This is an intricate text, and rather than promoting irrationality, it redefines cognition in ways that evoke Martha Nussbaum's argument for the cognitive components in affect (Nussbaum 1990: 41).

The protagonists of *The Sorrows of an American* experience this. "*I'm bruised*" (Hustvedt 2008: 160; emphasis original), Erik's internal voice says and thus expresses an unconscious knowledge of emotional pain which relies on a corporeal metaphor and links him to Lisa's injured dolls in the logic of the novel. In these patterns reading, but also recognition, are transformed into a processual and interconnected act which relies on emotionality. This is particularly noteworthy because one of the most influential theories of embodied metaphor, by Lakoff and Johnson, omits this emotive component which is part of cognition. Their argument that conceptual meaning is largely metaphorical whilst also being grounded in embodiment has had a groundbreaking impact on theories of cognitive metaphor. However, when Burke suggests that concepts like affectivity and emotionality need to complement this otherwise exclusive focus on physical embodiment (Burke 2002: 391), he strikes a point that is crucial in *Sorrows of an American*. The metaphors which this text works with enhance the affective quality of cognition not despite, but because of their origin in corporeality. Affect, after all, is a "living discourse" (Green 1999: 231) which mediates between the body and language.

The metaphoric patterns of this novel therefore take its epistemological potential beyond the interdisciplinary assemblage of cultures of knowledge which the protagonists represent. They add a structure that is dream-like when the central tropes reoccur on various planes of reality and in different guises, and through which runs an apprehension[2] of vulnerability. Where the novel's tangible cultures of knowledge are concerned, these patterns of variation and return underline the narrative qualities shared by all these discourses, be it medical sciences or philosophy.

The fall is one of these conceptual metaphors. A generally prevalent trope in the context of trauma, it has become even more so after the terrorist attacks on September 11, 2001, which figure in *The Sorrows of an American*. The multiple dimensions of this trope establish close interconnections between a literal fall taken by a body falling from height and its literary transformation. From an epistemological perspective, even this first conceptual metaphor therefore makes tangible the affective and embodied quality which characterizes the way in which human experience becomes knowable in *The Sorrows of an American*.

The novel ends in a fall. Eggy, Miranda's daughter, falls from a window and into a coma, from which she awakes, but the impact forcefully exposes the bodily vulnerability of the spirited child. It is the same "precarious life" (Butler 2004), as Butler succinctly phrases this in a 9/11 context, that is at the root of Sonia's trauma. The human bodies in free fall between life and death which she witnesses on this morning are never directly directly linked to Eggy's fall, but the textual hints are so strong that the girl's "blank eyes and her mouth tight" (Hustvedt 2008: 47) become telling gestures towards this hundredfold fall from the towers. True to her literary talents, Sonia builds on the indirect referentiality of trauma poetry to express this memory, which otherwise remains dissociated from expression. She uses the image of policemen looking for body parts on rooftops, thus transforming the height of Manhattan buildings to the low ground of human mortality (Hustvedt 2008: 120).

These falls thus materialize the ephemerality of human existence and underline gravity, the force towards death which is an inevitable component of embodied being. In both cases, moreover, this apprehension emanates from physical injury, which itself eludes clear understanding. When Sonia falls silent after

---

[2] I here draw on Butler definition of apprehension as "a form of knowing, […] bound up with sensing and perceiving, but in ways that are not always – or not yet – conceptual forms of knowledge" (Butler 2009: 5).

9/11, and Miranda faces the "nameless monitoring equipment" (Hustvedt 2008: 281) inserted into her daughter's wounded body, the knowledge of these falls moves beyond the alleged reliability of vision or the security of medical data. It is empathic affectivity, which mediates between the fallen body and language, which constitutes the only possibility to know, in a primary sense, the experience of these falls.

There is one more way of falling in the novel, though, and this one uproots the habitual categories of understanding in an equally radical but completely different way. Mr. T.'s literary history engulfs him in an imploded space, the non-dimensionality of which lacks even the most rudimentary baselines for orientation. His writing is also a Babelian tour de force, but it does more than evoking this biblical precursor to the falling towers of our contemporaneity. In the "Rage Page" (Hustvedt 2008: 90) of his poetry, language itself is in free fall and suspends both reference and logical understanding. The reason why Mr. T.'s precarious existence is so crucial to the interrelation between knowledge and trauma emerges when considering the referentiality of what he says. His intertextual nightmare recycles an eclectic range of the epitomes of philosophy and literary thought, such as Goethe or Buddha, into phrases that evoke Dadaist experiments. He detaches fragments of what was formerly upheld as cultural wisdom into statements like "Lavinia in Slovenia is slipping into schizophrenia" (Hustvedt 2008: 89). Referentiality or any truth claims thus collapse, but what remains is the potential of language, however nonsensical it might seem from a logical point of view, to express traumatic collapse. This makes Mr. T. the central instance in the project of defining post-traumatic practices of knowledge beyond the rational. He expresses the – in his case truncated – potential of literary, metaphoric language to generate an affective and embodied form of meaning. From this suspension, the rhyming and onomatopoetic materiality of his multiple languages becomes the basis of a different system of meaning. Martha Nussbaum's "learning to fall" (Nussbaum 1990: 274), which requires the self to rely on knowledge beyond evidence, recurs here in a renewed form. The post-traumatic falls in *The Sorrows of an American* are particularly striking because they deconstruct the purely rational cognition which Hustvedt generally takes issue with. Their embodied nature foregrounds the perspectivity of knowledge which Zapf detects in *What I Loved* as well (Zapf 2008: 179).

The scars, another metaphoric pattern, underline this when they build their ambivalent referentiality on this suspended apprehension of vulnerability, and foreground the materialization of metaphor in *The Sorrows of an American*. A trace that marks a violent occurrence but does not contextualize or explain, the scar initially turns the epistemology of the fall on its head. It is not knowledge beyond evidence, but to the contrary it is pure proof of the fact that something happened, if not how or what that occurrence was. This almost indexical referentiality, though, is more complex in the novel itself. Like the falls, the scars in *The Sorrows of an American* interconnect bodily injury with metaphoric, artistic transformations of inner and outward bruising.

Lisa Odland is a scar in Erik's father's memoir as such, a trace of an occurrence that remains unspoken. For Lisa herself, though, "the body keeps the score" (Van der Kolk 1996: 215) as van der Kolk would phrase it. Her neck is marred by the scars of a fire she survived as a small child, and which she only learned about when she was grown up. This makes Lisa's body the carrier of a memory that, for a long time, remained enigmatic, but it is only via the dolls she makes that the impact of this becomes apparent. "Telling but not telling" (Hustvedt 2008: 189), these figures are embodiments of stories of pain and warp the notion of testimony. The realism of the bruises or pained expressions on these dolls subverts the factual truth claims inherent in testimony in a very subtle way. They are emanations of fictional stories, after all, so that their referent is imaginative; testimony therefore is positioned in a liminal space between imagination on the one hand and reality on the other hand. This includes realism as a representational mode, but also reality as a potential occurrence, a story that might have been real. Any claim to know these stories of suffering therefore has the bruised body as its sole basis, which actualizes a pain that otherwise remains elusive.

The other body artist of the novel, Jeffrey Lane, radicalizes this epistemological ambivalence. By cutting out the eyes in photographs, Lane achieves an emotionally disturbing effect that is also a comment on what Inga, in an otherwise unconnected episode in the text, calls the "ocular bias" (Hustvedt 2008: 34) of Western culture. When Miranda sees these scarred photographs of herself without eyes, this has a paradoxical effect: she sees that she does not see, and with the empirical connotations of the visual sense thus subverted, it is – again – affectivity through which Lane's photographs are witnessed. That trauma and mental illness generally becomes an artistic stance for Lane is a pungent side effect which he shares with Lisa Odland. The collapse of trauma is what allows them to express the violent turmoil that they perceive underneath the surfaces of people's lives, and they explicitly stage trauma as an artistic performance and a trajectory into hidden layers of experience. The ethics of this, especially when considering the troubling effect both have on the lives of others, may be questionable. What this shows, however, is that trauma as a "crisis of truth" (Felman 1995: 16) is one nodal point at which pathological suffering converges with the sense that the precariousness of human life eludes any such epistemological categories which rely on a stark differentiation between factuality and imagination. The embodied affectivity of the scar is a mode of apprehension, artistic and emphatic, that points towards a new category of making sense of such events.

Other metaphoric patterns in the text, such as the returning trope of the fugue, differentiate this further. This is most clearly embodied by Erik's father, who in sudden spurts walks off his pain for hours and during the night. This literal act of fleeing, however, also denotes the elusiveness of secure knowledge. One traumatic event in the novel shows this particularly clearly. In WWII, Erik's father witnesses the shooting of a soldier who is kneeling in a position that might suggest prayer, or reaching for a hand grenade. In this case, this knowledge would make the difference between life and death, but it remains elusive. It is this ambivalence that makes it traumatic, but in the embodied gesture of prayer, it has a deep impact on the young soldier and thus, again, roots this memory in affect. The "hidden and oblique shadow" (Hustvedt 2008: 30) in *The Sorrows of an American* therefore represents not only pain and trauma, but also a practice of knowledge that eludes conventional categories of factuality or truth, but is perceptible through its embodiment and intuitive emotionality.

The conceptual metaphors which structure *The Sorrows of an American* therefore entwine figurative language with the affective materiality of human existence. They develop a multidimensional practice of knowledge that cannot be grasped in a simple rational-irrational duality, but which constitutes a new mode of cognition. The power of metaphor to combine the subjective perspectivity of corporeality with the interconnected reach of these dreamlike, figurative patterns is the key point in Hustvedt's approach. Not despite of, but because she chooses the novel and thus an imaginative form of expression can this epistemology of material metaphors develop.

3. Conclusion: The Post-Traumatic Knowledge of Literature

This assertion of the potential of imaginative literature to engage with questions of knowledge is one of the most fascinating points in *The Sorrows of an American*. Such a potential has, of course, been hinted at frequently– for instance by Walsh in her assertion of the "triumphant intelligibility" (Walsh 1969: 71) of literature. Hustvedt, however, goes beyond the connotations of epiphany which this concept carries. Her approach uses empirical study, it appreciates logical analysis and yet ascertains that both these modes only have meaning when they integrate affectivity and acknowledge embodiment. What the associative patterns of *The Sorrows of an American* thus engender is a form of cognition that is created by metaphors steeped in the materiality of human existence. Where Eaglestone sees a change in language from a direct, inherent connection to the discourse of the modern period (Eaglestone 2014: 19), Hustvedt's post-traumatic fiction is one prism for another change. Understanding and reference move with and beyond deconstruction to a language of embodied metaphor and intuitive analysis, a form of cognition, that is, which completely breaks apart the dualisms of a two-culture-thesis. Sense perception, memory, and inference can become instances of knowledge, as Lackey reminds us (Lackey 2006: 4), and this is exactly the point where the novel format proves its epistemological potential. The patterned processes of discovery onto which narrative embarks shape the world from the point of view of trauma, in which habitual categories do not hold anymore. It is through the multi-dimensional interaction between memory and imagination, empiricism and fiction, that the metaphoric language of literature uncovers the inherent interconnection between rationality affect, corporeality, and intuition. Through the multi-dimensional patterns of several conceptual metaphors, *The Sorrows of an American* establishes the possibility of cognition beyond the rational.

Works Cited

American Psychiatric Association (ed). 2013. *Diagnostic and Statistical Manual of Mental Disorders*. 5th ed. Washington, DC: American Psychiatric Association.

Burke, Michael. 2002. "Touching from a Distance: Emotion, Culture and Cognitive Metaphor." In: Joyce Goggin and Michael Burke (eds.). *Meaning, Frame and Metaphor*. Amsterdam: ASCA Press. 391–409.

Butler, Judith. 2004. *Precarious Life: The Powers of Mourning and Violence*. London/New York: Verso.

Butler, Judith. 2009. *Frames of War: When is Life Grievable?* London/New York: Verso.

Caruth, Cathy. 1996. *Unclaimed Experience: Trauma, Narrative, and History*. Baltimore/London: The Johns Hopkins University Press.

Caruth, Cathy (ed.). 1995. *Trauma: Explorations in Memory*. Baltimore/London: The Johns Hopkins University Press.

Craps, Stef. 2005. *Trauma and Ethics in the Novels of Graham Swift: No Short-Cuts to Salvation*. Brighton/Portland: Sussex Academic Press.

Eaglestone, Robert. 2014. "Knowledge, 'Afterwardsness' and the Future of Trauma Theory." In: Gert Buelens, Sam Durrant and Robert Eaglestone (eds.). *The Future of Trauma Theory: Contemporary Literary and Cultural Criticism*. London/New York: Routledge. 11–22.

Everson, Stephen. 1990. *Epistemology*. Cambridge: Cambridge University Press.

Felman, Shoshana. 1995. "Education and Crisis, or the Vicissitudes of Teaching." In: Cathy Caruth (ed.). *Trauma: Explorations in Memory*. Baltimore/London: The Johns Hopkins University Press. 13–60.

Freud, Sigmund. 1969 [1914]. "Erinnern. Wiederholen, Durcharbeiten." In: Anna Freud (ed.). *Sigmund Freud: Gesammelte Werke.* Bd. V. London: Imago. 125–136.

Green, André. 1999. *The Fabric of Affect in the Psychoanalytic Discourse.* London/New York: Routledge.

Horvitz, Deborah M. 2000. *Literary Trauma: Sadism, Memory and Sexual Violence in American Women's Fiction.* New York: State University of New York Press.

Hughes, Robert. 2010. *Ethics, Aesthetics, and the Beyond of Language.* Albany: State University of New York Press.

Hustvedt, Siri. 2008. *The Sorrows of an American.* New York: Picador.

Hustvedt, Siri. 2010. "The Analyst in Fiction: Reflections on a more or less Hidden Being." *Contemporary Psychoanalysis* 46.2: 224–234.

Kolk, Bessel A. van der. 1996. "The Body Keeps the Score: Approaches to the Psychobiology of Posttraumatic Stress Disorder." In: Bessel A. van der Kolk, Alexander C. McFarlane and Lars Wiesaeth (eds.). *Traumatic Stress: The Effects of Overwhelming Experience on Mind, Body, and Society.* New York/London: Guilford Press. 214–241.

Lackey, Jennifer. 2006. "Introduction." In: Jennifer Lackey and Ernest Sosa (eds.). *The Epistemology of Testimony.* Oxford: Oxford University Press. 1–21.

Lakoff, George and Mark Johnson. 1999. *Philosophy in the Flesh: The Embodied Mind and its Challenge to Western Thought.* New York: Basic Books.

Laub, Dori. 1992. "Bearing Witness, or the Vicissitudes of Listening." In: Shoshana Felman and Dori Laub (eds.). *Testimony.* New York/London: Routledge. 57–74.

Luckhurst, Roger. 2010. "The Trauma Knot." In: Richard Crownshaw, Jane Kilby, and Antony Rowland (eds.). *The Future of Memory.* New York/Oxford: Berghahn Books. 191–206.

Marks, Christine. 2014. *"I Am Because You Are": Relationality in the Works of Siri Hustvedt.* Heidelberg: Winter.

Musselman Green, Elizabeth. 2006. *Nervous Conditions: Science and the Body Politic in Early Industrial Britain.* Albany: State University of New York Press.

Novitz, David. 1987. *Knowledge, Fiction & Imagination.* Philadelphia: Temple University Press.

Nussbaum, Martha C. 1990. *Love's Knowledge: Essays on Philosophy and Literature.* Oxford: Oxford University Press.

Porush, David. 1993. "Voyage to Eudoxia: The Emergence of a Post-Rational Epistemology in Literature and Science." *SubStance* 22.2/3: 38–49.

Ricœur, Paul. 1986. *The Rule of Metaphor: Multi-Disciplinary Studies of the Creation of Meaning in Language.* London: Routledge.

Rothberg, Michael. 2000. *Traumatic Realism: The Demands of Holocaust Representation.* Minneapolis: University of Minnesota Press.

Walsh, Dorothy. 1969. *Literature and Knowledge.* Middletown, CT: Wesleyan University Press.

Zapf, Hubert. 2008. "Narrative, Ethics, and Postmodern art in Siri Hustvedt's *What I Loved.*" In: Astrid Erll, Herbert Grabes and Ansgar Nünning (eds.). *Ethics in Culture: The Dissemination of Values Through Literature and Other Media.* Berlin/New York: De Gruyter. 171–194.

Katja Sarkowsky
"The wounded psyche is not a broken leg": Illness, Injury, and Writing the Self in Siri Hustvedt's Work

In an essay entitled "The Analyst in Fiction," Siri Hustvedt quotes a discarded passage from *The Sorrows of an American* in which her protagonist and narrator Erik Davidsen (himself a psychoanalyst) states the seemingly obvious: "The wounded psyche is not a broken leg" (Hustvedt 2012: 152). He refers to the difficulty of identifying, categorizing, let alone 'healing' the wounds of the psyche, but he also expresses his anxiety over where his profession is going: "'Disorder' is the word of choice these days. Mental illness is a state of chaos and the job of mental health professionals is to restore order by all means at their disposal" (Hustvedt 2012: 152–153). In the medical profession, the restoration of 'order' at all costs, he implies, is a banishment of ambiguity that concerns not only the illness, but also the very sense of the patient's self. However, Davidsen as well as other characters in Hustvedt's work – including Hustvedt herself – seeks ways to come to terms with the ambivalence of life experience and life stories rather than banish it.

The representation of impaired bodies and shaken and wounded souls abounds in Siri Hustvedt's fiction. *The Blindfold*'s (1992) protagonist not only works as a research assistant for a medical historian, "filling up index cards with information about great diseases" (Hustvedt 1992: 9), she is also hospitalized for severe migraine (one of the many autobiographical facets of the novel). In *The Enchantment of Lily Dahl* (1996), Martin Petersen is obsessed with the protagonist and their shared past to the point of delusion and finally kills himself. *What I Loved* (2003) presents one of the characters, Violet, in her continuous academic engagement with hysteria, eating disorder, and personality disorder. As Caroline Rosenthal has argued, "[o]ne function of depicting hysteria in *What I Loved* is to show how the boundary between the body as an imaginary space and the body as a real space visibly begins to shift" (2011: 106), and Violet's books about eating and personality disorders serve as forums for academic discussions about the cultural implications of the body represented also in the art produced by one of the male characters in the novel (Rosenthal 2011); another character in the same novel, Mark, illustrates this shift in his inability to articulate his personal boundaries. The already mentioned I-narrator of *The Sorrows of an American* (2008) is a psychiatrist and psychoanalyst, and many of the sessions with his suffering patients as well as his own struggles are recounted in the novel; what is more, Erik Davidsen's reflections about his own life, the impact his patients have upon him, and his dealing with his father's death highlight the fluidity and blurriness of the line that ambiguously separates 'illness' from 'health.' *The Summer without Men* (2011) begins with the protagonist Mia's recollection of herself 'going mad' and being put in a hospital after her husband's separation from her: "In the end, Dr. P. diagnosed me with Brief Psychotic Disorder, also known as Brief Reactive Psychosis, which means that you are genuinely crazy but not for long. If it goes on for more than one month, you need another label" (2011: 1); while this depiction rests on a heavy dose of self-irony, this initial 'madness' and the protagonist's creative writing work with teenage inpatients of a mental hospital also stress the difficulty to separate the 'normal' from the 'abnormal.' And in the most recent *The Blazing World*, not only does Hustvedt include with 'The Barometer' a character whose boundaries between his internal and the external world are so permeable that his everyday interactions with others are impaired – her protagonist Harriet Burden, whose story is told retrospectively after her death, has died of cancer. Cancer, but also anorexia and hysteria have been heavily metaphorized in American culture, and the latter two in particular maneuver the ambivalent and permeable boundary between the physical and the psychological (Sontag 1978); and *The Sorrows of an American* and *What I Loved* have been discussed by critics as 'neuronovels' (Morton in Kucharzewski 2013) and 'brain novels' (Stedman 2008) respectively, that is as novels that take up to explore recent neurological theories and their implication for the conception of the self.

This interest in the impaired body and the shaken psyche also finds a manifestation in Hustvedt's essays and her autobiographical writings. *The Shaking Woman* (2010) is a complex text both in context and form. It presents an example of what Thomas Couser has called an "impairment memoir" (2011: 232), a text that explores the effect of a bodily (or mental) impairment upon the self without presenting this impairment as the basis of an identity as 'disabled.' Couser expresses a fundamental uneasiness with the lack of political commitment manifest in such narratives, a commitment to the betterment of the situation of people afflicted by physical or mental 'impairments.' While I do not share this uneasiness, I regard his identification of a difference between memoirs that claim a particular disability as the basis of their identity and that seek an alignment "with a community of people sharing their condition" (2011: 232) on the one hand, and memoirs that probe into the effect of such impairments upon their sense of self, that try to explain and understand it without seeking that sense of identity on the other as crucial. Couser's categorization refers to memoirs, but it offers an important aspect for the understanding of illness and injury in Hustvedt's fictional writing as well: while illnesses of various kinds appear frequently in her prose, either as afflicting characters directly or as something characters are professionally concerned with (e. g. Erik Davidsen in *Sorrows* or Violet Blom in *What I Loved*), they are not presented as something to be dealt with, done away with, or claimed, but instead fundamentally question the possibility of the individual to create a coherent narrative of life and self – that is, the possibility to create 'order.'

It is thus, I want to propose, no accident that there is no sense of 'healing' in Hustvedt's fictional and non-fictional work. The emphasis on psychoanalytic and neurophysiological paradigms – both in content and structure – suggests that the various illnesses and impairments be read not merely as depictions of 'real life afflictions' but more importantly as metaphors through which to investigate "how mind, brain, body, and culture interact to create or perform selfhood" (Tougaw 2012: 174). Reading Hustvedt's fictional and autobiographical work side by side is not meant to propose an easy conflation of the two, even though her fiction is heavily infused with autobiographical aspects, but rather to highlight the similar narrative strategies deployed by Hustvedt in her complex investigations of the profound ambiguities of selfhood. Illness, mental and/or physical impairment, in this context most pronouncedly serves to explore the porosity and fragility, but also the necessity of a boundary between self and other.

While this, as briefly illustrated, plays a crucial role in all of Hustvedt's work, the function of illness and its metaphorical implications in the narrative construction of self (both fictional and autobiographical, problematic as this blunt juxtaposition may be) has shifted. In the following, I will briefly look at the ways in which selves are narratively constructed in Hustvedt's work, before I move on to the use of illness and impairment for such constructions and argue that, most recently, Hustvedt has begun to explore the impact of a broader variety of illnesses; while most of her work so far has been dominated by an engagement with various forms of personality disorders and with illnesses often associated with images of femininity – anorexia, migraine, hysteria –, in *The Blazing World* (2014) she tackles with cancer yet another, heavily metaphorized type of disease. In this latest novel as well as in the autobiographical *The Shaking Woman* (2010), Hustvedt not only takes on the question of the metaphorical function of illness for self-construction, but she also explores the ramification of this function for life writing, both fictional and autobiographical.

1. "I am multitudes": Narratives of the Relational Self

The importance of seeing and art, of intertextuality, and of doubles or alter egos in Hustvedt's work has been frequently emphasized. These are all aspects of a relationality to be understood on various levels, referring on the one hand to the relationship between the text and the reader and intertextually to that between Hustvedt's and other texts. On the other hand, it refers intratextually to the relationship between individual characters or characters and their environment. While these aspects concern distinct types of relationality, they nevertheless coalesce in the construction of self as relational, and in the importance of narrative for this construction. As Christine Marks has summed up in her study on the role of relationality in Hustvedt's work, "[h]ighlighting the self's need for a coherent narrative structure of personal experience, Hustvedt gives expression to the other's significance in the narration of the self" (2014: 213). This, as Marks points out, goes hand in hand with Hustvedt's interest in the recent developments in neuroscience, such as the discovery of mirror neurons (2014: 210–212). Taking this a step further, this leads to a reading of Hustvedt's work, both fictional and non-fictional, as a fundamental investigation into relationality as such and into structures of life writing.

Both relationality and the narrative construction of the self are by now a critical commonplace. Contemporary theories of life writing take the genre as one of self-construction rather than self-expression; this construction is a narrative process, embedded in a speaking position shaped by factors such as gender, class, or ethnicity, and in direct or indirect dialogue with others and their conception of the self. As Judith Butler has argued in *Giving an Account of Oneself*,

> the "I" does not stand apart from the prevailing matrix of ethical norms and conflicting moral frameworks. In an important sense, this matrix is also the condition for the emergence of the "I," even though the 'I' is not causally induced by those norms. [...] When the "I" seeks to give an account of itself, it can start with itself, but it will find that this self is already implicated in a social temporality that exceeds its own capacities for narration; indeed, when the "I" seeks to give an account of itself, an account that must include the conditions of its own emergence, it must, as a matter of necessity, become a social theorist. (2005: 7–8)

So this account of the self is necessarily social and a narrative. Narratives, as Paul John Eakin has put it, are an integral part of who we are (2008: 1), and they depend crucially on our relationship to others, the environment in which we are located, and the set of rules that governs these relationships. "When we talk or write about ourselves," Eakin writes, "we participate in a rule-governed discourse that establishes us as normal individuals in the minds of others" (2008: 2). These rules include the conduct between people as well as genre conventions. "We know the identity protocols by heart," he continues. "The working of the system becomes visible, however, when memory fails and narrative competence collapses, or when self-narration is deliberately refused" (2008: 23). One such potential diffusion is the experience of illness. So while many autobiographies seek to construct a more or less coherent (but not necessarily unified) sense of self, often against the background of reflections on the fragmentation of the self, narratives of illness centrally deal with the 'unsettled self,' more prone to the idea of re-establishing coherence as 'lost' in the face of bodily or mental disintegration, a coherence that is, as Eakin and others have pointed out, directly connected to common notions of 'normalcy' (2008: 30).

While illness interrupts notions of normalcy, potentially casting body and/or mind into a state of 'otherness' (as can be observed throughout Hustvedt's work), it nevertheless is a common experience: each of us can easily and unexpectedly be affected. In *Illness as Metaphor*, Susan Sontag comments:

> Illness is the night-side of life, a more onerous citizenship. Everyone who is born holds dual citizenship, in the kingdom of the well and in the kingdom of the sick. Although we all prefer to use only the good passport, sooner or later each of us is obliged, at least for a spell, to identify ourselves as citizens of that other place. (1978: 3)

This powerful metaphorization is then in the course of the book debunked: for Sontag, illness is precisely not metaphorical, and Ann Jurecic has highlighted that even though this is one of the most cited and influential metaphors for illness, it is equally frequently misread (2012: 67). But two crucial aspects are upheld throughout the text: the commonality of the experience of illness, that nevertheless results in being perceived (and more often than not perceiving oneself) as 'other' to normalcy – at least in part a result of metaphorization in Sontag's reading; and the juxtaposition of illness and wellness as two distinct states of being. Contemporary writing about the experience of illness and impairment – both fictional and non-fictional – particularly since the 1990s often questions this stark juxtaposition and insists on the arbitrariness of the very categories of 'illness' and 'health' and – depending on the particular affliction – on the subjectivity of the experience: a person with a disease might not feel 'ill,' and a 'healthy' person might nevertheless experience his or her mental or bodily state as impaired. Disability narratives in particular have challenged the notion of 'normalcy' underlying common definitions of 'health' or 'disability' and attribute experiences of marginalization or stigmatization to the social environment, not the individual bodily state.

This has important implications for the reading of 'illness' and its function for narrative constructions of the self in Hustvedt's work. Even though much of the current research in this area focuses on writing that is presented as autobiographical, the strategies of depicting, the challenges to notions of 'normalcy,' and the importance of relationality apply to Hustvedt's fictional as well as her non-fictional and autobiographical work and the ways in which she negotiates experiences of illness. Caroline Rosenthal has pointed to the shifting boundaries of the body in Hustvedt's *What I Loved* (2011: 105), and I would like to argue that the experience of illness, of bodily impairment and mental unsettling, serves as the primary testing case for these boundaries and, by extension, the boundaries between self and other – their porosity, but also their necessity despite the undoubted significance of relationality.

This significance for the narrative construction of self finds its manifestation not only in the depiction of relations in the text or in intertextual references, but also in the text's specific form. My contention is that particularly *The Shaking Woman* and *The Blazing World* take up questions of illness, as the other texts do, in order to investigate fundamental questions of the self as relational and to debunk concepts of normalcy, but that they also in their specific textual form take these issues further to include an exploration of the possibilities of writing (a) life.

2. "Health is tolerant of ill health": *The Shaking Woman*

The Shaking Woman is a text difficult to categorize in terms of genre; a personal story complemented by theoretical discussions and extensive endnotes of philosophical, neurological, literary, historical, and psychoanalytic references, it is "part essay and part autobiographical memoir, plays with the expectations of a 'traditional' feminist audience, turning the anxiety of authority into self-determination, and the 'desire for wholeness' into multiplicity" (Thiemann 2013: 367). It is thus also a text that investigates the possibility of telling one's life in light of an affliction the origin and exact diagnosis of which remain unclear.

As highlighted earlier, Hustvedt throughout her work does not address illness as something always clearly identifiably distinct from non-ill states, and certainly not as something that can be always 'cured.' Nevertheless, in this text more so than in her fictional writing, she seeks not only a sense of narrative coherence but also of closure and acceptance; the final sentence of the text, "I am the shaking woman" (2010: 199) clearly signals an identification with and acceptance of a particular bodily state initially experienced as 'alien.'

When the autobiographical narrator gives a speech in her father's honor on the campus of St. Olaf College where he had taught for decades, she unexpectedly begins to shake.

> [...] I looked out at the fifty or so friends and colleagues of my father's who had gathered around the memorial Norway spruce, launched into my first sentence, and began to shudder violently from the neck down. My arms flapped. My knees knocked. I shook as if I were having a seizure. (2010: 3)

The memoir has, in effect, two beginnings: while the memory of the death of her father is the beginning of the autobiographical narration, this unexplainable occurrence at her father's commemoration is the beginning of a self-exploration and the attempt to understand her affliction. "Intellectual curiosity about one's illness," she writes self-reflexively a little later in the text, "is certainly born of a desire for mastery. If I couldn't cure myself, perhaps I could at least begin to understand myself" (2010: 6). The desire for self-knowledge and a form of control through narrative order are common aspects of autobiographical motivation, both reflected and unreflected. What is remarkable in this passage, as Tanja Reiffenrath argues, is "the fact that so early in the narrative, the idea of 'cure' is supplanted by 'understanding,' since Hustvedt makes clear that in lieu of a cure for her condition, she seeks insight and knowledge" (n.p.).[1] In light of the text's ending, understanding 'herself' and understanding 'her illness' become one and the same.

Illness might thus even be seen as a particular path to self-understanding. Hustvedt appropriates a psychoanalytic emphasis on the relationship between understanding the dynamics of a particular affliction and a potential for either overcoming or productively integrating it into one's life and self-understanding. So on the one hand, psychoanalytic and neurological theories serve as interlocutors that are meant to provide explanations – indeed, seemingly, 'information as control.' Hustvedt searches for an explanation of what has happened in the first place, and this search is doubly genealogical: the subtitle of the book, *A History of My Nerves*, already points the reader to both the personal history of migraine and earlier seizure-like experiences of the autobiographical narrator, as

---

[1] I would like to thank Tanja Reiffenrath for allowing me to quote from her unpublished dissertation manuscript.

well as to the history of concepts that attempted to frame and explain these experiences.

But of course, information comes also as a narrative, and not only does the text attest to this, the autobiographical narrator also reflects it throughout. So on the other hand, psychoanalysis in particular is more than a reference, it serves as the text's basic rationale, and in some instances, Hustvedt addresses this self-ironically. A central example for this is the self-diagnosis undertaken by the autobiographical narrator: reading her violent shaking as an outlet for repressed memories, if not even a symptom of repressed mourning for her father, she identifies her predicament as a conversion disorder, as a form of hysteria. Here, she builds among other sources clearly on Freud and, in an almost self-ironic move, even imagines herself in psychoanalysis, telling the story of a cure:

> My imaginary analyst is a man. I choose a man because he would be a paternal creature, an echo of my father, who is the ghost somehow involved in my shaking. After listening to my story, my analyst would surely want to find out about my father's death and my relationship to him. […] We would talk, and through the exchange the two of us would hope to discover why a speech I delivered in front of a pine tree turned me into a shivering wreck. […] In the end, – there is supposed to be an end – we would have a story about my pseudoseizure, and I would be cured. That is, at least, the ideal narrative of an analysis, which is a peculiar form of storytelling. (2010: 20–21)

Note that the diagnosis precedes the imagined analysis; while psychoanalytic theories form the basis of her self-diagnosis as hysterical, the imagining of psychoanalysis as therapy both follows and seems to confirm that diagnosis. Marks has read the obvious irony of this passage as a counter-narrative to 'classical' psychoanalytical discourse (2010: 79), and it certainly functions as such. However, the irony is not only a criticism but also a self-irony that takes up the autobiographical I's own internalization of (and hope in) a dominant narrative of 'the talking cure'; just as the different concepts referenced in the following investigate and in part deconstruct one another, so does the story of the 'actual' visit to a psychoanalyst undo the earlier self-diagnosis:

> My fantasy story about the shaking woman doubles back on itself as, one by one, living persons replace my imaginary doctors. […] Unlike my phantom analysis, Dr. C. is a woman. Like my figment, she has a kind and intelligent face. She listens patiently as I tell her the story of my shaking. When I suggest conversion disorder, she shakes her head gently, a rather sad smile on her face. She does not believe I am hysterical. (2010: 153)

This passage to some extent undoes the possibility for an easily categorizable story of the unexplainable shaking. A story of repression and unacknowledged mourning promised not only coherence, but also a happy ending – a cure.

What exactly this cure ideally consists of is not made clear; but, even though Hustvedt self-ironically pokes fun at the 'ideal' narrative of a psychoanalytic process, the underlying assumption is nevertheless that by bringing to light the causes for the repeated shaking, assumed to be unfinished or unacknowledged mourning, the shaking would eventually stop.

Besides the double narrative, the title also points, in its shift from 'the shaking woman' to a 'history of *my* nerves,' to an act of appropriation. Early on in the text, the autobiographical narrator remarks: "I have come to think of the shaking woman as an untamed other self, a Mr. Hyde to my Dr. Jekyll, a kind of double" (2010: 47), the double being a crucial element also in Hustvedt's fiction. The process narrated throughout the text, in dialogue with scientific as well as (to a lesser degree) literary references, is one of recognition of this double, this other self as part of one's own self that is embodied story. In an interview, Hustvedt remarks, "I no longer think of her – the shaking woman – as a sort of monster alien. She has become part of my story" (Biever 2015: n.p.). This act of narrative incorporation turns the shaking woman from the 'alien within' into a part of the self; Hustvedt's phrasing 'part of my story' highlights the narrative approach to identity that underlies the entire account. It is thus not the actual explanations investigated and discussed by Hustvedt through referencing a wide range of scientific texts, but the act of searching, the act of trying to find an explanation without actually finding one, as some reviewers somewhat frustratedly pointed out, that marks the function of the referenced texts.

The ending, then, is the retelling of a moment of recognition by simply recounting the event, not by further seeking to explain it. The moment of acceptance cited earlier is preceded by a matter-of-factly rendering of 'what happened,' an attempt to capture in narrative a sequence that does not suggest a cause:

> In May 2006, I stood outside under a cloudless blue sky and started to speak about my father, who had been dead for over two years. As soon as I opened my mouth, I began to shake violently. I shook that day and then I shook again on others days. I am the shaking woman. (2010: 199)

This statement presents a departure from a psychoanalytic narrative of repressed mourning. Nevertheless, while psychoanalysis did not provide the hoped-for cure, the narrative per se seems to function as a 'writing cure,' only that 'cure' does not imply an end to the affliction. Rather, as Hustvedt quotes D.W. Winnicott (and this is another of the many psychoanalytic references used by Hustvedt), "we need now to remind ourselves that a flight to sanity is not health. Health is tolerant of ill health; in fact, health gains much from being in touch with ill health in all its aspects" (2012: 80). Thus, the recognition of herself experienced as 'unsettled' that form the memoir's ending can be seen as the kind of integration of conflict identified by Winnicott with 'health.' In the same essay quoted by Hustvedt, he sets out to define the 'healthy individual': "The life of the healthy individual is characterized by fears, conflicting feelings, doubts, frustrations, as much as by the positive features. The main thing is that the man or woman feels *he or she is living his or her own life*" (1990: 27; emphasis original).

The 'shaking' as a specific, situational experience and as an affliction grounded in the individual history of nerves and body provide both the stimulus for and the center of the narrative; at the same time, the individual narrative is embedded in a historical development of conceptualizing the experience of illness. Early on in the narrative, Hustvedt reflects upon the specific 'character' of illnesses, highlighting both the role of concepts and of feeling for this specificity:

> Every sickness has an alien quality, a feeling of invasion and a loss of control that is evident in the language that we use about it. No one says 'I am cancer' or even 'I am cancerous,' despite the fact that there is no intruding virus or bacteria; it's the body's own cells that have run amok. Neurological and psychiatric illnesses are different, however, because they often attack the very source of what one imagines is one's self. (2010: 6–7)

With the insistence on the importance of language and metaphor in the experience of illness, Hustvedt clearly connects to Sontag's already cited argument in *Illness as Metaphor*. Cancer, the disease to which Harriet Burden in *The Blazing World* has succumbed, is not prominently discussed in *The Shaking Woman*, but it nevertheless is significant for the way in which the text combines the exploration of illness, narrative, and the production of self and self-knowledge. The autobiographical narrator relates a dream in which she is diagnosed with inoperable and incurable cancer (2010: 128); the tumors protrude around her neck and throat, threatening to cut off her ability to speak (Reiffenrath 2015: n.p.). The threat to life and the treat to the ability to speak appear conflated here; however, the passage is followed by an interpretation of the dream: "Even before I crawled out of bed, I understood that my dream tumors referred to the malignant tumor the doctors removed from my father's thigh, which left his leg stiff and useless" (2010: 128); through a chain of associations, the cancer dream becomes subsumed in a narrative of a split self: "A sick neck served as the perfect dream image of my symptom: *From the chin up, I was my familiar self. From the neck down, I was a shuddering stranger*" (2010: 129; emphasis original). I am less interested in the interpretation itself than in the narrative shift performed here: from cancer as an (life-threatening) affirmation of connection and identification with the (dead) father to cancer as an image of the boundary between the familiar and the alien. As such, it provides an insight not only into the kind of self-exploration of and through illness presented in the text, but also illustrates the self-exploration as narrative self-construction. The interpretation of the dream is the very storytelling that would have been cut short by cancer and provides a condensed version of the reflection about the dynamics of life writing that the text provides on a larger scale. Early on in the memoir, Hustvedt reflects on the genre when she argues that "true stories can't be told forward, only backward. We invent them from the vantage point of an ever-changing present and tell ourselves how they unfolded" (2010: 38). The interpretation of the cancer dream with all its facets and its unsuccessful attempts at closure is the attempt to create order; at the end of the text, Hustvedt once again reflects about memory and narrative: "We order our memories and link them together, and those disparate fragments gain an owner: the 'I' of autobiography, who is no one without a 'you'" (2010: 198). The 'you' addressed in the memoir is multiple: it includes the self 'as another' – to use Ricoeur's term – as well as the multiplicity of discourses with which the narrating I engages.

3. "The 'I' has nothing to do with it": *The Blazing World*

While *The Blazing World* is a novel, it nevertheless can be read also as an investigation into strategies of life writing as an attempt to create a narrative unity, even if – or particularly when – it captures experiences of fragmentation. Forms and degrees of fictionalization are part of this strategy, not only in texts that are marketed as fiction, but also in autobiography. As Paul Ricoeur has argued,

> [i]t is precisely because of the elusive character of real life that we need the help of fiction to organize life retrospectively, after the fact, prepared to take as provisional and open to revision any figure of emplotment borrowed from fiction or from history. (Ricoeur 1992: 162)

At the same time, fiction may borrow modes of emplotment from autobiography, both conventional and experimental. This is clearly the case in *The Blazing World*, which relies heavily not only on postmodern autobiographical conventions, but also to an extent on the autobiographical subgenre of 'pathography' (Anne Hawkin's term). While many of the frequent themes in Hustvedt's fiction – art and seeing, doubles, gender performance, the porous boundary of the relational self – are addressed in this most recent work as well, I want to argue that her equally frequent interest in the connection between illness and the narration of the self is investigated in ways that link this novel strongly to *The Shaking Woman*.

The Blazing World is presented as a work edited by a scholar, I. V. Hess, trying to sketch the life of the artist Harriet Burden. By the time Hess begins with his or her work on the book (the gender of the scholar remains undisclosed), Burden has already died of cancer. Terry Castle in her controversial review of *The Blazing World* sees the strategy as a variant of Nabokov's *Pale Fire* (2014: 35); however, it appears reminiscent rather of more recent ventures into experimental life writing, most notably J.M. Coetzee's *Summertime* (2009). The 'edition' combines interviews on her life with friends, lovers, and her children, but also with acquaintances, enemies, and other members of New York's artistic community; art reviews of the work she staged with three male artists as her 'masques' and excerpts from Burden's own notebooks. The life of Harriet Burden is thus narrated through different, often contradictory perspectives (including her own), creating a fragmented, polyvocal narrative which through its institutional framing – the editor, the footnotes etc. – not only presents versions of her life, but critically investigates the very process of narratively constructing a life.

While *The Shaking Woman* appears interested in the re/construction of a subjective truth about the narrating I's life, body, and experience of self, *The Blazing Woman* posits the question as to the contingency of truth claims and the possibility of truthfulness in life writing. Marks has highlighted that coherence of the narrative in *The Shaking Woman*, arguing that the 'chaos' of body and experience is not manifest in the memoir's form (2010: 81); *The Blazing World*, despite its fragmentation and polyvocality, nevertheless gives the appearance of a similar attempt to 'keep narrative order' in face of chaos. In both texts, 'illness' is crucial for this investigation into narrating the self as coherent, for it poses a threat to that coherence, which, as Hustvedt points out in *The Shaking Woman*, "does not do away with ambiguity" (2010: 198). The same certainly is true for *The Blazing World*. In the following, I will focus on the overall structure of the novel as well as the fragments particularly towards the end, which tell of the protagonist's death of cancer.

Harriet Burden's notebook fragments during her last year appear to illustrate Hustvedt's above-cited distinction between diseases such as cancer and neurological or psychiatric illnesses: while the latter potentially affect the subject's sense of herself, the former are experienced as an outside force, an intrusion of the body. "Birth, like illness, and like death is not willed. It simply happens. The 'I' has nothing to do with it" writes Burden in her notebook 'T' (2014: 354). While the protagonist seeks to affirm the boundary between the illness as event and the 'I' as a non-agent in this event, the structure of the text and the way in which cancer features in Harriet Burden's fictional life story appears to suggest a different picture: while Castle's summary, according to which Harriet "succumbs soon enough to the cancer that will kill her" once the hopes she put into her sham have been blasted (2014: 36) is flippant, the chronology of events indeed seems to suggest that cancer is consuming Harriet once her ploy has not resulted in her desperately desired and long denied recognition as an artist, but had her even further humiliated. The excerpts from the notebooks – each of which is labeled with single letters only – are not reprinted in each notebook's logic but chronologically as to reconstruct an order of events. As Sidonie Smith and Julia Watson among others have suggested, chronology is a seemingly natural, but after all only one way of ordering the past, and it is clearly the dominant structural mode in autobiography as well as biography, implying a meaning either inherent in or assigned to temporal sequence. The choice of sequence, thus, either suggests or risks the reading of Harriet's cancer as at least in part a result of her body being 'taken over' by disease after her long-plotted revenge on a sexist and self-congratulatory art world has failed.

Indications of the disease are mentioned in a fragment of 'Notebook O' for the first time.

> My belly is always bloated, even though I am thin. I eat alone, and the food doesn't look as good as when he's with me. I have pains, vague abdominal aches that I wonder about. Sometimes at night they scare me, but in the morning I chide myself for hypochondria. (2014: 343)

Here, as in the following fragments there is a discernible attempt to address the experience of the illness coherently; the memory fragments that make up the last excerpts from 'notebook T' appear scattered, but they put together an 'I' that is self-coherent and self-identical. 'Notebook I' – the 'I' being, as the editor suspects,

> the first-person pronoun in English" (2014: 10) – remains missing, but the narrating I of the notebooks remains coherent – even while commenting on her narrative demise, the last sentence of the chosen excerpt being "Even my thoughts are not my own anymore. (2014: 361)

Who or what is left as one's own, as oneself, this implies, but the feeling, suffering, dying body? Sontag has juxtaposed the metaphors of cancer to those of tuberculosis, arguing that the former are exclusively corporeal: "Cancer, as a disease that can strike anywhere, is a disease of the body. Far from revealing anything spiritual, it reveals that the body is, all too woefully, just the body." (1978: 18) Hustvedt's earlier cited distinction between diseases such as cancer and neurological illnesses comes to mind, in which she regards the latter as challenges to the sense of self; however, when the novel is understood as an exploration of 'auto-bio-graphy,' of 'self-life-writing' (Smith and Watson), this distinction does not hold: the very experience of being thrown back onto the body and its vulnerability poses a threat to the self; if the self ceases to be 'tellable,' this might indeed constitute an attack on "the very source of what one imagines is one's self" (2010: 7), for, as Eakin has argued, "narrative is not merely a literary form but a mode of phenomenological and cognitive self-experience, while self – the self of autobiographical discourse – does not necessarily precede its constitution in narrative" (1999: 100). Thus, while on one level Hustvedt's distinction between cancer as an example for a bodily disease and neurological disorders finds a fictional rendering in the way in which Harriet Burden's experience of cancer is narrated in *The Blazing World* on the content level, the structure of the novel, its imitation of modes of postmodern life writing, foregrounds the threat presented by the suffering body to the possibility to narrate one's own self. The relationality of the self that is so crucial to Hustvedt's work is tested to the limits of its possibility by *The Blazing World*'s polyvocality. She can neither tell of her suffering nor of her death; but she insists on the importance of coherence as a kind of order with a tolerance of ambiguity. At the same time, her *editor* appears to conflate coherence with chronology, thus in effect silencing the voice of the protagonist by a narrative of a 'forced relationality.' He or she is not unlike the medical professionals criticized by Erik Davidsen in the passage that never made it into *The Sorrows of an American*: "Mental illness is a state of chaos and the job of mental health professionals is to restore order by all means at the disposal" (2012: 152–153). In *The Shaking Woman* and *The Blazing World*, different as the texts are in genre, style, and structure, Hustvedt explores the potential function and effect of disease on the possibilities of life writing as a form of order. The 'I' – in its multitude, its relationality, its narrativity, and its fragility – has everything to do with it.

Works Cited

Biever, Celeste. 2010. "Meet Siri Hustvedt, the Shaking Woman." *NewScientist* February 3. <http://www.newscientist.com/blogs/culturelab/2010/02/memoir-of-a-puzzling-mind.html> [accessed 15 March 2015].

Butler, Judith. 2005. *Giving an Account of Oneself*. New York: Fordham University Press.

Castle, Terry. 2014. "The Woman in the Gallery." *The New York Review of Books* September 24. 34–37.

Couser, Thomas. 2011. "Introduction: Disability and Life Writing." *Journal of Literary & Cultural Disability Studies* 5.3: 229–241.

Eakin, Paul John. 1999. *How Our Lives Become Stories*. Ithaca: Cornell University Press.

Eakin, Paul John. 2008. *Living Autobiographically: How We Create Identity in Narrative*. Ithaca: Cornell University Press.

Hawkin, Anne Hunsaker. 1993. *Reconstructing Illness: Studies in Pathography*. West Lafayette: Purdue University Press.

Hustvedt, Siri. 2010. *The Shaking Woman, Or, A History of My Nerves*. London: Sceptre.

Hustvedt, Siri. 2012. "The Analyst in Fiction. Reflections on a More or Less Hidden Being." *Living, Thinking, Looking*. London: Sceptre. 152–165.

Jurecic, Ann. 2012. *Illness as Narrative*. Pittsburgh: University of Pittsburgh Press.

Kucharzewski, Jan. 2013. "Survival of the Sickest? Cognitive Disorders and the Question of Agency in Contemporary American Fiction." In: Alfred Hornung (ed.). *American Lives*. Heidelberg: Winter. 521–535.

Marks, Christine. 2010. "The Ill Self, Memory, and Narrative Identity in Siri Hustvedt's *The Shaking Woman, or, A History of My Nerves*." In: Mita Banerjee et al. (eds.). *Living American Studies*. Heidelberg: Winter. 75–93.

Marks, Christine. 2014. *"I am because you are": Relationality in the Works of Siri Hustvedt*. Heidelberg: Winter.

Reiffenrath, Tanja. 2015. "Rewriting the Diagnostic Narrative: Siri Hustvedt's *The Shaking Woman, or, A History of My Nerves*." Memoirs of Well-being: Rewriting Discourses of Illness and Disability. Unpublished dissertation manuscript.

Ricoeur, Paul. 1992. "The Self and Narrative Identity." *Oneself as Another*. Trans. Kathleen Blamey. Chicago: University of Chicago Press. 140–168.

Rosenthal, Caroline. 2011. *New York and Toronto Novels after Postmodernism: Explorations of the Urban*. Rochester: Camden House.

Smith, Sidonie and Julia Watson. 2010. *Reading Autobiography. A Guide for Interpreting Life Narratives*. 2nd ed. Minneapolis, MN: University of Minnesota Press.

Sontag, Susan. 1978. *Illness as Metaphor*. New York: Farrar, Straus, and Giroux.

Stedman, Gesa. 2008. "Brain Plots: Neuroscience and the Contemporary Novel." In: Jürgen Schlaeger and Gesa Stedman (eds.). *The Literary Mind*. Tübingen: Narr Francke Attempto Verlag. 113–124.

Thiemann, Anna. 2013. "Shaking Patterns of Diagnosis: Siri Hustvedt and Charlotte Perkins Gilman." In: Carmen Birkle and Johanna Heil (eds.). *Communicating Disease: Cultural Representations of American Medicine*. Heidelberg: Winter. 365–386.

Tougaw, Jason. 2012. "Brain Memoirs, Neuroscience, and the Self: A Review Article." *Literature and Medicine* 30.1: 171–192.

Winnicott, Donald W. 1990. "The Concept of a Healthy Individual." *Home Is Where We Start From: Essays by a Psychoanalyst*. New York: Norton. 21–38.

Christopher Schliephake
Embodied Memories, Embodied Meanings: Mind, Matter, and Place in the Works of Siri Hustvedt

In *The Poetics of Space*, his now classic phenomenological study of how ordinary and intimate spaces inform our thoughts, memories, and dreams, the French philosopher Gaston Bachelard wrote about the significance of early childhood places for later orientation and development:

> [...] over and beyond our memories, the house we were born in is physically inscribed in us. [...] We are the diagram of the functions of inhabiting that particular house, and all the other houses are but variations on a fundamental theme. The word habit is too worn a word to express this passionate liaison of our bodies, which do not forget, with an unforgettable house. (Bachelard 1994: 14–15)

Bachelard's topophilic exploration of our environments is a stark reminder of how we become bonded to abstract spaces. Yet, rather than attributing this close bond to a specific meaning attached to a space, for instance through a narrative, his account depicts this intricate relationship as a prereflective one. If there is meaning attached to a space, it is, for Bachelard, an embodied one, a feeling rather than a reflective or cognitive process. Lived or inhabited places have, in their materiality, a presence that acts on us, whereas our bodies, in turn, act on our environments and become their own agents of memory that "retain habitualized patterns" and "reproduce pleasurable, traumatic, and indifferent experiences that we have undergone in the past" in relation to a place (Trigg 2012: 12).

Bachelard's observations are remarkable in their own right, yet, they also help to illustrate a recent trend in (cultural) memory studies that puts new emphasis on embodiment and the significance of bodily and perceptual experience for acts of remembering (or forgetting). What had once been dominated by approaches that underlined the social constructedness of both individual and collective memories and had conceptualized memory as a predominantly cognitive capacity of our brains that was often rendered in analogy to computers, has turned into a debate where the body resurfaces as a container of and a "ground for the past to reappear" (Trigg 2012: 13). Next to the linguistic and symbolic medialization or narrativization of what once was, thus stands a prelinguistic and pre-reflective account of the past that is highly ambiguous: Not only because it may be hard to put into words, but also because it is both subjective (stored in the living organism of an individual body) and intersubjective (situated at the border zone between the matter of the body and the matter of the world).

One contemporary writer who has repeatedly explored the relationship between embodiment, memory, and our storied and material worlds is Siri Hustvedt. In the following, I want to look at the role that the notion of body memory plays for her writings in order to show that the process of meaning-making in her work – both of the past and of oneself – follows a dialogical principle, combining an embodied take on the past and an encounter between the self and the (non-)human world. Before I will illustrate this argument with an analysis of *The Shaking Woman* and *The Sorrows of an American*, I will briefly sketch out recent theories of body memory and relate them to Hustvedt's essayistic work that can itself be seen as a highly innovative and important addition to (cultural) memory studies.

1. The Architecture of Memory between Mind and Matter

For more than two decades, memory studies have become one of the dominant thematic strands of literary and cultural studies as well as of historiography. They have blossomed into a vibrant field of interdisciplinary inquiry with manifold publications dedicated to the subject that are dominated, in part, by widely different approaches to an individual (and social) phenomenon which seems to elude any neat categorization or definition (cf. Schliephake 2014a: 303–312). For although it may seem clear enough what memory is – we all have a memory or can confidently say 'I remember' – the issue of how we store past experiences within our minds, how we retrieve them and how we ascribe meaning to them is another story altogether, leading to complex epistemological and ontological questions. The subject of memory is, after all, bound up with two fundamental problems that both the humanities and the sciences have been grappling with since at least the Cartesian divide, namely: *who* are we and *what* are we? On a subjective level, cognitive psychologists have underlined the significance of episodic or autobiographical memories for a personal sense of self or identity. For a long time, memory was viewed as a relatively stable mental faculty, situated in the realm of the mind. While this view has come under attack from both psychoanalysis and recently from neuroscience and has been replaced by a dynamic-functional model of memory, it has also been substituted by one that highlights the material and embodied fabric of this faculty (cf. Hahn 2010). The dualism that had long dominated the debate seems to increasingly give way to a more unified approach that thinks mind and bodily matter together in order to explore how our human actions or capacities – like memory – function and how they can be seen as processes that are at the same time cognitive, emotive, and embodied (cf. Schliephake 2014b). As Bianca Maroia Pirani and Ivan Varga put it, "the memory of the body is an impressive refutation of the dualism of consciousness and the physical body" (Pirani and Varga 2011: xxx), while memory is now

> conceived as a complex and diffuse mental faculty which does not reconstruct the past faithfully, but instead is responsible for a continuing process producing individual memories that depend on the meaning ascribed and the emotions linked to the embodied experience of the individual. (xii–xiii)

Only two decades ago, when cultural memory studies became a key topic in cultural studies and historiography, this definition would hardly have fitted into the dominant theoretical
frameworks of the day. Originating against the background of overall demographic shifts and political sea changes – above all, the slow disappearance of the generation that had survived the Holocaust and the fall of the Soviet Union – memory studies followed, at least in the humanities, a predominantly constructivist agenda: Rather than constituting an intrinsic mental faculty, memory was seen as a collective cultural phenomenon, socially produced and externalized in different media that made up, in their interplay and in how they interpreted the past, the topography of memory of a society. Especially European scholars like Pierre Nora (1989) and Jan Assmann (1992) conceptualized memory as a normative category with which social systems ascribe meaning to historic sites and construct a collective sense of identity, leading to a fundamental change in how history was seen: instead of forming a coherent chronological set of events with an unambiguous narrative, history came to the fore as a multi-layered and complex social phenomenon in which the imagination plays a central role. Accordingly, the focus shifted from the question of *what* happened in the past to *how* this past is actively remembered, symbolized, and collectively shared. Cultural memory studies, then, can be defined as a strand of cultural studies that explores the collective frameworks of individual remembering not as a primarily mental operation, but rather as a context-dependent social undertaking in which culturally decoded frames of meaning (e.g. narrative patterns, metaphors, symbols) play a fundamental role.

It was only towards the end of the millennium that this social constructivist view was broken up in favor of a more subjective conceptualization that highlighted the role of the individual in negotiating, selecting, and interpreting the past from a wide array of sources that could be both social and private. This also led a to re-surfacing of authors like Henri Bergson (2004) or Aby Warburg

(2010) in a debate that had thus far rather been dominated by the writings of French sociologist Maurice Halbwachs (1992). While the latter defined memory as a capacity that depends on the "social frameworks" (Halbwachs 1992: 35) in which we remembered the past and the way we made sense of our experiences through social interaction, the former highlight the role of the individual in making sense of his/her own past – a past that although it had to be made sense of through language, may not be integrated easily into the collective frameworks of the social surroundings that could, in the end, attain its meaning against dominant systems. Again, predominantly European scholars like Sigrid Weigel (1994) or Aleida Assmann (1999) underlined the subjective and bodily aspects of memory and laid emphasis on the affective and emotive character of remembering, thus also turning towards the repressed, subconscious or traumatic traces of the past engrained in an individual or social body. In fact, in their insistence on the material processing of memory through the matter, including also the neurons and nerve cells of the body, recent cultural memory studies can also be seen as being influenced by the so-called "material turn" that is currently re-shaping the humanities (cf. Schliephake 2013). In sum, the focus has shifted from a memory that is socially constructed to one of lived experience, thereby also opening the debate to an interdisciplinary dialogue with neuroscience, phenomenology, or psychoanalysis.

I would argue that it is exactly in this context that a writer like Siri Hustvedt can both enrich and broaden the debate (cf. Schliephake 2014b). Especially in her essayistic work, Hustvedt has repeatedly written about the role of memory in creative encounters with the world, in constructing a sense of self (incoherent though it may be), and in making sense of a past that may resist any clear interpretation. In her latest collection of essays, *Living, Thinking, Looking*, she sketches out a highly complex conception of memory that is, at the same time, narrative, material, intersubjective, and imaginative and moreover draws on a wide array of sources, at once consolidating the field and at the same time signaling new directions for future research. Thereby, her writings are not situated within any narrow disciplinary frameworks, but can rather be regarded as intellectual and discursive hinges or connecting links between various disciplines. In her insistence on the role of storytelling and the power of the imagination, she not only manages to offer vivid and accessible accounts of the subject within a de-pragmatized medium, but frames her remarks within the one medium that is itself central to how we make sense of the past: Whenever we tell of a past experience or retrieve it in our minds, we frame it in a symbolic or linguistic way in order to ascribe meaning to it and make it coherent. Whenever we remember, we inevitably *story* the past, just like we *story* ourselves.

As Hustvedt puts it herself,

as embodied beings we live in a world that we explore, absorb and remember – partially, of course. We can only find the *out there* in the *in here*. [...] Our thinking, feeling minds are not only made by our genes but also through our language and culture. (Hustvedt 2012: 31–32; emphasis original)

One of the primary ways by which our culture – as memory studies have shown over and over again – influences our individual acts of remembering is by providing us with narrative patterns, story structures or symbolical frameworks that help us in situating our past experiences within a meaningful setting that can be productively used for identity-shaping processes and for sharing with others. What is, however, important to note in Hustvedt's writing is that this process involves more than mere cognition but is already taking place on a level that is pre-reflective, or prelinguistic. Her insistence on the embodiment of all meaning, of all storied acts as it were, puts this claim into a new perspective and also problematizes a clear sense of self: "We become ourselves through others, and the self is a porous thing, not a sealed container. If it begins as a genetic map, it is one that is expressed over time and only in *relation* to the world" (70). Hustvedt's account of memory is one of bodily and sensual immersion in a world of intersubjective encounters, where we become open to both human and nonhuman others (343) that shape our sense of who we are. Memory, then, is both engagement and encounter – with others but also with oneself as another:

> [...] self-conscious narrative memories gain their flexibility – motion in time – and their mutability – they are not reliable but continually reconstructed over a lifetime – in language. They depend on our ability to see ourselves as others see us. (210)

Conscious episodic or autobiographic memories are therefore, for Hustvedt, as much situated in the realm of the imaginary as they are in the traces of past experiences in the material world. Recovering these traces is never an arbitrary, stable process, but a highly creative and dynamic undertaking in which we become the agents of and within our own storied worlds: "Memory, like perception, is not passive retrieval but an active and creative process that involves the imagination" (95). What neuroscientists refer to as a "reconsolidation of memory" in the light of present contexts and interpretations of past experiences (94; 254–258), is for Hustvedt an indication that fictions and memories derive from the same imaginative and embodied impulses that are not so much cognitive or even conscious but rather emotional and subconscious: "Like episodic memories and dreams, fiction reinvents deeply emotional material into meaningful stories" (195). It is especially in instances like these that Hustvedt offers new perspectives on thinking about memory and how it relates the inner workings of the mind to the outer social contexts in which we live. Like the "imagination" itself, it becomes "a bridge between a timeless core sensorimotor affective self and the fully self-conscious, reasoning and/or narrating linguistic cultural self, rooted in the subjective-intersubjective realities of time and space" (195).

And Hustvedt's own writings become a bridge between cultural scientific approaches to the subject that perceive memory as a primarily social phenomenon and those that underline its material and bodily undercurrents. Hustvedt can be seen as an intermediary between both positions, but her value as an interdisciplinary thinker does not stop here. Rather, in her wide reading and integration of phenomenological philosophy, psychoanalytic readings, and neuroscientific findings she has broadened the debate from crucial vantage points and has successfully combined empirical and narrative approaches. As she reminds us in *Living, Thinking, Looking*, "mind is matter" (28) and "all human states [...] are of the body" (27). Yet, rather than giving in to a mere medical materialism or neurological determinism, Hustvedt thinks sensory information is processed through chemical filters in our brains together with the imaginative and emotive interpretation of that very information, thus relegating the question of consciousness and creativity to another realm altogether, namely that of "feeling" (Hustvedt 2013: 114). Memory, too, although it is seen as a primarily mental faculty, "is consolidated by emotion" (2012: 103). And it is in this context that we have to account for memories that do not depend on active retrieval, that resist narrative structuring or sequencing and that are not rooted within a specific time or place: traumatic flashbacks and sensomotoric memories do not only involve bodily states of tension or anxiety, but are often clouded by feelings of fear, pain, or disorientation (192 and 212). They are clearly pre-reflective and pre-conscious and they illustrate that memories are embodied traces of the past, written into the material fabrics of the body that can re-surface involuntarily and at any time. The slightest sensory perception – no matter if it is a color, a smell, a space or if it is even unconscious – can lead to both episodic memories and flashbacks. It is this embodied and perceptual dimension of memory that I will turn to in the next section in the discussion of *The Shaking Woman*.

2. Shaking Up the Past: Embodied Memories in *The Shaking Woman*

Siri Hustvedt's *The Shaking Woman, or, A History of My Nerves* is her 2010 book, a "hybrid work that is part essay and part autobiographic memoir" (Thiemann 2013: 367) and an intimate exploration of her own mind and body "in which she underscores the self's embodied identity and its interrelatedness to the environment" (Marks 2014: 55). Starting with the account of a seizure from the neck down, which occurred during a memorial for her deceased father, and dealing with the involuntary, nervous shaking of parts of her body during subsequent public appearances, her book is a deeply personal exploration of the inner workings of the self and a probing quest for meaning. Based on an impressive presentation of the historical and philosophical issues that underlie the modern science of the mind – from psychoanalysis over psychiatry to neurology and neuroscience – her writing is a double helix of a narrative that fuses scientific discourses with personal memories and family history in a compelling intellectual odyssey that offers no easy answers. Rather than evading complex issues or controversial problems like the split between mind and body, she tackles them head on and sketches out an erudite narrative of questions that cannot only be dealt with in specialized scientific inquiries but also in storytelling. Hustvedt thus presents what one could call an embodied account of the self in which public discourses and the external material world interact with the personal psyche of the mind that is at once porous and dynamic. Instead of constituting a coherent or stable sense of self, we are constantly adapting to our surroundings and bodily feelings or motions. Once our bodies react in ways that are involuntary or unplanned, we have to make sense of their deviant behavior or symptoms. While these may be part of a larger socio-cultural clinical picture, identified and described by (socially constructed) scientific accounts, Hustvedt makes clear that they have their own history, embedded in personal narratives and memories that transcend any scientific sense-making. Their meaning, it becomes clear, often arises against or in opposition to conscious or linguistic frameworks, taking on a presence that is at once embodied and pre-reflective.

This could, in fact, be seen as an appropriate definition of the phenomenon of body memory, which indeed looms large in Hustvedt's writing. Body memory can in this context be defined as a memory that "embraces the totality of our subjective perceptual and behavioral dispositions, as they are mediated by the body" (Summa et. al. 2012: 418). Thereby it is an implicit form of memory "rather than [...] a re-presenting or presentifying act of recollection," which "designates the pre-thematic impact of preceding bodily experiences on the meaningful, and yet implicit, configuration of our actual experience" (418). It is also "a form of lived experience, which is constantly re-actualized and implicitly lived through by a bodily subject" (425). Body memory designates learned patterns of bodily movement, abilities or habits, a form of practical, pre-reflective form of knowledge – like walking or riding a bicycle – as well as implicit forms of remembering which are not processed cognitively or linguistically. The "life-long learning history of the body" (424) thus incorporates our earliest contacts with other beings – parents, siblings, relatives – that are sometimes referred to as "intercorporeal" or "incorporative" (424). Traumatic incidents, too, that deactivate explicit, declarative forms of memory and activate implicit, procedural memory (432) are stored in the body (sometimes visibly in the form of a scar) and are acted out rather than being narrated. Instead of simply being implicated in the "formation of bodily habitualities," body memory thus "embraces the different modalities of our situational and intersubjective being in and interacting with the world" and "is based on the co-relation between subjectivity and the world" (438). Resisting the computational metaphor that understands the mind as an information processor, body memory introduces the person as an embodied agent, where ideas and memories, too, are embodied and integrated into the brain.[1]

Although the involuntary shaking of Hustvedt during public appearances is not a form of body memory per se, there is clearly a memory involved that triggers a conscious sense of distress and nervousness, maybe even a fear of a loss of control. As she remarks herself in *The Shaking Woman:* "Everything associated with performance made me anxious and distressed. At any moment, the unruly saboteur inside me might appear and disrupt the proceedings" (Hustvedt 2010: 39). The mere anticipation of an external context – that of a public lecture, for instance – or the perception of an external stimulus activates a neurological reaction that translates into a bodily movement, namely that of the shaking of the limbs. What had suddenly started without warning has been processed through cognition and has turned into a fear of it happening again. As Hustvedt puts it: "Having to speak in public has become my tone or clap of thunder, and if there is a memory involved, it is implicit, not explicit, and the shaking itself doesn't involve my higher self-reflexive consciousness" (115). Although the reason for her shaking is never entirely clarified, it is nevertheless characterized as a form of body memory, and the interaction between self, cognition, body, and world is repeatedly problematized as one of intersubjectivity and self-reflective processing of information. The narrative pattern of *The Shaking Woman*, which is marked by a series of starts and stops, may be a way of interpreting her symptoms through storytelling. Yet, the body has entered the picture as an interpreter of signs too – of thoughts, feelings, and external settings. As Pirani and Varga claim,

> by inserting itself into every situation, the body carries its own past into the surroundings as a procedural field. Its experiences and dispositions permeate the environment like an invisible net that projects from its sense and limbs, connects us with the world and renders it familiar to us. (Pirani and Varga 2011: xxx)

---

[1] António Damásio's somatic marker theory can be seen as one example that highlights the integration of bodily states in the brain and shows how past experiences become emotionally coded. Cf. Damásio 2005.

Instead of presenting an objective account of a bodily symptom, the shaking woman then comes closer to what Shaun Gallagher calls "a brief indication of how bodily movement and the motor system influence cognitive performance – how the body shapes the mind" (Gallagher 2006: 9).

That this shaping does not necessarily lead to a coherent sense of self but can rather disrupt a sense of identity is underlined by Hustvedt herself when she points out that "the shaking woman cuts me in two," causing "disruption and division" between "my narrating first-person subject" and "my recalcitrant body" (Hustvedt 2010: 165). Instead of belonging to that realm of episodic memory that can be revisited and reconsolidated over time in order to meet present concerns or needs of self-identity (58–66; 108–113), body memory eludes any such cognitive reworking, questioning the power of language to determine who and what we are. Yet, it would be wrong to interpret this agency of the body as a sign of the mind/body dualism that Hustvedt has repeatedly grappled with in her works. Not only is "the issue [...] one of perception and its frames, disciplinary windows that narrow the view" (79), but also one of accounting for a sense of subjectivity which "must," as Hustvedt, reminds us, "include more than the narrating 'I'," also involving "an *actual material* body" (Hustvedt 2013: 121). In *The Shaking Woman*, bodily perception, memory, and narrative are brought into conversation with one another, leading to a highly complex and multi-layered account of the self. The self is, in this sense, not seen as an enclosed entity, but rather as a dynamic, ever-emergent phenomenon that originates in connection to the world and to others. It

> develops from our early prelinguistic, intersubjective, emotionally coded encounters into increasingly flexible symbolic forms, through which we become others to ourselves and project ourselves into multiple imaginary selves and locations. (124)

The body is, against this background, a contact zone between the self and the world, where perceptual modes of information processing and cognitive interpretations merge and encounter a world where the body situates itself in relation to other bodies.

This may also be the reason why spatial perception and setting play such a fundamental role in remembering (cf. Schliephake 2012). Once a temporal and spatial anchor is missing, a memory – most often a trauma – cannot be integrated into narrative patterns. Ever since ancient mnemonic techniques, the close relationship between spatial organization and sequential memory has been underlined. In Nora's words, "memory attaches itself to sites" (Nora 1989: 22) and environmental psychologists, too, stress the importance of memories of (childhood) places as "psychic anchors" (Marcus 1992: 89) for the formation of self-identity. Carter, Donald, and Squires (1993) define place as "space to which meaning has been ascribed" (xii), while the development of "place attachment involves an interplay of affect and emotions, knowledge and beliefs, and behaviors and actions in reference to a place" (Low and Altman 1992: 5).[2] For Hustvedt, "places have power" (Hustvedt 2010: 99) and it is no coincidence that the place where her shaking began was an intimate place for her, the campus where her father had worked as a professor and where she had spent much of her early childhood (3). She relates how, days prior to the memorial, she had felt the presence of her dead father; a feeling that may have gotten stronger in the actual place that was intricately connected to her father's life – including a memorial pine tree that had been planted in his honor. The return to this place is equated with a return of the past; the affective visit of the place is both a bodily as well as a mental undertaking, where a remembered past and a material presence (or absence) converge. And it is here that the body joins in the process of remembering a lost loved person. That this process of remembering her father, of facing his ghost, is for Hustvedt not merely a process that is acted out in a bodily manner is made clear in her 2008 novel *The Sorrows of an American* that I will turn to in the last part of my essay to explore how her experience of loss is explored in storytelling.

3. Body and Place Memory in *The Sorrows of an American*

Siri Hustvedt's 2008 novel *The Sorrows of an American* is a deeply moving story about the return of the past, the agency of places, and the inherent meanings and secrets stored within material traces that include both bodies as well as objects. It is at once obsessed with memory and can be read as a dialogue with the dead. At the center of the novel stands Erik Davidsen, an aging and divorced psychoanalyst who is suffering from increasing loneliness as he tries to come to terms with the death of his father, Lars, a World War II Veteran and former university professor. He narrates the events that mark the year which followed his father's death and which led to the retrieval and the unearthing of various family histories, past traumas, and personal stories about loss. Interweaving multiple

---

[2] Modern neuroscience has come up with the concept of the cognitive map, where complex information is constantly ordered and re-ordered, so that in the end, the retrieval of memory can be said to be a creative process (Kandel 2007: 321–332) in which fragmented aspects of past experiences are retrieved and become reactivated based on present needs and concerns.

storylines, settings, and time layers, the narrative is both fragmented and striving for coherence, illustrating the imaginative and episodic character of memory and how it relates to the present as well as how it can come back to haunt daily life routines and disrupt a personal sense of identity. It is also a story of love and interpersonal encounter set against the background of a sociopolitical climate dominated by anxiety and insecurity in the aftermath of the terroristic attacks on the World Trade Center and the subsequent war in Iraq. Dominated both by present concerns and by the absence of what once was, *The Sorrows of an American* is, in the end, a moving meditation on how the imagination constantly works to transcend the barriers that separate the dead from the living, the past from the present, and others from the self – and how our memories inhabit the border zones in-between.

At various instances, Siri Hustvedt has hinted at the deeply personal and autobiographic background of her novel. In *The Shaking Woman* she relates how the character of Erik Davidsen became the version of an "imaginary brother," "the boy never born to the Hustvedt family" (Hustvedt 2010: 5). During the writing process she immersed herself in a broad array of neuroscientific and psychoanalytic literature and opened herself to the imaginary other that was as much a product of her mind and the texts she had read as of the pre-reflective realm of the embodied emotions and feelings that are intricately connected to our ideas and memories: "[...] [W]riting novels is nevertheless a form of open listening to those imagined others, one that draws on memories, transmuted by both fantasies and fears. And it is an embodied act, not an intellectualization" (2012: 165). This personal immersion in the story does not lead to an autobiographical reflection of real persons or events, but to an imaginative transformation of internal impulses that are bound up with real life experiences. Thus, *The Sorrows of an American* was written during the last years of her father's life and the final result grew "*out of* his death" (163; emphasis original). Accordingly, some sections of a memoir that her father had written found its way into the novel as a dialogue with the life story of her father and as a presence that was revived in the act of narrating. As Hustvedt puts it, "I now know I used those passages as a way to revive him, if only as a ghost" (39). Rather than a merely cognitive enterprise, this dialogue with the written autobiographical memory of the father became an embodied process. Thus, Hustvedt "typed [...] letters" her father had written "in order to feel them" and the "typing allowed his words to take on a physical reality beyond what I would have experienced by just reading them. My fingers can listen, too" (125). In a novel that is in many ways concerned with the importance of listening to the stories of others and the inner loudness that can come from loneliness, this practice found its way into the structure and contents of the fictional narrative. "The words of the text I had written fell somewhere between us," Hustvedt writes about the speech she had planned for her father's memorial, filling the absence or void left behind by the beloved deceased: "I felt his remembered voice" (2010: 125). And these embodied memories have become a dominant theme of *The Sorrows of an American*, a novel that is haunted as much by his ghost as by the traces that the memories of him and the grief about his death left in the body of the writer. Creativity and creation are therefore to be seen as embodied acts themselves that are connected to non-conscious, emotional processes: "[T]he book can know more than the writer knows, a knowing that comes in part from the body, rising from the preverbal, rhythmic, motor place in the self [...]" (2012: 39).

The dominant theme of how memories, the imagination, and matter interact as well as of how an absent past stays with us in the present is introduced right at the beginning of the novel (2008: 1–5). Erik and his sister Inga, a widowed writer whose life story shows striking similarities to Hustvedt's own life, including a nervous shaking disorder, go through their father's study, sorting out what had been accumulated in the course of a career, and unearth old letters and a memoir that hint at aspects of Lars's biography which had thus far been unknown to his children. They set in motion a narrative whose trajectory spans almost a century and ranges from the Great Depression over the Second World War into the terror-ridden present. Lars's writings that are embedded at crucial points in the narrative also suffuse it with ethnic details (in this case, of a Scandinavian community) and with predominantly rural places remote from the hectic city life of New York City, the primary setting of the novel. Early on, it becomes clear that these places connected to the life story of the father and his family take on their own powerful presence, reaching out into the present generation. The "particular smell" (2) and atmosphere of Lars's office influences memory processes and functions as a perceptual placeholder of the absent father as much as the old family farm, where Erik meets his father in dreams (230–231; 250–252). Objects and places seem to possess their own mnemonic aura or agency that affects the living and that can be felt by coming into contact with them – for instance, in her old family home, Erik's mother "feels Lars" and her "mother" who "are both with me in this place" (186). Along with the writings of Erik's father, they function as material storehouses of memory, as embodied presences that carry the marks and traces of those people, long gone, that had come into contact with them. Places function as meeting points between the living and the dead and memories bound up with them have an auratic quality, accompanied by bodily feelings. Thus, "the memory" of a walk "across the Martin Luther College," where his father had taught as a professor, "carries," for Erik, "a trace of dry, sun-colored leaves lifted by the wind and a few intermittent snowflakes, tiny and hard against my face" (88). Place memories are therefore also environmental memories, "that fire the internal weather of our pasts" (159) and that can become, on a metaphorical level, the expression of inner feelings and emotions attached to past events.

The deep emotional quality of memories stored in the body is made apparent at various points in the narrative. They are typically bound up with intersubjective experiences, moments of inner turmoil as well as traumatic events that cannot be integrated into the linguistic structure of episodic memories and that somehow remain outside of narrative elaboration – articulating themselves mainly through body language. When Eric remembers how his father left for long walks during the night, without anyone in the family knowing why or where he went, the recollection of the sound the door made is present as "a memory in my body" (32). Although this is not a traumatic memory per se, it is nevertheless connected to a feeling of anxiety and confusion, originating in the fear of a young child being left behind by his father. The narrative symbol of drawers is, within the narrative, brought together with memories and pasts locked within the bodies of the characters. Instead of stabilizing the self or a sense of identity (80; 144), these are memory fragments that physically "hurt" (48; 195). Erik's niece Sonia, who witnessed the terror attacks on the World Trade Center from her school, has been traumatized by the event ("she had silent ghosts inside her," 65) and has a breakdown shortly before its anniversary while standing at a window. As Erik explains the incident: "The second anniversary opened an internal crack in Sonia, a fissure through which she released the explosive feeling that had horrified her for two years" (230). This is a moment when the body revolts against and resists internal (or external) images, official narratives or explanations of events and finds its own expression that cannot be controlled by mere cognition or rationality. This is a past moment that is relived in the present, that is acted out rather than told. Lars, who had himself been tormented by his experiences during fighting in the Philippines (69–70; 83–85) and by a family history haunted by loss, also relates a flashback and an uncontrollable trembling he suffered during a concert of the college choir after his return from the war in his memoirs (136–137). Like wounds that can hurt or maim a body externally, these are incidents or memories that hurt the body internally – the literal meaning of "trauma." As *The Sorrows of an American* makes clear, while there can be no complete healing of this kind of wounds, they can nevertheless be integrated – if only in a painstaking and long process – within a narrative. And although this is often done in solitary retrospection, it is, like the conversations of Erik with his patients or the integration of Hustvedt's father's memoir into her fictional narrative, often a dialogical process, where the fragmented "I" depends on a "you" for coherence.

Works Cited

Assmann, Aleida. 1999. *Erinnerungsräume: Formen und Wandlungen des kulturellen Gedächtnisses*. München: Beck.
Assmann, Jan. 1992. *Das kulturelle Gedächtnis: Schrift, Erinnerung und politische Identität in frühen Hochkulturen*. München: Beck.
Bachelard, Gaston. 1994. *The Poetics of Space*. Boston, MA: Beacon Press.
Bergson, Henri. 2004. *Matter and Memory*. Trans. Nancy Margaret Paul and W. Scott Palmer. Mineloa, NY: Dover Publications.
Carter, Erica, James Donald and Judith Squires. 1993. "Introduction." In: Erica Carter, James Donald and Judith Squires (eds.). *Space and Place: Theories of Identity and Location*. London: Lawrence and Wishart. vii–xv.
Damásio, António. 2005. *Descartes' Error: Emotion, Reason, and the Human Brain*. Putnam: Penguin.
Gallagher, Shaun. 2006. *How the Body Shapes the Mind*. New York: Oxford University Press.
Hahn, Alois. 2010. *Körper und Gedächtnis*. Wiesbaden: VS Verlag für Sozialwissenschaften.
Halbwachs, Maurice. 1992. *On Collective Memory*. Trans. Lewis A. Coser. Chicago: University of Chicago Press.
Hustvedt, Siri. 2008. *The Sorrows of an American*. London: Sceptre.
Hustvedt, Siri. 2010. *The Shaking Woman, or, A History of My Nerves*. London: Sceptre.
Hustvedt, Siri. 2012. *Living, Thinking, Looking*. New York: Picador.
Hustvedt, Siri. 2013. "Borderlands: First, Second, and Third Person Adventures in Crossing Disciplines." In: Alfred Hornung (ed.). *American Lives*. Heidelberg: Winter. 111–135.
Kandel, Eric. 2007. *In Search of Memory: The Emergence of a New Science of Mind*. New York: Norton and Company.
Low, Setha M. and Irvin Altman. 1992. "Place Attachment: A Conceptual Inquiry." In: Irvin Altman and Setha Low (eds.). *Place Attachment*. London: Plenum. 1–12.
Marcus, Clare Cooper. 1992. "Environmental Memories." In: Irvin Altman and Setha Low (eds.). *Place Attachment*. London: Plenum. 87–112.
Marks, Christine. 2014. *"I am because you are." Relationality in the Works of Siri Hustvedt*. Heidelberg: Winter.
Nora, Pierre. 1989. "Between Memory and History: Les Lieux de Mémoire." *Representations* 26: 7–25.
Pirani, Bianca Maria and Ivan Varga. 2011. "Introduction." In: Bianca Maria Pirani (ed.). *Learning from Memory: Body, Memory and Technology in a Globalizing World*. Newcastle: Cambridge Scholars Publishing. xi–xxxiii.
Schliephake, Christopher. 2012. "Memory, Place, and Ecology in the Contemporary American Novel." In: Timo Müller and Michael Sauter (eds.). *Literature, Ecology, Ethics*. Heidelberg: Winter. 95–112.
Schliephake, Christopher. 2013. "The Materiality of History and the Shifting Shapes of Memory in John Hersey's *Hiroshima* and Alain Resnais' *Hiroshima Mon Amour*." *Ecozon@* 4.1: 61–77.
Schliephake, Christopher. 2014a. "Textualität und 'Vergangenheitsbewirtschaftung': Überlegungen zum kulturwissenschaftlichen Erinnerungsparadigma anhand von Iris Hanikas 'Das Eigentliche.'" In: Christian Baier, Nina Benkert and Hans-Joachim Schott (eds.). *Die Textualität der Kultur*. Bamberg: University of Bamberg Press. 303–324.

Schliephake, Christopher. 2014b. "Körpergedächtnis und Kulturökologie in der zeitgenössischen *graphic novel*." In: Andrea Bartl and Hans-Joachim Schott (eds.). *Naturgeschichte, Körpergedächtnis: Erkundungen einer kulturanthropologischen Denkfigur*. Würzburg: Königshausen und Neumann. 347–369.

Summa, Michela, Sabine C. Koch, Thomas Fuchs and Cornelia Müller. 2012. "Body Memory: An integration." In: Sabine C. Koch, Thomas Fuchs, Michela Summa and Cornelia Müller (eds.). *Body Memory, Metaphor and Movement*. Amsterdam: John Benjamins Publishing. 417–444.

Thiemann, Anna. 2013. "Shaking Patterns of Diagnosis." In: Carmen Birkle and Johanna Heil (eds.). *Communicating Disease: Cultural Representations of American Medicine*. Heidelberg: Winter. 365–386.

Trigg, Dylan. 2012. *The Memory of Place: A Phenomenology of the Uncanny*. Athens: Ohio University Press.

Warburg, Aby. 2010. "Mnemosyne Einleitung." In: Martin Treml, Sigrid Weigel and Perdita Ladwig (eds.). *Aby Warburg: Werke*. Frankfurt am Main: Suhrkamp. 629–639.

Weigel, Sigrid. 1994. *Bilder des kulturellen Gedächtnisses: Beiträge zur Gegenwartsliteratur*. Dülmen-Hiddingsel: Tendel.

Heike Schwarz
"We have different selves over the course of a life, but even all at once": The Multiple Self and Cultural Multiple Personality in Siri Hustvedt's *The Blazing World*

> I felt a Cleaving in my Mind –
> As if my Brain had split –
> I tried to match it – Seam by Seam –
> But could not make it fit.
> Emily Dickinson (opening quote in *The Shaking Woman*, 2010)
>
> I am a double creature.
> (Marianne Werefkin, painter)[1]

Psychological and psychiatric theories on and literary transformations of the so-called multiple personality disorder (MPD) seem as controversial as fascinating. The uncanniness of secondary selves or identity states, in MPD theory also called "alters," and their unexplainable control over a person's behavior has influenced fiction on doppelgangers, somnambulism, hysterical states, traumatic dissociation, and inner plurality. The syndrome of MPD comprehends the occurrence of two or more distinct identities that take control of a person's behavior paired with an inexplicable memory loss. The renaming of MPD into dissociative identity disorder (DID) in the mid-1990s signified another episode of the discourse of MPD/DID that found its topical explanation in the current *Diagnostic and Statistical Manual of Mental Disorders, DSM-V*.[2] Siri Hustvedt's books, especially *What I Loved* (2003), *The Sorrows of an American* (2008), her non-fiction book *The*

---

1 My translation (Berger 1987: 195).
2 MPD referred to the literal multiplicity of alters as complex entities or *persons* in one body, whereas DID attempts to stress an internal fragmentation of one person experiencing identity states. Such differences are often not perceived by popculturalized hollywoodizations of films using many actors and twist endings (*Fight Club, Identity, Secret Window, The Machinist*). This differentiation is relevant as the disorder was renamed to stress the trauma mechanism of dissociation inside rather to emphasize the development of more and more alters defined as complex entities. For further reference see the various editions of the *Diagnostic and Statistical Manual of Mental Disorders (DSM)* which can be also viewed as narratives in a cultural contexts. Each edition contains another definition of the disorder in reference to cultural changes, discourses, and even controversy (especially cf. *DSM-IV* 1994).

Shaking Woman (2010), and *The Blazing World* (2014), carefully and critically investigate various psychological theories on inner plurality such as "multiplex personalities" (Myers 2006 [1896]: 168), newer concepts of a multiple sense of the "true and false inner self" (Winnicott 2006 [1965]: 140), and MPD/DID.³ Her fiction negotiates variations of approaches to self-concepts of literary characters and the narrative structure itself, so that especially the multi-voiced *The Blazing World* can be marked as clever variation of the multiple personality genre and its subgenres.⁴ Ever since the establishment of dynamic psychology and the "discovery of the unconscious" (cf. Ellenberger 1970: i), the concomitantly acknowledged multidimensionality of processes in the human mind has produced a wide range of psychological and psychiatric theories of self, identity, and personality as well as related labeled disorders such as "hysteria," "double-consciousness,"⁵ "dédoublement de la personnalité" (Binet 1896: ix), "désagrégation"/"dissociation" (Janet 1920: 4), and later MPD or DID.⁶ These concepts have in common the emphasis on the multi-dimensional rather than the one-dimensional perception of the self, although MPD often works with stereotypical alters and a reintegration into one single self.⁷ In accordance with Hustvedt's own words, this essay will focus on the use of "psychiatric diagnoses and the innumerable mental disorders that afflict human beings" (Hustvedt 2010: 5). Analogously to Hustvedt's own reasoning on the stance that mental functions that where formerly labeled as mental disorders or dysfunction may overlap with comprehensible and complex expressions of altered self-perceptions and variations of selfhood, new approaches to identity games, multiplicity and varied self-perceptions may be created. "But I understood that beneath the self I

---

3 With MPD/DID the popcultural interchangeability of the two concepts is stressed.
4 I argued elsewhere that several sub-genres of MPD/DID fiction can be clearly detected. Such subgenres include the "Devil Inside" (demon possession stories), the "Spy Inside" (spy thrillers), the "Killer Inside" (usually serial killer stories), and the "Protector Inside" (dissociation as coping mechanism). Contemporary novels by Margaret Atwood or Siri Hustvedt blend those genres and add critical comments (Schwarz 2013).
5 W.E.B. DuBois later employs William James's psychological term.
6 Henri Ellenberger's seminal work *The Discovery of the Unconscious: The History and Evolution of Dynamic Psychiatry* (1970) includes various theories such as psychoanalysis or then almost forgotten concepts of double-consciousness and multiple personality and painstakingly traces the development of "depth psychology" or the manifold notions of psychological concepts of identity, self and personality. He is, however, not too critical about some concepts such as multiple personality. Cornelia Wilbur developed her definition of multiple personality disorder after reading Ellenberger. Her only MPD case *Sybil* was published in the form of a novel in 1973 written by journalist Flora Rheta Schreiber with whom Wilbur cooperated (Schreiber 1973).
7 As the alters supposedly were classified as having their own memory, the goal of therapy was to reintegrate memory aspects into one original personality.

had believed in was another person who wandered in that parallel world," states narrator Erik Davidsen in *The Sorrows of an American* (Hustvedt 2008: 228). *The Blazing World*, Hustvedt's sixth novel, sensibly continues the already introduced negotiation of the plural inner world of artist characters and their MPD artistry, such as Jeff Lane's photo installations in *The Sorrows of an American* or the *Maskings* project by central character Harriet Burden in *The Blazing World*. The essay will investigate these inner/outer parallel worlds of Hustvedt's characters, show which concepts of MPD appear in her latest novels, how *The Blazing World* even mimics MPD by using the narrative technique of polyphony, and how her recurrent intertextual references emphasize a multidimensional sense of the self.

1. Double-Consciousness and Multiple Personalities: Approaches to the Multi-Self

The literary canon knows many multiple characters: Robert L. Stevenson's Dr. Jekyll wanted to release his hidden self (1886), Robert Bloch's Norman Bates reveals his tripartite self in *Psycho* after the final twist (1959), Matt Ruff confronts two multiples in *Set this House in Order* with each other (2003), Chuck Palahniuk's *Fight Club* (1996) presents a secondary self idolized by an unnamed narrator. The template for late twentieth century stories is *Sybil*, the pseudonym of a case reported and later fictionalized by psychiatrist Cornelia Wilbur who first detects and names sixteen persons inside patient Shirley Mason, first diagnosed with anxiety disorder, and later integrates them back into a singular person with only one self called "the Blonde" (cf. Schreiber 1973: 433). The sixteen selves, female and male alters of different age, temper and knowledge of Sybil 's past, seem one-dimensional whatsoever, as they represent various stages of Sybil's life and character traits. Alters, *Sybil* shows for later stories, emerge after a traumatic experience as patients dissociate trauma and display unexplainable memory loss. However, the reintegrated Sybil as "the Blonde" is a creation of the psychiatrist – she can be criticized as being too one-dimensional.[8]

---

[8] Shirley Jackson's pre-*Sybil* novel *The Bird's Nest* (1954) already addresses such a one-dimensional notion of a healthy self as questionable as it only represents social gender conventions of the 1950s. In Jackson's novel the male psychiatrist renames the female patient and does not permit any autonomous agency. In *Sybil* there are no references to Jackson. Other one-dimensional or stereotypical alters appear in non-fiction books on MPD such as Truddi Chase's *When Rabbit Howls* (1987) or Cameron West's *First Person Plural* (1991).

The term of the "self" seems a rather confusing one rooted in a "conceptual morass" of mushroomed definitions (Leary and Tangney 2003: 3) of which the most basic might be that a "possession of the self allows people to direct their conscious attention to themselves" (9). William James' groundbreaking classification of the consciousness of the self has already three parts: firstly its constituents, subdivided into material, social, spiritual self and the pure Ego, secondly its feelings and emotions, and finally its actions such as self-preservation (James 1890: 292). As several philosophical schools (pragmatism or communitarianism) and psychological theories (psychoanalysis, behaviorism) have introduced further complexity, it seems essential to stress the social embeddedness; hence the self is also understood as a "psycho-social dynamic processing system" (Mischel and Morf 2003: 15–17). Intrapsychic processes and subsequent motivations are influenced by social entanglements, societal circumstances, rituals, gender roles, constructions and behaviors, which in turn create various or "multiple self-concept categories" (Showers and Zeigler-Hill 2003: 49). These categories "typically correspond to distinct roles, contexts, relationships, activities, traits, states, and the like" and allow for a "self-complexity" with the addition of time factors (past, present, future) multiplying categories which are also measurable in empirical studies (49).[9] Given a coherent consciousness of literally *oneself* as conjoining core, the potential variety of self-concepts diverts from one-dimensionality of a single-self that might lack any opportunities or potentialities. Translating all these concepts into her fictional narratives, Hustvedt lets psychiatrist Erik Davidsen in *The Sorrows of an American* state that "[w]e have different selves over the course of a life, but even all at once" (Hustvedt 2008: 303). In *The Blazing World* the MPD concept artist Harriet Burden is influenced by these categories but not a dissociation normally connected to the disorder despite the missing notebook titled "I," and her secondary persons or alters are used as masks. While her first mask Anton Tish is a naïve artist, Harriet's other masks become more complex, already with the second being the homosexual Afro-American Phineas Q. Eldridge. He is much more professional and moreover familiar with posing and performance. The last mask is Rune, a smart and admired artist, who almost outdoes Harriet when he stages the ultimate sensation with his video recorded suicide.

In Hustvedt's works endogenous and exogenous factors influence the negotiation of self-conception. Therefore it is relevant that subjectivity in Hustvedt's

---

9 According to Showers and Zeigler-Hill two types of measures approach the multiple self-concept categories: firstly using self-descriptive attributes (being energetic, being lazy during various life stages such as being at school etc.), and secondly the self-concept at categorical levels such as intellectual/academic ability, physical ability etc. (49–51).

novels leads always to an intersubjectivity which highlights the interconnection of individuals and their interrelationship with each other as well as their environment that is composed of societal codes and cultural influences. While the exogenous factors stress the perception of the self as seen and foremost "interpreted" by others, endogenous factors promote the idea of the self as being flexible, fluid, thus plural and, also, in a psychological sense, multiple. One-dimensionality of the self is no option and so Hustvedt's characters act and react in terms of constant reflection of the self as being not only singular but defined by several complex layers: self-perception versus perception by others, the self during various stages of life, and experiences which may be traumatizing and somehow paralyzing or invigorating and stimulating.

Philosophical approaches to what counts as "reality" and therefore sole truth, or what may only be defined as perception of reality, include theories of mind and consciousness and lead in Hustvedt's narratives to the idea of the multiple self interpreting and negotiating these theories. As a consequence, the concept of a literal MPD (rather than DID) as "disruption of ordinary selfhood" (Hustvedt 2010: 12), as another variation of the multi-layered self is applied in diverse ways: the psychological concept and definitions with its controversies, the multiple selves invented by the media, the transgressive or transvestite other self, the transformation of MPD theory into artworks, or the structure of a novel itself. While the MPD/DID psychology is, for example, connected to a minor character in the novel *The Sorrows of an American* (2008), the patient Ms. L, and also used by the compulsive artist Jeff Lane in his art projects, it is theoretically framed within the non-fiction book *The Shaking Woman*, in which the theories of a variety of relevant psychologists are being negotiated next to the controversy of MPD/DID, and personal concepts of "multiple personality" or "double-consciousness" (cf. Hustvedt 2010: 46).

2. Harry/Harriet: The Portrait of an Artist Playing the Game of Multiplicity

The novel *The Blazing World*, structured as an anthology, shows a posthumously published collection of texts on a female artist's work on perception and prejudices. She uses three male artists as masks who exhibit her own installations. Hustvedt's literary translations of the multiple self are not stuck in stereotypical representations of MPD in popular culture although some of her artists, Jeff Lane and Harriet Burden, use them. Yet Hustvedt always includes a critical approach. Hence in *The Blazing World*, psychiatrist Rachel Briefman offers her professional explanation of MPD as social hysteria or its "hystories" (cf. Showalter 1997: 5) when she mentions the manufacturing of "subliminal material" (Hustvedt 2014: 237). She functions as the now typical 'correctional character' in MPD fiction. As such a correctional character she certainly has to mention the controversy around MPD and the renaming of the disorder into DID, the false memory movement and the epidemic during which patients housed "whole populations inside a single body" with "dozens of personalities" (Hustvedt 2014: 236). In *Sorrows of an American*, narrator Erik calls it one of the "clichés of popular culture" (Hustvedt 2008: 234). Hustvedt is also not tempted to use the concept of multiple personality either as disorder or mere metaphor, while Harry/Harriet might be prone to a more metaphorical application. Harriet follows certain stereotyped patterns when she attempts to view herself as being multiple with different writing styles in her simultaneously kept journals or when she expresses her fascination with the syndrome.

Hustvedt uses a genderless editor, the art historian I. V. Hess (a reference to Eva Hesse?), to frame the book's numerous voices of art historians, journalists, friends and family, two male artists and Harriet's own journal entries. Explanations of *Maskings*, Harriet Burden's tripartite art project that relies on disguise, are introduced with Hess's interpretation: "Not only to expose the anti-female bias of the art world, but to uncover the complex workings of human perception and how unconscious ideas about gender, race, and celebrity influence a viewer's understanding of a given work of art" (Hustvedt 2014: 1–2). The editor's authority here, however, is already undermined by Harriet's own explanations that come with a text she wrote under the pseudonym Richard Brickman, who claims to have received a letter by the artist in which she reveals her real identity as the sole creator of the three exhibitions. Masked as male scholar she presents her own view, hence she does not accept other interpretations and already claims authority by using again a male name she seemingly considers as more reliable than a female scholar writing about a female artist. The artist's application of the masks as 'poetized personality' (Kierkegaard) is understood by Hess as "a visual elaboration of a 'hermaphroditic self'" (Hustvedt 2014: 2), a term that emphasizes the fluidity and plurality of the self. Hess writes a book called *Plural Voices and Multiple Visions*, discusses philosophers such as Søren Kierkegaard, his usage of several pseudonyms and his identity questioning work *Either/Or*,[10]

---

[10] Published in 1843 under the pseudonym Victor Eremita and written under various other names (such as A or B), Kierkegaard refers to two life styles which he calls aesthetic, understood as merely being superficial and immature, versus the ethical as sincere existence full of moral responsibility and critical self-reflection. Hustvedt uses references to *Either/Or* already in *The Sorrows of an American*.

and provides intertextual references to Margaret Cavendish and her novel *Blazing World*, to philosophers such as Edmund Husserl, Paul Virilio and Guy Debord, John Milton, Edith Stein, Mary Shelley, Emily Dickinson, Sigmund Freud and Josef Breuer, Anna O., and others who already appeared in earlier novels and texts.

The difference between Kierkegaard's game with pseudonyms, Harriet's masks, and concepts of MPD lies in the sometimes occurring loss of a core self in the latter.[11] Harriet retains a strong ego center, yet she is seriously thrown off balance when her experiment with Rune gets out of control, no matter how dominant her negotiation of self/selves and masks might seem. The missing "I" notebook, however, indicates that the core self is not totally detectable. In the end she desires to unmask the illusion and teach the audience a lesson of perception disorder and suggestibility while demanding "sole stardom" (Hustvedt 2014: 108) for her now acknowledged masterwork. Jamie Lorentzen classifies Kierkegaard's creation of pseudonyms as "poetized personalities" (a term adopted by Harriet) as a means "to offer a plentitude of metaphoric points of illumination regarding various stages of existence" (Lorentzen 2001: 38). According to Kierkegaard, in modern times the singular I is abolished, which requires a construct of a plural personality:

> Therefore I regard it as my service that by bringing poetized personalities who say *I* (my pseudonyms) into the center of life's actuality I have contributed, if possible, familiarizing the contemporary age again to hearing an *I*, a personal *I* speak. (quoted in Lorentzen 2001: 38–39)

– hence leading again to Harriet's consistent core of the *I* as the sole creator of poetized and constructed masks.

The complexity of the modern self as well as the sometimes favored interrelation of postmodernism and the plural self (cf. Glass 1993) both influence Harriet's artistic approach. This is obviously underlined by the very structure of the novel itself with its many points of view as polyphonic panorama with multiple internal focalizations put together to decipher Harriet Burden's works of art. The heteroglossia of the novel can be classified with Lorentzen's Kierkegaard study which uses a fitting interpretation of Kierkegaard, who is influenced by Schleiermacher's "idea of using persons as representatives (or metaphoric vehicles) for various tenors of lifeviews" (Lorentzen 2001: 39). Kierkegaard's own words may describe how the novel works:

---

[11] In the very popular non-fiction book of the heydays of MPD *When Rabbit Howls* (1987), more than 90 alters replace the former core self.

> [...] he constructs a host of personalities out of the book itself and through them illuminates their individuality, as that instead of being faced by the reviewer with various points of view, we get instead many personalities who represent these various points of view. (qtd. in Lorentzen 2001: 39)

These various positions illuminate Harriet's inner life and landscape of plural selves and foreground the examination of perception as well as the identity diversion Hustvedt adapts here.

Despite the somehow stereotypical characters in the novel such as esoteric Sweet Autumn Pinkney, there is no oversimplified equation between postmodern and multiple personality (disorder). Some theories on MPD regard it as postmodern disease per se (cf. Hawthorn 1983; Mergenthaler 2008), some understand the alters as complex and real persons (Wilkes 1988; Gunnarsson 2010), some deny this and stress traumatization and fragmentation (cf. Glass 1993), and others question the validity of the diagnosis altogether (cf. Acocella 1997; Borch-Jacobsen 1997; Hacking 1995; Kenny 1986; McHugh 2008; Piper 1997; Rieber 2006; Spanos 1996). Some of Hustvedt's characters discuss the contested concept of MPD/DID. Briefman connects it to "hysterical contagion" when talking with Harry about the fluidity of the self, which uncovers the suggestibility of mass (media) society being prone to epidemics of psychiatric diagnoses and belief systems that are influenced by "a mixture of suggestion, mimicry, desire, and projection" (Hustvedt 2014: 235). The multi-layeredness of memory, its reconstruction or rewriting, the question of influences of the "multiple personality epidemic" as "mass hypnosis" (Hustvedt 2014: 236) make Harriet question her singularity: "Were we just one person or were we all many?" (237). For Harriet the idea of the multiple self works on the one hand as opportunity for self-development concerning artistry, and also as catalyst to take revenge on the misogynist art scene on the other. In this sense her "trilogy of personas" is what she calls – in Briefman's memory and viewpoint – a "personified possibility" (again a term by Kierkegaard, Hustvedt 2014: 237) to let a darker self take control: "*The thing, the person – whatever it is – is ruthless, cocky, loud, cold, superior, cruel, dismissive, and untouchable. The thing is not polite. It has never been polite*" (Hustvedt 2014: 238; emphasis original). As Briefman explains:

> That's why she was interested in multiple personalities, because she thought plurality was human, she explained. She didn't get dizzy, black out, or lose people inside her. She knew perfectly well that she was Harry, but she had discovered new forms of her self, forms she said that most men take for granted, forms of resistance to others. (Hustvedt 2014: 243)

This resistance is Harriet's feminist revenge and conviction that multiplicity could also work as form of defense or even disguise in a male dominated society:

> Why do you suppose, she said, *that over ninety percent of all reported cases of multiple personality have been women? Bend and sway [...]. The pull of the other [...]. Girls learn to read power, to make their way, to play the game, to be nice.* (Hustvedt 2014: 243; emphasis original)

For the female artist Harriet Burden this game of social and gender roleplay can be fulfilled with the application of the self as multiple. After constructing the masks Anton Tish, Phineas Q. Eldridge, and Rune, under the pseudonym Richard Brickman she attempts to rewrite herself, similar to Harriet's feminist understanding of Berta Pappenheim, Breuer's patient Anna O., mentioned by I. V. Hess in a footnote: "They rewrote her. She would rewrite them" (Hustvedt 2014: 64).

3. The Art Scene – Artificiality versus Authenticity

Harriet Burden is a consequent development of the artist in Hustvedt's oeuvre who works with concepts of MPD/DID. In *The Sorrows of an American* the photo installations in the exhibition titled "Jeff's Lives: Multiple Fictions, or an Excursion into DID" by the manic Jeffrey Lane deal with the personal, the internal and notions of dissociation and fragmented identity viewed by the psychiatrist Erik Davidsen (Hustvedt 2008: 260–262). Harriet Burden exercises her games with identity and masks in order to literally unmask the artificiality and the superficial celebrity culture of the art world. The presented misogynistic dynamics of the art scene is understood as force that transforms Harriet into the troubled mastermind behind three installations, while she cannot enjoy her share of stardom. Her purpose is hence to prove that the art world only responds when male artistry is presented. Accordingly, the novel starts with a strong statement by Harriet as Richard Brickman: "All intellectual and artistic endeavors, even jokes, ironies, and parodies, fare better in the mind of the crowd when the crowd knows that somewhere behind the great work or the great spoof it can locate a cock and a pair of balls" (Hustvedt 2014: 1). While Harriet is granted only postmortem fame, she will not be written out of art history. Despite successful life designs of female artists, Hustvedt is eager to present the pseudonym game, or rather the necessity of invention of pseudonyms by female artists who use a male name such as science-fiction writer Alice Bradley Sheldon who published as James Tiptree.

Acknowledgment and female fame still seem to be problematic issues. Analyzing the 1990s subculture movement of grunge music, Catherine Strong examines "the processes of remembering and forgetting the women involved" and how women, who did contribute to the grunge movement in a substantial way, eventually were "written out of historical accounts of music in order to re-inscribe the creative dominance of men in this field" which, paradoxically, was a "more gender-neutral scene" consisting of grunge style individuals both male and female (Strong 2011: 398). This very recent process of "writing out" female presence and transforming it into an obscured non-presence within art or music history can also be detected in former centuries. Many autobiographical writings by female artists show how throughout the centuries a stereotyping of the female artist and a definition of femininity in general was perceived as hindrance concerning the appreciation of the artworks (cf. Berger 1987). The attributes of femininity and well-received gracefulness – attributes that might not bother Harriet Burden, the "gigantic girl," although she intends to "expose the antifemale bias of the art world" (Hustvedt 2014: 1) – would allow female artists to arouse attention from the contemporary establishment, yet they simultaneously endanger a full acknowledgement postmortem since womanhood and artistic significance would contradict each other (Hustvedt 2014: 18). Judy Chicago, an American feminist artist, describes her "gender-troubles" during her university years as the sole female student in the art class in *Beyond the Flower* (1975). Neglecting femininity and womanhood seemed to be the prerequisite for approval as (gender-neutral) artist, yet for Harriet this does not work as she takes it a step further and uses male masks. In the introduction to her co-edited art book *Women and Art*, Judy Chicago, who was first and foremost a representative of second-wave feminism, states her personal experiences within the seemingly male-dominated art world:

> Later, I came to understand that some of the confusion I felt as a female child was the consequence of an art system that privileges male artists, as evidenced by the centuries of discrimination against women artists. (Chicago and Lucie-Smith 1999: 10)

This sexist art world of the late 1990s and early 2000s described in *The Blazing World* is essentially a cluster of hoaxes and fakes albeit it claims to present solely authentic artworks by artists who sell them by showcasing profound philosophical stances. Phineas Q. Eldridge, who functions as Burden's second mask, makes remarks on the nature of the superficial art scene seem relevant when he refers to Honoré de Balzac. He defines it as a postmodern vanity fair: "The grubby human comedy. Illusion upon illusion upon illusion" (Hustvedt 2014: 126). This reverberates with the analysis given by Chuck Palahniuk's character Tyler Durden in *Fight Club* (1996) when criticizing a consumer culture stuffed with simulacra and the subsequent vagueness of self-definition: "a copy of a copy of a copy" (Palahniuk 1996: 97). Hustvedt's complex tour de force challenges the quest for deciphering the true self of Harry/Harriet and her game of hide-and-seek within the artificiality of the art scene as major platform for individual yet stereotyped performances of its participants. These participants struggle at the same time with their own desire for authenticity or at least their own viability and survival as acknowledged individuals. The performance character within this habitat is obvious; individuals transform themselves into actors, and the world is their stage where performance and performativity rule:

> Isn't the world in thrall to actors, especially to those who press themselves to extremes, who starve themselves for authenticity, who rage and gnash their teeth and turn themselves into demented patients or idiot savants or leering, cannibal psychopaths? (Hustvedt 2014: 225)

For Rachel Briefman, "the art world was Harry's laboratory" (Hustvedt 2014: 235) where she can deconstruct the celebrity culture with her *Maskings* project. One prerequisite includes the inability of the audience to fully perceive and thus really understand and literally "see" the message behind her huge installations. The naïve Anton Tish is the first mask, who is interpreted as emerging late 1990s hipster artist and "bad-boy geek with a mystical underside" (Hustvedt 2014: 101). Tish's philosophical imbecility of explaining the installation *The History of Western Art*, a "gigantic sculpture of a woman spread out" (Hustvedt 2014: 41), is irrelevant; his performance even convinces himself and causes Briefman to ask: "But was Anton playing Harry – or was Harry playing Anton?" (Hustvedt 2014: 106). In the dialogue with Briefman Harriet clearly wants her "true self" to be revealed: "I will rediscover my lost purity, my authenticity" (Hustvedt 2014: 110). This demand for authenticity and acknowledgment is similar to the loss Anton Tish experiences after his performance as mask is over: "He didn't recognize himself anymore" (Hustvedt 2014: 108).

Harriet Burden is somehow evoking a paradox as she is desperately challenging authenticity while creating and using roles in order to tackle the artificiality of the art scene and confront it with its non-authenticity. A role is created to reveal the role playing. Subjectivity means a continuous engagement with influences, hence leading to intersubjective states of consciousness. In *What I Loved* Violet argues with her "mixing theory" when she interprets body symptoms and anorexia nervosa,[12] in *The Blazing World* the explanatory model again is given by Rachel Briefman when she states that "the inner world and

---

[12] In *What I Loved* Violet develops her theory of "mixing," outside influences shaping inner worlds: "Mixing is the way of the world. The world passes through us – foods, books, pictures, other people" (94).

the outer world can be difficult to separate" and that "fantasies are made between people, and the ideas about those people live inside us" (Hustvedt 2014: 111). In *The Sorrows of an American* all characters are constantly influenced by questions of identity and authenticity. Kierkegaard's *Either/Or* concept of the aesthetic and ethical life underline what he calls a double existence (Kierkegaard 1992: 725) and uncanny oscillations (791) disturbing the aesthetic principle of the superficial. Harriet therefore seems to deconstruct the aesthetic artificialities in order to reach and promote the ethical values of the real.

4. The Artist as Multiplayer

The art project *Maskings* not only challenges the idea of the plural self disguised with masks, concepts of gender roles, and performativity (Hustvedt has Hess cite Butler's *Gender Trouble* and Aby Warburg's theory on the *Pathosformel*, Hustvedt 2014: 272) as well as the artificiality of the art scene, it also questions the authority of the audience and its possible perception of the artwork. While the first installation *The History of Western Art* still enables the audience to walk around the sculpture in a way they desire, the second installation, *The Suffocation Rooms* with several connected rooms, and even more so the last labyrinthine installation with Rune called *Beneath*, do not allow for an autonomous movement of the audience – the artist leads the perception of the seen while the artist does not elucidate the meaning. Part of *Beneath* are video installations that are integrated into the opaque walls of the maze. Harriet appears in these video installations, disguised however, performing several scenes with Rune that almost disturb Harriet's ability to distinguish herself from Rune: "We'll change sex and play a game, a theater game" (Hustvedt 2014: 221). The identity games seem to almost blur the boundaries of self and staged self: "Are we not all malleable beings made of putty, who can be pulled and pressed and reconfigured?" (Hustvedt 2014: 225).

Harriet seems to be mixed up in the notions of the multiple self (earlier journals) and the trap of what is called the "reflected self." This concept emphasizes the ides "that people come to see themselves as they believe others see them" (cf. Tice and Wallace 2003: 91). Next to self-reflection and the creation of the reflected self, the context within cultures – in the case of Harry/Harriet it is not only the art world but literal gender trouble and the transition of American culture due to 9/11 – is reinforced by what can be called artificiality of (global) consumer culture. Contemporary approaches towards identity formation stress the resulting inner multiplications:

The problem of identity is more salient today than at any time in history. In market-oriented societies, which now dominate the globe, the range of possible identities available to most individuals is larger than ever, and the latitude given to individuals to pursue or enact different identities "appears" vast. (Ryan and Deci 2012: 225)

According to this the proliferating options (intensified through media and the internet as well as through cultural habits) have created a task for the modern self to find a convenient self-definition: "The concept is more salient and the struggle more obvious today, precisely because identity is so frequently an open question" (Ryan and Deci 2012: 226). An earlier concept of the reflected self shows how outside determination influences self-notion and thus creating a self as others define it from the outside. The determination from outside then becomes part of the inner self (cf. Tice and Wallace 2003: 91). "After all, we all play parts," stresses Harriet (Hustvedt 2014: 321).

If Harriet's tripartite project *Maskings* is classified not only as personal struggle of internal multiplicity but also as an outset to criticize the male-dominated art scene, the game of disguise and masks may best be elucidated by sociologist Erving Goffman's theory who concluded already in *Encounters* that we are constantly influenced by a "multiplicity of selves" (Goffman 1961: 132). Goffman's theory of face-to-face interaction understands human beings as social as long as the outside façade needs to be intact. He calls this presentation of the self "staging," that allows the individual to be a "fabricator of impressions" in every-day life performance (Goffman 1956: 23). Harriet's general notion of the actors in the art world corresponds with Goffman's "individual *qua* performer" (24). Goffman and his "staged self" form the pattern in which the masks can actually work as they emphasize the constructed celebrity culture and its constant performance as well as its marketing of artists as brands.

5. The True Self – Authenticity, Agency, and Authorship

Erving Goffman's performance theory and the staging of the self evoke a constant combat of what may count as authentic and to what extent the artificial or "social front" influences the definition of the self. Here he refers to Santayana, who states that "our animal habits are transmuted by conscience into loyalties and duties, and we become 'persons' or 'masks'" (qtd. in Goffman 1956: 37) in order to hide the "back stage" where "the image of the man behind the mask" can be revealed (135). In *The Blazing World* the mask functions as metaphor for the artificial layer and as instrument to unmask the celebrity culture of the art scene. The identity game of the maskings, however, shows that the distinction between mask and authentic self is fluid. Harriet is able to control Anton as a puppet but becomes more and more unable to distinguish herself from Rune. The mixing of identities and artistry construct a middle ground of what could count as authentic. Goffman's citation of Robert Ezra Park's writings on race and culture underlines the dynamics of such a process:

> In a sense, and in so far as this mask represents the conception we have formed of ourselves – the role we are striving to live up to – this mask is our truer self, the self we would like to be. In the end, our conception or our role becomes our second nature and an integral part of our personality. We come into the world as individuals, achieve character, and become persons. (Park qtd. in Goffman 1956: 12)

The character Harriet is multiple, layered, and dynamic – despite her hardened position of feminism and her personal rage. The structure of the novel itself offers with its polyphony another multiple formation that contains front play moments and insights into Harriet's "true self." This term by psychoanalyst Donald W. Winnicott translates Goffman's social façade into a "false self" with only artificial forced functions. For Harriet her identity travels from the expression of the true self in her early artwork to the false self as trophy wife and also to a multiple self-definition claiming authenticity, agency, and authorship. She is eager to stress in her late journals that she is "multitudes" (Hustvedt 2014: 340) aware of role play and staging as well as "undiscovered worlds inside" (Hustvedt 2014: 335). It seems to be a twist in the novel that of all characters it is Sweet Autumn Pinkney, a naïve and esoteric aura healer, who is not poisoned by the art world and who seemingly truly recognizes Harriet. Pinkney perceives the blazing truth of Harriet Burden's artwork as it literally shines for her, or it is the aura that Pinkney experiences. The art works Harriet created are for Pinkney "alive with the spirit" as they are "blazing hot and bright" (357).

6. Conclusion

Multiplicity, inner plurality – in terms of philosophical theories, pseudonym plays, and psychological and psychiatric concepts, most prominently MPD – is a major issue negotiated in Hustvedt's works. The self is additionally interpreted as embedded in social interaction as well as object of (false or plural) perceptions and self-presentation. While in the other Hustvedt novels this concept was slowly developed, secondary characters appeared with their own concepts of inner and social multiplicity, such as Violet in *What I Loved* and the artist Jeffrey Lane in *The Sorrows of an American*. Moreover, the non-fiction book *The*

Shaking Woman with references to self-perception, multiple selves, and inner plurality demonstrates Hustvedt's excellent knowledge of psychology, psychoanalysis, and neuroscience. With her latest novel *The Blazing World* Hustvedt accentuates the concept of the multiple self by creating the central character Harriet Burden, and she even works with a narrative structure that resembles the theory of multiple inner voices, which is reinforced by MPD references throughout the text.

Harriet Burden, also calling herself Harry and literally carrying a burden, struggles with her self as an acknowledged artist beside her socially accepted role as presentable wife of an extremely successful art dealer whose reputation among the incestuous New York art scene eventually seems to eliminate any artistic sparkle inside Harriet. After his death she can return to art with a vengeance. With the polyphony of *The Blazing World* – Hustvedt expressed in some interviews that during the writing process she felt like having multiple personality disorder (Redfer 2014; De Souza Schmidt-Madsen 2014) – the author consequently translates the syndrome of MPD into the cultural multiple self, providing a complex narrative which adds more depth into an otherwise stereotypically pop culturalized cliché.

Works Cited

Acocella, Joan. 1997. *Creating Hysteria: Women and Multiple Personality Disorder.* San Francisco: Jossey-Bass Publishers.
American Psychiatric Association. 1980. *Diagnostic and Statistical Manual of Mental Disorders.* 3rd ed. Washington, D.C.: American Psychiatric Association.
American Psychiatric Association. 1994. *Diagnostic and Statistical Manual of Mental Disorders.* 4th ed. Washington, D.C.: American Psychiatric Association.
Berger, Renate (ed.). 1987. "Und ich sehe nichts, nichts als Malerei": Autobiographische Texte von Künstlerinnen des 18.–20. Jahrhunderts. Frankfurt am Main: Fischer.
Binet, Alfred. 1896. *Alterations of Personality.* New York: Appleton and Company.
Bloch, Robert. 2000 [1959]. *Psycho.* Stuttgart: Reclam.
Borch-Jacobsen, Mikkel. 1997. "Sybil: The Making of a Disease: An Interview with Herbert Spiegel." *The New York Review of Books* April 24.
    ‹http://www.nybooks.com/articles/archives/1997/apr/24/sybil-the-making-of-a-disease/› [accessed 8 September 2009].
Butler, Judith. 1990. *Gender Trouble: Feminism and the Subversion of Identity.* New York: Routledge.
Chase, Truddi. 1987. *When Rabbit Howls.* New York: Berkley Book.
Chicago, Judy. 1996 [1975]. *Beyond the Flower: The Autobiography of a Feminist Artist.* New York: Viking.
Chicago, Judy and Edward Lucie-Smith (eds.). 1999. *Women and Art: Contested Territory.* London: Weidenfeld & Nicholson.

De Souza Schmidt-Madsen, Cida. 2014. "Siri Hustvedt." *Youtube* May 11.
⟨https://www.youtube.com/watch?v=oNMQ_IFrrbA⟩ [accessed 15 December 2014].

Du Bois, William E.B. 1997. *The Souls of Black Folk*. Boston: Bedford Books.

Ellenberger, Henri. 1970. *The Discovery of the Unconscious: The History and Evolution of Dynamic Psychiatry*. London: Fontana Press.

Glass, James M. 1993. *Shattered Selves: Multiple Personality in a Postmodern World*. New York: Cornell University Press.

Goffman, Erving. 1956. *The Presentation of Self in Everyday Life*. Edinburgh: University Press.

Goffman, Erving. 1961. *Encounters: Two Studies in the Sociology of Interaction*. New York: The Bobbs-Merrill Company.

Gunnarsson, Leif. 2010. *Philosophy of Personal Identity and Multiple Personality*. New York/London: Routledge.

Hacking, Ian. 1995. *Rewriting the Soul: Multiple Personality and the Science of Memory*. Princeton: University Press.

Hawthorn, Jeremy. 1983. *Multiple Personality and the Disintegration of Literary Character*. Melbourne: Edward Arnold.

Hustvedt, Siri. 2003. *What I Loved*. London: Hodder & Stoughton.

Hustvedt, Siri. 2008. *Sorrows of an American*. London: Hodder & Stoughton.

Hustvedt, Siri. 2010. *The Shaking Woman, or, A History of My Nerves*. London: Hodder & Stoughton.

Hustvedt, Siri. 2014. *The Blazing World*. New York: Simon & Schuster.

Jackson, Shirley. 1954. *The Bird's Nest*. London: Michael Joseph.

James, William. 1918 [1890]. *The Principles of Psychology*. Cambridge: Harvard University Press.

Janet, Pierre. 1920. *The Major Symptoms of Hysteria*. New York: The Macmillan Company.

Kenny, Michael G. 1986. *The Passion of Ansel Bourne: Multiple Personality in American Culture*. Washington: Smithsonian Institution Press.

Kierkegaard, Søren. 1992. *Either/Or: A Fragment of Life*. Penguin Books: London.

Leary, Mark R. and June Price Tangney (eds.). 2003. *Handbook of Self and Identity*. New York: The Guilford Press.

Lorentzen, Jamie. 2001. *Kierkegaard's Metaphors*. Macon: Mercer University Press.

McHugh, Paul. 2008. *Try to Remember: Psychiatry's Clash over Meaning, Memory, and Mind*. New York: Dana Press.

Mergenthaler, Jens. 2008. *Sollbruchstellen der Seele*. Marburg: Tectum-Verlag.

Mischel, Walter and Carolyn C. Morf. 2003. "The Self as Psycho-Social Dynamic Processing System: A Meta-Perspective on a Century of the Self in Psychology." In: Mark R. Leary and June Price Tangney (eds.). *Handbook of Self and Identity*. New York: The Guilford Press. 47–67.

Myers, Frederic. 2006 [1896]. "The Multiplex Personality." In: Roger Luckhurst (ed.). *Robert Louis Stevenson: Strange Case of Dr. Jekyll and Mr. Hyde, and Other Tales*. Oxford: University Press. 168–176.

Palahniuk, Chuck. 2006 [1996]. *Fight Club*. London: Vintage Books.

Piper, August. 1997. *Hoax and Reality: The Bizarre World of Multiple Personality*. Northvale: Jason Aronson.

Redfer, Chris. 2014. "Avenue Bookstore Podcast." *Youtube* Mar
⟨https://www.youtube.com/watch?v=utIHV8IVGXEch⟩ 23 [accessed 15 December 2014].

Rieber, Robert. 2006. *The Bifurcation of the Self: The History and Theory of Dissociation and its Disorders*. New York: Springer.

Ruff, Matt. 2003. *Set This House in Order*. New York: Harper Collins.

Ryan, M. Richard and Edward L. Deci. 2012. "Multiple Identities within a Single Self." In: Mark R. Leary and June Price Tangney (eds.). *Handbook of Self and Identity*. New York: The Guilford Press. 225–246.

Schreiber, Flora Rheta. 1995 [1973]. *Sybil*. New York: Warner Books.

Schwarz, Heike. 2013. *Beware of the Other Side(s): Multiple Personality Disorder and Dissociative Identity Disorder in American Fiction*. Bielefeld: transcript.

Showalter, Elaine. 1997. *Hystories: Hysterical Epidemics and Modern Media*. New York: Columbia Press.

Showers, Carolin J. and Virgil Zeigler-Hill. 2003. "Organization of Self-Knowledge: Features, Functions, and Flexibility." In: Mark R. Leary and June Price Tangney (eds.). *Handbook of Self and Identity*. New York: The Guilford Press. 47–67.

Spanos, Nicholas P. 1996. *Multiple Identities & False Memories*. Washington: American Psychological Association.

Stevenson, Robert Louis. 2006 [1886]. *Strange Case of Dr. Jekyll and Mr. Hyde*. Oxford: University Press.

Strong, Catherine. 2011. "Grunge, Riot Grrrl and the Forgetting of Women in Popular Culture." *The Journal of Popular Culture* 44.2: 398–416.

Tice, Dianne M. and Harry M. Wallace. 2003. "The Reflected Self: Creating Yourself as (You Think) Others See You." In: Mark R. Leary and June Price Tangney (eds.). *Handbook of Self and Identity*. New York: The Guilford Press. 91–105.

West, Cameron. 1999 [1991]. *First Person Plural*. New York: Hyperion.

Wilkes, Kathleen. 1993 [1988]. *Real People: Personal Identity without Thought Experiment*. Oxford: Clarendon Press.

Winnicott, Donald W. 1990 [1965]. "Ego-Distortion in Terms of True and False Self." In: Donald Woods Winnicott (ed.). *The Maturational Processes and the Facilitating Environment*. Karnac Books: London. 140–152.

Interview with Siri Hustvedt

Susanne Becker
"Deceiving the reader into the truth": A Conversation with Siri Hustvedt about *The Blazing World* (2014)

Siri Hustvedt's 2014 novel *The Blazing World* takes us straight into the dramatic story of an exceptional woman: talented, intellectual, ambitious – however, tragically kept outside by the world she openly desires to belong to, she initiates a bargain of Faustian dimensions. Harriet Burden, an artist ignored by the New York art scene, who is also the widow of an influential gallery owner, explores secrets of art and how we perceive and evaluate it by convincing three male artists to publish her work in their names. A radical and, as it turns out dangerous experiment – and a space for Siri Hustvedt's ironic and sometimes radical double-voice that has throughout her work exceeded expectable conclusions.

In *The Blazing World*, multiple voices narrate Harriet's story from different angles and degrees of involvement: her editor, her lover, her children, two of her artist-collaborators, her old teenie-friend, but also art critics, a gallery owner, an art dealer, journalists, scholars. The narrative is indeed Nabokovian, as American critics have quickly postulated (e.g. Eberstadt 2014) but it is also unreliable in the sense of Doris Lessing's intellectual heroine Anna's famously color-coded notebooks chronicling and fictionalizing a writer's life/lives (1962) as Harriet herself separates her own retrospective records into various alphabetically labelled notebooks. At the same time, Mary Shelley's ostracized creature from her gothic *Frankenstein* haunts Harriet's verbal and visual self-representations, especially the images of an outsider desperately looking into the longed for world, images that culminate in her fear that her *window*-artwork could have been stolen. Harriet is an avid reader of philosophical, feminist, theoretical thinkers, exploring questions of identity and perception, distrusting binary thinking and given Truth. Hustvedt's different narrating and answering voices explore subjectivity and perception, and the troubling – or liberating! – evasiveness of memory and the true story. They attack and blur boundaries of gender and identity, art and life. And the readers, much as we enjoy the play of satire and the energy of excess constructed by this dynamic choir, also sense the depth of tragedy around a talented and ambitious artist. In a sense, Harriet's power of love becomes a redeeming force that resonates beyond her death – but even more so a posthumous exhibition that seems to finally give her the public awareness she so longed for during her lifetime.

Siri Hustvedt has throughout her fictions extended her protagonists' worlds and possibilities and in all her work explored processes of story-telling, life-writing and perception. "Mixing" different artistic, scientific and philosophical discourses, her writing explores the flexibility of boundaries and the "zones between" in our world-views and self-images. Her novel's radical and overtly parodic play with expectations and presuppositions has evoked international praise as well as critical and scholarly exchange (e.g. Boyers 2014; Zapf 2014) – how tempting to mirror critical voices within and those outside Hustvedt's artfully border-blurring plot. Hustvedt has generously talked about her work, her life and the relationship between her art and her life (e.g. 1997, 2008, 2010), and *The Blazing World* once again seems to parodically evoke this relationship. But let us begin in the beginning.

Siri Hustvedt, you open The Blazing World *with a striking sentence: "'All intellectual and artistic endeavors, even jokes, ironies, and parodies, fare better in the mind of the crowd when the crowd knows that somewhere behind the great work or the great spoof it can locate a cock and a pair of balls.'"(Hustvedt 2014a: 1). How did it take shape for you? It is a quote attributed – within a complex double-layered construct – to your heroine Harriet Burden. Was it also the starting point for your novel? When in the process of writing did you actually compose it?*

Because I wrote the editor's preface after I had written the rest of the novel in sequence, the first sentence is a literal quotation from Richard Brickman's letter, which appears later in the text. In other words, I quoted a sentence I had already written as Richard Brickman, a male pseudonym of Harriet Burden, who is quoting "herself" or rather, quoting herself as Brickman in a 65-page letter she purportedly sent to him (the non-existent college professor), called "Missive from the Realm of Fictional Being" about her project *Maskings*. Brickman a.k.a Burden publishes a critical and much reduced version of that missive in *The Open Eye*, an academic journal devoted to perception and the arts. The sentence in the Brickman text, with its use of the word "crowd" is glossed by the editor, I. V. Hess, in a footnote as a reference to Kierkegaard, who also wrote under pseudonyms, a form he called "indirect discourse," which was a method by which he hoped to deceive his reader into the truth. Hess, the editor, goes on to suggest that the whole Brickman letter is a parody of academic writing, but because Burden is apparently quoting herself as herself, this particular sentence might be said to fall into direct discourse. Of course, all the reader knows as she or he begins reading the novel is that the editor is quoting someone. The sentence is provocative with its "cock and balls" at the end, but it is important to be alert to the phrase that qualifies "all intellectual and artistic activities": "even jokes, ironies, and parodies." From the very first sentence, the question: "Who is speaking and in what tone?" is addressed. At the same time, the reader is alerted to the possibility of irony, jokes, parody, all forms of double meaning.

As the book moves on, the reader discovers that Harry does believe there is a masculine enhancement effect, and she cites studies to back up her belief. Attach a man's name to a work, and it will be deemed better than if a woman's name is attached. Context affects perception.

Indeed. The novel starts from gender assumptions in our perception – and from the slowly growing uncanny recognition that by radically confronting them Harriet sets into motion uncontrollable, amazing, painful and horrific developments. Your artist-heroine is an impressive woman and her invisibility as an artist seems absurd and tragic. She confronts the "antifemale bias" by her own version of indirect discourses: the Maskings *trilogy, for which three male colleagues/competitors publish her work in their names. This project might at first seem playful, e.g. in the sense of William Boyd's hoax with "Nat Tate," an artist he invented (1998); it also recalls male pseudonyms of famous women writers, but Hess's "Editor's Introduction" clearly suggests dangerous and maybe even deadly consequences – "deception into truth" as a Faustian bargain. What would you say looms as largest danger behind* Maskings *and what is Harriet's greatest achievement – can* Maskings *become successful in her ambitious aim "to uncover the complex workings of human perception" (Hustvedt 2014a: 1)?*

Maskings is a game, a form of playing and competition, part of our world usually understood as male not female. Harry wants to open the field of play, to allow women to compete without prejudice. The Nat Tate hoax started and ended rather quickly, and it did not have a philosophical purpose. It was a sociological experiment. The pseudonyms used by Mary Anne Evans and the Brontës were purely a means of hiding their authorship behind male names. *Maskings* is far more ambitious because, from the beginning, Harry is aware that the pseudonym she adopts will affect the art she makes. The mask is a means of exploring aspects of her masculinity in ways she has never done before. The danger then lies in the place between Harry and the persona she dons, in the "mixing" of herself with the other. She exploits Anton Tish (Tisch), collaborates happily with Phineas Q. Eldridge, and loses herself in the opaque and dangerous persona of Rune, a loss that includes the discovery of her own sadism, played out in a game with literal masks. Harry's achievement is for the reader to decide. As a reader of my own book, I think there is force in Harry's work, a force that is recognized by the "world" only after she is dead. And yet, Sweet Autumn sees the vitality in Harry's work, feels it, and leaves her testimony.

The art assistant Sweet Autumn concludes the novel with the feeling – or rather knowledge – that "each and every one of those wild, nutty, sad things Harry had made was alive with the spirit. For a second there, I could almost hear them breathing." (357). The blur of borders between art and life. Manifold border-blurs characterize your work and they seem to be often set into motion through a specific type of "excess," e.g. in the sense that your early protagonists in The Blindfold *and* The Enchantment of Lily Dahl *extend borders and limitations in their processes of identity, self-representation, gender (see Becker 1999: 257). Harriet – Harry appears excessive and dynamic in this sense: the rich widow, thoughtful mother, desperate artist, torn lover, impressive woman, and more, she appears as excessive in a liberating sense, physically, creatively, emotionally, spiritually ... with her own various voices separated into notebooks that are not easily categorized, and as an artist creating a large woman figure. Feminine excess as a liberating dynamics, celebrating what is often used as a common reproach to women – that they are "too much": How did Harriet take this shape for you – can excess blur boundaries?*

I love Sweet Autumn. She feels with acumen, despite the fact that her interpretations of those feelings are often wacky. She gets the last word because she is wise in her own way and because she is removed from the intimacy that binds the other characters who are present at Harry's death.

I believe art can "breathe." We animate works of art because the relation between spectator-reader-listener and painting-book-music is an intersubjective one. The artwork is at once a thing and an other.

I wish I knew where Harry came from. She flew out of me. She was the Gorgon-Genius inside me, I guess. I do know we are accustomed to thinking of male heroes and male geniuses, not female ones, and I wanted Harry to be big and angry and terribly smart. Female genius is an oxymoron because for some reason the intellect, mind, and culture are still incessantly associated with masculinity and emotion, the body, and nature with femininity. So Harriet declares herself Odysseus, while admitting to having been Penelope, the one who waits for the hero to return home. Action is the province of men; waiting of women. But Harry desperately wants to explode those binaries, to move beyond them and by doing so, fly out of her former self. She is at once intellectual and passionate. She is "too much" in the way the characters in classical tragedy are too much. Furthermore, the emotions in those ancient tragedies are pure. Harry's fury is pure. I think of it as a keening high form of expression, which is why I find her anger invigorating, if exhausting. She could not have been the novel's sole narrator, but as an enraged, erudite writer of notebooks, who returns periodically, she becomes one presence among others. Creativity may always be a kind of excess, a need to burst out of various constraints and become another person. In literature, no doubt more than in life, excess can be enjoyed because we readers remain safely inside what I call the aesthetic frame. The monster is not going to jump out of the book and eat us.

Luckily not, but it helps Harriet in her ambitious spiel exploding binaries! It seems important how preoccupied Harriet herself is with monsters, dedicating her Notebook T to "teratology, the study of monsters" and arriving at a very feminine definition: "'But the monster is not always a Rabelaisian wonder of hearty appetites and boundless hilarity. She is often lonely and misunderstood'" (5). Monstrosity in the sense of Mary Shelley's Gothicism.[1] Harriet sees herself as an "other" in that sense after the opening of Rune's exhibition of her work: "Harry, a ghost outside her own opening [...] Why have I always been outside, pushed out, never one of them? What is it? Why am I always peering in through the window? I felt fault lines in my torso ready to split open" (Hustvedt 2014a: 271–272). And more "mixing" seems to be going on between emotional experience and the desire for or abjection of extreme, super-real experiences and media-constructions. There are neo-Gothic appearances, doubles (229), ghosts of former lovers (156) and those as which mothers are perceived (286). There is Rune, with his neo-baroque splendor, camera-addiction, violence, decadence, a seductive Byronic artist figure. Harriet's life seems to be haunted as well as invigorated by them. How do they help or hinder her project, or more specifically: how do you think our ghosts and such appearances of other worlds shape our lives?

I don't really think of *The Blazing World* as a neo-Gothic text, although I have always been interested in secrets and ghosts and the devices of suspense used in gothic texts. In all my books, however, there are natural explanations for these experiences. We all have ghosts, after all. The voices and faces of the dead live inside us. But I love to hint at transcendent otherness, at the possibility of ghosts and fairies and angels. Milton's *Paradise Lost* and his Satan, as well as Mary Shelley's use of Milton in *Frankenstein* run through the novel, not only as references, but in the language itself. The Barometer's "angel" whom Harry thinks is Rune, is a direct reference to Milton's fallen angel, and the Barometer lifts words from *Paradise Lost* while garbling the text, of course. "He's fallen, you

---

[1] Siri Hustvedt's earlier work reverberates with allusions to Shelley's abandoned creature, and Harriet Burden's notebooks recall e.g. Iris' explicit musings in *The Blindfold*: "Frankenstein's monster, a creation we chose to ignore" (Hustvedt 1992: 188) and Mia's intense shifts between an inside and an outside in her own subjective world-order in *The Summer without Men* is also often tied to different notions of "monstrosity" (see e.g. Hustvedt 2011: 65, 78 and 214).

know, fell from Heaven to here below, to keep us low, to build our ruin, but nothing broke when he fell, and now he roams through wood and waste, over hill and dale, to the place where Longitude meets Latitude [...]" (Hustvedt 2014a: 184). When Harry escapes to Nantucket after her breakup with Bruno, she reads *Paradise Lost* again. "I arrived at Eve's dreadful meal, the big turn in the old story. The flawed, stupid, vain woman has eaten the damned fruit. 'Greedily she engorg'd without restraint.' She has done it for knowledge, to know more, to be illuminated. How I understand it. Yes, light up my head. I will do anything to know, to know more" (324). The first Faustian bargain. The mythical in myriad forms *haunts* the book throughout.

Harry is a monster because she does not fit any category and like Frankenstein's monster, she is always outside looking in and that marginality, that lack of recognition, infuriates her. Harry is a person of immense appetite, but that appetite has been thwarted, not just by the world beyond her but by her own inhibition and repression. There's the rub.

Harry feels her own immensity, gifts, erudition, and wants others to see what she is, but no one can really follow her. (Hess does her/his best, but the editor is always several steps behind H.B.) Harry is a Kierkegaardian figure. Like S.K. she is too clever, too ironic, too brilliant for her own good and suffers because others cannot understand what she is up to. But she is also a director of her own performance theater, her own indirect discourses (à la Kierkegaard) through which she becomes her masks, and they in turn alter her character and the character of the work she makes. Rune is most dangerous because he is most inscrutable, a chameleon, but their game is about power. They both want it.

Søren Kierkegaard: his "indirect discourse" traces your work, e.g. in The Summer without Men, *when Mia enjoys her young neighbor Lola's directness (Hustvedt 2011: 69) – although: "The unspoken directed the evening" (69). In BW, her daughter Maisie Lord first talks about Harriet's continuous philosophical research and emphasizes Kierkegaard's influence (23); then, Harriet's notebook C ("C" for communication? – her memoir since Felix' death) confirms: "I wanted my own indirect communications à la Kierkegaard whose masks clashed and fought, works in which the ironies were thick and thin and nearly invisible" (34). Her editor Hess sums up her credo – albeit only in a footnote: "The path to the truth is doubled, masked ironic. This is my path, not straight, but twisted!" (34). Do you remember how you discovered Kierkegaard in this sense and realized that your protagonist could be related to his pursuit of truth? What does he mean to your work?*

I read *Fear and Trembling* when I was fifteen. I took it off the shelf in my parents' house and read it as if I were possessed by some demon (or angel). It was the first time I had run into a person who was as horrified by the Abraham and Isaac story as I was, a biblical tale that had sickened and horrified me as a girl. At the time, I made no distinction between Kierkegaard and his pseudonyms. I have read the book several times since then and am always surprised that I loved it so much as a teenager. I must have missed half of it, more than half of it. No doubt, I still miss a lot in S.K.'s work. Nevertheless, what I took with me then and continue to cherish now is the philosopher's passion, his belief that the stakes are high for each and every one of us. Only later did I come to love his ironies, his tricks, his metaphorical wildness and literary brilliance. Kierkegaard is so strong that other philosophers, Heidegger and Sartre especially, robbed the man blind. When I reread those two after having spent a couple of years reading and rereading Kierkegaard for a lecture I gave in Copenhagen in 2013, I was stunned by the degree to which they pillaged the great Dane. Harry and I share a love for S.K. and his "boys," his pseudonyms that take various perspectives on philosophical questions that are always rooted in actual human lives and ordinary experience. He is the novelist-philosopher par excellence. The older I get the more I feel that the route to understanding is twisted, not straight, multiple, not single.

Many modern writers satirize romantic love and friendship. In your work, and again in Harriet's life story, love can be strong and redeeming – can it balance out her dangerous project?

Harry loves in the novel. She loves Rachel, Felix, her children, her granddaughter, Aven, Phinny, even Sweet Autumn, but love is not what drives her story. Love is not her problem. Harry is driven by ambition. And love, most definitely, does not fill the emptiness of her voracious desire for recognition.

Recognition would be the job of the critics: their reactions seem to remain safely based within a system Harriet has long dissected as biased and self-perpetuating. Among the many parodic scenes in the art world in this novel, the critics also play their role. (Harriet once tries to write in a critical mode but gives up after a few lines). Has this reverberated in the reception of the novel in any way? In many reviews and interviews one of the central themes has long been the relationship of your art and your life and I wonder how this theme might be developing. And how is the reception of your work and of this new novel different in the US and in Europe?

I read lots of reviews of *The Blazing World*. Many of them were positive, but I did not read them to satisfy my vanity. After my first novel, I stopped reading reviews because, to be honest, they were mostly stupid, even the ones that were full of praise. However, with this novel, I realized that the reviews of the novel were embedded in and anticipated by the ideas of the novel itself. The reviews of *The Blazing World* by Siri Hustvedt became further "proliferations" of *Maskings* by Harriet Burden. Indeed, I quickly saw how individual reviewers revealed biases that were discussed in the text itself or buried in its structure. For example, one reviewer thought Rachel's perspective superior to all the others. This made me chuckle because the reader fell straight into the book's formal trap. Another reviewer expressed irritation at not knowing what I, the author, believed about the novel's artworks or story. She, too, wanted exactly what the novel refuses to give because it is *all* indirect discourse, "a moving target," and is intended to throw the reader back on herself. Others were alarmed by all the references in the book to other books. I have found that this criticism is more sharply aimed at women who write than at men who write. Male authors, such as Richard Powers and David Foster Wallace, are not criticized for their erudition or their citations of philosophy and science, at least not in the reviews I have read of their work. Some readers chose to condescend to the novel without knowing to what they were condescending, another tactic addressed in the text itself: The art critic Rosemary Lerner, who appears just once in the novel, articulates the problem this way: "Reviewers of every ilk like to feel they are above a work of art. If it puzzles them or if they are intimidated, they are more than likely to trash it" (68). I confess to a certain delight in watching the book rewrite itself before my eyes in its own reviews.

I have continually stressed that what I look for in my art is emotional truth, not literal truth. The fact that reviewers are constantly reducing my books to my life has become something of an irritant. It bespeaks a lack of imagination. I have not felt that there was a huge gap between the American and European reception of this book. Mostly, it has been well received on both sides of the Atlantic.

Throughout your work, you have developed fascinating excursions into memory, how we remember and tell (our) lives. There is the cruel and cynical summary of Iris's life and memoir "as a bad joke" by Paris in The Blindfold *(218), there is the recognition how a shared life can be remembered so differently by two people in* The Summer without Men *where remembering becomes aligned with repetition (e.g. 99), there are the memories tied to places in* The Shaking Woman *(e.g. 100) and here, in your new novel, Harriet's memory is gloriously unreliable in yet another way. How has your sense of remembering and telling lives changed and developed?*

I am obsessed by memory and by its role in our lives as a shaping fiction. In an early essay, "Yonder," I wrote: "Writing fiction is like remembering what never happened." Later, I unpacked the same sentence in another essay, "Three Emotional Stories," to argue that memory and imagination are essentially the same faculty (à la Vico). There is strong neurobiological evidence for this unity. Personal autobiographical memory is unconsciously edited and reedited over a lifetime, which means that we are continually rewriting our own stories. This further means we are all creatures of an imaginary past, which is a powerful idea when you think of it. At the same time, emotion consolidates memories. Indifference and forgetting are linked. I suspect that the emotional coloring of a memory is usually far more "accurate" than its details. Harry doubts her memories, recognizes their fictional quality and yet, it seems obvious that her father's inability to recognize her as an artist is a wound she has borne for years, one which plays a vital part in *Maskings*.

It seems that Harriet's notebook M indirectly encounters such wounds. When you introduced The Blazing World *in your lecture in Mainz University (June 17th 2014; Hustvedt 2014b), you read the passage from the notebook in which she exclaims: "I am a Riot. An Opera. A Menace!" (2014a: 208) and you linked this self-image to your concept of the "geographies of the self." More and more the novel's form feels like a spiral, circling in on this notebook entry and out again, as if it was the heartbeat of the story. Here appears Margaret Cavendish: "Duchess of Newcastle, that seventeenth-century monstrosity: female intellectual." (207) How did you first encounter her and how did the idea arise to use this title?*

I have read the passage from Notebook M aloud several times at public readings for the book because I love how the words feel in my mouth – the rhythm of the sentences, the crunching consonants and the singing vowels. Harry is writing at full steam, but you are right, it is also a moment of opening and/or spiraling in the text. I discovered Margaret Cavendish a number of years ago while I was making a return to seventeenth-century natural philosophy, rereading Descartes, and Hobbes, reading Gassendi for the first time, and returning to the mysterious but fascinating Vico. My endless puzzling over the mind/body problem led me back to the early modern period during which the arguments were very similar to the ones being made today. Anyway, Cavendish popped up, and I began to read her work and to read about her work. She is a brilliant natural philosopher, although not easy to read because she is not univocal. Her mature organicist, anti-dualist, anti-atomistic materialism, however, hews closely to my own ideas on the question, which have been shaped by the paradigm shift in cognitive science in 1990's influenced by phenomenology, Merleau-Ponty, in particular.

In *Philosophical Letters*, Cavendish invents an interlocutor, a lady with whom she corresponds. In her plays, she stages debates in which the characters air very different opinions and perspectives – without resolution. *The Blazing World* is sometimes referred to as an early work of science fiction. I read it as complex meditation on society in general, a critique of power, coupled with a fantasy of having power. (The Duchess of Newcastle was a Royalist and afraid of ceding power to the "rabble.") Nevertheless, Cavendish is a polyphonic writer, one who anticipates the many voices of what became the English novel. She was also a remarkable personality. She mingled men's with women's clothing in her dress. She published her work when women did not publish. She rebelled against the constrictions visited upon women, was most definitely a female intellectual, was regarded as a monstrosity, and suffered from intellectual loneliness. Her husband supported her, but she longed for a genuine dialogue with Hobbes, for example, (who was closely connected to her husband's intellectual circle). He snubbed her. In all of these respects, she is an early model for my Harry.

The novel's structure is continually circling in on itself; one text undermines and/or builds on the next. Although its deepest ironies are expressed in the Richard Brickman piece, the novel's emotional heart lies in Harry's outbursts, a good example of which is the one from Notebook M when she announces herself as a "riot."

As for the self, whatever it is, I do think of it as a kind of geography with murky borderlands between conscious and unconscious, between pre-reflective motor-sensory-affective terrains and reflective, linguistic ones. I am convinced that no self exists without other people or without a world beyond the self. That boundary, too, is continually blurred as we move through life.

Not only the title, also the form of the novel are linked to Harriet's understanding of Cavendish, when she says: "Polyphony is the only route to understanding, hermaphroditic polyphony." (208). A clue to the many-voiced novel about a life. Your protagonist uses all she has to go beyond (exceed, transcend) her femininity and herself uses different voices through her notebooks. At the same time, as Christine Marks has shown, your work explores the possibilities of "relational subjectivity" mixing processes of identity and multiple important discourses as in What I Loved *(2003) – does this also shape this novel's multi-voiced form?*

Christine Marks's book made a deep impression on me. It is strange to read about one's own work. Inevitably, one becomes a kind of stranger to one's self in the process. But Marks's take on "mixing" felt as if she had articulated my deepest impulses and put them into a new frame, which is to say that scholars often find and interpret what the writer herself can neither find nor interpret.

Cavendish as an early model for twenty-first-century Harry – incredible that she should encounter similar difficulties still. What would be the female monstrosity today? We still live in a world of gender bias, and although the women of the twentieth century in the Western world have reached so much, Harry's misery is no exception.

As for the female monster/intellectual, I think this remains a complicated business even today. I am hardly the first person to point out that the culture reinforces stereotypes and that we perceive the world through our expectations of it. This, too, has a neurobiological basis. Some scientists refer to the brain as an organ of prediction, that is, its fundamental function may be to predict the future through the learned repetitions of the past. A simple example of bias and expectation in terms of sex is one I have used before. When a man or woman is told that the beautiful, voluptuous young woman at a party is working on her second post-doctoral degree in molecular biology, that man or woman will inevitably be surprised. On the other hand, the dashing young man who is working on the same degree will not create a ripple of amazement. That is one reason why age is an ally of the female intellectual. Wrinkles and a fallen face inspire respect in ways that a smooth young face does not. Female youth, beauty, and fertility remain in opposition to female intellect. Rosemary Lerner comments on this phenomenon in the novel: "It is interesting that not all, but many women [artists] were celebrated only when their days as desirable sexual objects had passed." (69)

And, of course, style is important. A woman is still punished for presenting her ideas aggressively. And yet, if she hesitates, apologizes, is "soft," she is not taken seriously. It is still true that short of Herculean efforts, women are rarely taken as seriously as men. The condescension most women live with day in and day out is nothing short of infuriating, and yet, women and men have been lulled into a yawning acceptance of the way things are. (All the while, feminist theorists cannot agree on what a woman is, much less how to proceed.) The battles waged not so long ago in the West – should women be educated, should they vote, should they have credit cards in their own names? – are no longer battles to be won. No one I know of is proposing that suffrage be taken away from women.

As an artist, however, the only route to truth (note the small t) seems to be strangely non-ideological. When I was writing as Bruno, for example, a character I love, but who has less than equalitarian ideas about the sexes, I found myself not just sympathetic to, but actually believing in his benevolent sexism, in his rescue fantasies, in his argument that men suffer more from failure than women because the culture puts more pressure on them. One must write from belief, even if those beliefs shift from one character to another. That is the enchantment of the novel, but it is also the strangeness of "mixing," of the truth that identity at every level is relational, not fixed, including a writer's relation to her very own figments. They are not puppets. They act independently. Harry continually shifts person in her writing, from first to second to third because she takes different perspectives on herself. I wanted to write a restless book, to push against my own limits and inhibitions. By my own lights (which may not be the lights of others), I succeeded.

Elsewhere it is possible to violate women's bodies, lives, rights once again: a German journalist just published her study on women's lives in Afghanistan, Kongo and India, during her travels she realized regarding the fights these women take on in the face of suppression, that this often happens in the name of religion (Welser 2014). What do you think about that?

All three major religions are patriarchal, Islam no more than the others. I dare say polytheism was probably kinder to women than monotheism. The crimes against women committed in the name of Islam are part of a radical interpretation of the religion that was by no means a norm historically. Those radical interpretations are repugnant, however, and must be actively countered. Whether we know what a woman is or not, whether one believes she is mostly the result of social construction or biology or, as I believe, that the nature/nurture distinction is utterly false and to use such a frame for discussing what women are is absurd to begin with, it seems to me that there are countless human beings out there who are identified as women in various parts of the world and are suffering because of it. That fact turned me into a feminist when I was fourteen and that has kept me one at fifty-nine.

In conclusion, could we look at this moment in time, in your life. As this volume reflects, there are so many directions of thinking that have influenced your large spectrum of writing over the years and maybe your own "mixing" has unfolded ever new exciting, liberating and challenging "zones of focused ambiguity" (Hustvedt 2013a). Where would you say are you now, what is on your mind, your agenda? What is your strong interest right now – and where is it taking you?

I am finishing an essay (or a short book) at the moment called "The Delusions of Certainty." The truth is that although my reading in various subjects has certainly refined my ideas about what we human beings are, it has also led to myriad doubts and confusions. Doubt, however, is a fertile position while certainty is often, perhaps always, a sterile one. The so-called "life of the mind" might better be called "life as play" because intellectual inquiry is also corporeal and emotional and dynamic; it is a form of grownup fun, of tossing around ideas with others (even if those others take the form of books). The game only becomes deadly when it ceases to be fun, when one of the players claims to own the truth, so there is no use playing anymore. Dialogue ends. Violence and misery begin.

I would never have predicted when I was a child that my curiosity would lead me so far into the sciences. My interests were directed toward literature and the humanities. It turns out, however, that I love reading neurobiology and, more recently, genetics. I am a great fan of Evelyn Fox Keller, whose work I discovered six or seven years ago, and who has had a deep effect on me. After I finish this essay, I am embarking on a novel called *Losing Time*. I was also recently appointed lecturer in psychiatry at the Dewitt Wallace Institute for the History of Psychiatry, Department of Psychiatry, Weill Medical College of Cornell University. It's a long title! George Makari (psychiatrist, psychoanalyst, and medical historian), who is on the staff there, and I are hoping to codify a therapeutic writing program for psychiatric patients. My greatest ambition at the moment is just to stay alive. February 2015 is my sixtieth birthday. I am lusting after more time, more time to play.

Thank you so much for this conversation, Siri Hustvedt.

Works Cited

Becker, Susanne. 1999. *Gothic Forms of Feminine Fictions*. Manchester: Manchester University Press.
Boyd, William. 1998. *Nat Tate*. London: 21 Publishing Ltd.
Boyers, Robert. 2014. "'The Blazing World': An Exchange." *The New York Review of Books* September 25. <http://www.nybooks.com/articles/archives/2014/sep/25/blazing-world-exchange/> [accessed 25 September 2015].
Eberstadt, Fernanda. 2014. "Outsider Art." *The New York Times Sunday Book Review* March 30. BR1.
Hustvedt, Siri. 1992. *The Blindfold*. New York: Norton.
Hustvedt, Siri. 1996. *The Enchantment of Lily Dahl*. New York: Holt.
Hustvedt, Siri. 1997. "Im Schatten des Ruhms." Interview with *Die Zeit – Magazin* April 4: 18–21.
Hustvedt, Siri. 2006. "Yonder." *A Plea for Eros*. London: Picador.
Hustvedt, Siri. 2008. "Ich benutze mich selbst." Interview with *Spiegel online* April 14. <http://www.spiegel.de/kultur/literatur/autorin-siri-hustvedt-ich-benutze-mich-selbst/> [accessed 17 June 2014].
Hustvedt, Siri. 2010a. *The Shaking Woman, or, A History of My Nerves*. London: Sceptre.

Hustvedt, Siri. 2010b. *Ma Vie – Siri Hustvedt.* Dir. Nicola Graef. Arte-Biografie. WDR-ARTE. March 21.
Hustvedt, Siri. 2011. *The Summer Without Men.* London: Sceptre.
Hustvedt, Siri. 2012. "Three Emotional Stories." *Living, Thinking, Looking.* New York: Holt. 175–195.
Hustvedt, Siri. 2013a. "Borderlands: First, Second, and Third Person Adventures in Crossing Disciplines." In: Alfred Hornung (ed.). *American Lives.* Heidelberg: Winter. 111–135.
Hustvedt, Siri. 2013b. "On Love Faith Choice": an International Interdisciplinary Discussion on Kierkegaard at the Royal Library Copenhagen, Denmark. May 5.
Hustvedt, Siri. 2014a. *The Blazing World.* New York: Simon & Schuster.
Hustvedt, Siri. 2014b. "Vortrag und Lesung von und mit Dr. Siri Hustvedt." *Life Sciences – Life Writing.* Mainz: Johannes Gutenberg Universität/Universitätsmedizin. June 17.
Lessing, Doris. 1962. *The Golden Notebook.* London: Michael Joseph.
Marks, Christine. 2014. *"I am because you are": Relationality in the Works of Siri Hustvedt.* Heidelberg: Winter.
Shelley, Mary. 1965 [1818]. *Frankenstein.* New York: Signet Classics.
Welser, Maria von. 2014. *Wo Frauen nichts wert sind: Vom weltweiten Terror gegen Mädchen und Frauen.* München: Ludwig.
Zapf, Hubert. 2014. "An Accomplished Scholar and Intellectual." *The New York Review of Books* November 6. <http://www.nybooks.com/articles/archives/2014/nov/06/accomplished-scholar-and-intellectual/> [accessed 25 September 2015].

List of Contributors

Susanne Becker is a TV journalist with the ZDF Culture and Science Department and a lecturer in American Studies at the University of Mainz.

Britta Bein is a Ph.D. student at the Graduate Center for the Humanities and Social Sciences at the University of Marburg.

Carmen Birkle is Professor of American Studies at the University of Marburg.

Astrid Böger is Professor of American Studies at the University of Hamburg.

Rita Charon is Professor of Medicine and Executive Director of the Program in Narrative Medicine at Columbia University.

Françoise Davoine is a French psychoanalyst and Professor at the École des hautes études en sciences sociales in Paris.

Birgit Däwes is Professor of American Studies at the University of Flensburg.

Katharina Donn is a postdoc scholar in American literature at the University of Augsburg.

Petra Gelhaus is a physician and a faculty member at the Institute of Ethics, History and Theory of Medicine at the University of Münster.

Johanna Hartmann is lecturer and postdoc scholar in American Literature at the University of Augsburg.

Alfred Hornung is Professor and Chair of American Studies at the University of Mainz.

Siri Hustvedt is a writer and scholar living in Brooklyn. She has a Ph.D. from Columbia and is a lecturer in Psychiatry at the Dewitt Wallace Institute for History of Psychiatry at Weill Medical College of Cornell University.

Klaus Lösch is a senior lecturer in American Studies at the University of Erlangen-Nuremberg

Christine Marks is Associate Professor in the English Department at LaGuardia Community College (City University of New York).

Lucien Mélèse is a psychoanalyst and long-time member of the L'Ecole freudienne de Paris, now of société de psychoanalyse freudienne.

Heike Paul is Professor and Chair of American Studies at the University of Erlangen-Nuremberg.

Jean-Michel Rabaté is Professor of English and Comparative Literature at the University of Pennsylvania in Philadelphia.

Gabriele Rippl is Professor and Chair of Literatures in English/North American Literature and Culture at the University of Bern.

Susanne Rohr is Professor and Chair of American Studies at the University of Hamburg.

Caroline Rosenthal is Professor and Chair of American Studies at the University of Jena.

Katja Sarkowsky is Professor and Chair of American Studies at the University of Münster.

Carla Schulz-Hoffmann is art historian, curator, and retired vice director of the Bavarian States Collections in Munich.

Heike Schwarz is lecturer and postdoc scholar in American Literature at the University of Augsburg.

Christopher Schliephake is lecturer and postdoc scholar in Ancient History at the University of Augsburg.

Diana Tappen-Scheuermann wrote her dissertation on *Literary Narcissism* in English and American literature, including Siri Hustvedt's works, and publishes frequently in the field of English didactics.

Mark C. Taylor is Professor and Chair in the Department of Religion at Columbia University.

Anna Thiemann is lecturer and postdoc scholar at the University of Münster.

Jason Tougaw is Associate Professor of English at Queens College (City University of New York).

Hubert Zapf is Professor and Chair of American Literature at the University of Augsburg.

www.ingramcontent.com/pod-product-compliance
Lightning Source LLC
Chambersburg PA
CBHW070747230426
43665CB00017B/2279